SALLUST

BELLVM CATILINAE

EDITED BY
A. J. WOODMAN

CAMBRIDGE
UNIVERSITY PRESS

Shaftesbury Road, Cambridge CB2 8EA, United Kingdom

One Liberty Plaza, 20th Floor, New York, NY 10006, USA

477 Williamstown Road, Port Melbourne, VIC 3207, Australia

314–321, 3rd Floor, Plot 3, Splendor Forum, Jasola District Centre, New Delhi – 110025, India

Cambridge University Press is part of Cambridge University Press & Assessment, a department of the University of Cambridge.

We share the University's mission to contribute to society through the pursuit of education, learning and research at the highest international levels of excellence.

www.cambridge.org
Information on this title: www.cambridge.org/9781009371513

DOI: 10.1017/9781009371537

© Cambridge University Press & Assessment 2026

When citing this work, please include a reference to the DOI 10.1017/9781009371537

First published 2026

A catalogue record for this publication is available from the British Library

A Cataloging-in-Publication data record for this book is available from the Library of Congress

ISBN 978-1-009-37151-3 Hardback
ISBN 978-1-009-37149-0 Paperback

Cambridge University Press & Assessment has no responsibility for the persistence or accuracy of URLs for external or third-party internet websites referred to in this publication and does not guarantee that any content on such websites is, or will remain, accurate or appropriate.

For EU product safety concerns, contact us at Calle de José Abascal, 56, 1°, 28003 Madrid, Spain, or email eugpsr@cambridge.org

CAMBRIDGE GREEK AND LATIN CLASSICS

To
Xinyi and Raffael
the new generation

'The genius of Sallust'
(Macaulay)

CONTENTS

PREFACE

Sallust's *Bellum Catilinae* is an excellent text for students to read. It concerns a significant event in an important period of Roman history, it is a good story and of convenient length, and it is written in relatively straightforward Latin. Remarkably no student edition of the work has been published in Britain since the historical commentary of P. McGushin in 1980; any student wanting help with the Latin was obliged to go overseas to the valuable edition of J. T. Ramsey, which first appeared more than forty years ago in 1984. In the present book I have tried to provide linguistic aid and literary comment, while at the same time explaining the events which Sallust describes.

I owe a very considerable debt to two friends in particular. D. H. Berry very generously agreed to place at my disposal his unrivalled knowledge of the Catilinarian conspiracy, supplying me with copious notes on a draft of the volume, saving me from countless howlers, and answering my many queries in a whole series of patient emails. At a late stage F. Santangelo gave me much-needed encouragement by his spontaneous and very kind offer to read the final draft in its entirety, making numerous valuable suggestions and supplying me with much bibliographical information. For the support of both these friends I am extremely grateful.

In writing the commentary I also sought and received various kinds of help from the late J. N. Adams, S. Bartera, E. L. Bowie, J. D. Dillery, F. K. Drogula, J. Elliott, A.-M. Hutton, T. J. Keeline, P. T. Keyser, J. E. Lendon, J. M. Marincola, E. A. Meyer, H. Mouritsen, F. Muecke, K. S. Myers, J. Osgood, C. B. R. Pelling, G. Pezzini, J. T. Ramsey, M. D. Reeve, T. Reinhardt, A. Ring, K. E. Shannon-Henderson, B. D. Shaw, M. F. Smith, Z. Stamatopoulou, D. Sutton, K. Welch and T. P. Wiseman. I am most grateful to them, as also to A. Chahoud, C. B. Krebs, D. S. Levene, R. Maltby, R. G. Mayer and J. W. Rich, each of whom read a draft of the Introduction and suggested significant improvements; Professor Krebs in addition kindly sent me his discussion of Sallust's style in advance of publication.

As on previous occasions I am much indebted to the Editors of the green-and-yellow series, P. R. Hardie, S. P. Oakley and C. L. Whitton, not only for their very helpful and perceptive comments but also for a wide variety of other support and assistance. In writing the book I was greatly helped by the online resources provided by the University of Virginia, and I am much in the debt of Steve Snider, who with efficiency and good humour has guided me through many a technological challenge.

The commentaries on Sallust's *Bellum Catilinae* by K. Vretska and I. Mariotti each stretch to more than seven hundred pages, and there is now a further substantial commentary from L. Fezzi, which I have not seen (*Sallustio. La guerra di Catilina*, 2025). Given the scale of this scholarship, I am more than usually grateful for the opportunity of bringing out my own much more circumscribed work. This is the eighteenth book of mine to be published by Cambridge University Press, with which I have had the honour of being associated for over fifty years, and I owe much gratitude to the Press, and especially to Michael Sharp, for undertaking to publish yet another of my volumes.

15 January 2025   A. J. W.

REFERENCES AND ABBREVIATIONS

Sallust's works are abbreviated as *BC* (*Bellum Catilinae*), *BJ* (*Bellum Iugurthinum*) and *H.* (*Historiae*), although most references to the first omit *BC* altogether. References to the *Historiae* are given according to Ramsey's edition.

Cicero's *Catilinarians* are abbreviated as *Cat.* and usually omit the author's name.

Cicero's fragmentary speeches are numbered according to the edition of J. W. Crawford (²1994).

Livy's fragments are numbered according to the edition of D. S. Levene (2023).

Asconius is referenced according to the edition of A. C. Clark (1907).

Fragmentary historians are numbered according to the editions of T. J. Cornell (*FRHist* below) and H. Peter (repr. 1993).

For **Cato** I have used G. Manuwald, *Cato: Orations, Other Fragments* (Loeb edn, 2023).

The **grammarians** are cited from H. Keil, *Grammatici Latini.* Vols. 1–8 (1855–90, repr. 2009).

Cross-references. I use 'Intro.' to refer to the Introduction to the volume, and 'intro.' to refer to notes introducing sections of the narrative.

OTHER ABBREVIATIONS

BA	Talbert, R. J. A. (ed.) (2000). *Barrington atlas of the Greek and Roman world.* Vols. 1–2 and Maps. Princeton
BNP	*Brill's New Pauly.* Vols. 1–15. Leiden/Boston
CAH	Crook, J. A. et al. (edd.) (1989–94). *The Cambridge ancient history.* 2nd edn. Vols. 7–9. Cambridge
CGRH	Marincola, J. (ed.) (2007). *A companion to Greek and Roman historiography.* Malden, MA/Oxford/Carlton, Victoria
CIL	*Corpus Inscriptionum Latinarum*
CLE	Buecheler, F. and Lommatsch, E. (1895–1926). *Carmina Latina Epigraphica.* Vols. 1–3. Leipzig
CLL	Clackson, J. (ed.) (2011). *A companion to the Latin language.* Malden, MA/Oxford/Chichester
FRHist	Cornell, T. J. et al. (edd.) (2013). *The fragments of the Roman historians.* Vols. 1–3. Oxford
GL	Keil, H. (1855–80). *Grammatici Latini.* Vols. 1–8. Leipzig (repr. Cambridge 2009)

G&L	Gildersleeve, B. L. and Lodge, G. (1992). *Latin grammar.* 3rd edn. Repr. Walton-on-Thames
ILS	*Inscriptiones Latinae Selectae*
K–K	Keeline, T. and Kirby, T. (2019). 'Auceps syllabarum: a digital analysis of Latin prose rhythm', *JRS* 109.161–204
LH	Woodman, A. J. (2015). *Lost histories: selected fragments of Roman historical writers. Histos* Suppl. 2. Newcastle upon Tyne
LTUR	Steinby, E. M. (ed.) (1993–2000). *Lexicon Topographicum Urbis Romae.* Vols. 1–6. Rome
MRR	Broughton, T. R. S. (1951–86). *The magistrates of the Roman republic.* Vols. 1–3. New York/Atlanta
N–H	Nisbet, R. G. M. and Hubbard, M. (1970–78). *A commentary on Horace. Odes Book I* and *Odes Book II.* Oxford
NLS	Woodcock, E. C. (1959). *A new Latin syntax.* London
OCD	*Oxford Classical Dictionary.* 4th edn. Oxford
OCT	Oxford Classical Text(s)
OLD	*Oxford Latin Dictionary*
OLS	Pinkster, H. (2015, 2021). *The Oxford Latin syntax.* Vols. 1–2. Oxford
OR	Batstone, W. W. and Feldherr, A. (edd.) (2020). *Oxford readings in classical studies. Sallust.* Oxford
ORF	*Oratorum Romanorum Fragmenta*
PH	Woodman, A. J. (2012). *From poetry to history: selected papers.* Oxford
RDGE	Sherk, R. K. (1969). *Roman documents from the Greek East.* Baltimore
RIC	Sutherland, C. H. V. and Carson, R. A. G. (1984). *Roman imperial coinage.* Vol. 1. Rev. edn. London
RICH	Woodman, A. J. (1988). *Rhetoric in classical historiography.* London/Sydney/Portland
Rom. Stat.	Crawford, M. H. (1996). *Roman statutes.* Vols. 1–2. London
SCPP	*Senatus Consultum de Cn. Pisone Patre*
TLL	*Thesaurus Linguae Latinae*
TLRR	Alexander, M. C. (1990). *Trials in the late Roman republic 149 BC to 50 BC.* Toronto/Buffalo/London
W.[1]	Woodman, A. J. (1977). *Velleius Paterculus: the Tiberian narrative.* Cambridge
W.[2]	Woodman, A. J. (1983). *Velleius Paterculus: the Caesarian and Augustan narrative.* Cambridge
W.[3]	Woodman, A. J. (2014). *Tacitus: Agricola.* Cambridge

W.[4]	Woodman, A. J. (2017). *Tacitus: Annals V and VI.* Cambridge
W.[5]	Woodman, A. J. (2018). *Tacitus: Annals IV.* Cambridge
W.[6]	Woodman, A. J. (2021). *Horace: Odes III.* Cambridge
W–M	Woodman, A. J. and Martin, R. H. (1996). *The Annals of Tacitus Book 3.* Cambridge

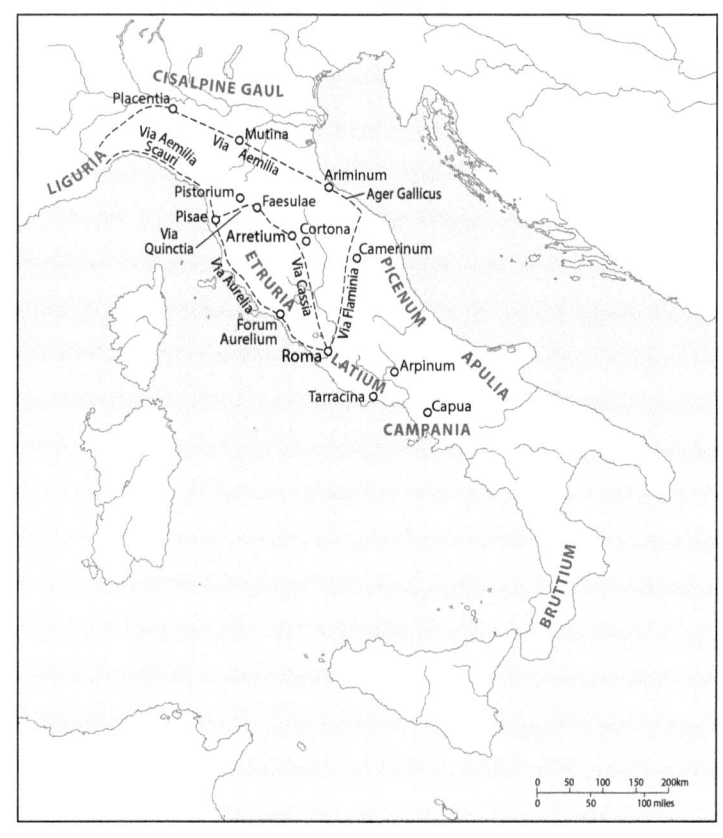

The Italian peninsula in the mid-first century BC

INTRODUCTION

Sallust's *Bellum Catilinae* describes the brief history of the so-called Catilinarian conspiracy up to its suppression in Rome in December 63 BC and the death of its eponymous leader on a distant Italian battlefield early in 62.[1] Sallust wrote his account about twenty years afterwards and it is the first work of Latin historiography that is extant.[2] Many historians had written during the previous century and a half, but their works have survived, if at all, only as fragments, sometimes consisting of no more than a single sentence or even a single word.[3] Most of these writers appear to have traced the history of Rome from its beginnings down to their own times, but some chose a different model: thus the *Origines* of the elder Cato (234–149 BC) seems to have been at least partly thematic, Coelius Antipater composed a monograph (c. 110) perhaps entitled *Bellum Punicum*, while some others restricted themselves to contemporary history. It is difficult to know what the early historians thought about the process of writing history, since little of this fragmentary material is programmatic or theoretical in nature, although Sempronius Asellio (c. 135) in two famous fragments (1–2) stresses the importance of historical explanation and assumes that one function of historiography is to encourage patriotism and morality in its readers.[4]

---

[1] Although the title of the work is given as *Catilinae Coniuratio* by Kurfess and as *De Coniuratione Catilinae* by Reynolds, the word *coniuratio* has no manuscript authority at all. Quintilian implies that the work was known as *Bellum Catilinae* (3.8.9 'C. Sallustius in bello Iugurthino et Catilinae'; cf. Aug. *Epist.* 138.16, Serv. *Aen.* 1.6), and throughout the monograph war is depicted as the goal of Catiline and his followers (see e.g. 17.6, 20.15, 21.2, 26.5, 32.1–2). Cf. e.g. Cic. *Cat.* 2.1 'iustum bellum geremus' (one of more than thirty such references); also W. W. Batstone, 'Word at war: the prequel', in B. Breed et al. (edd.), *Citizens of discord: Rome and its civil wars* (2010) 45–67, at 46 and n. 4.

[2] I am assuming that the historical writings of Julius Caesar, which are roughly a decade earlier, belong to the different genre of the *commentarius*, although this assumption is disputed (e.g. by D. Noussec, 'Genres and generic contaminations: the *Commentarii*', in Grillo and Krebs 103–8). The years 63–43 are the subject of K. Volk's *Roman republic of letters* (2021), but Sallust, says the author, 'does not belong to the period and cast of characters at the center of this book' (193).

[3] The fragments are available in three magnificent volumes (*FRHist*) under the general editorship of T. J. Cornell, where English translations and commentary may also be found. The first Roman prose historian is Fabius Pictor, a contemporary of the Second Punic War (218–201 BC), but whether he wrote in Greek (as usually thought) or Latin or both is disputed (see *LH* 4–22) and the exact period at which he wrote is unknown. We should remember that historical events also featured in epic poetry, such as the *Bellum Poenicum* of Naevius and the *Annales* of Ennius.

[4] For discussion see *LH* 28–37.

1 SALLUST

The birth of C. Sallustius Crispus at Amiternum, a town in Sabine country roughly 50 miles north-east of Rome, is generally thought to have taken place in 86 BC, the year given by St Jerome:[5] he was thus exactly twenty years younger than Cicero, born in 106, and an almost exact contemporary of Catullus, whose date of birth is conventionally given as 84. The so-called Social War between Rome and her Italian allies (*socii*) had ended shortly before Sallust's birth but was followed by an outbreak of civil war as the consuls of 87, Cn. Octavius and L. Cornelius Cinna, fought each other in the so-called 'Bellum Octauianum'. In the same year Sulla, who had been one of the consuls in 88, left Rome to campaign against Mithridates in the east, while at Rome his enemy Marius was elected consul for the seventh time. Although Marius died at the start of 86, the antagonism between supporters of the two men continued until Sulla returned to Rome and at the end of 82 defeated the Marians at the battle of the Colline Gate (5.6n., 11.4n.). In 81 Sulla as dictator introduced the proscriptions for which he was long remembered; he retired in 80 or 79 and died shortly thereafter. In 78 there followed another civil war whose chief features would find uncanny parallels in Catiline's war fifteen years later (4.4n.).[6]

Sir Ronald Syme, whose *Sallust* remains the standard anglophone discussion of the author after almost six decades,[7] set great store by historians who had political experience.[8] Sallust tells us himself that he was drawn to politics at an early age: his self-description (3.3 'studio ad rem publicam latus sum') closely resembles Plutarch's portrait of another ambitious non-metropolitan politician, the young Cicero (*Cic.* 5.1 ἐλπίδων μεστὸς ἐπὶ τὴν πολιτείαν φερόμενος, 'swept full of hope towards political life').[9] Both were

5 Jer. *Chron.* p. 151 Helm. Sallust's full name is given in various of the MSS (e.g. P, one of the two oldest) as well as elsewhere (e.g. *Bell. Afr.* 8.3, 34.1). There is an excellent brief account of his life and career in Ramsey (2013) xv–xxvii; a more detailed account is found in the early pages of Syme, *Sall.*, and in J. Malitz, *Ambitio mala. Studien zur politischen Biographie des Sallust* (1974). A valuable collection of source material on Sallust's life, career and the like has been assembled by Duursma 184–9.

6 For an account of the 80s and later see *CAH* 9; for the continuing memory of Marius and Sulla see Rosenblitt *passim*, also e.g. Morstein-Marx 110–13.

7 The book was reissued in 2002 with a new foreword by R. Mellor; equally wide-ranging is A. La Penna, *Sallustio e la rivoluzione romana* (1968). Selected discussions of aspects of Sallust's works have been reprinted in *OR*; brief accounts of his work will be found in C. S. Kraus and A. J. Woodman, *Latin historians* (*G&R* New Surveys in the Classics 27, 1997) 10–50. A. Feldherr, *After the past: Sallust on history and writing history* (2021), is a theoretically sophisticated study of Sallust's two monographs. A *Cambridge companion to Sallust* is forthcoming.

8 See e.g. 'The senator as historian' in *Ten studies in Tacitus* (1970) 1–10.

9 For origins outside Rome see 31.7n.

'new men' (*noui homines*), lacking all the advantages of a political pedigree and compelled to rely on their own merits if they were to make a success of their proposed careers: 'mihi spes omnes in memet sitae', as Marius, another *nouus homo*, is made to say in the speech attributed to him by Sallust (*BJ* 85.4).[10]

Sallust's first attested office at Rome is the tribunate of the plebs in 52;[11] whether he had previously held the quaestorship (usually the rank which secured admission to the senate) is unknown, but it is generally assumed that he did. Asconius, the first-century AD commentator on Cicero to whom a great deal of historical information is owed,[12] tells us that Sallust and two of his colleagues in the tribunate held public meetings (*contiones*) attacking T. Annius Milo, a candidate for the consulship who, in an episode which typified the violence and chaos of the times, had killed P. Clodius Pulcher on 18 January; since Cicero had agreed to defend Milo, he too was subjected to verbal attack (Ascon. 37.18–23).[13] Sallust perhaps had a personal reason for his antipathy towards Milo, since there was a story that he had been discovered in adultery with Milo's wife – the infamous Fausta, daughter of Sulla – and had been flogged by the injured husband.[14] Whatever the truth of the story, two years later, in 50, Sallust was expelled from the senate by the censor, Appius Claudius Pulcher, for reasons which are unknown (Dio 40.63.4);[15] it is perhaps this misfortune to which he makes oblique allusion with the statement that in his political career he found 'many things against me' (3.3).

Early the next year Julius Caesar with his army crossed the river Rubicon in northern Italy, marking the start of civil war and a series of famous battles. Sallust was commanding a legion for Caesar in Illyricum in that year and he shared in the general defeat suffered there by the Caesarian forces at the hands of the Pompeians.[16] Pompey himself was defeated in the summer of 48 at the battle of Pharsalus in central Greece.

[10] For everything relating to *noui homines* see Wiseman.
[11] *MRR* 2.236. See also D. C. Earl, 'The early career of Sallust', *Historia* 15 (1966) 302–11.
[12] The commentary by R. G. Lewis (2006) is due to be replaced by that of J. T. Ramsey; see also B. Santalucia, *Asconio. Commento alle orazioni di Cicerone* (2022). The evidence that Asconius wrote a life of Sallust (Pseudo-Acro on Hor. *S.* 1.2.41) is doubted by Syme (*Sall.* 282, 298).
[13] For violence see 14.1n.; for the incident itself see W. J. Tatum, *The patrician tribune: Publius Clodius Pulcher* (1999) 212–14, T. J. Keeline, *Cicero: Pro Milone* (2021), esp. 6–18.
[14] For this story, the details of which are complicated and confusing, see *PH* 116–20.
[15] It is usually assumed that the censor's motives were political. On the whole subject see L. C. Moore, *Ex senatu eiecti sunt: expulsion from the senate of the Roman republic, c. 319–50 BC* (Diss. London, 2013).
[16] *MRR* 2.266, 269.

The following summer Sallust, by now in Campania, was almost killed by
the mutinous troops with whom he was attempting to negotiate on
Caesar's behalf (App. *BC* 2.92.387); Dio adds that at the time he had
been elected to the praetorship for 46 'in order to recover his senatorial
rank' (42.52.2).[17] As praetor he was in Africa with Caesar, who sent him to
secure corn supplies from the island of Cercina off the coast (*Bell. Afr.*
34.3). After the battle of Thapsus in the spring of 46 Caesar appointed him
proconsular governor of Africa Nova, a new province constituted from
part of the former kingdom of King Juba of Numidia (*Bell. Afr.* 97.1,
App. *BC* 2.100.415).[18] We are told that in this role Sallust enriched himself
by extortion (Dio 43.9.2–3). Since as consul in 59 Caesar had carried
a new provincial extortion law,[19] and since as dictator he had removed
from the senate those who had been convicted of extortion (Suet. *DJ*
43.1), Sallust was in some danger of being expelled from the senate
a second time. Yet when on his return to Rome in 45 he was charged
with his malfeasance in Africa, he escaped another disgrace probably
through the influence of Caesar himself, whom he is alleged to have
bribed from his African profits (cf. [Cic.] *Sall.* 19, Dio 43.9.3, 43.47.4);[20]
nevertheless, when he says that he decided he should leave public life
(4.1), we may infer that there was no decision to make: his career in
politics was at an end.

That the *Bellum Catilinae* was Sallust's first work of history is clear from
the preface, where a defence of writing – as opposed to participating in –
history (1.1–3.2) is followed by an elliptical apologia for his own political
career (3.3–4.2). The defence of historiography is extremely elaborate,
leaving little doubt that, despite the dangers and miseries associated with
public life (4.1), he greatly regretted his enforced retirement from the
career of honours. We do not know when Sallust wrote the work, but
Caesar (d. March 44) seems no longer to be alive (cf. 53.6); whether
Cicero's death (December 43) had also taken place is unclear but seems
likely: indeed the killing of an admired leading statesman, with its implications for Sallust's own day,[21] may well have been a motivating factor in
his decision to write. Scholars assign publication of the work to 42
(the year Brutus and Cassius were defeated by Mark Antony and the future

[17] A. Mehl supports the view that Sallust never held the praetorship and that his
re-entry to the senate was effected by a second quaestorship (*Roman historiography* (2011) 85), but the evidence for this is no better than for a first
quaestorship (see Pina Polo and Díaz Fernández 307).
[18] See *MRR* 2.296, 298, 309.   [19] *MRR* 2.188.
[20] See *TLRR* 179 no. 383. His African profits are also thought to have made
possible the purchase of the famous *Horti Sallustiani* in Rome: see
K. Hartswick, *The gardens of Sallust* (2004).
[21] See 51.36n. (*alio*), evidence of the truism that 'all history is contemporary
history'.

emperor Augustus at Philippi) or a little later, followed within the next couple of years by a second monograph, the *Bellum Iugurthinum*.[22] The charismatic and ambitious Jugurtha was a Numidian prince whose murderous political intriguing eventually led to war with Rome (111–105 BC). Sallust introduces the work as follows (*BJ* 5.1–2):

> The war I am about to write is that which the Roman people waged with Jugurtha, king of the Numidians, first because it was great and frightening and of only spasmodic success, then because that was the first time the haughtiness of the nobility was confronted – and the latter struggle convulsed everything, divine and human alike, and advanced to such a point of derangement that the citizens' passions ended in war and the devastation of Italy.

The nobility's virtual monopoly of power, position and resources is one of Sallust's constant complaints and, in his view, led to the conflicts which he was witnessing in his own generation.[23]

Sallust's final work was the now fragmentary *Historiae*, a traditionally structured annalistic account of 'res populi Romani … militiae et domi gestas' (1.1).[24] Book 1 begins in 78 BC and described the mutual antagonism of the year's two consuls, M. Aemilius Lepidus and Q. Lutatius Catulus.[25] Lepidus was allotted one or both of the Gauls as his province for the following year,[26] but, after taking up his command, was summoned back to Rome thanks to the machinations of his enemies. His response was to assemble an army in Etruria and march on Rome, whereupon the senate decreed that the authorities 'should provide protection for the City and see to it that no harm come to the *res publica*' (*H.* 1.67.22). Lepidus found Catulus and other leaders waiting for him at the Mulvian Bridge, where he

---

[22] On which there is a heavyweight commentary in German by E. Koestermann (1971); the school edition by L. Watkiss (1971) is extremely helpful, as is the self-styled 'historical commentary' by G. M. Paul (1984); the commentary by M. Comber and C. Balmaceda (2009) has a facing English translation. J. Wisse and F. Santangelo are preparing a new commentary for the series Cambridge Greek and Latin Classics. See also *OR* 244–315.

[23] For a recent discussion of the *nobiles* see Mouritsen, *RE* 201–36.

[24] There is a modern (largely historical) commentary by P. McGushin (2 vols., 1992–4) and another in progress by A. La Penna and R. Funari (Vol. 1, 2015). See also *OR* 340–99, J. Gerrish, *Sallust's* Histories *and triumviral historiography: confronting the end of history* (2019), and Rosenblitt *passim*.

[25] It is thought likely that by starting in 78 Sallust was continuing from where a previous historian, Sisenna (cf. *BJ* 95.2), had left off (Marincola 291–2, Briscoe in *FRHist* 1.308). Sallust may have chosen his title because Sisenna's work too was called *Historiae* (C. B. Krebs, 'The buried tradition of programmatic titulature among republican historians: Polybius' Πραγματεία, Asellio's *Res gestae*, and Sisenna's redefinition of *Historiae*', *AJP* 136 (2015) 503–24, at 519–20).

[26] The matter is controversial: see Rafferty 175–7 for discussion.

was defeated and put to flight (cf. *H.* 1.70); subsequently he was declared an outlaw (*hostis*).[27] The latest event in the *Historiae* is dated to 67 and occurs in Book 5 (5.20); whether that year was Sallust's intended conclusion is uncertain.[28] It is widely assumed that the *Historiae* is a 'lost masterpiece',[29] but this assumption should not be allowed to downplay the interest and importance of the two earlier works. Sallust's death is placed in 36 or 35 by St Jerome,[30] a suspicious half-century after his birth.[31]

Sallust's transition from thematic to more strictly narrative historiography over the course of seven books is oddly reminiscent of the elder Cato, who in his seven-book *Origines* seems to have made a similar transition from the theme of origins to historical narrative;[32] but whether this similarity is a further manifestation of Sallust's well-known imitation of Cato (below) cannot be known. Cato enjoyed a reputation as a champion of moral rectitude, and each of Sallust's three works includes a fierce denunciation of contemporary society in contrast with the morality of earlier times.[33] The hypocrisy of this stance, from one whose own life scarcely

[27] The details of the crisis differ from source to source (see e.g. *CAH* 9.208–10, P. Burton, 'The revolt of Lepidus (cos. 78 BC) revisited', *Historia* 63 (2014) 404–21, Rosenblitt 45–79).
[28] The notion is supported by the fact that the earliest date in the main narrative of the *Bellum Catilinae* is the following year, 66 (18.2); for other possibilities see e.g. Syme, *Sall.* 191–2. Ausonius' reference to 'bis senos . . . annos' (*Protrep. ad Nepotem* 63) indicates merely the span of the work as he found it, not Sallust's intention. See further Stover and Woudhuysen.
[29] Syme, *Sall.* 179.
[30] Jer. *Chron.* p. 159 Helm. The entry appears under the year 36 accompanied by the words *quadriennio ante Actiacum bellum* (see Ramsey (2013) xvi–xvii).
[31] Also attributed to Sallust are (a) a short invective, *In M. Tullium Ciceronem Oratio*, to which the pseudo-Ciceronian *In C. Sallustium Crispum Oratio* is a response, (b) two short works under the title *Ad Caesarem Senem de Re Publica*. The Latin texts may be found in Reynolds' OCT of Sallust; the latter two are translated by J. M. Carter, *Sallust and Pseudo-Sallust* (LACTOR 6, 1970) 30–45, and Ramsey (2015) 473–527; see also A. A. Novokhatko, *The invectives of Sallust and Cicero: critical edition with introduction, translation, and commentary* (2009). Sallustian authorship is often doubted (see e.g. Fraenkel; R. G. M. Nisbet, *JRS* 48 (1958) 30–2; Syme, *Sall.* 313–51) and sometimes defended (see e.g. F. Pina Polo, *Hermes* 149 (2021) 177–205). It is perhaps to one or more of these works that reference is made at Sen. *Contr.* 3 *pr.* 8 'orationes Sallustii in honorem historiarum leguntur'. The invective against Cicero is self-evidently an *oratio*; the two works *Ad Caesarem* are conventionally described as 'letters' and entitled *Epistulae* by modern editors, but neither has formal epistolary markers and the first of them is indistinguishable from a speech (and was indeed entitled *Oratio* by H. Jordan in his edition). Seneca's words do not of course prove Sallustian authorship.
[32] Whether Cato devoted the first three books to origins and the remaining four to narrative, or adopted some other arrangement, is uncertain: for discussion of the various hypotheses see Cornell in *FRHist* 1.198–217.
[33] See Earl, *PTS*, esp. 45. For Cato see Levene, *OR* 215 and n. 5.

bore scrutiny, was not lost on later readers (e.g. Gell. 17.18, Dio 43.9.2–3, Macrob. 3.13.9).[34]

2 CATILINE

In the famous boat race in Book 5 of the *Aeneid*, one of the competitors is called Sergestus, 'from whom', says Virgil, 'the Sergian family derives its name' (121 'Sergestusque, domus tenet a quo Sergia nomen'). 'And Sergius Catilina belongs to it', adds Servius, the fifth-century commentator on Virgil ('et inde est Sergius Catilina').[35] Virgil, whose epic is full of such aetiologies,[36] was acknowledging a patrician *gens*, that is, a family from the most ancient aristocracy of Rome.[37] Republican history knows several Sergii, of whom the most distinguished was L. Sergius Fidenas in the fifth century BC,[38] although M. Sergius Silus, praetor in 197, was a disabled war hero (5.1n., 31.7n.). The latter was the great-grandfather of L. Sergius Catilina, the subject of the *Bellum Catilinae*: although the work contains details (whether true or false) about Catiline's personal life, as a general rule we have only scanty and inferential information about his origins and early career, involving allegations of murder (including fratricide), participation in the Sullan proscriptions, and sexual outrages.[39] If he held the praetorship in 68, as is usually assumed,[40] he will have been the same, or almost the same, age as his eventual nemesis, Cicero, born in 106.[41] An inscription records that on 17 November 89 one 'L. Sergius',

[34] The C. Sallustius Crispus who received an ode from Horace (2.2) and was a powerful minister of the emperor Augustus was Sallust's grand-nephew, whom he adopted. He died in AD 20 (Tac. *A.* 3.30.2–3 and W–M ad loc.).

[35] For Servius see Zetzel 131–42 and 262–3, whose work is an invaluable guide to the ancient grammarians and commentators.

[36] See J. J. O'Hara, *True names* ([2]2017) (pp. 109 and 160 for this example); Catiline himself appears once in the poem, as a great criminal being punished in the Underworld (*Aen.* 8.668).

[37] For patricians see Cornell, *BR*, esp. 242–71.

[38] See Ogilvie on Liv. 3.35.11 and 4.17.7; Urso 63–4. The *gens* effectively disappears from our records almost completely for around 150 years; when it resurfaces later, it is just a handful of figures holding mostly low-level offices.

[39] There is a slim biography by B. Levick, *Catiline* (2015), and a much fuller treatment by Urso; the most recent study is L. Canfora, *Catilina. Una rivoluzione mancata* (2023), which I have not seen. Note also Berry, *CC* 1–55, and the Commentary on 5.1–7 and 14–15.

[40] Since Catiline was eligible to stand for the consulship in 66 (Ascon. 89.6–11), his praetorship cannot be dated later than 68 (see *MRR* 2.138, 141 n. 7).

[41] So e.g. Brennan 2.545. A praetorship in 68 would normally mean a birth date no later than 108; but some scholars believe that patricians were entitled to hold the senior magistracies two years early (E. Badian, *Studies in Greek and Roman history* (1964) 140–56), which would bring Catiline's birth down to 106, the same year as Cicero.

presumably the young Catiline, was at Asculum in central Italy as
a member of the *consilium* of the consul, Cn. Pompeius Strabo (*ILS*
8888); also serving under Strabo at the same time was the young Cicero,
as he tells us himself (*Phil.* 12.27). In Sallust's fragmentary *Historiae* we are
told that an unnamed commander 'began the siege through the agency of
the legate, L. Catilina' (1.47 'obsidium coepit per L. Catilinam legatum').[42]
We are given neither the location of the siege nor its date nor the name of
the commander, although some have seen a reference to 82 BC, when the
Sullan forces under Q. Lucretius Afella successfully besieged Praeneste,
later to be a stronghold of the Catilinarians (Cic. *Cat.* 1.8).[43] In the
following year Sulla as dictator fell out with Afella because, despite having
held no previous magistracy, he 'was seeking the consulship against Sulla's
wishes in order to disrupt the *status ciuitatis*' (Ascon. 91.3–5 'consulatum
contra uoluntatem Sullae ad turbandum statum ciuitatis petentem'): Sulla
had him killed as he was campaigning in the forum. Neither Afella's ambition nor Sulla's method of operating would be lost on Catiline.

Asconius tells us (85.3) that Catiline governed the province of Africa
after his praetorship (cf. also Cic. *Cael.* 10). His governorship (67–66 BC)
was so rapacious that, even before his term of office was completed, envoys
were sent to the senate to complain of his behaviour (Ascon. 85.3–6), and
on his return to Rome he was duly charged with extortion. Catiline also put
himself forward for the consulship of 65, although his candidature was
disqualified on a technicality (18.3n.). It was at this point, according to
Sallust (18–19), that he embarked on the so-called 'First Conspiracy',
which most modern scholars, largely on the basis of a misreading of the
evidence, wrongly believe never to have taken place.[44] Catiline linked up
with P. Autronius Paetus, another disqualified consular candidate, and,
around 5 December 66, the two rejects, having communicated their plan
to a Cn. Piso, were preparing to murder the incoming consuls, L. Aurelius
Cotta and L. Manlius Torquatus, on 1 January 65, to seize the *fasces* for
themselves, and to send Piso to Spain to hold the two provinces there on
their behalf (18.5). But a failure of secrecy meant that they were obliged to
defer the coup to 5 February 65 (18.6), when they now intended to
murder not only the consuls but also numerous senators (18.7). But
Catiline gave the signal for the coup prematurely, the plot was abandoned
entirely (18.8) and he returned to his normal political activity. When his

[42] See *MRR* 2.72, 3.192.
[43] Everything about this fragment is controversial and disputed: see the notes of
McGushin ('Praeneste is out of the question') and La Penna and Funari,
whose numbering is respectively 1.46 and 1.51.
[44] See Woodman (2021a) 55–63, and the Commentary on 18–19.

trial for extortion took place in the second half of 65, he was 'scandalously' acquitted (Ascon. 89.16–17 'per infamiam').[45]

The First Conspiracy set the pattern for the three remaining years of Catiline's life, a detailed narrative of which is principally to be found in the *Bellum Catilinae*. Sallust depicts him as plotting military revolution from mid-64 onwards,[46] while at the same time putting himself forward as a candidate for the consulship of 63 (17, 20–3). It was evidently after the elections of 64, where Cicero and C. Antonius Hybrida were the successful candidates (24.1), that Catiline found himself on trial again, this time for complicity in the murder of those proscribed under Sulla: the prosecutor was L. Lucceius, who had perhaps been praetor in 67, but once more Catiline was acquitted.[47] In 63 he was a candidate for the consulship of 62 (26.1), but, when the elections were held in September of that year,[48] this third candidacy also ended in failure and he set in motion the civil war for which he had long been planning (26.5). The crisis which developed between October and December of that year may be followed both in the monograph of Sallust (27–55) and in the Catilinarian speeches of Cicero,[49] who as consul effected the red-handed entrapment of most of the ringleaders who were in the city (2–3 December): the senate voted for their execution, which was carried out with immediate effect (5 December), while Catiline himself, pursued and surrounded by the forces of the *res publica*, died in battle just north of modern Pistoia early in 62 (61.4).[50]

It will be noted that there exists a curious parallelism between Catiline and Sallust: both had progressed along the *cursus honorum* as far as the praetorship; both had proceeded thereafter to a governorship in Africa,

---

[45] *TLRR* 106–7 no. 212. The majority verdict was said to have been influenced by collusion between prosecution and defence (cf. Cic. *Att.* 1.2(11).1 and Shackleton Bailey ad loc.).

[46] Most modern scholars do not believe that Catiline was plotting as early as 64; *contra* Stone (1998), Woodman (2021a) 63–5.

[47] See *TLRR* 108–9 no. 217.   [48] For the date see Ramsey (2019).

[49] In Berry's opinion these speeches 'are later recreations by Cicero' which can be read 'entirely as productions of 60 BC', displaying 'contradictions and repetitions', and readers should 'suspend their critical faculties' when reading 'careless' passages (*CC* 87–8, 73, 174–5); but such judgements are hard to reconcile with the statement that these same speeches 'are certainly, as Cicero himself says, models of oratory for his young admirers' (Berry, *CC* 81, with ref. to *Att.* 2.1.3).

[50] In addition to Cicero and Sallust, the principal sources for the Catilinarian conspiracy are Suet. *DJ* 14, Plut. *Cic.* 10.3–12.1, 14.1–22.8, *Cato min.* 22–24.2, *Caes.* 7.5–8.5, App. *BC* 2.2.4–7.25, Dio 37.29–42. Note too Diod. 40.5–5a (discussed by G. Urso, 'Catilina "avant Salluste": remarques sur deux fragments de Diodore de Sicile', in O. Devillers and B. B. Sebastiani (edd.), *Sources et modèles des historiens anciens* (2018) 139–54).

where both had practised extortion on a scale which led to charges on their return to Rome; and both were political outcasts, Catiline having been repeatedly rejected at the consular polls, Sallust having experienced actual and threatened expulsions from the senate. Their moral trajectories as depicted by Sallust were the converse of each other, but therein too there lay interest: whereas Sallust confessed to having been corrupted by contemporary society (3.4–5), a familiar enough pattern, Catiline was someone whose innate evil and crookedness (5.1 'ingenio malo prauoque') did not prevent him from a brave and heroic death (60.4–61.4: see below). Whether these similarities had any bearing on Sallust's choice of subject is a matter for speculation, but 'transference' or 'automimesis' is a recognised feature of biographical writing,[51] a genre with which the *Bellum Catilinae* has much in common.[52]

3 THE *BELLVM CATILINAE*

Convinced that by his pre-emptive actions he had saved Rome from a terrible disaster, Cicero spent the remaining twenty years of his life reminding people of his achievement.[53] In addition to publishing his Catilinarian speeches,[54] in 62 he encouraged the poet Archias to complete a poem on the suppression of the conspiracy (*Arch.* 28), although by the summer of 61 the poem remained unfinished (*Att.* 1.16.15). On 15 March 60 Cicero sent his friend Atticus a *commentarius* of his consulship in Greek prose and promised that, if he wrote a Latin version, he would send that too (*Att.* 1.19.10; cf. 1.20(20).6).[55] In early June he wrote again to Atticus, explaining that he had sent a copy of the *commentarius* to the philosopher and historian Posidonius too in the hope – which was not to be realised – that he would use it as the basis of a more elaborate account of

[51] See T. Hägg, *The art of biography in antiquity* (2012) 5–6. Syme remarked that for such personalities as Catiline and Jugurtha 'Sallust betrays an insight verging on sympathy' (*Sall.* 269).

[52] Comparing Sallust's monographs with Tacitus' *Agricola*, Leo neatly said that 'Sallust has introduced biographical elements into history, Tacitus historical elements into biography', but he badly understated the extent to which Catiline is featured in the monograph (F. Leo, *Die griechisch-römische Biographie nach ihrer literarischen Form* (1901) 232).

[53] Some scholars have argued that the whole affair was fabricated by Cicero for his own self-glorification (K. H. Waters, 'Cicero, Sallust and Catiline', *Historia* 19 (1970) 195–215, R. Seager, 'Iusta Catilinae', *Historia* 22 (1973) 240–8), a hypothesis which flies in the face of common sense (see also E. J. Phillips, 'Catiline's conspiracy', *Historia* 25 (1976) 441–8). On 26 October 2023 a moot trial of Cicero was held in the UK Supreme Court, presided over by a Justice of the Court, at which he was accused of murder and misconduct in public office. He was acquitted.

[54] See Woodman (2021b) 1–3.   [55] See Drummond in *FRHist* 1.370–6.

his own (*Att.* 2.1.1). By the end of the year Cicero had written a three-book hexameter poem in Latin entitled *Consulatus Suus* (*Att.* 2.3.4),[56] but two years later, in 58, he was forced into exile by Clodius' law banishing anyone who had put Roman citizens to death without trial. Although this bitter experience lasted little more than a year, it made the great orator even more determined to argue the rectitude of his actions when consul. It was perhaps after his return from exile, as Dio suggests (39.10.2–3), that Cicero wrote another prose work, this time in Latin, to which modern scholars currently give the title *Consilia*.[57] The work, of which only one verbatim fragment survives,[58] was of a character that Cicero thought its publication best suppressed until after his death; although the scope of the work is unknown, it may safely be inferred that it included material on the year of his consulship. We know from letters of the mid-50s that Cicero wrote a second poem in Latin entitled *De temporibus suis* (*Att.* 4.8a.3, *Fam.* 1.9.23): since it dealt with his exile in 58, it is very likely that it included at least some reference to Catiline's war.

Posidonius was not the only writer to whom Cicero suggested his consulship as a literary theme. In the spring of 55 BC he wrote a letter to the same L. Lucceius who had prosecuted Catiline in 64 and who, having retired from politics, had now, like Sallust, turned to history (*Fam.* 5.12.1–6).[59] The now-famous letter, cajoling Lucceius to make Cicero the hero of a monograph on the Catilinarian episode, is a brilliant combination of flattery and humour and Cicero himself was very pleased with it (*Att.* 4.6.4), but, as far as is known, Lucceius did not succumb to his outrageous blandishments; the writer who took up the challenge was Sallust, and it was Catiline whom he decided to put centre stage.[60]

This decision, coupled with the fact that Sallust makes no explicit reference to any of Cicero's *Catilinarians* except the first (31.6),[61] has

---

[56] See Courtney, *FLP* 156–73; Berry, *CC* 158–62.
[57] See Drummond in *FRHist* 1.376–9, 2.770–3, 3.478–82.
[58] See *LH* 58–60.   [59] See Drummond in *FRHist* 1.335–7.
[60] Whether Sallust knew of Cicero's letter is uncertain. D. R. Shackleton Bailey acknowledges that letters of especial brilliance, such as *Fam.* 5.12, would be candidates for early publication (*Cicero's letters to Atticus* (1965) Vol. 1, pp. 59–73, at 60). One of Pollio's fragments (7C/5P) seems to echo *Fam.* 5.21.4 (*LH* 74).
[61] If Cicero delivered the *Fourth Catilinarian* when *introducing* the debate on 5 December (as argued by Woodman (2021b) 10), rather than halfway through (as is usually assumed), there is an oblique reference to the speech at 50.3 'consul ... refert quid de iis fieri placeat qui in custodiam traditi erant'; see also 48.1n. (*coniuratione*) for a possible allusion to the *Third Catilinarian*. For an extended discussion of the *Catilinarians* see Berry, *CC*, esp. 194–202; for their fame in antiquity see also T. J. Keeline, *The reception of Cicero in the early Roman empire* (2018) 80–1, 153.

led some scholars to infer that Sallust harboured a dislike of Cicero,[62] but the evidence of the work itself tells against this.[63] From the very start of his consulship Cicero is shown to be impressively supplied with intelligence about Catiline's plans (26.3) and always one step ahead of the enemies of the *res publica*. Thanks to Curius' information, Cicero is able to take precautions against being assassinated (28.2–3), thanks to Sanga's assistance he is able to involve the Allobroges (41.5), thanks to Gabinius he is able to set up the trap at the Mulvian Bridge (45.1). Throughout the course of events Cicero is 'fully informed' (45.1 'cuncta edoctus');[64] and, although he is allowed to reflect forebodingly on the future (46.2), the reflection is elliptical and fleeting: there is no reference anywhere in the narrative to Cicero's exile, no suggestion that the consul got what he deserved.[65] In the *Bellum Catilinae* Sallust 'aligned himself with Cicero, saviour of the Republic in 63 BCE and martyr to it in 43 BCE'.[66]

(a) Structure, Character, 'Political Thought'

Taking their cue from Cicero's letter to Lucceius, scholars once suggested that the *Bellum Catilinae* is structured like a Greek drama,[67] but, while the genres of historiography and tragedy undoubtedly had much in common,[68] the suggestion fails to accommodate various features of the narrative.[69] The more straightforward outline below seems a better reflection of the text: after the preface (1–16) the main narrative begins with a specific date in mid-64 BC (17.1) and continues in more or less strict chronological order until Catiline's last stand and death (59–61), which are known to have taken place in early 62 (Dio 37.39.1):[70]

---

[62] See the brief survey of opinion in La Bua 102–4, adding Y. Baraz, 'Lucan's Cicero', *CQ* 71 (2021) 721–40, at 724–5.

[63] Note esp. Sallust's treatment of the execution of Lentulus and the other conspirators (55.6): in general see the penetrating analysis by Stone (1999), esp. 53 and (on Lentulus) 72–5; also Berry, *CC* xxi–xxiii.

[64] See Pina Polo 325.

[65] 'No writer of antiquity implies that Sallust's portrayal of Cicero in the *Bellum Catilinae* was in any way malicious or unfair' (Syme, *Sall.* 287).

[66] Stone (2014) 248.

[67] E.g. R. Reitzenstein, *Hellenistische Wundererzählungen* (1906) 87–8, R. Ullmann, 'Essai sur le Catilina de Salluste', *Rev. Phil.* 42 (1918) 5–27, at 11–13. Cicero had referred to 'hanc quasi fabulam rerum euentorumque nostrorum', which 'habet ... uarios actus multasque mutationes et consiliorum et temporum' (*Fam.* 5.12.6).

[68] See R. Rutherford, 'Tragedy and history', *CGRH* 504–14.

[69] See e.g. Latte, *OR* 54–5, though his own analysis is also unconvincing.

[70] The broad chronological ordering should be clear, but there are local complications within some of the sections (see esp. 27–32.2 intro. n.).

No special claim is made for this outline, which is only one of many that have been proposed,[71] but it highlights a striking feature of the work as a whole. When deploring the failure of rewards or amnesty to encourage informers or deserters (36.5, 39.5), Sallust inserts a substantial digression on socio-political degeneration at Rome (37.1–39.4): this digression occurs at precisely the halfway point of the monograph and, although its placement immediately before (rather than immediately after) the end of a coherent sequence on informers and deserters is admittedly strange (39.5: see p. 226), it has the formal effect of dividing the monograph into two halves of identical length. The notion of such a division is encouraged by the fact that in each half there is a further formal digression (18–19 ~ 53.2–54.6) and in each there is a *hortatio* from Catiline (20–1 ~ 58). Yet the division of the work into two parallel halves, a division possibly suggested by Thucydidean practice,[72] is not merely formal: the central digression suspends the narrative at a crucial point in the story. Catiline, arming the *ager Arretinus* and arrogating to himself the role of consul, is declared a public enemy (*hostis*), while the consul Antonius is to pursue him with an army and the other consul (Cicero) is to protect the city of Rome (36.1–3); yet neither these measures nor the offers of rewards or amnesty encourage disloyalty in a single one of Catiline's followers (36.4–5). The momentum seems to be entirely in the Catilinarians' favour. It is only after the narrative resumes (39.5) that they make the fatal mistake of trying to enlist the help of the Allobroges (40.1) and the tide of events turns in favour of the *res publica*.

[71] See e.g. K. Vretska, 'Der Aufbau des Bellum Catilinae', *Hermes* 72 (1937) 202–22 (= V. Pöschl (ed.), *Sallust* (²1981) 74–101), F. Giancotti, *Strutture delle monografie di Sallustio e di Tacito* (1971) 15–84, Ramsey 21–3.
[72] Cf. H. R. Rawlings, *The structure of Thucydides' history* (1981).

Although the creation of suspense is repeated in a similar fashion at
53.2–54.6, when the execution of the conspirators is deferred by another
digression, the *Bellum Catilinae* may be thought to lack the narrative power
that is found in Livy or Tacitus.[73] But Cicero's letter to Lucceius is only one
of numerous texts from which we know that ancient historians were
expected to provide a pleasurable narrative for their readers (*Fam.*
5.12.4–5 'uoluptatis … ad delectationem lectoris … iucundae …
delectationem … iucunda … delectat … iucundissima lectionis
uoluptate'),[74] and Sallust's monograph has the individual elements of
a gripping story, none of which would be out of place in a modern thriller:
clandestine meetings (17, 20–21, 27.3–4, 40.5–6), a female whistle-blower
(23.4, 26.3, 28.2), murder plots (18.5–8, 28.1–3, 43.2), emergency legislation (29.2–3, 53.1), 'courtroom' confrontations (31.4–9, 51–2), a night-
time ambush (45) and a climactic battle (57.5–61.9). There are brilliant
character sketches (5.1–8 Catiline, 25 Sempronia, 54 Caesar and Cato)
and deft delineations of horrific scenes: the drinking of human blood to
seal a secret oath (22), the underground dungeon where executions are
carried out (55.3–4), the turning over of corpses for the purposes of
identification (61.7–9). Counterfactual reflection invites the reader to
consider how things could have turned out differently (39.4), while the
ebb and flow of events is represented by a series of the reversals which
Cicero mentioned in his letter (23.5–24.1, 31.1, 48.1–2, 60.5).[75] The most
significant of these reversals is the last, which takes place contrary to
expectation – παρὰ προσδοκίαν (*para prosdokian*), a key feature of
Thucydides' narrative[76] – while the decisive final battle is in progress.

Before the battle begins, Catiline summons his troops to a meeting
(57.6) and delivers a rousing *hortatio* (58). He acknowledges the difficult circumstances in which his men find themselves, and he urges
them to fight in accordance with the *uirtus* which they have always
shown in the past. The speech is replete with the customary commonplaces (see the Commentary ad loc.) and much of it could have been
delivered by any of Rome's great generals, but, since in the damning
assessment of Catiline at the start of the monograph we were told that
his mind was 'subdolus, uarius, cuius rei libet simulator ac dissimulator' (5.4), the reader's instinct is to dismiss the speech as just so much

---

[73] Of course one should make allowances for the difficulties of describing
simultaneous events in different theatres of action within a restricted period
of time (27–32.2 intro. n.).

[74] See W.[5] on Tac. *A.* 4.33.3; also *RICH* 229 (index 'entertainment').

[75] For the importance of περιπέτεια (*peripeteia* or 'reversal') in classical historiography see e.g. J. Marincola, 'Odysseus and the historians', *SyllClass* 18 (2007)
37–47.

[76] See J. H. Finley, *Three essays on Thucydides* (1967) 140–9.

verbiage. That Catiline's opponent, Petreius, is indeed dismissive is clear from his response: he sees no need for an answering *hortatio* (as would often be the case in a historical narrative) but simply has a few private words with individual soldiers in indirect speech (59.5–6). Yet Petreius has badly miscalculated, since, once the fighting starts, Catiline's performance is faultless (60.4): he offers support to weakened areas, provides reinforcements where needed, anticipates what will happen and even fights himself, often striking the enemy ('multum ipse pugnare, saepe hostem ferire'). Well might Sallust remark that 'he performed simultaneously the responsibilities of a keen soldier and a good general' ('strenui militis et boni imperatoris officia simul exsequebatur'). Petreius – and the reader along with him – is compelled to think again (60.5): 'Petreius, ubi uidet Catilinam, *contra ac ratus erat . . .*'.

When all is at last lost, Catiline hurls himself upon the enemy and dies fighting bravely (60.7), and it was then that one could see how much boldness there had been in his army (61.1 'quanta audacia . . . fuisset in exercitu Catilinae'). As for the leader himself, he displayed in his dying look the defiance of spirit which he had shown in life (61.4 'ferociam . . . animi quam habuerat uiuus in uultu retinens'): the unmistakable recall of his character sketch at the start of the book, where mention was made of his defiant spirit (5.7 'animus ferox'), serves only to highlight the contrast between the man 'of evil and crooked disposition' who was described then (5.1) and the commander who dies a heroic death in his final battle. Although scholars no longer believe that the ancients regarded one's character as fixed at birth and subsequently immutable,[77] nevertheless the suddenness with which Catiline at the end of the book changes from life-long villain to admirable hero seems designed to draw readers' attention and to challenge their preconceptions.[78] This challenge involves consideration of Sallust's so-called 'political thought'.[79]

The passages of the *Bellum Catilinae* from which scholars have extracted evidence for Sallust's political thought are principally his preface (1–16)

[77] Among many other discussions, see esp. C. Gill, 'The question of character-development: Plutarch and Tacitus', *CQ* 33 (1983) 469–87, who notes *BC* 14.5 'adulescentium . . . animi molles etiam et fluxi'.
[78] For discussion of paradox or inconsistency in the portrayal of character see esp. A. La Penna, 'Il ritratto "paradossale" da Silla a Petronio', in his *Aspetti del pensiero storico Latino* (1978) 193–221 (Catiline on pp. 212–13); Levene, *LHW* 73–4, 174–5, 180–6. There is a monograph by A. T. Wilkins, *Villain or hero: Sallust's portrayal of Catiline* (1994). Ledworuski regards the character sketch as one of Sallust's 'primary factual contradictions' (73–101).
[79] The classic work is that of Earl, *PTS*. See also J. A. Rosenblitt, 'Sallust', in V. Arena and J. Prag (edd.), *A companion to the political culture of the Roman republic* (2022) 136–45.

and the central digression (37.1–39.4).[80] The preface begins with the assumption, which Sallust takes for granted, that man's aim in life is to achieve *gloria* (1.3), a topic on which Cicero had been writing as recently as 44 BC,[81] and Sallust, like Cicero,[82] sees *gloria* as the product of *uirtus* (1.4; cf. *BJ* 1.3 'ad gloriam uirtutis uia'), which, no matter what one's walk of life, is therefore an essential precondition (2.7 'uirtuti omnia parent'). *uirtus* had been present in the Roman state from the very beginning (6.5), and in the early days of the republic it had taken control of everything (7.5 'uirtus omnia domuerat') and was the area in which citizens competed with one another (9.2 'ciues cum ciuibus de uirtute certabant'); there was also a competition in *gloria*, and everyone hastened to be seen striking the enemy or scaling an enemy wall (7.6 'gloriae maximum certamen inter ipsos erat: se quisque hostem ferire, murum ascendere, conspici dum tale facinus faceret properabat'). It was by *audacia* in war and by fairness in peacetime that citizens looked after both themselves and the state (9.3 'duabus his artibus – audacia in bello, ubi pax euenerat aequitate – seque remque publicam curabant').

Yet such societal morality was not to last. Sallust says that everything began to fall apart after the destruction of Carthage, Rome's rival, in 146 BC (10.1), which is no doubt a reference to the notion, made explicit in his two later works, that it was the fear of Carthage that had sustained Roman morality for so long (*BJ* 41.2 'ante deletam Carthaginem ... metus hostilis in bonis artibus ciuitatem retinebat'; cf. *H.* 1.10, 1.12).[83] Thereafter *auaritia* supplanted the earlier good qualities (10.4 'auaritia ... artes bonas subuertit') and *ambitio* compelled citizens to be duplicitous in their dealings (10.5 'ambitio multos mortales falsos fieri subegit, aliud clausum in pectore, aliud in lingua promptum habere'). The process of moral decline was given impetus in the aftermath of Sulla's domination (11.4, 37.6–11), and, although some politicians championed the people and some the senate, in reality everyone was competing for his own power under the pretence of the common good (38.3 'bonum publicum simulantes pro sua quisque potentia certabant'). By the mid-60s

---

[80] Similarly in the *Bellum Iugurthinum* the evidence is found in the preface (1–4) and a digression (41–2). The prefaces have been discussed by E. Tiffou, *Essai sur la pensée morale de Salluste à la lumière de ses prologues* (1974), the digressions by Shaw, although his discussion is discursive, as his subtitle implies ('Historiography and intellectual life at Rome'); these works are respectively more than 600 and 500 pages in length.

[81] Cicero's *De Gloria* (cf. *Att.* 15.27.2, 16.2.6, 16.3.1, 16.6.4, *Off.* 2.31) is unfortunately lost.

[82] E.g. *Mil.* 97 'ex omnibus praemiis uirtutis ... amplissimum esse praemium gloriam'; Hellegouarc'h 371.

[83] Some scholars dispute that the reference in 10.1 is to *metus hostilis* and the destruction of Carthage (*contra* Earl, *PTS* 13–15, 41–2; Levene, *OR* 224–6).

magistracies and provinces were in the hands of a few powerful individuals (39.1–2), the result being that within living memory – by which Sallust means roughly the two decades from Cicero's consulship in 63 BC to the time of writing – only two individuals, the younger Cato and Julius Caesar, displayed 'mighty *uirtus*' (53.6 'ingenti uirtute'): the former competed in *uirtus* with the keen (54.6 'cum strenuo uirtute ... certabat'), while the latter kept craving a new war in which his *uirtus* could shine (54.4 'bellum nouum exoptabat ubi uirtus enitescere posset'). On many occasions there was no one at all in Rome who was 'great in *uirtus*' (53.5 'multis tempestatibus haud sane quisquam Romae uirtute magnus fuit').[84]

There is little, if anything, that is original about this analysis. Sallust's more cerebral remarks are merely the tenets of popular philosophy, sometimes expressed in apparent allusion to one or more Greek authors,[85] while his moral code is derived from those of Roman aristocrats and of the *noui homines* who desired to rival them.[86] That Roman history was a process of decline had been voiced by Polybius (31.25.3) and Calpurnius Piso (F36C/34P, 40C/38P), although Sallust's choice of 146 BC as the key turning point seems to be his own.[87] Yet, despite its conventional nature, Sallust's analysis helps to explain his presentation of Catiline. Sallust's association of *ambitio* with duplicity (10.5) suggests that the duplicitous Catiline (5.4) was a man possessed of *ambitio*, a *uitium* which Sallust discusses further at 11.1–2:

> uitium propius uirtutem erat: nam gloriam, honorem, imperium bonus et ignauus aeque sibi exoptant; sed ille uera uia nititur, huic, quia bonae artes desunt, dolis atque fallaciis contendit.

> It was a *uitium* quite close to *uirtus*: for the good man and the base have a similar personal craving for glory, honour and power, but the former strives along the true path, whereas the latter, because he lacks good qualities, presses forward by cunning and falsity.

That Sallust's Catiline had the same cravings as the *bonus* is clear from the first speech which the historian puts into his mouth: he places before his men a vision of *gloria*, *honor* (in the form of magistracies and priesthoods)

---

[84] Many scholars have agreed with Syme that in Sallust's scale of estimation '*virtus* is paramount' (*Sall.* 268). In general see M. McDonnell, *Roman manliness: virtus and the Roman republic* (2006), C. Balmaceda, *Virtus romana: politics and morality in the Roman historians* (2017) (ch. 2 on Sallust).

[85] See e.g. the work of Perrochat (some further bibliography in Renehan, *OR* 104–15).

[86] For these see Earl, *MPTR*, Wiseman 107–16 on 'the ideology of *novitas*'.

[87] See Walbank on Plb. 18.35.1 and 31.25.3; Earl, *PTS* 41–59 (= *OR* 85–103); Williams, *TORP* 619–33; Lintott (1972). The latest study is G. Vassiliades, *La res publica et sa décadence: de Salluste à Tite-Live* (2021), a work of 700 pages.

and the consulship for himself (20.14, 21.2–3). Nor did he lack good qualities, as is evident from the final battle: he strikes the enemy (60.4 'saepe hostem ferire') as did men of earlier generations (7.6 'hostem ferire'); his keenness (60.4 'strenui militis') is a quality he shares with Cato the Younger (54.6 'strenuo'); and the military *audacia* which he imparts to his army (61.1) is one of the two key *artes* by which the republic was formerly distinguished (9.3 'audacia in bello'). At the end of the monograph Catiline emerges as a man of 'potential *uirtus*',[88] who because of his *ambitio* failed to choose the right path ('uera uia'). Cato in his speech had said that there was now no distinction between good men and bad (52.22 'inter bonos et malos discrimen nullum'): that was an exaggeration, but Catiline's behaviour in the final battle is deliberately presented so as to provoke readers into reflecting on the narrowness of the distinction and into asking wherein the distinction lay.[89]

(b) Words and Deeds

The proportions of the *Bellum Catilinae* are such that – after the preface, digressions and direct speech have been taken into account – scarcely more than half of the work is devoted to actually advancing the story of Catiline's conspiracy.[90] Direct speech occupies more than a quarter of the monograph, a very high ratio:[91] the most striking example is the pair of long speeches put into the mouths of Caesar (51) and the younger Cato (52.2–36). The remaining speech is given exclusively to the conspirators: in addition to his two *hortationes* at 20.2–17[92] and 58 and his brief outburst at 31.9, Catiline himself is also responsible for a letter (35).[93] Further direct speech comes from Manlius (33),[94] while a letter from Lentulus (44.5) plays a crucial role in the dénouement of the story (46.6–47.3).

---

[88] T. F. Scanlon, *Spes frustrata: a reading of Sallust* (1987) 35.

[89] Thus the *Bellum Catilinae* is 'open-ended' (see 56–61 intro. n.), like the *Bellum Iugurthinum* (see Levene, *OR* 272–305); openness is also noted by P. López Barja de Quiroga, 'Sallust as a historian of civil war', in C. H. Lange and F. J. Vervaet (edd.), *The historiography of late republican civil war* (2019) 160–84, at 162 n. 10.

[90] Ramsey in his analysis (21–3) tries to distinguish between the various elements but does not indicate the proportion of text devoted to each.

[91] The exact figure is c. 26.7 per cent: this compares with 21.8 per cent for Thucydides' work as a whole, although some individual books are significantly higher (1 = c. 30%, 3 = c. 32%, 6 = c. 38%). I owe the comparative figures to C. B. R. Pelling. Evidently the Augustan historian Pompeius Trogus (below, p. 33) criticised Sallust and Livy for their use of direct speech (Just. 38.3.11).

[92] The *hortatio* continues in indirect speech (21.2–4).

[93] His letter is preceded by another one in indirect speech (34.2).

[94] For the question whether 33 is a speech or a letter see K. F. Williams, *CP* 95 (2000) 160–71. A letter about Manlius is reported at 30.1.

These remarkable statistics seem to underline metatextually the importance of words, the point with which Sallust begins his monograph (1.1–3.2
dicere, scripsere, scribere, dictis, dicta).

Catiline's two *hortationes* can only be inventions by Sallust, since the
former was held in secret (20.1 'omnibus arbitris procul amotis') and the
latter, if ever delivered at all, had taken place twenty years earlier on
a battlefield 200 miles distant from Rome. But the circumstances of the
senatorial debate on 5 December were very different: Cicero is said to have
arranged for a transcript to be made of the speech which Cato delivered
(Plut. *Cato Min.* 23.3; cf. Cic. *Att.* 12.21.1). Nevertheless the likelihood that
Sallust's version of the speech bears any relationship to what Cato actually
said is deemed by scholars to be very slim;[95] even Syme was sceptical.[96]
One dimension of the speech's inauthenticity is that Cato's dialogue with
Caesar is recognised to be modelled on the opposing speeches of Cleon
and Diodotus in Thucydides' account of the Mytilene Debate, which took
place in 427 BC (3.37–48).[97] The closer the modelling, the less likely it is
that Sallust describes what actually happened; it may even be the case that
he has transposed Caesar's speech from one day to another in order to
contrive the 'Thucydidean' confrontation with Cato.[98] Sallust's allusive
presentation of the debate, like his putting into Catiline's mouth words
which he did not utter, helps to illustrate the conceptual gulf which
separates ancient historiography from modern.[99]

Almost twenty years later, in the spring of 45 BC, Cicero complained to
his friend Atticus that Brutus, who was writing an account of Cato, was
badly mistaken in his view of how the crucial debate of 5 December 63 had
progressed (*Att.* 12.21.1; cf. 13.46.2). Sallust, an exact contemporary of
Brutus, was in his early twenties at the time of the conspiracy and, when he
relied on his own or others' memory for the events of that critical
period,[100] no doubt he too could make mistakes. The historian was also
intimately familiar with Cicero's Catilinarian speeches, as is clear from the

---

[95] See e.g. R. Brock, 'Versions, "inversions" and evasions: classical historiography and the "published" speech', *PLLS* 8 (1995) 209–24, at 212–13.
[96] Syme, *Sall.* 73.
[97] See Scanlon 102–8, 233 n. 224; and the Commentary ad loc.
[98] See Woodman (2021b) 9.
[99] For this see *RICH*, esp. 70–116 (= J. Marincola (ed.), *Oxford readings in
classical studies: Greek and Roman historiography* (2011) 241–90). The views
argued there have recently been subjected to generous discussion in Shaw's
book on Sallust (51–65), although the notion that my work 'draws on . . . the
ideas of Hayden White in particular' (55) is demonstrably false, as I pointed
out in *Histos* 2 (1998) 312–13. This canard is repeated in A. Damtoft Poulsen
and A. Jönsson (edd.), *Usages of the past in Roman historiography* (2021) 2 n. 2.
[100] Cf. such expressions as 14.7 'scio fuisse nonnullos qui ita existimarent', 17.7
'fuere item ea tempestate qui crederent', 19.4 'sunt qui ita dicant', 22.1
'fuere ea tempestate qui dicerent', 48.7 'erant eo tempore qui existimarent'.

many verbal similarities between the texts,[101] and one reason why Sallust
may not have wished to afford the speeches more formal exposure (above,
pp. 11–12) is that they provided him with much of his information about
the conspiracy. Ancient historical writers, as is well known, rarely mention
their sources. Sallust will also have absorbed various of Cicero's other
works, some of which relate to Catiline or the conspiracy (such as the *Pro
Caelio* or *Pro Sulla*):[102] the *Pro Murena*, delivered a mere two weeks before
the collapse of the conspiracy, is a particularly good example.[103] Likewise
his admiration for the younger Cato (53.6–54.6) presumably means that
he was acquainted with at least some of the encomiastic literature on Cato
that sprang up after the man's death, including a eulogy from Cicero
himself (Plut. *Caes.* 54.5–6), to say nothing about the *Anticato* of Julius
Caesar, a man of whom he could speak from personal experience.[104]

On the other hand, it is no more likely that Sallust had first-hand
information about the final battle than he had about Catiline's pre-battle
hortatio, if there was one.[105] For his gripping account of Catiline's defeat by
the forces of the state (59–61) he relied on the process of rhetorical
inuentio, described by a modern expert as 'the "discovery" of what requires
to be said in a given situation, the implied theory being that this is
somehow already "there" though latent'.[106] The *descriptio pugnae* (Cic.
Or. 66) was a standard element in a young man's rhetorical education
and products of the system would know instinctively how a battle should be
described.[107] Thus Sallust's account is composed of battlefield commonplaces, conventional character traits and borrowings from Caesar's

---

    On one occasion he professes to have heard Crassus reminiscing (48.9
    'postea praedicantem').
[101] See Appendix II.
[102] The very choice of the Catilinarian conspiracy as his topic 'was in the final
    analysis a mistake of Sallust's from a historiographical point of view, the
    fundamental or primary mistake so to speak, since the material relating to
    Catiline was already badly manipulated through Cicero's writings'
    (Ledworuski 71, 365).
[103] See 38.8n., 52.11n., 23n., 24n., 54.4n.; the relationship of 36.4–39.4 to
    Cicero's works has been studied by Funari, *LPV* 15–61. It is very unfortunate
    that Cicero's speech *In Toga Candida*, attacking Catiline shortly before the
    consular elections of 64 in which both men were candidates, has survived
    only in a few fragments (see Crawford 159–99).
[104] For all these works see the Commentary on 53.2–54.6 (intro. n.), with
    further references.
[105] As a general rule ancient historians did not consult archival material
    (Marincola 103–6), and there is no evidence that Sallust consulted any
    report that may have been submitted to the senate.
[106] D. A. Russell, 'Rhetoric and criticism', *G&R* 14 (1967) 135. The application
    of *inuentio* to historiography is explained by Cic. *De Or.* 2.62–4, a text ana-
    lysed in detail in *RICH* 78–95.
[107] See *RICH* 89–90 and nn. 78–9, and esp. Lendon.

descriptions of quite different, more recent, battles (see ad loc.). Although readers are invited to be spectators at the scene (61.1n. *confecto*), there is not the slightest indication that Sallust had any eyewitness evidence at all. The climax of the *Bellum Catilinae* is imaginative fiction.

Modern readers may be tempted to see a conflict between *inuentio* and Sallust's promise at the beginning of his work that he would write 'as truthfully as possible' (4.3 'Igitur de Catilinae coniuratione quam uerissime potero paucis absoluam'), but *Igitur* shows that his promise is consequent upon the preceding statement that his mind was 'free from hope, fear and political partisanship' (4.2 'mihi a spe, metu, partibus rei publicae animus liber erat'). Sallust's promise of 'truth', in other words, consists in a claim to be unbiased, and he could make such a claim because he had retired from political life and had nothing to gain or lose from slanting his account in one direction or another.[108] Like many claims to 'truth' by ancient historians, *uerissime* relates to impartiality and is in no way inconsistent with the practice of *inuentio*.

4 READERS' RESPONSES

In antiquity Sallust was quoted more often than any other Latin prose author with the exception of Cicero. Moreover, since in the ancient world historians were appraised chiefly for their manner of expression, Sallust's 'style' (as we loosely refer to it) elicited direct or indirect literary comment from, among others, Asinius Pollio, Pompeius Trogus, the elder Seneca, Velleius Paterculus, the younger Seneca, Quintilian, Martial, Statius, Suetonius, Fronto and Aulus Gellius.[109] These names cover a variety of different genres and range across more than two centuries: the number and volume of their *testimonia* is highly unusual, if not unique. What was it about Sallust that attracted such attention?

The feature which provoked the most comment was Sallust's brevity (Sen. *Contr.* 9.1.13, Sen. *Ep.* 114.17, Quint. 4.2.45, 8.3.82, 9.3.12, 10.1.32, 10.1.102, Stat. *Silv.* 4.7.55, Gell. 3.1.6; also Macr. 5.1.7, Sidon. *Carm.* 2.190, 23.152). He was described as an archaiser (Suet. *Gramm.* 10.2, 10.6, 15.2) and as borrowing from the elder Cato (Quint. 8.3.29, Suet. *Gramm.* 15.2, *Aug.* 86.3, Fronto p. 56.21 vdH²). He was regarded as a neologist (Quint. 9.3.12, Gell. 1.15.18, 4.15.1) and bold with his metaphors (Suet. *Gramm.* 10.6). He was seen as abrupt (Sen. *Ep.* 114.17, Quint.

---

[108] Cf. *H.* 1.6 'neque me diuersa pars in ciuilibus armis mouit a uero'; see *RICH* 73–4. From Sallust's attested connections with Caesar it has often been thought that in the *Bellum Catilinae* he writes from a strongly pro-Caesarian point of view, but see the measured discussion of Shaw 196–206.

[109] See Kurfess xxvi–xxxi, Duursma 196–207.

4.2.45) and obscure (Suet. *Gramm.* 10.6), a second Thucydides (Vell. 36.2, Quint. 10.1.101). Almost none of this evidence is straightforward. A writer can be an archaiser and a neologist at the same time, but the combination is *prima facie* oxymoronic; and, while brevity and abruptness seem a natural pairing, Sallust's reputation for brevity seems belied by the innumerable times he uses two words where one would have done.[110]

(a) Brevity

Modern attempts at illustrating Sallust's brevity from his texts have not been especially convincing. It is true that he likes to omit forms of *esse* (as e.g. 16.5), but so do many other Latin authors; it is also true that he likes to omit various types of coordination, but his use of asyndeton (as it is called) seems largely to reflect that of contemporary political discourse.[111] Sallust's own statements of brevity are unhelpful, since they relate to narrative form rather than to manner of expression: in the preface to the *Bellum Catilinae* he promises a short work (4.3 'paucis absoluam'), and in his digression on the First Conspiracy he disavows long-windedness, as was conventional in digressions (18.2 'quam breuissime potero dicam'; cf. 19.6, 38.3, *BJ* 17.1 'paucis exponere', 19.2, 19.8, 42.5). In the elder Seneca's *Controuersiae* a Greek epigram (mistakenly attributed to Thucydides) is compared with its equivalent in Sallust (*H.* 1.49.24), whose version is declared superior because of its precision or verbal economy (9.1.13 'nothing can be deleted from Sallust's epigram without detriment to the sense'), while for Quintilian (8.3.82) Sallust's brevity lies in his suggestiveness: a vignette such as *Mithridates corpore ingenti, perinde armatus* (*H.* 2.63) implies more than it says, a regular definition of one type of brevity.[112]

In one of his letters the younger Seneca said that when Sallust's work was in fashion, his imitators fetishised his brevity (*Ep.* 114.17): 'Sallustio uigente

---

[110] For long lists of synonymous pairs see Skard (1964) 26–9, who quotes over ninety exs. from the *BC* (e.g. 1.4 'fluxa atque fragilis' (n.), 26.2 'dolus aut astutiae', 31.2 'festinare, trepidare').

[111] See Adams, *AILL* 553–87, 643. Some of the other possibilities are listed by Ramsey (12): 'long lists of words or clauses', 'frequent use of the historical infinitive', 'the use of polar opposites' and 'a decided preference for parataxis', but it is hard to see much relevance here to *breuitas* (more or less the same can be said of the discussion by A. Dziuba, '*Breuitas* as a stylistic feature in Roman historiography', in J. Pigoń (ed.), *The children of Herodotus: Greek and Roman historiography and related genres* (2008) 317–28). Summers (xix–xx) cites five exs. of 'compression of thought', but, even if all these exs. were certain (which they are not), they are quite overwhelmed by Skard's ninety cases of synonymous expressions (n. 110 above).

[112] For exs. see Berti on Sen. *Ep.* 114.1 (pp. 55–8).

amputatae sententiae et uerba ante exspectatum cadentia et obscura breuitas fuere pro cultu'. This is presumably the same feature which Quintilian detected in Sallust himself (4.2.45 'illa Sallustiana ... breuitas et abruptum sermonis genus'), but what is meant by *uerba ante exspectatum cadentia*? Seneca cannot mean that a Sallustian word will often end before you expect, since, especially in an inflected language such as Latin, it is impossible for a word to end unexpectedly:[113] *uerba* ... *cadentia* must refer to sequences of words. The latest commentator on the letter thinks that Seneca is referring to 'the sudden truncating of phrases owing to the search for *breuitas*',[114] but when the same habit amongst the imitators of Sallust (and Thucydides) is mentioned by Quintilian (10.2.17 'praecisis conclusionibus obscuri Sallustium atque Thucydiden superant'), the use of the term *conclusio* indicates that he is talking about the ends of sentences.[115] In what sense, then, can Sallust's sentences be said to 'end before you expect'? Since more than 80 per cent of Sallust's sentences end with a rhythmical clausula (and the figure could be even higher, depending on one's definitions and calculations),[116] almost all of Sallust's sentence-endings 'announce' themselves rather than take the reader by surprise.

If *uerba* ... *cadentia* refers to sentences, *amputatae sententiae* cannot mean 'amputated sentences', unless we are to accuse Seneca of a banal repetition: *sententiae* must mean 'thoughts'. And, since *amputatae* and *ante exspectatum cadentia* evidently refer to a similar phenomenon, the seeming antithesis between *sententiae* and *uerba* is a recognition of the fact that thoughts, if they are to be communicated, can only be expressed in words.[117] That is to say,

---

[113] Verbal forms comprising participle + *esse* (e.g. *ausi sunt*), from which *esse* can often be omitted, constitute a partial exception. At 5.4 Sallust perpetrates the (seemingly unique) tmesis *cuius rei libet* for *cuiuslibet rei*; some words in Latin have a short form where a long would be expected (e.g. *cura* for *curatio* in the sense of medical treatment at Cato, *Agr.* 157); and Quintilian refers to a *uitium barbarismi* which 'consists in adding or omitting a letter or syllable in any word you please' (1.5.10; cf. Arist. *Poetics* 1458a2–5; Lausberg 217–19 §462); but the context of Seneca's letter suggests that he cannot be referring to phenomena such as these.

[114] Berti ad loc.

[115] *Conclusio* has various different meanings (Lausberg 628 s.v.), including sentence-endings and complete sentences. For so-called 'periodic' sentences in Sallust see 45.3n. (*postquam*).

[116] It used to be thought that Latin historical prose was unrhythmical, but statistical analysis has shown recently that, 'while only some authors adhere to the Ciceronian rhythmic canon, every Latin author is "rhythmical" – they just choose different rhythms' (K–K 161). For Sallust's statistics see K–K 169 (I am including spondaic (22.24%) and heroic endings (11.49%) in these figures); some of his clausulae and their relative frequency are illustrated in the extract (8.1–9.1) quoted below.

[117] Cf. e.g. Cic. *De Or.* 2.93 'Pericles ... et Thucydides breues, sententiis magis quam uerbis abundantes' (with which compare Dion. Hal. *Thuc.* 24, quoted

amputatae sententiae ('amputated thoughts') and *uerba ante exspectatum cadentia* ('sentences ending before you expect') both refer to the same stylistic
phenomenon, though seen from different points of view, and this phenomenon results in *obscura breuitas*. What, then, is this phenomenon?
In his 'archaeology' of earlier Roman history (6–13) Sallust explains
how, when the monarchy was replaced by the republic, society was characterised by highly moral behaviour and *uirtus* was especially evident on the
battlefield (7.1–6): the historian could relate many Roman military victories won against the odds, except that it would take him too far from his
topic (7.7 'ni ea res longius nos ab incepto traheret'). There then follows
this passage (8.1–9.1):

Sed profecto Fortuna in omni rē dŏmĭnātŭr;[11.49%] ea res cunctas
ex libidine magis quam ex uero celebrat ōbscūrātquĕ.[22.24%] **2**
Atheniensium res gestae, sicuti ego aestimo, satis amplae magnificaeque fuere, uerum aliquanto minores tamen quam famā
fĕrūntŭr.[14.43%] **3** sed, quia prouenere ibi scriptorum magna ingenia, per terrarum orbem Atheniensium facta pro maximīs
cĕlĕbrāntŭr.[11.49%] **4** ita eorum qui fecere uirtus tanta habetur
quantum   eam   uerbis   potuere   extollere   praēclār(a)
īngĕnĭă.[18.56%] **5** at populo Romano numquam ea copia fuit,
quia prudentissimus quisque maxime negōtĭōsŭs ĕrăt;[9.57%] ingenium nemo sine corpore ēxērcēbăt;[22.24%] optimus quisque facere
quam dicere, sua ab aliis benefacta laudari quam ipse aliorum
narrārĕ mālēbăt.[9.57%]
   9.1 Igitur domi militiaeque boni mores colebantur...

The words *Sed...Fortuna...* lead the reader to expect that Sallust is about
to say that morality subsequently declined, but such a statement is not
forthcoming until 10.1 ('Sed ... saeuire Fortuna ac miscere omnia coepit'); instead we are told puzzlingly that Fortune praises and obscures
everything according to whim rather than according to reality ('celebrat
obscuratque'). Since this is not one of the usual manifestations of
Fortune's power, the reader expects an explanation, but Sallust next
(§2) introduces asyndetically – and seemingly out of the blue – the
Athenians, whose achievements are said to have been less than they are
reputed to be. This allegation appears to have no connection with anything, but in the following sentence (§3) we are told that, because Athens

below p. 26), Sen. *Vit. Beat.* 4.1 'potest ... eadem sententia non isdem
comprendi uerbis'. Ancient critics recognised a distinction between *figurae
sententiae* and *figurae uerborum*, for each of which they had a wide variety of
terms, but in practice the two are often difficult to distinguish: see Lausberg
272–3 §§602–3.

was blessed with a crop of talented writers, its achievements earn world-wide praise as being the greatest ('celebrantur'). The greatness of the Athenians' *uirtus* depends upon the excellence of their writers (§4). At last, helped by the repetition of the verb *celebrare*, it becomes clear what Sallust meant in §1: Fortune herself did not praise or obscure anything; it was Athens' literary superiority for which Fortune was responsible, but readers have to wait until §§3–4 to make this inference, and, even then, they remain in the dark as to why a reference to Athens appears in a narrative which had seemed to be about early Rome. In §5 we learn that the Roman people, to whom reference is finally made, had no comparable supply of talented writers, since all their best men preferred deeds to words and wanted those deeds to be celebrated by others rather than that they themselves should celebrate those of others. Only now, at the very end of the passage, does it become clear that the Athenians in §§2–4 have been a foil for the Romans in §5, much as the reference to Fortune in §1 was a foil for the Athenians;[118] but, since Sallust ends by saying that early republican historiography was virtually non-existent, the question is raised of how he can know about the Roman victories to which he referred earlier (7.7).

Each of Sallust's sentences in 8.1–2 'ends before you expect' in the sense that his 'thought is amputated': it is not until §3 that Sallust's initial meaning becomes clear, and §§3–4 are themselves not clarified until §5, which itself raises an unanswered question *vis-à-vis* 7.7. The procedure is almost identical to that described by Seneca earlier in the same letter (*Ep.* 114.11): 'Sunt qui sensus praecidant et hoc gratiam sperent si sententia pependerit et audienti suspicionem sui fecerit' ('there are those who cut short their thoughts and expect a favourable reaction if their expression is left hanging and provides the listener with only an inkling of it'); the difference is that in Sallust the reader cannot guess the author's intention from an individual *sententia* and so is left floundering. And, since the topic of social morality at 7.7 is not resumed until *Igitur domi militiaeque boni mores colebantur* at 9.1, it becomes clear that 8.1–5, as well as being unstraightforward in its internal articulation, constitutes a digression which cuts off the main narrative in mid-stream.[119] This entire section of Sallust's 'archaeology', both as a whole and in its individual elements, can be said to illustrate the *obscura breuitas* of which Seneca complained.

---

[118] This technique may explain Fronto's description of Sallust's writing as 'structe' (p. 134.1–2 vdH²): the adverb is unique in classical Latin and its meaning is disputed (see van den Hout ad loc.), but its derivation from *struere* presumably implies some form of build-up.

[119] Sallust frequently introduces a digression by *sed*, and *igitur* is regular to resume a main narrative (*OLD* 5).

The literary quality of *breuitas* was capable of many different meanings,[120] and the *breuitas* which was cultivated by the *Sallustiani* of the younger Seneca's letter was different from that discerned in Sallust by Seneca's father, which in turn differed from that discerned by Quintilian (and all of them differed from the *breuitas* to which Sallust himself laid claim). The very potentialities of Sallust's style were perhaps one reason why he attracted such attention.

(b) Thucydides

Velleius (36.2) and Quintilian (10.1.101) recognised that Sallust was an imitator of Thucydides,[121] and although it was no doubt Sallust's imitation of Thucydides' phraseology which these authors principally had in mind, the 'suspension of thought' or 'thematic anticipation' which we have just observed in Sallust's preface closely resembles the circular composition which is such a feature of Thucydides' own preface.[122] It is also interesting that, as has been pointed out,[123] the younger Seneca's remarks about the 'obscure brevity' of the *Sallustiani* resemble very closely the comments made about Thucydides' 'unclear brevity' by Dionysius of Halicarnassus, the historian and literary critic who was Sallust's younger contemporary: 'the most obvious of his characteristics is *the effort to express as much as possible in the fewest possible words and to combine many ideas into one* and **to leave the listener still expecting to hear something more … His brevity becomes unclear**' (*Thuc.* 24 ἐκδηλότατα δὲ αὐτοῦ καὶ χαρακτηρικώτατά ἐστι τό τε πειρᾶσθαι δι' ἐλαχίστων ὀνομάτων πλεῖστα σημαίνειν πράγματα καὶ πολλὰ συντιθέναι νοήματα εἰς ἕν, καὶ τὸ ἔτι προσδεχόμενόν τι τὸν ἀκροατὴν ἀκούσεσθαι καταλείπειν … ἀσαφὲς γίνεται τὸ βραχύ). The words in bold are strikingly similar to those used by the younger Seneca, but the italicised phrases seem more closely related to Sallustian brevity as discussed by Quintilian (8.3.82, above). The same combination recurs later in Dionysius' discussion, when, referring to

---

[120] See e.g. Lausberg 614–15 s.vv. *breuis, breuitas*.
[121] Thucydides was popular amongst some contemporary orators (Cic. *Brut.* 287, *Orat.* 30–2). For discussion of his relationship with Sallust see e.g. J. Robolsky, *Sallustius in conformanda oratione quo iure Thucydidis exemplum secutus esse existimetur* (Diss. Halle 1881), Perrochat 1–39, Scanlon, L. V. Pitcher, 'Thucydides in Greek and Roman historiography,' in P. Low (ed.), *The Cambridge companion to Thucydides* (2022) 233–5, 244–5, and numerous notes in the Commentary. Sallust gets rather short shrift from H. G. Strebel, *Wertung und Wirkung des thukydideischen Geschichtswerkes in der griechisch-römischen Literatur* (1935).
[122] For these terms see 2.3–6n., citing *inter al.* G. Williams, who makes the point that 'thematic anticipation' is closely related to ring composition. For Thucydides' preface see intro. n. to 1–16.
[123] See *RICH* 126–7, a discussion superseded here.

imitators of Thucydides, he points to the author's '**suspended thoughts**, . . . which **from amputation** *are intended to indicate many things* and **admit of a conclusion only after a long interval**' (*Thuc.* 52 τὰς ὑπερβατοὺς καὶ . . . ἐξ ἀποκοπῆς πολλὰ σημαίνειν πράγματα βουλομένας καὶ διὰ μακροῦ τὰς ἀποδόσεις λαμβανούσας νοήσεις): although the words in bold again suggest similarities with Seneca, the italics seem to relate to pregnancy of expression. The characteristics of *breuitas* detected in Thucydides seem very similar indeed to those detected in Sallust by his readers.[124]

Dionysius discusses Thucydides further in his *Letter to Pompey*, where he says (3) that the first and most essential task for historians is choosing a noble subject and one which will please their readers, but that Thucydides writes of a war that is neither noble nor fortunate; a historian should also choose the right starting point for his history, but Thucydides starts with the incipient decline of the Greek world, which should not have been done by a Greek and an Athenian; in his malice (φθονερῶς) he finds the overt causes of the war in the conduct of his own city. Dionysius continues:

> I will mention one other feature of the treatment of subject matter, a feature which in all histories we look for no less than any of those already mentioned. I mean the attitude (διάθεσιν) which the histor-ian himself adopts towards the events he describes . . . That of Thucydides is severe and harsh and proves that he had a grudge against his native country because of his exile. He recites a catalogue of her mistakes, going into them in minute detail; but when things proceed according to plan, he either does not mention them at all, or only like a man under compulsion.

It is striking how much of this analysis is applicable to the author of the *Bellum Catilinae*. His subject is not noble but a crime (4.4 *scelus*) and, although the architect of the crime was eventually defeated, the outcome of the final battle is presented as anything but fortunate (61.7–9). In various digressive passages Sallust goes out of his way to trace the decline of Rome (5.9–13.5, 37.1–39.4), and he too 'finds the overt causes of the war in the conduct of his own city' (see 14.1n.). As for the attitude which Sallust adopts towards the events which he describes,[125] the historian Granius Licinianus would later remark that 'he attacks his own times and criticises their failings' (36 'et tempora reprehendit sua et delicta carpit'). Finally, although Sallust was never exiled, he was of course cast out from

---

[124] Of course Sallust's critics may well have read his work with the criticism of Thucydides in their minds, as Christopher Krebs points out to me.
[125] For this aspect of a historian's work see J. Marincola, *Plutarch's* On the Malice of Herodotus *and the writing of history in the Greco-Roman world* (forthcoming Oxford, 2026), ch. 7.

the senate and, when readmitted, was in such danger of being cast out
again that he was compelled to turn to the writing of history. One could
almost substitute the name of Sallust for that of Thucydides in Dionysius'
analysis.

It has been said that 'the most famous characteristic of Thucydides'
style' is his *uariatio* (i.e. the deliberate avoidance of balanced
expression),[126] and Sallust too exhibits the same feature.[127] He will vary
pronouns (2.1 *pars... alii*, 38.3 *alii... pars*, 48.5 *alii... pars... plerique*,
48.7–8 *erant qui... alii... ego*, 61.8 *alii, pars... fuere qui*); he matches nouns
with clauses (~ indir. question 5.9; ~ acc. + inf. 10.4, 16.2, 30.2; ~ indir.
command 30.7) and makes prepositions correspond to a variety of syntac-
tical or grammatical features (~ clause 9.3, 33.1; ~ adv. 13.2, 42.2; ~ adj.
20.2; ~ gen. 17.3–4; ~ *quam* 17.6); adjectives can be matched with genitives
(~ partitive gen. 17.2; ~ descriptive gen. 18.4), abstract with concrete
(20.2); he seeks variety in cases (11.2 *ille* ~ *huic*, 33.1 *patriae* ~ *fama atque
fortunis*), number (7.7 *possum* ~ *nos*), tenses (32.2 *possent* ~ *confirment* ~
maturent ~ *parent*, 34.1 *uellent* ~ *discedant* ~ *proficiscantur*), conjunctions (1.6
priusquam ~ *ubi*, 3.2 *quod* ~ *quia*, 34.2 *non quo* ~ *sed uti*, 58.3 *quo* ~ *uti*),
prepositions (56.4 *per* ~ *ad* ~ *uersus*), construction (25.2 abl. ~ infin. ~ acc.;
40.1 participle ~ *quod*; 51.43 gerundive ~ indir. command), word order
(27.2: verbs). In addition he varies some standard expressions (14.2
alienum aes, 15.1 *sacerdos Vestae*, 29.3 *sine populi iussu*, 36.4 *ad occasum ab
ortu solis*, 53.2 *mari atque terra*). It is conventional to say that Sallust 'learned
from Thucydides' in this respect,[128] yet it is noteworthy that no ancient
critic remarks on his habit of *uariatio*. Perhaps the reason is that *uariatio*
was by no means exclusive to Sallust. Although we tend to think of it as
a feature which distinguishes him from his great contemporary Cicero,
uariatio is described by H. C. Gotoff, an expert in the analysis of Cicero's
stylistic technique, as 'central to Cicero's goal of avoiding predictable
balance and symmetry in his periodic style'. 'Cicero's characteristic practice', he says, 'is to establish the framework or suggestion of balance and
then to disappoint that expectation'.[129] He could have been describing
the habit of Sallust.

The similarities between Sallust and Thucydides should not lead us into
ignoring the differences between the two authors.[130] One can choose
almost any sentence at random from anywhere in the *Bellum Catilinae*
and it will be readily intelligible to a reader who has reached the

---

[126] J. S. Rusten, *Thucydides: The Peloponnesian War Book II* (1989) 26, with numerous examples and bibliography.
[127] See e.g. Ramsey 13–14.   [128] Syme, *Sall.* 265.
[129] H. C. Gotoff, *Cicero's elegant style* (1979) 241–2, 231.
[130] Grethlein, for example, has argued that Sallust's 'narratorial voice' reveals 'a
narrator very different from Thucydides' (322).

appropriate level of Latin.[131] The impression given by Thucydides' Greek, however, is one of significant difficulty. We are told by Dionysius that only a few readers could understand the whole of Thucydides, and some of these required the help of a linguistic commentary (*Thuc.* 51); and Cicero remarked that his speeches have 'so many obscure and latent thoughts that they can scarcely be understood' (*Orator* 30).[132] Here is a major difference between the two texts.[133]

(c) Archaising and the Elder Cato

Since Dionysius repeatedly draws attention to Thucydides' archaising language (*Thuc.* 24, 50, 52), it is of interest that Sallust too was said to archaise. Suetonius reports that a freedman called Ateius Philologus offered himself as a literary consultant to Sallust and, after Sallust's death, to Asinius Pollio, the distinguished politician and historian who was Sallust's younger contemporary by roughly ten years (*Gramm.* 10.6).[134] According to Suetonius, when Sallust and Pollio were starting to write their respective histories, Ateius produced for Sallust a comprehensive summary of Roman history from which he could select material at will ('breuiario rerum omnium Romanarum ex quibus quas uellet eligeret'); for Pollio he produced guidelines on how to write ('praeceptis de ratione scribendi'): since these guidelines evidently included the advice that Pollio 'should use familiar, ordinary and appropriate speech and avoid in particular the obscurity of Sallust and his daring metaphors' ('ut noto ciuilique et proprio sermone utatur uitetque maxime obscuritatem Sallustii et audaciam in translationibus'), Suetonius was surprised at Pollio's belief that Ateius had also been accustomed to collect *antiqua uerba* for Sallust ('antiqua eum uerba et figuras solitum esse colligere Sallustio').

Pollio had evidently revealed this belief in a book in which 'he criticised Sallust's writings for being sullied by an excessive pursuit of *prisca uerba*'

---

[131] For many years I taught the *BC* unproblematically to first-year undergraduates on both sides of the Atlantic.

[132] See e.g. C. C. De Jonge, 'Dionysius of Halicarnassus and the scholia on Thucydides' syntax', in S. Matthaios et al. (edd.), *Ancient scholarship and grammar* (2011) 451–78. It is odd to be told (Plut. *Cato Mai.* 2.5) that reading Thucydides helped the elder Cato to learn Greek at an advanced age.

[133] We must always remember that most of Sallust's *Historiae* has not survived: he may have become more 'Thucydidean' as his writing developed.

[134] For Pollio – who was also a consular, *triumphator*, patron of Virgil and playwright – see Drummond in *FRHist* 1.430–5, adding W.² on Vell. 78.2 and 86.3. For the fragments of his history see *FRHist* 2.854–67 and 3.521–30; for commentary on his famous obituary of Cicero (7C/5P) see *LH* 70–4; for general speculation about his history see *PH* 127–44. For Ateius Philologus see Kaster on Suet. *Gramm.* 10.1–2 and 10.6.

(Suet. *Gramm.* 10.2 'Sallustii scripta reprehendit ut nimia priscorum uer-borum affectatione oblita'). *prisca uerba* (sometimes in the singular) is quite a common expression in Latin (e.g. *Rhet. Her.* 4.15, Cic. *De Or.* 3.153, *Brut.* 83), to such an extent that it may be regarded as quasi-technical: an otherwise unknown Cincius, for example, wrote a book entitled *De Verbis Priscis* or 'On Archaic Words'.[135] Such terminology can be slippery because the concept of 'archaism' is relative: what was an archaism to Tacitus in the early second century AD may well not have been an archaism to Livy, writing a hundred or more years earlier. Since Pollio was a younger contemporary of Sallust, however, this difficulty is irrelevant: the two historians are likely to have had a similar perspective on what constituted archaising vocabulary.

Elsewhere Suetonius, quoting the emperor Augustus, refers more spe-cifically to *uerba* which Sallust 'culled from the *Origines* of Cato' (*Aug.* 86.3 'uerbis quae Crispus Sallustius excerpsit ex Originibus Catonis'), and Quintilian quotes an anonymous epigram to the same effect (8.3.29 'uerba antiqui multum furate Catonis'); to Fronto, later in the second century, Sallust is a 'regular follower' of the elder Cato (p. 56.21 vdH² 'frequens sectator'). Whether this evidence means that Sallust's borrow-ings from Cato *exemplified* his archaising, or whether they *constituted* his archaising, is a key question. Suetonius says that Sallust was attacked by one Pompeius Lenaeus, a contemporary, for being 'priscorum Catonisque uerborum ineruditissimum furem' (*Gramm.* 15.2). Unfortunately this statement is controversial. Since *prisca uerba* is a set expression, as we have seen, *priscorum* must be an adjective in agreement with *uerborum*, in which case the phrase will mean 'a very ill-informed thief of archaic – and in particular of Cato's – words'; but this interpretation is regarded as 'inconceivable' by Suetonius' editor, who agrees with those who think that -*que* should be deleted: in that case Sallust is being accused of stealing 'the archaic words of Cato'.[136]

As Skard pointed out, however, it is by no means easy to identify examples of Sallust's lexical 'stealing' from Cato.[137] None of his alleged Catonian idiolects is exclusive to Cato amongst pre-Sallustian authors.[138]

---

[135] For Cincius and the problems over his date and identity see *FRHist* 1.181.

[136] Thus R. A. Kaster, *Studies on the text of Suetonius* De Grammaticis et Rhetoribus (1992) 89–91, with ample discussion; in favour of the paradosis is Lebek 328 n. 83. On Lenaeus see Courtney, *FLP* 145 and in *BNP* 7.386 [2].

[137] Skard, *SV* 79–80.

[138] E.g. the rare noun *prosapia* ('lineage'), which Sallust uses at *BJ* 85.10 'ueteris prosapiae' and is described by Cicero as 'old' (*Tim.* 39; cf. Quint. 1.6.40, 8.3.26), is found once in the surviving fragments of Cato's *Origines* (21C/29P 'ueteres prosapia'); it also occurs twice in Plautus (*Curc.* 393, *Merc.* 634). *claritudo*, used twice by Sallust (*BJ* 2.4, 7.4), was also used by Cato (*Orig.* 28C/ 63P, 76C/83P), who is implied to have liked nouns formed with -*udo* (Gell.

Thus even *ferentarius* (60.2), which occurs in Cato (*Mil.* fr. 26 Manuwald) and which the grammarian Verrius Flaccus, Sallust's younger contemporary, explicitly associates with Cato (cf. Fest. 369 'Cato eos ferentarios dixit qui tela ac potiones militibus proeliantibus ministrabant'), occurs metaphorically in Plautus (*Trin.* 456): it seems more likely to be a rare technical term (cf. Varro, *LL* 7.57, quoting an inscription), its recurrence in Tacitus (*A.* 12.35.3) explained by its presence in Sallust. In view of this evidential difficulty, Skard suggested that Sallust was being criticised for his imitation of Cato's phraseology and manner, since, as he correctly pointed out, *uerbum* not only means 'word' but can also denote an expression or sentence.[139] Now it is indeed indisputable that Sallust, who in the preface to his *Historiae* praises Cato for his *breuitas* (1.3), alludes frequently to Cato's work in the *Bellum Catilinae*,[140] but that the critics are referring to anything other than vocabulary seems unlikely. Perhaps we should just conclude that Sallust's thieving would be more evident if a greater amount of Cato's *Origines* had survived; or perhaps his alleged thefts were simply the most striking aspect of the more general archaising to which Pollio referred.

Of what might archaising consist? The evidence for the *Bellum Catilinae* is listed in Appendix III: most of the seventeen items are individual words, a seemingly poor haul for roughly fifty OCT pages, but some of them occur more than once, and two of them (*foret/-ent* and *mortales*) account for no fewer than thirty-three occurrences.[141] The result is seventy-three archaisings in total, which is equivalent to three for every two OCT pages; whether such an average, with such repetitions, is deemed sufficient to justify a reputation for archaising is perhaps doubtful.[142] It is true that Lebek, after an in-depth analysis of *prisca uerba*, concluded that Sallust's archaising was significantly greater in the *Bellum Iugurthinum* than in the *Bellum*

17.2.19–20); it is also in Sisenna (15C/49P). An active form of the perfect of *soleo* occurs in Sallust (*H.* 2.54) and is said by Varro (*LL* 9.107) to have been in Cato and Ennius; it is also in Coelius Antipater (43C/45P). *tempestas* in the sense of *tempus* is frequent in Sallust (e.g. 7.1), is described by Cicero as an archaism (*De Or.* 3.153), and is in Cato at *Orat.* 123M; it is found regularly elsewhere too, including in an inscription of 189 BC (*CIL* 1².614). *socordia* ('sluggishness'), one of Sallust's favourite nouns (e.g. 4.1, 52.29, 58.4), is also attested in Cato's *Origines* (110C/117P), where it is said to have the different meaning of 'foolishness'; it also occurs in Accius, Plautus and Terence.

[139] Skard, *SV* 104–5. Good exs. of *uerbum* at Ter. *Ad.* 803–4, *And.* 426–7, *Eun.* 732.

[140] For Sallust and Cato see Levene, *OR* 214–43.

[141] There are twenty exs. of *foret/-ent* (I have excluded the infinitive from the statistics) and thirteen of *mortales* (of which four occur in Caesar's speech).

[142] To say that 'Archaism is the hall-mark of the Sallustian idiosyncrasy, patent and avowed' (Syme, *Sall.* 261) seems a considerable overstatement.

Catilinae, and greater still in the fragmentary *Historiae*,[143] and the impression created on readers by these two later works, perhaps coupled with the author's allusions to Cato, may account for the references to Sallust's archaising. Certainly the notion that archaic language served to recall the morality of ancient times (cf. Gell. 1.10.3 'quod honesta et bona et sobria et modesta sit') is likely to have appealed to Sallust, with his view that society had degenerated from an earlier moral age.[144] On the other hand, it is striking that, apart from Pollio, no one, not even Quintilian, commented on Sallust as an archaiser *tout court*. We must remember that Pollio was a notoriously grumpy critic who also complained about Caesar (Suet. *DJ* 56.4) and Livy (Quint. 1.5.56, 8.1.3):[145] since he shared with Sallust a literary consultant and had a similar manner of expression (see below), it would be perhaps understandable if Pollio resorted to exaggeration to distinguish himself from his famous predecessor. And modern readers have gone along with him because the orthography in our standard editions of Sallust seems to present us with an archaising text.[146]

5 *RERVM ROMANARVM FLORENTISSIMVS AVCTOR*

In Livy's preface, probably written shortly after Sallust's death, the author alludes to, and engages with, the preface to the latter's *Historiae*.[147] In the preface to a later book Livy claimed that his history had brought him fame (fr. 74L 'satis gloriae quaesitum'), a claim which is expressed via an apparent allusion to the preface of the *Bellum Catilinae*, where Sallust had said that one should aim for fame by using one's intellect (1.3 'ingenii . . . opibus gloriam quaerere').[148] Livy regarded Sallust as a rival, and he was accused by the elder Seneca of unfairness (*Contr.* 9.1.14 'tam iniquus Sallustio') when he contradicted the view that the epigram of Sallust at *H.* 1.49.24 was superior to an epigram attributed to Thucydides; but Livy allegedly thought he would beat Sallust more easily if the latter were already beaten by Thucydides ('facilius putat posse a se Sallustium uinci si ante a Thucydide uincatur').[149] Such rivalry is of course

---

[143] Lebek 310. His thesis is that Sallust was the first Latin historian to exploit systematic archaising.

[144] There was a view that literary style was a reflection of the age (e.g. Sen. *Ep.* 114.2).

[145] See e.g. Syme, *Sall.* 288 ('petulant'), Kaster on Suet. *Gramm.* 10.2 ('stern to the point of pedantry').

[146] On this see below, pp. 39–42.

[147] See *RICH* 128–34 (where it is argued that Livy wrote his preface before the battle of Actium in 31 BC).

[148] See *LH* 87–9 and Levene, *LFP* 1.274–6, on fr. 75L.

[149] On this complicated matter see Levene, *LFP* 1.283–5, on Liv. fr. 91L.

ubiquitous in Latin literature and allusions to Sallustian phraseology will be found throughout Livy's surviving volumes.[150]

Sallust's influence is also evident in contemporary verse. Virgil, for example, seems to have modelled an episode of the *Aeneid* (10.354–79) on the finale of the *Bellum Catilinae*.[151] Horace names Sallust amusingly in Book 1 of the *Satires* (1.2.48–9) and echoes Sallustian phraseology in Book 3 of the *Odes*.[152] When in the opening ode of Book 2 Horace pays tribute to the history which Asinius Pollio was in the process of writing, he shows his awareness of Sallust by indicating the close relationship between the works of the two historians.[153] Pollio's oratory was described by the younger Seneca as 'choppy and jerky and leaving off when you least expect it' (*Ep.* 100.7 'salebrosa et exiliens et ubi minime expectes relictura'): since this wording closely resembles what Seneca said about Sallust,[154] whose literary consultant Pollio had inherited (above, p. 29), it is perhaps legitimate to infer that the description was also applicable to Pollio's historiography.[155]

Contemporary with Livy and Pollio was Pompeius Trogus, whose world history itself has been lost but is mediated to us through the work of Justin some centuries later.[156] The loss of the original work makes it very difficult to discuss Trogus' language and possible allusiveness.[157] One might have expected Mithridates' speech (38.4–7), of which Justin seemingly claims to reproduce the Trogan original (38.3.11), to be indebted to Mithridates' letter in Sallust's *Historiae* (4.60), but the linguistic parallels are scarce (only two) and non-exclusive.[158]

By contrast, L. Arruntius (cos. 22 BC) wrote a history of the Punic War in which his enthusiasm for Sallust was on full display (Sen. *Ep.* 114.17–19):

[150] For the modelling of Livy's Hannibal (21.4.3–9) on Sallust's Catiline (*BC* 5.1–4) see 5.1–8n. The neat allusion at 22.29.8 to Sall. *BJ* 4.5 (see *PH* 386) is not mentioned by Briscoe and Hornblower ad loc.
[151] See Woodman (2022), with further references.
[152] See respectively *PH* 116–20 and W.[6] 261, 317, 319.
[153] See *PH* 129–44.
[154] Berti ad loc. thinks that at *Ep.* 100.7 Seneca is referring to clausulae.
[155] The one substantial fragment that survives (7C/5P) is Pollio's obituary of Cicero, where, as the elder Seneca recognised (*Suas.* 6.25), he was trying to out-Cicero Cicero (on the fragment see *LH* 70–4).
[156] For what is known of Trogus and Justin see J. C. Yardley and W. Heckel, *Justin:* Epitome *of the* Philippic History *of Pompeius Trogus*, Vol. 1 (1997) 1–13; also A. Borgna, *Ripensare la storia universale. Giustino e l'*Epitome *delle* Storie Filippiche di Pompeo Trogo (2018).
[157] See D. Levene, 'Pompeius Trogus in Tacitus' *Annals*', in C. S. Kraus et al. (edd.), *Ancient historiography and its contexts* (2010) 294–311. For the notion that Trogus was a Sallustian see M. Rambaud, 'Salluste et Trogue-Pompée', *REL* 26 (1948) 171–89.
[158] See J. C. Yardley, *Justin and Pompeius Trogus: a study of the language of Justin's* Epitome *of Trogus* (2003) 11–17, at 17.

L. Arruntius, uir rarae frugalitatis qui historias belli Punici scripsit,
fuit Sallustianus et in illud genus nitens. est apud Sallustium 'exercitum argento fecit' [*H. fr.* inc. 1], id est, pecunia parauit.
hoc
Arruntius amare coepit; posuit illud omnibus paginis: dicit quodam
loco 'fugam nostris fecere', alio loco 'Hiero rex Syracusanorum
bellum fecit', et alio loco 'quae audita Panhormitanos dedere
Romanis fecere'. gustum tibi dare uolui; totus his contexitur liber.
quae apud Sallustium rara fuerunt apud hunc crebra sunt et paene
continua, nec sine causa: ille enim in haec incidebat, at hic illa
quaerebat. uides autem quid sequatur ubi alicui uitium pro exemplo est. dixit Sallustius 'aquis hiemantibus'; Arruntius in primo
libro belli Punici ait 'repente hiemauit tempestas', et alio loco,
cum dicere uellet frigidum annum fuisse, ait 'totus hiemauit
annus', et alio loco 'inde sexaginta onerarias leues praeter militem
et necessarios nautarum hiemante aquilone misit'. non desinit
omnibus locis hoc uerbum infulcire. quodam loco dicit Sallustius
'dum inter arma ciuilia aequi bonique famas petit' [*H.* 1.78];
Arruntius non temperauit quominus primo statim libro poneret
ingentes esse famas de Regulo.

L. Arruntius, a man of rare frugality who wrote a history of the Punic
War, was a Sallustian and strained after that manner of his. There is
in Sallust's work 'he made an army with silver', that is, he procured
it with money. Arruntius began a love affair with this, putting it on
every page: in one place he says, 'they made flight for our men', and
in another 'hearing this made the Panhormitans surrender to the
Romans'. I only wanted to give you a taste; his whole book is shot
through with it. What was rare in Sallust's work is frequent and
almost constant in his, and not without reason: these things were
incidental for the former, but premeditated for the latter. But you
can see the consequence when someone takes a fault as his model.
Sallust said, 'with the rain turning wintry'; Arruntius in the first
book of his *Punic War* said, 'the weather suddenly turned wintry',
and in another place, when he wanted to say that the year was cold,
he said, 'the whole year turned wintry', and in another place 'from
there he sent sixty light cargo vessels in addition to the soldiery and
essential sailors, despite the north wind turning wintry'. There was
no stopping him cramming this word in everywhere. In one place
Sallust says, 'while he sought reputations for fairness and goodness
amidst the civil wars'; Arruntius couldn't refrain from writing, as
early as his first book, that the 'reputations' of Regulus were very
great.

Sallust does indeed like 'simple verbs' such as *facio*,[159] but *fugam facere* and *bellum facere* are common expressions,[160] while *facere* + acc. and inf. seems not to be found in extant Sallust. Seneca's problem with Sallust's *hiemare* appears to be not so much its unusualness but the fact that Arruntius used it everywhere.[161] The plural of *fama* is striking, being found elsewhere in classical Latin only in Plautus (*Trin.* 186).

When the historian Velleius Paterculus in AD 30 surveyed the prominent authors of the late republic and early empire, the only historians whom he singled out were Sallust and Livy (36.2–3). He describes Livy in the phrase 'consecutus Sallustium Liuius', by which he means not only that Livy was Sallust's successor but that he equalled Sallust's achievement,[162] and the pairing of the two historians becomes conventional, like that of Herodotus and Thucydides (e.g. Stat. *Silv.* 4.7.55–6). As in the case of their Greek predecessors, however, the purpose of the pairing is usually to contrast them (as by Servilius Nonianus ap. Quint. 10.1.102 'pares eos magis quam similes'). Such a contrast occurs in a famous passage where Quintilian is discussing the authors who should be read out in class by those students in their mid-teens who, having left the teaching of the *grammaticus*, are now beginning with the *rhetor* (2.5.18–20):

quod si potuerit optineri, non ita difficilis supererit quaestio qui legendi sint incipientibus. nam quidam illos minores, quia facilior eorum intellectus uidebatur, probauerunt, alii floridius genus, ut ad alenda primarum aetatium ingenia magis accommodatum. [19]ego optimos quidem et statim et semper, sed tamen eorum candidissimum quemque et maxime expositum uelim (ut Liuium a pueris magis quam Sallustium – et hic historiae maior est auctor, ad quem tamen intellegendum iam profectu opus sit). [20]Cicero, ut mihi quidem uidetur, et iucundus incipientibus quoque et apertus est satis, nec prodesse tantum sed etiam amari potest; tum, quem ad modum Liuius praecipit, ut quisque erit Ciceroni simillimus.

If this point can be carried,[163] there will remain the not-so-difficult question of who should be read by beginners. Some people, you see, have given their seal of approval to those lesser authors, because

[159] Syme, *Sall.* 262–3. See the Comm. on 4.5 (*de cuius*).
[160] The notes by Levick (*FRHist* 3.533–4) are misleading (see *LH* 126–7). *exercitum facere* seems not to be common but is found in e.g. Cicero (*Phil.* 5.23) and Livy (25.37.4).
[161] *aquis hiemantibus* is presumably a fragment from the *Historiae*, though it is omitted from standard editions seemingly on the grounds that Seneca has misremembered *hiemalibus aquis* from *BJ* 37.4.
[162] Cf. *OLD consequor* 3, 10.
[163] Quintilian has been talking about the involvement of the *rhetor* in classroom delivery.

understanding them seemed easier, while others have approved of the more florid type, as being more accommodated to nourishing youthful talent. My own preference, unhesitating and unwavering, would of course be for the best authors, but, all the same, I would prefer the clearest and most accessible of them (just as I would prefer Livy rather than Sallust in the case of boys – and the latter is the greater historical author, although at this stage one needs to progress to understand him). It is Cicero, at least as it seems to me, who is pleasant even for beginners and sufficiently approachable, able not only to be beneficial but also to be loved; thereafter, as Livy prescribes,[164] whoever is most like Cicero.

It has often been thought that Quintilian is saying here that Livy's Latin is the easier of the two authors', but this is counter-intuitive: few readers today would regard Livy's Latin as clearer and more accessible than that of Sallust.[165] I have argued elsewhere that the passage has been misunderstood and that Quintilian, while acknowledging that Sallust is the greater historian, is probably making the same point as he makes at 10.1.32, namely, that Livy has greater educational value.[166]

By the time of Augustus' death in AD 14, Sallust and Livy had each established for themselves a canonical status which meant that subsequent historians had two very different models to inspire them. Were historians to emulate Sallust, 'the historian of decline and fall',[167] with his Thucydidean inheritance and dissenting attitude? Given the pressures on free speech under the imperial dispensation, this seems the less likely alternative if a historian wished to trace the history of Rome into the present day. We cannot know for sure, since, with one exception, all such historians of the first century AD are lost; the exception is Velleius himself, much of whose history of Rome has survived.[168] Although he was

---

[164] Cf. Quint. 10.1.39 'apud Liuium in epistula ad filium scripta, legendos Demosthenem atque Ciceronem, tum ita ut quisque esset Demostheni et Ciceroni simillimus' = Liv. fr. 90L (Levene, *LFP* 1.60–3 (text and translation), 282–3 (commentary)).

[165] It is of course possible that ancient readers believed the opposite, but this seems to me implausible. Along with Terence, Cicero and Virgil, Sallust belonged to the quartet of ancient grammar school classics, the 'quadriga' of Arusianus Messius (cf. Cassiod. *Inst. Div.* 2.25).

[166] A. J. Woodman, 'Quintilian on Sallust and Livy', *Histos* 17 (2003) 198–204. For Livy's educational value see S. Hays, '*Lactea ubertas*: what's milky about Livy?', *CJ* 82 (1986–7) 107–16.

[167] Syme, *Sall.* 56.

[168] For recent discussion see T. J. Cornell, 'Roman historical writing in the age of Seneca the Elder', and S. P. Oakley, 'Point and periodicity: the style of Velleius Paterculus and other Latin historians writing in the early Principate', in M. C. Scappaticcio (ed.), *Seneca the Elder and his rediscovered Historiae ab initio bellorum ciuilium: new perspectives on early-imperial Roman*

heavily influenced by Sallustian phraseology,[169] his circuitous sentences and encomiastic attitude, especially towards Augustus and Tiberius, mean that he cannot be described as a Sallustian writer.[170]

If this perspective on the post-Augustan historians is correct,[171] Tacitus' arrival on the literary scene at the turn of the second century AD marks a significant change. He describes Sallust hexametrically as 'rerum Romanarum florentissimus auctor' (A. 3.30.2), and, however indebted to Sallust in his earlier historical works,[172] he began his *Annals* with a sentence ('Vrbem Romam a principio reges habuere') which expressly alludes to Sallust. *Vrbem Romam* ... *habuere* alludes to the sentence in the *Bellum Catilinae* where Sallust too begins an account of the earliest Roman history (6.1 'Vrbem Romam ... condidere atque habuere initio Troiani'); and, if Sallust in the preface to his *Historiae* (1.2) wrote *a principio*, as Servius says (*Aen.* 1.30), rather than *a primordio*, as Priscian says (3.188.16), then all but one of Tacitus' first six words are Sallustian. The sentence functions as a 'motto' or 'epigraph', alerting readers that they can expect a history written in a Sallustian manner and with a dissenting Sallustian attitude. The point is reiterated halfway through the six books devoted to the emperor Tiberius, where the words *repente turbare Fortuna coepit, saeuire ipse* at the start of Book 4 allude to *saeuire Fortuna ... coepit* at *BC* 10.1; and indeed much of the conspiracy of Sejanus against Tiberius seems intended to be seen as an action replay of the Catilinarian conspiracy.[173]

6 THE TEXT

The text of the *Bellum Catilinae* has been handed down to us in a large number of manuscripts, of which the two oldest, designated by the letters P and A, date from the ninth century, the former written somewhere near

---

historiography (2020) 9–28 and 199–234. Velleius has been the subject of much recent work: see the Introduction in A. J. Woodman, *Velleius Paterculus* (Loeb ed., 2024).

[169] See A. J. Woodman in *Hommages à M. Renard*, Vol. 1 (1969) 785–99.
[170] For such sentences cf. Quint. 10.2.17 'si quid modo longius circumduxerunt, iurant ita Ciceronem locuturum fuisse'.
[171] See also *RICH* 140–6, a book which goes unmentioned by V. Parker, 'Between Thucydides and Tacitus: the position of Sallust in the history of ancient historiography', *AuA* 54 (2008) 77–104.
[172] See W.³ 353 s.v. 'Sallust'; R. Ash, *Tacitus: Histories Book II* (2007) 406 s.v. 'Sallustian language'; C. B. Krebs, 'Tacitus and Sallust', in V. E. Pagán (ed.), *A companion to Tacitus* (2012) 333–4.
[173] See W.⁵ 4–9. Many of Tacitus' imitations of Sallust are noted throughout the Commentary.

Soissons, the latter probably at Auxerre.[174] They are now to be found
in the Bibliothèque nationale in Paris.[175] Another ninth-century manuscript, V, contains only speeches and is held in the Vatican.[176] Scraps of the
monograph are also found on a few papyri which are significantly older,
dating from the fourth and fifth centuries. But the picture is somewhat
complicated by the popularity which Sallust's works enjoyed long after his
death. During the second century AD, at the height of the so-called 'archaising movement',[177] his perceived archaising attracted the attention of
such writers as the belletrist Gellius and the consular historian-cum-
epistolographer Fronto, while in the late fourth and early fifth centuries
his severe moralising appealed to Christian writers such as St Jerome and
St Augustine.[178] Some idea of the extent to which these and other writers
quoted Sallust may be gathered from Kurfess' Teubner edition, where
such quotations, often very numerous, are usefully printed between the
main text and the apparatus criticus. It goes without saying that these
quotations, embedded in authors who have their own textual traditions,
sometimes differ from what is found in the manuscripts of Sallust
himself.[179] As is always the case, editors have to choose between the various
readings on offer, but one of the trickiest problems with which they will be
confronted is spelling.[180]

---

[174] For the textual transmission of Sallust's works see L. D. Reynolds (editor of
the Oxford Classical Text of Sallust) in id. (ed.), *Texts and transmission* (1983)
341–9.

[175] See   https://gallica.bnf.fr/ark:/12148/btv1b10547043p/f13.item.r=16024;
https://gallica.bnf.fr/ark:/12148/btv1b8514394x/f13.item.r=16025.

[176] See https://digi.vatlib.it/view/MSS_Vat.lat.3864.

[177] For this see e.g. L. Holford-Strevens, *Aulus Gellius: an Antonine scholar and his
achievement* ([2]2003) 1–8 and 354–63; it has been argued, however, that 'there
seems to have been an archaising trend throughout the first century AD'
(J. C. Bramble, *Persius and the programmatic satire* (1974) 176).

[178] See H. Hagendahl, *Latin Fathers and the classics* (1958) 292–4, and *Augustine
and the Latin classics* (1967) 225–44, 631–49.

[179] Quotations of one author by another are often referred to technically as the
'secondary' or 'indirect tradition' (see e.g. L. D. Reynolds and N. G. Wilson,
Scribes and scholars ([3]1991) 219–21). For example, the words *atque optima*
are inserted at 5.9 on the authority of St Augustine (*Civ. Dei* 2.18–19), and
the grammarian Diomedes (1.445.23) reads *breuissime* instead of the transmitted *uerissime* at 18.2. For Sallustian quotations in Nonius Marcellus see
P. T. Keyser, 'Nonius Marcellus' quotations of Sallust', *WS* 109 (1996)
181–226, who dates the lexicographer to the early third century AD; for
the fragments of Sallust which have been preserved on papyri see Funari
(2016).

[180] In general see G. Pezzini, 'Orthography', in de Melo and Scullion
(forthcoming).

Orthography

When Sallust started on the preface to his first work, what were its opening words? According to Reynolds' OCT (1991), they were *Omnis homines*, but according to Kurfess' Teubner edition (1957) they were *Omneis homines*. Since *decet* occurs later in the sentence, however, and the two words are accusative plural, we might perhaps have expected to find neither of these but *Omnes homines*, although Merivale in his school edition of 1870 seems alone in printing what to us in the modern world is the most familiar form of a third-declension adjective; the majority of editors, including Vretska and Mariotti in their major commentaries, agree with Reynolds in printing *Omnis*. Our initial question thus generates two others: from where do these three variants derive, and why do most editors choose to print *Omnis*?

Of our two oldest manuscripts, P reads *Omnis* and A reads (in abbreviated form) *Omnes*. The variant *Omneis* derives from the fourth-century grammarian Charisius (1.139.22–140.2), who quotes the first eight words of the preface in order to draw attention to the fact that, although Sallust writes *Omneis* in the preface, he writes *Omnes* when he again produces the same sequence of words *Omnes homines … decet* at 51.1. The alleged inconsistency should occasion no surprise. It is well known that Shakespeare was not consistent in the way he spelled his own name and that none of his versions corresponds to the style familiar today. As a crude rule of thumb, the third-declension accusative plural originally featured the 'digraph' *ei* (*omneis*), which was replaced in later times by a long *ī* (*omnis*) or a long *ē* (*omnes*); the latter eventually established itself as the standard form, although the *i*-form persisted for a period in verse and archaising prose writers such as Tacitus. Inscriptional and other evidence suggests that Sallust was writing at a time when there was no standardisation of orthography in the modern sense, and that all three of these variants coexisted, sometimes in the same text.[181] According to J. N. Adams the evidence for the use of *ei* is 'so overwhelming that its absence from a modern text of a republican author or from the manuscripts of that author must be suspect'; at the same time, we are told by Gellius (13.21.1–5) that Virgil had the choice of writing accusative plural *urbis* or *urbes* and on grounds of euphony chose the former at *G.* 1.25 and the latter at *Aen.* 3.106, while a late-republican papyrus preserves the famous fragment of Cornelius Gallus (fr. 2C/145H), in which three

---

[181] See Clackson in *CLL* 245–8, and esp. the comprehensive study of J. N. Adams (2024), and 'Ancient writing (Latin)', in de Melo and Scullion (forthcoming). J. M. Trappes-Lomax prints *loedere* for *ludere* at Catull. 17.1, and, on the highly questionable grounds that 'we may reasonably assume that Catullus was consistent in such matters', he 'restores' *loed-* also at 2.2, 2.9, 44.3, 50.5, 61.203–4 and 99.1 (*Catullus: a textual reappraisal* (2007) 69).

examples of *ei* in the last line coexist with *mihi* (rather than *mihei*) in the first line, where the older *quom* (rather than *cum*) is found alongside the more modern *maxima* (rather than *maxuma*) in line 2:

> Fata mihi, Caesar, tum erunt mea dulcia, quom tu
> maxima Romanae <pa>rs eris historiae
> postque tuum reditum multorum templa deorum
> fixa legam spolieis deiuitiora tueis.

Kurfess thus had every reason to follow Charisius in printing *Omneis* as the first word of Sallust's preface and *Omnes* at 51.1.

Yet Kurfess did not print *Omnes* at 51.1; despite the fact that some MSS (including A) agree with Charisius in reading *Omnes*, he, like Reynolds, prints *Omnis*, which is the reading of P. Why? What is the basis for their choice? The fact is that editors of Sallust, influenced by his reputation as an archaising writer, have been guided by their own view of archaic forms without asking whether these forms were archaic for Sallust and entirely ignoring the fact that Sallust also enjoyed a reputation for linguistic innovation which suggests that his alleged preference for the archaic was by no means straightforward.[182] Thus, since *omnes* became the standard form, many editors prefer *omnis* as being more archaic, and it was the same preference that led Kurfess to print *quom* instead of the conjunction *cum*, *quoius* for *cuius*, *lubido* for *libido*, *maxumus* for *maximus*, etc. If one asks why on the same principle editors do not prefer *Omneis* at 51.1, the answer is that for modern readers the intelligibility of a text decreases in proportion to the number and degree of its archaic forms.[183] Essentially we do not know how most classical Latin authors spelled their words, and editors go their own way.

Kurfess' Teubner text of 1957 is simply the latest edition of the text which A. W. Ahlberg produced in 1919 and in which he 'consistently wrote older forms' (p. viii 'uetustiores formas constanter scripsi'). Kurfess followed Ahlberg's spellings with a few exceptions (pp. xv–xvi), but according to Ramsey in his commentary of 1984 Kurfess' fondness for archaising forms 'is carried to an extreme' (p. 13 n. 12). Ramsey himself preferred to follow the 'more moderate course' set by the Budé edition of A. Ernout (1958), in which some archaising forms are adopted (e.g. *ignauos* for *ignauus*, *maxumus*, *lubido*, *aperiundum*) but not others (e.g. *quom* for *cum*, *quoius* for *cuius*). In his OCT of 1991, however, Reynolds adopted more or

---

[182] Cf. Gell. 1.15.18 'nouatori uerborum', 4.15.1 'uerborumque fingendi et nouandi studium'.

[183] Quintilian says (1.7.23, 9.4.39) that the elder Cato famously wrote *faciae* for *faciam* and *dicae* for *dicam*, yet no editor makes his most celebrated imitator use these forms at *BC* 4.5 and 18.2.

less the same practice as Kurfess, though he too balked at some archaising forms (pp. xxv, xxvi n. 1), including (as we have seen) *Omneis* at 1.1.[184] Yet Reynolds' implicit support for Kurfess did not persuade Ramsey to change his mind when he produced the second edition of his commentary in 2007 (see p. 12 n. 12); it was only in 2013–15, when he published his two-volume Loeb edition of Sallust, that Ramsey adopted the practice of Kurfess and Reynolds, now calling it 'traditional' rather than 'extreme' (Vol. 1, p. lxii).

Where is the real Sallust to be found? In Ramsey's commentary or in his Loeb edition or in neither? Editors routinely claim that 'traces' of these archaising forms are to be found in the best and oldest MSS, but a random check of P and A, two of the oldest and best MSS, suggests that this is not the case at all; these MSS present *cum, libido, maximus,* etc. and offer little justification for Reynolds' confident and comprehensive 'restoration' of archaising forms (p. xxv 'non dubitaui ... ubique reponere'). It is as certain as can be that Sallust himself was inconsistent in his orthographical practice, but nine centuries of scribal copying intervene between his autograph and our oldest MSS and we today cannot possibly know which form Sallust chose in which place. On two occasions (2.2, 7.7) Sallust wrote the accusative plural of *urbs*: although P and A offer *urbes* in both places, on each occasion editors assume that he wrote *urbis*; but who is to say that euphony did not lead him to write *urbes* on at least one of those occasions?

It would be possible to fashion certain principles to help decide orthographical questions. **Assonance** or **wordplay** would argue for <u>minume</u> ... <u>animum</u> rather than *minime* ... *animum* at 6.7, while **alliteration** is arguably more effective if one prints *si <u>uoluptatibus</u> <u>uostris</u> otium praebere <u>uol</u>tis* rather than *si <u>uoluptatibus</u> <u>uestris</u> otium praebere <u>uul</u>tis* at 52.5.[185] In the case of nouns ending in *-ius* or *-ium*, it is the more modern form of the genitive singular in *-ii* which produces the superior **clausula** of resolved molossus + cretic (18.56%) at 52.12 *fūrĭbŭs āerārĭī*, whereas it is the older form in *-i* which produces the favoured resolved cretic + trochaic (9.57%) at *cōnsĭl(ĭ) ăpĕrĭrĕm* at 58.3.[186] At 19.5 *Cn. Pompeii ueteres fidosque clientes*, the potentiality of the hexameter line – as it clearly is – cannot be realised unless *Pompeii* is spelled thus. Finally a case can be made that **external evidence**, such as that of the grammarian Charisius at 1.1, should be allowed to take precedence

---

[184] Ahlberg had in fact printed *Omnis* at 1.1; *Omneis* was Kurfess' own contribution.
[185] Latte maintains that in such cases there is 'more a visual than an aural effect' (*OR* 36 and n. 19).
[186] For these clausulae and the statistics see K–K 164 and 169.

over other considerations.[187] Yet there is no guarantee that in any of
these places the editorial decision would coincide with that of the
author: Sallust almost certainly admitted old-fashioned spellings, but
inconsistently, and we can never be sure where they were.[188] Like
Merivale in his edition of the *Bellum Catilinae*, and like many other
editors of Latin texts,[189] I have decided to print the forms with which
we are most familiar today: if nothing else, this should have the
advantage of not deterring potential new readers of one of the most
popular ancient historians.[190]

---

[187] This is one of the principles adopted by O. Skutsch in his commentary on
Ennius' *Annales* (*The Annals of Quintus Ennius* (1985) 68) and by R. Maltby
and N. W. Slater in their Loeb edition of Livius Andronicus, Naevius and
Caecilius, who naturally refer also to metrical considerations (*Fragmentary
republican Latin*, Vol. 6 (2022), xi); all three editors otherwise print regular
orthography as a general rule.

[188] Even the term 'old-fashioned' can be questioned: see Zair 10–15, who in his
work deals systematically with a wide range of orthographical changes including the evidence for e.g. *seruŏs/seruus* in Catullus, Sallust's exact contemporary (280–2).

[189] See B. J. Gibson in *CLL* 49–50. This is also the practice of G. Trimble in her
commentary on Poem 64 of Catullus.

[190] Sallust's remarkable popularity in later antiquity, the Middle Ages and the
Renaissance is beyond the scope of this volume: for some brief remarks see
Woodman (2007a) xxxiii–xxxiv, with further references, and note J. Elliott,
'Fortune's child: Sallust and the grammarians' (forthcoming in *The
Cambridge Companion to Sallust*).

APPENDIX I

TIMELINE FOR THE *BELLVM CATILINAE* (63 BC)

SEPTEMBER

(?) mid: Catiline's *ruina* speech in senate [*Mur.* 51 fin.]

(?) 21 or 22:   C. harangues supporters in his house [*Mur.* 50]

22:   Postponement of consular elections (due 23rd: cf. Ramsey (2019) 230–51) [*Mur.* 51 init.]

23:   Senate discusses Catilinarian crisis [Suet. *Aug.* 94.5]: C.'s 'two heads' speech; senate's 'insufficiently severe' decree [*Mur.* 51]

end: Consular elections [Sall. 26.5; Ramsey (2019) 232, 251]

OCTOBER

early: Manlius arrives back at Faesulae [Sall. 27.1~28.4]

(?) 21:   *senatus consultum ultimum* [Sall. 29.2, *Cat.* 1.3–4, 1.7, Ascon. 6.3–8]

27:   Manlius takes up arms [Sall. 30.1, *Cat.* 1.7, 2.14]

28:   C.'s intended urban coup thwarted [*Cat.* 1.7]

(?) end: C. interrogated by L. Paullus [Sall. 31.4, *Vat.* 25, Dio 37.31.3–32.2]

NOVEMBER

early: News of Manlius' actions on 27 Oct. reaches Rome [Sall. 30.1]

1:   C. had intended to seize Praeneste [*Cat.* 1.8]

6 (night):   Conspirators meet at Laeca's house [Sall. 27.3, *Cat.* 1.6, 1.8–9, 2.6, 2.13, *Sull.* 52]

7 (early):   Attempted murder of Cicero [Sall. 28.1–3, *Cat.* 1.9–10, 2.12, *Sull.* 52]

(day):	[1]Meeting of the senate: Cicero delivers the *First Catilinarian* [Sall. 31.6, *Cat.* 2.6, 2.12]
(night):	C. leaves Rome [Sall. 32.1, *Cat.* 2.1, 2.6, 2.14–16, 2.26, 3.3]
8:	Cicero delivers the *Second Catilinarian* at a *contio* of the people
(?) 13:	C. reaches Arretium [Sall. 36.1]
(?) 20:	Trial of Murena [cf. Ramsey (2019) 251]
late:	C. joins Manlius at Faesulae [Sall. 36.1]

DECEMBER

2:	C. and Manlius already declared *hostes* [Sall. 36.2] by this date [cf. Sall. 44.6]
3 (c. 3 a.m.):	Allobroges detained at Mulvian Bridge [Sall. 45, *Cat.* 3.5–6]
(morning):	Prisoners led to Cicero's house [*Cat.* 3.6–7], thence to the Temple of Concord [*Cat.* 3.21]
(day):	Meeting of the senate; prisoners under house arrest [*Cat.* 3.14, 4.5, 4.10]
(night):	Cicero delivers the *Third Catilinarian* at a *contio* of the people [*Cat.* 3.29]
4:	Meeting of the senate: rewards for the Allobroges [Sall. 50.1, *Cat.* 4.5, 4.10]; the prisoners' fate begins to be debated[2] [Sall. 50.3–4]
5:	Meeting of the senate: Cicero delivers the *Fourth Catilinarian*; prisoners' fate debated and decided; prisoners executed [Sall. 50.3, 55.5–6]
16:	Bestia to complain about Cicero at a *contio* [Sall. 43.1]
17 (night):	Arson, slaughter and the murder of Cicero planned [Sall. 43.2, *Cat.* 3.10, Plut. *Cic.* 18.2]

---

[1] Some scholars believe that this and the following events of 7–8 Nov. took place on 8–9 Nov.

[2] That the prisoners were discussed at a meeting prior to the famous one of 5 Dec. seems certain (cf. Sall. 50.3); whether this was the same meeting as that at which the Allobroges were rewarded is uncertain, and whether their fate began to be discussed at this earlier meeting is highly controversial (see the Commentary).

APPENDIX II

SOME PARALLELS WITH CICERO'S *CATILINARIANS*

Note. The following similarities are neither exhaustive (various motival or thematic similarities could be added) nor exclusive (some of the expressions occur elsewhere in Cicero or in other authors) but are intended cumulatively to show Sallust's deep familiarity with the *Catilinarians*. In each case the swung dash is preceded by Sallust and followed by Cicero.

1.3–4 quo mihi rectius esse uidetur ingenii quam uirium opibus gloriam quaerere et, quoniam *uita ipsa qua fruimur* breuis est, memoriam nostri quam maxime longam efficere. nam diuitiarum et formae *gloria* fluxa atque fragilis est, *uirtutis* clara *aeterna*que habetur ~ **3.28** mihi quidem ipsi quid est quod iam ad *uitae fructum* possit acquiri, cum praesertim neque in honore uestro neque in *gloria uirtutis* quicquam uideam altius quo mihi libeat ascendere?, **4.21** *aeterna gloria*

5.3 corpus patiens inediae, algoris, uigiliae, **5.7** inopia rei familiaris ~ **1.26** uigilare ... patientiam famis, frigoris, inopiae rerum omnium, **2.9** frigore et fame et siti et uigiliis perferendis, **3.16** nihil erat quod non ipse ... uigilare ...; frigus, sitim, famem ferre poterat

5.7 conscientia scelerum ~ **1.17** conscientia scelerum tuorum

5.9 quo modo rem publicam habuerint ~ **1.9** quam rem publicam habemus?

12.1 hebescere uirtus ~ **1.4** hebescere aciem horum auctoritatis

14.1 flagitiorum atque facinorum, **14.2** flagitium aut facinus ~ **1.13** quod facinus ... quod flagitium, **1.18** nullum ... facinus, nullum flagitium

14.2 quicumque *impudicus, adulter, ganeo,* **14.3** *omnes* undique *parricidae* ... quos *manus atque lingua* periurio aut sanguine ciuili alebat ~ **2.7** quis *parricida* ..., quis *ganeo* ..., quis *adulter* ..., **2.23** *omnes adulteri, omnes* impuri *impudici*que, **3.16** *neque lingua neque manus* deerat

15.2 *uacuam domum* scelestis *nuptiis fecisse* ~ **1.14** *nuptiis domum uacuefecisses*

15.5 color ... oculi ... uultu ~ **3.13** color, oculi, uultus

16.1 iuuentutem quam ... illexerat ~ **2.8** tanta ... iuuentutis illecebra fuit

16.4 *rapinarum* et uictoriae *ueteris* memores ~ **2.20** spem *rapinarum ueterum*

18.7 *iam* tum non consulibus modo sed plerisque senatoribus *perniciem machinabantur* ~ **1.2** *pestem* quam tu in nos omnes *iam* diu *machinaris*

45

20.9 quae quo usque tandem patiemini, o fortissimi uiri? nonne emori per uirtutem praestat . . .? ~ **1.1** Quo usque tandem abutere, Catilina, patientia nostra?, **1.2** fortes uiri, **1.3** uiri fortes, **1.20** si emori aequo animo non potes . . .?, **2.10** fortissimis uiris

21.1 quid ubique opis aut spei haberent ~ **3.16** omnes spes atque opes . . . concidisse

24.3 plurimos cuiusque generis homines asciuisse sibi dicitur ~ **2.8** nemo . . . oppressus aere alieno fuit quem non ad hoc incredibile sceleris foedus asciuerit

24.4 *seruitia* urbana *sollicitare* ~ **4.4** *sollicitantur* Allobroges, *seruitia* excitantur

26.4 praesidia amicorum ~ **1.11** amicorum praesidio

27.2 ipse cum telo esse . . . dies noctesque . . . uigilare ~ **1.8** iam intelleges multo me uigilare acrius ad salutem quam te ad perniciem rei publicae, **1.15** te . . . cum telo

27.4 Manlium praemisisse ~ **1.24** praemissos . . . praemissam

28.1 C. Cornelius *eques Romanus* operam suam *pollicitus* et cum eo L. Vargunteius senator constituere *ea nocte paulo* post cum armatis hominibus sicuti *salutatum* introire ad Ciceronem ac de improuiso *domi suae* imparatum confodere ~ **1.9–10** reperti sunt duo *equites Romani* qui . . . se *illa ipsa nocte paulo* ante lucem me in meo lecto interfecturos esse *pollicerentur . . . salutatum*, **1.32** insidiari *domi suae* consuli

31.5 in senatum uenit ~ **1.2** in senatum uenit, **1.16** uenisti . . . in senatum

32.1 urbem uigiliis munitam ~ **1.8** coloniam . . . uigiliis esse munitam

32.1 optimum factu credens (also **55.1**, **57.5**) ~ **1.29** si hoc optimum factu iudicarem

32.1 in Manliana castra profectus est ~ **1.10** proficiscere . . . Manliana castra, **1.30** in Manliana castra

32.2 propediem cum magno exercitu ad urbem accessurum ~ **3.8** ut ad urbem quam primum cum exercitu accederet

34.2 non quo sibi tanti sceleris conscius esset sed uti *res publica quieta* foret ~ **2.19** honores quos *quieta re publica* desperant perturbata se consequi posse arbitrantur

36.3 Cicero urbi praesidio sit ~ **2.26** mihi ut urbi . . . satis esset praesidii consultum atque prouisum est

37.5 Romam sicut in sentinam confluxerant ~ **2.7** hanc sentinam urbis (also **1.12**)

40.1 negotium dat uti legatos Allobrogum requirat ~ **3.4–5** legatos Allobrogum . . . negotium susceperunt

44.1 ab Lentulo, Cethego, Statilio . . . ~ **3.9** ab Lentulo, Cethego, Statilio . . .

44.5 *Qui sim ex eo quem ad te misi* cognosces. fac *cogites* in quanta calamitate sis, et memineris te *uirum esse!* consideres quid tuae rationes postulent. *auxilium* petas *ab omnibus, etiam ab infimis* ~ **3.12** *Qui sim* scies *ex eo quem ad te misi.* cura ut *uir sis et cogita* quem in locum sis progressus. et uide quid tibi iam sit necesse et cura ut *omnium* tibi *auxilia* adiungas, *etiam infimorum*

45.2 occulte pontem ... legati cum Volturcio ~ **3.5–6** occulte ad pontem ... legati ... unaque Volturcius

46.2 coniuratione patefacta (again at 36.5, 48.1, 57.1) ~ **4.5** coniurationem patefactam esse

46.2 ciuitatem periculis ereptam esse ~ **3.1** urbem ... e flamma atque ferro ac paene e faucibus fati ereptam

46.3 uocari ad sese ~ **3.6** ad me ... uocaui

46.6 magnaque frequentia eius ordinis Volturcium ... introducit ~ **3.7–8** senatum frequentem ... introduxi Volturcium

47.2 Cinnam atque Sullam antea: se tertium esse cui fatum foret urbis potiri ~ **3.9** se esse tertium ...; Cinnam ante se et Sullam fuisse

47.3 cum ... signa sua cognouissent ~ **3.10** signum cognouit ... cognouit et signum

47.3 senatus decernit uti abdicato magistratu Lentulus itemque ... in liberis custodiis habeantur ~ **3.14** censuerunt ut P. Lentulus, cum se praetura abdicasset, in custodiam traderetur, itemque ...

48.1 mutata mente ~ **1.6** muta ... istam mentem

48.4 de paratis incendiis, de caede bonorum ~ **2.10** eructant sermonibus suis caedem bonorum atque urbis incendia

49.4 magnam illi inuidiam conflauerat ~ **1.23** si mihi inimico ... tuo conflare uis inuidiam

50.3 eos paulo ante frequens senatus iudicauerat contra rem publicam fecisse ~ **4.5–6** multis iam iudiciis iudicauistis ... iudicastis ... de facto quid iudicetis

51.9 rapi uirgines, pueros ... matres familiarum pati ... ~ **4.12** tum lamentationem matrum familias, tum fugam uirginum atque puerorum

51.18 genus poenae nouum ~ **4.7** hoc genus poenae

52.24–5 *dux hostium* cum exercitu supra caput est; uos ... dubitatis quid *intra moenia* deprensis hostibus faciatis?, **52.35** *intra moenia atque* ... ~ **1.5** *ducem*que *hostium intra moenia atque* ...

APPENDIX III

ARCHAISING

antehac	25.4
ductare	11.5, 17.7, 19.3
foret/ -ent	14.7, 18.8, 20.2, 21.1, 22.2, 23.3, 23.6, 26.1, 29.1, 31.5, 32.1, 33.1, 34.2, 37.7, 38.3, 39.4, 40.1, 47.2, 50.4, 51.6
gerund + acc. object	4.1, 38.1, 42.2, 43.3, 54.3, 59.6
is (resumptive)	12.5, 20.4, 37.4, 58.16
luculentus	31.6
materies	10.3
(*multi*) *mortales*	1.5, 2.8, 6.3, 10.5, 12.4, 20.11, 33.4, 36.4, 51.11, 51.13, 51.15, 51.20, 52.7
patrare	18.8, 53.4, 56.4
plebes (fifth decl.)	37.1, 37.4
pollens (?)	6.3
-que . . . -que (?)	9.3, 14.2 (?), 36.4
reor	48.5, 55.1, 57.5, 60.5
supplicium 'supplication'	9.2, 52.29
tempestas 'time'	7.1, 17.7, 20.3 (?), 22.1, 24.3, 36.4, 53.5
tumulti (gen.)	59.5
ut 'because'	59.2

C. SALLVSTII CRISPI
BELLVM CATILINAE

C. SALLVSTII CRISPI
BELLVM CATILINAE

Omnes homines qui sese student praestare ceteris animalibus **1**
summa ope niti decet ne uitam silentio transeant ueluti pecora,
quae Natura prona atque uentri oboedientia finxit. sed nostra **2**
omnis uis in animo et corpore sita est: animi imperio, corporis
seruitio magis utimur; alterum nobis cum dis, alterum cum beluis
commune est. quo mihi rectius esse uidetur ingenii quam uirium **3**
opibus gloriam quaerere et, quoniam uita ipsa qua fruimur breuis
est, memoriam nostri quam maxime longam efficere. nam diui- **4**
tiarum et formae gloria fluxa atque fragilis est, uirtutis clara aeternaque habetur. sed diu magnum inter mortales certamen fuit uine **5**
corporis an uirtute animi res militaris magis procederet. (nam et, **6**
priusquam incipias, consulto et, ubi consulueris, mature facto opus
est: ita utrumque per se indigens alterum alterius auxilio eget.) **7**
igitur initio reges – nam in terris nomen imperii id primum fuit – **2**
diuersi pars ingenium, alii corpus exercebant. etiam tum uita
hominum sine cupiditate agitabatur: sua cuique satis placebant;
postea uero quam in Asia Cyrus, in Graecia Lacedaemonii et **2**
Athenienses coepere urbes atque nationes subigere, libidinem
dominandi causam belli habere, maximam gloriam in maximo
imperio putare, tum demum periculo atque negotiis compertum
est in bello plurimum ingenium posse. quod si regum atque imper- **3**
atorum animi uirtus in pace ita ut in bello ualeret, aequabilius
atque constantius sese res humanae haberent neque aliud alio
ferri neque mutari ac misceri omnia cerneres. nam imperium facile **4**
iis artibus retinetur quibus initio partum est; uerum, ubi pro labore **5**
desidia, pro continentia et aequitate libido atque superbia inuasere, fortuna simul cum moribus immutatur: ita imperium semper **6**
ad optimum quemque a minus bono transfertur.

Quae homines arant, nauigant, aedificant, uirtuti omnia parent. **7**
sed multi mortales, dediti uentri atque somno, indocti incultique **8**
uitam sicuti peregrinantes transiere; quibus profecto contra naturam corpus uoluptati, anima oneri fuit: eorum ego uitam

Bellum Catilinae *PK in subscriptionibus* (*cf. Quint. 3.8.9*)
1.1 Omnes *A*: -nis *P.* -neis *Charisius* **1.3** esse uidetur] uidetur esse *uel* uidetur **1.4** uirtutis *Woodman*: uirtus *codd.*

9 mortemque iuxta aestimo, quoniam de utraque siletur. uerum
enim uero is demum mihi uiuere atque frui anima uidetur qui
aliquo negotio intentus praeclari facinoris aut artis bonae famam
quaerit. sed in magna copia rerum aliud alii Natura iter ostendit.
3 pulchrum est bene facere rei publicae, etiam bene dicere haud
absurdum est: uel pace uel bello clarum fieri licet; et qui fecere et
2 qui facta aliorum scripsere, multi laudantur. ac mihi quidem,
tametsi haudquaquam par gloria sequitur scriptorem et auctorem
rerum, tamen in primis arduum uidetur res gestas scribere – primum, quod facta dictis exaequanda sunt; dehinc, quia plerique,
quae delicta reprehenderis, maleuolentia et inuidia dicta putant;
ubi de magna uirtute atque gloria bonorum memores, quae sibi
quisque facilia factu putat, aequo animo accipit, supra ea, ueluti
ficta, pro falsis ducit.
3   Sed ego adulescentulus initio, sicuti plerique, studio ad rem
publicam latus sum ibique mihi multa aduersa fuere. nam pro
pudore, pro abstinentia, pro uirtute audacia, largitio, auaritia uige-
4 bant. quae tametsi animus aspernabatur insolens malarum artium,
tamen inter tanta uitia imbecilla aetas ambitione corrupta teneba-
5 tur; ac me, cum ab reliquorum malis moribus dissentirem, nihilo
minus honoris cupido eadem qua ceteros fama atque inuidia uex-
4 abat. igitur ubi animus ex multis miseriis atque periculis requieuit
et mihi reliquam aetatem a re publica procul habendam decreui,
non fuit consilium socordia atque desidia bonum otium conterere
neque uero agrum colendo aut uenando seruilibus officiis inten-
2 tum aetatem agere; sed, a quo incepto studioque me ambitio mala
detinuerat, eodem regressus statui res gestas populi Romani carptim, ut quaeque memoria digna uidebantur, perscribere, eo magis
quod mihi a spe, metu, partibus rei publicae animus liber erat.
3   Igitur de Catilinae coniuratione quam uerissime potero paucis
4 absoluam (nam id facinus in primis ego memorabile existimo
5 sceleris atque periculi nouitate); de cuius hominis moribus pauca
prius explananda sunt quam initium narrandi faciam.
5   L. Catilina, nobili genere natus, fuit magna ui et animi et
2 corporis, sed ingenio malo prauoque: huic ab adulescentia bella
intestina, caedes, rapinae, discordia ciuilis grata fuere ibique iuuen-
3 tutem suam exercuit. corpus patiens inediae, algoris, uigiliae supra

---

3.2 auctorem] actorem   **3.5** honoris cupido *secl. Kraggerud*: honoris cupidum
Damsté

quam cuiquam credibile est; animus audax, subdolus, uarius, cuius 4
rei libet simulator ac dissimulator. alieni appetens, sui profusus;
ardens in cupiditatibus; satis eloquentiae, sapientiae parum. uastus 5
animus immoderata, incredibilia, nimis alta semper cupiebat. hunc 6
post dominationem L. Sullae libido maxima inuaserat rei publicae
capiendae; neque id quibus modis assequeretur, dum sibi regnum
pararet, quicquam pensi habebat. agitabatur magis magisque in 7
dies animus ferox inopia rei familiaris et conscientia scelerum,
quae utraque iis artibus auxerat quas supra memoraui. incitabant 8
praeterea corrupti ciuitatis mores, quos pessima ac diuersa inter se
mala, luxuria atque auaritia, uexabant.

Res ipsa hortari uidetur, quoniam de moribus ciuitatis tempus 9
admonuit, supra repetere ac paucis instituta maiorum domi militiaeque, quo modo rem publicam habuerint quantamque reliquerint, ut paulatim immutata ex pulcherrima <atque optima> pessima
ac flagitiosissima facta sit, disserere.

Vrbem Romam, sicuti ego accepi, condidere atque habuere 6
initio Troiani, qui Aenea duce profugi sedibus incertis uagabantur,
cumque his Aborigines, genus hominum agreste, sine legibus, sine
imperio, liberum atque solutum. hi postquam in una moenia con- 2
uenere, dispari genere, dissimili lingua, alius alio more uiuentes,
incredibile memoratu est quam facile coaluerint: ita breui multitudo diuersa atque uaga concordia ciuitas facta est. sed postquam 3
res eorum ciuibus, moribus, agris aucta satis prospera satisque
pollens uidebatur, sicuti pleraque mortalium habentur, inuidia ex
opulentia orta est. igitur reges populique finitimi bello temptare, 4
pauci ex amicis auxilio esse: nam ceteri metu perculsi a periculis
aberant. at Romani domi militiaeque intenti festinare, parare, alius 5
alium hortari, hostibus obuiam ire, libertatem, patriam parent-
esque armis tegere. post, ubi pericula uirtute propulerant, sociis
atque amicis auxilia portabant magisque dandis quam accipiendis
beneficiis amicitias parabant. imperium legitimum, nomen imperii 6
regium habebant. delecti, quibus corpus annis infirmum, ingenium sapientia ualidum erat, rei publicae consultabant; hi uel
aetate uel curae similitudine patres appellabantur. post, ubi regium 7
imperium, quod initio conseruandae libertatis atque augendae rei
publicae fuerat, in superbiam dominationemque se conuertit,

5.9 *post* pulcherrima *edd. suppl.* atque optima *ex Aug. Ciu. Dei 2.18–19* **6.2** ita
breui … facta est Π*4*, *Aug. Epist. 138.10* (*sed* facta erat): *deest in codd. plerisque*

immutato more annua imperia binosque imperatores sibi fecere:
eo modo minime posse putabant per licentiam insolescere animum
7 humanum. sed ea tempestate coepere se quisque magis extollere
2 magisque ingenium promptum habere. (nam regibus boni quam
mali suspectiores sunt semperque iis aliena uirtus formidulosa est.)
3 sed ciuitas incredibile memoratu est adepta libertate quantum
breui creuerit: tanta cupido gloriae incesserat.
4   Iam primum iuuentus, simul ac belli patiens erat, in castris per
laborem usum militiae discebat magisque in decoris armis et militaribus equis quam in scortis atque conuiuiis libidinem habebant.
5 igitur talibus uiris non labor insolitus, non locus ullus asper aut
arduus erat, non armatus hostis formidulosus: uirtus omnia
6 domuerat. sed gloriae maximum certamen inter ipsos erat: se
quisque hostem ferire, murum ascendere, conspici dum tale facinus faceret properabat: eas diuitias, eam bonam famam magnam-
que nobilitatem putabant. laudis auidi, pecuniae liberales erant;
7 gloriam ingentem, diuitias honestas uolebant. memorare possum
quibus in locis maximas hostium copias populus Romanus parua
manu fuderit, quas urbes natura munitas pugnando ceperit, ni ea
res longius nos ab incepto traheret.
8   Sed profecto Fortuna in omni re dominatur; ea res cunctas ex
2 libidine magis quam ex uero celebrat obscuratque. Atheniensium
res gestae, sicuti ego aestimo, satis amplae magnificaeque fuere,
3 uerum aliquanto minores tamen quam fama feruntur. sed, quia
prouenere ibi scriptorum magna ingenia, per terrarum orbem
4 Atheniensium facta pro maximis celebrantur. ita eorum qui fecere
uirtus tanta habetur quantum eam uerbis potuere extollere prae-
5 clara ingenia. at populo Romano numquam ea copia fuit, quia
prudentissimus quisque maxime negotiosus erat: ingenium nemo
sine corpore exercebat; optimus quisque facere quam dicere, sua
ab aliis benefacta laudari quam ipse aliorum narrare malebat.
9   Igitur domi militiaeque boni mores colebantur: concordia maxima, minima auaritia erat; ius bonumque apud eos non legibus
2 magis quam natura ualebat. iurgia, discordias, simultates cum hostibus exercebant, ciues cum ciuibus de uirtute certabant. in suppli-
3 ciis deorum magnifici, domi parci, in amicos fideles erant. duabus
his artibus – audacia in bello, ubi pax euenerat, aequitate – seque

---

7.1 promptum *Woodman*: in promptu *codd.*   **7.6** se] sic *uel* sic se   **7.7** possum]
possem

remque publicam curabant. quarum rerum ego maxima docu- 4
menta haec habeo, quod in bello saepius uindicatum est in eos
qui contra imperium in hostem pugnauerant quique tardius reuocati proelio excesserant quam qui signa relinquere aut pulsi loco
cedere ausi erant; in pace uero quod beneficiis magis quam metu 5
imperium agitabant et accepta iniuria ignoscere quam persequi
malebant. sed, ubi labore atque iustitia res publica creuit, reges 10
magni bello domiti, nationes ferae et populi ingentes ui subacti,
Carthago, aemula imperii Romani, ab stirpe interiit, cuncta maria
terraeque patebant, saeuire Fortuna ac miscere omnia coepit: qui 2
labores, pericula, dubias atque asperas res facile tolerauerant, iis
otium, diuitiae – optanda alias – oneri miseriaeque fuere.
   Igitur primum pecuniae, deinde imperii cupido creuit: ea quasi 3
materies omnium malorum fuere. namque auaritia fidem, probita- 4
tem ceterasque artes bonas subuertit: pro his superbiam, crudelitatem, deos neglegere, omnia uenalia habere edocuit; ambitio 5
multos mortales falsos fieri subegit, aliud clausum in pectore,
aliud in lingua promptum habere, amicitias inimicitiasque non ex
re sed ex commodo aestimare, magisque uultum quam ingenium
bonum habere. haec primo paulatim crescere, interdum uindicari; 6
post, ubi contagio quasi pestilentia inuasit, ciuitas immutata, imperium ex iustissimo atque optimo crudele intolerandumque factum.
   sed primo magis ambitio quam auaritia animos hominum exerce- 11
bat, quod tamen uitium propius uirtutem erat: nam gloriam, hon- 2
orem, imperium bonus et ignauus aeque sibi exoptant; sed ille uera
uia nititur, huic quia bonae artes desunt, dolis atque fallaciis contendit. auaritia pecuniae studium habet, quam nemo sapiens con- 3
cupiuit: ea, quasi uenenis malis imbuta, corpus animumque uirilem
effeminat, semper infinita, insatiabilis est, neque copia neque inopia minuitur. sed, postquam L. Sulla armis recepta re publica bonis 4
initiis malos euentus habuit, rapere omnes, trahere, domum alius,
alius agros cupere, neque modum neque modestiam uictores
habere, foeda crudeliaque in ciues facinora facere. huc accedebat 5
quod L. Sulla exercitum quem in Asia ductauerat, quo sibi fidum
faceret, contra morem maiorum luxuriose nimisque liberaliter
habuerat. loca amoena, uoluptaria facile in otio feroces militum
animos molliuerant. ibi primum insueuit exercitus populi Romani 6

10.3 primum *Woodman*: primo *codd.*   pecuniae *et* imperii *inter se transpos.* Nipperdey

amare, potare, signa, tabulas pictas, uasa caelata mirari, ea priuatim
et publice rapere, delubra spoliare, sacra profanaque omnia pol-
7 luere. igitur ii milites, postquam uictoriam adepti sunt, nihil reliqui
8 uictis fecere. quippe secundae res sapientium animos fatigant; ne
illi corruptis moribus uictoriae temperarent.

12 Postquam diuitiae honori esse coepere et eas gloria, imperium,
potentia sequebatur, hebescere uirtus, paupertas probro haberi,
2 innocentia pro maleuolentia duci coepit. igitur ex diuitiis iuuentutem luxuria atque auaritia cum superbia inuasere: rapere, consumere, sua parui pendere, aliena cupere, pudorem, <im>pudicitiam,
diuina atque humana promiscua, nihil pensi neque moderati
3 habere. operae pretium est, cum domos atque uillas cognoueris in
urbium modum exaedificatas, uisere templa deorum quae nostri
4 maiores, religiosissimi mortales, fecere. uerum illi delubra deorum
pietate, domos suas gloria decorabant, neque uictis quicquam
5 praeter iniuriae licentiam eripiebant; at hi contra, ignauissimi
homines, per summum scelus omnia ea sociis adimere quae fortissimi uiri uictores reliquerant – proinde quasi iniuriam facere, id
demum esset imperio uti.

13 Nam quid ea memorem quae nisi iis qui uidere nemini credibilia sunt, a priuatis compluribus subuersos montes, maria constrata
2 esse? quibus mihi uidentur ludibrio fuisse diuitiae: quippe quas
3 honeste habere licebat, abuti per turpitudinem properabant. sed
libido stupri, ganeae ceterique cultus non minor incesserat: uiri
muliebria pati, mulieres pudicitiam in propatulo habere; uescendi
causa terra marique omnia exquirere; dormire priusquam somni
cupido esset; non famem aut sitim neque frigus neque lassitudinem
4 opperiri, sed ea omnia luxu antecapere. haec iuuentutem, ubi
5 familiares opes defecerant, ad facinora incendebant: animus inbu-
tus malis artibus haud facile libidinibus carebat: eo profusius omnibus modis quaestui atque sumptui deditus erat.

14 In tanta tamque corrupta ciuitate Catilina (id quod factu facillimum erat) omnium flagitiorum atque facinorum circum se tam-
2 quam stipatorum cateruas habebat. nam quicumque impudicus,
adulter, ganeo, <quique> manu, uentre, pene bona patria lacerauerat, quique alienum aes grande conflauerat quo flagitium aut

---

12.2 <im>pudicitiam *van Veen* 14.2 impudicus, adulter, ganeo *secl. Leutsch,*
Sauppe (*cf. Fronto p. 145.18–19 vdH²*): impudicus, aleator, ganeo *Köchly*:
alii alia <quique> *Fronto loc. cit.* (*et cf. 146.1*)

facinus redimeret, praeterea omnes undique parricidae, sacrilegi, 3
conuicti iudiciis aut pro factis iudicium timentes, ad hoc quos
manus atque lingua periurio aut sanguine ciuili alebat, postremo
omnes quos flagitium, egestas, conscius animus exagitabat, ii
Catilinae proximi familiaresque erant. quod si quis etiam a culpa 4
uacuus in amicitiam eius inciderat, cotidiano usu atque illecebris
facile par similisque ceteris efficiebatur; sed maxime adulescen- 5
tium familiaritates appetebat: eorum animi molles etiam et fluxi
dolis haud difficulter capiebantur. nam, ut cuiusque studium ex 6
aetate flagrabat, aliis scorta praebere, aliis canes atque equos mercari, postremo neque sumptui neque modestiae suae parcere, dum
illos obnoxios fidosque sibi faceret. scio fuisse nonnullos qui ita 7
existimarent iuuentutem quae domum Catilinae frequentabat
parum honeste pudicitiam habuisse; sed ex aliis rebus magis
quam quod cuiquam id compertum foret haec fama ualebat.

Iam primum adulescens Catilina multa nefanda stupra fecerat, 15
cum uirgine nobili, cum sacerdote Vestae, alia huiusce modi contra
ius fasque. postremo captus amore Aureliae Orestillae (cuius prae- 2
ter formam nihil umquam bonus laudauit), quod ea nubere illi
dubitabat timens priuignum adulta aetate, pro certo creditur
necato filio uacuam domum scelestis nuptiis fecisse. quae quidem 3
res mihi in primis uidetur causa fuisse facinus maturandi: namque 4
animus impurus, dis hominibusque infestus, neque uigiliis neque
quietibus sedari poterat: ita conscientia mentem excitam uastabat.
igitur color ei exsanguis, foedi oculi, citus modo, modo tardus 5
incessus: prorsus in facie uultuque uecordia inerat.

   Sed iuuentutem, quam (ut supra diximus) illexerat, multis 16
modis mala facinora edocebat. ex illis testes signatoresque falsos 2
commodare; fidem, fortunas, pericula uilia habere, post, ubi
eorum famam atque pudorem attriuerat, maiora alia imperabat.
si causa peccandi in praesens minus suppetebat, nihilo minus 3
insontes sicuti sontes circumuenire, iugulare: scilicet, ne per
otium torpescerent manus aut animus, gratuito potius malus
atque crudelis erat.

   His amicis sociisque confisus Catilina, simul quod aes alienum 4
per omnes terras ingens erat et quod plerique Sullani milites largius suo usi rapinarum et uictoriae ueteris memores ciuile bellum

5 exoptabant, opprimendae rei publicae consilium cepit. in Italia
nullus exercitus, Cn. Pompeius in extremis terris bellum gerebat;
ipsi consulatum petenti magna spes, senatus nihil sane intentus.
tutae tranquillaeque res omnes, sed ea prorsus opportuna
Catilinae.

17 Igitur circiter Kalendas Iunias L. Caesare et C. Figulo consulibus
primo singulos appellare: hortari alios, alios temptare; opes suas,
imparatam rem publicam, magna praemia coniurationis docere.

2 ubi satis explorata sunt quae uoluit, in unum omnes conuocat
3 quibus maxima necessitudo et plurimum audaciae inerat. eo conuenere senatorii ordinis P. Lentulus Sura, P. Autronius, L. Cassius
Longinus, C. Cethegus, P. et Ser. Sullae Ser. filii, L. Vargunteius,
4 Q. Annius, M. Porcius Laeca, L. Bestia, Q. Curius; praeterea ex
equestri ordine M. Fuluius Nobilior, L. Statilius, P. Gabinius
Capito, C. Cornelius; ad hoc multi ex coloniis et municipiis domi
5 nobiles. erant praeterea complures paulo occultius consilii huiusce
participes nobiles, quos magis dominationis spes hortabatur quam
6 inopia aut alia necessitudo. ceterum iuuentus pleraque, sed maxime nobilium, Catilinae inceptis fauebat; quibus in otio uel magnifice uel molliter uiuere copia erat incerta pro certis, bellum quam
7 pacem malebant. fuere item ea tempestate qui crederent
M. Licinium Crassum non ignarum eius consilii fuisse: quia Cn.
Pompeius, inuisus ipsi, magnum exercitum ductabat, cuiusuis opes
uoluisse contra illius potentiam crescere, simul confisum, si coniuratio ualuisset, facile apud illos principem se fore.

18 Sed antea item coniurauere pauci contra rem publicam, in quis
2 Catilina fuit; de qua quam breuissime potero dicam. L. Tullo et M'.
Lepido consulibus P. Autronius et P. Sulla designati consules legi-
3 bus ambitus interrogati poenas dederant. post paulo Catilina pecuniarum repetundarum reus prohibitus erat consulatum petere,
4 quod intra legitimos dies profiteri nequiuerat. erat eodem tempore
Cn. Piso, adulescens nobilis, summae audaciae, egens, factiosus,
quem ad perturbandam rem publicam inopia atque mali mores
5 stimulabant. cum hoc Catilina et Autronius circiter Nonas
Decembres consilio communicato parabant in Capitolio Kalendis
Ianuariis L. Cottam et L. Torquatum consules interficere, ipsi
fascibus correptis Pisonem cum exercitu ad obtinendas duas

18.1–2 quis … breuissime *Diomedes* (*1.445.23*): quibus … uerissime *codd.*

Hispanias mittere. ea re cognita rursus in Nonas Februarias con- 6
silium caedis transtulerant: iam tum non consulibus modo sed 7
plerisque senatoribus perniciem machinabantur. quod ni Catilina 8
maturasset pro curia signum sociis dare, eo die post conditam
urbem Romam pessimum facinus patratum foret. quia nondum
frequentes armati conuenerant, ea res consilium diremit.

Postea Piso in citeriorem Hispaniam quaestor pro praetore 19
missus est, adnitente Crasso, quod eum infestum, inimicum Cn.
Pompeio cognouerat. neque tamen senatus prouinciam inuitus 2
dederat: quippe foedum hominem a republica procul esse uolebat,
simul quia boni complures praesidium in eo putabant et iam tum
potentia Pompeii formidulosa erat. sed is Piso in prouincia ab 3
equitibus Hispanis, quos in exercitu ductabat, iter faciens occisus
est. sunt qui ita dicant, imperia eius iniusta, superba, crudelia 4
barbaros nequiuisse pati; alii autem equites illos, Cn. Pompeii 5
ueteres fidosque clientes, uoluntate eius Pisonem aggressos: numquam Hispanos praeterea tale facinus fecisse, sed imperia saeua
multa antea perpessos. nos eam rem in medio relinquemus. de 6
superiore coniuratione satis dictum.

Catilina ubi eos quos paulo ante memoraui conuenisse uidet, 20
tametsi cum singulis multa saepe egerat, tamen in rem fore credens
uniuersos appellare et cohortari, in abditam partem aedium sece-
dit atque ibi omnibus arbitris procul amotis orationem huiusce
modi habuit:

'Ni uirtus fidesque uestra spectata mihi forent, nequiquam 2
opportuna res cecidisset, spes magna, dominatio in manibus frustra
fuissent; neque ego per ignauiam aut uana ingenia incerta pro
certis captarem. sed quia multis et magnis tempestatibus uos cog- 3
noui fortes fidosque mihi, eo animus ausus est maximum atque
pulcherrimum facinus incipere, simul quia uobis eadem quae mihi
bona malaque esse intellexi: nam idem uelle atque idem nolle, ea 4
demum firma amicitia est. sed ego quae mente agitaui omnes iam 5
antea diuersi audistis; ceterum mihi in dies magis animus accendi- 6
tur, cum considero quae condicio uitae futura sit, nisi nosmet ipsi
uindicamus in libertatem. nam postquam res publica in paucorum 7
potentium ius atque dicionem concessit, semper illis reges, tetrarchae uectigales esse, populi, nationes stipendia pendere; ceteri

---

18.8 Romam *fort. ut perperam additum secludendum* **19.3** quos in exercitu] quos
sine exercitu **20.2** *fort.* cecidisset <et>

omnes, strenui, boni, nobiles atque ignobiles, "uulgus" fuimus, sine
gratia, sine auctoritate, iis obnoxii quibus, si res publica ualeret,
8 formidini essemus. itaque omnis gratia, potentia, honor, diuitiae
apud illos sunt aut ubi illi uolunt; nobis reliquere pericula, repulsas,
9 iudicia, egestatem. quae quousque tandem patiemini, o fortissimi
uiri? nonne emori per uirtutem praestat quam uitam miseram
atque inhonestam, ubi alienae superbiae ludibrio fueris, per dede-
10 cus amittere? uerum enim uero – pro deum atque hominum
fidem! – uictoria in manu nobis est: uiget aetas, animus ualet;
contra illis annis atque diuitiis omnia consenuerunt. tantum
11 modo incepto opus est; cetera res expediet. etenim quis mortalium,
cui uirile ingenium est, tolerare potest illis diuitias superare, quas
profundant in exstruendo mari et montibus coaequandis, nobis
rem familiarem etiam ad necessaria deesse? illos binas aut amplius
domos continuare, nobis larem familiarem nusquam ullum esse?
12 cum tabulas, signa, toreumata emunt, noua diruunt, alia aedificant,
postremo omnibus modis pecuniam trahunt, uexant, tamen
13 summa libidine diuitias suas uincere nequeunt. at nobis est domi
inopia, foris aes alienum, mala res, spes multo asperior; denique
quid reliqui habemus praeter miseram animam?
14   'Quin igitur expergiscimini? en illa, illa quam saepe optastis,
libertas, praeterea diuitiae, decus, gloria in oculis sita sunt:
15 Fortuna omnia ea uictoribus praemia posuit. res, tempus, pericula,
egestas, belli spolia magnifica magis quam oratio mea uos horten-
16 tur. uel imperatore uel milite me utimini: neque animus neque
17 corpus a uobis aberit. haec ipsa, ut spero, uobiscum una consul
agam, nisi forte me animus fallit et uos seruire magis quam imperare parati estis.'
21   Postquam accepere ea homines quibus mala abunde omnia
erant, sed neque res neque spes bona ulla, tametsi illis quieta
mouere magna merces uidebatur, tamen postulauere plerique ut
proponeret quae condicio belli foret, quae praemia armis peterent,
2 quid ubique opis aut spei haberent. tum Catilina polliceri tabulas
nouas, proscriptionem locupletium, magistratus, sacerdotia, rapi-
3 nas, alia omnia quae bellum atque libido uictorum fert: praeterea
esse in Hispania citeriore Pisonem, in Mauretania cum exercitu
P. Sittium Nucerinum, consilii sui participes; petere consulatum

20.15 hortentur] hortantur

C. Antonium, quem sibi collegam fore speraret, hominem et familiarem et omnibus necessitudinibus circumuentum; cum eo se consulem initium agendi facturum. ad hoc maledictis increpabat 4
omnes bonos, suorum unumquemque nominans laudare: admon-
ebat alium egestatis, alium cupiditatis suae, complures periculi aut
ignominiae, multos uictoriae Sullanae, quibus ea praedae fuerat.
postquam omnium animos alacres uidet, cohortatus ut petitionem 5
suam curae haberent, conuentum dimisit.

   (Fuere ea tempestate qui dicerent Catilinam oratione habita, 22
cum ad ius iurandum populares sceleris sui adigeret, humani corporis sanguinem uino permixtum in pateris circumtulisse: inde 2
cum post exsecrationem omnes degustauissent, sicuti in sollemnibus sacris fieri consueuit, aperuisse consilium suum atque eo dictitasse facere quo inter se fidi magis forent, alius alii tanti facinoris
conscii. nonnulli ficta et haec et multa praeterea existimabant ab iis 3
qui Ciceronis inuidiam, quae postea orta est, leniri credebant
atrocitate sceleris eorum qui poenas dederant; nobis ea res pro
magnitudine parum comperta est.)

   Sed in ea coniuratione fuit Q. Curius, natus haud obscuro loco, 23
flagitiis atque facinoribus coopertus, quem censores senatu probri
gratia mouerant. huic homini non minor uanitas inerat quam 2
audacia: neque reticere quae audierat neque suamet ipse scelera
occultare; prorsus neque dicere neque facere quicquam pensi
habebat. erat ei cum Fuluia, muliere nobili, stupri uetus consue- 3
tudo. cui cum minus gratus esset quia inopia minus largiri poterat,
repente glorians maria montesque polliceri coepit et minari interdum ferro, ni sibi obnoxia foret, postremo ferocius agitare quam
solitus erat. at Fuluia insolentiae Curii causa cognita tale periculum 4
rei publicae haud occultum habuit, sed sublato auctore de
Catilinae coniuratione, quae quoque modo audierat, compluribus
narrauit.

   Ea res in primis studia hominum accendit ad consulatum man- 5
dandum M. Tullio Ciceroni. namque antea pleraque nobilitas inui- 6
dia aestuabat et quasi pollui consulatum credebant, si eum quamuis
egregius homo nouus adeptus foret; sed, ubi periculum aduenit,
inuidia atque superbia post fuere. igitur comitiis habitis consules 24
declarantur M. Tullius et C. Antonius.

22.2 dictitasse facere *Woodman*: dictitare fecisse *codd.*

2   Quod factum primo populares coniurationis concusserat; neque
    tamen Catilinae furor minuebatur, sed in dies plura agitare: arma
    per Italiam locis opportunis parare, pecuniam sua aut amicorum
    fide sumptam mutuam Faesulas ad Manlium quendam portare, qui
3   postea princeps fuit belli faciendi. ea tempestate plurimos cuiusque
    generis homines asciuisse sibi dicitur, mulieres etiam aliquot, quae
    primo ingentes sumptus stupro corporis tolerauerant, post, ubi
    aetas tantummodo quaestui neque luxuriae modum fecerat, aes
4   alienum grande conflauerant. per eas se Catilina credebat posse
    seruitia urbana sollicitare, urbem incendere, uiros earum uel
    adiungere sibi uel interficere.
25   Sed in iis erat Sempronia, quae multa saepe uirilis audaciae
2   facinora commiserat. haec mulier – genere atque forma, praeterea
    uiro, liberis satis fortunata – fuit litteris Graecis, Latinis docta,
    psallere, saltare elegantius quam necesse est probae, multa alia
3   quae instrumenta luxuriae sunt. sed ei cariora semper omnia
    quam decus atque pudicitia fuit; pecuniae an famae minus par-
    ceret, haud facile discerneres; libido sic accensa ut saepius peteret
4   uiros quam peteretur. sed ea saepe antehac fidem prodiderat,
    creditum abiurauerat, caedis conscia fuerat; luxuria atque inopia
5   praeceps abierat. uerum ingenium eius haud absurdum: posse
    uersus facere, iocum mouere, sermone uti uel modesto uel molli
    uel procaci; prorsus multae facetiae multusque lepos inerat.
26   His rebus comparatis Catilina nihilo minus in proximum annum
    consulatum petebat, sperans, si designatus foret, facile se ex uolun-
    tate Antonio usurum. neque interea quietus erat, sed omnibus
2   modis insidias parabat Ciceroni. neque illi tamen ad cauendum
3   dolus aut astutiae deerant. namque a principio consulatus sui multa
    pollicendo per Fuluiam effecerat ut Q. Curius, de quo paulo ante
4   memoraui, consilia Catilinae sibi proderet; ad hoc collegam suum
    Antonium pactione prouinciae perpulerat ne contra rem publicam
    sentiret; circum se praesidia amicorum atque clientium occulte
5   habebat. postquam dies comitiorum uenit et Catilinae neque peti-
    tio neque insidiae quas consulibus in Campo fecerat prospere
    cessere, constituit bellum facere et extrema omnia experiri, quo-
    niam quae occulte temptauerat aspera foedaque euenerant.

25.2 liberis ... Latinis ... saltare *Fronto pp. 100.23–101.1 vdH²*: atque liberis ... et
Latinis ... et saltare *codd. plerique*   **26.5** consulibus] -uli (consulibus *secl. Dietsch*)

Igitur C. Manlium Faesulas atque in eam partem Etruriae, **27**
Septimium quendam Camertem in agrum Picenum, C.
Iulium in Apuliam dimisit, praeterea alium alio, quem ubique opportunum
sibi fore credebat.

Interea Romae multa simul moliri: consulibus insidias tendere, **2**
parare incendia, opportuna loca armatis hominibus obsidere, ipse
cum telo esse, item alios iubere, hortari uti semper intenti paratique essent, dies noctesque festinare, uigilare, neque insomniis
neque labore fatigari. postremo, ubi multa agitanti nihil procedit, **3**
rursus intempesta nocte coniurationis principes conuocat per
M. Porcium Laecam, ibique multa de ignauia eorum questus **4**
docet se Manlium praemisisse ad eam multitudinem quam ad
capienda arma parauerat, item alios in alia loca opportuna qui
initium belli facerent, seque ad exercitum proficisci cupere, si
prius Ciceronem oppressisset: eum suis consiliis multum officere.
igitur perterritis ac dubitantibus ceteris C. Cornelius eques **28**
Romanus operam suam pollicitus et cum eo L. Vargunteius senator
constituere ea nocte paulo post cum armatis hominibus sicuti
salutatum introire ad Ciceronem ac de improuiso domi suae imparatum confodere. Curius ubi intellegit quantum periculum consuli **2**
impendeat, propere per Fuluiam Ciceroni dolum qui parabatur
enuntiat. ita illi ianua prohibiti tantum facinus frustra susceperant. **3**

Interea Manlius in Etruria plebem sollicitare egestate simul ac **4**
dolore iniuriae nouarum rerum cupidam, quod Sullae dominatione agros bonaque omnia amiserat, praeterea latrones cuiusque
generis, quorum in ea regione magna copia erat, nonnullos ex
Sullanis coloniis quibus libido atque luxuria ex magnis rapinis
nihil reliqui fecerat. ea cum Ciceroni nuntiarentur, ancipiti malo **29**
permotus, quod neque urbem ab insidiis priuato consilio longius
tueri poterat neque exercitus Manlii quantus aut quo consilio foret
satis compertum habebat, rem ad senatum refert, iam antea uulgi
rumoribus exagitatum. itaque – quod plerumque in atroci negotio **2**
solet – senatus decreuit darent operam consules ne quid res publica
detrimenti caperet. (ea potestas per senatum more Romano magis- **3**
tratui maxima permittitur: exercitum parare, bellum gerere, coer-
cere omnibus modis socios atque ciues, domi militiaeque

27.2 consulibus] -uli (consulibus *secl. Dietsch*)   **29.1** exagitatum *Cortius*: -tam
codd.: agitatam *Nipperdey*

imperium atque iudicium summum habere; aliter sine populi iussu
nullius earum rerum consuli ius est.)

30   Post paucos dies L. Saenius senator in senatu litteras recitauit
quas Faesulis allatas sibi dicebat, in quibus scriptum erat
C. Manlium arma cepisse cum magna multitudine ante diem VI
2 Kalendas Nouembres. simul – id quod in tali re solet – alii portenta
atque prodigia nuntiabant, alii conuentus fieri, arma portari,
3 Capuae atque in Apulia seruile bellum moueri. igitur senati
decreto Q. Marcius Rex Faesulas, Q. Metellus Creticus in Apuliam
4 circumque ea loca missi (ii utrique ad urbem imperatores erant,
impediti ne triumpharent calumnia paucorum quibus omnia hon-
5 esta atque inhonesta uendere mos erat); sed praetores
Q. Pompeius Rufus Capuam, Q. Metellus Celer in agrum
Picenum, iisque permissum uti pro tempore atque periculo exerci-
6 tum compararent; ad hoc, si quis indicauisset de coniuratione quae
contra rem publicam facta erat, praemium seruo libertatem et
sestertia centum, libero impunitatem eius rei et sestertia ducenta
7 [milia], itemque decreuere uti gladiatoriae familiae Capuae in
cetera municipia distribuerentur pro cuiusque opibus, Romae per
totam urbem uigiliae haberentur eisque minores magistratus
praeessent.

31   Quis rebus permota ciuitas atque immutata urbis facies erat. ex
summa laetitia lasciuiaque, quae diuturna quies pepererat, repente
2 omnes tristitia inuasit: festinare, trepidare, neque loco neque
homini cuiquam satis credere, neque bellum gerere neque pacem
3 habere, suo quisque metu pericula metiri. ad hoc mulieres, quibus
rei publicae magnitudine belli timor insolitus incesserat, afflictare
sese, manus supplices ad caelum tendere, miserari paruos liberos,
rogitare omnia, <omni rumore> pauere, <arripere omnia,>
superbia atque deliciis omissis sibi patriaeque diffidere.
4   At Catilinae crudelis animus eadem illa mouebat, tametsi praesidia parabantur et ipse lege Plautia interrogatus erat ab L. Paulo.
5 postremo dissimulandi causa aut sui expurgandi, sicut iurgio laces-
6 situs foret, in senatum uenit. tum M. Tullius consul, siue praesentiam eius timens siue ira commotus, orationem habuit luculentam
7 atque utilem rei publicae, quam postea scriptam edidit. sed, ubi ille

---

30.6 milia *secl. Carrio* **30.7** Capuae *Woodman*: Capuam et *codd.*: Capua [et]
Vretska **31.1** quis *Fronto p. 101.6 vdH²*: quibus *codd.*   lasciuiaque *Fronto p. 101.7*
vdH²: atque lasciuia *codd.*   **31.3** *uerba suppl. Fronto p. 101.13 vdH²*

assedit, Catilina, ut erat paratus ad dissimulanda omnia, demisso
uultu, uoce supplici postulare a patribus coepit ne quid de se
temere crederent: ea familia ortum, ita se ab adulescentia uitam
instituisse ut omnia bona in spe haberet; ne existimarent sibi,
patricio homini, cuius ipsius atque maiorum plurima beneficia in
plebem Romanam essent, perdita re publica opus esse, cum eam
seruaret M. Tullius, inquilinus ciuis urbis Romae. ad hoc maledicta 8
alia cum adderet, obstrepere omnes, hostem atque parricidam
uocare. tum ille furibundus, 'Quoniam quidem circumuentus', 9
inquit, 'ab inimicis praeceps agor, incendium meum ruina restinguam.' deinde se ex curia domum proripuit.   32
    Ibi multa ipse secum uoluens, quod neque insidiae consuli pro-
cedebant et ab incendio intellegebat urbem uigiliis munitam, optimum factu credens exercitum augere ac, prius quam legiones
scriberentur, multa antecapere quae bello usui forent, nocte intempesta cum paucis in Manliana castra profectus est. sed Cethego 2
atque Lentulo ceterisque quorum cognouerat promptam audaciam mandat, quibus rebus possent, opes factionis confirment,
insidias consuli maturent, caedem, incendia aliaque belli facinora
parent: sese propediem cum magno exercitu ad urbem
accessurum.
    Dum haec Romae geruntur, C. Manlius ex suo numero legatos 3
ad Marcium Regem mittit cum mandatis huiusce modi: 'Deos   33
hominesque testamur, imperator, nos arma neque contra patriam
cepisse neque quo periculum aliis faceremus, sed uti corpora nostra ab iniuria tuta forent, qui miseri, egentes, uiolentia atque crudelitate faeneratorum plerique patriae, sed omnes fama atque
fortunis expertes sumus. neque cuiquam nostrum licuit more
maiorum lege uti neque amisso patrimonio liberum corpus habere:
tanta saeuitia faeneratorum atque praetoris fuit. saepe maiores 2
uestrum, miseriti plebis Romanae, decretis suis inopiae eius opitulati sunt; ac nouissime memoria nostra propter magnitudinem aeris
alieni uolentibus omnibus bonis argentum aere solutum est. saepe 3
ipsa plebs, aut dominandi studio permota aut superbia magistratuum, armata a patribus secessit. at nos non imperium neque 4
diuitias petimus, quarum rerum causa bella atque certamina
omnia inter mortales sunt, sed libertatem, quam nemo bonus nisi

---

33.2 uestrum *Gell. 20.6.14*: uestri *uel* nostri *codd.*

5 cum anima simul amittit. te atque senatum obtestamur consulatis
miseris ciuibus, legis praesidium, quod iniquitas praetoris eripuit,
restituatis, neue nobis eam necessitudinem imponatis ut quaeramus quonam modo maxime ulti sanguinem nostrum pereamus!'
34 ad haec Q. Marcius respondit, si quid ab senatu petere uellent, ab
armis discedant, Romam supplices proficiscantur: ea mansuetudine atque misericordia senatum populi Romani semper fuisse ut
nemo umquam ab eo frustra auxilium petiuerit.
2   At Catilina ex itinere plerisque consularibus, praeterea optimo
cuique litteras mittit se falsis criminibus circumuentum, quoniam
factioni inimicorum resistere nequiuerit, fortunae cedere,
Massiliam in exilium proficisci, non quo sibi tanti sceleris conscius
esset sed uti res publica quieta foret neue ex sua contentione
3   seditio oreretur. ab his longe diuersas litteras Q. Catulus in senatu
recitauit, quas sibi nomine Catilinae redditas dicebat. earum exem-
35 plum infra scriptum est:
                    'L. Catilina Q. Catulo.
    Egregia tua fides – re cognita, grata mihi magnis in meis
2   periculis – fiduciam commendationi meae tribuit. quam ob
rem defensionem in nouo consilio non statui parare; satisfactionem ex nulla conscientia de culpa proponere decreui,
3   quam – me dius fidius – ueram licet cognoscas. iniuriis con-
tumeliisque concitatus, quod fructu laboris industriaeque
meae priuatus statum dignitatis non obtinebam, publicam
miserorum causam pro mea consuetudine suscepi, non quin
aes alienum meis nominibus ex possessionibus soluere non
possem (et alienis nominibus liberalitas Orestillae suis filiaeque copiis persolueret) sed quod non dignos homines honore
honestatos uidebam meque falsa suspicione alienatum esse
4   sentiebam. hoc nomine satis honestas pro meo casu spes
5   reliquae dignitatis conseruandae sum secutus. plura cum scri-
6   bere uellem, nuntiatum est uim mihi parari. nunc Orestillam
commendo tuaeque fidei trado: eam ab iniuria defendas, per
liberos tuos rogatus! haueto!'
36   Sed ipse paucos dies commoratus apud C. Flaminium in agro
Arretino dum uicinitatem antea sollicitatam armis exornat, cum
fascibus atque aliis imperii insignibus in castra ad Manlium

35.**6** tibi commendo V

contendit. haec ubi Romae comperta sunt, senatus Catilinam et 2
Manlium hostes iudicat, ceterae multitudini diem statuit ante quam
sine fraude liceret ab armis discedere praeter rerum capitalium
condemnatis. praeterea decernit uti consules dilectum habeant, 3
Antonius cum exercitu Catilinam persequi maturet, Cicero urbi
praesidio sit. ea tempestate mihi imperium populi Romani multo 4
maxime miserabile uisum est. cui cum ad occasum ab ortu solis
omnia domita armis parerent, domi otium atque diuitiae, quae
prima mortales putant, affluerent, fuere tamen ciues qui seque
remque publicam obstinatis animis perditum irent. namque duo- 5
bus senati decretis ex tanta multitudine neque praemio inductus
coniurationem patefecerat neque ex castris Catilinae quisquam
omnium discesserat: tanta uis morbi ac ueluti tabes plerosque
ciuium animos inuaserat.

– Neque solum illis aliena mens erat qui conscii coniurationis **37**
fuerant, sed omnino cuncta plebes nouarum rerum studio
Catilinae incepta probabat. id adeo more suo uidebatur facere: 2
nam semper in ciuitate, quibus opes nullae sunt, bonis inuident, 3
malos extollunt, uetera odere, noua exoptant, odio suarum rerum
mutari omnia student, turba atque seditionibus sine cura aluntur,
quoniam egestas facile habetur sine damno. sed urbana plebes, ea 4
uero praeceps erat de multis causis. primum omnium, qui ubique 5
probro atque petulantia maxime praestabant, item alii per dedecora
patrimoniis amissis, postremo omnes quos flagitium aut facinus
domo expulerat, ii Romam sicut in sentinam confluxerant. deinde 6
multi memores Sullanae uictoriae, quod ex gregariis militibus alios
senatores uidebant, alios ita diuites ut regio uictu atque cultu aetatem agerent, sibi quisque, si in armis foret, ex uictoria talia sperabat.
praeterea iuuentus, quae in agris manuum mercede inopiam toler- 7
auerat, priuatis atque publicis largitionibus excita urbanum otium
ingrato labori praetulerat. eos atque alios omnes malum publicum
alebat. quo minus mirandum est homines egentes, malis moribus, 8
maxima spe, rei publicae iuxta ac sibi consuluisse.

Praeterea, quorum uictoria Sullae parentes proscripti, bona 9
erepta, ius libertatis imminutum erat, haud sane alio animo belli
euentum exspectabant. ad hoc, quicumque aliarum atque senatus 10
partium erant, conturbari rem publicam quam minus ualere ipsi

36.2 condemnatos A^c **36.5** ac ueluti *Haupt*: atque uti *codd.*
plerisque *Shackleton Bailey*

11　malebant. id adeo malum multos post annos in ciuitatem reuer-
38　terat. nam postquam Cn. Pompeio et M. Crasso consulibus tribuni-
　　cia potestas restituta est, homines adulescentes summam
　　potestatem nacti, quibus aetas animusque ferox erat, coepere sena-
　　tum criminando plebem exagitare, dein largiendo atque pollici-
2　tando magis incendere, ita ipsi clari potentesque fieri. contra eos
　　summa ope nitebatur pleraque nobilitas senatus specie pro sua
3　magnitudine. namque (uti paucis uerum absoluam) post illa tem-
　　pora quicumque rem publicam agitauere honestis nominibus, alii
　　sicuti populi iura defenderent, pars quo senatus auctoritas maxima
　　foret, bonum publicum simulantes pro sua quisque potentia certa-
4　bant. neque illis modestia neque modus contentionis erat: utrique
39　uictoriam crudeliter exercebant. sed postquam Cn. Pompeius ad
　　bellum maritimum atque Mithridaticum missus est, plebis opes
2　imminutae, paucorum potentia creuit. ii magistratus, prouincias
　　aliaque omnia tenere; ipsi innoxii, florentes, sine metu aetatem
　　agere, ceterosque iudiciis terrere, quo plebem in magistratu pla-
3　cidius tractarent. sed ubi primum dubiis rebus nouandi spes
4　oblata est, uetus certamen animos eorum arrexit. quod si primo
　　proelio Catilina superior aut aequa manu discessisset, profecto
　　magna clades atque calamitas rem publicam oppressisset; neque
　　illis qui uictoriam adepti forent diutius ea uti licuisset quin defes-
　　sis et exsanguibus qui plus posset imperium atque libertatem
　　extorqueret. –
5　　　Fuere tamen extra coniurationem complures qui ad Catilinam
　　initio profecti sunt. in iis erat Fuluius, senatoris filius, quem retrac-
　　tum ex itinere parens necari iussit.
6　　　Isdem temporibus Romae Lentulus, sicuti Catilina praeceperat,
　　quoscumque moribus aut fortuna nouis rebus idoneos credebat aut
　　per se aut per alios sollicitabat, neque solum ciues sed cuiusque
40　modi genus hominum quod modo bello usui foret. igitur
　　P. Vmbreno cuidam negotium dat uti legatos Allobrogum requirat
　　eosque, si possit, impellat ad societatem belli, existimans publice
　　priuatimque aere alieno oppressos, praeterea quod natura gens
　　Gallica bellicosa esset, facile eos ad tale consilium adduci posse.
2　Vmbrenus, quod in Gallia negotiatus erat, plerisque principibus
　　ciuitatium notus erat atque eos nouerat. itaque sine mora, ubi

37.11 id adeo] ideo *uel* id

primum legatos in foro conspexit, percontatus pauca de statu
ciuitatis et quasi dolens eius casum requirere coepit quem exitum
tantis malis sperarent. postquam illos uidet queri de auaritia magis- 3
tratuum, accusare senatum quod in eo auxilii nihil esset, miseriis
suis remedium mortem exspectare, 'At ego', inquit, 'uobis, si modo
uiri esse uultis, rationem ostendam qua tanta ista mala effugiatis.'
haec ubi dixit, Allobroges in maximam spem adducti Vmbrenum 4
orare ut sui misereretur: nihil tam asperum neque tam difficile esse
quod non cupidissime facturi essent, dum ea res ciuitatem aere
alieno liberaret. ille eos in domum D. Bruti perducit, quod foro 5
propinqua erat neque aliena consilii propter Semproniam (nam
tum Brutus ab Roma aberat). praeterea Gabinium arcessit, quo 6
maior auctoritas sermoni inesset. eo praesente coniurationem
aperit, nominat socios, praeterea multos cuiusque generis innoxios, quo legatis animus amplior esset. deinde eos pollicitos operam
suam domum dimittit.

    Sed Allobroges diu in incerto habuere quidnam consilii caper- 41
ent. in altera parte erat aes alienum, studium belli, magna merces 2
in spe uictoriae, at in altera maiores opes, tuta consilia, pro incerta
spe certa praemia. haec illis uoluentibus tandem uicit Fortuna rei 3
publicae. itaque Q. Fabio Sangae, cuius patrocinio ciuitas pluri- 4
mum utebatur, rem omnem, uti cognouerant, aperiunt. Cicero per 5
Sangam consilio cognito legatis praecipit ut studium coniurationis
uehementer simulent, ceteros adeant, bene polliceantur dentque
operam, uti eos quam maxime manifestos habeant.

    Isdem fere temporibus in Gallia citeriore atque ulteriore, item 42
in agro Piceno, Bruttio, Apulia motus erat. namque illi quos ante 2
Catilina dimiserat inconsulte ac ueluti per dementiam cuncta simul
agebant: nocturnis consiliis, armorum atque telorum portationibus, festinando, agitando omnia plus timoris quam periculi effe-
cerant. ex eo numero complures Q. Metellus Celer praetor ex 3
senatus consulto causa cognita in uincula coniecerat, item in citeriore Gallia C. Murena, qui ei prouinciae legatus praeerat.

    At Romae Lentulus cum ceteris qui principes coniurationis 43
erant, paratis (ut uidebatur) magnis copiis, constituerant uti, cum
Catilina in agrum Faesulanum cum exercitu uenisset, L. Bestia

40.5 ab Roma] Roma **41.5** praecipit *Linker*: praecepit *codd.* **42.3** ulteriore
Cortius **43.1** Faesulanum *codd.*: Aefulanum *Rauchenstein* (ex agro Faesulano
Meiser)

tribunus plebis contione habita quereretur de actionibus Ciceronis
bellique grauissimi inuidiam optimo consuli imponeret: eo signo
proxima nocte cetera multitudo coniurationis suum quisque nego-
2 tium exsequeretur. sed ea diuisa hoc modo dicebantur: Statilius et
Gabinius uti cum magna manu duodecim simul opportuna loca
urbis incenderent, quo tumultu facilior aditus ad consulem ceterosque quibus insidiae parabantur fieret; Cethegus Ciceronis
ianuam obsideret eumque ui aggrederetur; alius autem alium,
sed filii familiarum (quorum ex nobilitate maxima pars erat) parentes, interficerent; simul caede et incendio perculsis omnibus ad
3 Catilinam erumperent. inter haec parata atque decreta Cethegus
semper querebatur de ignauia sociorum: illos dubitando et dies
prolatando magnas opportunitates corrumpere; facto, non consulto in tali periculo opus esse, seque, si pauci adiuuarent, languen-
4 tibus aliis impetum in curiam facturum. natura ferox, uehemens,
manu promptus erat, maximum bonum in celeritate putabat.

44   Sed Allobroges ex praecepto Ciceronis per Gabinium ceteros
conueniunt. ab Lentulo, Cethego, Statilio, item Cassio postulant
ius iurandum, quod signatum ad ciues perferant: aliter haud facile
2 eos ad tantum negotium impelli posse. ceteri nihil suspicantes
dant, Cassius semet eo breui uenturum pollicetur ac paulo ante
3 legatos ex urbe proficiscitur. Lentulus cum iis T. Volturcium quendam Cortonensem mittit, ut Allobroges, priusquam domum pergerent, cum Catilina data atque accepta fide societatem
4 confirmarent. ipse Volturcio litteras ad Catilinam dat, quarum
exemplum infra scriptum est:

5   'Qui sim ex eo quem ad te misi cognosces. fac cogites in quanta
calamitate sis, et memineris te uirum esse! consideres quid tuae
rationes postulent. auxilium petas ab omnibus, etiam ab infimis.'

6 ad hoc mandata uerbis dat: cum ab senatu hostis iudicatus sit, quo
consilio seruitia repudiet? in urbe parata esse quae iusserit: ne
cunctetur ipse propius accedere.

45   His rebus ita actis, constituta nocte qua proficiscerentur, Cicero
per legatos cuncta edoctus L. Valerio Flacco et C. Pomptino praetoribus imperat ut in ponte Muluio per insidias Allobrogum comitatum deprehendant. rem omnem aperit cuius gratia mittebantur;

44.3 Cortonensem *Forsythe*: Crotoniensem *codd.*   **45.1** comitatum *Wesenberg*: -us
codd.

cetera, uti facto opus sit, ita agant, permittit. illi, homines militares, 2
sine tumultu praesidiis collocatis, sicuti praeceptum erat, occulte
pontem obsidunt. postquam ad id loci legati cum Volturcio uener- 3
unt et simul utrimque clamor exortus est, Galli cito cognito consilio
sine mora praetoribus se tradunt; Volturcius primo cohortatus 4
ceteros gladio se a multitudine defendit, deinde, ubi a legatis
desertus est, multa prius de salute sua Pomptinum obtestatus,
quod ei notus erat, postremo timidus ac uitae diffidens uelut hostibus sese praetoribus dedit.

Quibus rebus confectis omnia propere per nuntios consuli declar- **46**
antur. at illum ingens cura atque laetitia simul occupauere: nam 2
laetabatur intellegens coniuratione patefacta ciuitatem periculis ereptam esse; porro autem anxius erat, dubitans in maximo scelere tantis
ciuibus deprehensis quid facto opus esset: poenam illorum sibi oneri,
impunitatem perdendae rei publicae fore credebat. igitur confirmato 3
animo uocari ad sese iubet Lentulum, Cethegum, Statilium,
Gabinium itemque Caeparium Tarracinensem, qui in Apuliam ad
concitanda seruitia proficisci parabat. ceteri sine mora ueniunt; 4
Caeparius, paulo ante domo egressus, cognito indicio ex urbe
profugerat.

Consul Lentulum, quod praetor erat, ipse manu tenens in sena- 5
tum perducit; reliquos cum custodibus in aedem Concordiae
uenire iubet. eo senatum aduocat magnaque frequentia eius ordi- 6
nis Volturcium cum legatis introducit; Flaccum praetorem scri-
nium cum litteris quas a legatis acceperat eodem afferre iubet.
Volturcius interrogatus de itinere, de litteris, postremo quid aut **47**
qua de causa consilii habuisset, primo fingere alia, dissimulare de
coniuratione; post, ubi fide publica dicere iussus est, omnia uti
gesta erant aperit docetque se, paucis ante diebus a Gabinio et
Caepario socium ascitum, nihil amplius scire quam legatos: tantummodo audire solitum ex Gabinio P. Autronium, Ser. Sullam,
L. Vargunteium, multos praeterea in ea coniuratione esse. eadem 2
Galli fatentur ac Lentulum dissimulantem coarguunt praeter litteras sermonibus quos ille habere solitus erat: ex libris Sibyllinis
regnum Romae tribus Corneliis portendi: Cinnam atque Sullam
antea: se tertium esse cui fatum foret urbis potiri; praeterea ab
incenso Capitolio illum esse uicesimum annum quem saepe ex

46.5 in senatum *ut glossema fort. eiciendum putat Summers*

3 prodigiis haruspices respondissent bello ciuili cruentum fore. igitur perlectis litteris, cum prius omnes signa sua cognouissent,
senatus decernit uti abdicato magistratu Lentulus itemque ceteri
4 in liberis custodiis habeantur. itaque Lentulus P. Lentulo
Spintheri, qui tum aedilis erat, Cethegus Q. Cornificio, Statilius
C. Caesari, Gabinius M. Crasso, Caeparius (nam is paulo ante ex
fuga retractus erat) Cn. Terentio senatori traduntur.

48 Interea plebs coniuratione patefacta, quae primo cupida rerum
nouarum nimis bello fauebat, mutata mente Catilinae consilia
exsecrari, Ciceronem ad caelum tollere: ueluti ex seruitute erepta
2 gaudium atque laetitiam agitabat. namque alia belli facinora praedae magis quam detrimento fore, incendium uero crudele, immoderatum ac sibi maxime calamitosum putabat, quippe cui omnes
copiae in usu cotidiano et cultu corporis erant.
3 Post eum diem quidam L. Tarquinius ad senatum adductus erat,
4 quem ad Catilinam proficiscentem ex itinere retractum aiebant. is
cum se diceret indicaturum de coniuratione, si fides publica data
esset, iussus a consule quae sciret edicere, eadem fere quae
Volturcius de paratis incendiis, de caede bonorum, de itinere
hostium senatum docet: praeterea se missum a M. Crasso qui
Catilinae nuntiaret ne eum Lentulus et Cethegus aliique ex coniuratione deprehensi terrerent eoque magis properaret ad urbem
accedere, quo et ceterorum animos reficeret et illi facilius
5 e periculo eriperentur. sed, ubi Tarquinius Crassum nominauit,
hominem nobilem, maximis diuitiis, summa potentia, alii rem
incredibilem rati, pars, tametsi uerum existimabant, tamen, quia
in tali tempore tanta uis hominis magis lenienda quam exagitanda
uidebatur, plerique Crasso ex negotiis priuatis obnoxii, concla-
mant indicem falsum esse deque ea re postulant uti referatur.
6 itaque consulente Cicerone frequens senatus decernit Tarquinii
indicium falsum uideri eumque in uinculis retinendum neque
amplius potestatem faciendam, nisi de eo indicaret cuius consilio
7 tantam rem esset mentitus. (erant eo tempore qui existimarent
indicium illud a P. Autronio machinatum, quo facilius appellato
8 Crasso per societatem periculi reliquos illius potentia tegeret; alii
Tarquinium a Cicerone immissum aiebant, ne Crassus more suo
9 suscepto malorum patrocinio rem publicam conturbaret. ipsum
Crassum ego postea praedicantem audiui tantam illam contumeliam sibi ab Cicerone impositam.)

Sed isdem temporibus Q. Catulus et C. Piso neque precibus **49**
neque gratia neque pretio Ciceronem impellere potuere uti per
Allobroges aut alium indicem C. Caesar falso nominaretur. nam **2**
uterque cum illo graues inimicitias exercebat – Piso oppugnatus in
iudicio pecuniarum repetundarum propter cuiusdam Transpadani
supplicium iniustum, Catulus ex petitione pontificatus odio incensus, quod extrema aetate, maximis honoribus usus, ab adulescen-
tulo Caesare uictus discesserat. res autem opportuna uidebatur, **3**
quod is priuatim egregia liberalitate, publice maximis muneribus
grandem pecuniam debebat. sed, ubi consulem ad tantum facinus **4**
impellere nequeunt, ipsi singillatim circumeundo atque ementiendo quae se ex Volturcio aut Allobrogibus audisse dicerent,
magnam illi inuidiam conflauerant usque eo ut nonnulli equites
Romani, qui praesidii causa cum telis erant circum aedem
Concordiae, seu periculi magnitudine seu animi mobilitate
impulsi, quo studium suum in rem publicam clarius esset, egredienti ex senatu Caesari gladio minitarentur.

Dum haec in senatu aguntur et dum legatis Allobrogum et **50**
T. Volturcio comprobato eorum indicio praemia decernuntur,
liberti et pauci ex clientibus Lentuli diuersis itineribus opifices
atque seruitia in uicis ad eum eripiendum sollicitabant, partim
exquirebant duces multitudinum, qui pretio rem publicam uexare
soliti erant. Cethegus autem per nuntios familiam atque libertos **2**
suos, lectos et exercitatos, orabat in audaciam, ut grege facto cum
telis ad sese irrumperent. consul ubi ea parari cognouit, dispositis **3**
praesidiis ut res atque tempus monebat, conuocato senatu refert
quid de iis fieri placeat qui in custodiam traditi erant.

Sed eos paulo ante frequens senatus iudicauerat contra rem
publicam fecisse. tum D. Iunius Silanus, primus sententiam rogatus **4**
quod eo tempore consul designatus erat, de iis qui in custodiis
tenebantur et praeterea de L. Cassio, P. Furio, P. Vmbreno,
Q. Annio, si deprehensi forent, supplicium sumendum decreuerat;
isque postea permotus oratione C. Caesaris pedibus in sententiam
Ti. Neronis iturum se dixerat, qui de ea re praesidiis additis referendum censuerat.

Sed Caesar, ubi ad eum uentum est, rogatus sententiam **5**
a consule huiusce modi uerba locutus est:

50.2 in audaciam *secl. Dietsch*   **50.4** dixerat *codd.*: dixit *Bussmann, Roscher*

51   'Omnes homines, patres conscripti, qui de rebus dubiis consult-
      ant ab odio, amicitia, ira atque misericordia uacuos esse decet.
2   haud facile animus uerum prouidet ubi illa officiunt, neque quis-
3   quam omnium libidini simul et usui paruit. ubi intenderis inge-
      nium, ualet; si libido possidet, ea dominatur, animus nihil ualet.
4   magna mihi copia est memorandi, patres conscripti, quae reges
      atque populi ira aut misericordia impulsi male consuluerint; sed ea
      malo dicere quae maiores nostri contra libidinem animi sui recte
5   atque ordine fecere. bello Macedonico quod cum rege Perse gessi-
      mus, Rhodiorum ciuitas magna atque magnifica, quae populi
      Romani opibus creuerat, infida et aduersa nobis fuit. sed, post-
      quam bello confecto de Rhodiis consultum est, maiores nostri, ne
      quis diuitiarum magis quam iniuriae causa bellum inceptum
6   diceret, impunitos eos dimisere. item bellis Punicis omnibus, cum
      saepe Carthaginienses et in pace et per indutias multa nefaria
      facinora fecissent, numquam ipsi per occasionem talia fecere;
      magis quid se dignum foret quam quid in illos iure fieri posset
7   quaerebant. hoc item uobis prouidendum est, patres conscripti, ne
      plus apud uos ualeat P. Lentuli et ceterorum scelus quam uestra
8   dignitas neu magis irae uestrae quam famae consulatis. nam si
      digna poena pro factis eorum reperitur, nouum consilium
      approbo; sin magnitudo sceleris omnium ingenia exsuperat, his
      utendum censeo quae legibus comparata sunt.
9   'Plerique eorum qui ante me sententias dixerunt composite
      atque magnifice casum rei publicae miserati sunt. quae belli saeui-
      tia esset, quae uictis acciderent enumerauere: rapi uirgines, pueros;
      diuelli liberos a parentum conplexu; matres familiarum pati quae
      uictoribus collibuissent; fana atque domos spoliari; caedem, incen-
      dia fieri; postremo armis, cadaueribus, cruore atque luctu omnia
10   compleri. sed per deos immortales, quo illa oratio pertinuit? an uti
      uos infestos coniurationi faceret? scilicet quem res tanta et tam
11   atrox non permouit, eum oratio accendet! non ita est, neque
      cuiquam mortalium iniuriae suae paruae uidentur; multi eas
12   grauius aequo habuere. sed alia aliis licentia est, patres conscripti.
      qui demissi in obscuro uitam habent, si quid iracundia deliquere,
      pauci sciunt: fama atque fortuna eorum pares sunt; qui magno
      imperio praediti in excelso aetatem agunt, eorum facta cuncti
13   mortales nouere. ita in maxima fortuna minima licentia est;

neque studere neque odisse, sed minime irasci decet; quae apud 14
alios iracundia dicitur, ea in imperio superbia atque crudelitas
appellatur. equidem ego sic existimo, patres conscripti, omnes 15
cruciatus minores quam facinora illorum esse. sed plerique mortales postrema meminere et in hominibus impiis sceleris eorum
obliti de poena disserunt, si ea paulo seuerior fuit.
     'D. Silanum, uirum fortem atque strenuum, certo scio quae 16
dixerit studio rei publicae dixisse, neque illum in tanta re gratiam
aut inimicitias exercere: eos mores eamque modestiam uiri cognoui. uerum sententia eius mihi non crudelis (quid enim in tales 17
homines crudele fieri potest?) sed aliena a re publica nostra uidetur. nam profecto aut metus aut iniuria te subegit, Silane, consulem 18
designatum genus poenae nouum decernere. de timore superua- 19
cuaneum est disserere, cum praesertim diligentia clarissimi uiri
consulis tanta praesidia sint in armis. de poena possum equidem 20
dicere, id quod res habet, in luctu atque miseriis mortem aerumnarum requiem, non cruciatum esse: eam cuncta mortalium mala
dissoluere; ultra neque curae neque gaudio locum esse. sed, per 21
deos immortales, quam ob rem in sententiam non addidisti uti
prius uerberibus in eos animaduerteretur? an quia lex Porcia 22
uetat? at aliae leges item condemnatis ciuibus non animam eripi,
sed exilium permitti iubent. an quia grauius est uerberari quam 23
necari? quid autem acerbum aut nimis graue est in homines tanti
facinoris conuictos? sin, quia leuius est, qui conuenit in minore 24
negotio legem timere cum eam in maiore neglegeris?
     'At enim quis reprehendet quod in parricidas rei publicae decre- 25
tum erit? tempus, dies, Fortuna, cuius libido gentibus moderatur.
illis merito accidet quicquid euenerit; ceterum uos, patres con- 26
scripti, quid in alios statuatis considerate. omnia mala exempla ex 27
rebus bonis orta sunt; sed, ubi imperium ad ignaros eius aut minus
bonos peruenit, nouum illud exemplum ab dignis et idoneis ad
indignos et non idoneos transfertur. Lacedaemonii deuictis 28
Atheniensibus triginta uiros imposuere qui rem publicam eorum
tractarent. ii primo coepere pessimum quemque et omnibus inui- 29
sum indemnatum necare: ea populus laetari et merito dicere fieri.
post, ubi paulatim licentia creuit, iuxta bonos et malos libidinose 30
interficere, ceteros metu terrere: ita ciuitas seruitute oppressa 31

51.24 neglegeris] neglexeris

32 stultae laetitiae graues poenas dedit. nostra memoria uictor Sulla
cum Damasippum et alios eius modi qui malo rei publicae creuerant iugulari iussit, quis non factum eius laudabat? homines sceles-
tos et factiosos, qui seditionibus rem publicam exagitauerant,
33 merito necatos aiebant. sed ea res magnae initium cladis fuit.
nam, uti quisque domum aut uillam, postremo uas aut uestimentum alicuius concupiuerat, dabat operam ut is in proscriptorum
34 numero esset. ita illi quibus Damasippi mors laetitiae fuerat paulo
post ipsi trahebantur neque prius finis iugulandi fuit quam Sulla
35 omnes suos diuitiis expleuit. atque ego haec non in M. Tullio neque
his temporibus uereor, sed in magna ciuitate multa et uaria ingenia
36 sunt: potest alio tempore, alio consule, cui item exercitus in manu
sit, falsum aliquid pro uero credi. ubi hoc exemplo per senatus
decretum consul gladium eduxerit, quis illi finem statuet aut quis
moderabitur?
37   'Maiores nostri, patres conscripti, neque consilii neque audaciae
umquam eguere; neque illis superbia obstabat quo minus aliena
38 instituta, si modo proba erant, imitarentur. arma atque tela militaria ab Samnitibus, insignia magistratuum ab Tuscis pleraque
sumpserunt. postremo quod ubique apud socios aut hostes idoneum uidebatur cum summo studio domi exsequebantur: imitari
39 quam inuidere bonis malebant. sed eodem illo tempore Graeciae
morem imitati uerberibus animaduertebant in ciues, de condem-
40 natis summum supplicium sumebant. postquam res publica ado-
leuit et multitudine ciuium factiones ualuere, circumueniri
innocentes, alia huiusce modi fieri coepere, tum lex Porcia aliaeque leges paratae sunt quibus legibus exilium damnatis permissum
41 est. hanc ego causam, patres conscripti, quo minus nouum consi-
42 lium capiamus, in primis magnam puto. profecto uirtus atque
sapientia maior illis fuit qui ex paruis opibus tantum imperium
fecere quam [in] nobis, qui ea bene parta uix retinemus.
43   'Placet igitur eos dimitti et augeri exercitum Catilinae? minime.
sed ita censeo: publicandas eorum pecunias, ipsos in uinculis
habendos per municipia quae maxime opibus ualent; neu quis de
iis postea ad senatum referat neue cum populo agat; qui aliter
fecerit, senatum existimare eum contra rem publicam et salutem
omnium facturum.'

51.42 in *secl. Woodman*

Postquam Caesar dicendi finem fecit, ceteri uerbo alius alii uarie **52**
assentiebantur. at M. Porcius Cato rogatus sententiam huiusce
modi orationem habuit:

'Longe mihi alia mens est, patres conscripti, cum res atque **2**
pericula nostra considero et cum sententias nonnullorum ipse
mecum reputo. illi mihi disseruisse uidentur de poena eorum qui **3**
patriae, parentibus, aris atque focis suis bellum parauere; res autem
monet cauere ab illis magis quam quid in illos statuamus consultare. nam cetera maleficia tum persequare, ubi facta sunt; hoc nisi **4**
prouideris ne accidat, ubi euenit, frustra iudicia implores: capta
urbe nihil fit reliqui uictis. sed per deos immortales uos ego appello **5**
qui semper domos, uillas, signa, tabulas uestras pluris quam rem
publicam fecistis: si ista, cuiuscumque modi sunt, quae amplexa-
mini retinere, si uoluptatibus uestris otium praebere uultis, expergiscimini aliquando et capessite rem publicam! non agitur de **6**
uectigalibus neque de sociorum iniuriis: libertas et anima nostra
in dubio est.

'Saepenumero, patres conscripti, multa uerba in hoc ordine feci, **7**
saepe de luxuria atque auaritia nostrorum ciuium questus sum,
multosque mortales ea causa aduersos habeo. qui mihi atque **8**
animo meo nullius umquam delicti gratiam fecissem, haud facile
alterius libidini malefacta condonabam. sed ea tametsi uos parui **9**
pendebatis, tamen res publica firma erat, opulentia neglegentiam
tolerabat. nunc uero non id agitur, bonisne an malis moribus **10**
uiuamus neque quantum aut quam magnificum imperium populi
Romani sit, sed haec, cuiuscumque modi uidentur, nostra an nobiscum una hostium futura sint. hic mihi quisquam mansuetudinem **11**
et misericordiam nominat? iam pridem equidem nos uera uocabula rerum amisimus: quia bona aliena largiri liberalitas, malarum
rerum audacia fortitudo uocatur, eo res publica in extremo sita est.
sint sane – quoniam ita se mores habent – liberales ex sociorum **12**
fortunis, sint misericordes in furibus aerarii; ne illi sanguinem
nostrum largiantur et, dum paucis sceleratis parcunt, bonos
omnes perditum eant!

'Bene et composite C. Caesar paulo ante in hoc ordine de uita et **13**
morte disseruit, credo falsa existimans ea quae de inferis memor-
antur, diuerso itinere malos a bonis loca taetra, inculta, foeda atque
formidulosa habere. itaque censuit pecunias eorum publicandas, **14**
ipsos per municipia in custodiis habendos, uidelicet timens ne, si

Romae sint, aut a popularibus coniurationis aut a multitudine con-
15 ducta per uim eripiantur – quasi uero mali atque scelesti tantummodo in urbe et non per totam Italiam sint aut non ibi plus possit
16 audacia ubi ad defendendum opes minores sunt! quare uanum
equidem hoc consilium est, si periculum ex illis metuit; si in tanto
omnium metu solus non timet, eo magis refert me mihi atque uobis
17 timere. quare, cum de P. Lentulo ceterisque statuetis, pro certo
habetote uos simul de exercitu Catilinae et de omnibus coniuratis
18 decernere. quanto uos attentius ea agetis, tanto illis animus infirmior erit; si paulum modo uos languere uiderint, iam omnes
feroces aderunt.
19   'Nolite existimare maiores nostros armis rem publicam ex parua
20 magnam fecisse. si ita esset, multo pulcherrimam eam nos haber-
emus: quippe sociorum atque ciuium, praeterea armorum atque
21 equorum maior copia nobis quam illis est. sed alia fuere quae illos
magnos fecere, quae nobis nulla sunt: domi industria, foris iustum
imperium, animus in consulendo liber, neque delicto neque libi-
22 dini obnoxius. pro his nos habemus luxuriam atque auaritiam,
publice egestatem, priuatim opulentiam. laudamus diuitias, sequi-
mur inertiam. inter bonos et malos discrimen nullum: omnia uir-
23 tutis praemia ambitio possidet. neque mirum: ubi uos separatim
sibi quisque consilium capitis, ubi domi uoluptatibus, hic pecuniae
aut gratiae seruitis, eo fit ut impetus fiat in uacuam rem publicam.
24   'Sed ego haec omitto. coniurauere nobilissimi ciues patriam
incendere, Gallorum gentem infestissimam nomini Romano ad
25 bellum arcessunt, dux hostium cum exercitu supra caput est; uos
cunctamini etiam nunc et dubitatis quid intra moenia deprensis
26 hostibus faciatis? misereamini censeo – deliquere homines adules-
27 centuli per ambitionem – atque etiam armatos dimittatis! ne ista
uobis mansuetudo et misericordia, si illi arma ceperint, in miseriam
28 conuertat. scilicet res ipsa aspera est, sed uos non timetis eam.
immo uero maxime. sed inertia et mollitia animi alius alium
exspectantes cunctamini, uidelicet dis immortalibus confisi, qui
29 hanc rem publicam saepe in maximis periculis seruauere. non
uotis neque suppliciis muliebribus auxilia deorum parantur; uigilando, agendo, bene consulendo prospere omnia cedunt. ubi
socordiae te atque ignauiae tradideris, nequiquam deos implores:
irati infestique sunt.

'Apud maiores nostros A. Manlius Torquatus bello Gallico filium 30
suum, quod is contra imperium in hostem pugnauerat, necari
iussit, atque ille egregius adulescens immoderatae fortitudinis 31
morte poenas dedit; uos de crudelissimis parricidis quid statuatis
cunctamini? uidelicet cetera uita eorum huic sceleri obstat. uerum 32
parcite dignitati Lentuli, si ipse pudicitiae, si famae suae, si dis aut
hominibus umquam ullis pepercit! ignoscite Cethegi adulescen- 33
tiae, nisi iterum patriae bellum fecit! nam quid ego de Gabinio, 34
Statilio, Caepario loquar? quibus si quicquam umquam pensi fuisset, non ea consilia de re publica habuissent.

'Postremo, patres conscripti, si mehercule peccato locus esset, 35
facile paterer uos ipsa re corrigi, quoniam uerba contemnitis. sed
undique circumuenti sumus: Catilina cum exercitu faucibus urget,
alii intra moenia atque in sinu urbis sunt hostes; neque parari neque
consuli quicquam potest occulte: quo magis properandum est.

'Quare ego ita censeo: cum nefario consilio sceleratorum ciuium 36
res publica in maxima pericula uenerit iique indicio T. Volturci et
legatorum Allobrogum conuicti confessique sint caedem, incendia
aliaque se foeda atque crudelia facinora in ciues patriamque parauisse, de confessis, sicuti de manifestis rerum capitalium, more
maiorum supplicium sumendum.'

Postquam Cato assedit, consulares omnes itemque senatus 53
magna pars sententiam eius laudant, uirtutem animi ad caelum ferunt, alii alios increpantes timidos uocant. Cato clarus
atque magnus habetur; senati decretum fit sicuti ille censuerat.

– Sed mihi multa legenti, multa audienti quae populus 2
Romanus domi militiaeque mari atque terra praeclara facinora
fecit, forte libuit attendere quae res maxime tanta negotia susti-
nuisset. sciebam saepenumero parua manu cum magnis legioni- 3
bus hostium contendisse; cognoueram paruis copiis bella gesta
cum opulentis regibus; ad hoc saepe fortunae uiolentiam toler-
auisse; facundia Graecos, gloria belli Gallos ante Romanos fuisse.
ac mihi multa agitanti constabat paucorum ciuium egregiam uir- 4
tutem cuncta patrauisse, eoque factum uti diuitias paupertas,
multitudinem paucitas superaret. sed postquam luxu atque desi- 5
dia ciuitas corrupta est, rursus res publica magnitudine sua
imperatorum atque magistratuum uitia sustentabat ac, sicuti

53.5 sua *codd.*: sui *Aug. Civ. Dei* 5.12

†effeta parentum†, multis tempestatibus haud sane quisquam
Romae uirtute magnus fuit.

6 Sed memoria mea ingenti uirtute, diuersis moribus fuere uiri
duo, M. Cato et C. Caesar; quos quoniam res obtulerat, silentio
praeterire non fuit consilium quin utriusque naturam et mores,
54 quantum ingenio possum, aperirem. igitur iis genus, aetas, eloquentia prope aequalia fuere; magnitudo animi par, item gloria,
2 sed alia alii. Caesar beneficiis ac munificentia magnus habebatur,
integritate uitae Cato. ille mansuetudine et misericordia clarus
3 factus, huic seueritas dignitatem addiderat. Caesar dando, subleuando, ignoscendo, Cato nihil largiendo gloriam adeptus est. in
altero miseris perfugium erat, in altero malis pernicies. illius facil-
4 itas, huius constantia laudabatur. postremo Caesar in animum
induxerat laborare, uigilare; negotiis amicorum intentus sua neglegere, nihil denegare quod dono dignum esset; sibi magnum imperium, exercitum, bellum nouum exoptabat, ubi uirtus enitescere
5 posset. at Catoni studium modestiae, decoris, sed maxime seuer-
6 itatis erat: non diuitiis cum diuite neque factione cum factioso sed
cum strenuo uirtute, cum modesto pudore, cum innocente abstinentia certabat; esse quam uideri bonus malebat: ita, quo minus
petebat gloriam, eo magis illum sequebatur. –

55 Postquam (ut dixi) senatus in Catonis sententiam discessit,
consul optimum factu ratus noctem quae instabat antecapere ne
quid eo spatio nouaretur, triumuiros quae id supplicium postulabat
2 parare iubet. ipse praesidiis dispositis Lentulum in carcerem dedu-
3 cit; idem fit ceteris per praetores. est in carcere locus quod
Tullianum appellatur, ubi paululum ascenderis ad laeuam, circiter
4 duodecim pedes humi depressus; eum muniunt undique parietes
atque insuper camera lapideis fornicibus iuncta; sed inculto, teneb-
5 ris, odore foeda atque terribilis eius facies est. in eum locum postquam demissus est Lentulus, uindices rerum capitalium, quibus
6 praeceptum erat, laqueo gulam fregere. ita ille, patricius ex gente
clarissima Corneliorum, qui consulare imperium Romae habuerat,
dignum moribus factisque suis exitum uitae inuenit. de Cethego,
Statilio, Gabinio, Caepario eodem modo supplicium sumptum est.

53.5 effeta parentum *locus desperatus: quidam* ui *uel ante uel post* parentum *suppl.*:
sicuti effeta <esse> partu *Kurfess: alii alia* 55.1 id *Gertz:* ad *uel* a̶d̶ *codd.* 55.3 as-
cenderis] descenderis 55.6 exitum uitae] exitium uitae (*secl.* uitae *illic*
Zimmermann, hic Nitzschner)

Dum ea Romae geruntur, Catilina ex omni copia quam et ipse **56** adduxerat et Manlius habuerat, duas legiones instituit. cohortes pro numero militum complet; deinde, ut quisque uoluntarius aut 2 ex sociis in castra uenerat, aequaliter distribuerat ac breui spatio legiones numero hominum expleuerat, cum initio non amplius duobus milibus habuisset. sed ex omni copia circiter pars quarta 3 erat militaribus armis instructa; ceteri, ut quemque casus armauerat, sparos aut lanceas, alii praeacutas sudes portabant. sed postquam Antonius cum exercitu aduentabat, Catilina per 4 montes iter facere, modo ad urbem, modo Galliam uersus castra mouere, hostibus occasionem pugnandi non dare. sperabat prope- diem magnas copias sese habiturum, si Romae socii incepta patrauissent. interea seruitia repudiabat, cuius initio ad eum mag- 5 nae copiae concurrebant, opibus coniurationis fretus, simul alie- num suis rationibus existimans uideri causam ciuium cum seruis fugitiuis communicauisse.

Sed postquam in castra nuntius peruenit Romae coniurationem **57** patefactam, de Lentulo et Cethego ceterisque quos supra memor- aui supplicium sumptum, plerique, quos ad bellum spes rapinarum aut nouarum rerum studium illexerat, dilabuntur; reliquos Catilina per montes asperos magnis itineribus in agrum Pistoriensem abdu- cit, eo consilio uti per tramites occulte perfugeret in Galliam Transalpinam. at Q. Metellus Celer cum tribus legionibus in agro 2 Piceno praesidebat, ex difficultate rerum eadem illa existimans quae supra diximus Catilinam agitare. igitur ubi iter eius ex perfu- 3 gis cognouit, castra propere mouit ac sub ipsis radicibus montium consedit, qua illi descensus erat in Galliam properanti. neque 4 tamen Antonius procul aberat, utpote qui magno exercitu locis aequioribus expedit<us impedit>os in fuga sequeretur. sed 5 Catilina, postquam uidet montibus atque copiis hostium sese clau- sum, in urbe res aduersas, neque fugae neque praesidii ullam spem, optimum factu ratus in tali re fortunam belli temptare, statuit cum Antonio quam primum confligere.

Itaque contione aduocata huiusce modi orationem habuit: 6 'Compertum ego habeo, milites, uerba uirtutem non addere: **58** neque ex ignauo strenuum neque fortem ex timido exercitum

---

56.3 portare *Seru. Aen. 11.682* **56.4** Galliam] in Galliam *uel* ad Galliam **57.1** Transalpinam *secl. Dietsch* **57.4** expedit<us impedit>os *Dietsch:* expeditos *codd.:* -us *Prisc. (3.343.22)*

2 oratione imperatoris fieri. quanta cuiusque animo audacia natura
aut moribus inest, tanta in bello patere solet. quem neque gloria
neque pericula excitant, nequiquam hortere: timor animi auribus
3 officit. sed ego uos quo pauca monerem aduocaui, simul uti causam
mei consilii aperirem.

4 'Scitis equidem, milites, socordia atque ignauia Lentuli quantam
ipsi nobisque cladem attulerit quoque modo, dum ex urbe praesi-
5 dia opperior, in Galliam proficisci nequiuerim; nunc uero quo loco
6 res nostrae sint iuxta mecum omnes intellegitis. exercitus hostium
duo, unus ab urbe, alter a Gallia obstant. diutius in his locis esse, si
maxime animus ferat, frumenti atque aliarum rerum egestas pro-
7, 8 hibet. quocumque ire placet, ferro iter aperiendum est. quapropter
uos moneo uti forti atque parato animo sitis et, cum proelium
inibitis, memineritis uos diuitias, decus, gloriam, praeterea liberta-
9 tem atque patriam in dextris uestris portare. si uincimus, omnia
nobis tuta erunt: commeatus abunde, municipia atque coloniae
10 patebunt; si metu cesserimus, eadem illa aduersa fient: neque
locus neque amicus quisquam teget quem arma non texerint.
11 praeterea, milites, non eadem nobis et illis necessitudo impendet:
nos pro patria, pro libertate, pro uita certamus, illis superuacua-
12 neum est pugnare pro potentia paucorum. quo audacius aggredi-
13 mini, memores pristinae uirtutis! licuit uobis cum summa
turpitudine in exilio aetatem agere, potuistis nonnulli Romae
14 amissis bonis alienas opes exspectare; quia illa foeda atque intol-
15 eranda uiris uidebantur, haec sequi decreuistis. si haec relinquere
uultis, audacia opus est: nemo nisi uictor pace bellum mutauit.
16 nam in fuga salutem sperare, cum arma quibus corpus tegitur ab
17 hostibus auerteris, ea uero dementia est. semper in proelio iis
maximum est periculum qui maxime timent; audacia pro muro
habetur.

18 'Cum uos considero, milites, et cum facta uestra aestimo, magna
19 me spes uictoriae tenet. animus, aetas, uirtus uestra me hortantur,
20 praeterea necessitudo, quae etiam timidos fortes facit. nam multitudo hostium ne circumuenire queat prohibent angustiae loci.
21 quod si uirtuti uestrae Fortuna inuiderit, cauete inulti animam
amittatis neu capti potius sicuti pecora trucidemini quam uirorum

58.10 sin *Kritz*

more pugnantes cruentam atque luctuosam uictoriam hostibus relinquatis!' Haec ubi dixit, paululum commoratus signa canere iubet atque 59 instructos ordines in locum aequum deducit. dein remotis omnium equis quo militibus exaequato periculo animus amplior esset, ipse pedes exercitum pro loco atque copiis instruit. nam uti planities 2 erat inter sinistros montes et ab dextra rupe aspera, octo cohortes in fronte constituit, reliquarum signa in subsidio artius collocat. ab 3 iis centuriones omnes et lectos euocatos, praeterea ex gregariis militibus optimum quemque armatum in primam aciem subducit. C. Manlium in dextra, Faesulanum quendam in sinistra parte curare iubet; ipse cum libertis et colonis propter aquilam assistit quam bello Cimbrico C. Marius in exercitu habuisse dicebatur.

At ex altera parte C. Antonius, pedibus aeger quod proelio 4 adesse nequibat, M. Petreio legato exercitum permittit. ille 5 cohortes ueteranas, quas tumulti causa conscripserat, in fronte, post eas ceterum exercitum in subsidiis locat; ipse equo circumiens unum quemque nominans appellat, hortatur, rogat ut meminerint se contra latrones inermes pro patria, pro liberis, pro aris atque focis suis certare. homo militaris, quod amplius annos triginta 6 tribunus aut praefectus aut legatus aut praetor cum magna gloria in exercitu fuerat, plerosque ipsos factaque eorum fortia nouerat; ea commemorando militum animos accendebat.

Sed ubi omnibus rebus exploratis Petreius tuba signum dat, 60 cohortes paulatim incedere iubet; idem facit hostium exercitus. postquam eo uentum est unde a ferentariis proelium committi 2 posset, maximo clamore [cum] infestis signis concurrunt: pila omittunt, gladiis res geritur. ueterani pristinae uirtutis memores 3 comminus acriter instare, illi haud timidi resistunt: maxima ui certatur. interea Catilina cum expeditis in prima acie uersari, 4 laborantibus succurrere, integros pro sauciis arcessere, omnia prouidere, multum ipse pugnare, saepe hostem ferire: strenui militis et boni imperatoris officia simul exsequebatur. Petreius ubi 5 uidet Catilinam, contra ac ratus erat, magna ui tendere, cohortem praetoriam in medios hostes inducit eosque perturbatos atque alios

59.2 rupe aspera] rupem asperam   **59.3** centuriones omnes lectos et euocatos *codd.* (et lectos *Courtney*): omnes euocatos et centuriones *Seru. Aen. 2.157* colonis] coloniis *uel* colonibus (calonibus *Putschius*)   **59.5** tumulti *Non. 489*: -tus *codd.*   **60.2** cum *codd., secl. Dietsch*: cuncti *Steuding*

alibi resistentes interficit; deinde utrimque ex lateribus ceteros
6 aggreditur. Manlius et Faesulanus in primis pugnantes cadunt;
7 <Catilina>, postquam fusas copias seque cum paucis reliquum
uidet, memor generis atque pristinae suae dignitatis in confertissimos hostes incurrit ibique pugnans confoditur.
61 Sed confecto proelio tum uero cerneres quanta audacia quan-
2 taque animi uis fuisset in exercitu Catilinae. nam fere quem quisque uiuus pugnando locum ceperat, eum amissa anima corpore
3 tegebat; pauci autem, quos medios cohors praetoria disiecerat,
paulo diuersius – sed omnes tamen aduersis uulneribus – concider-
4 ant. Catilina uero longe a suis inter hostium cadauera repertus est,
paululum etiam spirans ferociamque animi quam habuerat uiuus
5 in uultu retinens. postremo ex omni copia neque in proelio neque
6 in fuga quisquam ciuis ingenuus captus est: ita cuncti suae hostiumque uitae iuxta pepercerant.
7 Neque tamen exercitus populi Romani laetam aut incruentam
uictoriam adeptus erat: nam strenuissimus quisque aut occiderat in
8 proelio aut grauiter uulneratus discesserat. multi autem, qui
e castris uisendi aut spoliandi gratia processerant, uoluentes hostilia cadauera amicum alii, pars hospitem aut cognatum reperiebant;
9 fuere item qui inimicos suos cognoscerent. ita uarie per omnem
exercitum laetitia, maeror, luctus atque gaudia agitabantur.

60.7 Catilina *om. codd. antiquiores, suppl. recentiores*

COMMENTARY

1-16 PREFACE

The preface to the *BC* is exceptionally long in proportion to the main narrative, occupying more than a fifth of the entire work.[1] Taking for granted the importance of *uirtus* and *gloria*, S. begins by arguing that, since the mind is superior to the body, one can serve the *res publica* just as well by writing about events as by participating in them (1.1–3.2). He acknowledges that he himself was drawn initially to public life (3.3–5), but, when participation in politics proved too distasteful, he decided to write about them instead, selecting events on the basis of their memorability (4.1–2), and one of the most memorable was **the conspiracy of Catiline (A¹:** 4.3–4). But, before the main narrative can begin, this requires an exposition of Catiline's *mores* (4.5). **Catiline's evil character**, of which an account now follows (**B¹:** 5.1–7), was made worse by the corruption of society (5.8), which in turn requires S. to explain how Rome, once so great, has reached this nadir (5.9). In a so-called 'archaeology' he traces **societal corruption** at Rome from its rise to the present day (**C:** 6–13), when circumstances suited **a criminal like Catiline** and presented him with the opportunity for which he had been planning (**B²:** 14–16). That plan was **Catiline's conspiracy (A²:** 17ff.). Although a brief paraphrase cannot do justice to the complexity of S.'s argument, it will be seen how in the latter sections of the preface each successive topic arises out of a preceding topic until the author finally returns via ring composition to the point at which he started. The manner strikingly recalls that of Thucydides in his own preface (see e.g. N. G. L. Hammond, 'The arrangement of the thought in the proem and in other parts of Thucydides I', *CQ* 2 (1952) 127–41).

---

[1] From Quintilian's famous comment (3.8.9 'C. Sallustius in bello Iugurthino et Catilinae nihil ad historiam pertinentibus principiis orsus est'), which is misguided even on its own terms, it is possible to infer that he regarded the preface as consisting only of chh. 1–4. But S. himself says (4.5) that the *initium narrandi* will not take place until *after* the portrait of Catiline in ch. 5, and the apologia at 5.9 shows that the narrative cannot be regarded as starting with the 'archaeology' at 6.1–13.5. Since the wording of 14.1 suggests not an *initium narrandi* but rather a resumption of 5.9 after the intervening digression (see ad loc.), I understand the narrative proper not to begin until the formal dating at 17.1 (n.). Features of this arrangement were imitated by Tacitus at the beginning of his *Histories* (see e.g. 5.9n.).

85

1.1–4.2 Defence of Historiography

In the early days of Latin literature, the chorus of Ennius' tragedy *Iphigenia* was given some assonantal lines on the subject of *otium* (fr. 99J [= 199–202]/84G–M 'otio qui nescit uti | plus negoti habet quam cum est negotium in negotio . . .'). The elder Cato, Ennius' younger contemporary and S.'s Latin model, began his *Origines* by justifying the *otium* which permitted him to write it (2C/P 'clarorum uirorum atque magnorum non minus otii quam negotii rationem exstare oportere'). In the last days of the republic, Cicero too felt obliged to defend his *otium* when he was writing his *De Officiis* (2.2–6, 3.1–3). This repeated preoccupation with *otium*, which may seem strange to modern readers, was a quintessentially Roman characteristic (it was still a major topic for the younger Pliny a century and a half later) and arose from the aristocratic belief that an individual should engage actively in public life, whether in warfare or politics or both, and, in the course of doing so, should display *uirtus* and thus win *gloria*;[2] lack of active engagement, for whatever reason, required justification of one sort or another.

When S. was ignominiously forced into a second and final withdrawal from public life in the mid-40s BC, he had no intention of idling away his *bonum otium*, as he euphemistically calls it (4.1); he went from participating in politics to writing about politics, and the opening chapters of the *BC* (1.1–4.2) constitute his justification. S.'s apologia is skilfully managed, moving from universals (1.1 'Omnes homines') to his own situation (3.3 'Sed ego'). The popular philosophy with which he begins (1.1–4) is designedly commonplace, because such ideas, almost by definition, are difficult to gainsay and hence constitute persuasive premises.[3] The defence as a whole is articulated by a profusion of logical particles (*nam*, *sed*, *igitur* and the like), discouraging disbelief and advancing the argument, and the articulation is complemented by a series of synonyms (such as *animus*, *ingenium* and *anima*) and antitheses (such as *uis* and *uirtus*), combining insistence with variation. S. is particularly adept at insinuating into the reader's mind an idea which he does not develop at the time but to which he will return later, a technique which has been called 'suspension

---

[2] For *otium* see J.-M. André, *L'otium dans la vie morale et intellectuelle romaine, des origines à l'époque augustéenne* (1966); more recently, J. Osgood, *Caesar's legacy* (2006) 290–2; Y. Baraz, *A written republic: Cicero's philosophical politics* (2012) 27–35; Mouritsen, *RE* 124–41. For Pliny see R. K. Gibson and R. Morello, *Reading the Letters of Pliny the Younger* (2012) 169–99, 300. For the aristocratic code see e.g. Earl, *MPTR*; for *gloria* in particular, on which Cicero had written as recently as 44 BC (above, p. 16), see Hellegouarc'h 369–83.

[3] It is beyond the scope of the Commentary to repeat the scores of parallel passages with which S.'s statements have been compared by generations of scholars; interested readers are referred to the commentaries of Vretska and Mariotti.

of thought' (2.3–6n.). Since the intricacy of the whole has elicited from scholars much discussion of how the argument proceeds, it is a self-referential irony that 'every major step ... is accompanied by either a metaphor or a connotative association of "the way"'.[4]

S. was often acknowledged to be a follower of the elder Cato (Intro. pp. 29–31), and the preface duly begins with an allusion to the opening of Cato's *Origines* (1.1n.); and, as he was also recognised as an imitator of Thucydides (Intro. pp. 26–9), there are likewise allusions to the latter's history of the Peloponnesian War. Indeed his account of the difficulties of writing history (3.2) derives almost word for word from the beginning of Pericles' Funeral Speech (Thuc. 2.35.2). When he turns to give an account of himself and his own circumstances, as was conventional (3.3n. *Sed ego*), there is no mention of his two expulsions from public life (3.3–4.1); instead his tendentious self-portrait is modelled on the Seventh Letter attributed to Plato, as if to suggest that his enforced change from politician to historian resembled the virtuous Plato's self-motivated conversion from politics to philosophy (see esp. Renehan, *OR* 109–10).

1.1–2.6 S. begins by stating the self-evident truth that the mind is superior to the body (1.1–2). This being so, one should use one's mind to seek and acquire *gloria* and to be remembered by posterity (1.3). It is true that in very early times it was debated whether the mind or the body was key in military affairs, the area in which *uirtus* was most likely to result in *gloria* (1.5–2.1); but the success and growth of imperialism proved the superiority of the mind (2.2). If only rulers had been similarly guided in peacetime (2.3–6)!

1.1 O̲m̲n̲e̲s̲ *homines qui* **sese student praestare ceteris animalibus summa ope niti** decet ...[5] 'It is fitting that all persons who endeavour that they should surpass the other animals should strive with all their might ...': *omnes homines ... niti* is the regular acc. + infin. with *decet* (*NLS* 168 §210); for the evidence that S. wrote *omneis* here see Intro. p. 39. An acc. + infin. (*sese ... praestare*) with *studeo* (again at 37.3) is common in early verse (C. E. Bennett, *Syntax of early Latin* (1910) 1.381) and recurs in some other prose and verse texts contemporary with S., esp. the Ciceronian correspondence (cf. also *OLD studeo* 1c). The reflexive pronoun normally occupies an unemphatic position in its clause (as here, second place); a distinction between *se* and *sese* may have been discussed by Caesar, a linguistic expert, but, if so, the fragmentary evidence renders his point

---

[4] Krebs 591, who analyses the metaphor of 'the way' and illustrates the scholarly discussion.

[5] I use various typographical devices (such as italics and underlinings) *both* to point up verbal or phraseological similarities between texts *and* to indicate devices such as wordplay and alliteration.

unclear (Garcea 270–1). S.'s opening words function as a 'motto' or
'epigraph', alluding to the opening of Cato's *Origines* (1C/P 'Si ques
sunt *homines quos* delectat populi Romani gesta describere'), which, as
S.'s readers are expected to remember, is about the writing of history
(next n.). Cato's opening takes the form of a hexameter (*PH* 379),
a refinement which S. defers to the start of the 'archaeology' (6.1 and
n.). S.'s double juxtaposition of words denoting effort (*student praestare* ~
summa ope niti) is programmatic for his political thought (for the latter cf.
also 38.2, *BJ* 9.2, 31.17). Ennius in his *Annales* evidently talked of kings,
their quest for fame, their building and the effort involved (404–5 '*reges*
per regnum statuasque sepulcraque *quaerunt*, | *aedificant* nomen, summa
nituntur opum ui'), another passage which S. clearly had in mind (*reges* at
2.1, *quaerere* at 1.3, *aedificant* at 2.7).[6]

ne uitam silentio transeant: *uitam transire* (again at 2.8) is not found in
earlier extant Latin and does not recur in another author until the
younger Seneca, in whom it is common; it is the first of numerous references in S.'s preface to the metaphor of 'the way' (Krebs 583), frequent in
philosophical discourse. The immediate argument requires that *silentio* is
passive, 'in obscurity' (*OLD* 5), as is clear from *gloriam quaerere* below; but,
since it was a commonplace, esp. of cultural histories (2.1n. *etiam tum*),
that man is distinguished from animals by speech (Pease on Cic. *ND*
2.148), the active sense of the word (≈ 'without speaking') is impossible
to exclude (Woodman, *CQ* 23 (1973) 310). The two senses of *silentio* are
interdependent, since S. will later use the preface to argue that speech, in
the form of writing, is a legitimate way of avoiding obscurity. *silentio* is thus
an example in miniature of S.'s 'suspension of thought' (1.1–4.2 intro.).

ueluti pecora, quae Natura prona atque uentri oboediēntĭă fīnxīt 'like
livestock, which Nature has fashioned as [*or* to be] ...': the adjs. are
predicative (*OLD fingo* 2a), and despite 58.21, where there is an allusion
to Thuc. (n.), the generalised 'livestock' seems more appropriate than
'sheep' for *pecora* here: the contrast between downward-looking animals
and erect humans is a topos (see e.g. Vitr. 2.1.2; Pease on Cic. *ND* 2.140 or
Virg. *Aen.* 4.551). The 'semi-personification of the belly occurs in ...
vituperative and moral contexts' (Muecke on Hor. *S.* 2.7.104 'obsequium
uentris'; e.g. Plut. *Cato Mai.* 8.1): Hesiod actually described the unlettered
as 'mere bellies' (*Theog.* 26); the expr. *uentri oboedire* itself becomes common in later Latin (e.g. Vict. *Caes.* 4.1, of the emperor Claudius). The

---

[6] Observing how S.'s opening sentence differs from that of most other works of
history, D. Earl noted its similarity to the openings of Aristotle's *Nicomachean
Ethics, Politics* and esp. *Metaphysics* (Πάντες ἄνθρωποι τοῦ εἰδέναι ὀρέγονται φύσει, 'All
men by nature strive for knowledge') and argued that S. was reacting to the
recent arrival of Aristotle's works at Rome ('Prologue-form in ancient historiography', *ANRW* 1.2 (1972) 842–56).

heroic clausula, used only very rarely in the Ciceronian corpus, features more prominently in the *BC* (11.49%) than in the *BJ* (9.84%) or *Historiae* (8.94%); indeed the only other works to get into double figures are Cic. *Att.* 3, two letters attributed to Brutus (*Ep. Brut.* 1.16–17) and the texts of pseudo-Sallust (10.87%, 12.02%). The average for Livy is 7.55 per cent; no text of Tac. is higher than the defective *H.* 5 (8.49%). See K–K 169–70, 179–81, 188–9, whose work now supersedes that of H. Aili, *The prose rhythm of Sallust and Livy* (1979).

1.2 sed nostra omnis uis ... sita est: *sed* is by far the commonest adversative particle in S. (100×), occurring more than five times oftener (58%) than the next commonest, *at* (11%: statistics from E. Skard, *SO* 10 (1932) 77–8). Here it contrasts human power with that of animals, to whom humans were potentially *likened* in the previous sentence (*ueluti*); a similar point at *BJ* 2.1. *nostra*, 'of us human beings' (*OLD* 6d), modulates between the universalising *Omnes homines ... decet* (1.1) and the personal *mihi ... uidetur* below (1.3). *situs in* + abl. = 'dependent on' etc. (*OLD situs¹* 4a).

animi imperio, corporis seruitio magis utimur 'we rather avail ourselves of the dominion of the mind and the servitude of the body': the contrast between man and animals ('sed nostra ...') seems to be reinforced by *magis* (≈ 'unlike animals'). The metaphorical language is a philosophical commonplace, e.g. *BJ* 1.3, 2.3, Plato, *Phaedo* 80A 'When the soul and the body are joined together, nature directs the one to serve and be ruled, and the other to rule and be master' (Loeb trans.). *seruitium* in the abstract sense of 'slavery' (= *seruitus*) is common in S. (13×) but absent from Cicero, Caesar and Nepos; it occurs once each in Acc., Plaut. and Ter. but is common in the Augustan poets, relatively common in Livy and very common in Tacitus (Adams (1973) 128–9).

alterum nobis cum dis, alterum cum beluīs cōmmūn(e) ēst: *alterum ... alterum* seems to refer to the mind and body respectively (cf. Plato, *Phaedo* 80A 'the soul is like the divine and the body like the mortal'), but, whereas the second colon may be paraphrased 'like animals, we have bodies', the first suggests the meaning 'we share a mind with the gods', since it was Pythagorean and Stoic belief that humans have a share in the divine mind (see e.g. Powell on Cic. *Senec.* 78). *beluis* varies *pecora* and *animalibus* above, just as *ingenii* and *uirium* in the next sentence will vary the earlier references to *animus* and *corpus*. The proportion of double spondee clausulae in the *BC* (22.24%) is slightly less than in the *BJ* (25.10%) and *H.* (26.83%); the figure is not out of line with those of numerous other authors (e.g. Varro, Caesar). Ciceronian figures vary significantly from work to work (21.70% in *Rosc. Com.*, 2.79% in *Cat.* 2); Livy's average is very high (36.45%), while the figures for Tacitus are comparable with those for S. See K–K 169–70, 173–4, 181–2, 188–9.

1.3 quō mĭhĭ rēctĭŭs ēssĕ ŭĭdētŭr ... **gloriam quaerere:** in cases such as this, the adv. *quo* seems to combine the meanings of 'therefore' and 'all the more' (*OLD quo*² 1a–b); cf. 13.5n. (*eo*). *esse uidetur* is found in the two oldest MSS and one of the two next-oldest, of which the other reads *uidetur esse*; the *recentiores* omit *esse* altogether and are followed by all modern editors. It is true that S. does not elsewhere construct *uidetur* with *esse*, but is this sufficient reason for not printing it? In a work which exhibits so many hexametrical rhythms (see Koster), it is perhaps significant that the presence of *esse uidetur* (a favourite clausula of Lucretius) produces two thirds of a hexameter line. (Later, Horace would use both *mihi rectius* and *rectius esse* in his *Satires*, 1.4.134, 2.7.25.)

ingenii quam uirium opibus is to be taken with both *gloriam quaerere* and *memoriam ... efficere*. S. does not need to say that in the Roman world the surest way to achieve glory and to guarantee one's memory was through warfare (see Harris 17–34, with abundant evidence), an activity in which one might have assumed that physical strength was key (cf. Plb. 6.7.3). Hence warfare ('res militaris') is an absent presence in this sentence, and *ingenii quam uirium opibus* is potentially a paradox, to which S. returns at §5 below. The fact that memory requires a written record, a product of one's *ingenium*, remains inexplicit until 8.1–5.

For the spelling *ingenii* (that of the oldest MSS) rather than *ingeni* see Intro. p. 41. S.'s contemporary Varro evidently believed that the former was the correct form (Charis. 1.78.4–6; cf. 71.2–9, 141.6–7; Garcea 40, 140–7).

gloriam quaerere is a common phrase but its reappearance in one of Livy's prefaces (fr. 75L 'iam sibi satis gloriae quaesitum') perhaps indicates an allusion to this passage of S.'s preface: Livy has achieved the *gloria* which S. craved (*LH* 88–9). The verb suggests making for a destination on the journey through life (1.1n. *ne*): cf. e.g. Plaut. *Poen.* 691–2 'si mihi hospitium quaererem, ... irem ... recta uia'.

memoriam nostri quam maxime longam efficere: *memoria* is the posthumous extension of *gloria*; *memoria nostri* is almost a set phrase, e.g. Cic. *Senec.* 81 (the gen. is objective: G&L 233 §364 N. 2). Since 3.1–2 below is so clearly echoed by Pliny (*Ep.* 5.8.1–2), it seems very likely that the latter's words *aliorumque famam cum sua extendere* there are an allusion to *memoriam ... efficere* here. *maxime longam* instead of *longissimam* is extremely recherché. Caesar is said to have been the first to write *maximus* instead of *maxumus* (Quint. 1.7.21; also Garcea 148–52); we do not know which form was used by S. (Intro. p. 40).

1.4 nam diuitiarum et formae gloria fluxa atque fragilis est: *gloria* is qualified by adjs. which more naturally belong to *diuitiarum et formae*: since 'breakable' seems more applicable to a person's physique (Ov. *AA* 2.113

'forma bonum fragile est'), *fluxa* applies to riches (cf. Sen. *Phaedr.* 491 'fluxas opes'; *fragilis fauor* in 489); the transience of each recurs at *BJ* 2.2. The instability of riches anticipates S.'s numerous later references to riches, which attract his disapproval (e.g. 12.1–2) and are coveted by the conspirators (e.g. 20.14); the instability of beauty looks back to the transitoriness of life itself at 1.3 above. The accumulation of quasi-synonyms, often alliterating, is a marked feature of S. (long lists in Skard (1964) 26–7). Gellius (13.25.13–14) commented on this as a feature of the elder Cato's manner, quoting *Orat.* 163M 'secundis atque prolixis atque prosperis … superbiam atque ferociam' (see too Courtney ad loc.),[7] which also illustrates Cato's fondness for *atque* (commented on by Marcus Aurelius ap. Fronto, p. 34.20–1 vdH²; see Adams, *AIL* 11, 22). The colon as a whole acts as a foil for the permanence mentioned in the second colon, where *aeterna* looks back to *quam maxime longam.* Before *nam* we have to assume an ellipse, e.g. 'And the way to achieve this is through *uirtus,* for …'.

uirtutis clara aeternaque habetur: the two parts of the sentence are linked by adversative asyndeton, and, since *uirtus* is demonstrable above all in war (cf. 54.4), its mention here is natural after the implied reference to warfare in §3 (n. *ingenii*).

The transmitted text reads *uirtus* and is often translated as '<but> *uirtus* is a brilliant and eternal possession', for which 58.17 is quoted in support ('audacia pro muro habetur'); yet not only is the meaning there different (see n.) but *uirtus* can only be a possession during a person's lifetime, not for eternity. This interpretation is rightly doubted in *TLL* 6.3.2459.12. Alternatively S.'s own use of *haberi* + adjs. elsewhere (53.1 'Cato clarus atque magnus habetur', *BJ* 92.1 'maior atque clarior haberi coepit') has been taken to imply that the meaning here is '<but> *uirtus* is regarded as brilliant and eternal' (so *TLL* ibid.), but this too must be doubtful: *uirtus* cannot be 'regarded as' brilliant; it simply *is* brilliant.[8] I suggest that S. wrote *uirtutis,* with *gloria* understood from the preceding colon ('<but> that of *uirtus* is regarded as brilliant and eternal'): not only does the same idea recur at *BJ* 1.3 ('ad gloriam uirtutis^uia') but *uita ipsa qua fruimur* in the preceding sentence suggests that S. is thinking of the peroration of *Cat.* 3 (28 'mihi quidem ipsi quid est quod iam ad *uitae fructum* possit acquiri, cum praesertim neque in honore uestro neque in *gloria uirtutis* quicquam uideam altius quo mihi libeat ascendere?'). *gloria* is

---

[7] Cato is downplayed by B. A. Krostenko, 'Binary phrases and the middle style as social code', *HSCP* 102 (2004) 237–74, at 263–4; he does not quote Gellius.
[8] Do we have an example of adjectival hendiadys ('*uirtus* is regarded as eternally brilliant')? There seems to be no discussion of this phenomenon in Latin, but for Greek see D. Sansone, *Glotta* 62 (1984) 23.

often qualified by *aeterna* (*TLL* 6.2.2065.25–8), but again note esp. *Cat.* 4.21; for *clara* see Ov. *Ex P.* 3.2.36, Val. Max. 1.1.14, Sil. 14.654–5 (Ennius had famously written *gloria claret* at *Ann.* 365). The error will be due to a scribe who desired a subject for *habetur* and failed to recognise that *gloria* must be understood. The result is a sentence in which the contrasting genitives are fronted and one of S.'s complete hexameters is included ('frăgĭlĭs ēst, uĭrtūtĭs clār(a) āetērnăqu(e) hăbētŭr').

1.5 sed diu magnum inter mortales certamen fuit ... magis procederet: the implied context of §§3–4 is now mentioned explicitly: 'res militaris'. Although S. has stated as self-evident the superiority of the mind over the body (1.2–3), in the distant past men nevertheless debated whether war was prosecuted more successfully by physical than by intellectual power (1.5–2.1), a debate whose realism is attested by numerous passages in Greek literature (e.g. Eur. *Phoen.* 746–7, Plb. 1.35.4). This acknowledging of the opposite point of view is the rhetorical device of *concessio* (Lausberg 383 §856), allowing the writer an opportunity for refutation and thus making his own point all the stronger: in this case the warfare debate was settled in favour of the intellect by the persuasive cases of Cyrus, Sparta and Athens (2.2). S. adds 'between mortals' because in mythical times there had also been famous battles between the gods, and these battles too gave rise to the same debate, traces of which may be seen e.g. in Hor. *Odes* 3.4.65 'uis consili expers mole ruit sua'. *mortalis* (see further 2.8n.) also serves as a reminder that *uita ipsa ... breuis est* (1.3). *certamen* is regularly followed by an indir. question (*OLD* 4); for *procedo* = 'make progress, succeed' see *OLD* 13.

1.6 et, priusquam incipias, consulto et, ubi consulueris, mature facto opus est 'and there is need both for a decision/plan before you begin and for quick action once you decide/plan'. S. is in effect describing the qualities of an ideal general, like Agrippa, 'consultis ... facta coniungens' (Vell. 79.1 and W.²; see further 20.16n. below).

The indefinite second person singular subjunctive (*NLS* 90–1 §119) is frequent in the Latin historians and used for a variety of different reasons (see Gilmartin); here *incipias* places readers in the position of the general, thus making more immediate the issue facing him. Scholars differ on whether *consulueris* is also subjunctive or fut. perfect indicative: there is no formal distinction between the two forms 'and it is often difficult to tell what form one is dealing with' (*OLS* 1.491). At Thuc. 1.70.2, to which S. seems to be alluding (see below, 2.2n. *tum*), the author uses an aorist subjunctive in an indefinite rel. clause (ἃ ἂν γνῶσιν), which perhaps suggests the same mood in S.: if so, 'the perfect subjunctive is mainly used ... much in the same way as the present subjunctive' (*OLS* 1.491). Since the noun *factum* is the perf. part. passive of *facio*, it is regularly qualified by an adverb, as here (*OLD* 1a); for the resumption of a noun by a verb see Wills 327–8.

1.7 ita utrumque per se indigens alterum alterius auxilio eget 'thus each of the two, insufficient on its own, requires the help of the other': *alterum* is in apposition to *utrumque* but redundant, as in such English expressions as 'Each city fell, one after another' (= 'one city fell after another'): contrast Cic. *TD* 2.13 'ita est utraque res sine altera debilis'. Reciprocal polyptoton of the type *alterum alterius* is common (Wills 222–4). This use of *ita* in initial position (again at e.g. 2.6 below) is a mannerism of S. For compound verb followed by simple (again with *indigeo* ~ *egeo* at Cic. *Off.* 1.49) cf. Tac. *A.* 3.29.1 and W–M, Wills 319–20, 438–43; *egeo* is constructed with abl. or gen., and S. uses both. For *per se* see *OLD se*[1] 6b.

2.1 igitur initio reges . . . diuersi pars ingenium, alii corpus exercebant: Polybius (for whose possible relevance see 2.3–6n. *quod si*) rather differently maintains that the first kings were chosen because of their bodily strength and it was only later that excellence of judgement and reasoning became criteria for kingship (6.7.3). *pars . . . alii* (*uariatio* for *alii . . . alii* or *pars . . . pars*) are in apposition to *reges . . . diuersi* (cf. 1.7n. above). Except in speech (20.14, 51.43, *BJ* 31.18), *igitur* is always first word in S.'s monographs, as previously in Cato (*Orig.* 20C/28P, 78C/86P) and later in Tacitus (Adams (1973) 132–3): cf. Quint. 1.5.39; also Fraenkel 193. Here the particle resumes the argument of 1.5 after the parenthetic 1.6–7 (*OLD igitur* 5). *ingenium exercere* (earlier at *Rhet. Herenn.* 3.34) recurs at 8.5, *H.* 2.43.4; *corpus exercere* at *BJ* 71.1. *diuersi* = 'holding different views' (*OLD diuersus* 5d). According to Quintilian (1.7.25) Scipio Africanus was the first to start spelling such words as *diuersus* with an -*e*- instead of an -*o*- (see further Zair 106–8).

nam in terris nomen imperii id primum fuit: the priority of kingship was a commonplace (e.g. Thuc. 1.13.1, Arist. *Pol.* 1252b19–28, Plb. 6.4.7, Cic. *Off.* 2.41, *Leg.* 3.4). *in terris* seems oddly redundant but S. is alluding to Ennius' *Euhemerus* (cf. 7G–M/60–1V 'initio . . . primus in terris imperium summum Caelus habuit'), a (probably prose) work in which it was explained that Uranus, Cronos and Zeus were originally great kings and only subsequently worshipped as gods in heaven.

etiam tum uita hominum sine cupiditate agitabatur: numerous ancient authors, including S.'s contemporaries Lucretius and Diodorus Siculus, inserted into their works passages of cultural history, tracing the development of civilisation from its primitive origins to the modern day. These passages differ from one another in detail (see e.g. T. Cole, *Democritus and the sources of Greek anthropology* (repr. 1990)): since self-sufficiency, a characteristic feature of life in the Golden Age, is here said to have survived into the age of kings (a paradox pointed by *etiam tum*), it seems that S. was following a version such as that alluded to by Seneca, who attributes to Posidonius the notion that there were kings in the Golden Age (*Ep.* 90.5). The statement functions as a foil for what follows (2.2n. *postea*). S. uses *cupiditas* and *cupido* indifferently in *BC*, but the latter, never used by Cicero or Caesar,[9] exclusively in *BJ* and *H.*; nouns in -*do* are favoured by Cato for their greater *dignitas* (Gell. 17.2.19–20). *agitare*, a favourite verb of S., is also Ennian (*Ann.* 307 'qui t̲u̲m̲ uiuebant h̲o̲m̲i̲n̲e̲s̲ a̲e̲u̲u̲m̲que a̲g̲i̲t̲a̲b̲a̲n̲t̲') and in combination with *uitam* recurs in an interestingly primitivistic passage of Ovid (*F.* 2.291). Frequentative verbs in general are liked by Cato and Plautus (Adams, *AIL* 101).

sua cuique satīs plăcēbānt 'each person was content with his own property'. The clausula, much favoured in the *BC*, becomes less common in S.'s two later works (K–K 169).

2.2 postea uero quam ... coepere: the contrast with the preceding ('but, after ...') is double: the imperialism described in the *postquam*-clause contrasts with the contentedness of *etiam tum ... satis placebant*, while the priority of the *ingenium* in the main clause contrasts with its uncertain status in the sentence before that (*igitur... exercebant*). *postea uero quam*, again at *BJ* 29.1, is found twice each in Caesar (*BG* 4.37.4, *BC* 2.17.4) and Nepos (*Dion* 4.3, *Dat.* 3.5) and commonly in Cicero, esp. in the letters (9×). The third person plur. -*ere* in the perfect tense is an elevated alternative to -*erunt*; it is almost entirely avoided by Cicero (cf. *Orat.* 157; Garcea 43) and Caesar but is found in Cato (e.g. 76C/83P, with Courtney, *ALP* 75–6) and is so often preferred by S. (e.g. 2.5 *inuasere*, 2.8 *transiere*, etc.) that the -*erunt* form is relatively rare (only 5× in *BC*, e.g. 20.10); subsequently it is found also in Livy (esp. in the first decade) and Tacitus. See also Lebek 199, 362 (index).

urbes atque nationes subigere: in this phrase, the first element of an ascending tricolon, *urbes* applies to the Spartans and Athenians, while *nationes* applies to Cyrus: the clause is thus a chiastic example of correlative distribution (sometimes known misleadingly as 'double zeugma'), whereby 'in related pairs of terms each member of the succeeding pair corresponds only to one member of the pair preceding, though at first sight the pairs may seem wholly to correspond' (Goodyear on Tac. *A.* 1.55.1). In the sixth century BC the king of Persia, Cyrus the Great, defeated the peoples of Lydia in Asia Minor and also Babylonia, creating the largest empire the world had ever seen (*OCD* 407, *BNP* 4.17–20). The Peloponnesian League of city-states was created and dominated by Sparta from the sixth to the fourth centuries BC (*OCD* 1100–1, *BNP* 10.702–4); the Athenian equivalent, which started as the Delian League in 478, did not last beyond Athens' defeat by Sparta in 404 at the end of the Peloponnesian War (*OCD* 425–6, *BNP* 4.201–5).

---

[9] For full statistics of usage see *TLL* 4.1411.74–1412.19.

libidinem dominandi causam belli habere 'to regard the lust for domination as a motive/reason for war'. Astonishingly the expr. *libido dominandi* (*-ationis*) seems unparalleled in classical Latin.

maximam gloriam in maximo imperio putare: *sc. esse.* For the polyptoton see Wills 237–8.

tum demum periculo atque negotiis compertum est in bello plurimum ingenium posse: *tum demum* introduces the conclusion after the long *postea . . . quam*-clause (cf. Liv. 30.10.11, 38.48.12, [Quint.] *Decl.* 355.5). When *possum* is qualified by an internal accusative, as here by *plurimum* (which is not to be taken with *ingenium*), the meaning is 'to have ~ power/influence/importance' (*OLD* 8); again at 39.4, 52.15. Elsewhere the coupling of *pericula* and *negotia* suggests 'dangers and tasks' rather than a hendiadys (*Comm. Petit.* 49, Gell. 6.3.21, 13.28.3): see further below.

S.'s statement is elliptical, since he omits to explain how or why 'it was discovered that in war *ingenium* is of the first importance'. The reader has to remember that Cyrus was idealised as a ruler, most notably by Xenophon in his *Cyropaedia*, a work with which S. was familiar and where Cyrus is characterised by 'intelligent action' (1.1.3 ἐπισταμένως πράττειν). If *periculo atque negotiis* directs us to the Thucydidean speech in which the Corinthians explain the Athenian character to the Spartans (1.70.8 μετὰ πόνων . . . καὶ κινδύνων), that is where the Athenians are described as 'quick at forming plans and at accomplishing in practice what they decide' (1.70.2 ἐπινοῆσαι ὀξεῖς καὶ ἐπιτελέσαι ἔργῳ ἃ ἂν γνῶσιν, cf. 1.69.2, 70.7), exactly the capacity which S. has commended at 1.6 above. As for the Lacedaemonians, perhaps S. simply means that, since they defeated Athens in the Peloponnesian War, they must have enjoyed intellectual superiority in the end.

2.3–6 quod si . . . transfertur: having had the superiority of the mind confirmed (1.5–2.2), S. could have resumed his thoughts on *gloria* and *uirtus* at this point; but he chooses instead to digress by reflecting conversely that rulers tend not to maintain in peacetime the good qualities of intellect which they show in war (2.3–5), and as a result they find themselves replaced by someone else (2.6). The theory is analogous to, but not identical with, Polybius' 'cycle of constitutions' (6.9.10 πολιτειῶν ἀνακύκλωσις): according to this, monarchy is debased by its inheritors over the course of time and is replaced by an aristocracy, which eventually suffers the same experience and is replaced by democracy, to which the same thing happens; the cycle then starts again (6.5.4–9.9). In each of the three cases the inheritors are corrupted by their circumstances and give their fellow citizens no alternative but to react, a reaction which takes the form of the next stage of the cycle. (There is an excellent discussion of the anacyclosis and its possible sources in F. W. Walbank, *Polybius* (1972) 137–46.)

§§3–6 interrupt S.'s main argument and could have been omitted; but the equivalence of peace and war will return below at 3.1, while the deterioration in behaviour will be returned to later in the preface (5.9– 13.5). The technique, associated esp. but not exclusively with Lucretius, has been called 'suspension of thought' (Williams, *TORP* 720–1, and *Figures of thought in Roman poetry* (1980) ch. 5; T. P. Wiseman, *Cinna the poet* (1974) 33–4). It recurs often in the preface in various forms (see 1.1 (n. *ne*) and below), and I have suggested that it explains the 'amputatae sententiae' with which S. was associated by his ancient readers (see Intro. pp. 23–5): indeed 'suspension of thought' is almost a translation of the Latin phrase.

2.3 regum atque imperatorum: Sparta, like Persia, had been ruled by kings; at Athens military command was entrusted to *stratēgoi* (generals), who are regularly rendered in Latin as *praetores* (e.g. Nep. *Milt.* 4.4 'domi ... creant decem praetores'; *TLL* 10.2.1057.13–45); but S. has chosen the less technical *imperatores*, and, given that so much of §§3–6 seems relevant to S.'s own day, it is hard not to see the great Roman generals of the mid- to late republic behind his terminological choice here. That S. is not talking about the sixth and fifth centuries BC is indicated by the fact that the sentence is a present unfulfilled condition (*NLS* 148 §193).

aequabilius atque constantius: Cicero regularly couples these or cognate terms (e.g. *Orat.* 198 'aequabiliter constanterque') but never with *atque*, which recalls the practice of Cato (1.4n. *nam*);[10] S.'s exact wording is echoed by Tac. *A.* 15.21.4.

neque aliud alio ferri neque mutari ac misceri omnia cerneres 'and you would not have seen things being swept in different directions or everything changing and confused'. Another appeal to readers (1.6n.; for the imperf. tense see *OLS* 1.487–8), this time involving sight and inviting reflection on what they have witnessed personally. S.'s contemporary, Lucretius, often appeals to sight too (e.g. 2.456–7 'omnia ... cernis | diffugere'), and, although no single line of his appears to be in S.'s mind here, the words have a Lucretian *color* (e.g. 1.166 'sed mutarentur: ferre omnes omnia possent', 1.802 'sic alias aliis rebus mutarier omnes'); see further 2.8nn., 51.20–1nn., 24n. *omnia miscere*, here concluding a chiasmus, is a common phrase in contexts of political confusion (10.1; Landgraf on Cic. *Rosc. Am.* 91); together with *mutari* it anticipates the later themes of the preface (5.9–13.5 intro.).

2.4 nam imperium facile iis artibus retinetur quibus initio partum est: this idea (again at *BJ* 85.1) is conventional. In addition to the variants at Liv. 1.35.6 and Tac. *H.* 1.30.1, see e.g. W.² on Vell. 57.1 or Oakley on Liv. 7.33.3, who notes the elder Cato by way of illustration: unlike those who on

---

[10] Cf. also *Rhet. Herenn.* 3.21.

achieving honours 'adjust their future lives to the enjoyment of pleasurable ease', he did not rest on his laurels, but resembled 'men first taking up
public service and thirsting for honour and reputation' (Plut. *Cato Mai.*
11.3, Loeb trans.).

The noun *ars* is capable of numerous different meanings and in the
plural, when it = 'qualities, practices, behaviour' (*OLD* 4), is frequent in S.,
who likes to qualify it with the adjs. *bonae* (2.9 (and n.), 10.4, 11.3; and 6×
in *BJ*) and *malae* (3.4, 13.5, *BJ.* 41.1): see esp. Earl, *PTS* 11–12. Here
S. appears to mean the *bonae artes* associated with exercise of the *ingenium*.

**2.5 uerum, ubi pro labore desidia, pro continentia et aequitate libido
atque superbia inuasere, fŏrtūnă sĭmŭl cŭm mōrĭbŭs īmmūtātūr** 'but,
whenever instead of hard work there is an attack of idleness, and instead
of self-control and fairness there are attacks of lust and haughtiness, the
situation/status [*sc.* of rulers] changes along with their behaviour' (*OLD
fortuna* 11). Unlike Polybius (above, 2.3–6n. *quod si*), S. does not spell out
the circumstances in which rulers' behaviour degenerates, causing their
removal from their position of power; S. gives the impression that the three
vices just occur spontaneously, like idiopathic diseases (*inuasere:* see 10.6n.;
OLD 4a). The two pairs of abstract nouns are another ex. of correlative
distribution (2.2n.): since *continentia* contrasts with *libido* (as Cic. *Verr.* 4.115,
Plin. *Pan.* 3.4), *aequitas* must contrast with *superbia* by default (level ~ high).
The main clause is one syllable short of constituting a spondaic hexameter.
For the perf. tense in present generalising temporal clauses see *NLS* 175
§217 (2) (*c*); S. differs strikingly from Caesar, Nepos and Livy in his prefer-
ence for *ubi-* and *postquam*-clauses and his relatively infrequent use of *cum*
(M. Spilman, 'Cumulative sentence building in Latin historical narrative',
UCPCP 11 (1930–3) 153–247 (statistics at 238)).

libido atque superbia are vices esp. applicable to Tarquinius Superbus
and his son Sextus, the violator of Lucretia (6.7n. *in*). Both men would
illustrate excellently Polybius' anacyclosis as it applied to Rome (2.3–6n.)
quod si): after the benign reigns of earlier kings, they are the inheritors
whose corrupt behaviour caused the introduction of a different constitution (cf. 6.7).

2.6 ita … transfertur 'In those circumstances command always passes
to the best people from the less good person' (*OLD ita* 6a). The argument
is again extremely compressed, but Polybius explained that, on occasions
when monarchy changed into a tyranny, the first stage in the latter's
overthrow was conspiracy on the part of the subjects, 'not the work of
the worst men but of the noblest, most high-spirited and most courageous', who would replace the tyrant as leaders of the community (6.7.8–9).

2.7–3.2 Hitherto the discussion has focussed, either implicitly (1.3) or
explicitly (1.5–2.2), on warfare; now, after the moralising of 2.3–6,

S. makes the point that *uirtus* is operative in other spheres of activity as well. This allows him, after a parenthesis on those who do not use their mind and to whom *fama* (here substituting for *gloria*) does not apply (2.8–9), to introduce the activity of writing, which, as does not need to be said, is a product of the mind. Writing is as admirable as action (3.1): authors are as liable for praise as are doers, and, although they may not receive the same degree of *gloria*, the difficulties involved in writing history should not be underestimated (3.2).

2.7 Quae homines arant, nauigant, aedificant, uīrtūt(ī) ōmnĭă pārēnt: lists of occupations, e.g. Hor. *S.* 1.1.4–12, were something of a convention (see N–H on Hor. *Odes* 1.1, intro.). Unlike the public careers implied or mentioned above (1.3, 1.5–2.6), the three activities referred to here – arranged as an ascending tricolon and embracing the different elements of land and sea – are drawn from private life: this is because S.'s target topic, historiography, is also a private activity, albeit with a public dimension (3.1). *Quae* is an internal accusative (G&L 210 §333R. 2): 'whatever ploughing, sailing and building that men do ...'.[11] Most edd. understand *omnia* as nom. ('it is all subject to *uirtus*'), as Manil. 1.479 'certis ... legibus omnia parent', but some scholars, including an ancient grammarian who glosses *omnia* as *in omnibus*,[12] interpret it as an adverbial accusative ('they are subject to *uirtus* in every respect'), a construction sometimes found after verbs of obeying (Ter. *Ad.* 990, Stat. *Ach.* 1.660 'parebimus omnia matri', Gell. 2.7.3, 10). The former seems more natural.

2.8 multi mortales: the use of *mortales* for *homines* is choice and often pointed (e.g. 1.5n.; von Albrecht 68–70); the present expr., which occurs 9× in S., was discussed by Fronto (Gell. 13.29), who considered it poetical. It occurs in early Latin, including Cato (2× in *Orat.* 58M), 3× in Cicero and 10× in Livy's first decade (see Oakley on 6.16.4, who considers it archaic).

dediti uentri atque somno: *dediti ... somno* may derive from Lucr. 3.112 'somno dedita'; for *d. uentri* (varying *uentri oboedientia* of animals at 1.1) cf. *BJ* 85.41 'dediti uentri et turpissimae parti corporis' (see *PH* 384–5), Sen. *Ben.* 7.2.2 'uentri ac libidini deditos' (the remainder of this sentence imitates 16.3 below); similar phrases at Plin. *Ep.* 3.5.19 'somno et inertiae deditus', Tac. *G.* 15.1 'dediti somno ciboque', and cf. Plaut. *Pseud.* 175 'quae uentri operam det, ... quae somno studeat' (slightly different), Sen. *Ep.* 55.5 'ille sibi non uiuit, sed ... uentri, somno, libidini'. See also 13.3n. (*dormire*).

indocti incultique is picked up by Apul. *Deo Socr.* 22.3.

---

[11] Presumably we are not to imagine that men of S.'s class would actually plough or row, etc.

[12] *GL* 7.543.37 (the so-called Fragmenta Bobiensia, on which see Zetzel 331–2).

uitam sicuti peregrinantes transiere: the basic meaning of *peregrinari* is to be away from or leave one's home and it is often used metaphorically (*TLL* 10.1.1304.28–9, 1305.49ff., esp. 1306.70–5). S.'s point is that 'many mortals' are out of place in life and hence might just as well be dead (below: 'eorum ego uitam mortemque iuxta aestimo'). For *uitam . . . transiere* see 1.1n. (*Omnes*).

contra naturam . . . uoluptati: the 'unnatural' and pleasure will become important themes later in the preface (13.1–3).

anima oneri fuit: hitherto S. has been varying *animus* and *ingenium* as synonyms; here, somewhat in the manner of Lucretius (see Kenney on 3.94–7), he introduces *anima* as a further synonym, even though (or, more likely, because) he will use it in a different sense just below (9): 'suspension of thought' again. The statement is of course a paradox, since the mind is supposed to be 'light' (e.g. Sen. *Cons. Helv.* 11.6). *oneri* is a predicative dat. (*NLS* 49 §68) and a favourite of S. (again at 10.2, 46.2, *BJ* 14.4, *H.* 86.9).

iuxta 'equally' (*OLD* 2).

quoniam de utraque siletur 'because silence is kept about each of them' (*OLD sileo* 3a). There is a certain irony about the statement, because at 13.3 S. will wax eloquent about those who devote their lives to their stomachs and to sleep. Yet he cannot be accused of contradicting himself, since he names no names: no one is glorified or memorialised for their gluttony or somnolence.

2.9 uerum enim uero is demum mihi u̱iuere . . . u̱idetur 'on the other hand, *that* man seems to me to be truly alive . . .' (*OLD uiuo* 7a): *demum* is to be taken closely with *is* (*OLD* 2a); again at 12.5 and 20.4. For *uerum enim uero* see *OLD uerum*[3] 2.

frui anima is a Latin translation of χαρίζεσθαι ψυχῇ, which means 'to indulge oneself': S.'s point is that those who are 'devoted to their stomachs and to sleep' and who treat their 'bodies as a source of pleasure' are as much misguided in these respects as in their belief that they are truly living; true self-indulgence is experienced by the man 'qui . . . famam quaerit'. The only other ex. of the expr. seems to be Acc. 296R 'Sapimus animo, fruimur anima: sine animo anima est debilis'.

aliquo negotio intentus: *intentus*, a favourite word (20+ times in S.), is normally constructed with a dat. (including here, according to *TLL* 7.1.2118.52–3); but *aliquo* identifies the noun as abl., which is how it is understood by the fourth-century scholars Nonius Marcellus (483L) and Arusianus Messius (7.488.10).[13] Some have emended to *aliquoi*, but *intentus* is seemingly found again with an abl. at *BJ* 44.3. Perhaps a Sallustian idiosyncrasy (as if 'stretched by some task').

---

[13] On them see Zetzel 98–100, 231–2, 281–2.

praeclari facinoris aut artis bonae famam quaerit 'seeks a reputation for an outstanding deed or good quality' (chiastic). *facinus* in this neutral sense (as opposed to 'crime') is usually regarded as archaic, but for some doubts see Oakley on Liv. 8.24.9, who on 9.10.3 collects further exs. of its coupling with *praeclarus* (4× in S.). Despite Earl, *PTS* 11–12, S. is not the first to use *ars bona* (or variations thereof) in a moral sense (cf. e.g. Cic. *Cael.* 77). In other contexts the plural *bonae artes* often means 'cultural pursuits' etc. (*OLD ars* 6a); in view of the following argument (3.1–2), this is a further ex. of 'suspension of thought'.

sed in magna copia rerum aliud alii Natura iter ostendit: after the quasi-digressive remarks of §§8–9, S. returns to the point he had introduced in §7, namely that there is a diversity of occupations; but, whereas earlier he presented them in terms of *uirtus*, here he leaves it to be inferred from the preceding sentence ('famam quaerit') that he is now talking about reputation. This means that, when he brings in writing as yet another occupation (3.1–2), he need merely claim that the writer can achieve *gloria*, avoiding the invidious claim that it is an opportunity for *uirtus*. That this latter claim is nevertheless implicit may be inferred both from the repetition of §7 and from the metaphor of 'the ways' ('aliud . . . iter'), which inevitably reminds us of the Choice of Heracles (Xen. *Mem.* 2.1.21–34, a passage to which S. alludes at 13.3 below (n.); Krebs 585–6).[14] For road metaphors used of Natura cf. e.g. Cic. *Rep.* 2.30, *Leg.* 1.27.

3.1   pulchrum est . . . haud absurdum est: another chiasmus. *haud absurdum* seems defensive, acknowledging the superiority of *bene facere* (cf. Cic. *De Or.* 1.7 'quis enim est qui . . . non anteponat oratori imperatorem?'); the litotes recurs at 25.5 and (also + infin.) Vell. 38.1, Tac. *A.* 4.65, 12.24.1 (for *h. absurde* cf. Vell. 77.1, 83.3, Tac. *H.* 3.51.2).

bene facere rei publicae 'to do/act well for the advantage of the state': the only other ex. of this expr. is Cato's speech *De Sumptu Suo* (*Orat.* 173M): see Levene, *OR* 216–17.

bene dicere: *rei publicae* has to be understood from the phrase with which it is paired in the chiasmus, although some scholars dispute this. Because of his public eloquence Cicero was allegedly described by Caesar as 'bene de nomine ac dignitate populi Romani meritum' (*Brut.* 253–4); Cicero himself, in contrast to S., distinguished between his public service and his intellectual pursuits (*Off.* 2.3–4). When Camus, the French novelist, asked De Gaulle how a writer could serve France, the General replied that France was served by

---

[14] For the likelihood that the Choice of Heracles also featured in a preface of Lucceius, the historian whom Cicero tried to persuade to write the history of the Catilinarian conspiracy (*Fam.* 5.12), see *FRHist* 3.451–2, adding A. Ring, 'Heraclean historians', *SyllClass* 21 (2010) 41–3.

'Every man who writes and who writes well' (A. Malraux, *Fallen oaks: conversation with De Gaulle* (trans. I. Clephane, 1972) 80).

uel pace uel bello clarum fieri licet: the reader has already been nudged towards the equivalence of peace and war at 2.3 'in pace ita ut in bello'. *licet* is constructed with an acc. + infin. (*OLD* 1b), but the acc. subject has been omitted: 'that <a person> should become distinguished either in peace or in war is possible' (i.e. 'a person may become . . .'). *uel pace uel bello* is chiastic with *bene facere* and *bene dicere* above and with *qui fecere* and *qui . . . scripsere* below.

et qui fecere et qui facta <u>aliorum</u> scripsere, multi laudantur: Cicero's speech *Pro Archia* (62 BC) is eloquent testimony to S.'s statement. He argues, e.g., that generals like Pompey were accompanied on their campaigns by 'scriptores rerum suarum' (24), that in praising their patrons these writers were also praising the Roman People (22) and that the writers themselves received praise in their turn. Contrast the earlier period described at 8.5 (n. *optimus*). For the resumption of a verb by a verbal noun see Wills 327–8, whose first ex. is Homeric (*Il.* 18.200–1).

3.2 *mihi* **quidem** . . . *in primis* **arduum** *uidetur* **res gestas scribere** 'to me at least the writing of achievements seems especially steep' (*OLD imprimis* 1a). The implied logic of this sentence is that *gloria* is a lofty attainment and to be reached only with difficulty (cf. Ov. *Tr.* 4.3.74 'ardua per praeceps gloria uadat iter'; *OLD arduus* 3a, 4–5): since historiography is difficult (and doubly so: *primum* . . . *dehinc* below), it cannot be a disqualification for acquiring *gloria*. Numerous historians make explicit or implicit reference to the difficulty of their task, although the nature of the difficulty will vary from writer to writer (e.g. Thuc. 1.22.1, 1.22.3, Hirt. *BG* 8 *praef.* 1, Liv. *praef.* 4, Plin. *Ep.* 5.8.12, Just. *praef.* 2). S.'s sentence was echoed by Pliny in a famous letter (5.8.1 'quia *mihi* <u>pulchrum</u> *in primis uidetur* non pati occidere, quibus aeternitas debeatur, <u>aliorum</u>que famam cum sua extendere'); it was also defended by Gellius (4.15) against captious critics who objected to S.'s use of the adj. *arduum*, which is another of the 'journeying' metaphors found in the preface (Krebs 586–9; cf. W.[6] on Hor. *C.* 3.24.44).

tametsi haudquaquam par gloria sequitur scriptorem et auctorem rerum: Livy took it for granted that writing history would bring him a reputation (*praef.* 3 'mea fama') and he later admitted that he had amassed enough glory (1.3n. *gloriam*). One of the ambitions of Livy's contemporary, Pompeius Trogus, seems to have been to rival the glory of previous historians (Just. *praef.* 1 'aemulatione gloriae'), while a century or so later the younger Pliny acknowledged that historiography would prolong a writer's fame (*Ep.* 5.8.1, quoted last n.).[15] S. too sees historiography as an opportunity for glory, but he expresses himself in language which suggests

---

[15] For this letter see *PH* 223–42; for the historian's glory see Marincola 57–62.

through ambiguity that doing and writing are more equivalent than might
be thought. (a) His argument ('tametsi ...') requires the clause to mean
that the doer receives more *gloria* than does the writer, but *haudquaquam
par* is equally capable of meaning that the writer receives more *gloria* than
does the doer; (b) to describe the doer of deeds he has chosen a noun
which can mean 'writer' (e.g. Liv. 6.12.2 'harum rerum auctores'; *TLL*
2.1206.21ff., esp. 1207.25–1210.2) as well as 'doer' (e.g. *BJ* 1.4 'suam
quisque culpam auctores ad negotia transferunt', Liv. 40.11.2 'Quinctius
nunc est auctor omnium rerum'; *TLL* 2.1201.30–1204.29). The equivalence came naturally to the ancient mindset because (c) there was
a convention that the writer does what he describes (4.2n. *a quo*), (d)
the technique of vivid writing (*enargeia, demonstratio*), which was supposed
to turn readers into eyewitnesses of (or even participants in) the events
being described (*LH* 38), required that the writer himself should experience the necessary emotions of the situation (e.g. Quint. 6.2.29–31;
Lausberg 359–61 §§810–11). *gloria sequitur* (again at 54.6) is relatively
common (and cf. Otto 155); *tametsi ... tamen* is extremely common in S.,
Cicero and the Caesarian corpus but drops out of favour during most of
the first cent. AD.

primum quod facta dictis exaequanda sunt 'first because deeds have to
be matched by words'. *facta dictis exaequare* and similar phraseology is an
almost standard way of referring to the problem of describing men and
events in accordance with their deserts (e.g. Liv. 6.20.8 'facta dictis exae-
quando' with Oakley's n.): usually the problem is that of finding words
adequate to the great deeds being described (e.g. Isoc. *Pan.* 13 χαλεπόν
ἐστιν ἴσους τοὺς λόγους τῷ μεγέθει τῶν ἔργων ἐξευρεῖν),[16] although occasionally it will be that of adequately describing some heinous crime. The
historian's solution to these complementary problems is treated from
the reader's point of view in the second of S.'s causal clauses below.[17]
See also 8.3n. (*per*).

[16] Reversed in Pericles' speech at Thuc. 2.42.2 ἰσόρροπος ... ὁ λόγος τῶν ἔργων.
[17] Modern readers, familiar with the so-called 'linguistic turn' in historiography
(see e.g. E. A. Clark, *History, theory, text: historians and the linguistic turn* (2004)),
might assume that S. is referring to a problem of mimesis: namely, the difficulty
of representing reality in words. The sophists discussed this problem in the fifth
century BC (see e.g. G. B. Kerferd, *The Sophistic movement* (1981) 80–2), and that
it was a live issue in S.'s day is suggested by Diodorus when he writes that
'although the actual experience of the events contains the truth, yet the written
record ..., while presenting copies [μιμεῖσθαι] of the events, falls far short of
arranging them as they really were' (20.43.7, Loeb trans.). For *quae<que> in bello
gesta sint iterare* at Sempronius Asellio 2C/P see *LH* 32–7 and ref. there to
G. Lieberg, '*Iterare* ovvero sul rapporto fra parola e realtà', *Orpheus* 1 (1980)
411–21.

dehinc quia ...: the second causal clause consists of two parts, linked by adversative asyndeton: the first part (subject *plerique*+ relative clause) deals with readers' response to the historian's criticism of wrongdoing; the second (subject *quisque* + *ubi*-clause) deals with their response to the historian's praise of excellence. Both parts constitute a sustained allusion to the opening of Pericles' famous Funeral Speech in 431 BC as rendered by Thucydides, although only praise is dealt with (2.35.2): 'It is hard to speak appropriately in circumstances where even the appearance of truth can only with difficulty be confirmed. The listener who knows what has happened and is favourably disposed can easily think that the account given falls short of his wishes and knowledge, while the man lacking in experience may through jealousy think some claims exaggerated if he hears things beyond his own capacity. Praise spoken of others is bearable up to the point where each man believes himself capable of doing the things he heard of; anything which goes beyond that arouses envy and disbelief' (trans. P. J. Rhodes). *primum* ... *dehinc* seems uncommon but cf. *BJ* 5.1, Virg. *G.* 3.166–7, Ascon. 68, Apul. *Met.* 8.18.7, 10.24.5 (*primo* ... *dehinc* is only marginally more common).

plerique, quae delicta reprehenderis, maleuolentia et inuidia dicta putant: the antecedent has been incorporated into its relative clause: 'many people think that *the misdeeds which you have criticised* have been mentioned through ill will and resentment' (another ex. of the indefinite second person potential subjunc.: 1.6n.). For *maleuolentia et inuidia* cf. Cic. *Fam.* 1.1.1; for the wordplay *delicta ~ dicta* cf. Gell. 3.3.15 'delicta sua et petulantias dictorum'.

ubi de magna *uirtute atque gloria* bonorum memores: Tacitus alludes to this clause when he too is discussing the effect of historiography upon its readers *A.* 4.33.4 'etiam *gloria ac uirtus* infensos habet'). In his preference for *memoro* over *commemoro* (20:1) S. resembles Livy in his first decade (23:2, reversed thereafter by 24:34) and Virgil (34:0) and is predictably followed by Tacitus: for these and other statistics see J. N. Adams, *Antichthon* 8 (1974) 55.

quae sibi quisque facilia factu putat, aequo animo accipit: *sc. ea*: 'each person accepts equably <those things> which he regards as easy for himself to do' (*OLD puto* 5a). *facilis* + supine *factu* is a common *figura etymologica* (again at 14.1).

supra ea, ueluti ficta, pro falsis ducit: *supra ea*, introduced by a further asyndeton, seems to be elliptical for *quae supra ea sunt dicta*: '<but everything which is said> beyond that, as if fabrications, he considers as false'.

3.3 Sed ego ... ad rem publicam latus sum, ibique mihi multa aduērsă fŭērĕ: *sed* contrasts the career which S. *actually* chose (~ 3.1 *bene facere rei publicae*) with that which he has just been outlining (*bene dicere r.p.*). It became conventional for historians to mention the experience they brought to historiography (Marincola 133–48), but S.'s career (Intro. pp. 2–4) had been such that it required an apologia, and this sentence is the first of a series of allusions which in this section of the preface (3.3–4.2) S. makes to the autobiographical Seventh Letter attributed to Plato (Renehan, *OR* 109–10): cf. 7.324B–C 'Formerly, when young, I had the same experience as many others: I thought ... of entering immediately the public life of the city. And certain changes in the affairs of the city befell me ...'. S.'s diminutive (*adulescentulus*) and passive (*latus sum*) add to the exculpation, but he will have turned thirty when he entered upon the *cursus honorum* and became a senator – and been in his mid-30s when he was expelled from the senate (Dio 40.63.4), an ignominy to which *ibique mihi multa aduersa fuere* seems to be a euphemistic allusion.

pro ... audacia: for the triple anaphora of the preposition (again at 58.11) see Adams, *AILL* 31–2, who is unfortunately much more interested in pairs than in triples.

3.4 animus ... insolens mala*rum* a*r*tium 'my mind ... unaccustomed to wicked practices/behaviour' (*OLD insolens* 1). Since S. has hitherto been emphasising the crucial importance of the *animus*, it is significant that it portrays his own *animus* as innocent; his continued use of the passive voice, this time applied to his age (next n.), maintains the exculpatory stance. For *artium* see 2.4n. (*nam*).

imbecilla aetas ambitione corrupta tenebatur: *ambitione* has to be taken with both *corrupta* and *tenebatur* ('my feeble age, once it was infected by ambition, was kept in its grip'): for the illness metaphor cf. *OLD corrumpo* 2a, *teneo* 10; perhaps similar is Gell. 3.1.9 'auaritia mentem tenuit et corrupit'. It is significant that the one *uitium* to which S. admits is *ambitio*, 'quod ... uitium propius uirtutem erat' (11.1). The ref. at Hor. *S.* 2.2.85–6 'aetas | imbecilla' is to old age, not youth. S.'s dactylic rhythm is notable: 'ĭmbēcīll(a) āetās ∪ ∪ – – āmbĭtĭōnĕ'.

3.5 cum ab reliquorum malis moribus dissentirem: cf. Cic. *Font.* 30 'a ceterarum gentium more ac natura dissentiunt' (also 4.1n. *animus*, 10.1n. *reges*). For *cum* see 2.5n. (*uerum*).

honoris cupido eadem qua ceteros fama atque inuidia uexabat 'my desire for office afflicted me with the same notoriety and resentment with which <it afflicted> the others': the stirring up of *inuidia* 'was a major project of populist oratory at Rome' (Dyck on Cic. *Leg.* 3.25). S.'s illness metaphor continues (*OLD uexo* 4): *honoris cupido* is the primary condition, *fama* and *inuidia* are the secondary complications or attendant symptoms. *ceteros*, like *sicuti plerique* above (3.3), is exculpatory. But it cannot be denied that the sentence is awkward: *cupidum* was suggested by P. H. Damsté (*Mnem.* 21 (1893) 215–18), the deletion of *honoris cupido* by E. Kraggerud (*SO* 77 (2002) 110–13). For *cupido* see 2.1n. (*etiam tum*).

4.1 animus ... requieuit: the expr. was probably in Tacitus' mind at *A.* 6.38.1, although it had occurred elsewhere (Sen. *Ep.* 65.17, *Cons. Pol.* 8.1, Tac. *A.* 1.25.3). For *miseriis atque periculis* cf. Cic. *Font.* 46 (3.5n. *cum,* 10.1n. *reges*), Sen. *Contr.* 9.4.21, Val. Max. 7.2 *ext.* 5.
mihi reliquam aetatem a re publica procul habendam decreui: *sc. esse.* It is striking that S. now uses a first person active verb to refer to his enforced retirement from public life in dubious circumstances (again at *BJ* 4.3). In representing his move from politics as a conversion, S. is putting himself in the best possible light (for 'conversion stories' see Rutherford 103–7) and in particular is again following Plato (*Epist.* 7.325E–326A); but in fact his 'conversion' will soon be seen as a reversion (4.2n. *a quo*). S.'s metaphorical use of *procul habere* combines with *consilium* (next n.) to be imitated by Tacitus in the preface to the *Annals* (1.1.3 '*consilium mihi* ..., sine ira et studio, quorum causas *procul habeo*'): see Woodman, *Tacitus reviewed* (1998) 21–2.
non fuit consilium socordia atque desidia bonum otium conterere: the writing of history required *otium* (Cic. *Leg.* 1.9 'historia ... nec institui potest nisi praeparato otio, nec exiguo tempore absolui'), but *otium* was a condition of which the industrious Romans were deeply suspicious (1.1–4.2 intro.): S. later claimed that more advantage would accrue to the state on account of his *otium* than the *negotium* of others (*BJ* 4.4). *socordia* is one of S.'s favourite nouns; for its coupling with *desidia* cf. *Rhet. Herenn.* 2.35. *non fuit consilium* recurs at 53.6, *H.* 1.49.26.
neque uero *agrum colendo* aut uenando seruilibus officiis intentum aetatem agere: the construction with *non fuit consilium* now seems to change from a prolative infin. (*conterere*) to an acc. + infin. (*sc. me*), since otherwise *intentum* has nothing with which to agree. There seems to be no parallel for this constr., but S. likes an acc. + infin. where others would have a simple infin. (1.1n. *Omnes,* 7.6n. *se quisque*). Most scholars regard *seruilibus officiis* as referring to *agrum colendo aut uenando,* but this is puzzling: not only did the elder Cato proudly declare that he had spent his adolescence in the fields (*Orat.* 128M 'in parsimonia atque in duritia atque industria omnem meam adulescentiam abstinui *agro colendo*') but he also wrote a whole book *De Agri Cultura,* which he began by saying that farmers made the best soldiers (*praef.* 4 'ex agricolis et uiri fortissimi et milites strenuissimi gignuntur'). Hunting too was regarded as good training for warfare (Pease on Cic. *ND* 2.161; J. Aymard, *Les chasses romaines* (1951) 469–81). Kvíčala therefore took *seruilibus officiis intentum* together and interpreted the words as referring to the supervision of slaves as they went about their tasks (so too J. Delz, *MH* 42 (1985) 168–73); and, since *seruile* is to be taken literally on the few other occasions when it qualifies *officium* in Latin (e.g. Sen. *Contr.* 10.5.16), it seems that that is also the case here: '(it was not my intention) that I should spend my life in cultivating the land or in hunting,

attending to the tasks of my slaves'. *neque uero* = 'nor indeed' (*OLD neque* 9b); for the gerund + acc. object see 15.3n.

4.2 a quo incepto studioque me ambitio mala detinuerat, eodem regressus 'returning to the project and enthusiasm from which my wicked ambition had kept me': *eodem* is an adverb = 'to the same place' and refers to *incepto studioque*, which in turn looks back to *initio . . . studio* at 3.3; the *mala ambitio* is that by which his youthful self was gripped at 3.4. After the interval which followed his departure from political life (4.1 'ubi animus . . . requieuit'), and determined not to take up farming or hunting, S. has decided on a vicarious return to his original enthusiasm – politics via the medium of historiography. It was a regular conceit that the historian performs what he describes (Plb. 3.57.1, Dion. Hal. *Thuc.* 9, Liv. 10.31.10 'bella quae continua per quartum iam uolumen . . . agimus'; W.[4] on Tac. *A.* 6.38.1). (S.'s words are usually interpreted to mean that his original intention was to be a historian but that he was deflected by the lure of political life; but this seems highly unlikely in view of his remarks in 3.3, where no reference at all is made to historiography.) *ambitio mala* recurs at Hor. *S.* 2.3.77 and 2.6.18; for *detinuerat* cf. Colum. *RR* 1.1.19 'plerosque nostrum ciuilis ambitio saepe euocat ac saepius detinet euocatos'.

statui res gestas populi Romani carptim, ut quaeque memoria digna uidebantur, perscribere 'I decided to describe the affairs of the Roman people selectively, according as the topics each seemed worthy of record' (*quaeque* is neut. plur.). Statements of subject matter were expressed in a standard manner, with only slight variations, e.g. *H.* 1.1 'Res p.R ... gestas composui', Cato, *Orig.* 1C/P 'p.R. gesta describere', Semp. Asell. 1C/P 'res gestas a Romanis perscribere', Liv. *praef.* 1 'si a primordio urbis res populi Romani perscripserim', Hor. *Epi.* 1.3.7 'res Augusti scribere', Fest. 329L 'Agathoclis Siculi qui res gestas conscripsit'. *carptim* indicates that S.'s historiography will be selective, by which he means that he will treat individual topics in monograph form: obviously he is referring principally to the Catilinarian conspiracy (see §§3–4), but he may already have been thinking too of the Jugurthine War. *carptim* is explained further in the *ut*-clause: such phrases as *memoria digna* (equivalent to the Greek ἀξιόλογα, Thuc. 1.1.1) are usually deployed to promote the virtue of selectivity *within* a given narrative and hence to emphasise the importance of the *topics* selected (e.g. Tac. *A.* 13.31.1 'pauca memoria digna euenere'; Oakley on Liv. 7.10.5, W.[3] on *Agr.* 1.2, W.[5] on Tac. *A.* 4.32.1); here the reference is to selection from a list of potential *subjects*. Adverbs in *-tim* are a feature of early Latin (see J. Briscoe, 'The fragmentary republican historians', in T. Reinhardt et al. (edd.), *Aspects of the language of Latin prose* (2005) 55, 71), and Gellius (12.15) commented on their frequency in Sisenna, whose (now fragmentary) work was continued by S. in his *Historiae*. *carptim* is first attested here in extant Latin.

eo magis quod . . . animus liber erat 'all the more because my mind was free from . . .' (*OLD eo*³ 2). The first reason for S.'s decision to write history was that he did not plan to waste his retirement from public life (1); a further reason is that, because of his retirement, his vicarious return to politics will be free from the pressures of factionalism (*erat* adopts the perspective of S.'s future readers).

4.3–5.8 The Subject of the Work: Catiline (I)

After stating (4.3) and rationalising (4.4) the subject of his work, S. believes it necessary to say something about the character and personality of the man on whom the work will be focussed (4.5–5.8).[18] This was expected in historical writing (cf. Cic. *De Or.* 2.64 'hominumque ipsorum non solum res gestae sed etiam, qui fama ac nomine excellant, de cuiusque uita atque natura'), and S. will resume the theme (*Catiline (II)* at 14–16) after the intervening archaeology (5.9–13.5).

4.3 Igitur de C̲atilinae c̲oniuratione quam u̲erissime potero p̲aucis absoluam: the logic (cf. *Igitur*) is as follows: *de Catilinae coniuratione* implicitly picks up *quaeque memoria digna* (the connection will be made explicit by *in primis . . . memorabile* in the upcoming parenthesis); *paucis absoluam* picks up (somewhat paradoxically) *perscribere*; and *quam uerissime potero* picks up *animus liber*. In historical texts, references to 'truth' commonly denote impartiality or freedom from bias (e.g. *H.* 1.6 'neque me diuersa pars in ciuilibus armis mouit a uero', Cic. *Fam.* 5.12.3, Liv. *praef.* 5, Tac. *H.* 1.1.1–3, Lucian, *Hist. Conscr.* 39–40; *RICH* 70–4, 82–3, 233 (index s.v. 'truth'); T. J. Luce, 'Ancient views on the causes of bias in historical writing', *CP* 84 (1989) 16–31; Marincola 160–1). S.'s claim to impartiality seems to be based simply on his retirement from active politics (2 above); that S. in his narrative 'proves his refusal of narrow partisanship' is argued thoughtfully by Stone (1999) 50–2.

Although *absoluere* is used frequently of speech etc. (perhaps = 'to despatch, discharge'), it normally takes a direct object; *de* + abl. seems to be a Sallustian peculiarity. *paucis* (*sc. uerbis*) *absoluere* occurs elsewhere (e.g. 38.3, Pacuv. 181R, Liv. 33.12.2) but its use at *H.* 1.3 to describe the elder Cato invites the question whether it had been used in the *Origines* by Cato of himself. With *paucis absoluam* S. is claiming *breuitas*, by which is meant the self-imposed restriction on narrative length which is required by the monograph form (Intro. p. 22; see further *PH* 209–11, 213–20). For *igitur* see 2.1n.

---

[18] When Cicero was urging Lucceius to write a monograph about the Catilinarian conspiracy, he pointed out the advantage of focussing on a single personality (*Fam.* 5.12.2 'una . . . in persona') but of course was referring to himself.

4.4 nam id facinus ... memorabile existimo sceleris atque periculi nouitate: S.'s argument is chiastic: *memorabile* looks back to *memoria digna* (2), just as *animus liber* (2) was picked up by *quam uerissime* (3). It was important to claim novelty if one wanted to capture the interest of one's audience or readers (e.g. *Rhet. Herenn.* 1.7, Cic. *Inv.* 1.23, Quint. 4.1.33), and historians, who were expected to magnify their chosen subject (e.g. *BJ* 5.1 'magnum ... tunc primum'), were no exception (Hdt. 6.55 τὰ δὲ ἄλλοι οὐ κατελάβοντο, τούτων μνήμην ποιήσομαι ('I shall produce a record of what others have not taken for themselves'), Vitr. 5 *praef.* 1 'historiae per se tenent lectores: habent enim nouarum rerum expectationes'). S. does not specify exactly how the Catilinarian conspiracy qualified as novel,[19] and some key elements of the *bellum Catilinae* cannot have failed to recall Lepidus' 'war' in 78/7 (cf. *H.* 4.48 'belli Lepidani'): see Intro. p. 2 and esp. Rosenblitt 50–4. Each protagonist was associated with rebel forces at Faesulae (*H.* 1.59–60 ~ *BC* 24.2), each prompted the senate to pass the *senatus consultum ultimum* (*H.* 1.67.22 ~ *BC* 29.2), and each was declared *hostis* (Flor. 2.11(3.23).7 ~ *BC* 36.2); and, although Lepidus actually succeeded in marching on Rome with an army from Etruria (Flor. 2.11 (3.23).5), something which formed a major part of C.'s planning but which he failed to carry out (32.2, 44.6), the downfall for both came at the Mulvian Bridge, where reception parties were waiting (Flor. 2.11 (3.23).6 ~ *BC* 45). Perhaps S. means simply that elements of C.'s campaign were unprecedented in their intended destructiveness.

existimo regularly takes a predicate (*OLD* 2b); it is a favourite verb of S., as of Cato, who uses it 4× in the preface to his *De Agri Cultura* (see Courtney, *ALP* 50–2). See also 40.1n.

4.5 de cuius hominis moribus pauca prius explananda sunt quam initium narrandi faciam 'and a little must be straightened out about his behaviour before I can make a start on my narrative': *priusquam* (here in tmesis) is followed by the subjunc. because the temporal clause has the notion of purpose (*NLS* 184–5 §227, quoting this passage). Ancient historians might allow the personality of a protagonist to emerge gradually from the narrative (the so-called 'indirect' method of characterisation) or they might present the reader with a formal character sketch (the 'direct' method, which S. uses again at e.g. 25, 53.6–54.6 (a syncrisis), *BJ* 95.2). By placing the sketch of C. before the narrative begins, as does e.g. Polybius in

---

[19] The Bacchanalia episode of 186 BC is presented by Livy (39.8–19) in terms of the Catilinarian conspiracy (see Briscoe's commentary, p. 250) but seems in fact to have been altogether different. The elder Cato evidently delivered a speech on the episode which may have been entitled *De Coniuratione* (*Orat.* 68M), although it is not clear from the entry in Festus (who is attesting to Cato's use of the singular *precem*, the one word of the speech to survive) that those words are in fact a title.

the case of Scipio Africanus (cf. 10.2.1–2), S. allows his assessment to influence everything that follows.[20] It will therefore come as something of a surprise when at the end of the narrative C. dies a heroic death (61.1–4: Intro. p. 15); and there is some irony in S.'s putting his readers straight ('explananda') about an individual so crooked (5.1 'ingenio malo prauoque'). *pauca*, like *paucis* at 5.9 below, shows S. putting into practice the programme which he has just promised (4.3 *paucis*).

Scholars have remarked on S.'s liking for such 'simple' verbs as *facio* and *habeo* (Syme, *Sall.* 262–3). Often they feature as 'support verbs', i.e. they are combined with a noun which expresses the verbal idea, as here: *initium ... faciam* is a periphrastic equivalent to *incipiam*. For discussion see *OLS* 1.74–7, Spevak 250–4, Adams, *AIL* 70–1.

5.1–8 Since authors were often called upon to describe individuals either in praise or blame, theorists developed certain set methods for their description: thus Cicero offers a list of topical categories, starting with a person's name (*nomen*) before proceeding to e.g. *natura, uictus, habitus* and the like (*Inv.* 1.34), each of which is then explained in more detail (1.34–6); Menander Rhetor, like the second-century AD rhetorician Hermogenes (*Prog.* 7, p. 12 Spengel), orders the categories more chronologically (369.17–373.6), starting with origin and family before continuing through youth, accomplishments (ἐπιτηδεύματα) and deeds (πράξεις). See also Lausberg 106–7 §245, 174–5 §376. It is clear that these conventions have influenced S.'s description of C., which in its essentials resembles those found in Cic. *Cat.* (sometimes word for word) and elsewhere (e.g. *Sull.* 70); but on occasion, as required by circumstance, Cicero can be more nuanced (*Cael.* 12–14).[21] S.'s sketch acted as a model for Livy's of Hannibal (21.4.2–10: see J. J. Clauss, *MD* 39 (1997) 169–82; Levene, *LHW* 99–104) and for Tacitus' Sejanus (*A.* 4.1.1–3: see below, 5.3n. *corpus*).

5.1 L. Catilina: C. is formally named at the start of his sketch, the only occasion (apart from the letter quoted at 35.1) on which he is given *praenomen* as well as *cognomen*; Cicero sometimes uses both names in *Cat.* 2 but not in 1, 3 or 4 (see Dyck on 2.1.1–4). Neither author uses Sergius, C.'s *gentilicium*. For C.'s career see Intro. pp. 7–10.

nobili genere natus: so also *Comm. Petit.* 9. As M. Gelzer showed (*The Roman nobility* (Eng. trans. [2]1975) 27–40), only those with a consular

[20]   It is perhaps significant that Thucydides' habit in introducing persons is to 'tell us something we are supposed to need to know about this person *before* the moment in his life that Thucydides is choosing to write about' (G. T. Griffith, *PCPS* 7 (1961) 25). See also Williams, *TORP* 619–33, on 'the Roman view of historical explanation'.
[21]   R. G. Austin on Cic. *Cael.* 13 (3rd edn, p. 163) attributes to W. M. Calder the parallel of Plut. *Alcib.* 23.4–5 (not repeated by Dyck ad loc.). I am grateful to Dr P. T. Keyser for this reference.

ancestor in the male line could be described as *nobiles*. All that is known for
certain about C.'s ancestry is that his great-grandfather, M. Sergius Silus,
a famous disabled war hero, had been praetor in 197 (Urso 69–72, with
a convenient stemma). C.'s claim to *nobilitas* was probably based on his
supposed descent from one or more of the much earlier Sergii who
achieved the consulship or the military tribunate with consular power in
the fifth and fourth centuries BC (see Urso 63–8 for details). On *nobilitas*
see further e.g. Mouritsen, *RE* 218–36.

magna ui et animi et corporis: as e.g. Hermogenes (above) makes clear,
the two categories are standard in descriptions: 'and moreover the nature
of his spirit and body will be reviewed' (καὶ μὴν καὶ φύσις ψυχῆς καὶ σώματος
ἐξετασθήσεται). Each will be summarised chiastically below (3, 4–7), but
their combination here suggests that C. is potentially the ideal mentioned
at 1.6–7 above; the potential is frustrated by the intervention (both in real
life and in S.'s presentation) of C.'s *ingenium*. As with *ingenio* below, *magna
ui* is a descriptive abl. (*NLS* 31 §43 (6), 64–5 §83).

sed ingenio malo prauoque: *ingenium* here seems to mean 'temperament' or 'natural disposition'; it is the element which conditions C.'s *uis
animi* and it is illustrated and confirmed by *huic ... exercuit* immediately
following. For the expr. cf. Plin. *Ep.* 3.9.32. There are three exs. of
sentence-final *-que* in *BC* (again at 8.1, 15.1), seven in *BJ*; 'the sentence-
final enclitic was at home in the main stream of Latin historiographical
prose' (C. S. Kraus, 'How (not?) to end a sentence: the problem of *-que*',
HSCP 94 (1992) 321–9, at 329, with statistics).

**5.2 huic ab adulescentia bella intestina, caedes, rapinae, discordia
ciuilis grata fuere ibique iuuentutem suam exercuit:** a man was technically
a *iuuenis* until the age of forty-five: since at §6 below S. refers specifically to
the period from 80 BC (n. *post*), he is here referring to the decade before
that, stretching from C.'s late teens to his late twenties. There were numerous domestic wars during this period, but the precise number and nomenclature of Rome's various civil wars is disputed (P. Jal, *La guerre civile à Rome*
(1963) 43–55): the Social War, which began in 91, for example, can be
described by later authors as a civil war (Vell. 2.9.5, Flor. 2.6(3.18).1), and
may possibly have been so described by the historian Sisenna (E. Rawson,
Roman culture and society (1991) 366), who is mentioned by S. (*BJ* 95.2) and
perhaps participated in it. At any rate C. almost certainly participated in it,
as well as in the civil war at the end of the 80s (Intro. p. 8); Cicero said of
him *uigebant ... studia rei militaris* (*Cael.* 12). C. was also said to have
murdered various individuals, including his own brother and his sister's
husband, and to have overseen the murder of others, enriching himself in
the process (e.g. *Comm. Petit.* 9): hence *caedes* and *rapinae* (a regular duo,
e.g. Cic. *Cat.* 2.10). For the details see Berry on Cic. *Sull.* 70, *CC* 12–13.
S. reserves his adolescent *stupra* until 15.1–2 (nn.).

bellum intestinum is an extremely common phrase in Livy (it is also a term of Cicero's for the Catilinarian conspiracy: *Cat.* 2.28). *grata* is neut. plur. because, when combined subjects have different genders, neuter is the strongest gender when the subjects are things without life, as here (G&L 183 §286). *ibique* = 'and in those areas', a suggestive echo of 3.3 'Sed ego adulescentulus ... ibique ...' (Intro. pp. 9–10); *iuuentutem suam exercuit* = 'he spent his youth', though mysteriously Virg. *Aen.* 10.807–8 is given as the earliest ex. of the meaning 'spend' in both *OLD* (3c) and *TLL* (5.2.1377.50–60; cf. 1368.38–40, 1372.13–16).

5.3 *corpus* patiens inediae, algoris, uigiliae: *sc. fuit* or *erat*. These elements of C.'s public image, contrasting strongly with the vices of his contemporaries (13.3), were mocked and misrepresented by Cicero (*Cat.* 1.26 'uigilare ... patientiam famis, frigoris, inopiae rerum omnium', 2.9 'frigore et fame et siti et uigiliis perferendis', 3.16 'nihil erat quod non ipse ... uigilaret ...; frigus, sitim, famem ferre poterat'). *patiens* regularly takes the gen. (*OLD* 1a). See also 15.4n. (*animus*).

Tacitus had S.'s description in mind when he introduced Tiberius' henchman Sejanus (*A.* 4.1.3): '*corpus* illi laborum tolerans, *animus audax*, *sui* obtegens, *in alios* criminator; iuxta adulatio et superbia; palam compositus pudor, intus summa apiscendi *libido*, eiusque causa modo largitio et luxus, saepius industria ac *uigilantia*, | haud minus noxiae quotiens *parando regno* finguntur'.

supra quam cuiquam credibile est 'more than is credible to anyone': *supra* is an adverb, as e.g. Mela 1.72 'supra quam ut describi facile possit' (*OLD supra*[1] 6a). C.'s physical abilities are enhanced by the 'beyond belief' topos (W.[2] on Vell. 56.1, W.[1] on 130.1).

5.4 *animus audax,* subdolus, uarius: *sc. fuit* or *erat*. Plutarch's description of C.'s character is very similar (*Cic.* 10.3); *audax* is not just 'bold' or 'daring' but 'revolutionary', as argued by C. Wirszubski (*JRS* 51 (1961) 12–22, esp. 16),[22] and a natural epithet for C. (e.g. Cic. *Cat.* 1.1, 4, 7, 3.17, *Orat.* 129). Elsewhere S.'s adjs. are combined in literary contexts (Quint. 10.1.96 'uarius figuris et uerbis felicissime audax' (of Horace), Gell. 1.6.4 'sententiis ... audacibus ... subdolis').

cuius rei libet simulator ac dissimulator: it seems clear from the recurrence of *animus* at §5 below that at some point in the preceding clauses the subject must change from *animus* to C. himself; since the noun *animus* is often qualified by verbal formations in -*tor* (e.g. *BJ* 1.3, 2.3, 64.1 'contemptor animus'; W–M on Tac. *A.* 3.54.1, where many other exs. could be added), the likelihood is that the change of subject does not occur until *alieni*. The two verbal nouns here are quoted as a fine ex. of paronomasia

---

[22] Oddly not mentioned by P. Bruggisser, '*Audacia* in Sallusts "Verschwörung des Catilina"', *Hermes* 130 (2002) 265–87.

by Fronto (p. 97.2 vdH²); for the role played by pretence and dissimulation in S. see A. R. Hands, *JRS* 49 (1959) 56-60. The tmesis (for *cuiuslibet rei*) seems to be unique (*OLD quilibet*¹ a).

alieni _appetens_, _sui_ _profusus_ 'he was acquisitive of others' property, profligate with his own': *alieni* (*OLD alienum*) and *sui* (*OLD suus* B5a) are both nouns formed from adjs.; the gen. is regular with *appetens* (e.g. Cic. *De Or.* 2.135 'alieni appetens'; *OLD* 1b) but unique with *profusus*, although other such adjs. (e.g. *prodigus*) had long taken the gen. (cf. also 7.6n. *laudis*, 15.4n. *animus*). For *profusus* see further 13.5n. (*eo*).

ardens in cupiditatibus: Arusianus Messius (2.9n. *aliquo*) noted this ex. when listing the constructions taken by *ardeo* (7.449.14); it seems unparalleled in classical Latin (*TLL* 2.486.41-2). For *cupiditas* see 2.1n. (*etiam*).

_sa_tis eloquentiae, _sa_pientiae parum: *sc. ei erat* or *fuit*; the genitives are partitive (*NLS* 59 §77). This famous assonantal chiasmus too was noted favourably by Fronto (above, n. *cuius*). The two nouns are frequently coupled but cf. esp. Cic. *Inv.* 1.1 'ut existimem sapientiam sine eloquentia parum prodesse ciuitatibus, eloquentiam uero sine sapientia nimium obesse plerumque, prodesse numquam'. S. will put two formal speeches into C.'s mouth at 20.2-14 and 58.

5.5 uastus _ani_mus immoderata, _in_credibilia, _nimis_ _a_lta semper cupiebat: *uastus* is a suggestive adj. (W.³ on Tac. *Agr.* 38.2) whose meaning here has been debated: 'insatiable' or 'disordered'? According to C. Krebs (*CQ* 58 (2008) 682-6) it is equivalent to *uastatus*, 'devastated', and indicates that C. is a victim of the turbulent times. S.'s phrasing left its mark on Tacitus: cf. *A.* 4.38.5 'altissima cupere' (spoken by critics of Tiberius), 15.42.2 'incredibilium cupitor' (Nero).

5.6 post dominationem L. Sullae: L. Cornelius Sulla (Felix), who also features significantly in the *BJ* and *H.* (Book 1), was 'Sallust's obsession' (Rosenblitt 13). He arrived in Africa in 107 in support of the war against Jugurtha which was being fought by Marius (*BJ* 95.1), with whom Sulla would come to conduct a disastrous feud. As consul in 88 Sulla was forced to flee Rome on account of the violence which resulted from the manoeuvrings of his political opponents, principally Marius and his supporters; he then marched on Rome at the head of an army to reclaim his position, and, although Marius himself died at the start of 86, the antagonism between Sulla and the Marians persisted (11.4n. *postquam*). Having been elected dictator in 82, Sulla unleashed the proscriptions (11.4nn.), relinquished the dictatorship at the end of 81 and then retired into private life at the end of his second consulship in 80, dying in 78. See *MRR* 2.39-40, 69, 74-6, 3.73-6, *BNP* 3.825-9; A. Keaveney, *Sulla: the last republican* (²2005), F. Santangelo, *Sulla, the elites and the empire* (2007), Eckert and Thein. *dominatio Sullae* refers to Sulla's dictatorship: the expr. is first attested in the agrarian speeches of Cicero when consul (*Leg. Agr.* 1.21,

2.81), after which it appears in S. (again at 28.4, *H.* 1.44; the text at *H.* 1.43 is doubtful), from whom it was presumably taken by Tac. *A.* 1.1.1 'non Cinnae, non Sullae longa dominatio' (*Cinnae dominatio* being another expr. first attested in Cic.: cf. *Att.* 8.3.6, also Ascon. 23.24); see further Hellegouarc'h 562–3.

Little, if anything, is known of C.'s career between 82, when he was a legate under Sulla (*H.* 1.47), and 68, when he became praetor. In 67/6 he was propraetor in Africa (*MRR* 2.147), where he enriched himself successfully, and on his return to Rome he was arraigned for extortion (18.3n.). If Sulla was a role model for him, as he was said by Cicero to be for Pompey (*Att.* 8.11.2, 9.7.3), *post* will have an additional causal nuance (*OLD post²* 4): 'after and in view of'.

libido ... **rei publicae capiendae:** these words sum up the narrative of the monograph. *rem publicam capere*, surprisingly uncommon (but cf. Cic. *Dom.* 26, 129, *Pis.* 30), contrasts implicitly with *r.p. capessere*, a set phrase for embarking on public life (*OLD capesso* 8b). *libido inuadit* seems peculiar to S. (2.5, *BJ* 24.1, 84.3).

neque id quibus modis assequeretur ... **quicquam pensi habebat:** sentences or clauses involving the gen. of *pensum* ('weight') are difficult to deconstruct and it is probably best that each case (in S. again at 12.2, 23.2, 52.34, *BJ* 41.9) be treated on its merits: see *TLL* 10.1.1049.48–1050.7.[23] Although other interpretations are possible here, I think *habebat* (*OLD* 24 'to regard') is constructed with a gen. of value (*quicquam* being an adverbial acc.) and an indir. question, in the same way as *interest* (*OLD intersum* 8b), *refert* (*OLD refert* 1c) or indeed *pendo* (*OLD* 6b): 'nor did he attach any weight to the means by which he achieved it' (lit. 'and in no respect did he regard it as a matter of weight by what means ...'). *id* (viz. the seizure of the commonwealth, to be understood from *rei publicae capiendae* above) has been taken out of the clause to which it strictly belongs.

dum sibi regnum pararet 'provided that he obtained kingship for himself' (*OLD paro* 3a). Various individuals in the late republic were accused of wanting to establish *regnum* (see Hellegouarc'h 560–1), the most famous ex. being Julius Caesar (see e.g. Moles on Plut. *Brut.* 9.6); see also Lentulus at 47.2 (n. *Cinnam*). For *dum* = 'provided that' see *NLS* 178–9 §220.

5.7 agitabatur ... **animus ferox:** C.'s *ferocia animi* returns at 61.4 and frames the book (Intro. p. 15). *ferox/ferocia* often denotes defiance (as again at 38.1); see also Oakley on Liv. 6.23.3.

inopia rei familiaris et conscientia scelerum: each is imputed to C. by Cicero (*Cat.* 1.26 and 1.17 respectively): in the letter at 35.3 below C. denies that he cannot pay off his debts; for the significance of family deprivation see 13.4n. (*haec*). S. is attracted to the notion that *conscientia*

---

[23] *OLD pensum* is very misleading.

scelerum (a common phrase: Heubner on Tac. *H.* 4.56.1) makes people worse (*H.* 1.67.7 'flagrantes inopia ... scelerum conscientia exagitati'). See also next n.

quae utraque iis artibus auxerat quas supra memoraui 'each of which things he had increased by the behaviour which I recalled above'. A neut. plur. (*quae*) referring to two feminine antecedents is regular (see 20.2n. *Ni*); *utraque* makes it clear that *quae* does not refer to *scelerum*, the only preceding neut. plur. noun (for the plur. use of *uterque* see *OLD* 3). Nevertheless, although *inopia r.f.* and *conscientia scelerum* are formally the antecedents of *quae*, one would expect to be told that it was C.'s *scelera* which were increased, not his consciousness of them; it is as if *conscientia scelerum* meant 'self-acknowledged crimes' (cf. 8.3n. *scriptorum*). *supra memorare* is a Sallustian idiom (again at 57.1, *BJ* 12.2, 25.4, 28.4) which is imitated by Tacitus (W.³ on *Agr.* 18.3). See also R. J. Starr, 'Cross-references in Roman prose', *AJP* 102 (1981) 431–7.

5.8 incitabant praeterea corrupti ciuitatis mores: *sc. animum* or *Catilinam* as object. *corrupti* ('infected') anticipates the imagery of the *quos*-clause below; for *praeterea* see 14.3n.

quos pessima ac diuersa inter se mala, luxuria atque auaritia, uexabant: the imagery is that of disease (cf. Catull. 64.80 'quis angusta malis cum moenia uexarentur', Scrib. Larg. 182 'his malis uexantur'), regular in political discourse of all kinds and extremely frequent in S.: in addition to numerous notes in the Commentary, see e.g. Skard (1942) 145–6; *PH* 162–80; W–M on Tac. *A.* 3 p. 502 (index s.v. 'metaphors: disease and illness, cure and health'); W.⁴ on *A.* 5–6 p. 318 (index s.v. 'metaphors: disease'); Walters 153 (index s.v. 'disease'), to whose bibliography add K. Liong, 'Breathing crime and contagion: Catiline as *scelus anhelans* (Cic. *Cat.* 2.1)', *RhM* 159 (2016) 348–68. For the Greek background see R. Brock, *Greek political imagery* (2013) 69–82, 250 (index s.v. 'medical').

Livy (*praef.* 11) agreed with S. on the significance of 'auaritia luxuria-que', vices which he again coupled at 34.4.1 ('*diuersis*que duobus uitiis, *auaritia et luxuria*, ciuitatem laborare'); since the latter comes from a speech put into the mouth of the elder Cato, it is obviously possible that both S. and Livy are echoing Cato himself. The two vices are opposites because prodigality is demanded by *luxuria*, acquisitiveness by *auaritia*. For *pessima* qualifying *mala* cf. [Quint.] *Decl.* 18.6 'pessimum ... humanarum mentium malum est'; for the coordination of superlative and positive adjs. cf. *H.* 1.49.1 'maximi et clari'. For discussion of S.'s use of *luxuria* see F. R. Berno, *Roman luxuria* (2003) 41–8.

5.9–13.5 The 'Archaeology'

Thucydides' archaeology (1.2–19), the feature which S. is here imitating, was designed to minimise the significance of earlier Greek history in order to emphasise by contrast the importance of the Peloponnesian War, his chosen subject; S.'s archaeology, on the other hand, is designed to trace the degeneration of Roman society in order to demonstrate the corruption which produced a creature such as C. and in which his conspiracy, S.'s chosen subject, could flourish. The loss of so much pre-Sallustian historiography of Rome means that we cannot know whether any earlier Roman historian embedded a similar summary into his work, but it is known that Polybius in his sixth book, having explained his theory of the 'cycle of constitutions' (on which see 2.3–6n. *quod si*), proceeded to an archaeology of Rome of which only fragments now survive (see Walbank on 6.11a). Cicero, writing only a decade or more before S., incorporated an archaeology (admittedly of greater length) into Book 2 of his *De Re Publica*: his combination of moralising and history is not unlike S., who was perhaps challenged to write a shorter and alternative version.

The degeneration traced by S. happens in two stages. The first trigger is the destruction of Carthage in 146 BC (10.1), the second (11.4–8) is what Cicero called the 'Sullanum tempus', the years of Sulla's supremacy (88–80 BC). Since the significance of Carthage's destruction features in the history of Diodorus Siculus (10.1n. *Carthago*), and since Sulla was seen as a turning point also by Cicero (11.4n. *postquam*), it may be that in these respects too S. was reflecting contemporary thought.[24] The process of decline is seen in terms of contrasts between 'before' and 'after' (e.g. 7.4–5 ~ 10.2, 11.6), moral qualities replaced by immoral (10.2–6, 12.1–2, 12.5) and unnatural reversals (12.2, 13.1, 13.3). The changes and exchanges are themed by *immutata* (5.9, 10.6) and *miscere omnia* (10.1), which had also appeared proleptically earlier (2.3 'mutari ac misceri omnia').

It was commonplace in Greek and Roman thought that the present age represents a degeneration from an idealised past and that states and cities fall as surely as they rise. The role played by the destruction of Carthage in Rome's decline, repeated by S. in his two other works (10.1n. *Carthago*), became popular with later historians (Earl, *PTS* 47–9). It may be that the Sallustian historian Asinius Pollio was one of them; if so, he perhaps combined 146 BC with other turning points in the Sallustian manner, but whether he did so in an extended preface is unknown (*PH* 140–2).

---

[24] Whether these writers were correct in their diagnoses is naturally disputed by modern historians (see e.g. Lintott (1972)).

5.9 Res ... disserere: just as S.'s statement of topic (4.3–4) led to a programmatic apologia (4.5) which in turn introduced the description of C. (5.1–8), so here his reference at the end of that description to *ciuitatis mores* (5.8) leads to a second programmatic apologia 'de moribus ciuitatis' (5.9) which in turn introduces a summary history of Rome (6–13). A similar technique will be adopted by Velleius, an imitator of S., in a two-part digression (1.14.1, 16.1). For recent discussion of S.'s 'archaeology' see Shaw 119–69.

Res **ipsa hortari uidetur, quoniam de moribus ciuitatis tempus** *admonuit*, **supra repetere:** *sc. me* or *nos* with both *hortari* and *admonuit*: 'Because the moment has put me in mind of the community's morals, the subject on its own seems to urge me to a longer review' (*OLD ipse* 7, *supra*[1] 4, *repeto* 7a). *tempus* refers to the moment reached in the text (viz. 5.8 above): such phrases as *tempus est* in an actual speech (e.g. Claudius, *ILS* 212, col. II, line 20) are primarily temporal, but in a non-oratorical text (e.g. Quint. 11.3.61 'iam enim tempus est dicendi quae sit apta pronuntiatio') are primarily local (sometimes almost 'context'); at *BJ* 19.2 'quoniam alio properare tempus monet', the primary sense is temporal ('considerations of time') but metaphorical, because the monograph form requires a 'speedy' or 'brief' narrative (*PH* 208–11, 213–20). *res hortatur* and similar expressions are common; the constr. with the infin. is regular. *ipsa* insinuates that the subject is important enough not to infringe S.'s self-imposed rule of brevity (4.3n. *Igitur*): hence *paucis... disserere*, which follows. *repetere* is also the word used by Cicero to introduce his own 'archaeology' (*Rep.* 2.3); the addition of *supra* constitutes a Sallustian idiom (again at *BJ* 5.3 'pauca supra repetere') imitated by Tacitus (*A.* 16.18.1 'pauca supra repetenda sunt', *H.* 4.48.1; also W–M on *A.* 3.24.1), who pointedly alludes to S. at the equivalent moment in the preface to his *Histories* (1.4.1 'Ceterum antequam destinata componam, *repetendum uidetur* qualis ...') and then remodels S.'s whole sentence at *A.* 3.25.2 'ea *res admonet ut* de principiis iuris et *quibus modis* ... peruentum sit altius *disseram*'.

paucis ... disserere is imitated by Tacitus (*H.* 2.2.2) but without the extended hyperbaton. *disserere* is followed by an acc. and by three varied indir. questions.

domi militiaeque: the phrase (repeated at 6.5, 9.1) reflects the conventional division of much Roman historiography (cf. *H.* 1.1 'Res ... militiae et domi gestas'); in view of the adjacent allusion to Pericles' Funeral Speech (next n.), S. may also have in mind Thuc. 2.36.3 καὶ ἐς πόλεμον καὶ ἐς εἰρήνην ('both for war and for peace'). Livy in his preface may have looked back to S.'s sentence (*praef.* 9 'qui *mores* fuerint ... *domi militiaeque*').

quomodo <u>rem publicam habuerint quantamque reliquerint</u> renders Thuc. 2.36.2 κτησάμενοι ... ὅσην ἔχομεν ἀρχὴν ... ἡμῖν τοῖς νῦν προσκατέλιπον ('having taken possession of it, they [*sc.* our fathers] left to us today as great an empire as we now have'; cf. also 1.71.7, 144.4), except that *habuerint* seems to mean 'treated, administered'. S. may also intend an ironical allusion to Cicero's 'Quam rem publicam habemus?' (*Cat.* 1.9).

ut paulatim immutata ex pulcherrima <atque optima> pessima ac flagitiosissima facta sit: since S. elsewhere uses *immutare* absolutely (5×), it seems likely that *ex . . . optima* is to be taken with *facta sit*: 'how, changing gradually, it became so wicked and outrageous from having been so fine and noble' (*OLD ut* 1b, *ex* 13). St Augustine alluded to or quoted this clause three times (*Civ. Dei* 2.18–19) and on each occasion he wrote *pulcherrima atque optima*, although the words *atque optima* are not present in the principal MSS of the *BC*. Modern editors therefore insert *atque optima* into the text, generating a chiasmus. *pessima ac flagitiosissima* is imitated at Tac. *H.* 2.37.2 'bonum et innocentem principem pro pessimis ac flagitiosissimis expetitum'.

   6.1 V̄rbēm Rōmām, sīcŭt(i) ĕg(o) āccēpī, cōndidere atque *habuere* initio Troiani: Thucydides' archaeology is framed by first-person statements (1.1.3 ~ 1.20.1, 21.1), but, whereas he stresses his personal investigations, S. less expansively implies the virtue of selection. *sicuti ego accepi* (with *ego* seemingly emphatic, 'as *I* have understood': *OLD accipio* 21a) indicates that S. has chosen from amongst various alternative possibilities: the clause both claims the authority of tradition and disclaims personal responsibility for what the tradition says (for this see N. Horsfall, *The epic distilled* (2016) 111–34). The most notable alternative tradition was that which maintained that Rome was founded by Romulus (e.g. Cic. *Rep.* 2.4); the legends of Aeneas and Romulus were difficult to reconcile with each other (see T. J. Cornell, 'Aeneas and the twins', *PCPS* 21 (1975) 1–32), although Cato was one of the authors who tried (*Orig.* 14C/15P: see *FRHist* 3.73).[25] *habuere* combines the meanings of 'inhabit' and 'control' (*OLD* 8, 6a). S.'s sentence constitutes the 'motto' for Tacitus in the *Annals* (1.1.1 '*Vrbem Romam a principio reges habuere*'; Intro. p. 37); both authors display the hexametrical rhythm which is often found in historiographical openings (e.g. Cato, *Orig.* 1C/P (see 1.1n.), Sall. *BJ* 5.1, *H.* 1.1 (if *Marco* be spelled out); *PH* 379–80), although S.'s is almost unrecognisable and is one foot short of a complete spondaic hexameter.

   Aenea duce: Aeneas is again called *dux* at Liv. 1.1.8. The only other individual named in the archaeology is Sulla (11.4–5).

   sedibus *incertis* uagabantur 'had been wandering without any fixed abode' (*OLD sedes* 4a). S.'s words aptly summarise Aeneas' journey from Troy to Italy, which had featured variously in such earlier writers as Ennius and Naevius (*sēdĭbŭs īncērtīs* perhaps comes from some lost epic) and

---

[25] S.'s *sicuti ego accepi* is perhaps an echo of Cato's *ego . . . sic accepi* (*Orat.* 206M).

would be told in detail by Virgil in the *Aeneid*; but, since similar terminology is regularly used to describe primitive peoples (e.g. *BJ* 18.2 'uagi,
palantes', Cic. *Inv.* 1.2 'uagabantur', *Rep.* 1.40 'multitudo dispersa atque
uaga', *Sest.* 91 'dispersi uagarentur', Lucr. 5.932 'uolgiuago uitam tractabant more ferarum', Ov. *AA* 2.474 'tum genus humanum solis errabat in
agris'), it is as if the Trojan newcomers have something in common with
the native Aborigines (next n.).

cumque his Aborigines: *Aborigines* is the second subject of *condidere atque
habuere*, parallel to *Troiani*, and, as with the Trojans ('qui . . . uagabantur'),
their name is followed by a description ('genus . . . solutum'). In mentioning the Aborigines alongside Aeneas, S. is said by Servius (on *Aen.* 1.6) to
have been following the *auctoritas* of Cato in the *Origines* (63C/5P: see
FRHist 3.112), although Cato allegedly said that the Aborigines were
originally Greek (49C/6P) rather than, as S. seems to imply, native to
Italy (see *FRHist* 3.95–6). For a good summary of the various issues see *BNP*
1.26 'Aborigines'.

genus hominum agreste: the first element in a tripartite description of
the Aborigines which makes them out to be relatively uncivilised compared with the Trojans. *agreste* combines the notions of 'rustic' (it was
conventional for primitive peoples to be described as living off the land:
see e.g. Campbell on Lucr. 5.937ff., esp. 939) and 'uncivilised', but perhaps also hints at one of the etymologies of the people's name (Fest. 19
'Aborigines appellati sunt quod errantes conuenerint in agrum';
Maltby 2). *genus hominum* is a regular form of words, esp. in contexts
such as this (e.g., *BJ* 17.6), and often qualified by an adj., e.g. *BJ* 80.1
'genus hominum ferum incultumque', Curt. 7.3.6 'agreste hominum
genus et inter barbaros maxime inconditum'.

sine **legibus,** *sine* **imperio:** early peoples conventionally lacked law (Ov.
Met. 1.90 'sine lege'; Campbell on Lucr. 5.958–61; Horsfall on Virg. *Aen.*
7.203 'gentem . . . nec legibus aequam'; W–M on Tac. *A.* 3.25.2–28.2) and
it was only at a later stage of development that rulers arose (2.1n. *nam*):
compare the early inhabitants of Africa at *BJ* 18.1–2 'Africam initio
habuere . . . neque moribus neque lege aut imperio cuiusquam regeban-
tur'. For the anaphora of *sine*, a favourite of Livy, see Oakley on Liv. 7.2.4;
Adams, *AILL* 716 (index); also next n.

liberum atque *solutum:* the two adjs. are commonly coordinated, esp. in
Cicero (where they are usually in the opposite order), but also elsewhere.
solutus will mean principally 'unrestricted' (*OLD* 11) but also suggests
'loosely organised' (*OLD* 3b); some edd. have seen a chiasmus with *sine
legibus, sine imperio* above. Our whole passage seems recalled at Tac. *A.* 2.4.2
'*incerti solutique* et magis *sine* domino quam in libertate', although the
combination of asyndeton (last n.) and coordination is more exactly
mirrored at *A.* 3.15.2 (Adams, *AILL* 637).

6.2 **hi** is fronted as the logical subject of the sentence, although the main verb is actually *est*. The pronoun refers to both Trojans and Aborigines, as seems clear from *alius . . . uiuentes* below, but the implication of S.'s account is that the incomers civilised the indigenous population.

postquam in una moenia conuenere: *unus* is plural when it modifies nouns which are plural in form but singular in meaning, such as *castra* or *litterae* ('a letter'): see *OLD* 1b. The point of the clause is that both peoples came together within one set of walls, but, since the building of walls marked a recognised stage in the development of civilisation (e.g. Plb. 6.7.4, Cic. *Sest.* 91 'domicilia coniuncta . . . moenibus saepserunt', Varro, *RR* 3.1.3, Virg. *Ecl.* 4.32–3 'cingere muris | oppida'), the suggestion of a cultural history (2.1n. *etiam tum*) is continued. See further below.

dispari genere 'of different background' (as Caes. *G.* 7.39.1).

dissimili lingua: since the acquisition of language was a further stage in the development of civilisation (see e.g. Campbell on Lucr. 5.1028–90), we are to infer that the Aborigines were less primitive than has appeared hitherto. For the expr. cf. Plin. *NH* 6.15 'in eam [*sc.* the city of Dioscurias] CCC nationes dissimilibus linguis descendere'; the adj. is often coordinated with *dispar*, e.g. Sen. *NQ* 7.17.3 'dispares magnitudine, dissimiles colore'.

alius alio more uiuentes 'everyone living according to different customs': *uiuentes* agrees with *hi*, to which *alius* is in apposition: the *constructio ad sensum* (again at 6.5, 52.28) is difficult to reproduce in English (perhaps '. . . living, each man according to a different custom'). For problems caused by different customs see Tac. *A.* 6.32.2 and W.[4]

incredibile memoratu est is another Sallustian idiolect (cf. 7.3, *BJ* 40.3); it is impossible to say whether *memoratu* is abl. of the defective noun *memoratus* (*OLD memoratus²*) or the supine of *memorare*: each can be followed by an indir. qu., as here. For the 'beyond belief' topos see 5.3n. (*supra*).

ita . . . facta est 'in such circumstances it was only a short time before a disparate and nomadic crowd became a community through harmony' (*OLD ita* 6a). This sentence is missing from the principal MSS but a fifth-century scrap of Oxyrhynchus papyrus containing this part of the *BC* includes it (see Funari (2016) 148–51), and St Augustine quotes it (with *facta erat* instead of *facta est*) in such a way as to indicate that it comes from either Cicero or S. (*Epist.* 138.10).

breui: *sc. tempore.*

concordia: causal abl., looking back to *coaluerint* (cf. e.g. Liv. 1.11.2 'rem coalescere concordia posse'). See further 9.1n. (*concordia*).

6.3 **sed postquam** *res eorum* **ciuibus, moribus, agris** *aucta* **satis prospera satisque pollens uidebatur** 'but after their enterprise, reinforced by citizens, traditions and land, started to be seen as sufficiently prosperous and powerful'. *sed postquam,* a favourite of S. (13×), is also common elsewhere and is often used to mark a stage of decline (e.g. 11.4, 53.5, Catull. 64.397, where see Trimble's n.). *postquam* is constructed with the imperf. when the action continues into the time of the main clause (G&L 360 §562, *NLS* 176 §217 (5)), which I have tried to render by 'started to be seen'; the construction is rare in Cicero (Kinsey on *Quinct.* 70) and common only in the historians: for a rather different nuance see 56.4n. (*postquam*). *res* here is very difficult to translate: it seems to combine the notions of 'project' (*OLD* 12a) and 'state' (*OLD* 16a; cf. 17a). The three abls. (which seem to hover between abls. of respect and instrument) refer to the first three kings of Rome: Romulus, who increased Rome's population (see Ogilvie on Liv. 1.8.5); Numa, who introduced legal and religious systems (Tac. *A.* 3.26.4 and W–M); and Tullus Hostilius, who conquered Alba Longa and, by settling its inhabitants on Mons Caelius, 'legitimated Rome's rule over all of Latium' (*BNP* 6.534). For early Rome see G. Bradley, *Early Rome to 290 BC* (2020); it must be remembered that most of the very early 'events' belong to legend rather than to history. St Augustine quotes S.'s words but mistakenly substitutes *legibus* for the admittedly odd-looking *ciuibus* (*Civ. Dei* 3.10). S.'s wording is recognised as alluding to Cato, *Orig.* 117C/20P 'eodem conuenae et complures ex agro accessitauere: eo *res eorum auxit*', where *accessitare* is unparalleled and *augere* is used intransitively, but whether the contexts are the same is disputed (*FRHist* 3.145). This is the first appearance of the participial adj. *pollens* in extant Latin prose (again in S. at *BJ* 1.3, 6.1, 30.4): earlier it occurred in Naev. *Pun.* 8M–S, Plaut. *Capt.* 278, Licin. Calv. fr. 7C/32H and several times in Lucr.; subsequently it appears more in verse than in prose except Apul., who favours it (*TLL* 10.1.2539.42–2540.75; Lebek 300). Perhaps a choice lexeme rather than an archaism? *uidebatur* looks forward to *inuidia* in the main clause (n. below).

   sicuti pleraque mortalium habentur 'as is the way with many affairs of mortals' (the clause is prospective and relates to *inuidia . . . est*). *habere,* one of those 'simple' verbs which S. favours (4.5n. *de*), has a very wide range of different meanings (see *TLL* 6.3.2396.5–2462.11). Here the passive seems equivalent to *se habent* (which is at 2.3, 52.12; *OLD habeo* 21), perhaps imitated at Tac. *A.* 6.8.4 'quae coram habentur'. For *mortalium* see 2.8n. (*multi*).

   inuidia ex opulentia orta est: since *inuidia* is experienced when one *sees* the superior fortune of another (Maltby 311), the noun is often juxtaposed with forms of *uidere* (above); for a study see Kaster 84–103. Here the *inuidia* is external, as the next sentence makes clear, and not internal, as at 3.5 (n.) and elsewhere. S. has a liking for *opulentia* (again at 52.9, 52.22, *H.* 2.43.14) and is followed esp. by Curtius and Tacitus.

6.4 ĭgĭtŭr rēgēs pŏpŭlīquĕ | fīnĭtĭmī bēllō tēmptārĕ: *sc. eos.* In Cicero it is Romulus who 'bella cum finitimis felicissime multa gessit' (*Rep.* 2.15), and in Livy's first book the period between the death of Tullus Hostilius (6.3n. *sed postquam*) and the establishment of the consulship (6.7n.) is full of successive wars with various neighbouring peoples, esp. those of Latium, sometimes defensive (e.g. 1.32.3, 36.1), more often aggressive (1.35.7, 38.4, 53.2–4). Historic infinitives, which are even more common in the *BJ* than in the *BC*, are used 'in excited narrative to describe an unfolding scene, a state of feeling, or the beginning or repetition of striking actions' and they 'are seldom used singly' (*NLS* 15 §21). *temptare* is the first in a sequence of seven such infinitives: such clusterings are a mannerism of S. (e.g. 11.4, 27.2, 31.2–3, 60.4), though they also occur elsewhere (see H. Rosén, 'The Latin infinitivus historicus revisited', *Mnem.* 48 (1995) 536–64); the combination with *bello* ('to make an attempt on in war': *OLD tempto* 9a) is surprisingly rare (Cic. *Leg. Man.* 23, Ov. *Her.* 7.121, Tac. *A.* 2.79.2). For *igitur* see 2.1n.

pauci 'only a few': words for 'only' are often omitted in Latin.

metu perculsi a periculis aberant 'stricken with fear, they stayed clear of danger' (*OLD absum* 8): similar anagrams are at Liv. 7.10.10, Sen. *Ira* 1.12.1 'illas … periculi suspicio perculit'. *percello* is a favourite of S. (15×); its combination with *metu* (again at *BJ* 40.1, 58.2) is first found in early Latin tragedy (*TRF*[3] *Incert.* 7–8, p. 273/Enn. *Trag.* 52–3J) and then becomes common (esp. Livy).

6.5 intenti: although *intentus* is constructed with an infin. at *BJ* 49.3 (given in *TLL* 7.1.2118.68 as the only ex. in classical Latin), more probably it is used absolutely here, as often (ibid. 38–52), and to be taken closely with *domi militiaeque*; *contra* Woodman (2007a), followed by Adams, *AILL* 575–6.

festinare, parare '(the Romans) would be hurrying, making preparations': this absolute sense of *parare* is characteristic of S. (again at *BJ* 11.8 'moliri, parare', 60.1 'oppugnare aut parare', 76.4 'festinare, parare') but by no means exclusive to him (*TLL* 10.1.422.61–423.11).

alius alium hortari: this expr. recurs at Liv. 10.36.10, 26.9.5 (cf. *mutui hortatus* at Tac. *A.* 1.70.3).

libertatem, patriam parentesque armis tegere: although *tego = protego* is common (*OLD* 5), S. likes the simple forms of verbs, and the addition of *armis* (again at *BJ* 87.2 'armis libertatem, patriam parentesque et alia omnia tegi') is imitated at Tac. *A.* 6.2.4 (and W.[4]). *patria* and *parentes* is a very common doublet, but for the addition of *libertas*, which here (as in §6 below) must refer to freedom from outside interference, see also Plaut. *Amph.* 650–1 'Libertas, salus, uita, res et parentes, patria et prognati | tutantur'.

post, ubi pericula uirtute propulerant: the pluperf. indicates that *ubi* =
'whenever' (*NLS* 151 §194 *Note*), as confirmed by the generalising imper-
fects in the main clause. *periculum propulsare* is the more usual expr., but
S. here uses the regular form (as Liv. 40.11.10). *post* = 'afterwards'.
auxilia portabant: these words were used by Doederlein to defend his
emendation of Tac. *A.* 4.65 'cum auxilium . . . <por>tauisset' (described as
'attractive' by S. J. V. Malloch, 'The tradition about the *mons Caelius*',
Hermes 146 (2018) 454–69, at 455 n. 1).

magisque . . . amicitias parabant: seen as an allusion to Pericles' Funeral
Speech (Thuc. 2.40.4): 'we acquire friends not by receiving good from
them but by doing good to them' (see both Hornblower and Rusten ad
loc.). *beneficia* and *amicitia*, important concepts in ancient society, are
much discussed (e.g. Hellegouarc'h 48–54, 164–5; D. Konstan,
Friendship in the classical world (1997); K. Volk and J. E. G. Zetzel, *Cicero:
Laelius de amicitia* (2024), with large bibliography); here the terms anticipate the interstate relationships of the later republic (9.2, 9.5).

6.6 imperium legitimum, nomen imperii regium habebant 'They had
a statutory system of command and a name for the command, <viz.>
kingly'; the repetition *imperium . . . imperii* is strongly evocative of the *faux
naif* storytelling style that one often encounters in narratives of the
'archaeology' type and elsewhere, e.g. Hdt. 1.8.1 Οὗτος δὴ ὦν ὁ Κανδαύλης
ἠράσθη τῆς ἑωυτοῦ γυναικός, ἐρασθεὶς δὲ ἐνόμιζέ . . ., ὥστε δὲ ταῦτα νομίζων . . .,
Enn. *Euhem.* 4G–M 'sepulchrum eius est in Creta . . . inque sepulchro eius
est inscriptum . . .'.[26] The actual phrase *regium imperium* is used at §7 just
below. In §§6–7 the importance ascribed by S. to *imperium* resembles that
at the start of Book 3 of Cicero's *De Legibus* (see Dyck on 3.2–5 and 3.6.1
[pp. 431 and 440]), while its application to both kings and consuls
suggests the constitutional continuity implied by Cicero in Book 2 of his
De Re Publica (see Zetzel on 2.14–15). *i. legitimum* appears not to be
technical (Cic. *Phil.* 11.26, Liv. 8.35.7); Cicero's law code opens with the
words 'iusta imperia sunto' (*Leg.* 3.6), but the meaning there is 'orders'.

delecti . . . rei publicae consultabant 'Select individuals . . . would take
thought for the commonwealth': the verb alludes to the *regium consilium*
established by Romulus (Cic. *Rep.* 2.14 'in regium consilium delegerat
principes'). S.'s use of the frequentative with the same sense and construction as *consulo* is unique in classical Latin (*TLL* 4.594.3–4).

quibus . . . erat: the *consilium* is a proto-senate: the terms *senatores* and
senatus were conventionally associated with *seniores, senes, senectus*, etc. (e.g.
Cic. *Rep.* 2.50; Maltby 558–9): see further T. G. Parkin, *Old age in the Roman
world* (2003) 101–5. Cf. Cic. *Senec.* 17 'non uiribus . . . corporum res

---

[26] These exs. are taken from E. Norden, *Agnostos theos* (repr. 1974) 367–79.

magnae geruntur sed consilio, auctoritate, sententia'. Plutarch would later discuss the role of old men in public life (*Mor.* 783B–797F).

ei ... patres appellabantur: seniority is one of the explanations mentioned also by Dion. Hal. *AR* 2.8.1; *curae similitudo* is given by no other classical source (Maltby 455), but cf. Cic. *Rep.* 2.14 'appellati sunt propter caritatem patres'. As a political term *cura* features less prominently during the republic (Hellegouarc'h 252–3) than during the empire (W.[1] on Vell. 106.3), although it was often thought to be associated with the *curia*, where the senate met (Varro, *LL* 6.46 'ubi senatus rem p. curat'; Maltby 167).

6.7 regium imperium echoes Cicero's description of the consuls (*Leg.* 3.8 'regio imperio duo sunto' with Dyck's n.), further suggesting continuity between monarchy and republic.

conseruandae libertatis atque augendae rei publicae: gen. gerundives of purpose (*NLS* 165–6 §207 (4) *Note ii*). For *libertas* see 5n. above, although at Cic. *Rep.* 2.46 ('conseruanda ... libertate') the same phrase is used of L. Brutus' establishment of the republic (see below); note also *Fam.* 11.7.2. *augendae* refers esp. to geographical expansion (cf. e.g. Cic. *Sest.* 143, *Pis.* 27, *Off.* 2.85).

in *superbiam* dominationemque: hendiadys for *superbam dominationem*, and, like Virg. *Catal.* 9.37 'dominatus ... superbos', a reference to Rome's seventh king, Tarquinius Superbus (Liv. 1.50.3 with Ogilvie), whose exile from Rome brought an end to the monarchy (Liv. 1.60.2). See Y. Baraz, 'From vice to virtue: the denigration and rehabilitation of *superbia* in ancient Rome', in I. Sluiter and R. M. Rosen (edd.), *Kakos: badness and anti-value in classical antiquity* (2008) 365–97, and *Reading Roman pride* (2020). Also above, 2.5n. (*libido*), and below, 10.4n. (*pro his*).

immutato more 'with a change in convention': the *power* of the rulers remained the same; it was just differently arranged (next n.).

annua imperia binosque imperatores 'yearly commands and two commanders <each year>': *bini* is a distributive adj. (see *OLD*). S.'s continuing terminology is pointed: cf. Liv. 2.1.7 'libertatis autem originem inde magis quia annuum imperium consulare factum est quam quod deminutum quicquam sit ex regia potestate numeres'.[27] The establishment of the consulship is traditionally credited to L. Junius Brutus in 509 BC (Liv. 2.1.8, Tac. *A.* 1.1.1; *BNP* 6.1092–3 [I 14]), although the chief magistrates seem originally to have been called praetors, not consuls (see e.g. Ogilvie on Liv. 1.60.4, Oakley on 7.3.5, each with bibliography).

---

[27] Cf. Drogula, *CC* 14: 'the Romans believed that their earliest republican generals were annually elected magistrates, and their two different sets of responsibilities – those of the military general (*imperator*) and of the civilian magistrate (*magistratus*) – were combined in a single office, as they no doubt had been under the monarchy'.

eo *modo* minime ... *insolescere animum* humanum 'in that way they
thought there was the least chance of the human spirit becoming over-
bearing through licence'. Perhaps S. is thinking of Cato, *Orat.* 163M
(= Gell. 6.3.14) 'solere plerisque hominibus rebus ... prosperis *animum*
excellere atque *superbiam* ... augescere'; indeed the highly unusual *insolescere* may also derive from the same Catonian speech (cf. Gell. 6.3.15 'ne
Romani ... ad *superbiam* ferociamque et immodicum *modum insolescent*').
The verb is picked up by Tacitus (*H.* 2.7.2, *A.* 2.63.4, 75.2).

7.1 ea tempestate: *tempestas* in the sense of *tempus* is frequent in S., and
he has both *ea tempestate* (17×) and *qua tempestate* (2×). The latter is
described by Cicero (*De Or.* 3.153) as both archaic and poetic, and the
former is attested in 189 BC on an inscription (*CIL* 1².614). The usage is
common in Livy and Tacitus.

coepere: the verb is plural because *quisque* implies 'everyone' (G&L 148
§211R. 1 (*a*)).

magisque ingenium promptum habere: the MSS read *in promptu,* an
expr. which means either 'within easy reach, at one's disposal' and the
like or 'in full view' (*OLD promptus*² 1b, 2a). Clearly the former is
inappropriate here; but is *in promptu* correctly transmitted in the first
place? According to *TLL, in promptu habere* normally means 'to have
readily available'; this is the only case where it means 'to have in full
view' (10.2.1902.39–40). It is also suspicious that Tacitus, who so often
imitates S., thrice has the phrase *promptum ingenium* (*A.* 1.23.4, 1.29.4,
15.61.1), which also occurs at Quint. 11.2.46, Gell. *praef.* 12, Flor. 2.33
(4.12).59. Moreover S. is very fond of combining *habere* with an adj., e.g.
twice below at 10.5: 'aliud in lingua promptum habere, ... magisque
uoltum quam ingenium bonum habere'. The likelihood of scribal error
after the sequence *-nium* is high, and it may be suspected that *promptum* is
what S. wrote.

7.2 nam regibus ... aliena uirtus formidulosa est: from this parenthetic
generalisation, which explains why individuals could not realise their full
potential under the monarchy, it is clear that the self-promotion and
increased use of *ingenium,* referred to in the preceding sentence, constituted *uirtus.* For the commonplace that autocrats cannot tolerate excellence in others see Tac. *Agr.* 41.1 'infensus uirtutibus princeps' and W.[3].

7.3 sed ciuitas ... tanta cupido gloriae incesserat: *sed* both resumes the
argument after the brief digression (7.2) and contrasts the situation
during the republic ('adepta libertate') with that during the monarchy
('regibus'). *tanta cupido gloriae* repeats *coepere se quisque extollere* (7.1) in
different words and explains *ciuitas... quantum breui creuerit:* the individual
pursuit of personal glory is to be seen as directed towards the good of the
state as a whole. Thus begins a passage which 'is undoubtedly the most

thoughtful analysis of the imperialism of the middle Republic left to us by a Roman writer' (Harris 17 n. 4).

incredibile memoratu est: see 6.2n.

adepta libertate: *libertas* here, in contrast with 6.6–7 above, means the republic, as at Tac. *A.* 1.1.1; Livy uses the same phrase in the same context (2.1.4 'libertatem . . . adepta'), except that S., as again at *BJ* 101.9, gives the participle an unusual passive sense. The sequence of thought is curiously reminiscent of Hdt. 5.66.1 ('Athens had been great even before, but then, when it was rid of tyrants, it became greater. In it two men held preponderant positions . . .'): since S. mentions Athens at 8.2–4 below, this is perhaps another ex. of suspension of thought. For studies of *libertas* see C. Wirszubski, *Libertas as a political idea at Rome* (1950), Brunt 281–350, V. Arena, *Libertas and the practice of politics in the late Roman Republic* (2012), C. Balmaceda (ed.), *Libertas and Res Publica in the Roman Republic: ideas of freedom and Roman politics* (2020).

tanta cupido gloriae incesserat: S. could have written *tanta cupido gloriae incesserat ut ciuitas incredibile sit* . . ., but instead of a consecutive clause he has preferred parataxis: for this see Adams on *Rhet. Herenn.* 4.14 (*AIL* 129), with numerous exs. including *BJ* 84.3 'tanta lubido . . . inuaserat' (see also Liv. 10.25.1). *tanta cupido* is a line-end at Lucr. 3.1077, memorably repeated at Virg. *Aen.* 6.133 (cf. below, 7.5n. *non*). The usual expr. is *cupiditas gloriae* (many times in Cic.), but S. is predictably followed by Tacitus (*Agr.* 5.3 'intrauitque animum . . . gloriae cupido',[28] *A.* 4.50.2, *H.* 4.6.1); also Curt. 10.5.29, Sen. *Ep.* 74.21, Fronto p. 139.22 vdH². See above, 2.1n. (*etiam*). For *cupido* . . . *incesserat* cf. Liv. 1.56.10, 24.13.5, Val. Max. 1 *praef.*, Curt. 3.1.16, 4.8.3, 7.11.4, Tac. *H.* 2.2.2, 5.23.1.

7.4 iam primum 'To begin with', 'Initially'; the contrast comes only with *Sed* . . . *coepit* at 10.1, as is shown by the verbal links between the two passages (*laborem* . . . *labor* ~ *labores, asper* ~ *asperas, diuitias* . . . *diuitias* ~ *diuitiae*). This use of *iam primum*, again at 15.1, is different from *OLD iam* 8b.

simul ac belli patiens erat 'as soon as they were capable of enduring war'. S.'s sentence is quoted by Vegetius (1.4.4) when discussing the age at which military service should begin, which in the republic would be on one's seventeenth birthday (Tubero 4C/P with Oakley's n., *FRHist* 3.470). For *patiens* see 5.3n. (*corpus*).

usum militiae 'military experience' (Liv. 30.34.12, [Quint.] *Decl.* 352.1).

in decoris armis et militaribus equis: for the glitter of Roman weaponry see W.[3] on Tac. *Agr.* 26.1, 33.1, although it was also a feature of barbarian hordes (Oakley on Liv. 7.10.7). S.'s contemporary, Varro, notes that horses intended for military service need to be different from those used

---

[28] The whole paragraph is almost a personalised commentary on this passage of S.

for racing or other purposes (*RR* 2.7.15); *militaribus* implies that in contemporary Rome young men were interested in a different type of horse (cf. 14.6).

in scortis: unlike in C.'s day (14.6 'scorta').

7.5 nōn lăbŏr īnsŏlĭtūs: *sc. erat* from the second colon. *labor insolitus* recurs in Tacitus (*H*. 2.19.1; also Quint. 11.3.26), but, like *tanta cupido* above, it is also one of those metrical phrases in which Sallust's monographs abound (cf. Ov. *M*. 10.554 'sed labor insolitus'). The dactylic metre is continued in the next colon: – *non locus ullus* ∪ – – (*nec . . . locus ullus* is 3× in Ovid).

asper aut arduus: *asper* is the *mot juste* for rough terrain (59.2; *OLD* 4a) and is commonly combined with *arduus*, e.g. Cato, *Orat.* 19M.

uirtus omnia domuerat: *omnia* sums up the preceding list of obstacles (cf. Sen. *HF* 435 'uirtutis est domare quae cuncti pauent'). Other authors have *uirtute* less vividly in the abl. (Cic. *Sest.* 67 'qui . . . seruitia uirtute . . . domuisset', Sil. 15.186, Stat. *Theb.* 2.178); cf. 53.4n. (*ac*).

7.6 sed gloriae maximum certamen inter ipsos erat: this sentence is a form of conceit: they would compete without fear against an armed enemy (§5), *but* the greatest competition was amongst themselves – for glory. The *gloriae certamen* is to be seen in terms of the statement at §3 above (n. *sed*): this is competitive individualism for the collective good and is therefore different from that criticised at *BJ* 41.2 ('neque gloriae neque dominationis certamen inter ciues erat') and *H*. 1.8 ('semper in certamine libertatis aut gloriae aut dominationis agit'). Cf. Diod. 31.6 'Hence it is that among the Romans the most distinguished men are to be seen vying with one another for glory [ὑπὲρ δόξης ἀμιλλωμένους] . . . In other states men are jealous of one another, but the Romans praise their fellow citizens. The result is that the Romans, by rivalling one another in promotion of the common weal [ἀμιλλωμένους αὔξειν τὸ κοινῇ συμφέρον], achieve the most glorious successes' (Loeb trans.). More generally see J. E. Lendon, *Empire of honour* (1997), esp. 191.

se quisque hostem ferire . . . properabat 'each was impatient that he should strike the enemy'. *propero* + reflexive acc. and infin. is unique in classical Latin but the verb in this wider sense is constructed with a non-reflexive acc. and infin. at Virg. *Aen.* 7.56–7 (*OLD* 5c), and *sese student praestare* at 1.1 is analogous (n.). S. is also the only classical author to combine *propero* with a supine (*H*. 3.15.16 and 5.18). *hostem ferire* (again at 60.4, *BJ* 85.33) 'has the solemnity of a set phrase' (Skutsch on Enn. *Ann.* 234).

murum ascendere: scaling an enemy wall was a source of *gloria* (e.g. Prop. 4.3.63 'ascensis tanti sit gloria Bactris') and a *corona muralis* was awarded to the soldier 'qui primus murum subiit inque oppidum hostium per uim ascendit' (Gell. 5.6.16), a feat which Ti. Gracchus (trib. pleb. 133)

achieved at the siege of Carthage in 146, according to the historian
Fannius, who says that he accompanied him (4C/P). See also Oakley on
Liv. 6.20.7.

conspici dum tale facinus faceret 'to be seen while he was doing such
a deed': the subjunc. represents the thoughts of the ambitious soldier.
facinus facere is a common *figura etymologica* (e.g. 11.4, 53.2, Liv. 24.22.16
'facinus ... memorabile fecistis').

   eas diuitias ... putabant: *sc. esse* with each subordinate clause. *eas* and
eam, referring back to the three actions just mentioned, have been
attracted into the gender and number of the nouns which they qualify:
see *OLS* 1.1280 (k). For *diuitias* note Cic. *Parad. Stoic.* 51, *Off.* 3.63, Lucr.
5.1118–19, Prop. 3.13.25–6 'iuuentus | diuitiae quorum messis et arbor
erant'.

   laudis auidi, pecuniae liberales erant: *auidus* is regularly constructed
with the gen. (*l. auidus* is Ciceronian: *Leg. Man.* 7, *Att.* 1.15.1), but *liberalis* +
gen. seems unique in classical Latin (cf. 5.4n. *alieni*, 15.4n. *animus*). For
the two adjs. cf. Cic. *Rosc. Com.* 21.

   diuitias honestas: S. may be speaking non-specifically but the context
perhaps suggests that he is thinking of the spoils of war, which, while
honouring a victorious general, might also be used to finance some public
work (Oakley on Liv. 8.30.9). For *diuitiae* applied to spoils see Cic. *Leg. Agr.*
2.62.

   **7.7 memorare possum quibus in locis ..., quas urbes ..., ni ea res
longius nos ab incepto traheret:** *possem* is read by most MSS, *possum* by
a minority and by Servius (*Aen.* 12.230). When a modal verb such as *possum*
is found in the apodosis of a so-called 'unreal' condition, that verb often
remains in the indic. (*NLS* 156 §200 (i)); but, since it is very unusual for
a present indic. to be combined with an imperf. subjunc., *possum* is in fact
the reading more likely to be corrupted here and probably to be preferred
to *possem*. The meaning is: 'I am able to recall in what places ... and which
cities ..., <and I would be recalling them>, if the matter did not take us too
far from our project' (conceivably S. is repeating a Catonian mannerism:
cf. *Orat.* 185M 'dicere possum quibus ...'). S. does return briefly to this
topic at 53.3. *ni ... traheret* is an expr. of travel (cf. e.g. Liv. 21.53.10
'quanto longius ab domo traherentur'), and, when an author makes
reference to the length or brevity of his text, travel metaphors (as Sen.
Ep. 59.4 'non effert te oratio nec longius quam destinasti trahit', *Ben.*
7.13.1 'ne traham longius'; see also *OLD traho* 1d) are as common as
those of time (5.9n. *res ipsa*). Tacitus partially imitates S. at *A.* 6.22.4 'ne
nunc *incepto longius* abierim', where, however, the expr. is one of time (see
W.[4]). *nos* is an authorial plural, a common *uariatio* after the sing. *possum*
(W.[5] on Tac. *A.* 4.11.3, W.[3] on *Agr.* 43.2).

quibus in locis <u>ma</u>ximas hostium copias <u>p</u>opulus Romanus parua manu fuderit: like *ceperit* below, the verb takes its tense from *possum*. The reference to the Roman people is confirmation that S. sees the pursuit of individual glory as an intrinsic element in collective action (7.3n. *sed*, 7.6n. *sed*). The contrast between a numerous enemy and a few brave Romans is a commonplace (Oakley on Liv. 6.13.1 and Addendum (4.519)); for the expr. cf. Acil. 4C/5P 'quod parua manu innumerabiles exercitus fudisset' (= Liv. 35.14.7).

quas urbes natura munitas pugnando ceperit: *natura munitus* (again at *BJ* 54.3, 57.1, 87.1) is exceptionally common in, and almost exclusive to, Caesar, by whom S. was perhaps influenced (see also 60.1–2nn.). The seemingly inaccessible foreign fastness is a topos of military narrative (W.[5] on Tac. *A.* 4.46.3). *pugnando capere* (again at 61.2, *BJ* 28.7, Plaut. *Mil.* 267, *Bell. Afr.* 25.2) is also found in the elogium of C. Duilius, cos. 260 (*ILS* 65.4–5 'Macel[am … | p]ucnandod cepet').

8.1–5 S. interrupts his archaeology with a digressive passage on historiography, just as earlier (2.3–6) he had interrupted his defence of historiography with a digression which foreshadows the symptoms traced in the archaeology. The present digression, an extended example of 'suspension of thought' (Intro. pp. 24–5), reaffirms the Roman military achievements which S. has just declined to elaborate (7.7); but, since he stresses that earlier Romans concentrated on military action to the almost total exclusion of historiography (8.5), the question is raised of how he can know about those achievements in order to be in the position of declining their elaboration. He avoids this potential contradiction by claiming that the deeds were celebrated by persons other than those who performed them. It may seem strange that S. inserts a digression in which he risks contradicting himself, but the insertion functions as a narrative ellipsis: he substitutes textual time for an account whose details might have conflicted with his schematic survey of Roman history (e.g. 9.1n. *concordia*).

8.1 Sed <u>pr</u>ofecto <u>Fo</u>rtuna in <u>o</u>mni re <u>do</u>minatur: *Sed* introduces the digression; S. returns to the main narrative with *Igitur* at 9.1. The power of a whimsical Fortune (again at 51.25), who is regularly called 'domina' in Cicero (the verb at *Q.Fr.* 1.1.4 and again at Plin. *Ep.* 5.20.3), is of course conventional (Otto 143); S. is more specific in the next sentence (n. *ea*). In general on Fortuna see D. Miano, *Fortuna: deity and concept in archaic and republican Italy* (2018).

ea <u>res</u> cunctas ex libidine <u>magis quam ex uero</u> <u>c</u>elebra<u>t</u> obscuratque 'she celebrates and obscures everything according to her whim rather than according to reality': probably an allusion to Thuc. 2.41.2 οὐ λόγων… <u>κό</u>μπος τάδε <u>μᾶλλον ἢ ἔργων</u> ἐστὶν ἀλήθεια ('this is not verbal boasting rather than the truth of the facts'). S.'s statement is explained at §3 below: Fortune's power is manifested in the remarkable crop of writers who flourished at Athens – a point also made at Vell. 1.18.1 – and it is they who exaggerated Athenian achievements (*ex uero celebrat ~ pro maximis celebrantur*). *uerus* = real as opposed to a representation (*OLD uerus*[1] 2). *cunctus* is a regular adj. in contemporary writers but is used more selectively by early imperial authors, esp. historians (Adams (1973) 129–31); S. has *res cunctae* again at *BJ* 2.1. For sentence-final -*que* see 5.1n.

8.2–5 Atheniensium res gestae . . .: in the preface to his narrative of the Peloponnesian War, Thucydides argues that previous wars were relatively insignificant and that his was the greatest war, because the two sides were at the peak of their power and preparedness (1.1–23). During the course of his argument Thucydides introduces a contrast (1.10.2): if Sparta were depopulated and its surviving buildings were visited in later ages by some future traveller, he would have difficulty believing that the city had once been as powerful as its reputation suggests; but, if the same were to happen to Athens, the future visitor would assume that Athens' power was even greater than its reputation. 'It is not reasonable', concludes the historian, 'to examine the appearance of cities rather than their power'. S. in the present passage contrasts Athens with early Rome and in so doing alludes to his literary model, but with significant differences. He agrees with Thuc. that Athens was less great than its reputation, but this is not part of a larger argument that Athens was in fact supremely powerful; and the misleading element is not buildings but historiography.

8.2 satis amplae magnificaeque fuere, uerum aliquanto *minores* tamen quam fama feruntur: probably sc. *esse* in the latter clause (*OLD fero* 33 rather than 34a): 'were sufficiently impressive and magnificent, but still somewhat less than they are said to be by reputation', a reversal of Thuc. 2.41.3 μόνη . . . τῶν νῦν ἀκοῆς κρείσσων ἐς πεῖραν ἔρχεται ('alone of today's cities she [sc. Athens] is greater than her reputation as she faces her test'). For similar ideas cf. Liv. 45.27.5 'ad . . . uisenda . . . quae nobilitata fama maiora auribus accepta sunt quam oculis noscuntur', Hor. *Epi.* 1.11.3 'maiora minorane fama?' (both with ref. to buildings). *amplus* + *magnificus* is found first in Cicero (*II Verr.* 2.112, 4.62, *Fin.* 2.46), afterwards used by Livy (28.35.5, 42.3.1).

8.3 prouenere 'sprang up', a metaphor from plants or crops (again at Apul. *Apol.* 24.6 'uaria ingenia prouenere'; *OLD prouenio* 3), for which see esp. Plin. *Epist.* 1.13.1.

scriptorum magna ingenia is *either* to be explained as enallage, which is the transference to a governing noun (*ingenia*) of an adj. (*magna*) which more properly should be taken with an expressed dependent genitive (i.e. 'the talents of great writers'), *or* it is one of those cases where an abstract noun + gen. is equivalent to an adj. + noun in agreement ('greatly talented writers'): for such abstracts see e.g. Tac. *Agr.* 21.2, where *ingenia Britannorum* may mean 'talented Britons' and *conuiuiorum elegantiam* = 'elegant parties' (see W.[3] on the latter for discussion of the idiom). S. could be referring to Xenophon and Isocrates amongst other *scriptores*, but his numerous allusions to Pericles' Funeral Speech (see 5.9n. *quomodo*, 6.5n. *magisque*, 8.1n. *ea*, 8.2n. *satis*, 8.3n. *per*, 8.4n. *ita*, 10.1n. *cuncta*) make it very likely indeed that the plural is not to be taken literally but is a reference to Thucydides, who is assumed to identify with Pericles' views (for such plurals see Tac. *A.* 4.32.1 and W.[5]).

per terrarum orbem Atheniensium facta pro maximis celebrantur 'across the globe the Athenians' deeds are celebrated as being the greatest': in the light of *minores ... feruntur* (§2 above), this is a reversal of Thuc. 2.42.2 ἰσόρροπος ... τῶνδε ὁ λόγος τῶν ἔργων ('their fame equally balanced by their deeds'); see also 3.2n. (*primum*). The relationship with the *quia*-clause is underlined by forms of polyptoton (*magna ~ maximis*) and chiasmus (ABC ~ BCA); for the former see Wills 237–8. For *pro maximis* cf. Sen. *Ep.* 74.13 'quae pro maximis uolgus optat', Ben. 1.5.2 (*OLD pro*[1] 9). The order *terrarum orbis* is a great deal less common than the converse.

8.4 ita eorum qui fecere uirtus tanta habetur quantum eam uerbis potuere extollere praeclara ingenia 'Thus the *uirtus* of those who acted is regarded as being as great as outstanding talents were able to extol it in words': S. is referring to writers contemporary with the action (cf. *fecere*, *potuere*) and is perhaps reversing Thuc. 2.35.1 ἐμοὶ δὲ ἀρκοῦν ἂν ἐδόκει εἶναι ἀνδρῶν ἀγαθῶν ἔργῳ γενομένων ἔργῳ καὶ δηλοῦσθαι τὰς τιμάς ('I should have thought it sufficient, when men have been good in action, to show them honour also in action [*sc.* rather than in words]'). S.'s sentence is echoed by the emperor Verus in a letter to his historian, Fronto (p. 109.3–4 vdH[2] 'meae res gestae tantae ... uidebuntur quantas tu eas uideri uoles'; cf. 203.9–12), and Pliny in a famous letter to Tacitus says 'haec ... notiora, clariora, maiora tu facies' (*Ep.* 7.33.10). The sentence is also quoted at *HA Prob.* 1.1 (on which see *FRHist* 3.147–8).

8.5 at populo Romano numquam ea copia fuit 'But the Roman people never had such a possibility' or 'a possibility for that' (*OLD copia* 7). The most famous contrast between the cultural arts of the Greeks and the military arts of the Romans, underlined by the contrast *facere quam dicere* below, is of course Virg. *Aen.* 6.847–53: see Horsfall ad loc., adding Oakley on Liv. 8.22.8 and J. Marincola (ed.), *The collected papers of J. L. Moles* (2023) 1.492–502.

maxime negotiosus erat is explained by what follows: early Romans were doers, not writers.

ĭngĕnĭūm nēmō sĭnē cōrpŏrĕ ˘ ēxērcēbăt: a hexameter (if one allows the hiatus), with a spondaic fifth foot.

optimus quisque ... *sua ab aliis bene facta laudari* **quam ipse aliorum narrare malebat** 'all the best men ... preferred their own good deeds to be praised by others rather than themselves to narrate <those> of others'. S. is required to make this statement in order to avoid self-contradiction (8.1–5n.), but he is skating on thin ice. It is true that Roman historiography did not come into existence until late in the third century BC, before which there stretched five centuries of 'unwritten Rome';[29] it is also true that the exploits of M. Fulvius Nobilior (cos. 189 BC) were praised not by himself but by the poet Ennius, who accompanied him on campaign; but the early historians Fabius Pictor and Cincius Alimentus 'each gave, by virtue of personal experience, a detailed account of the events at which he himself was present', according to Dionysius of Halicarnassus (*Ant. Rom.* 1.6.2). And, although S. might dismiss these as minor figures (for the details see *FRHist* 1.160–90), the same cannot possibly be said of Cato the Elder, one of the most famous personalities in Roman history. Cato, consul (195) and censor (184), was both a successful soldier and the author of the *Origines*, and described by Livy as 'haud sane detractator *laudum suarum*' (34.15.9; cf. Plut. *Cato Mai.* 14.2). If Livy is alluding to our passage, as seems likely, he is demonstrating his awareness that S. has erased from the record the historian who constituted his Latin model – and who himself erased from his *Origines* the names of other Roman generals (Plin. *NH* 8.11).

9.1 Igitur resumes the main argument after the digressive 8.1–5.

concordia <u>m</u>**axima,** <u>m</u>**inima auaritia:** the chiastically arranged nouns look back to *domi* and *militiae* respectively, and much of what follows in 9.2–13.5 alternates between 'home' and 'abroad'. *concordia* was promoted by *metus hostilis* (cf. Diod. 34(35).33.5, Liv. 2.39.7 'externus timor, maximum concordiae uinculum'; Oakley on Liv. 6.27.7), which was removed by the destruction of Carthage (10.1n.). Such at least was the theory, but S.'s statement ignores entirely the 'Conflict of the Orders', the struggle between patricians and plebeians which lasted from the sixth to the early third century BC (see e.g. Cornell, *BR* 242–71). Contrast the summary of the same period at *H.* 1.10.

bonumque: 'what is morally good, right, or equitable', found 'esp. in conjunction with *aequum, ius,* etc.' (*OLD bonum* 6a).

non legibus magis quam natura: i.e. the laws were rarely enforced because moral behaviour came naturally – almost a 'golden age' feature (6.1n. *sine*).

9.2 <u>c</u>*iues* <u>c</u>**um** <u>c</u>*iuibus* **de uirtute** <u>c</u>**ertabant:** the notion of a *certamen uirtutis* is not uncommon (e.g. Cic. *Fin.* 5.71, Liv. 10.23.7, Vell. 26.2 'semper uirtutibus certatum erat') and represented in S.'s day by the

[29] Cf. T. P. Wiseman, *Unwritten Rome* (2008).

younger Cato (54.6 'cum strenuo uirtute ... certabat'). *ciues cum ciuibus* is an ex. of so-called 'battle polyptoton' (Wills 194–202).

in suppliciis deorum magnifici 'sumptuous in supplications to the gods'. This meaning of *supplicium* (again at 52.29, *BJ* 46.2, 55.2, 66.2; cf. Varro, *RR* 2.5.10 'ad deorum ... supplicia'; *OLD* 2) is found in Plaut., Acc. and Afran. and is absent from Cicero and Caesar, for whom the noun has its more familiar meaning of 'punishment, penalty' (as e.g. 49.2, 52.36); it is commonly said to be an archaism (cf. Fest. 308 'supplicia ueteres quaedam sacrificia a supplicando uocabant'). The contrast between public magnificence and private frugality is conventional: see N–H on Hor. *C.* 2.15.15, who quote *inter al.* Cic. *Mur.* 76 'odit populus Romanus priuatam luxuriam, publicam magnificentiam diligit'; add I. Gildenhard and C. Viglietti (edd.), *Roman frugality* (2020) chs. 5 (Gildenhard) and 6 (J. R. Patterson).

in amicos fideles 'loyal to allies' (*OLD amicus²* 4). The threefold division of the universe which S. implies in this sentence is perhaps also implicit in such passages as Cic. *Off.* 3.28 (*ciues ~ externi ~ di immortales*). For *fidelis in* + acc. cf. Ter. *Hec.* 472, Cic. *Mil.* 29, Sen. *Ag.* 180; S. has varied the construction with each of the three adjs.

9.3 duabus his artibus ... seque remque publicam curabant: *his* is prospective, signposting *audacia* and *aequitate*. *-que ... -que* ('both ... and') is the equivalent of τε ... τε and was perhaps introduced by Ennius (see Skutsch on *Ann.* 170): S. 'regarded it probably as archaic' (Fraenkel 193) and uses it again to coordinate pronoun and noun at 36.4, *BJ* 10.2, 85.37, 100.5; see also 14.2n. (*nam*). The interposition of *-que* between *rem* and *publicam* is regular. *rem publicam curare* is at Cato, *Orat.* 21M, though also in other authors.

audacia in bello, ubi pax euenerat, aequitate: chiastic with asyndeton and *uariatio* (prep. phrase ~ temporal clause). *ubi* = 'whenever' (6.5n. *post*).

9.4 maxima documenta haec habeo: another allusion to Pericles' speech (Thuc. 2.41.4 μετὰ μεγάλων ... σημείων, 'with great proofs'). *haec* is again prospective, signposting the two *quod*-clauses ('the fact that ...').

uindicatum est in eos qui contra imperium in hostem pugnauerant 'punishment was inflicted on those who had fought against the enemy contrary to orders' (*OLD uindico* 5b). A soldier was not allowed to leave the ranks, even to fight, without the permission of his commander (Oakley on Liv. 7.10.2); the most famous example of such punishment is Manlius Torquatus' killing of his son (52.30–1, Liv. 8.7.13–22).

quique tardius reuocati proelio excesserant 'and who had left the battle too slowly when summoned'. No exact instance of this seems to be known, but at Gergovia in 52 BC Caesar had to reprimand his troops 'quod ... neque signo recipiendi dato constitissent' (*BG* 7.52.1).

quam qui signa relinquere aut pulsi loco cedere ausi erant: *quam* follows *saepius* above, and *in eos* has to be understood before *qui*: 'than <on those> who had dared to abandon the standards or to withdraw from their position when beaten' (*or possibly* '… to withdraw when driven from their position'). The penalty was death (Plb. 6.37.11, Tac. *A.* 13.35.4) or, in the case of collective culpability, decimation (Front. *Strat.* 4.1.35). On punishments in the Roman army see G. R. Watson, *The Roman soldier* (1969) 117–26.

9.5 beneficiis magis quam metu imperium agitabant 'they exercised command more by acts of kindness than by fear': *imperium* here is the power of the Roman people over other nations etc. (Richardson 97). S. echoes the popular view of Roman imperialism (Liv. 26.49.8 'uenisse enim eos in populi Romani potestatem, qui beneficio quam metu obligare homines malit'); for other exs. of the antithesis cf. *BJ* 91.7, Liv. 22.22.11, [Sall.] *Ep. Caes.* 2.4.1, Tac. *A.* 13.26.3 (similar is Isoc. *Pan.* 80 'they won the Hellenic cities to themselves by doing kindness instead of subverting them by force' [Loeb trans.]). For *beneficium*, conventional in such contexts (e.g. Cato, *Orat.* 165M = *Orig.* 89C/95cP, Cic. *Q.Fr.* 1.1.26), see esp. Cic. *Off.* 2.26 'quam diu imperium populi Romani beneficiis tenebatur, non iniuriis' and Dyck's n. (also below, 11.8n. *ne illi*). *i. agitare* seems unique, but is imitated at [Sall.] *Ep. Caes.* 2.3.6 'dominationem … agitant' and cf. Just. 1.5.5 'agitato … regno'.

magis is not present in P or a few other MSS but is found in A and others. Since the omission of *magis* or *potius* is said to be a feature of both early Latin and historiography (see Skutsch on Enn. *Ann.* 130), should we follow P, as does Reynolds in the OCT? It seems suspicious that the ellipse does not occur elsewhere in S., and the omission is readily accounted for either by a scribe looking ahead to *malebant* or (more probably) by homoeoteleuton after *beneficiis*.

accepta iniuria ignoscere quam persequi malebant: this is the policy for which the elder Cato famously argued in his speech on behalf of the Rhodians in 167 BC (*Orat.* 163–9M = *Orig.* 87–93C/95P), a crisis mentioned by Caesar in his speech at 51.5 below. *iniuriam* (*-as*) *accipere* and *i. persequi* are both regular phrases.

10.1 ubi labore atque iustitia res publica creuit: *labore* perhaps refers back to 7.4–5, *iustitia* to 9.1–5. The *ubi*-clause continues as far as *patebant*.

reges magni bello domiti, nationes ferae et populi ingentes ui subacti: *sc. sunt* in each colon; *subacti* is to be taken with *nationes* as well as *populi*: its gender is determined not only by the nearest of the combined nouns but also by the fact that, in the case of things with life, masculine takes precedence (G&L 183 §286). *domiti* combines with *ferae* and *subacti* to portray these foreigners as wild animals tamed and subdued, as was conventional

(W–M on Tac. *A.* 3.47.4); for *ingens* of animals see *OLD* 1a. *magni* alludes to the fact that kings were often called 'the Great', e.g. Antiochus III, king of Syria, defeated at Magnesia in 190. The two verbs are coupled elsewhere (Liv. 3.28.10, Curt. 4.1.5, Flor. 1.18(2.1).1), but, since there are other phraseological similarities to Cicero's *Pro Fonteio* elsewhere (3.5n. *cum*, 4.1n. *animus*), see esp. *Font.* 12 'modo . . . subacti, modo bello domiti'.

Carthago, aemula imperii Romani, ab stirpe interiit: the three successive Punic Wars (264–241, 218–201, 149–146 BC) ensured that Carthage was regarded as the rival of the Roman empire (Diod. 34(35).33.5, Vell. 1.12.6, 2.1.1, Mela 1.34).[30] In the history of Diodorus, a contemporary of S., the elder Cato recommends the destruction of Carthage (cf. also Plin. *NH* 15.74, Flor. 1.31(2.15).4) but is opposed by Scipio Nasica, who argues for Carthage's preservation, predicting that otherwise a whole series of disasters would follow, ending in civil war (Diod. 34(35).33.3–5). The latter view is clearly reflected in S.'s two later works, where the destruction of Carthage in 146 represents a crucial turning point because, with the removal of an external threat ('metus hostilis'), Roman society started to fall apart (*BJ* 41.2 '*ante Carthaginem deletam* populus et senatus Romanus placide modesteque inter se rem publicam tractabant, neque gloriae neque dominationis certamen inter ciues erat: *metus hostilis* in bonis artibus ciuitatem retinebat', *H.* 1.10 'discordia et auaritia atque ambitio et cetera secundis rebus oriri sueta mala *post Carthaginis excidium* maxime aucta sunt', 1.12 '*remoto metu Punico*'); and, although there is no explicit reference to *metus hostilis* in the present passage, it is very difficult to believe that S. is not referring to the same phenomenon, which was evidently a matter of contemporary interest (so too e.g. Earl, *PTS* 13–15, 41–2; Levene, *OR* 224–6).[31] *a(b) stirpe*, a set expr. = 'from the base' (i.e. completely: see *OLD stirps* 1c), refers to the tradition that Carthage was razed to the ground (cf. e.g. Diod. 32.4.5, 32.14.1, Vell. 1.12.5 'funditus sustulit', Dio 21 = Zon. 9.30). For *aemula imperii* cf. also Tac. *A.* 15.13.2, Just. 8.4.9, 11.2.3, 21.1.3.

cuncta maria terraeque patebant seems a further allusion to Pericles' speech (Thuc. 2.41.4 πᾶσαν μὲν θάλασσαν καὶ γῆν ἐσβατὸν τῇ ἡμετέρᾳ τόλμῃ καταναγκάσαντες γενέσθαι, 'having compelled every sea and land to be accessible to our daring'); see also 53.2n. (*quae*). *cuncta* is to be taken with *terrae* as well as *maria* (5.2n. *huic*). *patere* is technical of open and

---

[30] Noting that the phrase *imperium Romanum* occurs first in S. (again at *H.* 3.2, 3.10.5), Richardson (99) alleges that *imperium* means 'power' here rather than 'empire'.

[31] This is now known in popular thought as 'Sallust's Theorem' (see N. Wood, 'Sallust's Theorem: a comment on "fear" in western political thought', *Hist. Pol. Thought* 16 (1995) 174–89).

accessible areas (*OLD* 3); the change of tense to the imperf. indicates the
ongoing state of affairs that was interrupted by Fortune.

saeuire Fortuna ac m͟i͟s͟c͟e͟r͟(e) ōmnĭă c͟o͟e͟pīt: after Rome's taming of wild
kings and peoples (above), *saeuire* may suggest the savaging of a wild
animal (*OLD* 2a), with *omnia* looking back meaningfully to 7.5 'uirtus
omnia domuerat', where the imagery is the same; but the turbulence of
a raging storm (e.g. Liv. 31.45.11 'saeuiente Borea'; *OLD* 3a) is suggested
rather by the coordination with *miscere* (e.g. German. 3.19 'omnia mis-
centur', Sen. *Ag.* 473–4), appropriate after the immediately preceding ref.
to seas and lands (above). *miscere omnia* (2.3n. *neque*) headlines the various
forms of confusion and change which are itemised in §§2–6 below. *miscere
omnia coepit* constitutes the second half of a hexameter line (cf. Virg. *Aen.*
9.296 'omnia coeptis'). Tacitus alludes to this passage for the turning
point of Tiberius' reign (*A.* 4.1.1 't͟u͟r͟b͟a͟r͟e͟ Fortuna coepit, saeuire ipse aut
saeuientibus uiris praebere').

   10.2 labores, pericula: for the various ways in which these two nouns
can be paired see Adams, *AILL* 504, 554, 574.
   dubias ... res has 'a traditional if not positively archaic flavour' (Horsfall
on Virg. *Aen.* 11.445), but the combination with *asperas* seems paralleled
only at Donat. *Aen.* 11.304 'in rebus dubiis asperisque'. *tolerare* is very
frequent in historical writers as an elevated synonym for *fero* or *perfero*
(Adams (1973) 133).
   eis otium, diuitiae – optanda alias – oneri miseriāēquĕ fŭērĕ: a double
paradox: peace (*otium*) is craved when one is fighting (Hor. *C.* 2.16.1ff.
'Otium diuos rogat', with N–H on line 5), but, once it is achieved, it
conventionally leads to idleness and associated vices (*TLL* 9.2.1177.3–
24); riches are craved when one is poor, but, once they are acquired,
they proverbially bring nothing but trouble (Hor. *S.* 2.6.79 with
Muecke's n.). *otium* and *diuitiae* are again coupled at 36.4. For *alias*
('otherwise') see *OLD alias* 3a; for the neuter *optanda* see 5.2n. (*huic*).
miseria is not elsewhere found combined with *onus* or used as a predic. dat.
(for *oneri* see 2.8n.); *-que fuerunt* is a reasonably common line-ending in
hexameter verse.
   10.3 igitur p͟rimum pec͟u͟niae, deinde imperii c͟upido c͟reuit: *pecuniae
cupido* is picked up by *auaritia* in §4, *imperii c.* by *ambitio* in §5. The MSS
here read *primo* ('there grew the desire first for money, then for power'),
but the sentence seems to conflict with 11.1 'Sed primo magis ambitio
quam auaritia animos hominum exercebat'.[32] Edd. suggest that S. intends
a contrast between *cupido* (the *desire* for money preceded the desire for

[32] That there is conflict is denied by D. F. Conley, *CP* 76 (1981) 121–5; see also his
   'The stages of Rome's decline in Sallust's historical theory', *Hermes* 109 (1981)
   379–82.

power) and *exercebat* (the *effects* of greed were felt later than those of ambition), but this seems very artificial; others point to an apparently similar sequence at Plb. 6.57.5–6 (K. Heldmann, *RhM* 136 (1993) 288–92), but it is not clear that that passage can defend the seeming contradiction in S. Since in 11–13 (below) the focus is almost entirely on wealth, we would expect S. to say 'the desire for money above all', but *primo* seems not to have the sense of *maxime* or *in primis* in classical Latin (*TLL* 10.2.1370.53–4); *primum*, however, commonly has this meaning (e.g. Cic. *Att.* 12.41.3 'si quaeris quid optem, primum Scapulae, deinde Clodiae'; *TLL* 10.2.1364.60–1365.3, *OLD primum*[2] 2), and confusion of the two adverbs would not be unusual (cf. 24.3, *BJ* 29.3). The resulting sentence produces a meaningful contrast with 11.1: *auaritia* was more of a problem than *ambitio*, but in fact it was *ambitio* whose effects were felt first.[33] For *cupido* see 2.1n.

ea quasi materies omnium malorum fuere 'they were (so to speak) the germ of every affliction'. The imagery is that of disease (*OLD malum*[1] 7b): cf. Apul. *Apol.* 50.1 'praecipua est materia morbi comitialis' (*Rhet. Herenn.* 2.34 seems different). S. is imitated by Horace (*C.* 3.24.49 'summi materiem mali'), where, however, the imagery is unclear. *materies* 'appears to have an archaic and poetic flavour' compared with *materia* (Brink on *AP* 131).

auaritia ... ambitio ...: the effect of *auaritia* is to undermine good qualities and replace them with bad ('pro his'), whereas that of *ambitio* (5) is to generate deception (cf. 11.2 'dolis atque fallaciis'). For the same duo cf. Thuc. 3.82.8 πάντων δ' αὐτῶν αἴτιον ἀρχὴ ἡ διὰ πλεονεξίαν καὶ φιλοτιμίαν ('the cause of all these things was <desire for> power, originating in greed and ambition'), Lucr. 3.59 'auaríties et honorum caeca cupido' (with Kenney's n.); also below, 11.1n. (*Sed*). For *auaritia* in particular see Tosi 809–10 §1811.

10.4 auaritia ... subuertit: the verb is perfect tense (cf. *edocuit* below). For the arrangement of the sentence (asyndeton bimembre + generalisation) see Adams, *AILL* 554–5. For *subuertit* cf. Sen. *Cons. Helv.* 10.1 'omnia subuertentis auaritiae'.

pro his ... edocuit: the syntax is most easily explained thus: *superbiam* and *crudelitatem* are the direct objects of *edocuit*, and with *neglegere* and *habere* we supply *homines* as object ('taught men to neglect ...'); some prefer to regard the infinitives as substantival, equivalent to the Greek τό + infin. ('taught neglect of the gods ...'). See also Adams, *AILL* 555. *superbia*, often a characteristic of Rome's enemies (famously at Virg. *Aen.*

---

[33] *Sed* at 11.1 seems to rule out Nipperdey's transposition of *pecuniae* and *imperii* at 10.3 (adopted by Woodman (2007a) 8).

6.853, Hor. *CS* 55), is now applied to the Romans; see also 6.7n. (*in superbiam*).

deos neglegere: in their dealings with allied peoples Romans would claim 'reverence for the gods' and refer to 'our high respect for the divine', as does the praetor M. Valerius Messalla in his letter to the city of Teos in 193 BC (*RDGE* 34.13 τῆς πρὸς τοὺς θεοὺς εὐσεβείας, 17 τὴν ἡμετέραν εἰς τὸ θεῖον προτιμίαν): see L. G. Driediger-Murphy, *ZPE* 189 (2014) 115-20. This too has now been reversed. In his *Antiquitates Rerum Diuinarum* (fr. 2) S.'s contemporary Varro complained about neglect of the gods (*ap.* August. *Civ. Dei* 6.2); a little later so did Livy (3.20.4; cf. 43.13.1); then Hor. *C.* 3.6.7-8.

omnia uenalia: the venality of republican politics (again at 30.4) is a Sallustian theme, esp. in *BJ* (cf. 8.2 'Romae omnia uenalia esse', 20.1, 31.26, 35.10): for a study see J. Hellegouarc'h, 'Vrbem uenalem ... (Sall., *Iug.* 35, 10)', *Bull. Assoc. Budé* 2 (1990) 163-74.

10.5 ambitio _m_ultos _m_ortales _f_alsos _f_ieri subegit: for *subigo* + infin. (again at 51.18) see *OLD* 6a; for *multos mortales* see 2.8n. (*multi*).[34]

aliud clausum in pectore, aliud in lingua promptum habere: for the wording of this semi-chiastic statement (ABC ~ ACB) cf. Cic. *Planc.* 34 'hic, quod cum ceteris a̱ṉi̱m̱o̱ sentiebat, id magis quam ceteri et *uultu promptum habuit* et *lingua*', and for *clausum* ~ *promptum* cf. (only) Cic. *Verr.* 4.42. The contrast between *pectus* and *lingua*, which goes back to Homer (*Il.* 9.313), is varied and frequent (e.g. Enn. *Ann.* 469-70S, Lucr. 1.413), but *clausus pectore* is relatively uncommon and almost exclusively in verse.[35] *promptum habere* recurs also at 7.1 (probably: see n. *magisque*) and Tac. *A.* 11.1.2.

magisque uultum quam ingenium bonum habere: the author of the 'Handbook on Electioneering' takes it for granted that his addressee will be open 'uultu ac fronte, quae est animi ianua' (*Comm. Petit.* 44): since the notion was commonly accepted (Otto 147), it was easy to deceive people.[36] The younger Cato preferred 'esse quam uideri bonus' (54.6), whereas Pompey was 'oris probi, animo inuerecundo' (*H.* 2.17). C. himself was a striking instance of falsity (5.4n. *cuius*). For the repeated *habere* see 4.5n. (*de cuius*).

10.6 haec ... uindicari 'At first these things developed slowly and were sometimes punished': S. changes to the historic infinitive (6.4n. *igitur*); *crescere* is consistent with the surrounding disease imagery (Cic. *Div.*

---

[34] For a stylistic analysis of 10.5-6 see von Albrecht 68-77.
[35] With the prep. *in* it seems to be found again only at *CLE* 2229.2.
[36] If this sounds simplistic, one should remember 'truth bias' and the like in the modern world (https://en.wikipedia.org/wiki/Truth-default_theory).

2.142). *post* in the next sentence responds to *primo . . . interdum* in adversative asyndeton.

post, ubi ̣contagio qu̱asi ̣pestilentia inu̱ası̣t, ̣ciuitas i̱mmutata: *sc. est*: '<but> after, when the infection, like a plague, had attacked, the community was changed'; for *inuado* of illness etc. see *OLD* 4a. Words of attack are used by Thucydides to describe the onset of the Athenian plague in 430 BC (2.48.2); that plague led to the collapse of socio-political values (2.53), whereas in S. a similar collapse is described in terms of a plague.

imperium ('the empire') contrasts with *ciuitas*: the two terms look back to *domi militiaeque* at 9.1.

factum: *sc. est.*

11.1 Sed primo magis a̱mbitio quam a̱uaritia a̱nimos hominum exercebat: for the logic of *Sed primo* see 10.3n. *ambitio* and *auaritia* are commonly juxtaposed, esp. in the younger Seneca (also above, 10.4–5n.); since the *quod*-clause shows that each is a *uitium* or 'disorder' (cf. Sen. *Ep.* 75.11 'morbi sunt inueterata uitia et dura, ut auaritia, ut ambitio'; *OLD uitium* 2b), *exercebat* is another illness word, often used of troublesome conditions (e.g. Cels. 1.6.1, 2.1.9, 2.1.18, 3.6.16, 4.24.2, 7.7.15D).

quod tamen ụitium propius ụirtutem erat 'a disorder which was nevertheless closer to virtue/to being a virtue': the antecedent has been included within the rel. clause, as often; for this pregnant use of *tamen*, implying a concession elsewhere in the context, see e.g. N–H on Hor. *C.* 1.15.19. *propius* is *either* the compar. of the prep. *prope* + acc. (so *TLL* 10.2.1962.47–8[37] but not *OLD prope* 11) *or* the neut. of the adj. *propior* (so *OLD propior* 6): if the latter, one might have expected the dat. (as Cic. *Off.* 2.22 'quae uirtuti propiores sunt'), but cf. *BJ* 49.1 'ipse propior montem', *al.* It was proverbial that 'there are vices adjacent to virtues' (Sen. *Ep.* 120.9 'Sunt . . . uirtutibus uitia confinia', *Clem.* 1.3.1 and Braund's n.; Otto 376, Tosi 763–4 §1708); perhaps Velleius had S. in mind when he wrote 'superatur . . . ambitio uirtute' (126.4).

11.2 bonus et ignauus: a Sallustian coupling (*BJ* 53.8, 57.6).

ille ụera ụia nititur 'the former struggles along the true path' (*OLD nitor*[1] 6a), viz. that of *uirtus* (*BJ* 1.3 'ubi ad gloriam uirtutis uia grassatur'), a common image (e.g. Hes. *WD* 287–92, Xen. *Mem.* 2.1.21; E. Fantham, *Comparative studies in republican Latin imagery* (1972) 70–1, Rutherford 176 and n. 138).

huic . . . contendit: in the interests of *uariatio* S. has written *huic* (which strictly belongs inside the *quia*-clause) instead of *hic*. The verb is

---

[37] In *TLL* it is assumed that with *propius* we have to understand *quam auaritia*, which seems impossible, since there was never any chance of *auaritia* being described in terms of proximity to *uirtus*. The understood comparison is 'than to being simply a *uitium*'.

understood to mean 'strive' in *OLD* (4), presumably picking up *nititur*, but 'compete' in *TLL* (4.668.83): cf. Lucr. 2.11–13 'certare ingenio, *contendere* nobilitate, | noctes atque dies *niti* praestante labore | ad summas emergere opes rerumque potiri'. But perhaps the meaning is 'march, hasten' (*OLD* 5), picking up *uera uia*: the *bonus* struggles along, but the *ignauus* has no trouble in simply forging ahead 'dolis atque fallaciis' (a common coupling).

11.3 auaritia pecuniae studium habet 'avarice means an enthusiasm for money': for *habeo* in the sense of 'to contain within itself' see *TLL* 6.3.2412.71–2413.57 (many exs.). Similar is Cato, *Carmen de Moribus* fr. 32 Manuwald 'auaritiam omnia uitia habere putabant'.

quam nemo sapiens *concupiuit* 'which [viz. money] no wise man ever desired', a gnomic perfect (G&L 160 §236 Note). If the upcoming image is one of food (next n.), the sense 'no man of taste' is perhaps also present (*OLD sapio* 5).

ea, quasi uenenis malis imbuta, corpus animumque uirilem effeminat 'as if drenched with harmful potions, it [viz. *auaritia*] feminises the manly body and spirit'; *uirilem*, its gender determined by the nearest noun, is to be taken also with *corpus* (G&L 183 §286). The discussion of this sentence at Gell. 3.1 omits to consider the image conveyed by the words *quasi ... imbuta*; unfortunately, however, 'the image is unclear', as remarked by Skard (1942) 145, who tentatively suggests that S. may be thinking of the cloak with which Nessus poisoned Heracles (cf. Ov. *Met.* 9.153). It is of course true that Heracles at one period during his career was forced to live like a woman and that the phrase *imbuta ueneno* is used of clothing at Enn. *Ann.* 476; but Heracles' cross-dressing had nothing to do with Nessus' cloak, and the combination of *imbuo* with *ueneno* (-*is*) is used in other contexts besides clothing (Acc. 535R, Liv. 39.11.2, Ov. *Tr.* 4.1.77). Since the *auarus* is always metaphorically hungry or thirsty (e.g. Hor. *C.* 3.16.18), perhaps the image is one of drugged food, which, once consumed, transforms the body and mind (cf. how Circe transforms Odysseus' men into pigs at Ov. *Met.* 14.273–90 by squeezing a drug into their drink). As well as meaning 'poison' (*OLD* 2), *uenenum* can mean any 'potent herb or other substance used for medical, magical, etc., purposes' (*OLD* 1a): hence the addition of *malis* (note esp. Cic. *Clu.* 148 'qui uenenum malum fecit, fecerit'). *effeminat* is picked up by *molliuerant* at §5 below; the contrast with *uirilem* anticipates the unnatural reversals of 12.2–13.3. For *effeminare* with *animum* cf. Caes. *BG* 1.1.3, Cic. *Fam.* 16.27.1, Sen. *Ep.* 51.10, 82.2; with *corpus* at Liv. 5.6.4, Cels. 1.9.6.

semper infinita, in*satia*bilis est, neque cō̆pia neque in-ō̆pia minuitur: S. now seems to see *auaritia* as hunger rather than as food. Avarice is self-evidently not diminished by *inopia*; nor is it diminished by *copia*, since avarice is proverbially never satisfied (Tosi 810–11 §1813). Wordplay such as *copia* ~ *inopia* is common (see esp. Tac. *Agr.* 30.4 '*auari ... ambitiosi ...*, quos non Oriens, non Occidens *satia*uerit: soli omnium opes atque *inopiam* pari adfectu *concupiscunt*'); among the various other effects note 'animumque ... effeminat ... infinita ... minuitur'. The asyndetic pairing of privative adjs. is common and in S. is often followed by *neque ... neque* (Adams, *AILL* 570, 585-7).

   11.4 sed: no wise man ever desired money (3 'nemo ... concupiuit'), *but*, during the Sullan proscriptions (next n.), everyone desired it ('omnes ... cupere' below).

   postquam L. Sulla armis recepta re publica bonis initiis malos euentus habuit: after leaving Asia (below, 5n.), Sulla invaded Italy in 83 BC and defeated the last of his opponents at the battle of the Colline Gate, in the north-eastern quarter of Rome, on 1 November 82 (*armis recepta re publica* seems to echo Cicero's words in early 80: *Rosc. Am.* 131 'imperii ... maiestatem quam armis receperat'). Elected dictator later that November, Sulla initiated a programme of political reforms and other measures (*MRR* 2.75, 3.74-5); but at the same time he instigated a series of proscriptions (next n.) which ended officially on 1 June 81 (Cic. *Rosc. Am.* 128; *MRR* 2.69). The reign of terror – itemised by the upcoming sequence of historic infinitives – ensured that Sulla became a byword for one whose initial achievements were overshadowed by the cruelty of his final period (51.32-4, *BJ* 95.4, Vell. 2.17.1, 27.5, Val. Max. 9.2.1, Juv. 1.16-17), and he is seen as a turning point in history also by Cicero (*Off.* 2.27 'post ... Sullae uictoriam': see Dyck's n.). *euentus (-um) habere* is common. *euentus* is almost always followed by a gen.; it is hard to tell whether *bonis initiis* is dat. (as Plaut. *Most.* 159 'euentus rebus omnibus') or a concessive abl. (either abs. or of attendant circumstances: see *OLD* 1.855). Or has *a* ('after') been lost after *publica*?

   rapere omnes, trahere, domum alius, alius agros cupere: 'The proscriptions were state-sanctioned plunder and killing of political enemies' (Dyck on Cic. *Rosc. Am.*, Intro. p. 2, with a convenient summary of the Sullan terror); for a full study see F. Hinard, *Les proscriptions de la Rome républicaine* (1985), with a lengthy list of those proscribed (pp. 327-411). *trahere* = 'plunder' (as *BJ* 41.5 'sibi quisque ducere, trahere, rapere'; *OLD* 5). For the historic infinitives see 6.4n. (*igitur*).

   neque modum neque modestiam 'neither limit nor restraint' (cf. 38.4, *BJ* 41.9, Plaut. *Bacch.* 613, Liv. 26.48.11).

   foeda crudeliaque in ciues facinora facere: the *figura etymologica* contrasts with its last occurrence (7.6n. *conspici*); the adjs. are coupled again at 52.36 and 3× in Cicero.

   11.5 huc accedebat quod ... 'To this was added the fact that ...' (*OLD* accedo 17b). S. now moves from the domestic scene in §4 to that abroad in

§§5–8, the passage as a whole contrasting with *domi militiaeque boni mores* (9.1) of earlier times.

exercitum … contra m̲orem m̲aiorum *luxuriose nimis*que l̲iberaliter habuerat 'had treated the army indulgently and too generously, contrary to ancestral custom' (*OLD habeo* 22): the tense is pluperf. because Sulla's Asian activities (next n.) preceded his dictatorship (4n. *postquam*). That S. once again has Cato in mind (*Orat.* 163M '*nimis luxuriose*') is suggested by the fact that Cato three times here uses the phrase *secundae res*, which occurs also at §8 below.

quem in Asia ductauerat: in 88 as consul for the first time Sulla had received Asia as his province and, with it, the command against Mithridates VI, which took him away from Italy until 83 (above, 4n. *postquam*): see *MRR* 2.40, 48, 55, 58, 61; B. C. McGing, *The foreign policy of Mithridates VI Eupator, king of Pontus* (1986). The use of *ductare* in connection with an army is a Sallustian idiolect (again at 17.7, 19.3 (n.), *BJ* 38.1, 70.2), described by Quintilian, who is concerned about the verb's double meaning, as archaic (8.3.44 'dicta sancte et antique'); it is picked up only by Tac. *H.* 2.100.2 'exercitui quem ipse ductauerat' (see Ash's n.; Lebek 298).

quo sibi f̲idum f̲aceret: it is often said that when *quo* introduces a purpose clause which does not contain a comparative (in S. again at 14.2 [?], 22.2, 33.1, 38.3, 48.4 [?], 58.3, *BJ* 37.4, 52.6, *H.* 1.49.1), the construction is archaic; but Oakley (on Liv. 9.10.9) has pointed out that there are many exs. in Cicero and several in other contemporary authors. *fidus*, avoided by Caesar and comparatively rare in Cicero, is preferred by S. to *fidelis* (12:4). Although Livy uses both adjs. equally, Tacitus follows S. (46:1). See Adams (1973) 139 n. 22. For the notion of generals currying favour with their troops see e.g. Liv. 39.7.3 'indulgentem ambitiosumque' of Manlius Vulso, Tac. *A.* 2.55.5–6, 3.12.3 of the elder Piso.

loca amoena, uoluptaria … feroces militum animos molliuerant: according to the common ancient belief in environmental determinism, 'soft lands breed soft men' (Hdt. 9.122), and the author of *Airs Waters Places* develops an extended contrast between the men of Europe and those of Asia (12–24), where 'pleasure rules supreme'. Asia was in fact famous for its *amoenitas* (e.g. Liv. 38.17.18 'uobis mehercule, Martiis uiris, cauenda ac fugienda quam primum amoenitas est Asiae', 38.49.4 'emollitum amoenitate Asiae', Tac. *A.* 3.7.1), and S. maintains that Sulla's troops were affected by their presence there: the soft locality contrasts with the 'rough terrain' to which their ancestors were inured (7.5 'locus … asper'). *locus* is regularly coupled with *amoenus*; for *uoluptarius* see Plaut. *Poen.* 601–3 'oraueris, | liberum ut commostraremus tibi locum et uoluptarium, | ubi ames, potes, pergraecere' (interesting similarities with S.), Fronto

p. 228.10 vdH²; for both adjs. together cf. Plaut. *Mil.* 641 'ex amoenis rebus et uoluptariis'. See further next n.

11.6 ibi primum insueuit exercitus populi Romani amare, potare ... 'It was there that an army of the Roman people first became accustomed to ...': the awfulness of the degeneration is underlined by the formal *exercitus p.R.* (as e.g. Liv. 9.8.15). *primum* indicates that this is an example of the ἀρχὴ κακῶν ('beginning of evils') motif (cf. 51.33), of which ancient historians are fond (W.⁵ on Tac. *A.* 4.6.1; *RICH* 63 n. 186): thus the return to Rome of Manlius Vulso from Asia (Piso 36C/34P 'primum', Liv. 39.6.7 'primum': see further next n.). The frequent combination of the verbs *amare* and *potare* (*TLL* 10.2.358.76–8) 'may have been an old expression of disapproval' (Adams, *AILL* 576). Not only was there a natural association between drink and sex (Otto 366) but S. is thinking of the *conuiuium*, where the two activities were (so to speak) formalised; the contrast is with 7.4, where the *maiores* took no pleasure 'in scortis atque conuiuiis'.

signa, tabulas pictas, uasa caelata mirari 'to admire statues, paintings and embossed vessels' (*OLD tabula* 2a). Livy remarks that the capture of Syracuse in 211 was the 'primum initium mirandi Graecarum artium opera' (25.40.2), and, when Manlius Vulso (cos. 189) celebrated his Asian triumph in 187, the event was notable for the display of luxury goods which he had brought back with him to Rome: Livy lists the items of precious furniture and the various female attractions and the like, all of which he saw as 'the origin of foreign luxury' (39.6.7). Since a similar list had appeared in the second-century historian L. Calpurnius Piso (last n.), it is obviously possible that, in positing a much later ἀρχὴ κακῶν, S. has been influenced by earlier descriptions of similar moments. See also Earl, *PTS* 41–6, T. J. Luce, *Livy: the composition of his history* (1977) 250–63.

ea ... rapere: *ea* refers to the three sorts of luxury items just mentioned; *priuatim et publice* could refer either to the source of the plunder (private and public property) or to the conditions under which the looting was carried out (both with and without official condonation).

delubra spoliare: for this and the surrounding context cf. Liv. 26.30.9 'spoliata deum delubra, dis ipsis ornamentisque eorum ablatis, nihil relictum Syracusis esse'. *delubrum* (again at 12.4 below) is a choice alternative to *templum*, with which it is often conjoined (e.g. 4× in Cic. *Cat.*).

sacra ... polluere: for the imagery see 23.6n. (*quasi*).

11.7 nihil reliqui uictis fecere 'they left nothing over for the defeated'. The noun *reliquum* is regularly found in the gen. (partitive) after neuter pronouns (*OLD reliquum* 2a–b), which could be the case here (equivalent to *nullum reliquum*, 'no residue'); but commentators prefer to see an example of the idiomatic *reliqui facere*, 'to leave over', where the gen. is equivalent to the adv. *super* (see Oakley on Liv. 7.35.8): the idiom is usually found in the negative, as here and 52.4, but not always (cf. Cic. *Sull.* 89).

On either interpretation the phrase is equivalent to *reliquere* and we have a case of S.'s favourite 'support verb construction' (4.5n. *de*).

11.8 secundae res sapientium animos fatigant: the sentence both constitutes a foil for *ne* ... *temperarent* and looks back to *nemo sapiens* at §3 above. *fatigant* = 'wear down' (*OLD* 5).

ne illi corruptis moribus uictoriae temperarent 'still less did those men of corrupt morality exercise moderation in respect of their victory' (*OLD tempero* 2a): for *ne* = *nedum* see *OLD ne*[1] 11c; in either case the subjunc. is regular. In view of the contrast with *sapientium animos*, it seems likely that *corruptis moribus* is an abl. of description rather than abs., but the distinction is almost impossible to make. *uictoriae temperare* is imitated by Tacitus (*H.* 3.31.3), who, like Velleius (85.6), also has *uictoriam temperare* (*H.* 4.1.3).[38] For the Romans' idealistic theory of imperialism cf. Cic. *Leg.* 3.9 'sociis parcunto', Virg. *Aen.* 6.853 'parcere subiectis et debellare superbos' (see Horsfall's n. for a vast bibliography; also above, 9.5n. *beneficiis*).

12.1 Postquam diuitiae ... et eas gloria ... sequebatur: *eas* is emphatic ('and it was them [riches] that glory, empire and power followed'); but S. warned at the beginning that 'diuitiarum ... gloria fluxa ... est': it was *uirtus* which was important. *honori* is predic. dat. (*NLS* 49 §68); for the tense of the verb see 6.3n. (*postquam*).

potentia: 'By comparison with *potestas*, which is the constitutional power of a magistrate, *potentia* is personal power, linked to the particular circumstance of each political personality. As a result, beside *potestas* (lawful power), *potentia* sometimes has the force of "unlawful personal power"' (Hellegouarc'h 242).

hebescere uirtus: the verb can mean 'become blunt' (like a sword), 'grow dim' (like a star) or 'weaken' (like an ailing body): that S. intended to exclude none of these is argued by C. Krebs (*HSCP* 104 (2008) 231–6); the same verb is used of *auctoritas* at Cic. *Cat.* 1.4, where the metaphor is expressly that of a blunted sword. *uirtus* is the first of three nominative abstracts, balancing those in the *postquam*-clause; each abstract contributes to a tricolon crescendo, arranged ABBABA.

paupertas probro haberi 'poverty (began) to be regarded as a disgrace' (*probro* is predic. dat.: *NLS* 49 §68): a reversal of Pericles' statement in his Funeral Speech that 'it is not shameful for anyone to acknowledge poverty' (Thuc. 2.40.1); cf. Hor. *C.* 3.24.42 'magnum pauperies opprobrium'.

innocentia pro maleuolentia duci coepit 'incorruptibility began to be regarded as malice' (*OLD pro* 9). *innocentia* here, as sometimes elsewhere

---

[38] At Cic. *Marc.* 8 the MSS are divided between *uicto, uictoriam* and *uictum*; the evidence of Arusianus Messius (see 2.9n.) strongly suggests that *uicto temperare* is the right reading (7.512.18).

(*BJ* 46.1; *TLL* 7.1.1707.1–10), is said to be a synonym for *abstinentia* in its sense of 'restraint in financial dealings' (*OLD abstinentia* 2: cf. 54.6 'cum innocente abstinentia certabat'): 'it was assumed that anyone who let slip a chance of enriching himself must do so in order to enjoy the equivalent pleasure of censuring those who had less scruple' (Summers ad loc.). Although there is no precise verbal correspondence, scholars have seen here the influence of Thuc. 3.82.4 (cf. 12.2n. *aliena*, 52.11n. *uera*). S. has not followed the passive *duci* with the passive *coepta est*, as would have been more normal (G&L 277 §423 N. 3).

12.2 igitur ex diuitiis iuuentutem ... **inuasere:** *ex* combines the notions of 'after' and 'as a result of' (*OLD* 10, 18a); *inuasere* again suggests the attack of a disease (2.5n. *uerum*, 10.6n. *post*). Young men played a significant role in contemporary public life and feature prominently in S.'s narrative (13.4, 14.5–7, 16.1–3, 17.6, 38.1): see Eyben 56–8; Lintott, *VRR* 213; E. Isayev, 'Unruly youth?', *Historia* 56 (2007) 1–13, esp. 8–11 on 'Youth and Catiline'; good bibliography in C. Laes and J. Strubbe, *Youth in the Roman empire* (2014).

rapere, consumere: thus the opposite of their ancestors, 'laudis auidi, pecuniae liberales' (7.6). The asyndeton belongs to 'a type expressing forceful seizure of something followed by its use, misuse or destruction' (Adams, *AILL* 576–7, comparing 20.12 below).

aliena cupere translates Thuc. 3.84.1 ἐπιθυμοῦντες τὰ τῶν πέλας ἔχειν.

pudorem, <im>pudicitiam ... **promiscua** ... **habere** 'they made no distinction between decency and indecency' (lit. 'they regarded ... as indistinguishable': *OLD habeo* 24); for the neuter see 5.2n. (*huic*). Most of those who retain the transmitted *pudicitiam* translate *promiscua* as 'worthless' here: not only is this meaning extremely doubtful in itself but *promiscua* clearly relates to the theme of confusion (5.9–13.5 intro. n.), and the context (*sua ~ aliena, diuina ~ humana*) seems almost to demand contrasting nouns. Adams suggests that *pudorem* 'may indicate a sense of shame arising from a wrongdoing' (*AILL* 556, comparing Cic. *Fam.* 14.3.2), but there seems to be no example where *pudor*, a particularly tricky term (Kaster 28–65), is contrasted with *pudicitia* (*TLL* 10.2.2483.55–64, 2497.4–48); on the contrary, the two are juxtaposed as synonyms at [Sall.] *Ep. Caes.* 2.8.8. On the other hand, the hypothesised omission of *im-* after *pudorem* is the easiest of scribal errors (so J. S. van Veen, *Hermes* 23 (1888) 160).

diuina atque humana promiscua ... **habere:** i.e. they made no distinction between the divine and the human. The context suggests the kind of behaviour of which Cicero accused Verres (*II Verr.* 1.47 'Apollinemne tu Delium spoliare ausus es? illine tu templo tam antiquo, tam sancto, tam religioso manus impias ac sacrilegas adferre conatus es?'). Cf. also *BJ* 5.2.

nihil pensi neque moderati habere: it is extremely difficult to know what these words mean. If *habere* continues to mean 'regard, consider', then the genitives seem to indicate worth: 'they considered nothing as worth weight or restraint'. On the other hand, if by the figure of syllepsis *habere* has a different meaning (*OLD* 4a, to have attached to one as quality etc.), the genitives will be partitive: 'there was nothing weighty or restrained in their behaviour' (lit. 'they had no element of weight or restraint'). On the principle that each expression involving *pensi* should be treated on its merits (5.6n. *neque*), the latter seems likelier than the former. See also *TLL* 10.1.1049.48–1050.7.

12.3 ŏpĕrāē prĕtĭ(um) ēst 'It is worthwhile ...' (*OLD opera* 3b, *pretium* 2b). The set phrase fits easily into hexameter verse (as Juv. 14.281), and Koster has pointed out (59) that an epic couplet can be formed out of *operae ... [4] decorabant.*

cum ... cognoueris 'when you become acquainted with ...': presumably another indefinite second person sing. subjunc., though one cannot be sure: fut. perf. indic. is a possibility (1.6n. *et*).

in urbium modum exaedificatas: S. 'often places long attributes, usually appositive, which consist for the most part of a participle and a few connected words, after a verb. The attribute performs much the same function as a relative clause ... This pattern is very rare in other types of Latin prose, but particularly common in Thucydides, from whom Sallust probably picked it up' (J. N. Adams, 'A type of hyperbaton in Latin prose', *PCPS* 17 (1971) 1–16, at 8). Other exs. of such 'verbal hyperbaton' at e.g. 28.4, 29.1. *in ... modum* = 'like' (*OLD modus* 11c). The villa of S.'s contemporary, Vedius Pollio, on the Bay of Naples was similarly described by Ovid (*F.* 6.641 'urbis opus domus una fuit'), and such descriptions were standard in the *conuicium saeculi* (Sen. *Contr.* 5.5 'urbium solo aedificatae domus'). Nero's house was notoriously said to be coextensive with Rome itself (Suet. *Nero* 39.2 'Roma domus fiet'). See further Coleman on Mart. *Spect.* 2.4; also below, 13.1n. (*Nam*).

uīsĕrĕ tēmplă dĕōrŭm: the verb = 'to go and look at or view' (*OLD* 2). Temples are a touchstone for social morality: see esp. Hor. *S.* 2.2.103–4 'quare | templa ruunt antiqua deum?' (written within a decade of the *BC*). *templa deorum*, naturally common (e.g. Cic. *Cat.* 1.12), is varied below by *delubra deorum* (11.6n.).

nostri maiores: this order of words, in contrast to *maiores nostri* (which is ten times more common: cf. 51.4n.), had virtually died out by the end of the republic.

12.4 domos suas gloria decorabant: since it was the custom to decorate the outside of houses and doorways with enemy spoils taken in battle (Plin. *NH* 35.7), *gloria* is almost a metonymy. For the expr. cf. Cic. *Acad.* 2.4 'gloria decorari' (45 BC).

praeter iniuriae licentiam 'apart from the licence to do harm'. *uictis* (above), like *sociis* (below), is the usual dat. after verbs of 'taking away' (*NLS* 44 §61).

12.5 per summum scelus: *per scelus* (again at *BJ* 14.7, 14.15, 14.25, *H.* 1.49.7) is a set phrase = 'criminally'; the addition of *summum* is imitated at [Sall.] *Ep. Caes.* 1.4.1.

omnia ea sociis adimere quae fortissimi u̲i̲r̲i̲ u̲i̲ctores reliquerant: thus M. Marcellus at Syracuse in 212 BC (Cic. *II Verr.* 2.4): 'urbem pulcherrimam Syracusas … non solum incolumem passus est esse, sed ita reliquit ornatam ut esset idem monumentum uictoriae, mansuetudinis, continentiae, cum homines uiderent et quid expugnasset et quibus pepercisset et quae reliquisset'. The useful term *socii* underlines the magnitude of the *scelus* (cf. M. Lavan, *Slaves to Rome* (2013) 25–72).

pro̲i̲nde quasi i̲n̲iuriam facere, i̲d̲ demum esset i̲m̲perio uti: 'the resumptive use of *is* without any intervening phrase is archaic, and rare in classical Latin' (Zetzel on Cic. *Rep.* 6.26; also Courtney, *ALP* p. 4): e.g. 20.4 'idem uelle atque idem nolle, ea demum firma amicitia est', Cic. *Fin.* 5.23 'ista animi tranquillitas, ea est ipsa beata uita' (with Madvig's n.), Ov. *Tr.* 5.14.24–5 'non se subducere nimbo, | id demum est pietas'. The effect is impossible to reproduce exactly in English: here perhaps 'just as if exercising power were precisely *that* – doing harm' (i.e. were equivalent to/the same as). Cf. also 37.4, 58.16. *iniuriam facere* and *imperio uti* function as nouns, respectively subject and predicate; for *proinde quasi* + subjunctive see *OLD proinde* 2b: in unreal comparative clauses the sequence of tenses is normally observed (52.15n.), as here. *demum* (here 'precisely') is to be taken closely with *id* (2.9n. *uerum*). The repetition of *iniuria* from §4 underlines the difference between then and now.

13.1 Nam quid ea memorem quae nisi eis qui uidere nemini credibilia sunt, a priuatis compluribus subuersos montes, maria constrata esse? 'Why should I call to mind those things which are credible to no one except to those who have seen them, namely, that mountains have been undermined and seas paved over by many private individuals?' *Nam* here indicates a 'lively or impatient' question (*OLD nam* 7a), as 52.34 'Nam quid … loquar?' *memorem* (deliberative subjunc.: cf. *NLS* 129–33 §§172–5) is followed both by *ea* and by the acc. + infin., which is in apposition to *ea*.

The sentence constitutes a *praeteritio* (for which *quid … memorem* is formulaic: Horsfall on Virg. *Aen.* 6.122–3): S. mentions the items which he professes to omit. *priuatis* pointedly implies that such extravagant building projects might be expected in *public* life, and, despite the plural form, it shows that S. is thinking principally of L. Licinius Lucullus (cos. 74 BC), who, because of his building works, was familiarly called the Roman Xerxes, after the fifth-century Persian king who famously bridged the Hellespont and cut a channel through Mt Athos (Hdt. 7.22-4, 33-6): see Vell. 33.4, Plin. *NH* 9.170, Plut. *Luc.* 39.3. Similar houses were built by others, most famously on the Bay of Naples (see J. E. G. Whitehorne, 'The ambitious builder', *AUMLA* 31 (1969) 28-39, J. H. D'Arms, *Romans on the Bay of Naples* (1970), M. Zarmakoupi, *Designing for luxury on the Bay of Naples* (2014)), and attracted the criticism of moralising writers on the ground that they upset the natural order of things (esp. Sen. *Contr.* 2.1.13 'aduersum naturam alieno loco aut terra aut mare mentita'). They therefore constituted marvels or wonders and, as such, defied belief ('nemini credibilia'), requiring a statement of autopsy on the part of the historian to vouch for their existence ('eis qui uidere'): see Marincola 82-6; K. E. Shannon-Henderson, 'Constructing a new imperial paradoxography: Phlegon of Tralles and his sources', in A. König et al. (edd.), *Literature and culture in the Roman empire, 96-235: cross-cultural interactions* (2020) 159-178, at 166-74. The present sentence, designed to elicit the indignation of readers, is the starting-off point for the discussion (by Grethlein, q.v.) of S.'s use of the first person in his narratives. See also 20.11n.

13.2 quibus mihi u̲identur ludibrio fuisse diu̲itiae 'and riches seem to me to have been a plaything for them': *ludibrio* (another predic. dat.) and *quibus* constitute a so-called 'double dative' construction; *mihi* is a regular indir. object with *uidentur*.

honeste ... per turpitudinem: the morality of wealth was an abiding philosophical topic (see e.g. M. Griffin, *Seneca: a philosopher in politics* (1976) 294-302, esp. 300-1); for the theme of immoral spending see e.g. Hor. *S.* 2.2.102 'quod superat non est melius quo insumere possis?' with Muecke's n. *honeste* contrasts with the ancestors, who 'diuitias honestas uolebant' (7.6); *per turpitudinem* (earlier at Cic. *II Verr.* 1.23, later at Sen. *Tranq. An.* 15.1) varies *turpiter* (at Cic. *Cat.* 2.21).

13.3 stupri, ganeae: imitated at Tac. *A.* 6.4.4 'inter ganeam et stupra'; see also 15.1n. (*multa*).

ceterique cultus: the noun is almost in ironical quotation marks: 'and other "refinement"'.

uiri mu̲liebria pati, mu̲lieres pudicitiam in propatu̲lo habere: in republican prose 'it is almost exclusively *mulier* that is used to place emphasis on the sex of a woman, both in explicit and implied contrasts with *vir*' (J. N. Adams, 'Latin words for "woman" and "wife"', *Glotta* 50 (1972) 242). Here S. extends to sexual practices the confusion of opposites seen earlier with the elements (1n.). *muliebria pati* denotes passive homosexuality (Adams, *LSV* 189-90). Since *in propatulo* ('generally available') literally means 'in the open' etc. (*OLD propatulus* 2a), the implication is that women are behaving like prostitutes, who would sit outside their establishment touting for business. The historic infinitives are the first in a series of six (6.4n. *igitur*).

uescendi causa terra marique omnia exquirere: thus Seneca too passes from unnatural buildings to foreign food (*Ep.* 89.22 'profunda et insatiabilis gula hinc maria scrutatur, hinc terras'; cf. Juv. 11.14–16 with Mayor's n). For food as an index of morality see E. Gowers, *The loaded table* (1993).

dormire priusquam somni cupido esset: after historic tenses *priusquam* takes the subjunctive 'when the action does not, or is not to, take place' (G&L 369 §577.1). Sleep, like eating, has already appeared as a moral indicator at 2.8 (n. *dediti*); here edd. point to Xen. *Mem.* 2.1.30 (Virtue speaking) 'You do not even wait for the desire of pleasant things but fill yourself with everything before you desire them ... It is not on account of work but on account of having nothing to do that you desire sleep'. See also next nn.

non famem aut sitim neque frigus neque lassitudinem opperiri: the criterion should be the needs of nature, not the requirements of pleasure (cf. Sen. *Cons. Helv.* 10.2 'corporis exigua desideria sunt: frigus summoueri uult, alimentis famem ac sitim extinguere; quidquid extra concupiscitur, uitiis, non usibus laboratur', *Ep.* 78.22; A. Oltramare, *Les origines de la diatribe romaine* (1926) 280). *frigus* regularly accompanies *fames, sitis* and *lassitudo* as an undesirable condition (*TLL* 6.1.1336.73–9); see also next n.

sed ea omnia luxu antecapere 'but they forestalled all those things because of indulgence': i.e. they ate before they were hungry and drank before they were thirsty; since sleep has already been mentioned, *lassitudinem* perhaps does not refer to one's bed but, as suggested by *neque ... neque*, has the same reference as *frigus*, presumably the baths (cf. e.g. Mart. 10.70.13, Ap. *Met.* 5.15.1). The language is choice. *luxus*, entirely avoided by Cicero and Caesar, is a rare and artificial variant for *luxuria*; though S. prefers the latter (14:6), Tacitus much prefers *luxus* (54:12). See W–M on Tac. *A.* 3.52.1. *antecapere*, a Sallustian favourite (again at 32.1, 55.1, *BJ* 21.3, 50.1), is also at Cic. *ND* 1.43 (45 BC), then not until Tac. *H.* 4.66.1.

13.4 haec iuuentutem, ubi familiares opes defecerant, ad facinora incendebant 'These things would inflame young men to crimes whenever their family resources failed': *ubi* + pluperf. indicates that the statement is generalising (6.5n. *post*). Impoverishment and debt (cf. 5.7) will feature strongly in the main narrative (14.2n. *alienum*). Here the relationship between impoverishment and crime is pointed etymologically (cf. Liv. 23.7.6 'si malum facinus quod a uetustissimis sociis consanguineisque defecissent forti ac memorabili facinore purgare uellent, ut interfecto Punico praesidio restituerent Romanis se').

animus imbutus malis artibus is imitated by Tac. *A.* 15.45.2 'animum bonis artibus non imbuerat'.

13.5 eo profusius omnibus modis quaestui atque sumptui deditus erat '*all the more* profligately, *therefore*, was it devoted to profit-making and expenditure by every means': in cases such as this (again at 48.4), *eo* seems to combine the meanings of 'therefore' and 'all the more' (*OLD eo*³ 1–2); cf. 1.3n. (*quo*). The verbal nouns *quaestui* and *sumptui* are modified by the adverbial *omnibus modis*; for the combination of the two nouns cf. Cic. *Quinct.* 94. *profusus* (*-e*) is frequently used in contexts of squandering and other immoral behaviour (*TLL* 10.2.1745.26–35, 51–6, 67–1746.12): see also 5.4, 20.11n. (*profundant*).

14–16 Catiline (II)

14.1 In tanta tamque corrupta ciuitate: these words pick up via ring composition those with which the archaeology was introduced at 5.8–9 '*corrupti ciuitatis* mores . . . *quantam*que reliquerint'.

id quod factu facillimum erat: for the parenthetical use of *id quod* ('something which . . .'), again at 30.2 and 51.20, see *OLD is* 9b. For *factu facilis* see 3.2n. (*quae*).

omnium flagitiorum atque facinorum . . . tamquam stipatorum cateruas habebat 'he had around him teams of every outrage and crime, like bodyguards': the sentence reads oddly in English but there was a long tradition of the personification of evil, e.g. of lawlessness by Hesiod (*Theog.* 230) and of *nefas* by Statius (*Theb.* 7.48): see further Horsfall on Virg. *Aen.* 6.274–89. The present conceit is helped by the fact that *facinus*, if not *flagitium*, could be used as a term of abuse (e.g. Cic. *Phil.* 11.10 'Lucium . . . quod facinus, quod scelus!'; *OLD* 2b). The alliterating nouns are coupled elsewhere (W–M on Tac. *A.* 3.50.2) but esp. apropos of the Catilinarian conspiracy (14.2, 23.1, 37.5, Cic. *Cat.* 1.13, 18, *Scaur.* 13, *Sull.* 16).

tamquam stipatorum implies the violence of contemporary Rome, where rival gangs, such as those mentioned at 50.1, went about 'in threatening massed groups . . . reflecting a disrupted political system' (I. Östenberg, 'Power walks: aristocratic escorted movements in republican Rome', in I. Östenberg et al. (edd.), *The moving city: processions, passages and promenades in ancient Rome* (2015) 13–22, at 22 (also 75–87), Lintott, *VRR passim*, Gruen 433–48). The cognate *stipatus* implies a different slur at Cic. *Mur.* 49 'Catilinam . . . stipatum choro iuuentutis' (cf. *Cat.* 2.22–3), but violence is openly expressed when S. returns to the young men at 16.1–3 below.

14.2 nam quicumque impudicus, adulter, ganeo, <quique> manu, uentre, pene bona patria laceraverat: editors have questioned the paradosis for two principal reasons. (1) We expect a one-to-one correspondence between the two sets of three nouns, but this happens only with *uentre ~ ganeo* and *pene ~ adulter*; *impudicus*, which probably refers to homosexual passivity (cf. *OLD* 1b), and *manu* are each left high and dry. (2) When Fronto quotes the passage to illustrate word order, the three personal nouns are absent (p. 145.18–19 vdH²): 'Sallustius <ait>: "quique manu, uentre, pene bona patria lacerauerat"'. Two remedies have been sought. (1) Since Fronto was concerned only with the position of *pene*, he is said not to have intended to quote the passage in full: hence his omission of *impudicus ... ganeo* is irrelevant (*quique* is assumed to be a mistake for *quicumque*). Scholars of this persuasion seek emendation(s) amongst the list of personal nouns; on the assumption that *manu* refers to gambling with dice, the simplest is Köchly's change of *adulter* to *aleator*, although it produces neither a chiastic nor a sequential arrangement. (2) Since Cicero has a very similar list of hangers-on (*Cat.* 2.23 'in his gregibus omnes aleatores, omnes adulteri, omnes impuri impudicique uersantur'; cf. 2.7), Reynolds agreed with those who had assumed that, apart from the apparent substitution of *quique* for *quicumque*, Fronto's is an accurate quotation and that the three personal nouns originated as a marginal gloss by a scribe who remembered the Ciceronian passage.[39] (The scribe's omission of a term for 'gambler' is said to be explained by the fact that he failed to realise that *manu* related to the throwing of dice.)

Neither of these remedies is entirely persuasive in itself,[40] and there are two further considerations: (3) the supposition that Fronto has mistakenly substituted *quique* for *quicumque* is implausible unless the two words are synonymous, which they are not; (4) the parallel with Cicero can be turned on its head: since S. so often echoes the *Catilinarians* elsewhere (see Appendix II), it is worrying to delete the very words which recall Cicero here. I suggest that Fronto has accurately reported what S. wrote: on this hypothesis *quique* has been mistakenly omitted from S.'s text, perhaps by a scribe who failed to realise that the transmitted *quicumque* is here not a rel. pronoun ('whichever') but an adj. ('any'). If this argument is correct, what does the omitted *quique* mean? I suggest further that -*que* does not mean 'and' but that *quique* is coordinate with *quique* below and means 'both <the man> who ...'.[41] S.'s list of C.'s villainous followers moves from social outcasts (*quicumque ... ganeo*) to two parallel types of financial desperados (*<quique> manu ... quique alienum ...*), before proceeding to parricides and the rest (*praeterea omnes ...*): 'Any passivist, adulterer or glutton, both the man who had wasted ... and the man who had accumulated ...'.

---

[39] That there is something formulaic about such lists is suggested by Naev. *Com.* 89M–S 'audax, ganeo, lustro, aleo', Catull. 29.2 = 29.10 'impudicus et uorax et aleo'.

[40] For arguments in favour of the transmitted text see K. Muse, *Mnem.* 65 (2012) 40–61 and 69 (2016) 503–10.

[41] For this construction, often stated wrongly to be found first at Liv. 1.55.6, see Cic. *Leg.* 2.21 with Dyck.

No association of *manus* with gambling is attested before Ovid, and, since the word is capable of many different meanings (see *OLD*), *manu* is unlikely to refer *tout court* to gambling here; it perhaps refers to extravagant payments of some sort, whether bribery or the hiring of gangs. In the list of body parts which was translated from the Greek orator Lycurgus by the rhetorician Rutilius Lupus (*Schem.* 1.18 Halm), and which has the same three as S. and in the same order, the hand is associated with theft (*rapina*); this cannot be the case in our passage, where the context is of wasting one's inheritance ('bona patria laceraverat').

For *lacerare* = 'to waste' etc. *TLL* quotes Plaut., Cic., Flor. besides S. (7.2.826.48–54); edd. compare the Homeric κτήματα δαρδάπτουσιν, 'they waste your patrimony' (*Od.* 14.92, 16.315). Cicero said that *penis* is today 'in obscenis' (*Fam.* 9.22.2), but it is found in the historian Calpurnius Piso (42C/40P) as well as S., and Adams (*LSV* 35–6) maintains that neither author 'is likely to have tolerated an outright obscenity or vulgarism' and that 'at worst *penis* was probably a risqué colloquialism of educated speech'.

alienum aes grande conflauerat 'had accumulated a large debt' (again at 24.3): S. has varied the more normal order *aes alienum*, and *grandis* 'probably had a freshness which *magnus* may have lacked' (Brink on Hor. *Epi.* 2.2.178–9): see also 49.3n. In *TLL* (4.241.40) *conflo* here is rendered as 'assembled' *vel sim.*, but in *OLD* (7b) it is given the unique meaning of 'run up'. For debt, which motivated many of C.'s followers (*Cat.* 2.18–21 with Dyck), see further 16.4, 18.4, 20.11–13, 21.2, 23.3, 24.3, 28.4, 33.1–2, 35.3, 37.5, 40.1, 41.2, 49.3; 'the *Bellum Catilinae* is in essence a study of the corrosive effect of debt on human behaviour and social norms' (Mouritsen, *RE* 193, in the course of discussing 'politics and debt'): see also B. D. Shaw, 'Debt in Sallust', *Latomus* 34 (1975) 187–96; M. W. Frederiksen, 'Caesar, Cicero and the problem of debt', *JRS* 56, (1966) 128–41; Berry, *CC* 27–30, 271 (index 'debt').

quo ... redimeret 'with which to buy off an outrage or crime' (*OLD redimo* 8a): a rel. clause of purpose (*NLS* 109 §148), although *quo* could conceivably be a conjunction (11.5n.).

14.3 praeterea ... ad hoc ...: these are two of S.'s commonest sentence connections (27× and 10× respectively in *BC*).

parricidae: cf. *Cat.* 2.7 'quis tota Italia ueneficus, quis gladiator, quis latro, quis sicarius, quis parricida, quis testamentorum subiector, quis circumscriptor, quis ganeo, quis nepos, quis adulter, quae mulier infamis, quis corruptor iuuentutis, quis corruptus, quis perditus inueniri potest qui se cum Catilina non familiarissime uixisse fateatur?' (also 2.22); Cicero also applies the term to C. himself (*Cat.* 1.17 with Dyck's n., 29, 33): see too 31.8, 51.25, 52.31; Walters 101–20.

conuicti iudiciis aut pro factis iudicium timentes 'whether convicted by the courts or fearing judgement as punishment for their deeds' (*OLD pro*[1] 10): it is not clear whether the chiastically arranged *conuicti* and *timentes* modify *parricidae* and *sacrilegi* (as taken here) or whether they refer to two further groups of persons. The singular suggests, but does not prove, that *iudicium* has a different meaning from *iudiciis*; if that is correct, the repetition illustrates not only polyptoton but also a form of *distinctio*, i.e. the repetition of a word in different senses (Lausberg 296-7 §§660-2). For *conuicti iudiciis* cf. Cic. *Verr.* 3.135.

quos manus atque lingua periurio aut sanguine ciuili alebat 'those whom hand and tongue were feeding [*or perhaps* keeping alive] with perjury and citizen blood' (chiastic). Metaphors of feeding or nourishing are common, esp. with blood or slaughter (e.g. Cic. *Rep.* p. 89 Powell: 'quae sanguine alitur, quae in omni crudelitate sic exultat ut uix hominum acerbis funeribus satietur'). Here *manus* is clearly an 'instrument of violence' (*OLD* 8); for the combination with *lingua* see esp. *Cat.* 3.16 'erat ei consilium ad facinus aptum, consilio autem neque lingua neque manus deerat'.

egestas: 'the correlation between "want/neediness" and personal immorality and criminality became a well-established trope' (Mouritsen, *RE* 92: see further p. 320, index s.vv. '*egens/egestas*').

14.4 quod si quis etiam a culpa uacuus . . . inciderat, . . . ceteris efficiebatur 'And if anyone who was still free of guilt fell into friendship with him, by daily intercourse [*OLD usus* 10] and allurements he was easily made exactly the same as the others', a past general condition (*NLS* 149-51 §§193-4); *etiam* (*OLD* 1a) implies the unlikelihood that anyone was still guiltless; *cotidiano* is to be taken with *illecebris* as well as *usu* (as e.g. Cic. *De Or.* 3.82 'uitam tuam ac studia'; *OLS* 1.1275). Cicero repeatedly refers to C.'s allurements (*Cat.* 1.13, 2.8, *Cael.* 12); S.'s sentence as a whole is recognised as being similar to Theopompus' account of the court of Philip II of Macedon (F224 = Athen. 167B): εἰ δὲ καὶ μὴ τοιοῦτός τις <ὢν> ἐληλύθει, ὑπὸ τοῦ βίου καὶ τῆς διαίτης τῆς Μακεδονικῆς ταχέως ἐκείνοις ὅμοιος ἐγίνετο ('And if anyone was not of this type when he arrived, he quickly became like them because of the Macedonian lifestyle and practice'). For *a culpa uacuus* cf. Apul. *Met.* 10.10.2 (*culpa uacuus* at Tac. *A.* 6.16.3); for *in amicitiam incidere* cf. Cic. *Amic.* 42. *par* and *similis* are a regular coupling: it was proverbial both that like attracts like (cf. Cic. *Cat.* 2.6 'nisi uero si quis est qui Catilinae similis cum Catilina sentire non putet') and that the strongest friendship exists between the like-minded (Otto 264, Tosi 585 §1304, 600-1 §1335); see also 20.4n. (*ea*).

14.5 sed maxime a̲dulescentium familiaritates a̲ppetebat: similarly Cicero refers to the *adulescentuli* to whom C. appealed (*Cat.* 1.13), and he later had to defend M. Caelius against the charge that when an *adulescens* he had been a friend of C.'s (*Cael.* 10–14); see also above, 12.2n. (*igitur*).

eorum animi molles etiam et fluxi dolis haud difficulter capiebantur 'their *animi*, still malleable and unstable, were captivated without difficulty by means of stratagems'. The language is suggestive rather than the imagery clear. *molles* (often used of the *animus*) and *fluxi* perhaps suggest clay or wax for moulding;[42] *dolis . . . capiebantur* (a common expr.) seems to combine the notions of charming, bribing and deluding (*OLD capio* 17, 19–20). For *etiam* see 14.4n. (*quod*).

14.6 ex aetate 'because of his age' (*OLD ex* 18a).

scorta praebere: presumably this means that C. hired prostitutes from a *leno*, thereby acting as a kind of *leno* himself. Cf. *Cat.* 2.8.

canes atque equos mercari: hounds and horses symbolise 'gilded youth' (Sherwin-White on Plin. *Ep.* 9.12.1 'Castigabat quidam filium suum quod paulo s̲u̲m̲p̲t̲u̲o̲s̲i̲u̲s̲ *equos et canes* e̲m̲e̲r̲e̲t̲', possibly an allusion to S., who has *sumptui* in the next clause). Hounds would be used for hunting (Gratt. *Cyn.* 150–496); horses might also be used for hunting (ibid. 497–541), although racing too was an attractive sport (7.4n. *in decoris*). See also Eyben 102–3.

postremo neque sumptui neque modestiae suae parcere 'in short, he showed no consideration either to his resources or to his sense of decency' (*OLD postremo* 4), i.e. he spent extravagantly and behaved unrestrainedly.

dum illos obnoxios f̲idosque sibi f̲aceret 'provided that he made them subservient and loyal to himself'; for *dum* = 'provided that' see *NLS* 178–9 §220. *obnoxius*, frequent (8×) in S. (with *sibi* again at 23.3), seems more notable for its absence from Cicero and Caesar than for any archaising *color*, though it does occur in several early authors. For *fidos . . . faceret* see 11.5 (and n. *quo*).

14.7 scio fuisse nonnullos qui ita existimarent . . .: responsibility for the report of sexual activity is displaced to contemporaries. *ita* either looks forward to the following or. obl. (*OLD* 15b) or means 'therefore' (*OLD* 5), i.e. as a result of C.'s behaviour as described in the previous sentence.

parum h̲oneste pudicitiam h̲abuisse 'had treated their chastity rather dishonourably' (*OLD habeo* 22a): a euphemistic circumlocution for having passive sexual relations with C.

sed ex aliis rebus . . . haec fāmă uălēbāt 'but this rumour thrived for other reasons rather than because the matter had been discovered/ proved by anyone' (*OLD ex* 18a): presumably S. means that Cicero accused C. of homosexual relations, both active and passive (*Cat.* 2.4, 8, 23, *Red.*

---

[42] It is interesting that Horace, alongside listing young men's liking for horses and hounds and their spendthrift ways, uses the same image at *AP* 161–4, although he seems to be talking about youths who are a little younger.

Sen. 10, *Dom.* 62), but that such accusations were conventional in Roman invective, as indeed they were: see e.g. C. A. Williams, *Roman homosexuality* (1999) 149–50. For *fama ualebat* cf. Cic. *Mur.* 38, Liv. 8.17.6, 21.60.4, Tac. *A.* 15.59.1.

compertum foret has the same meaning as *compertum esset*. The use of *forem* instead of *essem* is common in S., although he uses *essem* an almost identical number of times: see Lowrance 183–5, who concludes: '*forem*, though doubtless in good literary standing in the time of Plautus, was later an archaic and colloquial word. Its use by subsequent writers, especially Sallust, smacks of archaism of the affected sort' (189). Tacitus, like Livy, imitated S. in this regard (W–M on *A.* 3.14.4). See further 23.3n. (*et minari*).

15.1 Iam primum is picked up by *postremo* (2). For the period referred to see below (n. *cum sacerdote*).

multa nefanda stupra: *stuprum* is 'an illicit sexual act, whether an adulterous liaison or a forcible violation'; the act might be homosexual or heterosexual, and the term 'is not necessarily used of a violation perpetrated against the will of the victim' (Adams, *LSV* 201). For *nefanda s.* cf. Sen. *Phaedr.* 726.

cum uirgine nobili: unknown; a different person from the Vestal (next n.).

cum sacerdote Vestae: the expression (again at Ov. *F.* 5.573, Gell. 10.15.31) varies *uirgine Vestali*, S. having used *uirgine* in the preceding colon. The Vestal's name was Fabia and she was the half-sister of Terentia, Cicero's wife; in 73 BC, when C. was in his mid-thirties, she was tried in the pontifical court on a charge of *incestum*, the technical term for the infringement of a Vestal's virginity and chastity (*OLD* 2; J. J. Lennon, *Pollution and religion in ancient Rome* (2013) 71) and was acquitted (*TLRR* 83 no. 167). Her case, and C.'s involvement in it, have generated far more discussion than this bald summary would suggest: see R. G. Lewis, 'Catilina and the Vestal', *CQ* 51 (2001) 141–9; Cadoux; Syme, *ARR* 158–61, 358–9 (Santangelo); also 35.1n. (*Egregia*).

alia huiusce modi contra ius fasque: *sc. fecerat* from above: '<and> he had done other things of just this kind …'; the context implies that S. is still referring to sexual malpractice. *fas* looks back to *nefanda* (similar repetitions at Virg. *Aen.* 2.155–8, Stat. *Theb.* 9.665–7, 12.97–8). *huiusce modi* (sometimes written as one word) is an extremely common expression and liked by S. (7× in *BC*); -*ce* is an enclitic particle affording a degree of emphasis and is also found when *huius* qualifies other nouns (thus 17.5 'consilii huiusce').

15.2 Aureliae Orestillae: C.'s real and alleged marital relations are baffling (brief summary by Lewis on Ascon. 91) and scholars have great difficulty in separating fact from fiction. If Aurelia Orestilla was the daughter of Cn. Aufidius Orestes (cos. 71), she was descended from a long line of consulars (cf. R. J. Evans, 'Catiline's wife', *Acta Classica* 30 (1987) 69–72); but an oblique statement in Cicero's now fragmentary speech *In Toga Candida* (fr. 19 'ex eodem stupro tibi et uxorem et filiam inuenisti') is explained by Asconius (91.27–92.3) to mean that C. married the daughter that resulted from his adulterous affair with her mother: the name of the mother is unknown, but the daughter is taken to be Orestilla. According to Asconius, the same allegation was made in speeches by L. Lucceius, the very man whom Cicero wanted to write a monograph on his consulship (Intro. p. 11); it reappears (without names attached) at Virg. *Aen.* 6.623 (see D. H. Berry, *CQ* 42 (1992) 419–20) and Plut. *Cic.* 10.3 (without mentioning marriage). Orestilla, who is thought to have married C. in the mid-6os, was still alive in 50 BC, when her daughter (mentioned at 35.3 below) was due to marry Q. Cornificius (Cic. *Fam.* 8.7.2), the poet and addressee of Catullus (38).[43] Orestilla, who was not C.'s first wife (see below), was doubtless related to Q. Mucius Orestinus, the tribune who in 64 vetoed a proposed *lex ambitus* aimed at C. (Ascon. 83, 85–6) but whose ancestry and relationship to the consul of 71 are unsure (D. R. Shackleton Bailey, *Two studies in Roman nomenclature* (1991) 78–9).

cuius praeter formam nihil umquam bonus laudauit: seemingly imitated at Vell. 74.3 'nihil muliebre praeter corpus gerens' (Fulvia), Tac. *A.* 13.45.2 'huic mulieri cuncta alia fuere praeter honestum animum' (Poppaea Sabina). *cuius* is to be taken ἀπὸ κοινοῦ (*apo koinou*, in common) with *formam* and *nihil.* E. Courtney's suggested insertion of *quisquam* is attractive but unnecessary (*RFIC* 133 (2005) 309).

timens priuignum adulta aetate: Syme accepted the evidence that C.'s first wife was one Gratidia, sister of M. Marius Gratidianus, the ex-praetor killed in a hideous manner in the late 8os (cf. *H.* 1.36–7); that C. was his killer (cf. Cic. *Tog. Cand.* frr. 5, 15) is disputed by B. A. Marshall, *CQ* 35 (1985) 124–33. Others think that C.'s first wife was the unnamed woman whom Cicero (*Cat.* 1.14) says that C. murdered in order to be free to marry someone else, presumably Orestilla. See Syme, *ARR* 154–7, 356–7 (Santangelo). Either way, C. evidently had a grown-up son of whom Orestilla was allegedly afraid, a reversal of the convention whereby the stepmother is the object of fear (P. A. Watson, *Ancient stepmothers* (1995)).

pro certo creditur necato filio uacuam domum scelestis nuptiis fecisse: *scelestis*, which means 'doom-laden' or 'cursed' (*OLD* 1a) as well as simply 'wicked', is explained by *necato filio*: since C. killed his son in order to

---

[43] For more on the interesting Cornificius see the commentaries on his poetic fragments by Courtney and Hollis. He was son of the homonym mentioned at 47.4 (n.).

facilitate his marriage to Orestilla, the marriage, when it took place, came accompanied by a curse. As we discover in §§4–5 below, the curse takes the form of deranged behaviour resembling madness. These various elements are the stuff of tragedy, and the similarity of S.'s wording not only to Cicero (*Cat.* 1.14 'cum morte superioris uxoris nouis *nuptiis domum uacuefecisses*') but also to Livy (1.46.9 'cum *domos uacuas* nouo matrimonio *fecissent*') persuaded Skard, *SV* 57–66, that the source of all three texts was a now-lost Latin tragedy. That S. was thinking in terms of tragedy seems certain, especially if the *cognomen* of C.'s latest father-in-law was Orestes; but Skard began from the premiss that, since S. only rarely alludes to the *Catilinarians*, he is unlikely to be alluding to Cicero here. As we see repeatedly, however, S. frequently alludes to these speeches (Appendix II), and it seems to me more likely that S. is describing the murder of the son in the terms used by Cicero to describe the murder of C.'s previous wife (*Cat.* 1.14, above) and that Livy in his turn was alluding to S. or Cicero or both (see Ogilvie on 1.46–8). Whether or not the story of the son's murder was actually true, scholars have seen it alluded to by Catullus at 64.401–2 ('optauit genitor primaeui funera nati | liber ut innuptae poteretur flore nouercae'), but the lines are controversial and the text disputed (see Trimble's n. and on 399–404). For such phrases as *scelestis nuptiis* see Ferri on *Octav.* 141–2.

15.3 quae quidem res ... facinus maturandi 'That circumstance above all seems to me to have been the reason for his hastening on the crime.' The statement is explained in the following sentences: unable to get the murder of his son out of his mind (*conscientia*), C. developed a form of mental hyperactivity which he could not control ('animus ... sedari poterat') and which resulted in his plunging into the conspiracy. This hyperactivity was akin to madness ('ita ... uecordia inerat') and constituted the fulfilment of the curse which he had brought upon himself by his marriage.

Solodow (102) sees this as an ex. of 'emphatic *quidem*' ('*That* circumstance above all ...'), comparing Caes. *G.* 1.53.6 'quae quidem res Caesari non minorem quam ipsa uictoria uoluptatem attulit'; I see it rather as an ex. of 'extending *quidem*' (Solodow 110–19): the preceding allegation is expanded by way of S.'s own view (*mihi*) before he returns to the main narrative at 16.1 below. The use of a gerund + acc. object (instead of a gerundive) is in general 'archaic and post-classical' but the construction is sometimes used 'to stress the verbal notion' (*NLS* 161–2 §206 *Note ii* (c)): here *maturandi* is the point.

15.4 animus impurus ... neque uigiliis neque quietibus sedari poterat 'his polluted mind ... could not be calmed by periods of either waking or sleeping'. This seems to mean that C. suffered from insomnia and no

amount of daytime activity would exhaust him sufficiently to bring on
sleep. There is no doubt a connection between this description and the
uigilia for which C. had a reputation (5.3n.). *animum sedare* is a favourite
expr. of Cicero (e.g. *Part. Or.* 67 'ad sedandos animos'); the rare plur.
quietibus (elsewhere only at Lucr. 1.405, Cic. *Off.* 1.103) presumably means
'periods of sleep' here, just as *paces* at *BJ* 31.20 means 'periods of peace'
(see Brink on Hor. *Epi.* 2.1.102); the usage is facilitated by coordination
with the regular *uigiliis* (cf. 5.4n. *alieni*).

dis hominibusque infestus means 'hostile to gods and men' (as Flor. 2.9
(3.21).12 'dis hominibusque infestus'), but one expects rather the meaning 'with gods and men against him', as if S. had written *infestis* (cf. 52.29).
Some edd. have therefore suggested that *infestus* is passive, 'hateful to' or
'hated by', but there is no parallel for this meaning applied to persons in
classical Latin (*TLL* 7.1.1410.41–3). Perhaps S. means that filicide itself
constitutes hostility to gods and men, in the same way as parricide at Cic.
Rosc. Am. 65 ('cum omnia diuina atque humana iura scelere nefario
polluisset'), a passage with some linguistic similarities to ours.[44]

ita conscientia mentem excitam uastabat 'to such an extent was his
awareness ravaging his excited mind': the awareness is that of the *res* in
§3, which in turn refers to his murder of his son; compare the effect of fear
on Jugurtha at *BJ* 72.2. For the paratactic construction instead of
a consecutive clause see 7.3n. (*tanta*); since *mens* is more normally governed by *excitare* than by *excire*, it is perhaps surprising that no one seems to
have suggested *exci<ta>tam*.

15.5 color exsanguis: the same phrase at Apul. *Met.* 5.18.5 indicates
fear, but paleness could also be a sign of madness (e.g. Cic. *Har. Resp.* 2
'exsanguis ... uecors ... sine colore', *Q.Fr.* 2.3.2 'furens et exsanguis').
The MSS offer *color*, although the grammarian Probus says that S. chose
the archaising *colos* (4.15.14, 23.34 'Sallustius "igitur colos exsanguis"';
also Sacerd. 6.446.11): see Intro. pp. 41–2.

foedi oculi: the adj. is taken to connote bloodshot eyes, a symptom of
madness (Fraenkel on Aesch. *Ag.* 1428), but, since the eyes are a door to
the soul (Otto 147), it also denotes C.'s foulness (~ *animus impurus*). The
chiastic arrangement with *color exsanguis* is repeated in the next colon.

citus modo, modo tardus incessus: Cicero recommends that an even
pace of step indicates propriety and self-control (*Off.* 1.131); according to
Seneca (*Ira* 1.1.3) *citatus gradus* is a sign of insanity. For *modo modo* see
56.4n.

prorsus in facie ͜uultuque ͜uecordia inerat 'in a word, insanity was present
in his demeanour and face' (*prorsus* sums up: *OLD* 4b). *facies* and *uultus* are
often combined, and Latte thinks they are synonymous here (*OR* 27, 31);

---

[44] Prof. C. L. Whitton kindly drew this passage to my attention.

but Gellius (13.30) says that *facies* can refer to the whole body rather than just the face: if so, then *uultu* seems to look back chiastically to *color...oculi*, and *facie* to *citus...incessus*. Cicero stresses C.'s 'madness' (*furor, amentia*) from the very beginning of the *Catilinarians* (e.g. 1.1, 2, 8, 22, 25); cf. esp. *Mur.* 49 'uultus erat ipsius plenus furoris'. S. likes this use of *inesse* to refer to qualities or characteristics (*OLD* 3); elsewhere it is used with the dat. (17.2, 23.2, 40.6, 58.2) or absolutely (25.5).

   16.1 sed iuuentutem...illexerat: *sed* is resumptive; *supra* refers to 14.5–6: for cross-references see 5.7n. (*quae*). S. has in mind *Cat.* 2.8 'quae tanta umquam in ullo iuuentutis illecebra fuit quanta in illo?', and is in turn imitated at Tac. *A.* 6.45.3 'iuuenem illicere' (cf. also Liv. 3.47.7).

   iuuentutem...mala facinora edocebat: for the double acc. with verbs of teaching see *NLS* 10–12 §16.

   16.2 commodare 'he provided'. *falsos* qualifies *testes* as well as *signatores*. Cf. *Cat.* 2.7.

   fidem, fortunas, pericula uilia habere: some take *habere* as a second historic infin. after *commodare*, but the statement 'he regarded their loyalty...as cheap' is unsurprising, whereas 'he commanded them...to regard loyalty, fortunes and dangers as cheap' makes the point that his followers were compelled to rethink their natural assumptions. *habere* (*OLD* 24b) depends on *imperabat* below (*OLD impero* 4d).

   post...maiora alia imperabat 'afterwards, when he had effaced their reputation and sense of shame, he commanded other, more significant things': the construction after *imperabat* is now varied (*OLD* 2a).

   16.3 si causa peccandi in praesens minus suppetebat 'If the pretext for wrongdoing was temporarily less available' (*OLD causa* 5a, *minus* 4a). *in praesens* is deeply cynical: if there was not a pretext at the moment, there soon would be – but why wait?

   nihilo minus...iugulare 'none the less he would frame the innocent in the same way as the guilty and kill them' (*OLD circumuenio* 6). Of course the 'guilty' are not guilty at all; they are simply individuals of whom C. wanted rid. *insons* (again at *H.* 3.15.10) had mostly dropped out of use by S.'s time, although it is preferred to *innocens* by Livy and increasingly by Tacitus (J. N. Adams. 'The language of the later books of Tacitus' *Annals*', *CQ* 22 (1972) 357–8).

   scilicet, ne per otium torpescerent manus aut animus, gratuito potius malus atque crudelis erat 'evidently, to prevent muscle or spirit from becoming sluggish through idleness, he was gratuitously evil and cruel instead', i.e. instead of the non-gratuitous evil and cruelty which he displayed as a matter of course: *potius* (*OLD* 3) is to be taken closely with *gratuito*. C. is often described by Cicero as a 'general and leader' (e.g. *Cat.* 1.5, 10, 27, 2.14); here he behaves like a warped version thereof, inventing tasks to maintain fitness and morale (e.g. Frontin.

Strat. 4.1.15; Malloch on Tac. *A.* 11.20.2): *scilicet* (*OLD* 4) underlines the continuing cynicism. *gratuito* normally means 'without charge'; only here in classical Latin does it mean 'without reason' (*TLL* 6.2.2247.80–1). *per otium . . . animus* seems imitated at Sen. *Ben.* 7.2.2 'animus inerti otio torpet' (the preceding words imitate 2.8, where see n. *dediti*); S. prefers *torpesco* (again at *BJ* 2.4) to the much commoner *torpere*, which he does not use at all.

16.4 aes alienum: see 14.2n. (*alienum*).

largius s̰ṵo̰ ṵs̰i 'having exploited their own property too extravagantly' (*OLD suus* B5, *utor* 8a). At *Cat.* 2.17–27 Cic. lists various categories of C.'s followers (see Dyck's nn.) and in §20 deals with the veterans whom Sulla had rewarded by placing them in colonies (see below, 28.4n. *nonnullos*); S.'s present sentence is almost a paraphrase of Cicero's passage: here compare 'se . . . sumptuosius insolentiusque iactarunt'.

rapinarum et ṵictoriae ṵeteris memores: *ueteris* is to be taken with *rapinarum* as well as *uictoriae* (*OLS* 1.1274–5): see esp. Cic. *Cat.* 2.20 'spem *rapinarum ueterum*'. For the period these men are recalling see 11.4–6 and nn.

opprimendae rei publicae: picked up at 39.4 'rem publicam oppressiset': C.'s 'effect is identified with his intention' (Stone (1999) 55). Compare the ambition of Q. Lucretius Afella (Intro. p. 8): 'ad turbandum statum ciuitatis'.

16.5 in Italia nullus exercitus: recent decades had seen Italy at the mercy of powerful men such as Sulla and Lepidus at the head of an army (see e.g. *CAH* 9.165–228), but by 64 BC, the time in question (see below), this was no longer the case.

Cn. Pompeius in extremis terris bellum gerebat: in 64 BC (17.1n.) Pompey advanced from Pontus into Syria as part of his campaigning in the Third Mithridatic War, which would be concluded in 63 by the death of Mithridates VI (11.5n. *quem*): see *MRR* 2.163–4. The opportuneness of Pompey's absence is mentioned also by Plut. (*Cic.* 10.2) 'in words very close to the phraseology of Sallust' (C. Pelling, 'Plutarch and Catiline', in *Plutarch and history* (2002) 47).

ipsi consulatum petenti refers to C., who was a candidate in 64 for the consulship in the following year; the others were P. Sulpicius Galba, C. Antonius (21.3n.), L. Cassius Longinus (17.3n.), Q. Cornificius (47.4n.), C. Licinius Sacerdos and of course Cicero (cf. Ascon. 82.4–9). *petere* is a technical term (*OLD* 9a).

senatus nihil s̰a̰n̰ḛ intentus: in mid-64, the date which S. is about to mention (17.1), Cicero had spoken of the danger posed by C. (*Tog. Cand.* fr. 21: see Woodman (2021a) 57–8) and later would complain repeatedly that the senate had not taken C.'s threat seriously enough (e.g. *Cat.* 1.30, *Mur.* 51). *nihil sane* = 'in no way at all' (*OLD sane* 4b).

<u>tutae</u> <u>tranquillaeque</u> res omnes, sed ea <u>prorsus</u> <u>opportuna</u>
Catilinae: S. adheres to the rule that 'the last item in a preface ought to be
that to which the beginning of the next section can most conveniently be
linked' (Quint. 4.1.76). *prorsus* ('absolutely') intensifies *opportuna* (*OLD*
2a). The association of *opportunus* with *portus* (Fest. 190 'opportune dicitur
ab eo quod nauigantibus maxime utiles optatique sunt portus') suggests
that S. is thinking in nautical terms (cf. Cic. *Planc.* 94 'an ... si ... petat
portum ... non minus tutum atque tranquillum, cum tempestate
pugnem ...?', Petron. 123, line 236 'tuta ... tranquillaque litora');
C. will take advantage of the favourable conditions, like any sailor (cf.
Liv. 45.30.4 'maritimas quoque opportunitates ei praebent portus ad
Toronen ... alii ad Hellespontum opportune uersi'), but only to disrupt
them himself. *ea* (neut. plur.) refers back to *res omnes* (10.1–2nn.).

17–22 THE SECRET MEETING: c. 1 JUNE 64

The main narrative of the *Bellum Catilinae* begins appropriately with
a secret meeting of conspirators in mid-64 BC, when C. was a candidate
for the consulship of 63 (cf. 16.5, 20.17, 21.5), although the story is
interrupted by a digression on an earlier conspiracy in 66–65 BC (18–
19). The centrepiece of the main episode is C.'s speech in *oratio recta*
(20.2–17), which is preceded by a list of his conspiratorial auditors
(17.3–7) and followed by a supplementary speech in *oratio obliqua* (21).
The episode is formally concluded by ring composition (21.5 *conuentum* ~
20.1 *conuenisse* ~ 17.3 *conuenere*), after which a parenthetical paragraph
(22) separates this episode from the next.

   C.'s speech, which is dated (17.1) to a similar period as Cicero's *In Toga
Candida* and may perhaps be regarded as a counterpart to it,[45] is defined as
a military *hortatio* but contains elements more appropriate to a campaign
speech (20.1n. *in rem*). Many scholars believe that it is implausible that
C. should be plotting revolution before the elections of 64 were decided
(for which cf. 24.1).[46] They therefore conclude that S. has retrojected to
mid-64 a conspiracy which did not form until after C.'s second electoral
rejection in mid-63 and in particular that C.'s speech at 20–1 has been
transposed to the present moment from the *contio domestica* 'that belongs
to the electoral season of 63' (Syme, *ARR* 166, referring to Cic. *Mur.* 50).
There are two seemingly fatal flaws in this hypothesis. First, not only is

---

[45] Cicero's now-lost speech was delivered a few days before the consular elections
   of 64 (Ascon. 82.1, 83.11–12) and did in fact provoke C. into responding
   (Ascon. 93.24–5), although the speeches which he is given by S. here are clearly
   quite different in nature.
[46] A laudable exception is Stone (1998).

C. made to stress his candidature in both speeches (20.17, 21.3, 5) but he also makes revolutionary plans in 63, when he was a consular candidate for 62 (cf. 26.1). Historiography had to be plausible, and, as a contemporary of events, S. evidently saw no inconsistency between conspiracy and consular candidature. According to Appian, C. 'announced his candidature for the consulship with the intention of making this his route to tyranny' (*BC* 2.2.4). Second, the revolutionary speech mentioned at Cic. *Mur.* 50 was delivered *before* the elections of 63, a fact obscured by Syme's deliberately vague reference to 'the electoral season of 63'. See further Woodman (2021a) 63–5.

17.1 circiter Kalendas Iunias L. Caesare et C. Figulo consulibus: 1 June 64 BC, the first of five dated days in the work (cf. 18.5–6, 30.1);[47] the consular dating formula in the abl. abs. is appropriate at the start of the narrative proper,[48] but the Kalends are not those of January, as might have been expected in a 'normal' annalistic history: see R. Cowan, 'Not the consular year: perverting annalistic time in Sallust', *Histos* 14 (2020) 70–115, at 85–6. Although most scholars believe that the meeting which S. is about to describe did not take place in 64 (see intro.), they nevertheless infer from the reference to June that in the year 64 the consular elections were expected in July: see Ramsey (2019) 218, 255–6; also below, 24.1n. (*comitiis*). L. Julius Caesar (a distant relative of the future dictator) was brother-in-law of the conspirator P. Lentulus Sura (below, 3n.), who was the second husband of his sister Julia:[49] see *BNP* 6.1054–5 [I 6]. Little is known about C. Marcius Figulus: see *BNP* 8.311 [I 12]. Both consuls supported the execution of the conspirators (Cic. *Att.* 12.21.1); neither is mentioned by S. again. *circiter* is here a prep. + acc.

primo singulos appellare 'he first accosted/addressed individuals' (*OLD appello*[2] 1), perhaps with the extra implication that he called them by name (cf. 21.4), an important task both for generals (59.5n.) and for electoral candidates (*Comm. Petit.* 28, 41–2). *primo* and *singulos* are picked up by *ubi satis explorata sunt* and *in unum omnes conuocat* respectively below (2).

hortari alios, alios temptare 'he encouraged some, tried to influence others' (*OLD tempto* 6): the (chiastic) words are explanatory of *singulos appellare*. Cf. also 20.1 and n.

opes suas ... docere 'he told them about ...' (*docere* + acc. is regular). C. had enriched himself as governor of Africa in 67–66 (18.3), but he is described as a spendthrift (14.6) and in debt (Cic. *Cat.* 1.14), 'having

---

[47] In the narrative of the main conspiracy this is also the only date which is not to be found in (and hence is not dependent on) Cic. *Cat.*

[48] It is much more common at this period still to pair the consuls' names in asyndeton, as at *H.* 1.1, but S. coordinates again at 18.2 and 38.1 and elsewhere.

[49] Her first husband had been M. Antonius Creticus and one of their offspring was Mark Antony.

reduced himself to poverty in order to gratify his ambition' (App. *BC* 2.2.4).

imparatam rem publicam 'the *unpreparedness of* the commonwealth': one could supply *esse* ('that the commonwealth was unprepared'), but this is probably an ex. of the so-called '*ab urbe condita* idiom', of which S. is fond (e.g. 18.1, 31.7) and in which 'the noun together with the predicative participle forms an abstract noun-phrase wherein the leading idea is conveyed by the participle' (see *NLS* 75–6 §95). For the lack of preparation see 16.5n. (*senatus*).

17.2 quibus maxima necessitudo et plurimum audaciae inerat 'who were possessed of the greatest need and the most radicalism' (*OLD insum* 3; above, 15.5n. *prorsus*). The distinction between *necessitudo* and *necessitas* is discussed at Gell. 13.3. Both nouns can mean 'need' in various senses; the former commonly means 'bond, tie' too, a meaning which *necessitas* very rarely has: S. greatly prefers the former (10×) to the latter (which is only in *H.*: 2×), perhaps because nouns in -*do* were regarded as having greater *dignitas* (2.1n. *etiam*). For some statistics on each noun see Lebek 224–5 and 303. Even if ours is not the only passage in any author where *necessitudo* means 'poverty' (so *OLD* 4), the meaning is certainly very rare (cf. *TLL* 9.1.394.75, 395.16–24). For *audacia* cf. 5.4n. (*animus*). S. has varied the constr. by using the relatively rare *plurimum* + gen.

17.3-4 For discussion of the list of conspirators see Gruen 418–22, Syme, *ARR* 166–8 (elliptical, even by Syme's standards), 361–2 (Santangelo). Comparable lists are given by Cicero (*Cat.* 3.14 with Dyck, *Sull.* 6–7 with Berry); conspiracy narratives tend to begin by listing the conspirators (cf. Liv. 39.17.6, Tac. *A.* 15.49–50), as do battle narratives with catalogues of forces (W.[5] on Tac. *A.* 4.4.3, with bibliog.).

17.3 eo refers to the location implied by the set phrase *in unum* (2), viz. the house mentioned at 20.1.

senatorii ordinis: S. seems to be using this description to include ex-senators, since not all of the eleven men listed here were currently senators (see nn. below). See Ryan 256–7.

P. Lentulus Sura: P. Cornelius Lentulus Sura, brother-in-law of one of the year's consuls (1n.), was an important participant: consul in 71 with Aufidius Orestes (15.2n. *Aureliae*), he had been expelled from the senate in 70 but would regain his rank in 63 by serving as praetor in that year (Plut. *Cic.* 17.1, Dio 37.30.4; *MRR* 2.166). He is mentioned frequently by Cicero in the *Catilinarians*, and in S. is the most frequently named of the conspirators after C. himself. He is led to execution by Cicero personally at 55.2. See *BNP* 3.815 [I 56] and esp. Stone (1999) 72–5.

P. Autronius: P. Autronius Paetus had been designated as consul for 65 together with P. Cornelius Sulla but both were then accused of *ambitus*

(18.2) and expelled from the senate. Frequently mentioned by Cicero (*Sull.*), he was exiled in 58 and died some years later. See *TLRR* 113 no. 229; *BNP* 2.419 [2].

L. Cassius Longinus had been praetor in 66; since in 64 he was a rival candidate with Cicero and C. for the consulship, scholars have argued that he joined the plot only later, after his candidacy had failed. Longinus used a delaying tactic to disguise his flight from Rome (44.2) and later was sentenced to death in his absence (50.4). His fate is unknown. See *BNP* 2.1167 [I 13].

C. Cethegus: according to a *later* plan, C. Cornelius Cethegus would be detailed to murder Cicero at his house (43.2 and n.); he was one of those executed (55.6). See Berry on Cic. *Sull.* 53; *BNP* 3.809–19 [I 12].

P. et Ser. Sullae Ser. filii: these two brothers are mentioned together at Cic. *Sull.* 6; they were prosecuted after the suppression of the conspiracy and seemingly condemned (*TLRR* 113–14 nos. 230 and 233). Publius is not to be confused with his better-known namesake, P. Cornelius Sulla, nephew of the dictator and consul designate for 65 (above and 18.2n.): see Berry on *Sull.* 6 and Appendix I; L. E. Reams (*CJ* 82 (1986–7) 301–5) points out that S.'s only reason for using the description 'Ser. filii' was to distinguish the conspiratorial P. Sulla from P. Sulla the consul designate. Servius recurs at 47.1 below.

L. Vargunteius: he and the *eques* C. Cornelius (4 below) took it upon themselves to murder Cicero at his house on the morning of 7 November 63, although Cicero was forewarned and the plot thwarted (28.1–3). Although Vargunteius is again described as a senator at 28.1, Cicero himself refers to *both* would-be assassins as *equites* (*Cat.* 1.9): scholars mostly assume that Vargunteius, who is known to have been accused of *ambitus* (Cic. *Sull.* 6), had been expelled from the senate after conviction and that this explains the discrepancy between S. and Cicero (see *TLRR* 102 no. 202 and n. 1). The outcome of his trial for conspiracy seems unknown but was presumably conviction (*TLRR* 114 no. 232). See Berry on Cic. *Sull.* 6, Dyck on Cic. *Cat.* 1.9, Syme, *ARR* 361 (Santangelo).

Q. Annius: the name here and at *Comm. Petit.* 10 is used to emend *Q. Manlium Chilonem* to *Q. Annium Chilonem* at Cic. *Cat.* 3.14.

M. Porcius Laeca lived 'inter falcarios' (Cic. *Cat.* 1.8, *Sull.* 52), i.e. in the scythe-makers' quarter (its location is now unknown). It was at his house that the conspirators met on the night of 6–7 November 63 (27.3–4); he was later convicted of conspiracy (*TLRR* 114 no. 231).

L. Bestia: L. Calpurnius Bestia was trib. pleb. in 62, having entered upon that office on 10 December 63; one week later his role in the conspiracy would be to attack Cicero in a public speech, a signal for mayhem to follow (43.1). There is no other explicit evidence of his participation in the plot, although he and his colleague in the tribunate, Q. Metellus Nepos, attacked Cicero on 29 December, his last day of office, for his role in the punishment of the conspirators and prevented him from delivering the speech customary for an outgoing consul (Plut. *Cic.* 23.1–3). See Berry on Cic. *Sull.* 31 and 34. Syme has suggested that S., for reasons of personal animosity, has 'shoved in Bestia', adding his name to the list of conspirators after the man's death (at an unknown date) and in the process transposing his attack on Cicero from one context to another (*Sall.* 131–3, *ARR* 128–36).

Q. Curius: his principal function in the narrative is as Cicero's informant (26.3, 28.2). For his problematic identity and status see on 23.1–4, where he is described as having been expelled from the senate.

17.4 ex equestri ordine varies the gen. *senatorii ordinis* above (3).

M. Fuluius Nobilior: 'the knight with a name redolent of history' (Syme, *ARR* 167). Although this Fulvius does not recur in S.'s narrative, there are 'Fulvia the spy' at 23.3 and Fulvius the victim of filicide at 39.5: 'Sallust had a certain interest in the Fulvii, a great domestic house of the plebeian *nobilitas* now in decay, but high in notoriety' (Syme, ibid.; also 182–5). Cicero in 54 writes that 'M. Fuluius Nobilior condemnatus est' (*Att.* 4.18 (92).3); perhaps identical with the conspirator.

L. Statilius, P. Gabinius Capito: both feature prominently in S.'s narrative (e.g. 43.2) and are executed (55.6). Cicero calls the latter 'Cimber' (*Cat.* 3.6), but whether this is an insulting nickname or an alternative *cognomen* is disputed (see Dyck ad loc.).

C. Cornelius: along with L. Vargunteius (above), he volunteered to murder Cicero on 7 November (28.1); Plutarch (*Cic.* 16.1) understandably confuses him with C. Cornelius Cethegus, a would-be murderer of Cicero on a later occasion (above, 3n.). The outcome of his trial is uncertain but was presumably conviction (*TLRR* 113 no. 228). See further Cic. *Sull.* 6, 18 (and Berry ad locc.), 52; *BNP* 3.808 [I 3].

ex coloniis et municipiis: this doublet (again at 58.9 and common in Cic., e.g. *Cat.* 2.24) is 'constantly used of Italian towns, and so comes to be an equivalent for "Italy"' (H. J. Cunningham, *CQ* 8 (1914) 132). Originally the distinction between the two types of community was that a *colonia* had been set up by Rome, whereas a *municipium* was an independent town incorporated into the Roman state.

domi nobiles is an otherwise rare expr., used by Cicero esp. in the *Verrines* (6×), for persons who were dignitaries in their local communities. Cf. Liv. 8.19.4 'uir non domi solum sed etiam Romae clarus'.

17.5 dominationis spes hortabatur: *d. spes* is picked up by Tacitus (*A.* 12.8.2, 14.2.2); *hortari* with an abstract noun as subject (*TLL* 6.3.3008.25–39) recurs at 20.15, 58.19.

17.6 quibus in otio ... **copia erat** 'for whom it was possible to live at leisure in magnificence or comfort' (*OLD copia* 7, more normally with the gen. than an infin.). *uiuere* is modified by *magnifice* again at Cic. *Fin.* 4.69, *Off.* 1.92 and by *molliter* at Cic. *Off.* 1.106, Ov. *Tr.* 3.1.24, Sen. *Ep.* 82.2.

incerta pro certis, bellum quam pacem malebant: such contrasts (again at 20.2, 41.2) are proverbial (Otto 81, Tosi 773 §1731) and appealed esp. to Tacitus (e.g. *H.* 2.86.3 'pro certis et olim partis noua, ambigua, ancipitia malebat' with Ash's n., *A.* 4.3.4 and W.[5]). S. has varied the contrasts by *pro ~ quam.*

17.7 fuere item ea tempestate qui crederent M. Licinium Crassum non ignarum eius consilii fuisse 'There were in addition some at that time who believed that M. Licinius Crassus had not been unaware of the plan': after such expressions as *sunt qui, est qui,* etc. (again at 19.4, 22.1, 36.4, 48.7, 61.8) the subjunctive is regular (*NLS* 118 §158, G&L 404 §631.2) but not universal (39.5n. *Fuere*). *item* (*OLD* 4) refers back to §5: some *nobiles* were secret members of the plot, but Crassus' membership was only a matter of belief. The tenses are important: *ea tempestate* refers to late 63, when the conspiracy had become public knowledge and measures were taken against it (cf. 48.5 'pars ... uerum existimabant'), and *fuisse* refers to the summer of 64, which S. is currently describing. Like C. himself, Crassus had served under Sulla in 83–82, recruiting forces, conducting sieges and then enriching himself during the proscriptions (*MRR* 2.65, 71). After successfully defeating the rebel Spartacus in 72, he was elected consul in 70 (cf. 38.1) and joined Pompey and Caesar in a political alliance ten years later in 60/59; he was consul again in 55 and was responsible for the notorious Roman defeat by the Parthians at Carrhae in 53, where he died (*MRR* 2.126, 214–15, 230). For him see *BNP* 7.524–5 [I 11]; A. M. Ward, *Marcus Crassus and the late Roman Republic* (1977); M. T. Schettino, *Marcus Licinius Crassus: pratique et conception du pouvoir* (2023). On his appearance in S., Syme, *ARR* 158–65, 358–61 (Santangelo); also below, 18.1 (n. *Sed*), 48.4–9. For *ea tempestate* cf. 7.1n. (*ea*).

quia Cn. Pompeius ... **ductabat:** the verb is indic. either because the clause is a factual comment by S. or (more likely) because S., like Livy and Tacitus, sometimes retains the indic. in subordinate clauses in indir. speech (e.g. 27.4). For Pompey's army see 16.5n.; for *ductare* see 11.5n. (*quem*), 19.3n. (*ab*).

inuisus ipsi 'whom he [*sc.* Crassus] hated'.

cuiusuis opes uoluisse ... **crescere:** *uoluisse* is infin. because the or. obl. continues after *crederent* above; Crassus continues as subject: '(they believed) that he had wanted anyone's influence to grow in opposition to that man's powerfulness'. For *potentia* see 12.1n.

simul confisum ... **prīncĭpēm sē fŏrĕ** 'being at the same time confident that, if the conspiracy succeeded, he would easily be the chief amongst them'. *ualuisset* (*OLD* 7) represents a fut. perf. indic. in direct speech. The double cretic clausula is a Sallustian favourite (K–K 169).

18–19 Digression. The First Conspiracy: 66–65 BC

These two chapters constitute a retrospective digression, framed programmatically by ring composition (18.1–2 'Sed <u>antea</u> item <u>coniurauere</u> pauci ... *de qua quam breuissime potero dicam* ~ 19.6 *de* <u>superiore coniuratione</u> *satis dictum*). S.'s subject is the first Catilinarian conspiracy, which, in the opinion of Syme and of most other modern scholars, never happened (*Sall.* 88–102);[50] but I have argued elsewhere that the evidence relating to the First Conspiracy has been misinterpreted and that there are no good grounds for rejecting what S. says (Woodman (2021a) 55–63). Syme also said that the digression 'is not well placed' and would have had 'a better lodgment' before 17.1 (*Sall.* 99–100), but that is not at all the case. Since at the start of the conspiracy C. was only an inconsiderable participant (18.1) and it was the changing circumstances which saw him cast in a leading role (18.2–5), the brilliant transition from 16.5 ('sed ea prorsus opportuna Catilinae') to 17.1 ('Igitur ...') would have been rendered impossible. As it is, the digression is motivated formally by the reference at 17.7 to Crassus and his antipathy to Pompey, since Cn. Piso, a member of the first conspiracy (18.4), was known by Crassus to be an enemy of Pompey (19.1), who may have been involved in Piso's death, the point at which the digression ends (19.5).

18.1 Sed ... pauci: no mention is made of Crassus in the following list of conspirators, but it seems that Cicero, in a work perhaps entitled *Consilia* and not published until after his death, accused Crassus of being the architect of the first conspiracy (F4C = Ascon. 83 'eius quoque coniurationis quae ... facta est a Catilina et Pisone arguit M. Crassum auctorem fuisse' with Drummond ad loc. in *FRHist* 3.479). Crassus' alleged involvement here would lend credence to the stories of his involvement in 64 (17.7). The use of *sed* to introduce the digression somewhat resembles its use at 8.1 or 53.2.

18.1–2 ... in quis Catilina fuit; de qua quam breuissime potero dicam: the fourth-century grammarian Diomedes cites S.'s words thus in order to illustrate the *constructio ad sensum* whereby the antecedent of *qua* is *coniuratione*, understood from *coniurauere pauci* above

---

[50] S. 'describes the so-called First Conspiracy ... as historical fact', says Ledworuski (366), who regards it (167–86) as the most substantial of the many factual and chronological mistakes which she alleges in the *BC* and, with accompanying graphs and tables, classifies according to numerous different categories.

(1.445.23);[51] the MSS universally have *quibus* instead of *quis* and *uerissime* instead of *breuissime*. Editors have generally printed *quis* but retained *uerissime*, but this is somewhat paradoxical (Woodman (2007b) 221–2). Although *quis* for *quibus* recurs only once in the *BC*, at 31.1, where it depends on a quotation by Fronto (n.), it is frequent in *BJ* and *H*. It is true that the same phrase *quam uerissime potero* was used by S. earlier at 4.3; but there the words are part of a larger argument (4.2) in which he is presenting himself as an unbiased writer, for which *ueritas* and its cognates are standard terms (n.). It is not obvious that bias is in question in the present digression, and I suspect that editors have preferred *uerissime* both because they think it refers straightforwardly to 'truth' and because it suits the common view that there is something strange about the first conspiracy. Brevity, on the other hand, is a standard requirement in digressions (Quint. 4.2.104); the phrase *quam breuissime potero* (*potui* etc.) seems almost formulaic (e.g. Cic. *ND* 2.3, *Div.* 1.70, Vitr. 10.8.1, Quint. 1.10.1, 5.7.37, Apul. *Apol.* 48); and S. concludes his account with an implicit affirmation of brevity (19.6 'de superiore coniuratione satis dictum'), picking up *breuissime* at the start. Mariotti prints *breuissime* (but not *quis!*) and notes that S.'s later digression on Africa is framed similarly (*BJ* 18.2 'quam paucissimis absoluam' ~ 19.8 'de Africa … satis dictum').[52] The letters *b* and *u* are frequently confused in MSS.

18.2 L. Tullo et M'. Lepido consulibus: once again, as at 17.1 (n.), S. begins with a consular date (66 BC). L. Volcacius Tullus was the consul in charge of the consular elections from which C. was disbarred (Ascon. 89.9–12: see below, 3n. *post paulo*); neither he nor M'. Aemilius Lepidus recurs in the narrative.

P. Autronius et P. Sulla, designati consules, legibus ambitus interrogati, poenas dederant: Autronius was one of the conspirators (17.3n.); P. Cornelius Sulla, the man defended in 62 by Cicero in the *Pro Sulla*, is not to be confused with his lesser-known namesake, brother of Servius and also a conspirator (17.3n.). The two designates were successfully prosecuted for bribery by L. Aurelius Cotta and the L. Manlii Torquati (father and son) respectively (see *TLRR* 100–1 nos. 200–1): see further below, 5n. (*Kalendis*). *legibus* (*lege*) *interrogare* is a set phrase = 'to arraign, indict' (*OLD interrogo* 4).

---

[51] Diomedes, on whom see Zetzel 294–5, cites the whole of the first sentence but omits the words *contra rem publicam*.

[52] Kurfess in his Teubner edition (Addenda, pp. 198–9) came round to thinking that *breuissime* was probably the correct reading.

18.3 post paulo pecuniarum repetundarum reus, prohibitus erat consulatum petere quod intra legitimos dies profiteri nequiuerat: this sentence raises numerous problems. (a) Although S. clearly states that C. offered himself as a consular candidate only for the re-run election of 66 ('post paulo'), numerous scholars (e.g. Syme, *Sall.* 88, 91, 100) refuse to accept this and maintain that he stood as a candidate at the first election, something for which there is no evidence and contradicted by Cic. *Sull.* 68. (b) S. says that C. was disqualified from standing as a candidate because he failed to submit his name within the specified period ('quod ... nequiuerat'). Other scholars refuse to accept this and maintain that C. was disqualified because he 'had not been a candidate at the first election' (Seager (1964) 338). This interpretation is inexplicable.

(c) During his governorship of Africa in 67–66 C.'s financial depredations had been so extortionate that the locals sent envoys to Rome to complain even before he left to return to Rome (Ascon. 85.3–6; *MRR* 2.147, 155). Since the reason for C.'s disqualification as a consular candidate is explicitly provided by *quod ... nequiuerat*, S.'s reference to extortion ('pecuniarum repetundarum reus') seems unlikely to be causal; and indeed scholars generally accept that a charge of extortion (as opposed to actually being on trial for extortion) did not disqualify a candidate from standing for office (see e.g. G. V. Sumner, 'The consular elections of 66 BC', *Phoenix* 19 (1965) 226–31, at 227–8; B. A. Marshall, 'Catilina: court cases and consular candidature', *SCI* 3 (1976–7) 127–37). Since C.'s trial for extortion did not take place until the second half of 65, twelve months later (*TLRR* 106–7 no. 212), *reus* cannot mean that C. was literally 'a defendant' in 66 but must refer to some kind of quasi-formal preliminary charges, such as those brought by the African envoys: the adj. gives the circumstances in which C. offered himself as a candidate and was disqualified (cf. Ascon. 89.11–12 with J. T. Ramsey, *HSCP* 86 (1982) 122–5). For *profiteri* = 'to submit one's name as a candidate' see *OLD* 2b; *reus* + gen. of the charge is regular. *post paulo* recurs in Caesar, Sallust (56.3, *BJ* 74.1, 106.3), Livy, Horace and Quintilian; *paulo post*, the normal order in Cicero, is also found in S. (28.1, 51.34, *BJ* 36.2, 71.5), Caesar and Livy.

18.4 Cn. Piso, adulescens nobilis: little is known of Cn. Calpurnius Piso apart from what we are told in this digression. Syme noted 'the malignant care with which the historian attaches the label of noble birth to disreputable characters' (*ARR* 174, quoting also 5.1, 23.3, 43.2, 55.6).

audaciae: see 5.4n. (*animus*).

egens: see 14.3n. (*egestas*).

18.5 cum hoc Catilina et Autronius ... parabant: *cum hoc* is fronted because it is to be taken in common (*apo koinou*) with *communicato* and *parabant*. The date of 5 December, which goes with *communicato*, is otherwise unattested, but it would be on the same day three years later that the conspirators were executed (55.2–6). It will be noticed that C., having been only one of several conspirators at 18.1, is now playing a leading role along with Autronius. For *circiter* see 17.1n.

Kalendis Ianuariis L. Cottam et L. Torquatum consules interficere: L. Aurelius Cotta and the elder L. Manlius Torquatus were elected consuls for 65 only after the original designates, Autronius and P. Sulla, had been disqualified for bribery (18.2n.; *MRR* 2.157). Neither Cotta nor Torquatus is mentioned again in the narrative; in 62 P. Sulla would be accused by Torquatus' son of participation in the Catilinarian conspiracy and defended successfully by Cicero in the *Pro Sulla*. Some scholars have thought that the proposal for Cotta and Torquatus to be murdered on 1 January 65 and replaced by C. and Autronius (below) is a mistaken inference from Cic. *Sull.* 68, where Cicero repeats an allegation that P. Sulla plotted to kill the elder Torquatus and to make himself consul on 1 January, presumably with Autronius as his colleague (so Dyck on Cic. *Cat.*, Intro., pp. 2–3). The real plan, according to this scenario, was to kill the consuls designate on 29 December 66 (see further below, 6n. *ea re*), thus leaving their positions vacant the following morning; but, while such a plan may seem more practical, it lacks the dramatic symbolism of a coup on 1 January.

ipsi fascibus correptis ...: i.e. C. and Autronius would appoint themselves consuls (36.1n. *cum*).

Pisonem ... ad obtinendas duas Hispanias mittere: at this time there were two Spanish provinces, Citerior (down the eastern side of the Iberian peninsula) and Ulterior (along the south); in the event Piso would take charge (*OLD obtineo* 3, a technical term) only of the former (see 19.1 and nn.). The sending of a governor to Spain would evoke memories of Q. Sertorius, who had been sent there to govern two decades previously but, having been ousted subsequently, embarked on a rebellion which despite the best efforts of Pompey (who was despatched to oppose him) lasted until his murder in 73 (*BNP* 13.322–3). Sertorius features often in the fragments of S.'s *Historiae*.

18.6 ea re cognita rursus in Nonas Februarias consilium caedis transtulerant: the date of 5 February occurs in no other source and is seemingly accepted as genuine even by those scholars who think that the rest of S.'s account is pure fiction (e.g. Seager (1964) 345). *rursus* is difficult to translate but combines the notions of 'so as to restore things as they were before' and 'in repetition of an action' (*OLD* 2–3).

According to Cicero, speaking in early November 63 (*Cat.* 1.15), it was common knowledge that on the last day (29th) of December 66, C. had stood in the Comitium armed with a weapon and had assembled a group of men for the purpose of killing the consuls and community leaders. Scholars who deny that there was a first conspiracy are anxious to maintain that C.'s armed presence (which they accept) had nothing to do with a plot to murder the new consuls the next day but was connected with C. Manilius' trial for extortion (*TLRR* 103 no. 205), which was due to begin on 29 December and which C. was anxious to prevent (Seager (1964) 344–5). Yet C.'s armed presence on the eve of a murderous plot seems too much of a coincidence, and not everyone has been convinced by the hypothesis of Manilius' trial. S.'s statement nevertheless seems totally implausible: if 'the matter was detected' ('ea re cognita'), how is it that C. and Autronius were not apprehended immediately but were left free to defer their plan to a later date? The likelihood is that when C. equipped himself with a sword on 29 December, he did *not* intend it to be seen by the general public (carrying a weapon with criminal intent was illegal: 27.2n. *ipse*); but such was his incompetence as a plotter – which would be amply demonstrated on 5 February 65, when he gave the signal prematurely – that the sword *was* seen: those who saw it would no doubt have deduced some criminal intent, but, since they would not have known what the intent was, he and Autronius were free to defer their murder to early February. It was only later, when C.'s aims were better understood, that people put two and two together and realised why he had been carrying a sword on 29 December 66: this explains why Cicero, writing almost three years after the event, was able to refer to common knowledge, and why S., writing two decades after that, was able to write *ea re cognita*. See further Woodman (2021a) 60–1.

18.7 iam tum … plerisque senatoribus perniciem machinabantur: Cicero would refer to 'caedem optimatum' (*Tog. Cand.* fr. 21), which Asconius interpreted as 'caedem senatus' (92.17), and to 'consilium senatus interficiendi' (*Mur.* 81). S.'s sentence appears to be a reworking of *Cat.* 1.2 'pestem quam tu in nos omnes *iam* diu machinaris', where Cicero seems also to refer to the First Conspiracy. With *tum* S. contrasts the present version of the plan (§§6–7) with the earlier (§5), while *iam* anticipates the later plans for more widespread murder in the main conspiracy. *perniciem machinari* is unparalleled and *pestem m.* recurs at Cic. *ND* 3.66.

18.8 quod ni Catilina maturasset … facinus patratum foret 'And, if C. had not been precipitate in giving the signal to his associates in front of the senate house, on that day there would have been perpetrated the worst deed/crime since the foundation of the city of Rome.' The drama and effectiveness of this sentence are heightened in four ways. (1) The counterfactual presentation, as e.g. *BJ* 53.7 'paene imprudentia admissum facinus miserabile, ni utrimque praemissi equites rem explorauissent', Tac. *Agr.* 37.4 'quod ni … iussisset, acceptum aliquod uulnus … foret'; Chausserie-Laprée 597–617. (2) The focus on 'the day' itself (see e.g.

Oakley on Liv. 6.25.3, Murgatroyd on Tib. 1.7.3–4, Harrison on Virg. *Aen.*
10.508, W.² on Vell. 86.1), a device used by Cicero too for the same
occasion (*Tog. Cand.* fr. 21 'paene acerbum et luctuosum rei publicae
diem'). (3) The reference to the foundation of Rome, as e.g. Tac.
H. 3.72.1 'id facinus post conditam urbem luctuosissimum foedissimum-
que rei publicae populi Romani accidit'. (4) Since the first syllable of
patratum may be either long or short, it is not clear whether the clausula
is molossus + cretic or double cretic, but each is a favourite of Ciceronian
oratory (K–K 176).

C.'s premature signal gave Syme 'grounds for scepticism or ridicule'
(*Sall.* 95), but it is confirmed by Asconius (92.18–20 'quod prius quam
parati essent coniuratis signum dedisset'): after C.'s lateness in submitting
his name as a candidate in 66 (§3), S. is surely making the point that the
incompetent ringleader had a problem with timekeeping.[53] For the '*ab
urbe condita* idiom' see 17.1n. (*imparatam*). No other ex. of the *post conditam
urbem* formula includes the name *Romam*, which perhaps originated as
a marginal gloss. *maturo* + infin. normally means 'to hurry to ~' but here
has the extra nuance of being 'too quick' (*OLD* 2b). For *facinus* see 2.9n.
(*praeclari*); *patrare*, liked by S. and other historians but otherwise relatively
uncommon, is discussed alongside *ductare*, and for the same reason, by
Quintilian (8.3.44), who regards both as archaising (see 11.5n. *quem*, and
Malloch on Tac. *A.* 11.28.2, with other exs. of *patrare facinus*). *foret = esset*
(14.7n. *sed*).

quia nondum frequentes armati conuenerant 'Because the armed men
had not yet assembled in force' (*frequentes* is predicative).

ea res: i.e. the premature signal and the absence of armed men.

19.1 Postea Piso … missus est: if *postea* is to be taken literally, he was
despatched after 5 Feb. 65; by the summer of the following year he would
be dead (19.3n.). See *MRR* 2.159, 163.

quaestor pro praetore: i.e. quaestor with praetorian rank (*OLD praetor*
2d), an appointment confirmed epigraphically (*ILS* 875 'Cn. Calpurnius
Cn. f. Piso quaestor pro pr. ex s.c. prouinciam Hispaniam citeriorem
optinuit'): see Pina Polo and Díaz Fernández 228.

adnitente Crasso: this is a good ex. of an 'appendix sentence' facilitated
by an abl. abs., a phenomenon which becomes esp. common in Tacitus
(see e.g. W.³ on Tac. *Agr.*, pp. 32–3). The role of Crassus is generally
accepted (e.g. by Syme, *Sall.* 88–9, 100, *ARR* 358–9 (Santangelo)), but

---

[53] It is obviously possible that C.'s armed presence in the Comitium on the day
preceding the planned murder on 1 January has become confused with his
premature signal in front of the Curia in February. The Comitium was in front of
the Curia, and on both alleged occasions C.'s presence resulted in the planned
murder being abandoned.

his was a personal hostility towards Pompey (next n.) and to be distinguished from the more general fear experienced by the senate and others
(§2).

quod eum in̲festum, in̲imicum Cn. Pompeio cognouerat: for Crassus'
hostility to Pompey see e.g. Plut. *Crass.* 12.2, *Pomp.* 22.2–3; Gruen 40–1. It
is difficult to know whether S.'s alliterative words are two adjs. in asyndeton
('hostile and unfriendly') or adj. + noun ('a hostile enemy'). The latter
type of pleonasm in expressions of hostility is not uncommon (e.g. *BJ* 23.2
'hostem infestum [*sc.* esse]', Tac. *Agr.* 7.1 'hostiliter populatur'), but
asyndeton seems more likely, given the frequent coupling of *infestus* and
inimicus, esp. in Cicero (e.g. *II Verr.* 1.12 'infesto atque inimico'), and the
general popularity of asyndetic privatives in *in-*. Adams (*AILL* 571) is
undecided.

    19.2 quippe … esse uolebat: although Suetonius and Dio agree that
the senate wanted Piso out of Rome, the reason they give is that he had
revolutionary aspirations (Suet. *DJ* 9.3 'ob suspicionem urbanae coniurationis', Dio 36.44.5 'When Piso's revolutionary stance continued even so
[ἐθρασύνετο], the senate was afraid that he would cause disturbance and
immediately sent him to Spain').[54] It seems very odd to bestow an official
posting to Spain, of all places (18.5n. *Pisonem*), on a man whose revolutionary tendencies were known and feared, but this is not the version of
events which appears in S. He does not specify of what Piso's 'foulness'
(*foedum*) consists, but explains that the *boni* (next n.) saw in Piso
a counterbalance to the power of Pompey. 'There need be no doubt',
writes Gruen, 'that some men feared civil war from Pompey at so early
a time. Even earlier, in the winter of 75–74, he had sent a menacing
dispatch to the senate from Spain' ('Pompey and the Pisones', *CSCA* 1
(1968) 155–70, at 161, quoting Sall. *H.* 2.86.10 'exercitus hinc et cum eo
omne bellum Hispaniae in Italiam transgredientur'). It is of course ironical that Piso was sent officially to the very region where C. and Autronius
had wanted to send him (*in … Hispaniam … missus est ~ 18.5 ad …
Hispanias mittere*), but this is exactly the kind of thing that happens in
conspiracies: *ex hypothesi* C.'s intentions were not yet generally known
(18.6n. *ea re*), and their subsequent revelation perhaps explains the references to Piso's revolutionary ambitions in Suetonius and Dio.

    quia boni complures praesidium in eo putabant: *sc. esse.* The *boni* were
elite Roman citizens, defined principally by their wealth, although wealth
was deemed to imply possession of moral qualities (which were therefore
assumed to characterise any *uir bonus*); sometimes *boni* is used to refer to
a certain section within the elite; and, while the term can refer to persons
who were neither senators nor *equites*, it can also be used of persons

[54] The text of Ascon. 92 is unfortunately corrupt.

belonging to each of these *ordines*. See Mouritsen, *RE passim* (esp. pp. 35–
57 'Who were the boni?'); also Hellegouarc'h 484–93, Paananen 59–64.
praesidium is another political term (Hellegouarc'h 172–3).

et iam tum . . . **erat** explains *boni* . . . *putabant*. Pompey's *potentia* picks up
17.7 before the flashback.

19.3–5 C.'s alleged accomplice was not the first Piso to be killed in
Spain (the son of the historian Piso died there in perhaps 112 BC: cf. Cic.
Verr. 4.56 'cum esset in *Hispania praetor*, qua *in prouincia occisus est* . . .'), and
he would not be the last: S.'s episode is the model for the murder of a later
Piso in Spain in AD 25 (Tac. *A.* 4.45): '*facinus* atrox in *citeriore Hispania*
admissum . . . *praetorem prouinciae* L. *Pisonem* . . . *in itinere* adortus uno
uulnere in mortem affecit . . . Piso Termestinorum dolo caesus habe<ba>-
tur, qui pecunias e publico interceptas acrius quam ut tolerarent *barbari*
cogebat' (see W.⁵ ad loc.).⁵⁵ A Caesarian would accuse the Spanish of
multiple attacks (*Bell. Hisp.* 42.4): 'uos . . . more barbarorum populi
Romani magistratibus sacrosanctis manus semel et saepius attulistis'.

19.3 Piso . . . **occisus est:** Asconius (92.20–1; cf. 82.1, 83.11–12) says
that Piso was already dead when Cicero delivered his speech *In Toga
Candida* a few days before the elections of 64, which presumably took
place some time in July (17.1n. *circiter*).

ab equitibus Hispanis quos in exercitu ductabat has to mean something
like 'by Spanish horsemen of whom he was in command as part of his
army', although *in exercitu* admittedly seems superfluous with *ductabat*. The
sense is unlikely to be 'whom he was leading in his army' (the meaning of
ductare at *BJ* 38.1) because the presence of other soldiers would presumably have deterred the assassins: it is no doubt to head off this interpretation that two MSS present the tempting alternative *quos sine exercitu*
(printed by Dietsch). For *ductare* see further 11.5n (*quem*).

19.5 alii: *sc. dicunt*; the indirect speech continues to *perpessos*.

Cn. Pompeii ueteres fidosque clientes is a hexameter line, if *Gnaei* is
spelled out in full; cf. *H.* 1.1 (6.1n. *Vrbem*). For *ueteres fidosque* cf. Mart.
2.30.3, 2.43.15, 5.19.9.

uoluntate eius 'with his [i.e. Pompey's] approval' (*OLD uoluntas* 3b).

nos eam rem in medio relinquemus 'We shall leave the matter
undecided' (a set phrase: see *OLD medium* 7). *nos* is a plural of authorship
(as 22.3).

19.6 de superiore coniuratione satis dictum: Cicero describes the first
conspiracy in the same words (*Sull.* 14, 67 'in illa . . . superiore coniuratione'). *satis dictum*, a common transitional phrase, here signals the end of
the digression.

---

⁵⁵ It is possible that Livy too remembered S.'s passage when he described the death
of Hasdrubal in Spain (21.2.6 'barbarus eum quidam palam . . . obtruncat').

**20.1 Catilina, ubi eos ... conuenisse uidet, tametsi cum singulis ...
appellare et cohortari:** the return to the main narrative of ch. 17 is marked
by ring composition (~ 17.1–3 'primo *singulos appellare: hortari* ... eo
conuenere ...') and underlined by an explicit cross-reference ('quos ...
memoraui': see 5.7n. *quae*). A historic present tense is rare in a temporal
clause except in the historians: the conjunction is usually *ubi*, as here, and
the verb is usually one of perceiving, also as here (*NLS* 175 §217 (3)).
Again at 21.5, 57.5, 60.1, 5, 7.

   multa saepe egerat 'he had often discussed many things' (*OLD ago* 40a).

   in rem fore credens uniuersos appellare et cohortari: *in rem esse* + infin. =
'to be advantageous to ~' (*OLD res* 13b). *appellare* may simply mean 'to
address' (as 17.1; cf. Caes. *BG* 5.33.2 'in appellandis cohortandisque
militibus'), but may also have the extra meaning of 'to appeal to for
support/call on' (*OLD appello*² 2): either way, *cohortari* (and cf. §15 'hortentur') defines the following speech as a *hortatio*, like C.'s final pre-battle
speech (58), with which it has phrases in common (57.6n. *huiusce modi*);
for such self-referential definitions (again at 51.1n. *Omnes*, 58.n. *nequiquam*, 59.5n. *hortatur*) see e.g. W.³ on Tac. *Agr.* 15.5. After the speech,
however, his listeners demand more details (21.1), and that is because
C. has left key aspects deliberately vague (3 'maximum atque pulcherrimum facinus', 5 'quae mente agitaui', 17 'haec ipsa ... agam'): although
there are passing references to dying with courage (9) and the spoils of war
(14–15), much of the speech is straightforwardly political (5–8, 11–13)
and would not be out of place in an electoral campaign.⁵⁶ Scholars believe
that in ancient Rome campaign speeches from electoral candidates were
the exception rather than the rule (see the convenient summary of the
evidence by Tatum 43–5), but C. was of course a consular candidate at the
time (cf. §17), a matter on which he is more explicit in the second speech
which S. gives him (21.3, 5).

   in abditam partem aedium: domestic meetings are 'very much
a Catilinarian motif' (Oakley on Liv. 6.14.11, quoting 27.3, 40.5, Cic.
Cat. 1.8–9, 3.8). The owner of the house is not known; perhaps
C. himself (cf. Cic. *Mur.* 50).

   arbitris ... amotis: *amotis* is a unique variant on the commoner *remotis*
(for numerous exs. of which see Oakley on Liv. 7.5.4).

   orationem huiusce modi habuit: since there were no witnesses to C.'s
speech (above), S. knows only what is likely to have been said (*huiusce
modi*). Readers of historical texts expected authors to compose speeches
that were appropriate to the occasion (Cic. *Orat.* 66 'interponuntur etiam
contiones et hortationes'), as we are explicitly told in the case of S. (Gran.

⁵⁶ Berry calls it an 'election address' (*CC* 30); the speech 'parodies the style of
a would-be popular champion addressing the people' (Rosenblitt 52).

Licin. 36 'contiones inserit'). There is a vast literature on this subject, e.g.
J. Marincola, *CGRH* 118–32.

20.2 Ni ... spectata mihi forent 'If your courage and loyalty were not
known quantities to me' (*OLD spectatus* 1): the neut. plur. *spectata* referring
to two feminine abstract nouns is regular (cf. 5.7, 31.1, *BJ* 38.8, 41.3, 52.4
'plerosque uelocitas et regio hostibus ignara tutata sunt', 68.1; G&L 183
§286.3, though the statement that 'this usage does not appear' in S. is
mistaken); *forent = essent* (14.7n. *sed*).

nequiquam opportuna res cecidisset: *opportuna* seems to be predicative
(cf. 49.3 'res autem opportuna uidebatur'): 'in vain would the situation
have turned out opportune' (*OLD cado* 17b). The favourability of the
situation is one of the topoi of the *hortatio* (e.g. *BJ* 56.4; Harto Trujillo
118).

dominatio in manibus 'the domination within your grasp': *in manibus*,
which varies and alliterates with *magna*, constitutes an 'adnominal prepositional phrase', for which see Spevak 236ff. For this meaning of *in manibus*
(*manu*), again at §10 below, see *OLD manus*¹ 16d; C. has a similar expression, with a different meaning, in his speech at 58.8 (n. *memineritis*). For
the doubling of *nequiquam* and *frustra* cf. Catull. 77.1, Liv. 22.20.8,
24.36.8–9, Virg. *Aen.* 11.715–16.

neque ego per ignauiam aut uana ingenia incerta pro certis captarem:
these words make no sense as a third apodosis to *Ni ... forent*; they are an
independent conditional sentence in which the protasis is contained
within the phrase *per ignauiam aut uana ingenia* (cf. G&L 379 §593.3):
'and I would not be aiming at uncertainty instead of certainty, with
cowardice and unreliable characters to help me' (i.e. 'if I had
cowardice ...'). The articulation of §2 as a whole would be greatly aided
by the insertion of *et* after *cecidisset*, making it clear that only *nequiquam ...
frustra fuissent* comprises the apodosis to *Ni ... forent*.[57] Typical of S. are the
uariatio (abstract ~ concrete), alliteration and quasi-anagrammatism of
ignauiam ~ uana ingenia, which look back to *uirtus* and *fides* respectively;
incerta pro certis (17.6n.) adds to the paronomasia, and the position of *ego* is
emphatic ('I'm not the man to ...'). For *uana ingenia* cf. Liv. 1.27.1,
29.23.6, 34.36.4.

20.3 uos cognoui fortes fidosque mihi repeats *uirtus fidesque uestra ...
spectata mihi.* Storms ('tempestatibus') are a common political metaphor
(*OLD* 4), e.g. Vell. 72.5 and W.².

eo 'for that reason', correlative with *quia* above (*OLD eo*³ 1b); again at
52.11.

---

[57] Syme tried to clarify the text by reading *aut uano ingenio* (*Philol.* 106 (1962) 300–2).

simul quia . . . **intellexi** '<and> at the same time because I have realised that your views of good and evil are the same as mine'; for the datives of reference see G&L 225–6 §352.

20.4 ea demum firma amicitia est '*that* is solid friendship': *ea* instead of *id* is the result of attraction into the gender of *amicitia*, a regular phenomenon; for the resumptive use of *ea* see 12.5n. (*proinde*), and for *demum* see 2.9n. (*uerum*). The definition of friendship (again at e.g. Catull. 8.7 'quae tu uolebas nec puella nolebat') is proverbial (Tosi 589–90 §1310); see also 14.4n. (*quod*).

20.5 quae mente agitaui . . . **audistis:** 'The relative is not unfrequently used where we should expect the interrogative, especially when the facts of the case are to be emphasised' (G&L 297 §467.2). It is hard to know whether *agitaui* = 'planned' or 'pondered' (*OLD* 16–17); *iam antea diuersi* refers back to 17.1.

20.6 nisi nosmet ipsi uindicamus in libertatem: the language (again at *BJ* 42.1; cf. *H*. 3.22) is that of freeing from servitude (*OLD uindico* 3): it is found also in Cicero, the Caesarian corpus, Nepos and Livy, after whom it does not recur until Trajan and Florus (once each). Its most famous occurrence is in the *Res Gestae* of Augustus (1.1 'rem publicam . . . in libertatem uindicaui'), who was styled 'Libertatis P.R. Vindex' on coins of 28 BC (*RIC* 1².79 no. 476). See Hellegouarc'h 550–5. Self-proclaimed freedom fighters in the modern world usually foresee themselves as future masters, and so it is with C. here (cf. *dominatio* at 2 above).

Since *futura sit* represents a vivid future condition in indirect speech, we should have expected the perf. subjunc. here (i.e. a fut. perf. indic. in direct speech: see *NLS* 236 top); *uindicamus* is thus doubly emphatic: C. speaks as though his auditors are already actively engaged in what he is urging them to do.

20.7 postquam res publica in paucorum potentium ius atque dicionem concessit: *ius* and *dicio* are regularly combined to express the notion of total control; *pauci* and *potentes* (here a noun: *OLD* 4c) are terms common in the late republic (see also last n.), and usually used pejoratively to describe one's opponents (Hellegouarc'h 442–6): in S.'s works '*pauci* refers to a power-holding clique whose members were, in practice, *nobiles*' (Paananen 51): *pauci potentes* recurs at *BJ* 31.19 and *H*. 1.12 'dum pauci potentes, quorum in gratiam plerique concesserant, . . . dominationes affectabant'; the variant *potentia paucorum* at 39.1 and 58.11. For *concedo* + *in* and acc., 'to pass into a new state or condition', see *OLD* 2a.

reges, tetrarchae uectigales esse: for the number and types of asyndeta in C.'s speech see Adams, *AILL* 557–8, 577, 581. Tetrarchs 'were minor eastern kings under Roman protection' (Ash on Tac. *A*. 15.25.3, where

again, as often, the term is coupled with the more important *reges*).
uectigales = 'tax-paying' (*OLD* 1b).

stipendia pendere: the *figura etymologica* is fairly common from Enn.
Ann. 215 onwards.

strenui, boni: these two words (again at 60.4, *BJ* 7.5, 67.2 [cf. 22.3],
H. 4.5, Cael. ap. Cic. *Fam.* 8.9.4, Liv. 4.3.16, [Sall.] *Ep. Caes.* 1.1.6, 2.11.4,
Gell. 4.8.2) are first coupled by the elder Cato (*Orat.* 18M, *Orig.* 41C/73P):
'*strenuus* is quite a favourite word of Cato, who was himself notably energetic' (Courtney, *ALP* 52). For rhetorical purposes, and to enhance the
contrast with the *pauci*, C. is here aligning himself with the *boni* (19.2n.
quia), who here are seen more in moral terms as upstanding citizens. Cf.
21.4 (n. *increpabat*).

nobiles . . . fuimus 'known and unknown, we were simply "the masses"':
for a positive adj. combined with a negative (these two again at e.g. Cic.
Inu. 2.30) see Wills 451-4. Of course C. himself was *nobilis* too in a more
technical sense (5.1n. *nobili*), but that is not the point here.

sine gratia, sine auctoritate 'without favour, without influence' (respectively from and over others). For the repeated *sine* see 6.1n.

quibus . . . formidini essemus: C.'s speech is marked by several predic.
datives (9 *ludibrio*, 21.4 *praedae*, 5 *curae*); this one seems paralleled only at
Sen. *Ira* 2.11.4 in classical Latin.

20.8 pericula, repulsas: the former are perhaps not just 'risks' but the
danger incurred in criminal trials (*OLD* 3), in which case *iudicia* (below)
will be the adverse verdicts; *repulsae* are 'electoral defeats'. C. is speaking
from some personal experience here (Intro. pp. 8-9).

20.9 quae quo usque tandem patiemini, o fortissimi uiri?: in early
November 63 Cicero famously began his *First Catilinarian* by directing at
C. the question 'Quo usque tandem abutere, Catilina, patientia nostra?'
(*Cat.* 1.1);[58] here S. puts into the mouth of C. a modified version which in
early June 64 he allegedly directed at his own treacherous followers, whom
he then addressed with the same terms Cicero had used for fellow loyalists
(*Cat.* 1.2 'fortes uiri', 1.3, 2.10 'fortissimis uiris').[59] Scholars have debated
whether the question in S. is parody (Renehan, *OR* 107-8), a tribute to
Cicero (D. C. Innes, *CQ* 27 (1977) 468), a restoration to C. of his own words
which Cicero had parodied (D. A. Malcolm, *CQ* 29 (1979) 219-20,
endorsed by Berry, *CC* 92-3) or something far more complicated still (A.
Feldherr, 'Free spirits: Sallust and the citation of Catiline', *AJP* 134 (2013)

---

[58] For an analysis see C. B. Krebs, 'Painting Catiline into a corner: form and
content in Cicero's *In Catilinam* 1.1', *CQ* 70 (2020) 672-6.

[59] It must be admitted that *uir fortis* is ancient and common and in Cicero's
speeches is worked 'almost to death' (Vretska).

49–66).[60] *quo usque* = 'for how long . . .?' (*OLD quousque* b); with the addition of *tandem* (as again at Liv. 6.18.5) the meaning is 'for how much longer . . .?'

nonne emori per uirtutem praestat quam uitam miseram atque inhonestam . . . per dedecus amittere? 'Is it not better to die with courage than to lose a wretched and unhonoured life in disgrace?' (*OLD praesto*² 4c); *emori* featured in another question directed by Cicero at C. (*Cat.* 1.20 'si emori aequo animo non potes'). The contrast (here chiastic) between a glorious death and an inglorious life goes back to Achilles (Hom. *Il.* 9.410–16) and became proverbial (e.g. *Rhet. Herenn.* 4.57 'cum possis cum summa uirtute et honore pro patria interire, malle per dedecus et ignauiam uiuere'); its deployment is obviously appropriate in a military *hortatio* (cf. Harto Trujillo 131–3). *per dedecus* (first at Cato, *Orat.* 58M) is quite common (see esp. Cic. *Rosc. Am.* 30 'per summum dedecus uitam amittere'), as is the contrast between *uirtus* and *dedecus*.

ubi alienae superbiae ludibrio fueris 'in which you become a laughing stock for the arrogance of others' (similar is *BJ* 31.2). *fueris* is the 'generalising' second person subjunctive (1.6n.).

20.10 pro deum atque hominum fidem: *pro* is an interjection, which may be found alone or with a nom., voc. or (as here) exclamatory acc.; *pro fidem* is a common combination, to which *deum* and/or *hominum* may be added (*OLD pro*² 1b): 'good heavens!', *vel sim.*

in manu nobis est 'is within our grasp' (as at §2 above: n. *dominatio*), as seems clearly indicated by the context.

contra illis annis atque dīuĭtĭīs ˘ ¯ ˘ ōmnĭă cōnsĕnŭērŭnt: *illis* (dat. of disadvantage, separate from the causal abl. *annis atque diuitiis*) contrasts with *nobis* above ('but in their case everything has withered through age and riches') and the contrast is repeated through §§11–13 below. Speaking ill of one's opponents is customary in the *hortatio* (Harto Trujillo 114–17). The dactylic rhythm is notable.

tantummodo incepto opus est: the proverbial 'beginning is half the battle' (Otto 117, Tosi 374–5 §802) is naturally to be found in a *hortatio*.

cetera res expediet 'the undertaking <itself> will facilitate everything else'. The words have been invoked to explain Tac. *A.* 1.49.1 'cetera fors regit' (see Goodyear's n.).

---

[60] A. J. Sillett in his discussion seems unable to decide between the various interpretations ('*Quousque tandem*: the reception of a catchphrase', in F. R. Berno and G. La Bua (edd.), *Portraying Cicero in literature, culture, and politics* (2022) 267–82, at 273–5). Cf. also Sall. *H.* 1.67.17 'quo usque . . . r.p. intutam patiemini', Tac. *A.* 1.13.4 'quo usque patieris', Quint. 1.5.63 'quo usque patitur decor', and esp. Diod. 14.65.4 μέχρι τίνος οὖν καρτερήσομεν ταῦτα πάσχοντες, ὑπὲρ ὧν οἱ ἀγαθοὶ χάριν τοῦ μὴ λαβεῖν πεῖραν ἀποθνήσκειν ὑπομένουσιν; ('For how long, then, shall we endure suffering these things, for which good men endure to die in order not to experience them?', speech of Theodorus, 396 BC).

20.11 cui uirile ingenium est varies the proverbial 'si uir es(t)' (Otto 373, Tosi 63 §140) and it appeals to the *uirtus* which his audience has already shown (2, cf. 9): cf. 40.3n., 44.5n. For *u. ingenium* cf. Sen. *Ep.* 92.35.

illis diuitias superare ... deesse: the acc. + infin. is dependent on *tolerare* (*OLD* 4, seemingly unique); *illis* contrasts with *nobis*.

profundant has the sense of 'squander' (*OLD* 8b), but *in exstruendo mari* activates the notion of the wealthy actually pouring money, as if it were concrete, into the sea for their building works (cf. Hor. *C.* 3.1.34–5). Whether the subjunc. is that of purpose or characteristic is unclear.

in exstruendo mari is said to mean 'in building on the sea' (*OLD exstruo* 3, *TLL* 5.2.1940.79–80), but the few alleged parallels seem to me not quite the same, and 'in building up the sea' (*sc.* with mansions), though surreal, would be much more vivid. For extravagant building see 13.1n. (*Nam*).

rem familiarem 'private means'.

binas aut amplius domos continuare 'that they join together two or more houses', as Clodius wanted to do a few years later (Cic. *Dom.* 115 'habitare laxe et magnifice uoluit duasque et magnas et nobiles domos coniungere'); *binas* is, as it were, distributive: each of the individuals being talked about (*illos*) has two or more houses at his disposal. The emperors were later examples of the practice, e.g. Vell. 81.3 'contractas emptionibus complures domos ... quo laxior fieret ipsius' (Augustus). For the quasi-adjectival use of *amplius* = 'a greater number' see *OLD* 2.

larem familiarem: the *Lar familiaris* was the tutelary god of the hearth or home; here the expr. is used by metonymy for the home itself (*OLD Lar* 2). See H. I. Flower, *The dancing Lares and the serpent in the garden* (2017) 355 and 388 (index).

20.12 cum ... toreumata emunt: *tamen* (below) shows that *cum* = 'although', for which the subjunc. is normal in classical Latin; but the indic. is regular in comedy (e.g. Plaut. *Most* 858 'cum culpa carent, tamen malum metuunt') and recurs in Cicero (e.g. *De Or.* 2.192) and later authors. A *toreuma* – the Greek word suggests the cultural pretensions of the owners – is 'an embossed cup or other piece of plate, particularly of silver' (Nisbet on Cic. *Pis.* 67): for some exs. almost contemporary with C.'s speech see A. Oliver, 'A set of ancient silverware in the Getty Museum', *The J. Paul Getty Museum Journal* 8 (1980) 155–66.

noua diruunt, alia aedificant: perhaps the inspiration of Hor. *Epi.* 1.1.100 'diruit, aedificat, mutat quadrata rotundis'. Caesar once demolished a new villa of his because it failed to live up to his expectations (Suet. *DJ* 46). For building coupled with buying (above) cf. Nepos' praise of Atticus (*Att.* 13.1): 'nemo illo minus fuit emax, minus aedificator'.

pecuniam trahunt, uexant 'they plunder <and> ravage their money' (*OLD traho* 5a, *uexo* 3a–b): the image of warfare is sustained in the main clause (*uincere*).

tamen summa libidine diuitias suas uincere nequeunt 'nevertheless despite the extreme nature of their desire they are unable to get the better of their wealth', i.e. no matter how much they spend, they never exhaust their fortunes.

20.13 foris aes alienum: if you stay at home, the moneylender 'installs himself there and keeps knocking at your door' (Plut. *Mor.* 828E).

mala res, spes multo asperior 'a grim circumstance <and> an expectation much harsher' (*sc.* than the *mala res*): the two (chiastically arranged) phrases refer back to *domi inopia* and *foris aes alienum* respectively. The paronomasia (again at Stat. *Theb.* 11.715 'spes aspera mortis') is perhaps intended to suggest 'an expectation much more hopeless', as if *a-* were a negative prefix like a Greek ἀ- (as Lucian, *Hermot.* 51 ἀνέλπιστα ἐλπίζοντα).

denique 'in fine' (*OLD* 3).

miseram animam 'a wretched existence'.

20.14 Quin igitur expergiscimini? 'Why not therefore rouse yourselves?', as Apul. *Apol.* 25 'quin igitur tandem expergiscimini?'

en illa, illa quam saepe optastis, libertas: Cicero's speeches 'abound' with geminated demonstrative pronouns, 'especially in answer to rhetorical questions' (Wills 76), as here.

Fortuna omnia ea uictoribus praemia posuit 'Fortune has held out to the victors all these things as prizes for them': *uictoribus* is to be taken *apo koinou* (15.2n. *cuius*) with *praemia* and *posuit*; the expr. *praemium (-a) ponere* is not uncommon but the meaning varies depending on context; here it seems to have the sense of the compound *proposuit* (*OLD propono* 7a–b), as again at Gell. 10.18.5, 18.2.3, 8. The rewards of victory are a commonplace of the *hortatio* (58.8n. *memineritis*).

20.15 res, tempus ... belli spolia magnifica magis quam oratio mea uos hortentur: *tempus* suggests the 'decisive moment' topos of the *hortatio* (e.g. *BJ* 49.3 'illum diem'; Harto Trujillo 117). The verb forms a closural ring with *cohortari* (20.1); it is not clear why edd. prefer the minority reading *hortantur* to the jussive subjunctive *hortentur*, read by the majority of MSS and much superior in sense.

20.16 uel imperatore uel milite me utimini: neque animus neque corpus a uobis aberit: as before (7.3n. *tanta*), S. has preferred vivid parataxis (*uel... uel...* + imperative) to hypotaxis (*siue... siue...* + indic.: 'Whether you employ me as commander or as soldier, neither my mind nor my body will let you down'). By the very fact of delivering this speech C. has assumed the role of commander, but the ideal commander combined his intellectual role with the physical role of soldier (W.² on Vell. 85.5) and it was

natural that C., who in the final dénouement proved as good as his word
(60.4 'strenui militis et boni imperatoris officia simul exsequebatur'),
should end his speech with this promise (cf. *BJ* 85.47 'in agmine aut in
proelio consultor idem et socius periculis uobiscum adero', Marius'
speech). See also 1.6n. (*et*). For the meaning of *aberit* see *OLD absum* 2b.

20.17 haec ipsa, ut spero, uobiscum una consul agam 'These are the
very things, I hope, which as consul I shall do together with you.'

seruire magis quam imperare parati estis: the conventional antithesis
between *seruire* and *imperare* and their cognates (e.g. 1.2n. *animi*) is to be
expected in a rousing speech (e.g. *H.* 1.49.10 'seruiendum aut imperitan-
dum', Cic. *Phil.* 6.19 'populum Romanum seruire fas non est, quem di
immortales omnibus gentibus imperare uoluerunt'). *animus fallit* (above)
is a set phrase (*OLD fallo* 2a).

21.1 quibus ... ulla 'who had every misfortune in abundance but
neither resources nor any good hope' (*OLD abunde* 1).

tametsi illis quieta mouere magna merces uidebatur 'although to them it
seemed a great reward to disrupt the tranquillity' (for which cf. 16.5 'tutae
tranquillaeque res omnes'). *magna merces* (again at 41.2, *BJ* 33.2) is a set
phrase; *quietus* is almost technical of settled political circumstances etc.
(*OLD* 4b), while *mouere* is likewise regular of causing political turmoil (*OLD*
11). It is possible that S. is rendering a Greek expr. such as τὰ καθεστῶτα
κινεῖν (Plb. 2.21.3).

quae condicio belli foret 'what the nature of the war would be', as Just.
38.7.6 (*OLD condicio* 8); rather different are Caes. *BC* 3.78.3 and Tac. *Agr.*
27.1.

quid ubique opis aut spei haberent 'what resources or hope they would
find anywhere' (*OLD ubique* 1); *opis aut spei* (partitive genitives after *quid*)
pick up *neque res neque spes bona ulla* above. After C.'s departure to Manlius'
camp in Nov. 63 (32.1), Cicero would assure his fellow citizens 'omnes
spes atque opes ... concidisse' (*Cat.* 3.16).

21.2 tabulas nouas: lit. 'fresh accounts', i.e. the cancellation of debt
(*OLD tabula* 7b). 'For Catiline's followers *tabulae novae* were a major,
perhaps *the* major issue' (Dyck on *Off.* 2.84, where Cicero remarks that
pressure for this measure was never greater than during his consulship). In
the *Catilinarians* Cicero poured scorn on C.'s promise (2.18 'quid enim
exspectas? ... an tabulas nouas? errant qui istas a Catilina exspectant') and
helped defeat a tribunician proposal in 63 to cancel debts (Dio 37.25.4).
See also Berry, *CC* 29–30, Mouritsen, *RE* 180–2.

proscriptionem locupletium: C. is promising to be a second Sulla
(11.4n. *rapere*).

sacerdotia: the four most important *collegia sacerdotum* were the *pontifices*,
augures, *quindecimuiri sacris faciundis* and *epulones* (Rüpke 7–8). 'Roman
priests were merely a sub-group of the Roman political elite, who acted as

religious advisers on religious matters and carried out or supervised particular rituals and sacrifices. The same men, by and large, filled the roles of leading politicians and state priests' (M. Beard and M. Crawford, *Rome in the late republic* (^{2}1999) 30). The asyndetic pairing of *sacerdotia* with *magistratus* 'belongs in the category of asyndeta describing officials/offices' and recurs at Liv. 34.7.2 and in an Umbrian prayer (Adams, *AILL* 251, 266, 558).

alia omnia quae . . . libido uictorum fert: expressed more specifically at 51.9 'matres familiarum pati quae uictoribus collibuissent' (Caesar's speech). For *libido . . . fert* cf. Ter. *Heaut.* 573, Cic. *Verr.* 3.56.

21.3 praeterea esse in Hispania citeriore Pisonem: the narrative moves into indirect speech (a verb of saying has to be understood from *polliceri* above). Piso had died before the elections of 64 (cf. 19.3n. *Piso*), but we do not know how long before. Since C. is imagined as speaking around the start of June (17.1n. *circiter*), it is likely (but not certain) that Piso was already dead when C. made the statement here attributed to him; but S. cannot have intended to portray C. as pulling a fast one over his audience: if C. knew of Piso's death, then his audience will have known of it too. Besides, S. himself may not have been aware of any chronological discrepancy, if indeed there was one.

in Mauretania cum exercitu P. Sittium Nucerinum: P. Sittius from Nuceria, a town in Campania, was an adventurer and leader of a private army called 'the Sittians' (App. *BC* 4.54.230–1). He was indeed in Mauretania in 64 (Cic. *Sull.* 56); whether he already had an army there at this date is uncertain: Shackleton Bailey (on Cic. *Fam.* 5.17(23), a letter to Sittius) thinks that Appian is evidence that he had, but Appian seems to be referring to events of a later period, which Syme believes have been retrojected by S. to 64 (*Sall.* 100–1). See Berry on Cic. *Sull.* 56; J. W. Rich, 'Warlords and the Roman republic', in T. Ñaco del Hoyo and F. López Sánchez (edd.), *War, warlords, and interstate relations in the ancient Mediterranean* (2018) 283 and n. 58; L. Pfuntner, 'Provincial brokers in Roman civil wars', in D. García Domínguez, J. García González and F. Santangelo (edd.), *Connected histories of the Roman civil wars 88–30 BCE* (2024) 258–63.

C. Antonium, quem sibi collegam fore speraret: C. Antonius Hybrida, son of the famous orator M. Antonius (cos. 99) and uncle of Mark Antony, had been praetor in 66. C.'s confidence that he would have Antonius as his consular colleague was based on such extensive bribery by both of them that the senate proposed a new law increasing the penalties for *ambitus* (Ascon. 83.1–12). But the proposal was vetoed by Q. Mucius Orestinus, tribune of the plebs (and C.'s brother-in-law), to which Cicero's response was the speech *In Toga Candida Contra C. Antonium et L. Catilinam Competitores*, of which only fragments now survive (Crawford 159–99). In the event it was Cicero and Antonius who were elected (24.1), Antonius going on to serve as proconsul of Macedonia in 62–60 (*MRR* 2.151–2, 165–6, 175–6, 184, 358, 3.18). An infirmity is said to have prevented him from taking personal command in the final battle against C. in early 62 (59.4).

hominem ... circumuentum 'a man who was both a friend and hampered by every constraint': *necessitudinibus circumuentum* presumably refers to Antonius' extensive debt (Asc. 84.23–5).

21.4 increpabat omnes bonos: the early placed indic. signals the return to narrative after the or. obl. (3). *bonos* is here not imagined as being spoken by C. (cf. 20.7n. *strenui*) but is the term used by S. to describe the wealthy elite with whom C. contrasted his own followers (*egestatis, cupiditatis, praedae* below).

nominans laudare: the infin. is historic; for *nominans* see 17.1n. (*primo*).

suae here refers not to the subject of the sentence but to *alium* (G&L 195 §309.2); see also 28.1n. (*domi*).

complures periculi aut ignominiae '(he reminded) several of their risk or disgrace' (*admoneo* + gen. is regular: see *OLD* 1). *ignominiae* refers to convictions or the like; for *periculi* see 20.8n.

multos uictoriae Sullanae, quibus ea praedae fuerat '(he reminded) many, to whom it had been a source of plunder, of Sulla's victory': see 11.4n. (*postquam*). *praedae* is another predic. dat. (*TLL* 10.2.529.19–28).

21.5 postquam ... uidet: for the historic present see 20.1n. (*Catilina*).

cohortatus ut petitionem suam curae haberent, conuentum dimisit: *cohortatus* looks back to 20.1 'cohortari', while *conuentum* looks back to 20.1 'conuenisse' (~ 17.3 *conuenere*). *curae habere* (again at e.g. Cic. *Fam.* 8.8.10, Liv. 43.1.6) is yet another predic. dat.

22.1 Fuere ea tempestate qui dicerent ...: the paragraph which is thus introduced is parenthetic and is used to separate the preceding episode from the following (for this technique see W–M on Tac. *A.* 3.16.1). S.'s cautious language is repeated at the end and reflects the implied horror of what is described. For *ea tempestate* see 7.1n.; for *fuere ... qui* see 17.7n.

populares sceleris sui 'the partners in his crime' (*OLD popularis*[2] 1b), as 24.1, 52.14. S. does not use *popularis* in its political sense and does not use its antonym *optimates* at all: see H. Mouritsen, *Politics in the Roman republic* (2017) 123–6, on 'Sallust: politics without "optimates" and "populares"'. *adigo* is technical of binding persons to an oath (*OLD* 9a).

22.2 sicut in sollemnibus sacris fieri consueuit 'as is accustomed to happen in solemn rituals': the perf. is used in a present sense, but the impersonal constr. seems unusual (*OLD consuesco* 2b). In many periods and across many cultures blood is a traditional element in oaths of allegiance and the like: see e.g. Hdt. 1.74.5 (Persia) and 4.70 (Scythia), with the respective nn. of Asheri and Corcella. Plutarch (*Cic.* 10.4) and Dio

(37.30.3) say that the blood passed round by C. resulted from a human
sacrifice, a practice which had been outlawed at Rome in 97 BC (*MRR* 2.6);
though S. makes no explicit reference to such an outrage, it seems implied
by *humani corporis* and would explain the caution with which the story is
expressed. The painting of the scene by Salvator Rosa in 1663 (*La congiura
di Catilina*, Florence, Museo di Casa Martelli) features incised right arms,
not human sacrifice.

consilium suum: i.e. the practical details of his plot, as opposed to the
grandiose aims and ambitions mentioned in the two speeches.

atque eo dictitasse facere quo inter se fidi magis forent 'and that he had
said repeatedly that he was doing so precisely in order to increase their
mutual trust'. The MSS here read *atque eo dictitare fecisse*, which makes no
sense and was deleted in its entirety by Ritschl and Reynolds. But it is
difficult to see what is wrong with *atque eo*, and *dictitare* alone was deleted by
Selling and Ramsey and emended to *dicationem* by Kurfess. My simpler
suggestion is to transpose the infinitival tenses (Woodman (2007b) 222):
it is generally true that S. is less keen on the omission of *se* in or. obl. than
are other historians, but the *quo*-clause already presents *se* with a different
reference, the sense is perfectly clear, and for another exception cf. *BJ*
102.13. For *eo* introducing a purpose clause see *OLD eo*³ 1c; *forent = essent*
(14.7n. *sed*).

alius alii tanti facinoris conscii 'one man sharing knowledge of the great
crime with another': *conscii*, with which *alius* is in apposition (cf. 1.7n. *ita*),
agrees with the implied subject of *forent*; *alii* is of course dative (*OLD
conscius* 1a).

22.3 nonnulli ... dederant 'Many thought that both this and much
besides had been fabricated by those who believed that the resentment
at Cicero, which arose afterwards, would be softened by the enormity of
the crime of those who had been punished': *leniri* is present for future, as
often (*OLS* 1.533). Before his consulship Cicero was already attracting
resentment on account of his *nouitas* (23.6), but after the execution of the
Catilinarian conspirators (*postea*), for which he was held personally responsible, he incurred even greater *inuidia*. The incoming tribunes,
Q. Metellus Nepos and L. Calpurnius Bestia, prevented him from delivering the customary speech on his last day as consul, his repeated self-
congratulation was greatly disliked, and eventually in 58 he was forced
into exile by P. Clodius Pulcher, who also ensured that the great man's
various villas and properties were destroyed (see e.g. Plut. *Cic.* 23.1–24.1,
Dio 37.38.1–2; *MRR* 2.174). *atrocitas* is used 'esp. of criminal offences' but
also hints at barbarism (*OLD* 3, 2). For *lenire inuidiam* cf. Liv. 5.21.15, Tac.
H. 4.44.3, Suet. *Dom.* 11.3, Amm. 29.1.41.

parum comperta est is an expr. favoured by S. (again at *BJ* 67.3, 113.1)
and thus also by Tacitus (Kraus on *Agr.* 11.1), but is found also at Liv.

30.45.6, Quint. 2.4.42. *nobis* (dat. of agent) is a plural of authorship (as 19.5); *pro magnitudine* = 'considering its gravity'.

23–6 CATILINE'S ELECTORAL FAILURES: JULY 64–SEPTEMBER 63

This section records C.'s second (24.1) and third (26.5) failed attempts at becoming consul, respectively in 64 and 63 BC, each failure increasing his resentment and his determination to resort to revolution (24.2, 26.5). But the section also introduces us to two women, the patriotic Fulvia (23.3) and the charismatic Sempronia (25.1), and although it is the latter who is given a brilliant and extended character sketch (25.2–5), she plays almost no further part in the story (cf. 40.5); it is Fulvia whose actions now become crucial throughout: informed of the conspiracy by her lover, Q. Curius (23.1–3), she is indirectly responsible for Cicero's electoral success in 64 (23.4–6) and thereafter ensures that as consul in 63 Cicero is kept up to date with all the conspirators' plans (26.3; cf. 28.2).

23.1 Sed both resumes the main narrative after the parenthesis, as often (cf. 7.3), and contrasts the preceding secrecy (20.1) with Curius' upcoming revelation.

Q. Curius … flagitiis atque facinoribus coopertus, quem censores senatu probri gratia mouerant: these words, very similar to the description in Appian (*BC* 2.3.8), imply, but do not guarantee, that Q. Curius was no longer a member of the senate in 64 BC: the assumption would be that he was one of the 64 members who were expelled by the censors in 70 BC (Liv. *per.* 98). Yet he was described as being 'senatorii ordinis' at 17.3: either he is one of the ex-senators at 17.3 to whom this phrase applies (see ad loc.) or, like Lentulus Sura in 63, he had held some magisterial office in the intervening period which entitled him to readmission, as is perhaps implied by *Comm. Petit.* 10 'ex curia Curios'. Who is he? He is usually said to be identical with the man described as a 'hominem quaestorium' by Cicero in 64 (*Tog. Cand.* 27), who according to Asconius (93.19–23) was a notorious gambler, in illustration of which he quotes a fragment of Licinius Calvus (1C/34H) where a Curius is said to be expert at dice. There is a seeming plausibility to this identification. *quaestorium* might imply the recent holding of a quaestorship, enabling readmission to the senate; and gambling had been legislated against since the third century BC (Plaut. *Mil.* 163–4), perhaps providing a reason for the man's initial expulsion (as Asconius' *damnatusque postea est* perhaps implies: cf. Cic. *Phil.* 2.56). Yet there is no certainty about this identification; not only could *quaestorium* refer to a quaestorship before 70 (cf. *MRR* 2.122) but the word has sometimes been deemed corrupt; Calvus may have been referring to a Manius Curius, equally well known for his gambling

(Quint. 6.3.72); and in any case the legislation against gambling was routinely flouted (J. P. V. D. Balsdon, *Life and leisure in ancient Rome* (1969) 154–6, C. Edwards, *The politics of immorality in ancient Rome* (1993) 190–1). In short, Q. Curius is something of a mystery (see further B. A. Marshall, *Ant. Class.* 47 (1978) 207–9, Ryan 259–61, C. Bur, *Rev. Phil.* 87 (2013) 37–58). For *flagitiis atque facinoribus* see 14.2n.; *coopertus* + abl., again at *BJ* 14.11, is idiomatic for being overwhelmed by crime, misery, etc. (*OLD cooperio* 2). Gen. + *gratia* here = 'as a result of' (*OLD* 7e).

23.2 uanitas seems explained by the next main clause and hence to combine the notions of 'unreliability' and 'foolish pride' (*OLD* 1b, 2b). Another ambiguity at 23.4 below. For *inerat* see 15.5n. (*prorsus*).

prorsus neque dicere neque facere quicquam pensi habebat 'in a word, he placed no weight at all on either speaking or acting' (5.6n. *neque*), i.e. he would say or do what he liked. For *prorsus* cf. 15.5n.

23.3 Fuluia, muliere nobili: Plutarch agrees on her nobility (*Cic.* 16.2), but for Florus she is 'uilissimum scortum' (2.12(4.1).6). The two verdicts might be reconciled if, as Syme believes, she is identical with the 'well known' Fulvia who in 52 BC, for the entertainment of the consul and tribunes, acted as a prostitute in a faux brothel at a banquet (Val. Max. 9.1.8). 'Sallust, it will pertinently be recalled, was one of the tribunes' (*ARR* 181). Her identity is otherwise unknown; she is to be distinguished from the more famous Fulvia, wife of Mark Antony, who is more normally assumed to be the Fulvia featured in Val. Max.'s anecdote.

stupri ... consuetudo: cf. Curt. 4.10.31, Suet. *Cal.* 24.1, *Otho* 2.2, Just. 8.6.6, Eutrop. 6.22.2. For *stuprum* see 15.1n. (*multa*).

minus ... minus: the former is an adv., the latter either an adv. or a noun.

maria montesque polliceri: the expr. is not exactly paralleled, though said to be proverbial (cf. Tosi 779 §1744), as 'promettere mari e monti' (equivalent to our 'promise the earth') still is in Italy. Curius evidently expected to profit from the conspiracy.

et minari interdum ferro, ni sibi obnoxia foret 'and he would threaten her sometimes with a sword if she would not submit to him'. S. might have followed *minari* with e.g. *usurum se ferro*, but instead he has used a simple instrumental abl. (a less usual construction, first in Plaut., for the more normal acc. and dat.: see *TLL* 8.1028.11–24). *ni ... foret* represents the protasis of a vivid future condition in secondary indirect speech, for which the impf. subjunc. is regular (Curius is imagined as having said 'if you will not submit to me'): S. could therefore have written *esset* instead of *foret*, but the latter, formed as it is from the alternative fut. infin. *fore*, can have a future aspect which is useful here. This is thus a slightly different case from some others (14.7n. *sed*); see Lowrance 184–5.

Since S. much prefers *nisi* to *ni*, it is tempting to agree with those MSS which have *nisi* and to think that *ni* in others is accounted for by haplography before *sibi*; but our sentence is quoted by Gell. 6.17.7, who has *ni*. For *minari* see 49.4n. (*egredienti*), for *obnoxia* see 14.6n. (*dum*).

ferocius agitare quam solitus erat 'he behaved more defiantly than he had been used to' (*OLD agito* 12b); imitated at Tac. *A.* 4.46.1 'ferocius agitabant'.[61]

23.4 insolentiae looks back both to *quam solitus erat* and to *glorians . . . polliceri*: hence it combines the notions of 'strangeness' and 'arrogance' (*OLD* 2, 4). Cf. *uanitas* at 23.2 above.

_causa cognita: we have already been told (§2) that Curius could not keep his mouth shut.

haud occultum habuit 'did not keep secret' (as e.g. Plaut. *Aul.* 131; cf. *TLL* 9.2.368.58–62). In Tacitus' account of the Pisonian Conspiracy it is again a woman – the virtuous Epicharis – who reveals the plot, but the motive and circumstances are quite different (*A.* 15.51).

sublato auctore de Catilinae coniuratione . . . compluribus narrauit: *sublato auctore* is elliptical for 'suppressing <the name of> her source' (*OLD tollo* 12a, *auctor* 10a); *de C. coniuratione* may be taken either with *auctore* (an 'adnominal prepositional phrase': 20.2n. *dominatio*) or with *narrauit*. Since we are told later that Cicero was given information by Q. Curius and Fulvia (26.3, 28.2), we must infer from the present sentence that Cicero got to hear of Fulvia's unattributed revelations (5n. *Ea res*) and arranged for her to provide him with more details, including the name of her source.

quae quoque modo audierat . . . narrauit means *either* 'she described <the things> which she had heard and the manner in which <she had heard them>' (i.e. the antecedent of the second relative has been incorporated into the rel. clause) *or* 'she described <the things> which she had heard by each means'. The latter has a suggestion of sexual techniques ('honey-trapping') which is not necessarily present in the former, but, though seemingly more complicated, the former perhaps makes the better sense; for rel. clauses instead of indir. questions see 20.5n. (*quae*). There is perhaps a distant echo of this passage at Tac. *A.* 3.19.2 'quoquo modo audita'.

23.5 Ea res refers to Fulvia's revelations and implies that they received wide circulation (cf. 29.1 'uulgi rumoribus'). Most scholars dismiss such evidence because of their conviction that S. has retrojected to 64 events which belong to 63; but according to Appian (*BC* 2.2.4–5) C. 'announced his candidature for the consulship with the intention of making this his

---

[61] Tacitus may also have remembered this passage at *A.* 13.44.1–3 'promittens . . . modo *minitari . . . ferrum*'.

route to tyranny, but ... was beaten off because of this very suspicion (διὰ
τὴν ὑποψίαν τήνδε)'. Whether Cicero in his mid-64 speech *In Toga Candida*
alluded to C.'s intentions is unfortunately unknown, but he knew of C.'s
movements almost as soon as they happened (*Tog. Cand.* fr. 1 'superiore
nocte ... Catilinam et Antonium cum sequestribus conuenisse') and he
could also have made inferences from the First Conspiracy, to which he
did refer (Asc. 83.23–4).

ad consulatum mandandum M. Tullio Ciceroni: although this is not
Cicero's first mention (cf. 22.3), he is given his full name on his first
appearance as a participant in the story. *mandare* is a technical term
(*OLD* 4b); *ad* + gerund(ive) after *studium* is an alternative to the more
usual gen. (*OLD studium* 2).

23.6 pleraque nobilitas inuidia aestuabat ... homo nouus adeptus foret:
attacks on Cicero's *nouitas* were made by his electoral rivals Antonius and
C. (Ascon. 93.25–94.1 'inuecti in nouitatem eius'), as well as by the
tribune Q. Mucius Orestinus (Cic. *Tog. Cand.* 25 'me esse dignum consulatu negabas'), and his status as a *nouus homo* is a major theme of the
Comm. Petit. (esp. §§2–14: see Tatum 166–8), which may be contemporary
with Cicero's electoral campaign (Tatum 51–66). A *nouus homo* himself,
S. was alert to such sneers (cf. *BJ* 63.6–7 'consulatum nobilitas inter se per
manus tradebat; nouus nemo tam clarus neque tam egregiis factis erat
quin indignus illo honore et quasi pollutus haberetur'); see Wiseman 100–
7; also below, 31.7n. (*inquilinus*). *pollui* is again pres. for future (cf. 22.3);
adeptus foret = adeptus erit in direct speech (cf. 23.3n. *et*).

quasi pollui consulatum: the imagery of pollution is a favourite (11.6, *BJ*
15.5, 41.9, 63.7, *H.* 1.49.11; Skard (1942) 145); see also W–M on Tac.
A. 3.29.4.

ubi periculum aduenit: imitated at Tac. *Agr.* 11.3 'ubi aduenere [*sc.*
pericula]'.

post fuere 'took second place'. This use of *post* to express relative
importance etc. is extremely rare and is again coupled with *esse* only at
Ter. *Ad.* 262 (*TLL* 10.2.163.21–4).

24.1 comitiis habitis: the Comitia Centuriata, the popular voting assembly responsible for the election of consuls, usually met in the Campus
Martius (cf. J. R. Patterson, *Political life in the city of Rome* (2000) 8–11). It is
not known when the elections of 64 were actually held, although it is
inferred from the reference to 1 June at 17.1 (n. *circiter*) that they were
expected to take place in July.

consules declarantur M. Tullius et C. Antonius: since Cicero topped the
ballot, an achievement of which he was appropriately proud (*Pis.* 3, *Leg.*
Agr. 2.4, 2.7, *Vat.* 6), his name appeared first on the *fasti*. Antonius pipped
Catiline to second place (Ascon. 94.3–5, Plut. *Cic.* 11.2). Cf. A. M. Stone,

'Three men in a hurry: the consular elections of 64 BC', *Classicum* 19 (1993) 2–4.

primo populares coniurationis concusserat: the pluperf. tense implies that the supporters' shock ended quickly, when they saw that the *furor* of their leader was undiminished (see *OLS* 1.456–7). For *populares* see 22.1n.

24.2 neque tamen Catilinae furor minuebatur: C.'s *furor* is mentioned twice by Cicero in the first paragraph of the *First Catilinarian* (1.1–2); see also 15.5nn. *minuit furorem* recurs in Horace's famous Cleopatra ode (1.37.12).

in dies plura agitare 'he became daily more active'.

arma per Italiam locis opportunis parare: the reference is probably to arms caches, but strategically placed groups of armed men (*OLD arma* 7, *paro* 5a) are also possible (cf. 27.4, Plut. *Cic.* 14.2).

pecuniam sua aut amicorum fide sumptam mutuam: *mutuum sumere* is a technical expr. = 'to borrow' (*OLD mutuus* 1a): hence 'money borrowed on his own or his friends' credit'.

Faesulas ad Manlium quendam: Faesulae (mod. Fiesole) in Etruria, the location of Manlius' camp (32.1), was perched on a hillside at almost 1,000 ft above the R. Arno: it was roughly 170 miles N of Rome on the Via Cassia (*BA* Map 42: A1) and a place where Sulla had settled some of his veteran soldiers (Cic. *Cat.* 3.14, *Mur.* 49); see also Dyck on *Cat.* 1.5. The area will play an increasingly important part in the narrative from now on. Gaius Manlius (his *praenomen* is given at 27.1) features often in the *BC*: he was a former centurion in Sulla's army and now leader of those disillusioned veterans who were 'dreaming again of raiding and plundering readily available riches' (Plut. *Cic.* 14.2–3). On 27 October 63 he took the initiative in starting hostilities (30.1): cf. *princeps* below.

24.3 ea tempestate: 7.1n.

plurimos cuiusque generis homines asciuisse sibi dicitur: cf. *Cat.* 2.8 'nemo ... oppressus aere alieno fuit quem non ad hoc incredibile sceleris foedus asciuerit' (in 63 BC).

mulieres etiam aliquot: cf. Tac. *A.* 15.48.1 'feminae etiam' (the Pisonian conspiracy).

ingentes sumptus ... tolerauerant 'had supported their huge expenditures' (as Ter. *Heaut.* 544, Cic. *Q.Fr.* 1.1.25): huge expenditure was implied apropos of Fulvia at 23.3. For *stupro* see 15.1n.

post, ubi aetas tantummodo quaestui neque luxuriae modum fecerat 'after, when age had placed a limit only on their profitability but not on their extravagance'. Unless these women have aged overnight, their careers as mistresses ('quae ... tolerauerant') must have predated C.'s conspiracy by quite some time. For Syme they are 'veteran mondaines' (*ARR* 174).

aes alienum grande conflauerant: see 14.2n. (*alienum*).

24.4 seruitia urbana sollicitare: the recruitment of slaves was a policy on which C. would eventually have second thoughts (56.5). No one knows the slave population of Rome at this time: perhaps c. 300,000 (W. Scheidel, *JRS* 95 (2005) 67). For *seruitia* = 'slaves', again at 44.6 and Cic. *Cat.* 4.4 'sollicitantur Allobroges, seruitia excitantur', see *OLD* 3b; *sollicitare* = 'incite to disloyalty, revolt etc.' (*OLD* 5a–b).

uiros earum uel adiungere sibi uel interficere: 'he collected a great deal of money from many women who hoped that their husbands would get killed in the rising' (App. *BC* 2.2.6).

25.1 Sed *in* iis *erat* Sempronia, quae multa saepe uirilis audaciae facinora commiserat: the *last* of C.'s associates to be mentioned is a woman of manly boldness, like Artemisia, who *concludes* Herodotus' list of Xerxes' allies (7.99 ὑπὸ λήματός τε καὶ ἀνδρηίης, 'because of her courage and manly spirit'),[62] or Penthesilea, *last* of the pictures in Dido's temple (Virg. *Aen.* 1.493 'audetque uiris concurrere uirgo') or Camilla herself, whose description *ends* Book 7 of the *Aeneid* (803–17).[63] Some have thought Sempronia's sketch disproportionate to her almost total absence from the remainder of the narrative (her one further mention (40.5) is as host of a conspiratorial meeting in the house she shared with her husband, D. Junius Brutus, the consul of 77), but no one disputes its brilliance: 'Sempronia is present for the sake of a wonderful character-portrait' (Stone (1999) 53). Her family background has been much discussed, to no general agreement: see Syme, *ARR* 173–81, 363–6 (Santangelo);[64] C. E. Schultz, *Fulvia* (2021) 11–13.

Tacitus had S.'s description in mind when he introduced Nero's second wife (*A.* 13.45): '*erat in* ciuitate Sabina Poppaea . . . *huic mulieri* cuncta alia fuere praeter honestum animum. quippe mater eius . . . *formam* dederat . . . *sermo* comis nec *absurdum ingenium*: modestiam praeferre et lasciuia uti . . . *famae* numquam *pepercit*, maritos et adulteros non distinguens; neque affectui suo aut alieno obnoxia, unde utilitas ostenderetur, illuc *libidinem* transferebat'.

25.2 *haec mulier* . . . luxuriae sunt: editors see two sentences here: they punctuate (e.g. with a semi-colon) after *fortunata fuit* and then debate the various ways in which the second sentence may in theory be construed (see

---

[62] Herodotus' phrase is rendered by *uirilem audaciam* in Justin's description of Artemisia (2.12.24).

[63] On these figures see further B. W. Boyd, '*Virtus effeminata* and Sallust's Sempronia', *TAPA* 117 (1987) 183–20, and 'Virgil's Camilla and the traditions of catalogue and ecphrasis', *AJP* 113 (1992) 213–34.

[64] Santangelo also summarises bibliography on the more 'literary' aspects of Sempronia's sketch; add e.g. M. Loar, 'Sempronia, Q. Curius, and the decline of Roman *gentes* in Sallust's *Bellum Catilinae*', *Histos* 13 (2019) 146–57, Shaw 307–14.

COMMENTARY: 25.2   191

Ramsey's n.). I prefer to see a single sentence of the type Subject (*haec mulier*) Copula (*fuit*) Predicate (*litteris ... sunt*): this type, often used in definitions, lends itself to 'thematic statements' such as character sketches (J. N. Adams, *Wackernagel's Law and the placement of the copula esse in classical Latin* (1994) 14, 63–8); S. had used a simple form of it to describe C. at 5.1 'L. Catilina, nobili genere natus, fuit ... prauoque'. On this reading *genere ... fortunata* is in apposition to *haec mulier* and, in telling us nothing that we do not expect of a society lady, is relatively less important; but *fuit* focusses what follows, namely the three different specialisms (cf. *docta*) in which this woman (*haec mulier*) illustrates further the paradox introduced in the previous sentence (*uirilis audaciae*). Each of these three specialisms is given its own construction depending on *docta* (see nn. below).

liberis satis fortunata: this statement has been used as an argument against the theory that D. Junius Brutus (cos. des. 42), one of the murderers of Caesar, was connected (e.g. son or stepson) with Sempronia – Caesar being someone whom S. idealised (53.6): cf. T. J. Cadoux, 'Sallust and Sempronia', in B. Marshall (ed.), *Vindex humanitatis* (1980) 103–4. For the asyndetic pairing of family members see Adams, *AILL* 167–70, 558; for *fortunatus* + abl. cf. Ter. *Hec.* 601, Cic. *Senec.* 29, Ov. *Met.* 15.97–8, Auson. 19.27 (p. 141G) 'nec fortunata marito'.

litteris Graecis, Latinis docta: for cultured women see E. A. Hemelrijk, *Matrona docta: educated women in the Roman elite from Cornelia to Julia Domna* (1999). The abl. is regular, e.g. Cic. *Brut.* 169 'docti et Graecis litteris et Latinis'. For the asyndeton see Adams, *AILL* 571.

psallere, saltare elegantius quam necesse est probae '(expert) at playing [*sc.* on the cithara] and dancing more elegantly than is necessary for a moral woman': although *doctus* + infin. is found in prose (e.g. *BJ* 85.33 'illa multo optima ... doctus sum: hostem ferire' (not quite the same), Tac. *A.* 14.60.2 'canere per tibias doctus'), it is much commoner in verse: see esp. Hor. *C.* 4.13.7 'doctae psallere', an allusion which shows that Horace understood *psallere, saltare* as depending on *docta* and not as historic infinitives.[65] The Grecism *psallere*, first here in extant Latin, complements *litteris Graecis* above; for this further asyndeton see Adams, *AILL* 577. For the dubious morality of dancing see J. P. V. D. Balsdon, *Roman women* (1975) 274–5; consorting with dancers was also questionable (Plin. *Ep.* 7.24.4 'habebat illa pantomimos fouebatque effusius quam principi feminae conuenit').

multa alia quae instrumenta luxuriae sunt: '(expert) in many other things that are aids to extravagance'. Verbs which in the active take two accusatives (e.g. Cic. *Balb.* 15 'ea quae nos libri docent', 'the things *which*

[65] At *Epi.* 2.1.33 Hor. has *psallimus* and *doctius*, which seems to confirm his remembering of S.

books teach *us*'; 16.1n. *iuuentutem*) may retain an accusative in the passive
(e.g. Colum. *RR* 3.3.2 'hoc primum docendi sunt', 'they must be taught
this first'); but *doctus* also came to be regarded as an adj. in its own right
('expert, learned'), and on such occasions the acc. functions rather as an
acc. of respect (e.g. *H.* 1.132 'doctus militiam', 'expert in military matters'
(so Ramsey (2015) 113)). See also 45.1n. (*cuncta*). For *i. luxuriae* cf. Ov.
F. 5.279, Plin. *NH* 9.39, Just. 30.1.9, *HA Heliog.* 28.6.

25.3 decus atque pudicitia 'decorum and chastity' (*OLD decus* 4): *pudicitia* was regarded as a woman's glory (*decus* in another sense: cf. Sen. *Contr.*
2.7.9, Sen. *Cons. Helv.* 16.4), especially if she was married (S. Treggiari,
Roman marriage: iusti coniuges from the time of Cicero to the time of Ulpian
(1991), 218–20, 236–7).

pecuniae an *famae* minus *parceret* haud facile discerneres 'you could not
easily have discerned whether it was her money or her reputation that she
spared less'. The indefinite second person singular subjunctive (1.6n. *et*) is
often used in descriptions of character, e.g. Liv. 21.4.3 'haud facile discerneres utrum imperatori an exercitui carior esset'; Gilmartin 112–14.
famae parcere is found elsewhere apart from Tac. *A.* 13.45.3 (above, 1n.):
cf. 52.32, Cic. *II Verr.* 2.49, *Tull.* 3, Prop. 1.16.11, Ov. *Am.* 3.14.36.

***libido* SIC accensa *ut* SAEPIUS peteret uiros quam peteretur:** compare
and contrast Prop. 2.20.27 'cum te tam multi peterent, tu me una petisti',
Ov. *AA* 1.277–8, Liv. 39.9.6 'ultro … appetitus … erat' (of the young man
and his virtuous *scortum*). S.'s *sententia* is oddly reapplied by Aufidius Bassus
in his obituary of Cicero (2C/P 'uixit sexaginta et tres annos ITA ut SEMPER
aut peteret alterum aut inuicem peteretur'), seemingly a 'false echo' (for
this concept see K. Maurer, '*Notiora fallaciora*: exact, non-allusive echoes in
Latin verse', *Studies in Latin literature and Roman history* 11 (2003) 121–56).

25.4 saepe antehac fidem prodiderat, creditum abiurauerat 'often
before this she had betrayed trust, forsworn debt'. *antehac* (only here in
S.) is found twice in Ennius and Turpilius, common in Ter. and (esp.)
Plaut., once each in Cornelia (mother of the Gracchi), Lucr. and Hor.,
and rare in Cic.; it is almost entirely absent from the first cent. AD but
returns in Tac. *A.*, so a likely archaism.

25.5 haud *absurdum*: see 3.1n. (*pulchrum*).

posse uersus facere: Sempronia is the 'first Latin woman described as
actually having written poetry' (J. Stevenson, *Women Latin poets* (2005) 33).

iocum mouere seems to mean 'produce a joke', although in the only
other instance of the expr. (Hor. *Epi.* 1.19.20) the meaning is 'provoke
a jest' *vel sim.* (perhaps cf. *OLD moueo* 18); for other exs. of phrases which
can have more than one meaning see Conington on Virg. *Aen.* 10.396 and
Housman on Manil. 2.617–18 (and pp. 126–7).[66] It is said of Licymnia at

---

[66] I owe these references to Prof. R. G. Mayer.

Hor. *C.* 2.12.18 that she is not ashamed 'certare ioco', but the reference there seems to be different (see N–H or Harrison ad loc.).

sermone uti uel modesto uel molli uel PROcaci: the opposites *procaci* ('ribald': cf. Catull. 61.119–20 'procax … iocatio') and *modesto* do not help clarify the meaning of *molli*, which perhaps, since the referent is a woman, means simply 'gentle' *uel sim.*

PROrsus multae facetiae multusque lepos inerat 'in a word, she possessed considerable wit and considerable charm': for the coupling of the two nouns cf. Catull. 12.8–9, 50.7–8, Cic. *Clu.* 141, *De Or.* 1.17, 1.242, 2.219, 2.225; there is much discussion of them in B. A. Krostenko, *Cicero, Catullus, and the language of social performance* (2001). For *prorsus* and *inerat* see 15.5n.

26.1 His rebus comparatis refers back to 24.2–4. For the expr. cf. Caes. *BG* 7.8.1.

in proximum annum: i.e. for 62 BC. He was supported in his candidature by the conspirator L. Cassius Longinus, who, to judge from the inscription on a bowl now in the Museo Nazionale in Rome (*CIL* 6.40897 CASIVS LONGINV QVEI CATILINAE [SV] SVFRAGATVR), provided food for the voters in an effort at persuading them to support C.: see Berry, *CC* 20–5 and 240–5 for discussion; also 37.7n. (*priuatis*).

si designatus foret would be fut. perf. indic. in direct speech; for *foret* 23.3n. (*et*).

facile se ex uoluntate Antonio usurum: *ex uoluntate* = 'at will' (*OLD uoluntas* 2d). According to Plutarch, Antonius was 'a man who on his own was capable of leading others neither to the good nor to the bad but who would contribute to the power of anyone else who did take the lead' (*Cic.* 11.1, trans. Moles).

omnibus modis insidias parabat Ciceroni: this plot against Cicero's life was being hatched in the first half of 63 (as inferred from *namque a principio consulatus sui* at §3 below) and is the first of S.'s three references to such attempts. The second is during the consular elections of 63 (5 below), the third on 7 November 63 (27.4–28.3). Cicero himself reports a still earlier plot in the second half of 64 (cf. Cic. *Cat.* 1.11 'quam diu mihi consuli designato, Catilina, insidiatus es' and 15, to which Dyck mistakenly thinks our passage corresponds). See also 27.4n. (*eum*); Woodman (2021a) 64–5.

26.2 dolus aut astutiae: the point seems to be that the morality of these two resources (coupled again at Plaut. *Asin.* 546, *Epid.* 375) depends upon the purpose to which they are put.

26.3 a principio consulatus: the First Conspiracy (18–19) had alerted Cicero to the danger posed by C.

multa pollicendo per Fuluiam effecerat ut Q. Curius … sibi proderet: the spread of Fulvia's revelations seems first to have alerted Cicero to C.'s present intentions, and the consul then persuaded her to disclose the name of her source (23.4n. *sublato*): hence Fulvia, who was interested in money (23.3), is likely to have been a beneficiary of Cicero's promises as well as Curius; and our passage suggests too that it was she who conveyed Cicero's promises to her lover.

On *pollicendo* see *NLS* 160 §205 (d): 'A gerund in the instrumental ablative is sometimes used so vaguely that it is almost equivalent to a present participle in agreement with the subject.'

de quo paulo ante memoraui: at 23.1–4. For cross-references see 5.7n. (*quae*); for *memoro* cf. 3.2n. (*ubi*).

26.4 pactione prouinciae: when consuls were elected, they decided by lot the provincial commands which had been assigned by the senate for the year after their consulship: Macedonia, a rich province, fell to Cicero, while Gallia Cisalpina fell to Antonius. Initially the two men exchanged commands, to the satisfaction of both, but later Cicero renounced Cisalpina altogether (Cic. *Pis.* 5, Plut. *Cic.* 12.4; *MRR* 2.166; Rafferty 106, 185).

ne contra rem publicam sentiret: the expr. is elsewhere only at Cic. *II Verr.* 2.113; perhaps S. intends us to understand *cum Catilina* (cf. *Cat.* 2.6 'cum Catilina sentire').

circum se praesidia amicorum atque clientium occulte habebat: an entourage of lictors carrying *fasces* would escort consuls when they went about in public, a privilege which alternated between the consuls on a monthly basis, the senior consul, who in 63 was Cicero (24.1n.), starting the process in January (cf. A. J. Marshall, *Phoenix* 38 (1984) 127–32, esp. 131 and n. 41); but the escort was perhaps more ceremonial than anything else, and Cicero would later make a point of saying that, when as consul he presided over the elections at the Comitia Centuriata in 63, he was protected by a bodyguard of *amici* (*Cat.* 1.11 'cum proximis comitiis consularibus me consulem in campo et competitores tuos interficere uoluisti, compressi conatus tuos nefarios amicorum praesidio et copiis', *Sull.* 51 'ego tectus praesidio firmo amicorum'). He was countering his enemy's deception (cf. 5 *quae occulte temptauerat*) with his own (*occulte habebat*). For *occulte habebat* cf. Front. *Strat.* 3.10.8.

26.5 dies comitiorum: the date of the consular elections in 63 has caused much discussion. Alarmed by reports of a *contio domestica* which C. was said to have held, Cicero persuaded the senate that, in order to have time to discuss the Catilinarian crisis, the elections, scheduled for the following day, should be postponed (*Mur.* 50–1). Some scholars have identified the scheduled day as 23 September, the day the emperor Augustus was born, since we know from Suetonius that his birth coincided with a meeting of the senate at which the Catilinarian crisis was discussed (*Aug.* 94.5). The case is argued in great detail, with much supporting

evidence, by Ramsey (2019), who concludes that 'the consular elections in
63 were almost certainly held towards the end of September' (232).
**Catilinae neque petitio neque insidiae quas consulibus in Campo fecerat
prospere cessere:** those elected were D. Junius Silanus, who would vote to
execute the conspirators (50.4n.), and L. Licinius Murena, who would be
successfully defended against electoral bribery by Cicero in the *Pro Murena*
two weeks before the collapse of the Catilinarian conspiracy. The consular
elections were presided over by a consul (Cic. *Att.* 9.9.3; Pina Polo 287–8),
and Cicero twice refers to C.'s murderous designs on him personally at the
elections (*Mur.* 52, *Sull.* 51); at *Cat.* 1.11 he adds C.'s fellow candidates as
potential victims too (see 26.4n. *circum*); Dio refers to 'Cicero and some
others of the leading men' (37.29.2). No other author seems to say that
C. intended to kill both consuls (again at 27.2), and some MSS here offer
consuli rather than *consulibus*. The reference to both consuls is odd, given (i)
that elsewhere (27.4; cf. 32.1–2) C. is made to refer to Cicero alone as the
main obstacle to his plans and (ii) that he had hoped to make an ally of
Antonius, Cicero's consular colleague (26.1). On the other hand, Antonius
would be opposed to C. in the final battle (59.4). *Catilinae* is dat. with *cessere*
(*OLD cedo*[1] 7a 'to turn out' for one); for the ending in -*ere* see 2.2n. (*postea*).
prospere perhaps anticipates the imagery of *aspera foedaque* below (n.).
    in Campo: *sc. Martio* (24.1n. *comitiis*).
    extrema omnia experiri: *experior* is commonly coupled with *omnia*
or, slightly less commonly, *ultima* = 'to leave nothing untried' (*TLL*
5.2:1668.3–32); there appears to be no parallel for the substitution of the
latter by *extrema* or of the conjunction with *omnia*, but cf. Liv. 3.15.9 'omnia
extrema temptaturum' (perhaps an echo of S., who has *temptauerat* just
below). Statements of 'unqualified assertion' such as 'all' and 'last' are
common in passages of closure (B. H. Smith, *Poetic closure* (1968) 182–6),
as here at the end of the episode.
    quae occulte temptauerat presumably refers to the *insidiae* planned for
Cicero.
    aspera fōĕdăqu(e) ēuēnĕrānt: the adjs. are not coupled elsewhere, but,
since each can be used of storms etc. (*OLD asper* 13c, *foedus*[1] 2), perhaps
S. is returning to the imagery which C. had used at the start of his first
speech (20.3). The double cretic clausula is one of Cicero's favourites (K–
K 176).

27–32.2 DEVELOPMENTS IN ETRURIA AND ROME:
OCTOBER–NOVEMBER 63

S.'s focus now narrows down to the last months of Cicero's consulship,
when developing events and the different areas of operation illustrate the
difficulty, mentioned by S.'s contemporary Diodorus (3.2n. *primum*), of

representing actions through the medium of a text. The first problem is
one of chronology. The five events which can be securely dated appear as
follows in S.'s narrative:

(i)   the conspirators met at Laeca's house (27.3–4) during **the night of
      6–7 November**;
(ii) the assassination of Cicero (28.1–3) was attempted on **the morning
      of 7 November**;
(iii) the *senatus consultum ultimum* (29.2) was passed on **21 or
      22 October**;
(iv) Manlius resorted to arms (30.1) on **27 October**;
(v)   Cicero delivered his *First Catilinarian* (31.6) on **7 (or 8) November**.

It will be seen that S. interrupts the crucial November period (27.3–28.3,
31.6) by inserting events (iii) and (iv), which had taken place in the
previous month (29.2, 30.1).

The second problem is geographical. After a single sentence in which
attention is directed to three different areas of Italy (27.1), the scene shifts
to Rome (27.2 'Interea Romae ...') and in particular to an attempt on
Cicero's life (27.2–28.3). After the attempt is thwarted, however, there is
another single sentence on Italy (28.4 'Interea ... in Etruria ...'), before
we are returned to Rome for the remainder of the episode, which culmin-
ates with Cicero's *First Catilinarian* and its sequel (29.1–32.2).

Whether we accuse S. of ineptitude or (like Syme, *Sall.* 79–81) argue
that he has done his best with difficult material, the arrangement of the
narrative redounds to Cicero's credit. The separation of the attempted
assassination (ii) from the delivery of the *First Catilinarian* (v) absolves
Cicero of the charge that his attack on C. represented a personal vendetta
rather than the statesman-like speech he alleged that it was.

27.1 C. Manlium Faesulas ... **dimisit:** S. has omitted to tell readers that
Manlius had left his base at Faesulae (24.2 and n.) to come to Rome to
support C. in his bid to be elected consul (Plut. *Cic.* 14.3). According to
Orbis, routine private travel from Rome to Faesulae up the Via Cassia in the
autumn would take over a week.

Septimium quendam Camertem in agrum Picenum: Picenum, a region
NE of Rome on the Adriatic coast, will recur in the narrative (30.5, 42.1,
57.2); since Septimius (of whom nothing else is known) came from
Camerinum in the eastern foothills of the Apennines (*BA* Map 42: E2),
he could perhaps be expected to have some local knowledge. See Berry on
Cic. *Sull.* 53.

C. Iulium in Apuliam: Apulia, a region in the SE of Italy (*BA* Map 45),
will also recur (30.2–3, 42.1, 46.3); nothing else is known of the man (cf.
MRR 2.115–16n. 6).

alium alio: *sc. dimisit* ('he despatched one man to one place, another to another').

quem ubique opportunum sibi fore credebat: the antecedent of *quem* is *alium*, but Eng. prefers a transposition of terms: '*wherever* he thought *anyone* would be advantageous/available for him' (*OLD ubique* 1 'anywhere', *opportunus* 1, 4; cf. 2). Cf. Cic. *Cat.* 1.9 'distribuisti partes Italiae, statuisti quo quemque proficisci placeret'.

27.2 Interea Romae: S. now turns to the first main event of this section of narrative. Although *interea Romae* is not exclusive to S. (cf. Cic. *Mur.* 42, *Quinct.* 29), it seems very likely that S.'s phrase is in Tacitus' mind at *A.* 11.22.1, introducing an episode where an armed man is discovered waiting to pay his respects to the *princeps* – exactly as in our passage.

moliri: the first of ten historic infinitives (6.4n. *igitur*): the arrangement of the first five is chiastic, that of the second five alternating. C. is the subject throughout.

consulibus insidias tendere: *i. tendere* is a common metaphor derived from hunting (*OLD tendo* 4); for the plur. *consulibus* see 26.5n. (*Catilinae*).

opportuna loca armatis hominibus obsidere 'he held strategic points with armed men': the instrumental abl. is used of persons 'if they are regarded as the mere instruments in the hands of another' (*NLS* 32 §44, quoting Cic. *Att.* 4.3.2 'armatis hominibus expulsi sunt fabri de area nostra'). It is impossible to know whether the verb is *obsĭdeo* or *obsĭdo* (cf. *TLL* 9.2.220.45, 222.4–5); each produces a favoured clausula (K–K 169).

ipse cum telo esse: *cum telo* is a set expression (*OLD telum* 3c), often legal, and carrying a weapon with criminal intent contravened the Sullan law *de sicariis* (cf. Cic. *Mil.* 11 'lex … quae … esse cum telo hominis occidendi causa uetat', with Keeline's note; *Rom. Stat.* 2.749–53): when C. was in the forum on 29 December 66 (18.6n. *ea re*), he was 'cum telo' (*Cat.* 1.15).

item alios iubere 'he ordered others <to do> likewise'.

uti semper intenti paratique essent: *uti* is the older form of *ut*, 'increasingly rare after Cic. but affected by archaising writers such as Sal., and in poets metri gratia' (*OLD*); the form is quite common in *BC*. The coupling of *intentus* and *paratus* (again at *BJ* 49.3) is found sprinkled throughout the historians but is also at Cic. *Mil.* 67, Gell. 13.28 *init.*

dies noctesque festinare, uigilare, neque insomniis neque labore fatigari: this is a complicated example of correlative distribution (2.2n. *urbes*), in that *festinare* refers back to *dies* and is picked up chiastically by *labore*, while *uigilare* refers back to *noctes* and is picked up chiastically by *insomniis*. See also Adams, *AILL* 577–8. For *uigilare* cf. *Cat.* 1.8 (addressing C.) 'iam intelleges multo me uigilare acrius ad salutem quam te ad perniciem rei publicae'.

27.3 ubi multa agitanti nihil procedit 'when, despite much activity on his part, no progress was being made' (for the expr. cf. Cic. *Att.* 10.12.1

'cui nihil procedit'). *multa agitanti* (*sc. Catilinae*) looks back to 24.2 'plura agitare'.

rursus intempesta nocte coniurationis principes conuocat per M. Porcium Laecam: *nox intempesta* (again at 32.1) is a set expr. in prose and verse for 'the dead of night' (*OLD intempestus* 1); night was the traditional time for making plans (Oakley on Liv. 9.3.1), and nocturnal meetings and the like are a staple of conspiracies (42.2, Cic. *Cat.* 1.1, 1.6, 1.8, 2.26; W. Nippel, *JRS* 74 (1984) 24), which is why they were allegedly prohibited in the Twelve Tables (cf. *Rom. Stat.* 2.694–5). The meeting at the house of Laeca (17.3n.) took place on the night of 6–7 November (Cic. *Sull.* 52; cf. *Cat.* 1.8–9, 2.13). *per* seems almost = 'thanks to' (cf. *OLD* 15a); the usage is odd, and not rendered any easier by the following *ibique*, from which we have to infer that S. is referring to Laeca's house. Dietsch prints the emendation *penes*, but it is not clear that *penes* is an equivalent of *apud*. Cicero stresses C.'s presence at the meeting (*Cat.* 1.9 'fuisti . . . apud Laecam illa nocte, Catilina') and his domination of the proceedings, of which S. provides an apt impression. The meeting was followed immediately by the attempt on Cicero's life (28.3) and by the delivery in the senate of the *First Catilinarian* (31.5n. *in senatum*). 'Quid proxima, quid superiore nocte egeris, . . . quos conuocaueris, quid consilii ceperis quem nostrum ignorare arbitraris?' (*Cat.* 1.1, addressing C.). *rursus* indicates that this was not the first such meeting, and we know that, just before the day scheduled for the consular elections (which was probably 23 September: 26.5n. *dies*), C. had harangued his supporters in a private house (Cic. *Mur.* 50 'in contione domestica'); see also 20.1n. (*in*), 43.1n. (*Lentulus*).

27.4 multa . . . questus: *multa* is an adverbial acc. (*OLD queror* 1d). C. will repeat his complaint at 58.4 (n.).

Manlium praemisisse: cf. Cic. *Cat.* 1.24 'praemissos . . . praemissam'.

eam multitudinem quam ad capienda arma parauerat: cf. 24.2.

seque ad exercitum proficisci cupere, si prius Ciceronem oppressisset: a form of fut. condition in *oratio obliqua* (*oppressisset* = fut. perf. indic. in direct speech): 'and he wanted to [i.e. he would] set off for his army, if he first crushed Cicero'.

eum suis consiliis multum officere: S.'s own high opinion of Cicero (Intro. p. 12) is here 'endorsed by – of all people – Catiline', says Stone (1999) 56; in the opinion of the conspirator, 'Cicero's life and death are the difference between failure and success'. For *consiliis . . . officere* cf. Liv. 2.30.2.

28.1 igitur . . . confodere: this sentence closely follows *Cat.* 1.9–10.

C. Cornelius . . . L. Vargunteius . . . constituere: see 17.3–4nn. for the assassins. *operam suam* is ironic, since performing the *salutatio* (next n.) was a client's *opera* (Mart. 3.46.1). *constituere* could be either historic infin. or perf. indic.; the latter seems more likely since the dependent verbs *introire* and *confodere* are infinitives.

ea nocte paulo post … sicuti salutatum introire ad Ciceronem: the *salutatio* or reception, at which a great man would receive callers paying their respects, took place early in the morning (*BNP* 12.909–10); the visit on 7 Nov. is timed similarly by Cicero (*Cat.* 1.9 'illa ipsa nocte paulo ante lucem'). *sicut* = 'as if', as regularly with single words (*OLD* 6b); *salutatum* is supine of purpose (as Amm. 14.6.12 'si … salutatum introieris'): cf. Plut. *Cic.* 16.1 'as if to greet Cicero'. S. does not explain how the armed men would have been deployed in the planned scenario, though *salutationes* could evidently be scrum-like (Cic. *Ep. Brut.* 2.4.1 'ipsa in turba matutinae salutationis'). *introire ad* + acc. is rare (Plaut. *Most.* 422, Ter. *Hec.* 551).

domi suae: the locative takes the possessive adj. in the genitive (G&L 266 §411. R4), as Cic. *Cat.* 1.32 'insidiari domi suae consuli'. The reflexive here does not refer to the subject of the sentence; *suus* 'is especially used in this way when it is emphatic' (*OLS* 1.1132): the plan was to attack Cicero *in his own home* – an outrage both in itself (Cic. *Sull.* 18 'in meis sedibus, in conspectu uxoris ac liberorum meorum') and against the *ius amicitiae* (ibid. 52).

28.2 impendeat: for the tense after a governing verb in the historic present see 32.2n. (*mandat*).

propere per Fuluiam Ciceroni dolum qui parabatur enuntiat: Cicero said that information had reached him almost before C.'s meeting broke up (*Cat.* 1.10); Fulvia as informant (23.3–4nn.) reappears in Plutarch (*Cic.* 16.2), who, however, does not refer to Curius (23.1n.). For the indic. *parabatur* cf. 17.7n. (*quia*).

28.3 ianua prohibiti 'kept from the door'. According to Gellius, larger houses had a vestibule-like area between the street and the main door in which would-be callers would be detained before admittance (16.5.8–9): see S. Speksnijder, 'The elusive *vestibulum*', in J. A. Baird and A. Pudsey (edd.), *Housing in the ancient Mediterranean world* (2022) 322–53, esp. 326. Cicero explains his counter-measures (*Cat.* 1.10): 'domum meam maioribus praesidiis muniui atque firmaui, exclusi eos quos tu ad me salutatum mane miseras'.

28.4 Interea Manlius in Etruria: the narrative now returns to the point at which we left it (27.1).

plebem sollicitare: the noun *plebs*, which occurs here for the first time in the work, may mean 'the general body of citizens at Rome (as distinct from the patricians), the plebeian class, the commons' (*OLD* 1); it may also mean 'the common people, mob, common herd, the masses' (*OLD* 2). Often the distinction between these two becomes blurred, and the meaning in each case needs to be determined by the context: see Paananen 23–7, 37–43, and in general Mouritsen, *PP* 1–17. In the present case the latter meaning seems foremost, as the following description suggests. *p. sollicitare* recurs at *BJ* 19.1 and was reused at Liv. 23.15.3; for the verb see 24.4n. (*seruitia*).

egestate simul ac dolore iniuriae nouarum rerum cupidam: the *plebs'* suffering and revolutionary enthusiasm are alike explained by the following *quod*-clause; *nouarum rerum cupidus* (again at 48.1, *BJ*66.2) is a common expr., and the *plebs'* sympathy for revolution is a topos (37.1n.). *dolor* = 'indignation' (*OLD* 4), as often with *iniuriae*; for the coupling with *egestas* cf. Cic. *Fin.* 4.72, *Off.* 2.38, Sen. *Ira* 1.16.4, *Ep.* 85.41. For the 'verbal hyperbaton' after *sollicitare* see 12.3n. (*in*).

quod Sullae dominatione agros bonaque omnia amiserat: Sulla's veteran settlements (below) often meant expropriating local people.

latrones cuiusque generis 'bandits of every type'.

nonnullos ex Sullanis coloniis, quibus libido atque luxuria ex magnis rapinis nihil reliqui fecerat: whether these are a separate group or a subdivision of the *latrones* ('numbers <of them> from the Sullan *coloniae*, whose lust and luxury . . . had left them with nothing over') is not certain; for *nihil reliqui fecerat* see 11.7n. (*nihil*). *ex magnis rapinis* is almost impossible to translate because it is to be taken *apo koinou* (15.2n. *cuius*) both with *libido atque luxuria*, where it = 'resulting from' (*OLD* 18a), and with *nihil reliqui fecerat*, where, as at 31.1, it = 'after' and indicates reversal as well as time (*OLD* 10; cf. 13a). See esp. Cic. *Cat.* 2.20 (with some overlap of vocabulary) and Dyck's nn. Sulla is thought to have settled between 80,000 and 120,000 of his soldiers on the land. In addition to rewarding his veterans, he seems also to have chosen his locations with a view to revenge on his former enemies and strengthening certain areas of the country. The known *coloniae* are Faesulae (24.2n.) and Arretium (Cic. *Mur.* 49, *Att.* 1.19(19).4) in Etruria, where there was also a settlement at Volaterrae (Cic. *Att.* 1.19(19).4); Praeneste (Cic. *Cat.* 1.8 with Dyck, *Agr.* 2.78) in Latium; Pompeii (Cic. *Sull.* 60–2 with Berry) and Urbana (Plin. *NH* 14.62) in Campania; and Aleria on Corsica (Plin. *NH* 3.80). The Sullan settlements have caused considerable scholarly discussion, e.g. A. Thein, 'Sulla's veteran settlement policy', in F. Daubner (ed.), *Militärsiedlungen und Territorialherrschaft in der Antike* (2010) 79–100, A. Keaveney, '*Paludes et silvae*: the ruin of the veteran', in Eckert and Thein 89–103. *libido* (of which the older form *lub-* would maximise the alliteration) and *luxuria* (again at *BJ* 89.8) and their cognates are commonly combined.

29.1 ea cum Ciceroni nuntiarentur, ancipiti malo permotus, quod neque urbem . . . neque exercitus Manlii . . .: *ea* refers to the activities of Manlius just described at 28.4; the *anceps malum* with which Cicero was confronted is explained by *neque . . . neque*: first there is his need of more support to deal with C.'s measures at Rome as described at 27.2, second there is his ignorance of what Manlius' activities implied. In S.'s view these two problems are the reason (*quod*) why Cicero convened the senate (*rem ad senatum refert* below) on 21 or 22 October (2n. *senatus*).[67]

neque ... longius ... poterat 'neither could he any longer ...' (*OLD longe* 3a).

priuato consilio is a set phrase whose precise meaning will depend upon context: here perhaps 'personal decision-making'. See also next n.

neque exercitus Manlii quantus aut quo consilio foret satis compertum habebat 'nor had he found out with sufficient certainty how big Manlius' army was or what its intentions were': *exercitus Manlii* has been extracted from the indirect questions and fronted in order to contrast directly with *urbem* above. *compertum habere* (again at 58.1) is a set phrase (*OLD compertus* c) and here used pointedly: Cicero's claims to knowledge (e.g. *Cat.* 1.10 with Dyck ad loc., 27) were such that the verb *comperire* was later used to taunt him (*Fam.* 5.5.2, *Att.* 1.14.5); but Cicero's claims were in fact limited (e.g. *Sull.* 12 'nihil comperi' with Berry's n.), and here S. reminds readers that Cicero did not pretend to knowledge which he did not have. *quo consilio* is an abl. of description, the meaning of the noun being different from that in the preceding colon (14.3n. *conuicti*). *foret* again = *esset*.

rem ad senatum refert: technical wording for referring a matter to the senate for debate (*OLD refero* 7).

iam anteā uūlgī rūmōrĭbŭs ēxăgĭtātŭm: this is a tricky passage. The MSS read *rumoribus exagitatam*, but, despite *TLL* 5.2.1154.55–61, there is no clear example of *exagito* = 'discuss' (as opposed to 'criticise, attack'). Nipperdey's *agitatam* is very strongly supported by Tac. *A.* 3.9.1 'eaque res agitata rumoribus', but Cortius' *exagitatum* ('roused, agitated'), though unparalleled with *rumoribus* (-*re*), is an easier change, preserves the favoured clausula, and perhaps gives better sense (for the verbal hyperbaton see 12.3n. *in*). *uulgi rumor(es)* is common in Tacitus (5×), though found occasionally elsewhere (Liv. 44.34.4, Sil. 4.9). The association of rumours and the crowd goes back to Homer (*Il.* 2.93–4); see also below, 30.2n. (*alii*).

29.2 quod ... solet: *sc. fieri* or similar. *quod* is parenthetical (*OLD qui*[1] 13a) and refers to *senatus decreuit*.

---

[67] S. does not mention the story about Crassus as reported by Plutarch (*Cic.* 15, *Crass.* 13.4) and Dio (37.31.1): allegedly Crassus had received from an anonymous source several letters, including one addressed to himself, in which he was advised to leave the city because of the bloodshed planned by Catiline. Crassus had taken the letters (the others unopened) to Cicero, who next day convened the senate and obliged the addressees to read out the contents there and then. Since these other letters agreed with that of Crassus, the senate was persuaded by the evidence to pass the *senatus consultum ultimum* (2n. *senatus*).

senatus decreuit darent operam consules ne quid res publica detrimenti caperet: Asconius, whose text at the key point (6.4–6) is defective, is understood to be saying that Cicero delivered his *First Catilinarian* on the eighteenth day after the *senatus consultum ultimum* was passed, but (a) it is not known whether Asconius was counting inclusively, (b) the date of Cicero's speech is itself uncertain (31.5n.). Scholars conventionally assign the *s.c.u.* to 21 or 22 October. In surviving references to ultimate decrees of the senate the wording *ne quid . . . capiat* (*caperet*) is very frequent indeed, although the introductory formula admits of more variation (see S. Mendner, 'Videant consules', *Philol.* 110 (1966) 258–67, at 263–4).

29.3 ea potestas . . . habere: although in surviving texts a *senatus consultum* is first described as *ultimum* at Caes. *BC* 1.5.3 'decurritur ad illud extremum atque ultimum senatus consultum', the measure itself had been in existence since 121 BC, when it was used against Gaius Gracchus: there was thus no real need for S. to insert an explanatory parenthesis, but the device is narratologically effective in emphasising the gravity of the step taken (see also next n.). The various infinitives are dependent on *potestas* (*OLD* 5a): 'That is the greatest power permitted to a magistrate, <namely, the power> to assemble an army . . .'. For discussion see e.g. Lintott, *CRR* 89–93; G. K. Golden, *Crisis management during the Roman republic* (2013) 104–49, esp. 125–33; Straumann 88–100, 129–30; P. Buongiorno (ed.), *Senatus consultum ultimum e stato di eccezione: fenomeni in prospettiva* (2020).

domi militiaeque imperium atque iudicium summum: although it is difficult to be sure (as also at Cic. *Leg. Agr.* 2.34 'summo cum imperio iudicioque rerum omnium'), it seems plausible to regard these words as a chiasmus, in which *domi militiaeque* corresponds to *summum* in the same way as *imperium* corresponds to *iudicium*: the point is not that *imperium* is *summum* (a common expr.) but that *imperium* could be exercised *domi* (which was unusual): the expression *domi militiaeque imperium* is in fact exceptionally rare (for discussion see Drogula, *CC* 88–92, 121–5). If this analysis is correct, it follows that *summum* qualifies only *iudicium*: this too is an exceptionally rare expr., and, although its significance is severely downplayed by Drummond 79–81, in the context of the Catilinarian conspiracy it is difficult not to see a reference to the passing of a sentence of *summum supplicium*.

aliter sine populi iussu nullius earum rerum consuli ius est 'otherwise the consul has the right to none of those matters without an order from the people' (*OLD aliter* 6a). *iussu* is found only in the abl. and its combination with *populi* is very common; its unparalleled governance by *sine* seems a Sallustian variation for the common *iniussu populi*.

30.1 L. Saenius: not mentioned anywhere else.

litteras ... **Faesulis allatas:** a routine journey from Faesulae to Rome would take over a week (27.1n.); according to *Orbis*, a horseman could do it in under five days, while a relay of horsemen would take just over a day. **ante diem VI Kalendas Nouembres:** 27 October, the same date as given at Cic. *Cat.* 1.7, where it is described as a prediction on Cicero's part.

30.2 id quod ... **solet:** *sc. fieri* or similar. For the parenthetical use of *id quod* ('something which ...') see 14.1n.: the parenthesis logically applies only to the announcement of portents and prodigies.

alii portenta atque prodigia nuntiabant: *portentum* and *prodigium* are 'essentially synonymous terms' (Pease on Cic. *Div.* 1.93) and quite frequently coordinated (e.g. Cic. *Tog. Cand.* fr. 11 'Te uero, Catilina, consulatum sperare aut cogitare non prodigium atque portentum est?'). *nuntiare* is the regular word for the reporting of prodigies and the like (e.g. Liv. 22.1.8 'augebant metum prodigia ex pluribus simul locis nuntiata'; *OLD* 6–7), and Cicero devotes a whole section of the *Third Catilinarian* to the topic (18–19); but the generalisation *id quod ... solet* suggests very strongly that S. is not referring to anything specific but to a phenomenon which is common to all wars. See esp. Fussell 115–25.[68]

Capuae ... **seruile bellum moueri:** the slave revolt of 73–71 BC under the leadership of the gladiator Spartacus had started in Capua before spreading across Italy: see B. D. Shaw, *Spartacus and the slave wars* (2001), T. Urbainczyk, *Spartacus* (2004). See also 30.7n. (*uti*).

30.3 senati decreto: the old-fashioned gen., mentioned at Quint. 1.6.27 as an alternative to *senatūs*, is usually found dependent on *decretum/-a* (as at 36.5, 53.1, *BJ* 40.1, *H.* 1.62) or *consultum/-a* (as at Sisenn. 38C/17P, 78C/119P and often in Cicero), but not always (e.g. *BJ* 25.11 'senati uerbis'). See also Lebek 271; 59.5n. (*quas*).

Q. Marcius Rex ... **Q. Metellus Creticus:** the former (cos. 68) had been proconsul in Cilicia; the latter (cos. 69) on Crete, which he established as a Roman province (hence his *cognomen*): see *MRR* 2.168–9.

in Apuliam circumque ea loca '(was sent) into Apulia and around that area': the only other ex. of this phrase is in the Caesarian corpus (*BC* 1.37.1 'quas Narbone circumque ea loca hiemandi causa disposuerat'; cf. *Bell. Hisp.* 20.1 'castra mouit Vcubim uersus et circum ea loca castella disposuit').

30.4 ii utrique ad urbem imperatores erant 'each of those two were near the City as "imperatores"' (*OLD ad* 13a). Not only were both men present as army commanders, but each had also been saluted as

---

[68] Fussell quotes from Marc Bloch, *The historian's craft* (Eng. trans. 1954) 108–9, who noted that during the First World War there was 'a prodigious renewal of oral tradition, the ancient mother of myths and legends'; Bloch in turn seems to be remembering the preface to Thucydides (1.23.3 'the stories of former times, handed down by oral tradition, ceased to be incredible').

'imperator' by his army (*MRR* 2.145, 154). For the rules associated with requesting a triumph see M. Beard, *The Roman triumph* (2007) 187–218. Metellus Creticus was obliged to wait until 62 for his triumph (*MRR* 2.176); Marcius Rex died untriumphed in 61. The plural *utrique* can be used of individuals when they form 'a natural pair' (*OLD* 3b).

calumnia paucorum quibus omnia honesta atque inhonesta uendere mos erat: by the Lex Gabinia (67) and Lex Manilia (66) Pompey had succeeded to the commands of Marcius and Metellus with superior powers (*MRR* 2.144–6, 153–5), and his supporters (*paucorum*) maintained that the two had been in effect his subordinates and so not entitled to a triumph (see also Epstein 77–8). For the juxtaposition of positive and negative adjs. (*honestus ~ inhonestus* recurs at *BJ* 31.12, 80.4 and is quite common, e.g. Ter. *Andr.* 797–8) see 20.7n. (*nobiles*): S.'s clause is imitated at Tac. *A.* 2.38.4 '*quibus omnia* principum, *honesta atque inhonesta*, laudare *mos est*'. For venality see 10.4n. (*omnia*).

30.5 Q. Pompeius Rufus … Q. Metellus Celer: *sc. missi sunt.* The former, who did not advance beyond the praetorship, is not mentioned again; the latter, who became consul in 60, was currently praetor (42.3) and is mentioned also at 57.2 (*MRR* 2.166, 3.37). According to Cicero (*Cat.* 2.5, 26), Celer was sent not just to Picenum but also to the *ager Gallicus*, that being the area immediately to the north (*BA* Map 42: D1–F3). The view that Celer's wife Clodia was Catullus' beloved Lesbia is now largely dismissed (see Ian Du Quesnay and Tony Woodman (edd.), *The Cambridge companion to Catullus* (2021) 3).

30.6 indicauisset: the pluperf. subjunc. (= fut. perf. indic. in direct speech) is explained by the fact that we are now in virtual indirect speech after *decreuere* (next n.).

praemium … sestertia ducenta: *decreuere* has to be understood from the following sentence (it would have been a great deal easier if S. had written *decreuere itemque* rather than the other way round): 'In addition, if anyone revealed …, they decreed freedom and 100,000 sesterces as reward for a slave, and immunity for the matter and 200,000 sesterces for a free man'. When Cicero's informant, Q. Curius, subsequently alleged that Julius Caesar had been one of the conspirators, Caesar prevented him from receiving the reward (Suet. *DJ* 17.1–2). *sestertia* is a neut. plur. adj. with *milia* understood (*OLD* 3b). For the genitive of the offence, again at *BJ* 31.19, see *TLL* 7.1.723.8–27.

30.7 uti gladiatoriae familiae Capuae in cetera municipia distribuerentur pro cuiusque opibus: the construction with *decreuere* now changes from dir. object to indirect command, a common variation. *familiae* (*OLD* 3a) is the technical term for troops of gladiators, who were kept and trained in a *ludus* (see G. G. Fagan, 'Training gladiators: life in the *ludus*', in L. L. Brice and D. Slootjes (edd.), *Aspects of ancient institutions and geography*

(2015) 122–44). Gladiatorial schools would be owned by individuals such as Julius Caesar (Caes. *BC* 1.14.3, Cic. *Att.* 7.14.2, Suet. *DJ* 10.2), C. Porcius Cato (Cic. *Q.Fr.* 2.5.3) or Atticus (Cic. *Att.* 4.4a.2). The potential support of gladiators for C. is mentioned several times in Cicero's *Second Catilinarian* (2.7, 9, 19, and esp. 26), and the policy of dispersing a school's gladiators as a public precaution would be adopted again in 49 BC (Cic. *Att.* 7.14.2; see also Oakley on Liv. 9.42.9). But, since there was at least one other gladiatorial school at Capua in addition to Caesar's (cf. Vell. 30.5), the transmitted acc. *Capuam* is very odd: how could gladiators be dispersed to Capua if they were already there? Vretska proposed to read abl. *Capua* and to delete the transmitted *et*, which follows: adnominal ablatives of origin or domicile are regular (Adams, *AIL* 565), e.g. Caes. *BC* 3.71.1 'M. Sacratiuirum Capua', but *Capuae* perhaps better explains the presence of *et* (cf. Liv. *per.* 95 'gladiatores Capuae ex ludo Lentuli profugerunt'). For the qualification *pro... opibus* cf. Tac. *A.* 3.2.2 'pro opibus loci uestem, odores aliaque funerum sollemnia cremabant' (also 51.43 below).

per totam urbem uigiliae haberentur: *uigiliae* are mentioned again at 32.1 (n.), and in both cases it is difficult to be sure whether the term is abstract ('watches') or refers more concretely to men on patrol: see *OLD* 1a–b, where the present passage is listed (probably correctly) as abstract, although Cicero's frequent references to *uigiliae* in his Catilinarian speeches are often taken as concrete (e.g. 1.1 'urbis uigiliae', listed under *OLD* 1b). Whether Rome had any form of police force in the republic is surprisingly controversial, but it seems from the Catilinarian crisis that patrols could be mounted at least on an ad hoc basis. See e.g. W. Nippel, *Public order in ancient Rome* (1995), C. J. Fuhrmann, *Policing the Roman empire* (2012).

minores magistratus: those below the rank of praetor, but esp. the *triumuiri capitales*, the three men responsible for the maintenance of public order (*BNP* 14.891–2).

31.1 Quis rebus permota ciuitas atque immutata urbis facies erat 'The community had been shaken by these developments and the face of the city altered.' The latter phrase suggests an earthquake image or similar (cf. Sen. *NQ* 6.4.1 'mille miracula mouet faciemque mutat locis', Plin. *Ep.* 6.20.18 'occursabant ... oculis mutata omnia', Tac. *A.* 4.67.2 'antequam Vesuuius mons ardescens faciem loci uerteret'); *permoueo*, unlike the simple form (e.g. *BJ* 41.10 'moueri ciuitas et dissensio ciuilis quasi permixtio terrae oriri coepit'), is not elsewhere used of earthquakes but is more normally applied to persons: hence *ciuitas* means in effect 'citizens' (*OLD* 2), their emotions illustrated in the sentences which follow. For *urbis facies* cf. Ov. *Tr.* 4.6.45, Plin. *Ep.* 2.17.27. *quis rebus* (again at *BJ* 105.1,

H. 1.29, 2.79.4, 3.10) rather than *quibus rebus* (which he also uses) seems unique to S.

ex summa l̲aetitia l̲asciuiaque: as at 28.4 (n. *nonnullos*), *ex* combines the notion of 'after' with that of transformation, here marking the *peripeteia* or 'reversal' which is one of the hallmarks of classical historiography (Intro. p. 14). Since edd. tend to adopt Fronto's quotation of this whole passage (§§1–3), it seems illogical not to adopt his *lasciuiaque* for the MSS' *atque lasciuia.* The alliterating nouns are contrasted at Tac. *A.* 14.21.3, but not otherwise combined until *Itin. Alex.* 43.

quae diuturna quies pepererat: *quae* is neut. plur., referring to *laetitia* and *lasciuia* (cf. 20.2n. *Ni*). *diuturna quies* (which recurs at Liv. 3.25.5) is odd: the war with Spartacus had ended less than a decade previously (30.2n. *Capuae*).

omnes tristitia inuasit: despondency is seen as a disease (*OLD inuado* 4a), as again at *BJ* 39.1 'metus atque maeror ciuitatem inuasere'.

31.2 trepidare: the first of four different words for fear in this paragraph, the others being *metu* (easily S.'s commonest word for fear: 62×), *timor* (12×), *pauere* (3×). The historic infin. is one of a series of six, closely followed by another series in the next sentence (6.4n. *Igitur*). *timor populi* is another theme which opens the *First Catilinarian* (1.1). For the coupling with *festinare* cf. Plaut. *Cas.* 432 (Adams, *AILL* 578).

neque loco . . . satis credere: the conspirators' threats of arson (e.g. 24.4, 27.2, 32.2) were seemingly well known (*Cat.* 1.3, 2.10 and Dyck's nn.), but in an earthquake too, to which the present circumstance is likened (1n. *Quis*), no refuge can be trusted (cf. e.g. Lucr. 6.596–600, Sen. *NQ* 6.1.4–5).

suo quisque m̲e̲tu pericula m̲e̲tiri: it seems possible that the opening words stuck in Tacitus' mind (*H.* 3.69.2 'suo quisque metu') but the dactylic rhythms (– ∪ ∪ – <∪> ∪ – ∪ ∪ – – – <–>) suggest a *sententia* drawn from epic.

31.3 mulieres, quibus rei publicae magnitudine belli timor i̲nsolitus i̲ncesserat: *insolitus* is to be taken closely with *magnitudine*: 'over whom there came a fear of war <that was> unaccustomed because of the greatness of the commonwealth'. Women and (below) children are standard elements in narratives of the 'disaster' type (e.g. Xen. *Cyr.* 3.3.67, Quint. 8.3.68–70); the novelty of their fear adds to its severity (Sen. *Ep.* 91.3 'nouitas adicit calamitatibus pondus'; Oakley on Liv. 9.24.8). *timor incedit* is common in Livy and the Caesarian corpus but is otherwise unknown; the verb is found with a variety of constructions (see *OLD* 6), here a dat. For *timor insolitus* cf. Prop. 1.3.29; for *mulieres* see 13.3n. (*uiri*); interestingly, *r. p. magnitudo* seems unparalleled.

afflictare sese 'they beat themselves', i.e. they beat their breasts.

rogitare omnia 'they queried everything'. *rogitare*, only here in S., is common in comedy, Livy and Tacitus, with occasional occurrences in intervening authors (e.g. Cic., Virg., Prop., Val. Flacc.).

<omni rumore> pauere, <arripere omnia>: the bracketed words appear in Fronto's quotation of this passage; their omission from the MSS is doubtless due, at least partly, to confusion arising from the repetition of forms of *omnis*. The two expressions are a deliberate paradox: the women 'took fright at every rumour and seized on every item [*sc.* of news]' (*OLD arripere* 4).

superbia atque deliciis omissis is suggestive rather than clear. At Hor. *Epi.* 1.6.30–1 *omissis . . . deliciis* (the only other occurrence of the expr. and presumably reminiscent of S.) the noun seems to mean 'delights' or 'pleasures' (cf. *TLL* 5.446.14–15); some think S. means 'luxuries' or 'adornments'; but the coordination with *superbia*, a conventional feature of the desired female (e.g. Ov. *F.* 1.419), suggests that *deliciis* may be personal, 'lovers' (cf. 13.3n. *uiri*): S. sees the women as *dominae*, who act imperiously towards their paramours. The sense is similar to, but not quite the same as, *delicias superbiamque* at Mart. 12.75.6.

31.4 praesidia parabantur: esp. on Cicero's initiative (*Cat.* 1.6, 4.18).
ipse lege Plautia interrogatus erat ab L. Paulo: Cicero, addressing C., said 'tu te ipse in custodiam dedisti' (*Cat.* 1.19 with Dyck's n.); the interrogation (*TLRR* 111 no. 223) presumably took place in the interval between the passing of the *s.c.u.* and the *First Catilinarian*. L. Aemilius Paulus (cos. 50) seems later to have issued coins celebrating the defeat of C. and his conspiracy (M. H. Crawford, *Roman republican coinage* (1974) 1.441, no. 415/1): see Berry, *CC* 53–4. The Lex Plautia de ui (*TLRR* 111 no. 223) is thought to have been carried by the tribune Plautius in 70 BC (*MRR* 2.128).

31.5 sui expurgandi '(for the sake of) clearing his name' (*OLD expurgo* 3); contrast Cic. *Mur.* 51 'non se purgauit'.

sicut iurgio lacessitus foret 'as if he had been provoked/challenged by/in a quarrel': this use of *sicut* + subjunc., again at 38.3, 50.3 (probably) and *BJ* 60.4, seems to be a Sallustian mannerism (*OLD* 6a). For the expr. cf. Liv. 38.33.6, Rut. Lup. 2.7, Tac. *A.* 14.49.1. *foret* again = *esset*. It is very suspicious that, on the only two occasions in the *BC* where the principal MSS offer *sicut* rather than *sicuti*, the following word begins with *i-* (cf. 37.5 'sicut in').

in senatum uenit: so too Cicero in the *First Catilinarian* (2 'in senatum uenit', 16 'uenisti . . . in senatum'). The date of the speech, and hence of C.'s presence in the senate, is disputed. In support of 7 November see Berry on Cic. *Sull.* 52 and *CC* 35 n. 61; in support of 8 November see Dyck on Cic. *Cat.*, appendix 2. In the *Second Catilinarian*, which was delivered on the day after the First, Cicero says this (2.12): 'hesterno die, cum domi

meae paene interfectus essem, senatum in aedem Iouis Statoris conuocaui, rem omnem ad patres conscriptos detuli'. Since the attempted
murder of Cicero is agreed to have taken place in the morning of
7 November, I do not see how this passage does not confirm that the
First Catilinarian was delivered on the same day.[69]

31.6 praesentiam eius timens: Cicero's fear is not for himself but for
the state (*Cat.* 1.10 'magno me metu liberabis, modo inter me atque te
murus intersit', 18, 2.17).

orationem habuit luculentam atque utilem rei publicae: this is S.'s only
explicit reference to a Catilinarian speech; its seemingly understated
description as 'utilem rei publicae' is pointed, as 'Sallust everywhere
assumes Cicero's commitment to *res publica*' (Stone (1999) 59; see his
brilliant discussion, pp. 55–60). *luculentus* is common in Plautus and other
archaic authors and is a favourite of Cicero, but it is almost non-existent in
the first century AD, only reappearing in Gellius and Apuleius – a familiar
pattern. A month later, on 5 December, Cicero chose the phrase *uerba
luculentiora* (*Att.* 12.21.1) to describe the speech of Cato (52.2–36).

quam postea scriptam edidit: the question whether Cicero's published
speeches accurately represent their oral originals has become in recent
years 'the most debated topic in Ciceronian oratory' (Berry, *CC* 56). Berry
in a long discussion (56–82) argues that in most cases the published
speeches 'are reasonably close approximations of what Cicero actually
said' but that in the case of the *Catilinarians* they were not published
until almost three years after delivery (cf. *Att.* 2.1.3, June 60 BC) and that
in the interval they had been revised, sometimes extensively: it is possible
'to read the speeches entirely as productions of 60 BC' (88). Yet a three-
year interval between delivery and publication would be 'unparalleled' (G.
La Bua, *Cicero and Roman education* (2019) 29), and I have argued elsewhere that *Att.* 2.1.3 has been misread and that Cicero did not delay in
publishing the most important speeches of his life (Woodman (2021b) 1–
3). The wording of S.'s clause (with which cf. Postum. Alb. 4C/P 'in eo
uolumine quod de aduentu Aeneae conscripsit atque <e>didit', if that text
is right) implies that he took the *First Catilinarian* to be what it purports to
be, viz. a written version of what Cicero said on 7 (or 8) November. There
is no hint of revision.

31.7 assedit: *assīdĕre* is the *mot juste* for sitting down after delivering
a speech (*OLD* 1a; Oakley on Liv. 9.8.2). In its perfect forms (again at
53.1) it is indistinguishable from *assīdēre* ('to sit beside').

---

[69] Supporters of 8 November are obliged to say that *hesterno die* refers only to
conuocaui and *detuli* and not also to *cum … interfectus essem*: such is the practice
of Dyck, who omits the passage from his discussion of what he misleadingly
describes as 'the evidence'; but the fronted position of the phrase strongly
suggests otherwise.

Catilina, ut erat paratus ad dissimulanda omnia: this use of *ut*, not quite the same as that at 59.2 (n.), is quasi-causal: 'prepared as he was to dissemble everything' (cf. e.g. *BJ* 7.4 'Iugurtha, ut erat impigro atque acri ingenio', Cic. *Mur.* 52 'ille, ut semper fuit apertissimus', Liv. 5.50.1, Curt. 6.6.27, Tac. *A.* 11.8.3 'ille, ut erat magnis ausis promptus', 15.42.2 'Nero tamen, ut erat incredibilium cupitor'). For C.'s *dissimulatio* see above and 5.4.

demissu uultu: a speaker's *uultus* was crucial in creating the right impression (Quint. 11.3.72 'dominatur maxime uultus. hoc supplices, ... hoc summissi sumus'). But C.'s charade does not last (9 'tum ille furibundus ...').

postulare a patribus coepit: this is not the impression given by Cic. *Orat.* 129 'a nobis homo audacissimus Catilina in senatu accusatus obmutuit': §§7–9, if not entirely invented, have been transposed here from accounts of speeches which C. is said to have made on earlier occasions (see below). S. makes no mention of the fact that C. was sitting all alone on the senate benches (*Cat.* 1.16, 2.12), as depicted dramatically by Cesare Maccari in his famous fresco of 1888.[70]

ea familia ortum: *ea* is equivalent to *tali* and, like *ita* below, signposts the following consecutive clause (*OLD is* 3): 'he had been born of such a family that ...'. Livy has Manlius Torquatus echo C.'s words when he seeks permission to fight the giant Gaul (7.10.3 'me ex ea familia ortum quae ...'). *ortus* instead of *natus* is often said to be elevated; the evidence (*TLL* 9.2.998.48–68) suggests that it depends on the context.

ut omnia bona in spe haberet: does *bona* agree with *omnia* or *spe*? It is difficult to be sure (see the *in spe* phrases collected by Shackleton Bailey on Cic. *Att.* 1.13(13).6), but the former perhaps makes better sense: 'that he had every advantage in prospect' (*OLD spes* 3d). The order is always *spes bona* when S. combines the two words elsewhere, as he does several times (e.g. 21.1).

sibi patricio homini ... perdita re publica opus esse: the usual *opus est* construction (dat. of the person, abl. of the thing required) is here extended by means of a perf. passive part. (*OLD opus* 12b), which forms another example of the *ab urbe condita* idiom (17.1n. *imparatam*): '(they should not think that) he, as a patrician, required *the ruin of* the commonwealth'. *sibi* is fronted because it begins an elaborate (chiastic) contrast with Cicero (ABC ~ CAB): identity (*sibi*), background (*patricio ... essent*), destruction (*perdita r.p.*) ~ protection (*eam seruaret*), identity (*M. Tullius*), background (*inquilinus ... Romae*). See next n. but one.

---

[70] Scholars have pointed out that Maccari wrongly depicts Cicero as older than C. and places his speech in the senate house rather than in the temple of Jupiter Stator.

ipsius atque maiorum plurima beneficia in plebem Romanam: scholars have questioned the expr. *plebem Romanam* here. Paananen (26) suggests that *plebs* has a different meaning with each genitive: with *maiorum* C. is referring to the time of the Conflict of the Orders and the struggle between patricians and plebeians; with *ipsius* he means the lower classes of his own time, to whom he was trying to appeal with his revolutionary programme. The latter hardly strikes the exculpatory note required in the circumstances. The former is given point by the contrast with *patricio homini*, but what is the evidence that the early Sergii conferred *beneficia* on the *plebs*? M. Sergius Silus, C.'s presumed grandfather (Urso 71), served in the war against king Perseus in 168 BC (Liv. 44.40.5), while his great-grandfather performed with remarkable bravery in the Second Punic War (Plin. *NH* 7.104–5); these *maiores* would be well worth referring to, but their beneficiaries were the *populus Romanus* as a whole (as Gruter proposed to read here).

cum eam seruaret M. Tullius: the clause is ironical and means the opposite of what it says: C. means that Cicero is *failing* to protect the commonwealth: hence, if C. wanted to destroy it (something which of course he denies), there would be no need for him to do so. The allegation of Cicero's weakness perhaps derives from the riddling allegorical contrast with C. himself which the latter drew at an earlier meeting of the senate (cf. Cic. *Mur.* 51, Plut. *Cic.* 14.6).[71]

inquilinus ciuis urbis Romae: *inquilinus* ('lodger') and *ciuis* are in apposition to each other, and the effect is underlined by the formality of *urbis Romae* (Spevak 283): 'a lodger-citizen of the city of Rome'. Cicero, like Marius, came from Arpinum, a small town in the western foothills of the Apennines about 60 miles SE of Rome (*BA* Map 44: E2). His non-metropolitan origins were the cause of considerable snobbery (see Berry on Cic. *Sull.* 22); C.'s famous jibe (reported also by App. *BC* 2.2.5) is applied defensively to the elder Cato at Vell. 128.2. See also 23.6n. (*pleraque*).

31.8 hostem atque parricidam uocare: each noun is a regular term of abuse (e.g. Cic. *Sull.* 19 'illi hosti ac parricidae', of Autronius), but C. will formally be declared a *hostis* of the state very shortly (36.2). The Catilinarians are called *parricidae* by Caesar (51.25) and Cato (52.31) and in the *Catilinarians* (e.g. 1.19).

31.9 furibundus: adjs. in *-bundus* are regarded as vivid and appropriate for dramatic moments; S. also uses *praedabundus* (*BJ* 90.2) and *uitabundus* (*BJ* 38.1, 60.4, 101.9, *H.* 3.25). Usually they accompany verbs of motion

---

[71] The meeting to which Cicero and Plutarch refer is that which took place on the day originally scheduled for the consular elections of 63, viz. 23 September (as argued by Ramsey (2019)): see 26.5n. (*dies*).

(W.[3] on Tac. *Agr.* 37.5), which is not quite the case here (cf. *se* ... *proripuit* below). *furibundus* is esp. common in poetry.

Quoniam quidem circumuentus ... **ab inimicis praeceps agor:** *circumuenio* here = 'frame, accuse falsely' (*OLD* 6): as at 34.2, C. claims to be a victim of the procedure which earlier he himself had used against others (16.3n. *nihilo*); *praeceps ago(r)* is a set phrase = 'to (be) drive(n) headlong'. *ab inimicis* is to be taken in common with both participle and finite verb. *quoniam quidem*, esp. common in Cic., Val. Max., Colum. and Sen., 'is usually no more than a strengthened *quoniam*' (Solodow 134).

incendium meum ruina restinguam: S. has transposed to 7 (or 8) Nov. a threat which C. had evidently delivered almost two months earlier.[72] At a meeting of the senate 'a few days before' that of 23 September (Cic. *Mur.* 51 'paucis diebus ante'), C., who evidently liked speaking allegorically (31.7n. *cum*), had given Cato this reply: 'si quod esset in suas fortunas incendium excitatum, id se non aqua sed ruina restincturum' (Cic. *Mur.* 51; cf. Otto 172–3). The reference is to knocking down buildings to prevent a fire spreading (Tac. *A.* 15.40.1 'finis incendio factus, prorutis per immensum aedificiis'). S. is followed in his transposition by Val. Max. 9.11.3 and Flor. 2.12(4.1).7.

32.1　se ex curia ... **proripuit:** cf. *Cat.* 2.1 'L. Catilinam furentem ... uerbis prosecuti sumus. abiit, excessit, euasit, erupit'. *curia* is here metonymy for *senatu* (cf. Cic. *De Or.* 3.167), since the senate meeting of 7 (or 8) November had been held in the Temple of Jupiter Stator at the foot of the Palatine Hill (*Cat.* 2.12). For the symbolism and significance of the place see Vasaly 41–59 (map on p. 44).

ibi ... **profectus est:** the sentence is periodic, with the subject (*ipse*) almost at the very beginning and the main verb at the very end (for S.'s preference for terminal verbs see A. M. Devine and L. D. Stephens, *Latin word order* (2006) 216–18). Within this frame there are: a present participle (*uoluens*), a two-part causal clause (*quod neque* ... *et* ...), and a second present participle (*credens*), on which depends an accusative + infinitive incorporating a temporal clause (*priusquam* ...).

multa ipse secum uoluens: S. cannot possibly have known this; debates with oneself are a regular feature of emotive writing, both verse and prose (e.g. Liv. 26.7.3 'multa secum ... uoluenti'; Pease on Virg. *Aen.* 4.533). See also Rutherford 14–21.

neque insidiae consuli procedebant et ab incendio intellegebat urbem uigiliis munitam: these words look back to the first two of C.'s aims as itemised at 27.2 (~ *consulibus insidias* ... *incendia*), which explains why *ab*

---

[72] A nineteenth-century suggestion that C. made the threat on two separate occasions is rightly rejected by Ledworuski 240 n. 102.

incendio is fronted: as a result, *intellegebat* occurs within the clause which depends on it. *neque* ... *et* ... is regular, e.g. *BJ* 1.5, 20.5 *al.*

neque insidiae^consuli procedebant: the dat. is not to be taken with *procedebant* (as 27.3) but with *insidiae*, a construction evidently influenced by the verb *insidiari*, which takes a dat.

ab incendio intellegebat urbem uigiliis munitam: *sc. esse*; cf. *Cat.* 1.8 'illam coloniam ... uigiliis esse munitam' (of Praeneste), the only other ex. of the expression; for *uigiliae* see 30.7n. *muniri ab* is not very common but is found in both verse and prose (e.g. Lucr. 3.820, Hor. *C.* 3.16.3, Colum. 1.8.9, 11.3.2, Curt. 6.8.9). For *uigiliis* see 30.7n. (*per*).

optimum factu is a set phrase (55.1, 57.5, Cic. *Cat.* 1.29): *sc. esse* or *fore*.

priusquam legiones scriberentur: the impf. subjunctive here represents a present subjunctive in direct speech: C. is imagined as having said 'before the legions *can be* enrolled' (*NLS* 185 §227 'the subjunctive became obligatory ... when the action of the main clause must of necessity ... precede that of the temporal clause'). For *scribo* = 'enroll, muster' see *OLD* 7b.

multa antecapere: for the verb see 13.3n. (*ea*).

nocte intempesta 'at dead of night' (27.3n. *rursus*). Since C. had left Rome by the time Cicero delivered his *Second Catilinarian* (*Cat.* 2.1, 26 'hac nocturna excursione Catilinae'), which was on the day following the delivery of the First, the night in question must, on the present reckoning (31.5n. *in senatum*), be that of 7–8 November.

cum paucis: 'parum comitatus', according to *Cat.* 2.4, although Plut. mentions 300 followers (*Cic.* 16.6).

in Manliana castra profectus est: cf. Cicero's statement at the end of the *First Catilinarian* (1.30): 'intellego, si iste quo intendit, in Manliana castra, peruenerit, neminem tam stultum fore qui non uideat coniurationem esse factam' (cf. 1.10, the only other ex. of *Manliana castra*).

32.2 ceterisque quorum cognouerat promptam audaciam: *sc. esse* ('the others whose revolutionary spirit he knew to be keen'); C. had earlier complained about the *ignauia* of his supporters (27.4; cf. 28.1) and his complaints would later be echoed by the impatient Cethegus (43.3 'ignauia sociorum'). For *audaciam* see 5.4n. (*animus*); for *promptam aud.* cf. Curt. 8.11.11, 9.6.10, Amm. 17.12.8. For Cethegus and Lentulus see 17.3nn.

mandat ... confirment: *sc. ut*, as often (*OLD mando*[1] 6b); *quibus* seems equivalent to *quibuscumque*: 'he ordered that they should reinforce the resources of their faction by whatever means they could'. After a governing verb in the historic present, the subordinate verbs may be either primary sequence (as 28.2) or historic; here, as at 34.1, we have both (see *OLS* 1.559–61). For the meaning of *factio* here (*OLD* 4a) see Seager (1972) 57.

caedem, incendia ... **parent:** the two nouns (again at 43.2, 48.4, 51.9, 52.36) are commonly combined in various authors in various ways and esp. by Cicero and in the *Catilinarians* (e.g. 1.3, 2.6 'uideo ... quis sibi has urbanas insidias caedis atque incendiorum depoposcerit', 2.10): see Adams, *AILL* 559.

propediem cum magno exercitu ad urbem accessurum: *sc. esse.* The 'great army' is that which C. was on his way to Manlius to collect (above, 1), but *propediem* ('shortly', 'any day') is an empty promise: it would take a considerable length of time to reach Manlius and return to Rome with an army (36.1n. *paucos,* 43.1n. *cum*). C. is reminded of his vow by Lentulus at the start of December (44.6 'ne cunctetur ipse propius accedere'; cf. Cic. *Cat.* 3.8 'ut ad urbem quam primum cum exercitu accederet').

32.3–39.5 PLEAS, PROTESTATIONS AND PITY: (?) NOVEMBER 63

This section features messages from two of the main protagonists: Gaius Manlius and C. himself. In 32.3–33.5 Manlius sends to his would-be opponent, the ex-consul Q. Marcius Rex, a pre-emptive message, presented in direct speech, protesting that his recourse to armed conflict was not treasonable and pleading that the senate should take pity on the plight from which his men were suffering on account of the debts for which they were liable. The message is a *tour de force*, quite belying the reputation for inarticulateness which was imputed to military men (W.[3] on Tac. *Agr.* 9.2). Manlius begins by focussing on his followers (1 *nos*), to whom, by way of anaphoric references to the *maiores* (2 'saepe maiores uestrum') and the *plebs* (3 'saepe ipsa plebs'), he returns at the end (4 'at nos'). The circular movement of the argument is reinforced by verbal links (1 ~ 5: *testamur ~ obtestamur, imperator ~ te, miseri ~ miseris, lege ~ legis, praetoris ~ praetoris*), and the repeated reference to 'the pitiable' identifies the message as a *miseratio* or 'appeal to pity'. Marcius' reply, presented in indirect speech, is brief and to the point (34.1): armed threats were unacceptable and pleas to the senate should be made in the proper way.

In 34.2 C. writes to various ex-consuls and others protesting his innocence and alleging that he was going into voluntary exile in Massilia to save the commonwealth from any further disruption. But this brief summary in indirect speech is then matched by the letter, in direct speech, which C. sent to the ex-consul Q. Catulus. This letter too is constructed on a ring basis, being framed by pleas that Catulus should look after Orestilla, C.'s wife (1 *tua fides ... commendationi meae ~ 5 commendo tuae ... fidei*); the ominous fatalism of this plea is given substance in the body of the letter, where C. talks resentfully of his political rejection and declares that he is taking up the cause of the pitiable ('miserorum causam'). But his claim to be telling the truth is belied by the illogicality of his argument (35.2n.), and his letter is otherwise replete with strange examples of wordplay (*priuatus* ~ *publicam*; *alienum* ~ *alienis* ~ *alienatum*; *nominibus* ~ *nominibus* ~ *nomine*; *honore honestatos* ~ *honestas*).

It will be clear that the format of the narrative is chiastic (two extended messages in direct speech enclose two brief passages of indirect speech) but that the dynamics are in parallel: Manlius' elaborate address is rebuffed by Marcius' brief reply, while the falsity of C.'s circulars is shown up by his own quite different letter to Catulus. This double 'reality check' sets the scene for three senatorial decisions: the declaration of C. and Manlius as 'hostes', an amnesty for anyone leaving their army, and the roles allotted to the two consuls, Cicero and Antonius, for dealing with the enemy (36.2–3).

These roles will be described in detail in the second half of the book (respectively 39.6–55.6 and 56–61); in the meantime, by way of concluding the first half, S. uses the Catilinarians' rejection of the amnesty to illustrate the pitiable state of contemporary society ('imperium ... miserabile'). Although Rome ruled the world and was richer than ever before, there were still some citizens who wanted to destroy everything (36.4): not a single member of the conspiracy betrayed it for a reward or even abandoned C.'s side (36.5); on the contrary, there were those outside the conspiracy who set off to join it (39.5). These two latter statements frame a digression on socio-political decline (37.1–39.4), the insertion of which emphasises the division between the first half of the monograph and the second (Intro. p. 13).

32.3 Dum haec ... geruntur: this formula (again at *BJ* 32.2) is esp. common in the Caesarian corpus (17×) and Livy (35×); see also 56.1n. (*Dum*) and in general Oakley on Liv. 9.32.1.

ad Marcium Regem: Marcius Rex had been despatched to Manlius' base at Faesulae (30.3n.).

33.1 Deos hominesque testamur, imperator: when a speaker was making an appeal to pity (intro.), an 'invocation to the gods' might be found effective (Quint. 6.1.34). *deos hominesque testari*, which is found with a variety of constructions (here the acc. + infin.) or none, is a regular expr. (*OLD testor* 1 'To invoke as a witness'); in Livy's story of *Manlius Capitolinus*, where 'Catilinarian motifs' have been detected (Oakley on 6.11.1 (pp. 481–4) and 6.14.11), the unique *deos atque homines obtestantem* (6.14.5, where the meaning is 'implore') seems to combine allusions to *Deos hominesque* at the start of Gaius *Manlius'* message and to *obtestamur* at the end (§5); for others see below. *imperator* is a 'respectful address to a Roman general of the republican period, from his own subordinates or others' (E. Dickey, *Latin forms of address* (2002) 331); for Marcius Rex as *imperator* see 30.3–4.

nos arma neque contra patriam cepisse neque quo . . . sed uti . . . sumus: *arma capere* is a set phrase (*OLD capio*[1] 1b); the emphasis of the sentence seems to fall on the contrasting purpose clauses and hence on Manlius' emotive description of his followers.

neque quo periculum aliis faceremus: although *arma . . . cepisse* almost certainly means 'that we have taken up arms', a primary perfect is sometimes followed by a dependent imperfect subjunctive in letters (Whitton on Plin. *Ep.* 2.5.2). *quo* varies the prepositional phrase *contra patriam* and (as again at 58.3) is itself varied by *uti* below; for *quo* = *ut* see 11.5n. (*quo*). *aliis* is a nicely oblique hint at the existing danger from which Manlius' supporters are suffering (cf. 20.8n.).

uti corpora nostra ab iniuria tuta forent: although *corpora* here refers to 'the body regarded as denoting the whole man, one's person, one's very self' (*OLD* 8a), thus leading neatly into the masculine rel. pronoun *qui* (a *constructio ad sensum*), nevertheless the very reference to 'bodies safe from injury' implies that Manlius sees himself and his followers as slaves at physical risk from their creditors (see further below). *forent* = *essent*, but again with its useful future aspect (23.3n. *et*). *tutus ab* is regular (*OLD* 1a).

uiolentia atque crudelitate faeneratorum: causal abls. For *c. faeneratorum* cf. again Liv. 6.14.3 '*crudelitate faeneratorum* et miseriis *plebis*' (also 8.28.1, 5). For debt see 14.2n. (*alienum*), 21.2n. (*tabulas nouas*).

miseri, egentes: this belongs to the category of asyndeton bimembre in which the first term (on which see 35.3n. *publicam*) is expanded or illustrated by the second. Manlius' whole sentence is analysed and discussed by Adams, *AILL* 571–2.

plerique patriae, sed omnes fama atque fortunis expertes sumus: *plerique* and *omnes*, which contrast with each other, are in apposition to *qui*. Normally *expers* is constructed with a gen. but can also take an abl.: S. characteristically has both in the same sentence (*uariatio*). *patriae . . . expertes* (an unparalleled expr.) refers to exile, but it is unclear whether S. means that men fled Italy to escape debt or that men were so heavily in debt that they were as good as stateless: the latter seems suggested by what follows, in which case there is grim irony in the allegation that such persons could be fighting *contra patriam* (1). *fama* and *fortuna(e)* are very commonly combined (again at 51.12, *H.* 2.43.5); perhaps the present combination influenced Tac. *A.* 6.17.3 'multique *fortunis* prouoluebantur; euersio rei familiaris dignitatem et *famam* praeceps dabat' (of the debt crisis in AD 33).

neque cuiquam nostrum . . . lege uti: the Lex Poetelia et Papiria of 326 BC had abolished *nexum* or debt-bondage (see Oakley on Liv.

8.28.1–9), but in §5 Manlius says that the protection of the law had been removed with official blessing. *nostrum* is the form used when the genitive is partitive (G&L 55 §100 R.2); see further below, 2n.

neque amisso patrimonio liberum corpus habere 'nor (could any of us) live a free life after losing our property'. *liberum corpus*, seemingly a set phrase (first in Cato, *Orat.* 212M) and found also in Livy's Manlius episode (6.11.8), continues the implication (see above) of slavery brought on by debt (cf. Liv. 3.56.8 'qui liberum corpus in seruitutem addixisset'). *habere* is a 'support verb' (4.5n. *de*).

tanta saeuitia faeneratorum atque praetoris fuit: the urban praetor was the official who dealt with matters of debt (cf. *Cat.* 1.32, Tac. *A.* 6.17.2 'strepere praetoris tribunal'; Brennan 1.130–3); his 'savagery', like his *iniquitas* at 5 below, consisted of his favouring creditors over debtors. In 63 the urban praetor is thought to have been L. Roscius Otho (F. X. Ryan, *Hermes* 125 (1997) 236–40), and it has been suggested that his treatment of debtors explains why in July 63 he was the victim of a popular demonstration at the Apolline Games which as urban praetor he sponsored (so J. T. Ramsey, *Ciceroniana Online* 5.1 (2021) 22–4). For the paratactic construction see 7.3n. (*tanta*).

33.2 saepe maiores uestrum: the plur. *uestrum* means men like Marcius Rex, the ex-consul to whom the letter is addressed. The noun *maiores* is usually accompanied by the possessive adj. (e.g. *BJ* 31.6 'saepe maiores uestri', 17); its unique combination with the gen. of *uos* is attested by Gell. (20.6.14), who says that in his day readers of S. had already started to cross out *uestrum* and replace it with *uestri*. *saepe* is repeated in anaphora at §3 below: the repeated words itemise the two antithetical groups of forbears, who act as foils for the return to *nos* below (4). The very repetition of a word was deemed to be effective in the *miseratio* (*Rhet. Herenn.* 4.38).

miseriti *plebis* Romanae: the participle gestures towards Manlius' message being a *miseratio* (32.3–36.3n.) and was perhaps picked up by Livy in the Manlius Capitolinus episode (see above, 1n. *uiolentia*).

decretis suis inopiae eius opitulati sunt: if Manlius is not referring to debt, which is mentioned in the next sentence, he is perhaps referring to such legislation as that of Gaius Gracchus in 123, establishing the basic right of every Roman citizen to a ration of corn at a cheap rate below the normal market price (cf. Rickman 48–9, 158–61). Wordplay on *inopia* and cognate words is common (e.g. 11.3n. *semper*); for Seneca *opitulari* is a 'Ciceronian word' (*Ep.* 17.2).

memoria nostra ... argentum aere solutum est 'within living memory ... silver was redeemed by bronze' (*OLD soluo* 19). This is taken to allude to 86 BC, when C. was in his early 20s: the suffect consul L. Valerius Flaccus carried a law by which repayment of 25 per cent was deemed to cancel a debt entirely (Vell. 23.2), and, since a quarter of a silver sesterce was a single bronze *as*, S.'s reference to silver and bronze would be explained. Five years earlier M. Livius Drusus as tribune had alloyed silver with an eighth part of bronze (Plin. *NH* 33.46 'octauam partem aeris argento miscuit'), but this is less likely to be S.'s reference, since *soluere* seems not to be used of alloying. For *memoria nostra* cf. 51.32, 53.6 (*OLD memoria* 6b). *magnitudo aeris alieni* is something of a standard expr.

uolentibus omnibus bonis: *uolentibus* may be an allusion to 89 BC, when creditors were *un*willing, killing A. Sempronius Asellio who as praetor had tried to relieve the burdens of debt (see *MRR* 2.33, 3.188; Brennan 2.443). For the *boni* see 19.2n. (*quia*).

33.3   saepe ipsa plebs . . . armata a patribus secessit: *ipsa* looks back to *plebis* (2) and emphasises what the *plebs* did of its own accord as opposed to relying on the pity of others. There were three principal 'Secessions of the Plebs', in 494 (Liv. 2.31.7–33.3 with Ogilvie), 449 (Liv. 3.50.1–54.5 with Ogilvie) and c. 287 (Liv. *per.* 11.6 with Levene, *LFP* 2.219–22): see further *CAH* 7.2.212–17, 227–35, 400; *BNP* 13.184–5. *plebs armata* is a standard description on these occasions (*H.* 1.10.4, 3.15.1, Liv. 3.52.7, 4.9.8, Val. Max. 8.9.1, Flor. 1.17 = 1.23.1).

aut dominandi studio permota aut superbia magistratuum: the Secessions were revolts against the ruling powers and attempts at achieving some political influence; at least the First and Third are associated with the problem of debt. For *superbia* see 6.7n. (*in*); *s. magistratuum* recurs at Liv. 4.56.12, 43.2.2.

33.4   non imperium neque diuitias: the two nouns look back chiastically to §§3 and 2 respectively. C. had said exactly the opposite in his speech at 20.14–17 'diuitiae . . . in oculis sita sunt: . . . imperare', and Cicero for one had no illusions (*Cat.* 2.19): 'quamquam premuntur aere alieno, dominationem tamen exspectant'.

libertatem . . . nemo bonus nisi cum anima simul amittit: Manlius' words foreshadow C.'s death (61.2 'amissa anima'). The nom. *nemo bonus* is otherwise exclusively Ciceronian (4×).

33.5   obtestamur is here constructed without *ut* (*OLD* 2): 'we implore . . . that you should . . .'. The verb is picked up at Liv. 6.14.5 (above, 1n.).

legis praesidium quod iniquitas praetoris eripuit: for the law see above, 1n. (*neque cuiquam*). *legis/-um praesidium* is frequent in Cicero and uncommon elsewhere; *i. praetoris* is a Ciceronian phrase (*Quinct.* 9, *Tull.* 38); for *eripuit* cf. Sen. *Ep.* 18.10 'quod eripere nulla fortunae iniquitas possit'.

neue nobis eam necessitudinem imponatis ut quaeramus quonam modo maxime ulti sanguinem nostrum pereamus 'and that you do not place upon us the necessity of seeking how best we may avenge our blood by dying' (the speech ends with an 'heroic' clausula). *pereamus* represents a deliberative question in direct speech, but the main idea is expressed by

the participle *ulti* (a favourite device of Horace: see W.[6] on *C.* 3.10.1–2):
Manlius knows that, if it comes to a battle (*eam necessitudinem*), his side is
outnumbered and will be cut to pieces (*sanguinem nostrum*); the question is
how many of their opponents they can take with them when they die. The
threat is repeated by C. at the end of his final speech (58.21 'cauete inulti
animam amittatis'). *eam* (*OLD is* 2b) signposts the consecutive clause (see
also below, 34.1n. *respondit*).

34.1 respondit: Marcius throws Manlius' idioms back at him: he too
omits *ut* from introducing an indir. command and adopts the same use of
a pronoun to signpost a consecutive clause ('ea ... ut ... petiuerit'). As at
32.2, S. varies the tenses in the indir. speech ('uellent ... discedant ...
proficiscantur'). This is the last we hear about Marcius Rex, which is odd,
given that he had been despatched to Faesulae (30.3); perhaps his army
was incorporated into that of the consul Antonius when he was subsequently given the command to pursue C. (36.3): it is Antonius who is
mentioned in the final operations (56.4, 57.4–5).

mansuetudine atque misericordia: abls. of description. For the same
combination see 52.11n. (*hic*); the two nouns are contrasted at Sen.
Clem. 2.5.1.

senatum populi Romani: for this expr. cf. Cic. *Red. Sen.* 18, *Pis.* 18, Plin.
NH 35.28, Gell. 17.21.48, Fronto p. 119.15–16 vdH².

ut ... petiuerit: after a secondary main verb, consecutive clauses regularly exhibit a perfect subjunc. (*OLS* 1.575–7), which is retained even after
a secondary verb introducing indirect speech (*NLS* 225 §273 *Note*).

34.2 ex itinere 'while travelling' (*OLD* 3); he had set off on the night of
7–8 (or 8–9) Nov. (32.1).

optimo cuique: see 19.2n. (*quia*).

**se falsis criminibus circumuentum, quoniam factioni inimicorum resis-
tere nequiuerit:** C. repeats the protestations he made in the senate on 7
(or 8) Nov. (31.9 and n.). The suicide note of the elder Piso begins
similarly (Tac. *A.* 3.16.3): 'conspiratione *inimicorum* et inuidia *falsi criminis*
oppressus, quatenus ...'. Using the term *factio* of one's opponents is
common (famously at e.g. Caes. *BC* 1.22.5 'ut se et populum Romanum
factione paucorum oppressum in libertatem uindicaret', *Res Gestae* 1.1
'rem publicam a dominatione factionis oppressam in libertatem uindicaui'), but the exact meaning is not always clear: here 'intrigue', 'influence' or 'faction' are possible (Seager (1972) 55). Indirect speech is
regular after *litteras mittere* (*OLD littera* 7b).

Massiliam in exilium proficisci: on 8 (or 9) Nov., Cicero (*Cat.* 2.14, 16)
refers to the rumour that C. was going, not to Manlius' camp, but into exile
at Massilia (mod. Marseille), the place of exile of Verres in 70 and of Milo
some years later (Dio 40.54.3). Both then and on the previous day Cicero
talks of C. leaving Rome by the Via Aurelia (*Cat.* 1.24, 2.6), which runs up

the north-western coast of Italy and is the route one would take if Massilia were the destination. But Cicero knew full well (cf. *Cat.* 1.30) that this was a feint and that C. was on his way to join Manlius at Faesulae: 'triduo ... audietis' (*Cat.* 2.15).[73]

non quo sibi tanti sceleris conscius esset sed uti res publica quieta foret 'not because he was complicit in such a great crime but in order that the commonwealth should be undisturbed': *sibi*, often found with *conscius* (*OLD* 3a), is not translated in English; for *quo* to express a rejected reason see *OLD quo²* 4: the *uariatio* with a purpose clause is common. The purpose is of course the opposite of what C. really wanted (Cic. *Cat.* 2.19 'honores quos quieta re publica desperant perturbata se consequi posse arbitrantur').

seditio oreretur is a common expr.; as well as the third-conjugation form of the verb (again at *BJ* 72.1) S. also uses the fourth-conjugation form (*BJ* 6.3).

34.3 Q. Catulus: Q. Lutatius Catulus had been consul in 78 and represented the conservative faction in the senate; he is mentioned several times in S.'s *Histories* (1.1, 1.58, 1.67.6, 19, 22, 3.15.9): see *MRR* 2.85, 90, 157, 3.131. For his connection with C. see 35.1n.

nomine Catilinae 'on C.'s authority' (*OLD nomen* 14a, not 13a).

earum exemplum infra scriptum est 'A copy of it is written below.' Such phraseology is frequent in Cicero's correspondence (e.g. *Att.* 8.2.1, 8.6.2 'earum exemplum infra scripsi', *Fam.* 6.8.3 'earum litterarum exemplum infra scriptum est'). S. repeats the formula at 44.4, where the letter in question (44.5) shares some wording with the version quoted by Cicero (*Cat.* 3.12): whether we can infer from this evidence the authenticity of the present letter is uncertain, since there is no comparandum; nevertheless, on the grounds that 'the style and language of the letter are not Sallustian', Berry maintains that this 'is the only text to give the actual words of Catiline, or possibly a lightly edited version of them' (*CC* 38–9; cf. 238–9). 'Here speaks the authentic Catilina,' says Syme (*Sall.* 72).[74] But, whereas the *Catilinarians* were surely the source of the letter at 44.5, as

---

[73] *triduo* cannot refer to 'the estimated time for word to be brought back from Faesulae', as Dyck ad loc. says. (a) It would be very odd indeed to refer to the return journey, thereby ignoring entirely the outward journey, which had scarcely even begun. (b) Faesulae is c. 170 miles from Rome: travelling at a speed of almost 60 miles a day would have been impossible. Either Cicero is using *triduo* loosely to mean 'in no time at all' or, more probably, he is referring to the time it would take for C.'s true destination to become clear, either because C. would soon need to change route to the Via Cassia or because Cicero had knowledge of C.'s letter to Catulus (34.3).

[74] L. Canfora infers authenticity from the coincidence of *miserorum* at 35.3 and *miserorum ... miser* at Cic. *Mur.* 50 ('La lettera di Catilina: Norden, Marchesi, Syme', *HCS* 1 (2019) 128–34).

of much of S.'s other information about the conspiracy, where would he have found a copy of this one twenty years later? The techniques of ethopoeia and prosopopoeia were part of the rhetorical education of an elite Roman, and many ancient historians invented letters just as they did speeches. No one believes that Pompey's letter to the senate at *H.* 2.86, still less Mithridates' letter to King Arsaces at *H.* 4.60, are authentic documents, and there must be at least a possibility that S. is likewise resorting to *inuentio* here.

35.1 L. Catilina Q. Catulo: the words *salutem dicit* (often abbreviated to 'S.D.') are to be understood.

Egregia tua fidēs – rē cōgnĭtă, grātă mĭhī māgnīs in periculis: C.'s liaison with the Vestal Virgin, mentioned at 15.1 (n.), had led to his being brought before the pontifical court in 73 on a charge of *incestum* from which, according to the fifth-century AD historian Orosius, he was acquitted thanks to the influence of Catulus (6.3.1 'eodem anno ... Catilina incesti accusatus quod cum Fabia uirgine Vestali commisisse arguebatur Catuli gratia fultus euasit'). Since Catulus was a *pontifex* and may even have chaired the pontifical court in 73 (Cadoux 167), Orosius' evidence, if true, would explain the opening words (chiastically arranged and hexametrically rhythmical) of C.'s letter: *magnis in periculis* certainly suggests the danger of being a defendant on trial (20.8n. *pericula*).

commendationi meae: C. means the entrusting of his wife to Catulus (*OLD* 1, not 2a), to which he returns at the end of the letter (5). For *fides ~ fiduciam* (very common) see W–M on Tac. *A.* 3.11.2.

35.2 quam ob rem ... proponere decreui 'Therefore I have determined not to prepare a defence in the matter of [*OLD in* 42] my new plan <but> I have decided, not from any consciousness of guilt, to put forward an explanation': the new plan seems to be a reference to C.'s intention of joining Manlius rather than going into exile at Massilia. *satisfactionem* is translated as 'apology, excuse' in *OLD* (2), which gives a less than cogent antithesis to *defensionem*; at [Quint.] *Decl.* 301.3, the only other ex. where the two terms are contrasted, Shackleton Bailey translates as 'explanation'. *quam ob rem* is explained by C.'s confidence in Catulus' goodwill: because of Catulus' assumed *fides*, C. does not need to embark on an elaborate defence of his proposed course of action. *ex* is causal (*OLD* 18). It is easiest to regard *de culpa* as equivalent to an objective genitive, as translated, but J. N. Adams (*SVLL* 266) has noted that the preposition here 'can be given one of its basic classical meanings ("concerning, about")'; *conscius* can take *de* as well as a genitive (Cic. *Att.* 2.24.3). Since C. clearly uses epistolary tenses in §§3–5 below, it seems likely that *statui* and *decreui* strictly mean 'I determined' and 'I decided', though in Eng. it is more natural to translate them as perfects with 'have'. For *defensionem ... parare* cf. Tac. *A.* 13.15.5.

In *BC ob* is used only in the formulaic *quam ob rem* (again at 51.21), whereas the prep. is extremely common in *BJ* and *H*.; the equivalent *propter* (4× in *BC*) is relatively much less frequent in *BJ* and entirely absent from *H*. A predilection for *ob* is usually interpreted as evidence of archaising.

quam – me dius fidius – ueram licet cognoscas 'which, as I call god to witness, you can recognise is true' (*quam* refers to *satisfactionem*); the clause is compressed for 'quam licet cognoscas ueram esse': *licet* + subjunctive ('it is permitted that ...') is regular (*OLD* 1c), although elsewhere S. prefers an infinitive constr. (e.g. 13.2, 36.2).

In fact C.'s explanation is entirely spurious. In almost the exact centre of his letter he declares that his plan is to champion the cause of the poor, as he has always done (3 'publicam ... suscepi'); but his stated reasons, which both precede ('iniuriis ... concitatus') and follow ('sed quod ... sentiebam') his declaration, have nothing to do with the poor; his logic works only if he himself is one of the impoverished, something which he expressly denies ('non quin ... persolueret'). The illogicality of his position is underlined by the contradiction between *pro mea consuetudine* (3) and *nouo consilio* (2). No wonder he feels obliged to fortify his explanation by an oath. With *me dius fidius* (variously spelled: see *OLD Fidius*) one has to supply a verb (*iuuet* is commonly mentioned, although there seems to be no actual instance of it). Evidently Dius Fidius was 'the Italic god of good faith' (Berry on Cic. *Sull.* 83); the oath, very common in Cicero, is appropriate in a letter framed by *fides* (32.3–36.3n.). See also Maltby 233.

35.3 iniuriis <u>contumeliisque</u> <u>concitatus</u>: injustices are denoted by the former noun, insults by the latter, and the combination of the two (esp. common in Cicero and Seneca) has something of our 'adding insult to injury' (cf. Pacuv. 279–80R, Cic. *Inv.* 1.105 'cum iniuria contumelia iuncta' (as a means of rousing *indignatio*), Phaedr. 5.3.5 'iniuriae qui addideris contumeliam'). Each looks forward to the *quod*-clause (next n.).

quod ... statum dignitatis non obtinebam: the clause explains *concitatus*. *status dignitatis*, which is found elsewhere in republican Latin only in Cicero's correspondence (*Att.* 1.20.2, *Fam.* 4.9.3, *Q.Fr.* 3.6.1; cf. Sen. *Ep.* 115.17), is in itself a vague expression (the two nouns can each mean 'rank, status'), but its combination here with *non obtinebam* seems to point directly to C.'s recent failure to be elected consul. I therefore think that *status* here is almost equivalent to *gradus* ('stage, grade') and that the meaning is 'because I did not gain the ranking in status', *sc.* 'that I deserved for my *labor* and *industria*' (*OLD status*² 9a, *dignitas* 3a, *obtineo* 9a),[75] rather than 'since I ... was unable to maintain the position of my prestige' (Ramsey). *fructu priuare* is Ciceronian (*Verr.* 3.48, *Att.* 1.5.1, *Fam.*

---

[75] Cf. Liv. 6.11.6 'postquam inter patres non quantum aequum censebat excellere opes suas animaduertit' (of Manlius), perhaps one of Livy's numerous allusions

5.20.4; cf. Vitr. 8.3.28); *fructus laboris* (*-um*) is common, esp. in Cicero and Seneca; *f. industriae* is significantly less common, but for both together cf. Cic. *I Verr.* 32 'mei laboris, industriae diligentiaeque capiam fructum'.

publicam miserorum causam pro mea consuetudine suscepi is echoed at Liv. 7.41.1 'ut causam miserorum ciuium susciperet', where Oakley comments that *miseri* is 'quite often applied to the poor and debt-ridden'. *publica causa* ('the official cause') is a very common expr. in various contexts; *pro mea consuetudine*, again at Cic. *Arch.* 32, = 'in conformity with my usual custom' (*OLD pro*[1] 14a).

non quin aes alienum meis nominibus ex possessionibus soluere possem 'not because I cannot [lit. "could not"] pay off from my possessions the debt against my own accounts': for *non quin* = 'not because … not …' see *OLD quin* 7a; *possem* is subjunctive because it is a rejected reason (*NLS* 199–200 §243): for the imperf. tense see 33.1n. (*neque*). *meis nominibus* appears to be an abl. loosely attached to *aes alienum* (cf. 30.7n. *ut*) and refers to entries under C.'s name in a ledger of loans (*OLD nomen* 22a). *ex* indicates the source of payment (*OLD* 14b).

et alienis nominibus liberalitas Orestillae suis filiaeque copiis persolueret: *aes alienum* has to be understood from above as object of *persolueret* (which seems to be a potential subjunctive): 'and the generosity of Orestilla could pay off from her own and her daughter's resources <the debt> against the accounts of others'. For the repetition of a simple verb by its compound see Wills 443–5, Courtney on Cato, *Agr.* 156.1.

sed quod … uidebam meque … sentiebam: the two parts of the clause look back to *iniuriis* and *contumeliis* respectively.

non dignos homines honore honestatos: C. means above all Cicero, the *nouus homo*, as compared with himself, a *nobilis* and patrician: cf. Cic. *Tog. Cand.* 25 'me esse dignum consulatu negabas' (to the tribune Orestinus). For the *figura etymologica* cf. Plaut. *Capt.* 247, 356.

alienatum esse 'treated as an enemy, made an outcast' (*OLD* 6b); *falsa suspicione* is a causal abl.

35.4 hoc nomine … sum secutus 'For this reason I have followed the hope – honourable enough, given my circumstance – of preserving what status is left to me.' For *nomen* = 'reason' see *OLD* 26a ('perh. always abl. with pron. adjs.'); for *pro* see *OLD pro*[1] 13; for *reliquus* see *OLD* 3a.

35.5 plura cum scribere uellem: *plura scribere* is a common formula in letters, both verse and prose; for *uellem* cf. Fronto p. 31.1 vdH[2] 'uolo ad te plura scribere'.

35.6 nunc Orestillam commendo tuaeque fidei trado 'As it is [*OLD nunc* 11a], I entrust and commit Orestilla to your tutelage' (*OLD fides*

to S.'s account of the conspiracy (Oakley on 6.11.1, p. 483 n. 6; above, 33.1n. *Deos*).

1a). These two verbs are combined several times elsewhere and seem formulaic (e.g. 5× in Cicero's correspondence); *commendo* is frequently combined with the dat. *fidei* (e.g. Cic. *Mur.* 2, *Att.* 3.20.2, Liv. 42.44.4): it therefore seems more likely that *tuae . . . fidei* here is to be taken with both verbs than that we have to understand *tibi* (which is actually written in MS V) with the first of them. This form of *apo koinou* (15.2n. *cuius*) is perhaps less common in prose (e.g. Cic. *De Or.* 2.6 'et ingeniis et magna laude dicendi') than in verse (e.g. Catull. 56.2 'dignamque auribus et tuo cachinno'; W.[6] on Hor. *C.* 3.1.12–13), but the postulated exs. often give rise to textual doubts (*OLS* 1.1275–6). For *fidei trado* cf. Fronto p. 111.22–3 vdH[2] 'hunc a me fidei tuae atque opi traditum tuearis peto'.

per liberos tuos rogatus: Catulus had a daughter, Lutatia, grandmother of the emperor Galba (*liberi* can be used of a single offspring: *OLD* a). For appealing to someone by invoking their offspring see Watson on Hor. *Epo.* 5.5–6.

haueto 'Greetings!' (*h*) *aue* is indeclinable (*OLD aue*), though treated by Latin authors as if there were a verb *aueo*, which explains the unparalleled form here (≈ future imperative); (*h*) *auete* and (*h*) *auere* are also found. See e.g. Henriksén on Mart. 9 *praef.*

36.1 paucos dies commoratus apud C. Flaminium in agro Arretino . . . in castra ad Manlium contendit 'having delayed a few days with C. Flaminius in the territory of Arretium . . . he marched to join Manlius in his camp': as *ad* shows, *in* indicates the intended destination (as Cic. *Att.* 8.11D.1 'iter ad te in Apuliam facere'; *OLD in* 8a), not the fact of arrival. Arretium (mod. Arezzo) was a town in Etruria just over 120 miles north of Rome on the Via Cassia (*BA* Map 42: B2), a journey which *Orbis* estimates at about six days for routine private travel, but we know that, when C. left Rome on the night of 7–8 November, he pretended he was going into exile in Massilia (34.2) and so travelled up the Via Aurelia as far as Forum Aurelium, where, as prearranged, he joined up with an armed force (*Cat.* 1.24). From there he presumably made his way across country to the Via Cassia, picking up other followers *en route* (App. *BC* 2.3.11 στρατολογῶν), until he reached the *ager Arretinus*. The initial feint, the company of an armed force and the *en route* recruiting will all have added to the time of the journey (see also 57.1n. *reliquos*). It is impossible to know how long the 'few days' delay' around Arretium lasted, but, since C. spent his time arming the locals (below), it is unlikely to have been short.[76] Since Faesulae is 50 miles from Arretium, it would have taken several further days to complete the journey,[77] which seems likely to have taken him into

---

[76] *paucis ante diebus* at *Cat.* 3.3 refers to a period of three and a half weeks.

[77] The Schlieffen Plan assumed a rate of march of 12 miles a day (J. Keegan, *The First World War* (1998) 37–8), which corresponds fairly closely to the average

the last week of November. Nothing is otherwise known about Flaminius, whose name does not recur.

dum uicinitatem antea sollicitatam armis exornat: the metonymy of *uicinitas* 'neighbourhood' (= local inhabitants) is common (*OLD* 3); *antea* is a reference back to 28.4. For *armis exornat* cf. Luc. 6.256–7.

cūm fāscĭbŭs ātqu(e) ălĭīs īmperii insignibus: the appurtenances are mentioned also by Cicero (*Cat.* 2.13, *Sull.* 17), Appian (*BC* 2.3.11) and Plutarch (*Cic.* 16.6) and are surely intended to imply consular status (cf. 18.5): C. is obsessed with the magistracy to which he had thrice failed to be elected. See further T. C. Brennan, *The fasces* (2022) 85–7.

36.2 haec ubi Romae comperta sunt, senatus … hostes iudicat: the outlawing of C. and Manlius (attested only by S.) took place at some point before 2 December (cf. 44.6); Ramsey (2019: 247 n. 82) suggests that the actual date was 17 or 18 November, but his estimates of journey times seem optimistic. For *hostis* declarations see Allély, Straumann 88–100; also below, 50.3n. (*sed*).

ceterae multitudini diem statuit ante quam liceret sine fraude ab armis discedere '<and> for the rest of the crowd it appointed a day before which it was lawful <for them> to lay down their arms with impunity'. Either *ceterae multitudini* is to be taken also with *liceret* or we have to supply e.g. *iis* or similar. *sine fraude* is a technical legal expr. (*OLD* 2).

praeter rerum capitalium condemnatis 'apart from those condemned on capital matters' (it is unclear whether the dat. is to be taken with *diem statuit* or *liceret*). *praeter*, normally a preposition + acc., is highly unusual: for the grammarian Probus (4.149.8–9) and *TLL* (10.2.1002.46–8) it is an adv. here, but for *OLD* (9) it is a disjunctive conjunction.[78] There are similar cases at Ov. *F.* 6.406, Just. 13.5.2 'exules praeter caedis damnati restituebantur'. The gen. of the charge is regular (*OLD condemno* 1a).

36.3 Antonius cum exercitu Catilinam persequi maturet: that Antonius was in active pursuit of C. is inferred by scholars from Cic. *Mur.* 84, a speech delivered in late November (Ramsey 2019: 248–51), although that is not a necessary inference from the passage. For *maturo* + inf. see *OLD* 2b.

Cicero urbi praesidio sit: cf. *Cat.* 2.26 'mihi ut urbi … satis esset praesidii consultum atque prouisum est', *Mur.* 79 'consulem … de urbis

---

distance of 10–12½ miles between Agricola's marching camps in Scotland (D. J. Breeze, 'The logistics of Agricola's final campaign', *Talanta* 16–19 (1987–8) 7–22, at 11). K. Raaflaub and J. T. Ramsey calculate that Caesar's army marched on average 15½ miles a day ('Reconstructing the chronology of Caesar's *Gallic Wars*', *Histos* 11 (2017) 1–74, at 5–11).

[78] 'Many words are sometimes conjunctions & sometimes adverbs' (H. W. Fowler, *Modern English usage* (1934) 603).

praesidio ... deturbari uolunt'. *praesidio* is a common predicative dat. (*TLL* 10.2.887.17–64).

36.4 Ea tempestate m̲ihi imperium populi Romani m̲ulto maximē m̲īsĕrābĭlĕ uīsūm (e)st: *imperium p.R.* (again at 52.10) is a favourite expr. of Cicero and here seems to mean 'state' or the abstract 'empire' (cf. also 10.1n.). No doubt Virgil (*Aen.* 1.111) was responsible for the popularity of *miserabile uisu* in the hexameters of later poets, but S.'s wording perhaps suggests that both authors were indebted to Ennius (yet not mentioned by Skard, *ES*). For *multo* + superl. (again at 52.20) see *OLD multo*[1] 1b; for *tempestate* see 7.1n.

cui refers back to *imperium* and is to be taken with both *parerent* and *affluerent* (albeit slightly differently in each case).

ad o̲ccasum ab o̲rtu solis o̲mnia d̲omita armis 'to the setting from the rising of the sun ...': the imperialist topos 'from east to west' (W.[1] on Vell. 126.3) provides a more impressive contrast with *domi* below than would e.g. *foris*; for the transposition of the 'natural order' (Quint. 9.4.23) cf. Ov. *Tr.* 4.9.21 'ad occasum ... ab ortu'. For *domita armis* cf. Liv. 7.32.9 'omnia ... domita armis', 28.39.14 'qua terrarum ultimas finit Oceanus domitam armis habeatis'.

domi seems to be in play with *domita* (cf. Plaut. *Men.* 105, Lucr. 5.1334).

otium atque diuitiae, quae prima mortales putant, affluerent: whether *prima* is a noun = 'the most important things' (so *OLD primum*[1] 6a) or an adj. is immaterial, since the meaning is basically the same either way. *otium* and *diuitiae* recur from 10.2 (cf. also Vict. *Caes.* 37.7); the central digression in *BJ* begins similarly (41.1 'earum rerum quae prima mortales ducunt'); for *mortales* see 2.8n. (*multi*). *diuitiae ... affluerent* (again at [Quint.] *Decl.* 14.2) suggests a river of gold like the Pactolus (cf. Hor. *Epo.* 15.20 'tibique Pactolus fluat'); with *otium* we have to understand a related but less specific verb such as *abundare* (e.g. Cic. *TD* 2.26), although *otium* elsewhere can be associated with flowing (e.g. W.[2] on Vell. 88.2 'otio ... fluens').

qui seque remque publicam ... perditum irent: the idea, repeated at 37.8, is closely related to C.'s threat at 31.9 (n.): for other exs. cf. W.[2] on Vell. 91.4. For *perditum ire* ('to set out to destroy') see 52.12n.; for *-que ... -que* see 9.3n.; *obstinatis animis* (or sing.) is a set expr. from Acc. *Trag.* 84 onwards.

36.5 duobus senati decretis 'despite two senate's decrees' (viz. those mentioned at 30.6 and 36.2, each referred to by *neque ... neque ...* below): the required sense is concessive, but it is hard to tell whether the abl. is abs. or of attendant circumstances (*OLS* 1.855). For *senati* see 30.3n.

neque p̲raemio inductūs coniurationem p̲atefecerat: *sc. quisquam* from the following colon. Curius' revelations (23) preceded the offer of a reward (30.6).

tanta uis morbi ac ueluti tabes plerosque ciuium animos inuaserat 'such
was the violent disease and (so to speak) the decay which had attacked very
many of the citizens' minds': the MSS read *atque uti*, but *ut(i)* rarely, if ever,
has the required sense of 'as if'; Haupt's *ac ueluti* is more or less guaranteed
by *BJ* 32.4 'tanta uis auaritiae in animos eorum ueluti tabes inuaserat', the
latter echoed by Sulp. Sev. *Chron.* 1.23.5 'tanta … animos eorum habendi
cupido ueluti tabes incessit' (cf. also Liv. 42.5.7 'contagione uelut tabes in
Perrhaebiam quoque id peruaserat malum', Petron. 119, line 54 'ueluti
tabes'). For the parataxis see 7.3n. (*tanta*). *uis morbi* is a regular expression
(cf. also *OLD uis* 9b); for the association with *tabes* cf. Liv. 3.24.4, Manil.
1.880, Plin. *NH* 17.232, Tac. *A.* 11.6.2, Gell. 19.5.3. *inuado* is frequently
used of diseases (2.5n., 10.6n., 12.2n.). *plerosque* is perhaps an example of
enallage (8.3n. *scriptorum*), found unacceptable by Shackleton Bailey, who
emends to *plerisque* (*Mnem.* 34 (1981) 351–2).

37.1–39.4 Digression. Plebs *and Politics*

S.'s attraction by the theme of socio-political decline was already evident in
the preface (5.9–13.5); here, marking the halfway point of the book, he
inserts into his narrative a digressive passage resuming the same theme,
just as he would do in the *Bellum Iugurthinum* (41–2). But whereas the
latter digression is concluded by means of a conventional formula, clearly
distinguishing the passage from the surrounding narrative (*BJ* 42.5 'ad
inceptum redeo'), no such clarification is available here. Editors agree
that the present digression ends with the two following sentences (39.5):
'Fuere tamen extra coniurationem complures qui ad Catilinam initio
profecti sunt; in iis erat Fuluius, senatoris filius, quem retractum ex itinere
parens necari iussit.' Yet not only is the reference to filicide entirely anti-
climactic, but *tamen* is logically inexplicable, since there is nothing in the
preceding context with which a contrast may be generated. This curiosity
requires an explanation, and it is to be found at the point where the
digression begins. At 36.5 S. says that despite two senatorial decrees no
one from within the conspiracy ('ex tanta multitudine') betrayed it and no
one from within C.'s camp ('ex castris Catilinae') abandoned it – and it is
at this point that it makes sense to say 'Nevertheless there were many
outside the conspiracy who initially set off to *join* it.' The statements at
36.5 and 39.5 correspond to each other and frame the digression, and the
relationship between them suggests that S. has, as it were, inserted into his
history one of those 'transferable commonplaces' about decline which are
mentioned later by the elder Seneca (*Contr.* 1 *praef.* 23 'quae … satis apte
et alio transferuntur, tamquam quae … de saeculo … dicuntur'). No
doubt he was inspired by the famous digression on *stasis* which

Thucydides incorporated into his third book (82–3) and to which S. makes unmistakable allusions (38.3nn.).

The digression divides into two halves: the first (37.1–8) is an analysis of the *plebs*, the second (37.9–39.4) recounts how, in the years 70–63, the tribunes tried to manipulate the *plebs* and attack the senate. The turmoil of the period is well brought out: the profiteers from Sulla's victory prompted revolutionary ambitions in others (37.6), while the victims of that victory wanted revenge for themselves (37.9); Pompey's legislation in 70 increased the power of the tribunes (38.1), but his departure in 67 conversely weakened them (39.1–2). Everyone was seeking power for themselves (38.3).

The *plebs'* support for C.'s revolution, with which the digression begins (37.1 'nouarum rerum studio'), is returned to at the end (39.3 'nouandi spes'), where, in a brief excursion into 'counter-factual history', S. reflects powerfully on what would have happened if C. had not been defeated (39.4).

37.1 aliena mens in late Latin denotes madness, *alienatio mentis* (*OLD alienatio* 3), e.g. Auson. *Epist.* 13.11 'inspirant uacuos aliena mente poetas' (p. 209G): cf. *TLL* 1.1575.77–83. So too here (*OLD alienus*[1] 12); it is one of the symptoms of the *morbus* mentioned above.

sed omnino cuncta plebes: *sed omnino* ('but actually') is a favourite idiom of Cicero (Nisbet on *Pis.* 64). *cuncta plebes* means the common people anywhere in Italy (such as those in Etruria at 28.4), including the *plebs Romana*. If the evidence of MSS can be trusted, S. uses the third-declension nom. *plebs* at 33.3 and 48.1 but here and at 4 below uses the fifth-declension form *plebes*, which is said to be archaic (Prisc. 3.475.37–8): it outnumbers *plebs* in *BJ* (5:2) and is used exclusively in the fragments of *H*. For *cunctus* see 8.1n.

nouarum rerum studio: a Sallustian expr. (again at 57.1) picked up by Tacitus (3×).

37.2 id adeo more suo uidebatur facere 'and what is more [*OLD adeo*[2] 6b], its behaviour was clearly conforming to type' (lit. 'it was seen to be doing it in accordance with its own habit') – 'a moralizing rehash of typical ancient prejudices about the fickle mob and its readiness for revolution' (Rosenblitt 52). *more suo*, a common expr., is abl. of attendant circumstances. See further e.g. Cic. *Sest.* 99; P. A. Brunt, 'The Roman mob', *Past & Present* 35 (1966) 3–27, Scanlon 56–9, Shaw 222–8.

37.3 quibus opes nullae sunt: *sc. ei* as antecedent: 'those whose resources are non-existent'.

bonis: see 19.2n. (*quia*).

uetera ōdere, noua exoptant; ŏdio suarum rerum mutari omnia student: theme and variation, pointed by the resumption of *odere* by *odio* (for which type see Wills 327–8). For *studeo* + acc. and inf. see 1.1n. (*Omnes*); for *mutari omnia* cf. 2.3 (n. *neque*). S. is imitated at Tac. *H.* 2.8.2 '*rerum nouarum cupidine* et *odio praesentium*'.

turba atque seditionibus sine cura aluntur 'they are nourished by disruption and mutinies without caring': the metaphor of feeding (as Cic. *Sest.* 99 'discordiis ciuium ac seditione pascantur') is pointed when applied to those who cannot afford to eat (again at 37.7). *turba atque seditionibus* (again at *H.* 1.12) is, like the two further exs. at 5 below, another of S.'s 'Catonian' pleonasms (1.4n. *diuitiarum*); the two nouns are also coupled at Cic. *Clu.* 103, Liv. 3.68.11, 23.10.10, Quint. 2.16.2, Tac. *A.* 1.19.2.

quoniam egestas facile habetur sine damno 'because want is easily maintained without loss' (since the poor have nothing to lose); *sine damno* interacts with *sine cura*. S. is imitated at Tac. *H.* 2.38.1 'nam rebus modicis aequalitas *facile habebatur*' (*OLD habeo* 15c).

37.4 sed urbana plebes, ea uero praeceps erat de multis causis: the resumptive use of *is* (12.5n.) emphasises the words *urbana plebes* and hence the contrast with *cuncta plebes* above; *urbana*, a regular epithet for *plebs* (*TLL* 10.1.2383.62–9), is a derogatory substitute for *plebs Romana*, which S. uses elsewhere. *de multis causis* contrasts with *more suo* above (the 'many reasons' are itemised in §§5–8 immediately below): this use of *de* with *causis* is extremely frequent (e.g. Caes. *BG* 6.1.1 'multis de causis'). *praeceps* = 'acting precipitately, impetuous' (*OLD praeceps*¹ 3).

37.5 primum omnium 'first of all' (a set phrase). The sequence is continued by *deinde* (6) and *praeterea* (7).

qui ... praestabant: *sc. ei* as antecedent: 'those who were outstanding everywhere for their shame and self-entitlement' (*a petendo petulantia*: Cic. *Rep.* 4 fr. 8P).

alii per dedecora patrimoniis amissis 'others who had lost their property for disgraceful reasons': the abl. abs. seems to function as an abl. of description. *per dedecus* is relatively common (20.9n. *nonne*), but the plural is elsewhere only at Tac. *A.* 5.6.2.

flagitium aut facinus: 14.2n.

ii Romam sicut in sentinam confluxerant: *sentina* here means a ship's bilge, the place where water collects at the bottom of the vessel and stagnates, an appropriate sump for those whom Cicero described as 'infimam faecem populi' (*Q.Fr.* 2.5.3); Cicero used *sentina* himself at *Cat.* 1.12 and 2.7, where, however, it means 'bilge water': for the imagery and more general discussion see Jenkyns 164–5. The resumptive pronoun is used differently from 4 above. For *sicut* cf. 31.5n.

37.6 Sullanae uictoriae: 82 BC (11.4n. *postquam*). The implied notion of wanting the days of Sulla to return perhaps derives from *Cat.* 2.20 (see also 16.4nn.).

ex gregariis militibus alios senatores uidebant, alios . . . **diuites:** *sc. fieri* or *factos esse* or equivalent; *ex* = 'from being' (*OLD* 13). *gregarii milites* are common soldiers (*OLD gregarius* 2). In 81 Sulla created 300 new senators, doubling the membership: Dion. Hal. says that the beneficiaries were 'ordinary people' (*Ant. Rom.* 5.77.4 ἐκ τῶν ἐπιτυχόντων ἀνθρώπων), other sources mention only equestrians (*MRR* 2.74). The parvenu who achieves rank and/or riches is a commonplace figure (see Watson on Hor. *Epo.* 4).

regio uictu atque cultu: the two nouns are often combined; the abls. are of attendant circumstances: for *regio uictu* cf. Liv. 45.32.5, for *r. cultu* cf. Nep. *Dat.* 3.1, Val. Max. 3.2 *ext.* 9, 5.1 *ext.* 4, Curt. 5.12.20, Tac. *A.* 12.51.4.

quisque is in apposition to *multi* above (cf. 2.1n. *Igitur*).

si in armis foret 'if he were in arms': *foret* represents a vivid or remote future in direct speech.

37.7 quae in agris manuum mercede inopiam tolerauerat 'who had withstood the hardship of poverty by being paid for manual labour in the fields' (*OLD manus* 6b, *merces* 1a, *tolero* 5). What the actual level of wages might have been seems impossible to determine (W. Scheidel, 'Real wages in early economies: evidence for living standards from 1800 BCE to 1300 CE', *Journal of the Economic and Social History of the Orient* 53 (2010) 425–62, esp. 444–5; W. V. Harris, 'The Roman economy in the late republic', in his *Rome's imperial economy: twelve essays* (2011) 257–68; B. D. Shaw, *Bringing in the sheaves* (2013) 79–88). For more on the *iuuentus* see 14.5–7, 16.1–3; their convergence on the capital mirrors that of the renegades above (§5).

priuatis atque publicis largitionibus excita 'drawn away by private and public largesse'. Electoral candidates were expected to provide food for potential voters: when campaigning for the tribunate, for ex., the younger Cato seems to have supplied food-bowls for the voters in the same way as did L. Cassius Longinus (26.1n. *in*, 54.3n. *nihil*). Monthly distributions of grain to the poor had been established by successive laws, of which the most recent was in 73 (*MRR* 2.109; see Rickman 158–72; also Pelling on Plut. *Caes.* 8.6–7 with further refs.).

urbanum otium: the expr. has 'the tang of paradox: for the better sort, Rome was where business was done and the country was for retreat and relaxation, but for their inferiors the reality was increasingly the opposite of this' (Jenkyns 82).

ingrato labori: cf. Virg. *G.* 3.97–8 (of a horse).

malum publicum 'the public affliction/disorder' (*OLD malum* 7b). The expr. (again at e.g. *H.* 1.67.13, Cato, *Orat.* 173M = 203M, Coel. Ant. 17C/ 23P, Sisenn. 92C/111P) reactivates the illness metaphor introduced at 36.5 (n.); *alebat* looks back to *largitionibus*: the young men came to the city for food, but what nourished them was the prospect of revolution (cf. 37.3).

37.8 quo minus mirandum est 'And *therefore* it is *all the less* to be wondered at . . .': for *quo* doing double duty see 1.3n. (*quo*). For *miror* + acc. and infin. see *OLD* 2b; the wording is Ciceronian (*Mur.* 38, *Div.* 1.45).

rei publicae iuxta ac sibi consuluisse 'were no more concerned about the commonwealth than about themselves' (lit. 'as concerned . . . as . . .': *OLD iuxta* 2): the words look back to 36.4 'qui seque remque publicam . . . perditum irent' (n.).

37.9 Praeterea: since the proscribed, whose offspring are about to be mentioned, tended to be significant figures (11.4nn.), the adverb seems to indicate that S.'s subject is no longer the *plebs* as such.

quorum . . . imminutum erat: *sc. ei* as antecedent; *erant* has to be supplied with *proscripti* and *erepta*. According to Plutarch, this 'seemed the greatest injustice of all': Sulla 'took away all civil rights from the sons and grandsons of the proscribed and confiscated the property of all' (*Sull.* 31.8); see further Pelling on Plut. *Caes.* 37.2. This effect of the Sullan victory is, as it were, the converse of that mentioned in §6.

haud sane alio animo 'with no very different an outlook', i.e. from the category of individuals mentioned in §8. *haud sane*, again at 53.5, = 'not very' (*OLD sane* 4a).

37.10 quicumque aliarum atque senatus partium erant 'whoever belonged to a different party/faction than the senate's' (*OLD atque* 13a, *pars* 16).

conturbari rem publicam quam minus ualere ipsi mālebant 'preferred the commonwealth to be disabled than to thrive less themselves': the contrast with *ualere* suggests that *conturbari* is to be taken in a quasi-medical sense (*OLD* 1).

37.11 id adeo mālum multos post annos in ciuitatem reuerterat 'Such was the affliction which had returned into the community after many years.' *adeo* here seems to emphasise *id . . . malum* (as Liv. 2.29.10 'id adeo malum . . . natum', a somewhat similar context) and hence to have a different meaning from §2 above (n.); *id* seems to look forwards (cf. 38.1 *nam*) as much as backwards. *malum* continues the metaphor of disease, the continuity emphasised by alliteration (51.4n. *sed*); for *reuerto(r)* of recurrence cf. Cels. 4.20.4 'id malum . . . reuertitur'.

38.1 postquam . . . tribunicia potestas restituta est: 'Whenever the tribunate appears, Sallust portrays it negatively' (Shaw 231). There were ten *tribuni plebis*: their power of vetoing legislation (*intercessio*) had been limited in 81 by Sulla as consul, who had also removed their right to initiate legislation and to hold further office (*MRR* 2.75); in 70 Pompey and Crassus as consuls, despite their personal animosity, cooperated in restoring the tribunes' powers (*MRR* 2.126). S. himself had been tribune in 52 (Intro. p. 3). See Lintott, *CRR* 210–13, Mouritsen, *PP* 136–47.

homines adulescentes ... quibus aetas animusque ferox erat: *homines adulescentes* is a set combination, usually plural (sing. at *BJ* 6.2) and in that order, though sometimes varied with the diminutive *adulescentuli* (as 52.26); it is found in comedy and earlier Latin, but seems to have dropped out of currency after Livy, returning only with Gellius. Most tribunes were in fact in their thirties (as was S. himself when tribune in 52), but *adulescens* is a flexible term and could be used by Cicero of himself as consul, when he was 43 (*Phil.* 1.22 with Ramsey's n., 2.118); it could also be used derogatively depending on context, as here (cf. Eyben 56–65): see also 49.2n. (*quod*). *ferox* often denotes defiance (5.7n.).

senatum criminando: the tribunes' activities during this period are illustrated by Wiseman in *CAH* 9.329–38. S. seems echoed by Liv. 22.34.3 'tribunus plebis ... criminando non senatum modo sed etiam augures' (217 BC). For the gerund + object see 15.3n. (*quae*).

plebem exagitare, dein ... magis incendere: *dein ... magis* suggests a relationship between *exagitare* and *incendere*, the latter being an intensification of the former: evidently the *plebs* is seen as a torch or firebrand being shaken into flame in the hands of the tribunes (cf. Sen. *Contr.* 2.2.8 'fax ... exagitata reddat ignes') and then burning (cf. Cic. *Phil.* 2.91 'faces incendisti'), before being applied to the *res publica*. The verbs are perhaps similarly used at Catull. 64.94–7 'exagitans immiti corde furores | ... incensam ... mente puellam', but there are textual problems (see Trimble ad loc.). Tacitus alludes to our passage but changes the image (*A.* 3.27.2 'tribunis reddita licentia quoquo uellent populum agitandi').

largiendo atque pollicitando: this is probably a reference to agrarian legislation (cf. Liv. 2.52.2 'tribuni plebem agitare suo ueneno, agraria lege'): the tribune P. Servilius Rullus, who took office on 10 Dec. 64, proposed to buy up land and distribute it to the impoverished (*MRR* 2.168), but he was opposed by Cicero as consul, who represented such measures as *largitio* or bribery (e.g. *Leg. Agr.* 1.4, 2.10, 12, 16, 76, *al.*); for *pollicitando* cf. e.g. *Leg. Agr.* 2.10 'si qui agros populo Romano pollicentur'. See Brunt 240–80.

clari potentesque: a frequent combination (e.g. again at *BJ* 1.3, 8.1, 16.2).

38.2 summa ope nitebatur: see 1.1n. (*Omnes*).

senatus specie pro sua magnitudine: phrasal adversative asyndeton: 'under the specious cover of the senate <but in fact> on behalf of their own importance' (*OLD species* 7c, *magnitudo* 6). The former phrase is echoed by Tacitus (*H.* 1.74.2 'copias specie senatus misit'). For *nobilitas* see Intro. p. 5 and 5.1n. (*nobili*).

38.3 uti paucis uerum absoluam: *uerum* refers to impartiality between the two groups about to be mentioned (*alii ... pars ...*): cf. 4.2–3 'mihi a ...

partibus rei publicae animus liber erat ... quam uerissime potero paucis
absoluam' (and nn.).

quicumque rem publicam agitauere honestis nominibus: the usual translation is 'whoever disturbed the commonwealth under honourable
names', although *agitauere* could be neutral: 'occupied themselves with
politics' (*OLD* 11). S. is remembering Thucydides' digressive passage on
civil war (3.82.8): 'The leading men in the cities used respectable-
sounding names [μετὰ ὀνόματος ... εὐπρεποῦς] on each side' (trans.
Rhodes). See also next n. but one and 12.1n. (*innocentia*). For *honestis*
nominibus cf. also Cic. *II Verr.* 2.142, Hor. *S.* 1.3.42, Tac. *A.* 2.33.4, 14.21.1,
14.39.3; for a compound verb (1 *exagitare*) followed by its simple form see
1.7n. (*ita*).

alii ... pars ...: both are in apposition to *quicumque*. For *quo* = *ut* see
11.5n. (*quo*).

bonum publicum simulantes pro sua quisque potentia certabant:
S. continues his allusion to Thuc. 3.82.8 (see above): 'and while nominally
cherishing public interests [τὰ μὲν κοινὰ λόγῳ θεραπεύοντες] they in fact set
them up as prizes, and, using every means in their competition
[ἀγωνιζόμενοι] to get the better of their opponents ...'.

38.4 neque ... modestia neque modus: see 11.4n. (*neque*).

uictoriam ... exercebant: in this expr. the verb 'often approximates to
"exploit" or "make use of"' (Oakley on Liv. 6.22.4, with exs.).

39.1 postquam ... missus est: the Lex Gabinia of 67 BC empowered
Pompey to rid the Mediterranean Sea of pirates (*MRR* 2.146), while the
Lex Manilia of 66 gave him command of the war against Mithridates (*MRR*
2.155): see further 16.5n.

opes 'influence' (*OLD* 2b). For Pompey as a supporter of the *plebs* cf.
H. 4.32 'uolenta plebi facturus habebatur', 4.37 'multitudini ostendens
quam colere plurimum, ut mox cupitis ministrum haberet, decreuerat',
Cic. *Att.* 2.1.6.

paucorum potentia: see 20.7n. (*postquam*). The phrase (again at 58.11,
BJ 3.4) recurs at Hirt. *BG* 50.2, Cic. *Fam.* 12.15.4, Tac. *A.* 13.4.2.

39.2 ii magistratus ... tenere: *magistratus* is acc. plural; *tenere*, like *agere*
and *terrere* below, is a historic infin. (6.4n. *igitur*). Cf. C.'s speech at 20.7.

ipsi ... florentes is echoed at Tac. *A.* 1.1.2 and 3.40.3. *innoxii* is passive,
'unharmed' (*OLD* 4).

ceteros iudiciis terrere quo plebem in magistratu placidius tractarent
'terrorised the others by means of the courts in order that, when in office,
their management of the people should be calmer'. *ceteros* = would-be
tribunes, as indicated by *quo ... tractarent*; their office was not strictly
a magistracy, but S. uses the word similarly elsewhere (*BJ* 37.2, *H.* 3.15.3
'inani specie magistratus'). *iudiciis* refers to court proceedings against
tribunicii, of whom several were prosecuted in the period between

Pompey's mission against the pirates in 67 (§1) and C.'s conspiracy in 63; only two are known certainly to have been condemned, viz. C. Licinius Macer in 66 for *repetundae* (*TLRR* 98 no. 195) and C. Manilius in 65 for *maiestas* (Ascon. 60.13–14; *MRR* 2.153, 3.134, *TLRR* 105 no. 210). *terrere* of course embraces acquittals as well as convictions, as shown when the tribune of 67 was subsequently brought to trial (Ascon. 60.16–17 'Cornelius perterritus Manili exitu'; *MRR* 2.144, *TLRR* 104–5 no. 209). See the discussion in Gruen 260–8. For *placidius* (*OLD placide* 2) see *BJ* 41.2 'placide modesteque . . . r.p. tractabant'; S.'s sentence is perhaps echoed at Tac. *A.* 4.33.2 'quibus modis temperanter haberetur' (the subject is the people).

39.3 ubi primum . . . nouandi spes oblata est, uetus certamen animos eorum arrexit: *eorum* refers back to *plebem* (a *constructio ad sensum*); *a Catilina* is to be understood with *oblata est*: the sentence completes a ring with *cuncta plebes nouarum rerum studio Catilinae incepta probabat* at the start of the digression (37.1; cf. also 48.1). *nouandi spes* appealed to Livy, though always with the accusative *res* (28.36.5, 29.12.3, 29.36.10, 35.17.9); the absolute use of the verb is imitated at Tac. *A.* 4.18.2. For *uetus certamen* cf. Liv. 27.8.1 (patricians vs. *plebs*).

39.4 quod si primo proelio . . .: for 'counter-factual history' (intro. n.) see e.g. *PH* 342 n. 13. Since the 'first battle' is that described at the end of the book (59–61), the clause illustrates 'narrative prolepsis'.

aut aequa manu 'or at least on equal terms' (*OLD aut* 6b, *manus* 9e).

profecto 'without question', a regular 'correlative' to *si* (*OLD profecto* 2a).

clades atque calamitas: the same pairing at Plaut. *Capt.* 911. Two abstract nouns in combination, when conceived as a unit, take a singular verb (G&L 182 §285.2).

neque illis . . . extorqueret 'and those who won [lit. "would have won"] the victory would not have been allowed to enjoy it for too long, before someone more powerful extorted [*or* without someone more powerful extorting] *imperium* and freedom from them in their exhausted and debilitated state'. *illis qui . . . forent* refers to those who would have inflicted *clades atque calamitas* on the *res publica* (the ruination would have constituted the consequence of their victory); the pluperfect subjunc. takes its cue from *licuisset*, the regular apodosis of a past unfulfilled condition. *quin*, difficult to explain and translate at the best of times, here seems to introduce a result clause after the negative *neque . . . diutius . . . licuisset* (G&L 357 §556). In such sentences it is conventional to resort to the English 'without' (as Cic. *Att.* 10.8(199).6 'nullo enim modo posse . . . stare istum diutius quin ipse per se . . . concidat', 'he cannot last very long without falling by his own impulse' (trans. Shackleton Bailey)), but in our passage 'before' will serve equally well (as Caes. *BG* 3.24.5 'exspectari diutius non oportere quin ad castra iretur', 'there should be no longer delay before there was an advance on the camp').

qui plus posset = aliquis potentior (*sc. quam uictores*): see 2.2n. (*tum*) for the expression. The verb is subjunctive 'because the reference in *qui* is not to a definite individual, but to any one fulfilling the condition of "being stronger"' (Neatby and Hayes ad loc.). The particular power struggle to which reference is made never took place (C. was defeated and killed 'primo proelio'), but S. knew from hindsight that Pompey and Caesar had both enjoyed their periods of dominance and had been killed, a pattern of events likely to continue. One might expect *imperium* and *libertatem* to be antithetical, but cf. e.g. Caes. *BG* 7.64.3, Cic. *Phil.* 3.37, 4.8, 5.37, Liv. 2.23.2; the combination brings the digression to an emblematic conclusion.

39.5 Fuere tamen extra coniurationem complures qui ... profecti sunt: this sentence picks up the narrative of 36.5, framing the digressive 37.1– 39.4 (see intro. n. there): an extreme example of one of S.'s *amputatae sententiae* (Intro. pp. 24–5). After *est qui* and the like, where the subjunc. had become regular (cf. 17.7n. *fuere*), the indic. may be used in 'statements of definite facts' (G&L 405 §631.2R. 1); in comedy the indic. is common (see e.g. Christenson on Plaut. *Pseud.* 462).

Fuluius, senatoris filius, quem retractum ex itinere parens necari iussit: this example of *patria potestas* in action is mentioned also by Val. Max. 5.8.5 and Dio 37.36.4, but the individuals are otherwise unknown (*MRR* 2.491). See also 48.3 for another returnee.

39.6–48.2 THE ALLOBROGES:
NOVEMBER–DECEMBER 63

It is doubly ironical that the threat of *domesticum bellum* against the Roman republic was averted by the agency of foreigners who had every reason to encourage it rather than to thwart it.[79] Ever since the sack of Rome by the Gauls in 390, fear of Gallic militarism had been endemic in the Roman psyche (40.6n.), and its dangers will have been brought home vividly to S. and his contemporaries more recently when they read Caesar's *commentarii* on his Gallic exploits during the 50s.[80] Representative of this militarism were the Allobroges (40.1), as Horace would later acknowledge (*Epo.* 16.6). Defeat by Rome in 121 had led to their incorporation into the

---

[79] *domesticum bellum* is Cicero's preferred term for the conflict with C. (Dyck on *Cat.* 2.1); the very name 'Allobroges' meant 'foreigners' (Schol. Juv. 8.234: see D. E. Evans, *Gaulish personal names* (1967) 132–3, 158–9).

[80] Cf. e.g. J. F. Gardner, 'The "Gallic menace" in Caesar's propaganda', *G&R* 30 (1983) 181–9.

province of Gallia Transalpina, but within fifty years they were so heavily in debt to Rome that they sent a deputation to protest; the governor, M. Fonteius, was defended successfully by Cicero in his *Pro Fonteio* (69 BC). The Allobroges had revolted vainly in 66 and would do so again in 62/1 (*MRR* 2.154, 176). In late 63 a second deputation had come to Rome to seek from the senate some remission of their debt; but the legates' request was rejected (40.3), and the Catilinarians, thinking that they could capitalise on the Gauls' failure, asked them to join the conspiracy.

The Allobroges now had the opportunity to avenge their injustices and to reverse the defeat of 66, and it is interesting to speculate what might have happened if they had agreed to the conspirators' approach; but, although initially the legates promised their support (40.6), they were in fact uncertain about where their advantage lay and, after debating the matter amongst themselves (41.1–2), they decided – perhaps surprisingly – against joining the conspiracy. Instead, in a move which S. attributes to *Fortuna rei publicae* (41.3), the Gauls offered their services to Cicero, who, hoping thereby to acquire incriminating evidence, encouraged them to feign support for the conspirators (41.5).

At the moment of this dramatic *peripeteia* S. interrupts his main narrative in the interests of suspense and diverts first to developments elsewhere in Italy (42) and then to the conspirators' proposals for carnage and arson in Rome (43). When the main narrative resumes (44.1 *Sed*), Cicero is colluding with the Allobroges to elicit written evidence from the conspirators, whose lack of suspicion (44.2) contrasts strongly with the masterminding of the well-informed consul (45.1). In the famous ambush at the Mulvian Bridge, even the Allobroges are initially taken by surprise, but they soon realise the situation, and the written evidence is secured (45.3–4).

With the operation completed successfully, it was now Cicero's turn to debate how best to proceed (~ 41.1–2), since punishment of the conspirators might have unfortunate implications for himself (46.2); but any personal risk was outweighed by concern for the *res publica* (~ 41.3), and he summoned the conspirators to the senate, where, at a dramatic meeting on 3 December, they were confronted with the evidence against them. The evidence was irrefutable, and the conspirators were placed under house arrest (46.3–47.4).

The narrative concludes with an elegant coda in which S. describes the delight of the *plebs* at this outcome and their praise of the consul who had brought it about (48.1–2), an implied allusion to Cicero's *Third Catilinarian*, in which, delivered before the people at an evening *contio* (*Cat.* 3.29), he provided many of the details on which S.'s narrative relies.[81]

---

[81] For a comparison of 39.6–47.4 with *Cat.* 3.3–15 see Berry, *CC* 138–49.

39.6 Isdem temporibus Romae Lentulus, sicuti Catilina praeceperat ...: this picks up the narrative of 32.2 'Lentulo ... mandat' (the night of 7–8 Nov.).

quoscumque moribus aut fortuna nouis rebus idoneos credebat ... **sollicitabat:** *sc. esse* or *fore*: 'was soliciting/trying to solicit ... whoever he believed were/would be suitable for revolution on account of their behaviour or situation'; *moribus aut fortuna* are causal abls. For *sollicitare*, the verb also used by Cicero (*Cat.* 3.4), see 24.4n. (*seruitia*).

sed cuiusque modi genus hominum, quod modo bello usui foret 'but humankind of every type, provided that it would be useful for the war'. *genus hominum* is a set phrase (*OLD genus*[1] 4b), here used derogatively; a rel. pronoun + *modo* (again at *BJ* 64.5) = 'provided that he/she/it/ they ...' (*OLD modo*[1] 3b): the subjunctive expresses both purpose and characteristic.

40.1 P. Vmbreno: described by Cicero as a freedman (*Cat.* 3.14), he is unknown outside the Catilinarian conspiracy. *umbra* and cognates seem not to have the connotation that 'shady' has in English; there is another Umbrenus at Hor. *S.* 2.2.133. For sentence-initial *igitur* see 2.1n.

negotium dat uti legatos Allobrogum requirat 'gave the task of seeking out the Allobroges' legates'. The Allobroges, a Gallic tribe in the province of Gallia Transalpina, occupied a large swathe of territory on the eastern side of the Rhone Valley, from south of Vienna (mod. Vienne), their capital (Strabo 4.1.11, Plin. *NH* 3.36), north-eastwards to the southern shore of Lake Geneva (*BA* Map 17); see Watson on Hor. *Epo.* 16.6, Malloch 142–3 on *Tab. Lugd.* II.9–10. The present deputation, consisting of two legates (Plut. *Cic.* 18.4), was in Rome to seek relief from their debts, much as Africa had sent envoys to Rome during C.'s governorship there in 67–66 (18.3n. *Post*). For more on the problem of Gallic debt see Cic. *Font.* 11 and Dyck's n. *negotium dare* is regularly constructed with a defining clause (*OLD negotium* 5a); *negotium* and *legatos Allobrogum* are also in Cic., but not in the same sentence (*Cat.* 3.4–5). *requirere* (*OLD* 1) has a different meaning from §2 below (the figure *distinctio*: cf. 14.3n. *conuicti*).

eosque: the Allobroges, not their legates.

existimans: the participle recurs at 52.13, 56.5 and 57.2 and is also liked by Caesar (11×); see also 4.4n. (*nam*). For the 'appendix' arrangement see 19.1n. (*adnitente*).

oppressos is a genuine participle (expressing cause and varied by *praeterea quod*): 'overwhelmed by debt both communally and individually'.

quod natura gens Gallica bellicosa esset: the warlike character of the Gauls (again at e.g. 53.3, *BJ* 114.2, Cato, *Orig.* 33C/34P, Liv. 5.36.4) featured often in Caesar, who considered it weakened if they associated with traders (e.g. *BG* 1.1.3); see further Williams, *BRRG* 88–93.

40.2 quod in Gallia negotiatus erat 'because he had conducted business in Gaul'. According to Cicero, 'referta Gallia negotiatorum est, plena ciuium Romanorum' (*Font.* 11, where see Dyck). *negotiatus* looks back to *negotium*: Umbrenus was a man who could do deals.

notus ... nouerat: for such variation (again at *BJ* 70.1) see e.g. Tac. *Agr.* 5.1 'noscere ... nosci', *H.* 3.24.1; W–M on *A.* 3.45.1.

percontatus pauca de statu ciuitatis et quasi dolens eius casum: *status* can mean 'financial status' (W–M on Tac. *A.* 3.28.3), but, since it can also be used of one's physical condition (*OLD* 5), it suits the surrounding language of illness and medicine: *casus* is technical in medical writers to describe a 'case' of illness (e.g. Cels. *praef.* 68 'non eadem omnibus etiam in similibus casibus opitulantur'; *TLL* 3.578.79ff.). The metaphors continue below. *casum dolere* (again at *BJ* 14.22) is otherwise exclusively Ciceronian apart from Calp. Flacc. *Decl.* 14.

quem exitum tantis malis sperarent: although *sperare* can of course take a direct object (e.g. Sen. *Ep.* 22.6 'sperat ... salutarem exitum'; *OLD* 1a), the dat. is most easily explained by assuming the ellipse of *fore*. 'what they hoped/expected the outcome would be to their great afflictions' (cf. *BJ* 14.24 'utinam emori fortunis meis honestus exitus esset'). Cf. 4.4n. (*postquam*) on *euentus*. The illness metaphor continues with *malis* (cf. 37.7n.).

40.3 queri de auaritia magistratuum: such complaints are frequent (e.g. Liv. 43.2.2 'de magistratuum Romanorum auaritia superbiaque conquesti' (Spain, 171 BC)): for Gaul see above, 40.1n. (*negotium*). For *uidet* see 20.1n. (*Catilina*).

accusare senatum quod in eo auxilii nihil esset: evidently the legates had already failed in their appeal to the senate.

miseriis suis remedium mortem exspectare: each infin. has been followed by a different construction: *de*+ abl., *quod* and, here, two accusatives. *remedium* keeps alive the sustained metaphor.

si modo uiri esse uultis 'if you really want to be men' (*OLD modo*[1] 3a), another variation on the proverbial 'si uir es(t)' (cf. 20.11n. *cui*): perhaps the unimpressed senators, in rejecting the Gauls' appeal, played on the meaning of *Galli* as 'not manly' (*OLD Gallus*[4]), and Umbrenus is capitalising on the legates' indignation. At any rate he is given direct speech for this pivotal moment in the dialogue.

rationem ... qua tanta ista mala effugiatis: *rationem* combines the notions of 'method' and 'scheme' (*OLD* 14, 10); the noun is very frequent in Celsus and, when combined with *mala*, suggests medical language (e.g. Cels. *praef.* 47 'ipsam curandi rationem'); *effugio* is regularly used of escaping illness or disease (*TLL* 5.2.209.21–7). The subjunc. expresses purpose. For *mala effugere* cf. Sen. *Ira* 2.12.6, Tac. *A.* 5.6.3, Just. 39.3.5.

40.4 ut sui misereretur 'that he should take pity on them': the gen. is regular (*OLD misereo(r)* 1a).

nihil . . . esse: a verb of saying has to be understood from *orare*.

dum . . . liberaret 'provided that it freed . . .' (*NLS* 178–9 §220). The verb is often used of being released from debt (*OLD* 4a).

40.5 in domum D. Bruti: *domus* takes a preposition both when the meaning is 'house' rather than 'home' and when the actual building is meant (*NLS* 6 §9 (i)): each condition is met here, although the nuance changes with *aliena* below. Brutus was consul in 77 and husband of Sempronia (25.1nn.).

neque aliena consilii 'and not unconnected with the plot': in classical Latin *alienus* + gen. is regular but not common (*TLL* 1.1581.18–20); contrast the dat. at Hor. *S.* 1.9.49–50 'domus . . . | nec magis his aliena malis'.

nam tum Brutus ab Roma aberat: the majority of MSS read simply *Roma* here, but two of them have been corrected to read *ab Roma*, which is also read by several grammarians in their discussions of the use of prepositions (Prob. 4.150.21, 26; Prisc. 3.66.15; Serg. 4.511.30; Aud. 7.355.8). The grammatical 'rule' for 'from + town name' is that the plain abl. is used, but S. again uses *ab* at *BJ* 104.1 'ab Tucca', and in Livy *ab Roma* is frequent and regular: for discussion of this complicated matter see Adams, *SVLL* 328–32. In theory S.'s parenthetical explanation could imply that Brutus too was a conspirator, for whom his wife was substituting during his absence from Rome; but there is no evidence of Brutus' involvement and it is much more likely that this is an elliptical use of *nam*: '<the venue was safe>, for Brutus was away from Rome at the time'.

40.6 Gabinium arcessit: Gabinius was an *eques* (17.4n.): hence he had *maior auctoritas* than Umbrenus (below). Cf. *Cat.* 3.14.

nominat . . . multos . . . innoxios: this was a dangerous tactic: if the Allobroges acted on their own initiative, they might mistake innocent persons for conspirators and hence betray the plot. S. is perhaps thinking of Cicero's client, P. Sulla (17.3n.): see 41.5n. (*ceteros*).

pollicitos operam suam: Umbrenus had asked them to stir up a *tumultus Gallicus*, of which the Romans had a deep-seated terror (Oakley on Liv. 7.9.6), and to provide cavalry (*Cat.* 3.4, 9), in which the Gauls specialised (Caes. *BG* 7.68.3). See also 52.24n. (*Gallorum*).

domum: the same word at 44.3 refers to the legates' homeland in Gaul, but here it may refer to their lodging in Rome.

41.1 in incerto habuere quidnam consilii caperent 'they regarded it as uncertain what policy they should adopt': there is no exact parallel for *in incerto habere* + indir. qu., although the passive is found at *BJ* 46.8 'ut, absens an praesens, pacem an bellum gerens perniciosior esset, in incerto haberetur' ('with the result that it was regarded as uncertain whether . . .'). See also *OLD incertus* 8a. *caperent* represents a deliberative subjunc. in direct speech. *quisnam* is little different from *quis*.

41.2 in altera parte ... in altera ... 'On the one hand ... on the other ...' (*OLD pars* 14, not 15).
incerta ... certa: cf. 17.6n. (*incerta*).

41.3 uicit Fortuna rei publicae: there was no cult of or temple to Fortuna Rei Publicae, yet the expression, which is common (esp. in Cicero), is not simply a manner of speaking: the logic of the next sentence – result (*itaque*) rather than explanation (*nam* or *enim*) – implies that some kind of divine providence was in operation. Likewise Cicero (*Cat.* 1.15 'sceleri ac furori tuo ... Fortunam populi Romani obstitisse', addressing C.; cf. 3.22). See also Oakley on Liv. 6.30.6.

41.4 Q. Fabio Sangae: the patronage of outside communities etc. by individual Romans was a regular practice (*BNP* 10.627, *OCD* 1094). Sanga is scarcely otherwise known, but his name suggests a connection with Q. Fabius Maximus, who took the name Allobrogicus when as consul in 121 BC he defeated the Allobroges and other peoples in Transalpine Gaul (*MRR* 1.520–1).
uti cognouerant '(exactly) as they had learned of it'.

41.5 per Sangam consilio cognito: *per* = 'thanks to, through the agency of' (27.3n. *rursus*): Sanga's contact with Cicero seems to have involved L. Licinius Murena, the consul designate (cf. Cic. *Dom.* 134). See Dyck on *Cat.* 3.4; Berry, *CC* 43.
studium ... simulent: cf. Tac. *H.* 4.86.2, Suet. *Dom.* 2.2.
ceteros adeant 'they should accost the others [i.e. the other conspirators]'; *adire* here means to accost a person 'for a purpose indicated or implied by the context' (*OLD adeo*¹ 4b). It is known from Cicero (*Sull.* 36–9) that at some point the Allobroges were in contact with L. Cassius Longinus (17.3n.), as a result of which they wrongly named Cicero's client, P. Sulla, as a member of the conspiracy.
bene polliceantur 'they should make the appropriate promises' (*OLD bene* 3).
dentque operam uti eos quam maxime manifestos habeant: *dare operam ut* is a regular expr. (*OLD opera* 2a), but the required sense of *habeo* + two accusatives seems impossible to parallel: 'and they should do their best to render them [the conspirators] as red-handed as possible'. S. returns to the Allobroges at 44.1 (n.); §§42–3 are digressive.

42.1–2 Isdem fere temporibus ... quos ante Catilina dimiserat: S. here looks back to 27.1 'Septimium ... in agrum Picenum, C. Iulium in Apuliam dimisit, praeterea alium alio', the timing of which seems to have been after the consular elections in late September (26.5n. *dies*). Since we are now in late November, that would allow roughly two months for the activities which S. is about to describe.

42.1 in Gallia citeriore atque ulteriore: alternative names for Cisalpine and Transalpine Gaul. The former stretched from the River Rubicon to the Alps; the latter was the area to the north and west of that.

Bruttio is, like *Piceno*, an adj. agreeing with *agro*. The area is in the 'toe' of Italy.

42.2 inconsulte ac ueluti per dementiam: the *uariatio* of adv. ~ prep. phrase follows immediately upon that of proper adjs. ~ proper name in §1. *ueluti per dementiam* (cf. 36.5) seems echoed at Tac. *A.* 6.24.2 'quasi per dementiam'.

portationibus: the noun is found elsewhere only at Vitr. 10.1.5, Scrib. Larg. 101.

festinando: since S. almost always uses this favourite verb absolutely, the likelihood is that *omnia* is the object only of *agitando* (so too Adams, *AILL* 578).

42.3 Q. Metellus Celer had been sent to Picenum and the *ager Gallicus* (30.5n.), a responsibility which in a letter to him of January 62 Cicero flatteringly described as a division of labour with himself (*Fam.* 5.2(2).1 'mihi tecum ita dispertitum officium fuisse in rei publicae salute retinenda ut ego urbem a domesticis insidiis et ab intestino scelere, tu Italiam et ab armatis hostibus et ab occulta coniuratione defenderes'). See further 57.2n.

ex senatus consulto: when Cicero renounced Gallia Cisalpina as his province for 62 (26.4n. *pactione*), he wanted Celer to take his place as proconsul there, as he told him in his letter (§3: last n.). In the same letter (§4) Cicero refers to a *senatus consultum* which evidently had relevance to Celer (see Rafferty 106–7), but whether that is the *s.c.* to which S. refers here is unclear. Presumably *ex senatus consulto* refers both to *causa cognita* and to *in uincula coniecerat*.

causa cognita 'after the hearing of the case' (*OLD cognosco* 4a).

item: *sc. complures in uincula coniecerat.*

in citeriore Gallia C. Murena, qui ei prouinciae legatus praeerat: it is possible that S. is in error here (see Ledworuski 262–3). In 63 C. Licinius Murena was said by Cicero to be legate in *Transalpine* Gaul (*Mur.* 89), where his brother L. Murena was the proconsul: when the latter returned to Rome for the consular elections (26.5n. *Catilinae*), he left his brother in charge. Cortius changed *citeriore* to *ulteriore* to remove this alleged mistake. It has nevertheless been argued (by W. Allen, *CP* 48 (1953) 176–7) that L. Murena inherited from his predecessor, C. Calpurnius Piso (cos. 67), the governorship of *both* provinces (see 49.2n. *oppugnatus*), and hence that C. Murena was indeed in charge of Cisalpine Gaul (as well as Transalpine) at the time. Nevertheless other scholars either ignore S. entirely (so, seemingly, Rafferty 183–5) or accept Cortius' emendation (see *MRR* 3.123).

43.1 At Romae recurs in classical Latin only in Tacitus, for whom the transitional phrase is a mannerism (12×).

Lentulus cum ceteris . . . constituerant: a singular subject combined with another word by *cum* is rarely treated as a plural by earlier writers but the *constructio ad sensum* becomes more common in S. (e.g. *BJ* 101.5), Livy and later authors (G&L 183 §285 N. 2). There had been an earlier meeting on 6 Nov. at Laeca's house at which C. had assigned tasks to the various conspirators (27.3n. *rursus*), but S. is here referring to a later meeting at which, in C.'s absence (next n.), Lentulus as the senior conspirator evidently presided and the assignment of tasks was updated in the light of developments in the interval (43.2n. *sed ea*).

cum Catilina in agrum Faesulanum cum exercitu uenisset 'when C. arrived in the territory of Faesulae with an army' (*uenisset* represents a fut. perf. indic. in direct speech). Since some scholars assume that the clause refers to C.'s approaching Rome in fulfilment of the promise he made at 32.2, they are troubled by the mention of the *ager Faesulanus*, which is 170 miles north and the Catilinarians' base (24.2n.). But, since C. will not have reached Faesulae until late in November (36.1n. *paucos*), there is no chance that he would be anywhere near the vicinity of Rome; when Lentulus and the others had taken their decisions (last n.), C. had probably not even reached Faesulae, or, if he had, the news had not yet reached Rome. The point is made more clearly at App. *BC* 2.3.11 Λέντλῳ δὲ καὶ τοῖς συνωμόταις ἔδοξεν, ὅτε Κατιλίναν ἐν Φαισούλαις πυνθάνοιντο γεγενῆσθαι . . ., 'Lentulus and his co-conspirators decided that, when they learned that C. had arrived at Faesulae . . .'). It would take a horse rider the best part of five days to reach Rome from Faesulae, although a series of relay riders would cover the distance faster (30.1n. *litteras*). *cum exercitu* refers not to the army which C. had promised to bring to Rome but to that which he had been gathering on his march to Faesulae (36.1n.).

L. Bestia tribunus plebis: the tribunician elections of 63 had probably taken place in July (Plut. *Cato Min.* 21.3: see Ramsey (2019) table 2), but, since tribunes did not assume office until 10 Dec., a date not yet reached in the narrative, Bestia was currently tribune designate. S.'s phrase must mean 'L. Bestia *as* tribune of the people', looking forward to a moment on or later than 10 Dec. (see below). For Bestia see further 17.3n.

contione habita quereretur de actionibus Ciceronis: the words are heavy with irony, since Bestia *would* 'complain about the actions of Cicero' under completely different circumstances at the very end of December (17.3n.). A *contio* was a public meeting summoned by a magistrate or priest (*OLD* 1a), such as those at which Cicero delivered his second and third Catilinarian speeches. Since Bestia's complaints were to be voiced *during* his proposed meeting, *habita* is a so-called 'aoristic' or timeless participle (*NLS* 81–2 §103, *OLS* 1.548). For *actio* = 'deed, action' see *OLD* 2a.

bellique grauissimi inuidiam optimo consuli imponeret 'and that he
should saddle the best of consuls with resentment at [i.e. caused by] the
gravest of wars'. *optimus consul* is a phrase almost exclusive to Cicero, who
uses it to describe statesmen of whom he approved (e.g. *Sull.* 11); it is
unclear here whether the phrase is being voiced by the conspirators (in
which case it is ironical) or is authorial (in which case it repeats the praise
of 31.6). When Brutus many years later publicly described Cicero himself
with the same words, the great man's reaction was to complain of faint
praise (*Att.* 12.21.1); but S. is unlikely to have known of this, since the
letters to Atticus were unpublished. *inuidia* is not elsewhere constructed
with *imponere* (*OLD* 12b), but the gen. is regular.

proxima nocte: the Allobroges had evidently reported that the intended
timing was to be the Saturnalia, which began on 17 Dec. (*Cat.* 3.10, Plut.
Cic. 18.2).

cetera multitudo coniurationis: *multitudo* + gen. = 'a large number of' is
common (*OLD* 3a); *coniuratio* seems almost = 'conspirators' here (*OLD*
2b). *quisque* below is in apposition to *multitudo.*

43.2 sed ea diuisa hoc modo dicebantur: *ea* = *negotia*; with *diuisa* we
must understand *esse* ('to have been distributed'). Since Cicero says (*Sull.*
52, *Cat.* 1.8–9) that the various tasks had already been assigned on 6–7
Nov. at the meeting at Laeca's house (27.3n. *rursus*), the question arises
whether S. is here belatedly providing details of those earlier assignments,
in which case *sed* will introduce a digressive flashback, or whether he is
simply elaborating later decisions just mentioned in §1 (cf. *suum quisque
negotium*). That the latter is correct is suggested by the change in assignments: previously arson was the responsibility of Cassius Longinus (*Cat.*
3.14, 4.13, *Sull.* 53), who was now (or about to be) absent (44.2), and
Cicero's murder was to be undertaken by Vargunteius and the equestrian
C. Cornelius (28.1, *Sull.* 18), whereas here the arson is assigned to Statilius
and Gabinius and Cicero's murder to C. Cornelius Cethegus (although it
is to be noted that the two men named C. Cornelius are understandably
confused at Plut. *Cic.* 16.1). If revised assignments are being described, *sed*
seems to perform a similar function to that at 25.1, introducing an expansion of a topic just previously mentioned.

Statilius et Gabinius uti ... incenderent: the *uti*-clause is explanatory of
hoc modo, as often (e.g. Cic. *Rosc. Com.* 10 'ad iudicium hoc modo uenimus
ut totam litem aut obtineamus aut amittamus'); the subjects of the clause
precede the conjunction for the purposes of itemisation (cf. *Cethegus*
below).

quo tumultu facilior aditus ... fieret: *quo* is a relative adj. and the clause
is purposive: 'in order that, on account of this confusion, access ... should
be easier'. *ad ... ceterosque* can be defined either as an adnominal

prepositional phrase (Spevak 83; also 20.2n. *dominatio*) or as a support verb construction (as if *facilius ad consulem ceterosque adiretur.* see 4.5n. *de cuius*).

Cethegus: 17.3n.

alius autem alium, sed filii familiarum (quorum ex nobilitate maxima pars erat) parentes, interficerent: this seems to mean 'and there should be various killings, but <especially> by family sons (the majority of whom belonged to the nobility) of their parents'. A *filius familias* was 'a son under the paternal power (*in potestate*) of his father (*pater familias*)', and such sons 'had no power to own or manipulate property in their own right', becoming *sui iuris* only on the father's death (quotations respectively from A. Berger, *An encyclopedic dictionary of Roman law* (1953) 472, and S. Dixon, *The Roman family* (1992) 40).

caede et incendio ... ad Catilinam erumperent: C. had promised that, after equipping himself with a large army in Etruria, he would return to Rome as quickly as possible (32.2, 48.4; cf. 44.6). *caede et incendio* (a regular pairing: 32.2n.) refers chiastically to the preceding instructions.

43.3 semper querebatur de ignauia sociorum: at the meeting of 6–7 Nov. it was C. himself who had complained (27.4 'multa de ignauia eorum questus'), and later he will complain again (58.4 'ignauia Lentuli'). Cethegus' impatience is mentioned also by Cicero (*Cat.* 3.10).

dies prolatando 'by putting off the days [*sc.* of the uprising]' (*OLD prolato* 2).

facto, non consulto ... opus esse: imitated at Tac. *H.* 1.62.1 'ubi facto magis quam consulto opus esset'. Contrast 1.6.

impetum in curiam facturum: in the contemporary *Pro Murena* (c. 20 Nov.) Cicero refers to C.'s long-standing 'consilium senatus interficiendi' (81; cf. *Sull.* 53 'ut occuparet curiam [*Schliack*: etruriam *codd.*]', Ascon. 92.17 'caedem senatus'). When Cethegus' house was searched on Cicero's instruction, a hoard of weapons was found (*Cat.* 3.8, 10, Plut. *Cic.* 19.2).

43.4 naturā ferox, uehemens: cf. Cicero on Vatinius: 'nimium es uehemens feroxque natura' (*Vat.* 4). Cicero himself characterised Cethegus by *furor* (*Cat.* 3.16, 4.11). For *ferox* see 5.7n. (*agitabatur*).

manu promptus: this Sallustian phrase (again at *BJ* 7.1, 44.1) became popular with Livy (3×) amongst other authors: Velleius saw Sex. Pompeius as a second Cethegus (73.1).

44.1 Sed Allobroges ex praecepto Ciceronis ... ceteros conueniunt: the verb here means 'approached' (*OLD* 2) and the whole sentence picks up 41.5 'Cicero ... legatis praecipit ut ... ceteros adeant'; *sed* signals the return to the main narrative after the digressive §§42–3.

ab Lentulo, Cethego, Statilio ...: S. repeats *Cat.* 3.9 'ab Lentulo, Cethego, Statilio ...'; the three are named in order of rank.

ius iurandum quod signatum ad ciues perferant 'an oath which, sealed, they could take to their fellow citizens'. Each principal except Cassius wrote out the oath in his own hand on a set of *tabellae* (two hinged tablets forming a kind of two-page booklet): cf. *Cat.* 3.10 'tabellas ... quae a quoque dicebantur datae'. The tablets were then bound together with string and sealed with the individual's own seal, the whole ensemble representing their good faith (*fides*): see E. A. Meyer, *Legitimacy and law in the Roman world:* tabulae *in Roman belief and practice* (2004) 221-2; also below, 47.3n. The Allobroges' fellow citizens back in Gallia Transalpina are envisaged by Cicero as divided into 'senate and people' (*Cat.* 3.10).

aliter 'otherwise', 'if not' (*OLD* 6a).

44.2 dant: *sc. ius iurandum.*

eo is usually taken to mean 'to Gaul', but it seems quite implausible that Cassius should promise to leave the scene of the expected action; by *eo* ('to there') the suspicious Cassius was doubtless promising Gabinius, the go-between (44.1), that he would come to the Allobroges' meeting place in a short while, 'breui' <but later than his three co-conspirators>.

44.3 T. Volturcium quendam Cortonensem: this man is otherwise unknown. That he came from Cortona in northern Etruria rather than (as the MSS say) Croton in the 'toe' of Italy has been persuasively argued by G. Forsythe (*AJP* 113 (1992) 407-12): Etruria features prominently in the conspiracy, and names beginning with *Vol-* are above all associated with northern Italy, esp. Etruria.

ut Allobroges, priusquam domum pergerent, cum Catilina ... societatem confirmarent: C. will just have arrived at Faesulae (43.1n. *cum*), but was then expected to return to Rome with a reinforced army (32.2, 48.4, 44.6); evidently Lentulus' plan was that the Allobroges should meet him on the Via Cassia, after which the Allobroges would proceed home by taking the Via Quinctia west to join the Via Aurelia.

4 quarum exemplum infra scriptum est: the same phraseology is used to introduce a letter at 34.3, but, whereas the earlier letter resulted from S.'s imagination (see n.), the present letter is quoted, with some differences, also by Cicero (*Cat.* 3.12). The situation is thus similar to (but not identical with) that at Tac. *A.* 6.6.1, where Tacitus quotes a Tiberian letter which, with only the slightest difference in wording, is quoted also at Suet. *Tib.* 67.1. The letter is one of the various occasions on which Tacitus introduces direct speech with the words *his uerbis* or similar: 'Once all these examples have been assembled it becomes plain that we are dealing with a particular, and restricted, kind of recorded utterance. It is always the case that when Tacitus claims to be offering *ipsa uerba* it is not a long formal set speech he records, but a ... short sentence or two, pungent and illuminating' (R. Mayer, '*Ipsa verba*: Tacitus' verbatim quotations', in T. Fuhrer and D. Nelis (edd.), *Acting with words* (2010) 129-42, at 133).

We cannot know anything about the authenticity of Cicero's quotation, although presumably it is more likely than not to be genuine; the most that can be said of S.'s quotation is that, like so much else of his work (Appendix II), it surely derives from Cicero.

44.5   Cicero's version of the letter (*Cat.* 3.12) is as follows: 'Qui sim *scies* ex eo quem ad te misi. *cura ut* uir sis et cogita *quem in locum sis progressus. et uide quid tibi iam sit necesse et cura ut* omnium *tibi* auxilia *adiungas*, etiam infimorum.' Of the various differences (italicised) perhaps the most striking is S.'s elimination or reduction of repetition: *cura ut* (2×) has gone altogether, and the present subjunc. of *esse* has been halved (4× → 2×). Scholars say that *scire ex*, which S. has varied by *ex . . . cognoscere*, is colloquial, but there is no evidence for this: elsewhere he simply uses *cognoscere* far more frequently than *scire*. Another substitution is *auxilium petere* for *auxilia adiungere*: the former is extremely common and liked by S. elsewhere (6× in total), whereas the latter is much rarer and at home in military narrative (Liv. 27.8.16, 41.6.6, Tac. *H.* 1.79.1). Instead of the four original imperatives, each coordinated by *et*, S. has produced only one, followed by three jussive subjunctives, of which the last two are in asyndeton. For the bland *uide* S. has substituted *consideres*, a word which he twice puts into C.'s own mouth (20.6, 58.18), as if Lentulus were addressing C. in his own language. S.'s Lentulus does not mince his words: *in quanta calamitate sis* is more blunt than *quem in locum sis progressus*, while *quid tuae rationes postulent* appeals more to C.'s sense of responsibility than does the vague *quid tibi iam sit necesse*. It is perhaps for this reason that C.'s courage seems less in question in S. ('memineris te uirum esse') than in the original ('cura ut uir sis').

Qui sim: Lentulus cannot have been trying to hide his identity, which would have been obvious from his handwriting and seal (cf. *Cat.* 3.12): *qui sim* means not 'who I am', but 'what I am like' (*OLD qui*[1] 2), i.e. 'what my position is' (so F. Cairns, *Historia* 61 (2012) 78–82, esp. 80–1, where (n. 20) he supports the variant *qui* for *quis* in Cicero's version of the letter).

fac cogites 'make sure you reflect' (*OLD facio* 16a), a 'periphrastic imperative' form where there is an ellipse of *ut* (Kenney on Lucr. 3.421–4); *memineris, consideres* and *petas* are best understood as independent jussive subjunctives, a colloquial usage (*NLS* 96 §126 *Note* (ii)) and thus appropriate to a letter.

te uirum esse: see 20.11n., 40.3n.

tuae rationes 'your calculations' (*OLD* 10a).

ab infimis: a euphemism for 'slaves' (6 below).

44.6   ad hoc mandata uerbis dat 'In addition he issued oral instructions'; the following indirect speech is dependent on *mandata*; the relevant verbs (*iudicatus sit* etc.) are in primary tenses of the subjunctive because S. is resorting to the device of *repraesentatio*, reflecting 'more precisely the tenses as they were actually used in direct speech' (*OLS* 1.593, part of a long discussion). Lentulus is imagined as having said: 'Since you have been declared an enemy by the senate, for what reason are you rejecting (the) slaves? The things you ordered are ready in the city; you must not hesitate to come nearer.'

cum ab senatu hostis iudicatus sit: C.'s outlawing (36.2n.) was probably recent, i.e. shortly before the night of 2–3 Dec. (referred to at 45.1 just below).

quo consilio seruitia repudiet? cf. 56.5 'seruitia repudiabat'. For *seruitia* cf. 24.4n.

ne cunctetur ipse propius accedere: as C. had promised at 32.2 (n.).

45.1 constituta nocte qua proficiscerentur 'having decided the night on which they would set out': the verb is subjunc. because the clause is to be regarded as virtual indir. speech after *constituta*, and the imperf. is being used with reference to the future (*NLS* 136 §181). The subjects are the Allobroges and Volturcius; the night was that of 2–3 December (*Cat.* 3.5).

cuncta edoctus: *(e)docere* ('to teach, instruct') can take a double acc. (16.1n. *iuuentutem*); when in the passive it is accompanied by an acc. and means 'tell, inform', as here and *BJ* 112.2, it is difficult to know whether the acc. is retained ('having been told everything') or is one of respect ('informed about everything/in every respect'). 'One sometimes wonders whether a grammatical distinction almost impossible to make is really meaningful' (Goodyear on Tac. *A.* 1.18.3). See also 25.2n. (*multa*).

L. Valerio Flacco et C. Pomptino praetoribus imperat: Cicero issued his orders on 2 Dec. (*Cat.* 3.5). Flaccus had extensive military experience in Asia, Gaul, Cilicia, Spain, Crete and the Caucasus. In 59 he was charged with extortion after his administration of the province of Asia in 62/1 and was defended by Cicero in the *Pro Flacco* (*TLRR* 122–3 no. 247): see *BNP* 15.174 [I 24]. Pomptinus had fought against Spartacus in the slave wars of 71, and in 62/1 as governor of Gallia Transalpina he suppressed a revolt by the Allobroges (*MRR* 2.176, 3.167); ten years later he would be with Cicero at the battle of Mt Amanus in Cilicia (Cic. *Att.* 5.20.3; *LH* 43–5): see *BNP* 11.585.

ut ... Allobrogum comitatum deprehendant 'to intercept the Allobroges' party': the two legates no doubt had a retinue of attendants, but the point was to intercept the letters that were being carried: *comitatum* here cannot mean 'retinue, escort' (*OLD* 1) but must refer to the whole company (*OLD* 4) of which the legates were part (cf. *Cat.* 3.6 'in eo comitatu').[82] I have assumed that *comitatus* has been correctly emended to the singular, although the mistake is hard to explain.

---

[82] The meaning of *magno comitatu* at *Cat.* 3.6 is not clear.

in ponte Muluio: the Pons Mulvius spanned the Tiber to the north of Rome: it carried the Via Flaminia, from which the Via Cassia branched off. **rem omnem aperit cuius gratia mittebantur; cetera . . . permittit:** cf. *Cat.* 3.6 'res praetoribus erat nota solis, ignorabatur a ceteris'. *cuius gratia* = 'on account of which'; for the repetition of a simple verb by its compound see 35.3n. (*et alienis*).

cetera uti facto opus sit ita agant permittit 'he gave them permission to conduct other matters according to what action was needed' (*ut* can be omitted after *permitto*: see *OLD* 6a). The unspecific language is typical of orders which might subsequently have to be denied.

45.2 homines militares: cf. *Cat.* 3.5 'fortissimos . . . uiros'.

sine tumultu praesidiis collocatis, sicuti praeceptum erat, occulte pontem obsidunt 'they stationed guard posts without any disruption and, as they had been instructed, took secret possession of the bridge'. The events of this famous night are described by Cicero, who explains that his forces were stationed in houses on either side of the bridge (*Cat.* 3.5-6). *praesidium (-a) collocare* is a common military expr.

45.3 postquam ad id loci legati cum Volturcio uenerunt: the time was about 3 a.m. on 3 Dec. (*Cat.* 3.6 'tertia fere uigilia exacta . . . legati . . . unaque Volturcius . . .'). *ad id loci* = 'to that exact place' (partitive gen.: see *OLD locus* 25a); the expr. is found only with *uenire* in classical Latin (*BJ* 75.7, Cic. *Cael.* 18, Hyg. *Astr. praef.*): see further Oakley on Liv. 9.45.2. The action develops over two periodic sentences, the second (the unsuspecting Volturcius) markedly longer than the first (the complicit Gauls). After the *postquam*-clause, the first subject (*Galli*) is followed by an abl. abs. and terminal main verb; in the second sentence the contrasting subject (*Volturcius*) is fronted: his responses are twofold (*primo . . . deinde*), the second of them further divided (*prius . . . postremo*); the two main verbs are again terminal, and the subsidiary developments are expressed by an *ubi*-clause and a sequence of participles. See also 48.5, 49.4n., 57.5n.

utrimque clamor exortus est: 'a typical element of descriptions of battle-scenes' (E. Fraenkel, *Horace* (1957) 118, on the parody at Hor. *S.* 1.9.77 'clamor utrimque'): cf. e.g. Hirt. *BG* 8.42.4.

cito cognito consilio: they had not been warned in advance (*Cat.* 3.6), but they catch on quickly.

45.4 multa . . . Pomptinum obtestatus 'with much beseeching of Pomptinus' (*OLD obtestor* 2): *Pomptinum* is the direct obj., *multa* an adverbial acc. (as Liv. 23.26.2 'multum . . . obtestanti').

timidus ac uitae diffidens ueluti hostibus sese praetoribus dedit: Volturcius had not been included in the agreement between Cicero and the legates (*Cat.* 3.6). For *timidus ac . . . diffidens* (again at *BJ* 32.5) cf. Suet. *Claud.* 35.1 (the adverbs are first coupled at Cic. *Clu.* 1); *uitae* is dat., as

Caes. *BG* 6.38.2 'diffisus suae atque omnium saluti'. Since S. has a modest preference for the clausula – ∪ – – – (9.57%) over – ∪ – ∪ – (6.04%), the verb is perhaps more likely to be the present tense of *dedere* than the perfect of *dare* (cf. *tradunt* of the Gauls just above).

46.1 Quibus rebus confectis is found 3× in Caesar and 2× in Nepos but not elsewhere.

propere: it was roughly 3 miles from the Mulvian Bridge to the centre of Rome; Cicero says that it was already getting light when the apprehended men reached him (*Cat.* 3.6).

46.2 at illum ingens cura atque laetitia simul occupauere: the two emotions are explained chiastically in what follows (*laetabatur . . . anxius*). The antithesis *cura* ~ *laetitia* is not uncommon but S. is imitated by Tac. *A.* 1.52.1 'nuntiata ea Tiberium laetitia curaque adfecere'; *occupat cura* becomes a Livian idiom; for *laetitia* cf. Liv. 23.13.6.

The following narrative up to the execution of the Catilinarian conspirators has been discussed in learned and exhaustive detail by Drummond, whose approach – focussing particularly on the speeches of Caesar and Cato – is almost exclusively historical, constitutional and legal. To note each point as it arises is beyond the scope of this commentary; interested readers are advised to consult Drummond directly and to compare his discussion with S.'s narrative.

laetabatur intellegens 'he was delighted to know': the constr. with the participle is regular (*TLL* 7.2.881.16–22).

coniuratione patefacta: the expr. (again at 36.5, 48.1, 57.1) is almost exclusively Ciceronian (e.g. *Cat.* 4.5, *Sull.* 4).

periculis ereptam esse: *ereptam* (again at 48.1) features prominently in the first sentence of *Cat.* 3: 'urbem . . . e flamma atque ferro ac paene e faucibus fati ereptam'. *periculis* is dat. after a verb of 'taking away'.

porro 'on the other hand' (*OLD* 6c).

tantis ciuibus 'such great/important citizens', as Prop. 3.11.55 'hoc . . . tanto . . . ciue'.

poenam illorum sibi oneri . . . fore: when he attributes thoughts like these to Cicero, S. has the benefit of hindsight (although note such sentiments as *si qua est inuidia in conseruanda re publica suscepta* at *Cat.* 3.29); see also Stone (1999) 59–60. *oneri* is a regular predic. dat. (*NLS* 48–50 §68).

impunitatem perdendae rei publicae fore: formally the gerundival phrase could be either dat. or gen., respectively paralleling or varying *oneri*. A dat. would express purpose ('impunity would have the purpose of destroying the commonwealth'), which is obviously not the required sense. On the other hand, a genitive gerundive is sometimes found as the complement of *esse* and 'may be translated by *serve to*' (G&L 280 §428R. 2;

cf. *NLS* 66–8 §85), e.g. Cic. *II Verr.* 2.132 'quae res euertendae rei publicae solent esse' ('things which customarily serve to overturn the commonwealth'): hence 'impunity would serve to destroy the state'. The usage, which expresses a potential result, is to be distinguished from a gen. gerundive of purpose (6.7n.). Etymological plays on *poena* ~ *impunitas* and cognates are common from Enn. *Ann.* 1.94–5 onwards; here the two terms point the contrast between the two clauses (ABC ~ ACB).

46.3 confirmato animo: an abl. abs. liked by Cicero (*Red. Quir.* 19, *Quinct.* 77); otherwise only at Curt. 10.6.20.

uocari ad sese: cf. *Cat.* 3.6 'ad me . . . uocaui', where the context (3.7) implies that the venue is Cicero's house. For the various individuals see 17.3–4nn.

Caeparium Tarracinensem: named also by Cicero (*Cat.* 3.14), but otherwise unknown. Tarracina (mod. Terracina) is a coastal town c. 60 miles south of Rome.

46.4 sine mora ueniunt: they were unsuspecting (*Cat.* 3.6), but Lentulus 'tardissime . . . uenit', true to his name (Berry, *CC* 132). Cf. also 58.4n. (*socordia*).

indicio cannot refer to the actual letters, which Cicero was refusing to open until he was inside the senate, but Caeparius may have heard a similar rumour to that which drew some of the leading figures to Cicero's house that morning (*Cat.* 3.7 'audita re').

46.5–6 in senatum perducit . . . in aedem Concordiae uenire iubet. eo senatum aduocat . . . Volturcium cum legatis introducit: since *senatum* and *aedem* have the same reference, the sequence of verbs suggests that, when the senators assembled in the temple in response to Cicero's order, the consul and Lentulus were already there waiting for them. In Woodman (2007a) it was proposed to read *aduoc<ar>at* to avoid this oddity, but S. never uses a contracted form of the pluperfect. Perhaps Cicero relished the drama implicit in the paradosis.

46.5 consul Lentulum, quod praetor erat, ipse manu tenens in senatum perducit: the decision that Lentulus should resign his office had not yet been taken (cf. 47.3).

aedem Concordiae: the Temple of Concord stood at the NW end of the Forum (*LTUR* 1.316–20).

46.6 magnaque frequentia eius ordinis: so too *Cat.* 3.7 'senatum frequentem': the exact meaning of such phraseology (again at 48.6, 50.3) is disputed (see Kaster on Cic. *Sest.* 26), but clearly implies a large attendance. The abl. is that of attendant circumstances (*NLS* 31 §43 (5) (ii)).

Volturcium cum legatis introducit: contrast *Cat.* 3.8 'introduxi Volturcium *sine* Gallis', where the implication (3.9) is that the

Allobroges were introduced immediately afterwards. The verb is regular for bringing non-members into the senate.

47.1 quid aut qua de causa consilii habuisset 'what plan/intention he had had and for what reason'. The partitive gen. *consilii* follows *quid* (hyperbaton).

fide publica: a promise of immunity from prosecution (*OLD fides*[1] 2e), again at 48.4: cf. *Cat.* 3.8 'fidem publicam . . . dedi'.

audire solitum . . . esse: for the various individuals see 17.3nn.

47.2 Lentulum dissimulantem coarguunt praeter litteras sermonibus quos . . . solitus erat: *Lentulum dissimulantem* is an ex. of the '*ab urbe condita* idiom' with a present participle (see 17.1n. *imparatam*), and *praeter litteras* is quasi-parenthetic: 'they refuted Lentulus' dissembling by means of (apart from his letters) the conversations which he had been accustomed to hold'. *litteras* refers both to Lentulus' written oath and to his message to C. (44.1, 4–5).

ex libris Sibyllinis regnum Romae tribus Corneliis portendi 'that according to the Sibylline Books kingship at Rome was portended for three Cornelii' (*OLD ex* 20); the acc. + inf. depends on *sermonibus*. The Sibylline Books, reputed to derive from the Sibyl of Cumae, had been kept in the temple of Jupiter Optimus Maximus on the Capitol, but the temple was destroyed by fire in 83 BC (below) and the Books, which were under the charge of the *quindecimuiri sacris faciundis*, had to be reconstituted. See esp. Shannon-Henderson on Phlegon, *Mir.* 10 (intro. n.).[83] How Lentulus came to know of the Books' contents is unclear; Dyck (on *Cat.* 3.9) suggests that he may have been one of the *quindecimuiri*.

Cinnam atque Sullam antea: se tertium esse cui fatum foret urbis potiri: *sc. fuisse* with *antea*: 'there had been Cinna and Sulla previously: he was the third to whom it was fated to control the city' (cf. *Cat.* 3.9 'se esse tertium . . .; Cinnam ante se et Sullam fuisse'); for *fatum est* + inf. see *OLD fatum* 2a; *potior* takes a gen. rather than an abl. when the reference is to political power etc. (*OLD* 5a; W.[2] on Vell. 41.2). L. Cornelius Cinna had been consul four years running (87–84) and notorious for his cruelty (cf. Cic. *ND* 3.81 'omnium crudelissimus tam diu Cinna regnauit', *Phil.* 2.108); for Sulla, likewise associated with *regnum* (e.g. Cic. *Att.* 8.11.2, 9.7.3), see 5.6n. (*dum*), 6–13 intro. n. Being contemporaries and rivals, the two formed a natural pair (e.g. Cic. *Har. Resp.* 54, *Phil.* 5.17, Tac. *A.* 1.1.1).

ab incenso Capitolio: 83 BC (A. A. Barrett, *Rome is burning* (2020) 36–7 and nn. 37–8); for the '*ab urbe condita* idiom' see 17.1n. (*imparatam*).

quem saepe ex prodigiis haruspices respondissent bello ciuili cruentum fore 'which in the light of prodigies the soothsayers had often reported would be bloody on account of civil war' (causal abl.). In 65 soothsayers had explained lightning strikes on the Capitol as portending civil war; Cicero mentions these developments at a later point in his speech (*Cat.* 3.19), although his reference to the 'twentieth year' occurs at the same point in the proceedings as in S. (*Cat.* 3.9).

47.3 cum prius omnes signa sua cognouissent: the conspirators' recognition of their seals runs as a refrain through *Cat.* 3.10.

senatus decernit uti abdicato magistratu Lentulus itemque ... in liberis custodiis habeantur: cf. *Cat.* 3.14 'censuerunt *ut* P. *Lentulus*, cum se praetura *abdicasset, in custodiam* traderetur, *itemque* ...'. Whether Lentulus in fact resigned his office has been debated (see e.g. Berry, *CC* 72–3), but Cicero and others say that he did (*Cat.* 3.15 'magistratu se abdicauit', 4.5, Plut. *Cic.* 19.3, App. *BC* 2.5.16, Dio 37.34.2) and there is no evidence that he did not: see Woodman (2024). *libera custodia* is house arrest (4).

47.4 It is not clear why the assignments listed here are not mentioned by Cicero (*Cat.* 3.14), nor why these particular five men were chosen for their task. P. Lentulus Spinther would become consul in 57 (*MRR* 2.200); Q. Cornificius had been praetor in (?) 66 (*MRR* 2.152); Julius Caesar (50.5n.) was currently praetor designate; Crassus (17.7n.) had been consul in 70. Cn. Terentius is otherwise unknown.

48.1–2 The reversal to which this paragraph refers (see below) is elegantly described. In the first sentence, after the fronted subject, an abl. abs. + rel. clause is balanced by an abl. abs. + asyndetic historic infinitives. The final sentence incorporates a tricolon crescendo with interlaced alliteration (*in- c- imm- c-*).

48.1 coniuratione patefacta: the day's events in the senate were explained to the people by a triumphant Cicero in his *Third Catilinarian* (*Cat.* 3.29), to which *patefacta* (see also 46.1n.) is perhaps an allusion (cf. esp. *Cat.* 3.3 'quae quoniam in senatu illustrata, patefacta, comperta sunt per me, uobis iam exponam breuiter, Quirites'). The speech was delivered at a *contio* in the evening of 3 Dec. (*Cat.* 3.29): see Vasaly 60–87.

plebs ... primo cupida rerum nouarum ... Catilinae consilia exsecrari: a reversal (*peripeteia*) of 37.1 'plebes nouarum rerum studio Catilinae incepta probabat'. For the proverbial fickleness of the crowd see e.g. Tosi 477 §1025.

Ciceronem ad caelum tollere: *ad caelum* is regular in expressions of praise (53.1; *OLD caelum*² 3d), like Eng. 'praise to the skies', but some think that the *plebs* was actually calling their benefactor a god (C. Habicht, *Cicero the politician* (1990) 33–4).

ueluti ex seruitute erepta: the construction (again at Cic. *Parad. Stoic.* 41 'eripite nos ex seruitute') varies that at 46.2, where see n. on *ereptam*.

gaudium atque laetitiam agitabat: for the coordinated synonyms see 1.4n. (*nam*); the favourite verb here seems to mean 'experienced' or 'felt' (as 61.9). For the popular reaction see too Dio 37.34.3.

48.2 alia belli facinora ... fore: the *plebs*, being poor, were unlikely to be targets for looting but would themselves profit from looting the better-off. *praedae* and *detrimento* are predicative datives.

crudele, immoderatum: for these two adjs. in asyndeton cf. Cic. *Att.* 13.28.3 (Adams, *AILL* 572-3).

maxime: to be taken with *sibi* (*OLD maxime* 4). With *incendium* we have to supply *fore* from earlier.

quippe cui omnes copiae in usu cotidiano et cultu corporis erant 'since their resources all went on their daily life and bodily care' (*OLD in* 41). After *quippe qui* S. uses the indic. where Cicero and most later authors use the subjunc. (G&L 401 §626 N. 1): this is the only ex. in *BC* but it is common in *BJ* (e.g. 1.3, 7.6, 14.10).

48.3–49.4 CRASSUS AND CAESAR: 4 DECEMBER 63

Twin episodes contrast the ways in which two prominent politicians are affected by the conspiracy: Crassus, now in his early fifties and a former consul, and Julius Caesar, considerably younger, praetor designate, and recently elected *pontifex maximus*. Crassus, influential and immensely rich, is named as a conspirator by an unknown renegade who may have been put up to it by Cicero (48.3–9); Caesar, influential and greatly in debt, is accused by two distinguished ex-consuls but not named as a conspirator by Cicero (49). The charge against Crassus (which some believed to be true) sees his accuser imprisoned, but the charge against Caesar (which is described as false) sees the accused in danger of his life. The contrasting episodes interpose narrative suspense between the dramatic debates of 3 and 5 December, as well as serving to introduce Caesar, one of the two main speakers on the latter occasion (51) and himself the subject of a second and more famous syncrisis thereafter (54).

48.3 Post eum diem quidam L. Tarquinius ad senatum adductus erat: *eum diem* is 3 December; *ad senatum* refers to the meeting on 4 December at which rewards were decreed to the Allobroges and Volturcius (50.1n.). The pluperf. tense sets the scene before the meeting starts at §4. L. Tarquinius is otherwise unknown; his story is also at Plut. *Crass.* 13.2 and Dio 37.35.1–2, though there he is not named.

quem ad Catilinam proficiscentem ex itinere retractum aiebant: he thus resembles the equally obscure Fulvius (39.5 'ad Catilinam initio profecti sunt ... quem retractum ex itinere ...'), except that Tarquinius' brief history, like much of the Crassus episode, is a matter of report: 'aiebant', of which the subject is presumably unidentified contemporaries.

48.4 diceret ... **edicere:** for the repetition of a simple verb by its compound see 35.3n. (*et alienis*); here the interplay is linked by *indicaturum* and rounded off by *docet*.

si fides publica data esset 'if immunity were given to him' (47.1n. *fide*): the verb would have been fut. perf. indic. in direct speech.

de paratis incendiis, de caede bonorum: cf. *Cat.* 2.10 'eructant sermonibus suis caedem bonorum atque urbis incendia'.

hostium is already applicable to C. and Manlius (36.2n. *haec*); Lentulus and the others came close to being declared *hostes* at the meeting of 4 Dec. (50.3n. *sed*).

se missum a M. Crasso qui Catilinae nuntiaret ...: a rel. clause of purpose is often found after verbs of sending. 'The use of *ut* draws attention to the purpose in the mind of the subject of *mittit*, whereas *qui* draws attention to the means by which he achieves it' (*NLS* 108 §147). For Crassus cf. 17.7n.

ne eum Lentulus et Cethegus aliique ex coniuratione deprehensi terrerent 'that *the arrest of* Lentulus, Cethegus and others of the conspiracy should not scare him', another ex. of the so-called '*ab urbe condita* idiom' (17.1n. *imparatam*).

eoque magis properaret ad urbem accedere 'and <that> he should *therefore* hurry *all the more* to reach the city': *ut* has to be understood after the preceding *ne*; for the double meaning of *eo* see 13.5n. (*eo*). *ad urbem accedere* refers back to the promise C. made to his supporters on the night of 7–8 Nov. (32.2 'propediem ... ad urbem accessurum'). For *propero* + infin. see *OLD* 3b.

quo et ceterorum animos reficeret et illi facilius e periculo eriperentur: *periculo* refers to the plight of being a defendant (*OLD* 3) and indicates that by *illi* are meant the five under house arrest (47.4); *ceterorum* are the Catilinarians still at large: the transition from a general 'others' to a more specific subject is characteristically Greek and esp. typical of Herodotus (e.g. 6.49.1 Οἵ τε δὴ ἄλλοι νησιῶται διδοῦσι γῆν τε καὶ ὕδωρ Δαρείῳ καὶ δὴ καὶ Αἰγινῆται): see J. D. Denniston, *The Greek particles* (²1954) 255–6. The use of *quo* to introduce a purpose clause (cf. 11.5n. *quo*) is here influenced by the comparative in the second colon.

48.5 sed, ubi ... **uti referatur:** another periodic sentence: after an initial *ubi*-clause, each of the three subjects is variously qualified (respectively participle, *quia*-clause, adj.) before the two main verbs, each introducing brief indirect speech.

hominem nobilem: on *nobilitas* see 5.1n. (*nobili*): Crassus' father was P. Licinius Crassus, consul in 97 BC (*BNP* 7.526–7 [I 15]).

maximis diuitiis: the first of two abls. of description, varying *nobilem*. Crassus was famous for his immense wealth (e.g. Cic. *Off.* 1.25; F. E. Adcock, *Marcus Crassus, millionaire* (1966)), although the proverbial

'richer than Crassus' (Otto 96) seems to derive from another branch of
the Licinii whose *cognomen* was Dives (see Shackleton Bailey on Cic. *Att.*
1.4(9).3).

rem incredibilem rati: *sc. esse.* All forms of *reor* are entirely absent from
Caesar and from Cicero's speeches; the past participle is extremely rare
elsewhere in Cicero, in whose *De Oratore* (3.153) the form *rebar,* also
uncommon in Cicero, is described as archaic and poetic. Quintilian,
discussing archaisms, describes *reor* as 'tolerabile' (8.3.26). S. has *rebatur*
once (*BJ* 26.2) but *ratus* numerous times, though significantly less often
in *BC* (4×) than *BJ.* See further Lebek 31.

pars, tametsi uerum existimabant, tamen quia ... tanta uis hominis
magis lenienda quam exagitanda uidebatur 'others because, although
they considered it true, in such a crisis so violent/powerful a man
seemed to require soothing rather than arousing': contemporary sus-
picions of at least Crassus' knowledge of the conspiracy, if not of his
involvement in it, were already voiced at 17.7 (see also 29.1n. *Ea*); but
Crassus is chosen to supervise Gabinius' house arrest (47.4), and it
would be very odd to delegate such a responsibility to someone
regarded as a suspect. *tanta uis hominis* resembles the numerous
phrases in Greek epic and tragedy which combine a word for 'force'
with an adj. or genitive (thus at Hom. *Il.* 14.418 Ἕκτορος ... μένος, lit.
'the might of Hector' = 'mighty Hector'). Since the periphrasis is very
frequently used of animals (see Pease on Virg. *Aen.* 4.132), the contrasting gerundives (*OLD lenio* 2a, *exagito* 1c) perhaps suggest that
Crassus is seen as a dangerous beast who should not be provoked
out of his lair.[84] Other exs. of the expr. *uis hominis* (Cic. *Fin.* 5.43,
Lucr. 3.645, 4.1040) are rather different. For *existimo* see 4.4n. (*nam*);
pars (*OLD* 3b) is often followed by a plural verb. For *tametsi ... tamen*
see 3.2n. (*tametsi*).

plerique Crasso ex negotiis priuatis obnoxii '(very) many being in
Crassus' debt as a result of private/personal transactions' (*OLD obnoxius*
1a, *ex* 18a). Cf. Plut. *Crass.* 3.1.

deque ea re postulant uti referatur 'and they demanded that a motion
about the matter be placed [*sc.* before the senate]': *a consule* may, but need
not, be supplied with *postulant* or *referatur* or both; for *referatur* see 29.1n.
(*rem*). *-que* is very commonly attached to the prep. *de.*

---

[84] Cicero has three consecutive exs. of the idiom at *Cat.* 3.16: 'non mihi esse
P. Lentuli somnum nec L. Cassi adipes nec C. Cethegi furiosam temeritatem
pertimescendam', 'I would have nothing to fear from the lazy Publius Lentulus,
or the obese Lucius Cassius, or the reckless, insane Gaius Cethegus' (trans.
Berry).

48.6 consulente: the technical term for the consul's formal consultation of the senate (*OLD* 1b). See also Maltby 152.

frequens senatus: the use of this quasi-technical expression (46.6n *magnaque*) is perhaps pointed here, since on the following day (5 Dec.) Cicero publicly noted (*Cat.* 4.10) the absence of someone – evidently a prominent individual – who had been present the previous day, i.e. today.[85]

indicium falsum uideri: *uideri* represents the prudential language of senatorial decrees (e.g. the verb is 4× in lines 6–9 at the start of *SCPP*): see Oakley on Liv. 8.10.12 (*Addendum* 4.573).

neque amplius potestatem faciendam, nisi de eo indicaret cuius … esset mentitus: *sc. indicandi* with *potestatem*, and *esse* with *faciendam*: 'and the opportunity [*sc.* of giving information] should no longer be provided <to him> unless he gave information about the person at whose suggestion he had fabricated so great a matter' (*OLD amplius* 5b, *consilium* 2b, *potestas* 5, *mentior* 4 [rather than 3]). *indicaret* represents a fut. indic. in direct speech.

48.7–9 These sections constitute a digressive closure to Tarquinius' story. The *uariatio* of 48.5 ('alii … pars … plerique …') continues: 'erant … qui aestimarent … [8] alii … aiebant … [9] ego … praedicantem audiui'. As at the start of the episode (3 *aiebant*), the emphasis is on the reported word.

48.7 a P. Autronio machinatum: *sc. esse*: the passive use of *machinari* seems peculiar to S. (again at *H.* 3.10.3, 4.6); the case of Vitr. 10.1.4, quoted at *TLL* 8.18.6–7, is unclear. For Autronius see 17.3n.

quo facilius … illius potentia tegeret 'in order that, once Crassus had been named/accused, the man's powerfulness might protect the rest more easily through his association with their danger': either Crassus might deflect attention from the others or his involvement would deter further investigation. *appellare* regularly means 'mention by name' (*OLD* 11), which makes good sense here (cf. 5 'Crassum nominauit'), but the much rarer meaning 'charge, accuse' (*OLD* 5b) would be equally appropriate; likewise *periculi* may mean simply 'danger' but may more technically refer to the plight of the defendants (4 above). *societas periculi* (-*orum*), fairly frequent in Cic. (e.g. *Rab. Perd.* 21), is also at Nep. *Dion* 5.2, Curt. 9.4.15; for the quasi-personification of *potentia*, *TLL* compares *BJ* 30.2, Cic. *Dom.* 80, *Caecin.* 71, Curt. 10.10.18 (10.2.292.68–74).

48.8 more suo suscepto malorum patrocinio: Crassus had a reputation for 'helping to aid the wicked' (Plut. *Comp. Nic. Crass.* 1.2; cf. Syme, *ARR*

---

[85] Cicero is usually thought to have been referring to Crassus, whose absence is inferred from his omission from the list of consular voters at Cic. *Att.* 12.21 (260).1 (*contra* Drummond 14–15).

165, Drummond 19). *suscipere patrocinium* is a regular phrase (*TLL* 10.1.778.9–11).

48.9 ipsum Crassum ego postea praedicantem audiui: the participle makes it clear that S. heard Crassus in the act of making his declaration (cf. *BJ* 14.12 'praedicantem audiueram patrem meum'): he and Cicero disliked each other (cf. Cic. *Phil.* 2.7 with Ramsey's n.). The occasion must have pre-dated Crassus' departure for the east in Nov. 55. Autopsy enhances authorial credibility (Marincola 63–86 and his 'Source-citations in the classical historians' in J. Verheyden et al. (edd.), *On using sources in Graeco-Roman, Jewish and early Christian literature* (2022) 3–25, esp. 14); this is the only occasion in the work in which S. invokes it for his account of the conspiracy. Cf. also 13.1n. (*Nam*).

tantam illam contumeliam sibi a Cicerone impositam: *sc. esse*: 'that that great insult had been inflicted on him by Cicero' (*OLD impono* 12b): for the expr. cf. Cic. *Verr.* 4.20, Apul. *Flor.* 7.

49.1 isdem temporibus: the upcoming reference to the Allobroges indicates that the period in question is late Nov./early Dec.

Q. Catulus et C. Piso: for the former see 34.3–35.1 and nn.; C. Calpurnius Piso (42.3n. *in*) had been consul in 67 (*MRR* 2.142–3). Their motivations for wanting to attack Caesar are given chiastically below.

gratia 'influence'.

uti per … indicem … falso nominaretur: this episode is the counterpart of the former (~ 48.5 *nominauit … indicem falsum … indicium falsum*), except that here the allegation of falsity seems authorial.

49.2 uterque cum illo graues inimicitias exercebant: the sentence is extended beyond the main verb by *Piso* and *Catulus*, each of which is in apposition to *uterque*. For the personal enmity which S. mentions see Epstein 52, 102–3. *inimicitias exercere* (again at 51.16) is a regular expression; for *graues* cf. Vell. 45.1 'cum graues inimicitias cum M. Cicerone exerceret' (of Clodius).

oppugnatus … supplicium iniustum 'having been opposed [*sc.* by Caesar] in the extortion court for his unjust punishment of a Transpadane' (*OLD oppugno* 2a): Piso had been governor of Cisalpine and Transalpine Gaul in 66–65 (*MRR* 2.154, 159, 3.46); the trial must have taken place during 63, since Piso was defended by Cicero when he was consul (*Flacc.* 98): *iniustum* is not the view of the court, since Piso failed to be condemned. See *TLRR* 112 no. 225; Stone (1999) 70.

ex petitione pontificatus odio incensus 'burning with hatred on account of/after his candidature for the pontificate' (*OLD ex* 9–10, 18a, *petitio* 5). Catulus had been a member of the *pontifices* (21.2n. *sacerdotia*) for well over two decades and in 63 campaigned unsuccessfully for the office of *pontifex maximus*; his two rivals were Caesar and P. Servilius Vatia Isauricus (cos. 79): see Rüpke 778 §2308.

quod ... uictus discesserat: Catulus had been born in the 120s: in addition to his consulship (78), he had been given the task of restoring the temple of Jupiter on the Capitol (Gell. 2.10.2) and had recently (65) been appointed censor. Caesar had already been a *pontifex* for about ten years before his election as *pontifex maximus* (Rüpke 734–5 §2003): having been born on 13 July 100, he was now thirty-seven; men in their thirties could be described as *adulescentes* (38.1n. *homines*), but here the diminutive form ('a mere youth') is perhaps focalised by Catulus. *discedo* is here used of withdrawing from a contest *vel sim.* (*OLD* 4).

49.3 res autem opportuna uidebatur: the *res* in question is the attempt of Catulus and Piso to associate Caesar, who had run up immense debts, with C., whose plan included the cancellation of debt (21.2).

egregia liberalitate: see 54.2–3. The description of Caesar here balances that of Crassus at 48.5.

publice maximis muneribus: the lavish games (*OLD munus* 4a) which Caesar had put on as aedile in 65: for this and his other extravagances see Plut. *Caes.* 4.4–7, 5.8–9 and Pelling's nn.

grandem pecuniam seems almost to be a set expr. (Oakley on Liv. 10.46.10); see also 14.2n. (*alienum*).

49.4 Sed ubi ... minitarentur: another periodic sentence (45.3n.), this time with a centralised main verb (*conflauerant*), after which there is a consecutive clause which itself displays significant subordination.

singillatim circumeundo: as if *singulos*: 'by doing the rounds of individuals'.

ementiendo quae se ... audisse dicerent 'by fabricating what [i.e. the things which] they said they had heard ...': *dicerent* is an ex. of a so-called 'oblique' use of the subjunctive in 'sentences with a cognition verb that governs an accusative and infinitive clause': see *OLS* 1.620, where numerous other exs. are quoted, incl. Cic. *Phil.* 2.7 'litteras, quas me sibi misisse diceret, recitauit'. It is as if the subjunctive has been attracted into the acc. + inf. construction, an attraction facilitated by the fact that *ementiri* can itself introduce indirect speech.

magnam illi inuidiam conflauerat 'they had stoked up great resentment against him [i.e. Caesar]': *inuidiam conflare* is a Ciceronian idiom, e.g. *Cat.* 1.23 'si mihi inimico ... tuo conflare uis inuidiam'.

nonnulli equites Romani, qui praesidii causa cum telis erant circum aedem Concordiae: the temple of Concordia was where the senate met on 3 Dec. (46.5n.) and 5 Dec. (Cic. *Phil.* 4.14) and presumably on 4 Dec. too. There are numerous references to a force of equestrians who, led by Atticus (*Att.* 2.1(21).7), were stationed by Cicero in the vicinity for security purposes, although the details vary from author to author (cf. Cic. *Red. Sen.* 12, *Sest.* 28, *Phil.* 2.16, Plut. *Caes.* 8.2, Suet. *DJ* 14.2 'manus equitum Romanorum, quae armata praesidii causa circumstabat'; see further below);

but it is worth noting that a few weeks earlier, when Cicero delivered his *First Catilinarian* in the temple of Jupiter Stator (32.1n.), armed equestrians had also surrounded the senate and shown their support (cf. *Cat.* 1.21 'studia ... tela').

seu periculi magnitudine seu animi mobilitate impulsi: belief in the false rumours leads the *equites* either to think that Caesar poses a danger to the state or to change their minds about their function as a mere security presence (the alternatives are not mutually exclusive): for this sense of *animi mobilitas* cf. Caes. *BG* 2.1.3. *impello* has a rather different sense from its two earlier appearances in this paragraph (14.3n. *conuicti*).

quo studium suum in rem publicam clarius esset, egredienti ex senatu Caesari gladio minitarentur: the equestrians' threat is dated by Cicero to 5 December (*Red. Sen.* 12) and is described as their angry response to Caesar's speech on that day, in which he argued that the conspirators should not be executed (Plut. *Caes.* 8.2, Suet. *DJ* 14.2). Since S. in his narrative does not reach 5 Dec. until 50.3 and does not present Caesar's speech until 51.1–43, it may seem that he has misdated the threat; but, since 48.7–49.4 is (as it were) a 'timeless' section (cf. the vague *eo tempore* at 48.7 and *isdem temporibus* at 49.1) inserted into the senatorial session of 4 Dec. (48.3–6 ~ 50.1), the equestrians' threat is more properly seen as a 'narrative prolepsis'.[86]

The curious purpose clause here should be seen in the light of Cicero's remarks to the senators on 5 Dec. (*Cat.* 4.15 'equites Romanos ... qui uobis ita summam ordinis consiliique concedunt ut uobiscum de amore rei publicae certent'). The equestrians rival the senators in their *amor rei publicae*; the purpose of their threatening Caesar after the debate was to show that their *studium in rem publicam* was clearer than that of a senator who argued that traitors should not be executed. With *clarius* (*OLD* 4) we have to understand *quam Caesaris*. For the relationship between the *equites* and Cicero cf. D. H. Berry, *CQ* 53 (2003) 222–34, esp. 226.

minari is preferred to the frequentative form by the majority of authors; the most notable exceptions are Val. Max. and esp. Plaut. and Tac., although Cic. and Sil. use *minitari* liberally (*TLL* 8.1024.50–65): S. has 3 exs. of *minitari* and 2 of *minari*. The constr. (dat. + abl.) seems regular (*TLL* 8.1025.11–26).

50–5 DEBATE AND DEATH: 4–5 DECEMBER 63

The monograph ends with two set-piece descriptions, of which the first is devoted to the famous debate on whether the Catilinarian prisoners

---

[86] The two days seem to be confused by C. Davenport, *A history of the Roman equestrian order* (2019) 103–4.

should be put to death. The question was one of extreme gravity, and the matter of the prisoners' execution would haunt Cicero for the remaining twenty years of his life.

The principal sources for the debate, apart from S. himself, are Cicero (*Cat.* 4, *Att.* 12.21.1), Plutarch (*Cic.* 20.4–21.4, *Cato Min.* 22.3–23.3, *Caes.* 7.7–8.1), Appian (*BC* 2.5.18–6.21) and Dio (37.36), all of whom tell more or less the same story. D. Junius Silanus, the consul designate, spoke first and in favour of execution, and his proposal was supported by every subsequent speaker up to Julius Caesar, praetor designate, who proposed a form of imprisonment. He was supported by many senators, including some who now changed their minds. (Silanus, relying on the ambiguity of the term *supplicium*, maintained that he had never intended to propose execution in the first place.) But then Q. Lutatius Catulus, the consul of 78, and M. Porcius Cato, tribune designate, each argued that the prisoners should be put to death, and Cato's speech was so powerful that it persuaded the majority in favour of execution. Appian adds the detail that Caesar's speech was preceded by a proposal from Ti. Claudius Nero, who suggested that the prisoners should be kept under guard until C. was defeated in battle and the situation became more clear.[87]

S. in his account gives pride of place to the speeches of Caesar (51) and Cato (52.2–36), who in any case were the two contemporaries for whom he declared his principal admiration (53.6), but his introduction to the debate refers to an earlier meeting of the senate (50.3 'paulo ante frequens senatus') and can be read as implying that it was at this earlier meeting that Silanus and Caesar first made their respective proposals (50.4). Since this interpretation seems to receive support from Cicero (*Cat.* 4.7, 24), it will be argued in the following notes that the famous meeting of 5 December was the *second* of two meetings devoted to the question of the prisoners' fate; and according to S.'s account (50.4) it was Claudius Nero who suggested that there be a second meeting, a suggestion very much in keeping with the gravity of the matter with which the senators were confronted. See further S. J. Heyworth and A. J. Woodman, 'Sallust, *Bellum Catilinae* 50.3–5', *LCM* 11 (1986) 11–12; Woodman (2021b).

S.'s account of the Catilinarian debate recalls Thucydides' account of the Mytilenean Debate in 427 BC (3.36–50): the Athenians, enraged by a revolt at Mytilene and having decided to punish the city by killing all its men and enslaving all its women and children, then changed their minds and on the next day held a second debate at which Cleon's speech in favour of the original severity (3.37–40) was answered by Diodotus' speech against it (3.42–8). In S.'s account the two speeches are the other way

---

[87] For a reconstruction of the debate see Berry, *CC* 164–73, although he differs in various significant respects.

round, Caesar speaking first in favour of a milder punishment and Cato speaking second in favour of the death penalty; and, although in both authors the second speaker persuades his audience, once again the result is the converse of that in Thucydides. These are the kinds of adaptation which one expects in an allusive narrative, and it is clearly possible that the relationship between the two texts, which scholars have long recognised,[88] provides further support for the notion that in 63 BC too there were two debates rather than one.

When Caesar and Cato delivered their speeches, they each had much of their futures in front of them, but when S. wrote his monograph, both protagonists were dead (cf. 53.6 *fuere*) and the historian is able to benefit from hindsight. Although S. gives no hint of the feud between them which characterised the two succeeding decades,[89] Caesar's advocacy of a milder punishment seems to foreshadow his famous *clementia*, while Cato's support for the death penalty anticipates the severity with which his name became associated. Their speeches in S. differ from each other in structure and theme (50.5n., 52.1n.), but verbal similarities between them give the impression that Cato is responding to Caesar. Yet the relationship between the speeches is less straightforward than this antiphony suggests. While we might have expected Cato to echo Thucydides' Cleon (52.7n. *Saepenumero*) and Caesar to echo his Diodotus (51.2n. *facile*), it is perhaps less expected that Caesar should also echo Cleon (51.8nn.), and even less expected that it should be Caesar who alludes to the famous speech *Pro Rhodiensibus* that was delivered by Cato's revered great-grandfather and subsequently incorporated in the latter's *Origines* (51.5–7nn.). See esp. Levene, *OR* 227–43.

After Cato finishes his speech and the death penalty is decreed (53.1), S. at this crucial point in the story once again suspends his narrative, as at 36.5 (Intro. p. 13), and inserts a digressive passage on *uirtus* (53.2–6) which acts as a foil for the celebrated syncrisis of Caesar and Cato (53.6–54.6). It is only then that S. returns to the main narrative and the implementation of the death penalty in the terrible dungeon (55).

50.1 Dum haec in senatu aguntur et dum legatis Allobrogum et T. Volturcio ... praemia decernuntur: *haec* can only refer back to the proceedings of 4 Dec. described at 48.3–6, and, since the decision to

[88] See e.g. Scanlon 102–8. L. Canfora ('Thucydides in Rome and late antiquity', in A. Rengakos and A. Tsamakis (edd.), *Brill's Companion to Thucydides* (2012) 737–8) supports the view that S.'s paired speeches are 'based (and at times modelled)' on the speeches of Nicolaus and Gylippus on the fate of the Athenian prisoners in Diod. 13.20–32, but his account is variously confused.

[89] For the feud between Caesar and Cato see e.g. Drogula, *CY* 79–83, 119–31, 260–73.

reward the legates and Volturcius was taken at a senate meeting on 4 Dec. (cf. *Cat.* 4.5 '*hesterno die* praemia legatis Allobrogum Titoque Volturcio dedistis amplissima', 10), it seems inevitable that both *dum*-clauses refer to the same meeting.

diuersis itineribus 'along different streets'. The wording of this episode in Appian (*BC* 2.5.17) is almost identical; cf. also Dio 37.35.3.

in uicis 'in the neighbourhoods', an adnominal prepositional phrase (20.2n. *dominatio*) to be taken closely with *opifices atque seruitia*. For *uici* and their political significance see e.g. J. B. Lott, *The neighborhoods of Augustan Rome* (2004), H. I. Flower, 'Beyond the *contio*', in C. Steel and H. van der Blom (edd.), *Community and communication: oratory and politics in republican Rome* (2013) 97.

partim = *alii* (*OLD* 1a).

duces multitudinum, qui pretio rem publicam uexare soliti erant: *dux* is the regular term for rabble-rousers, and *multitudo* can mean a 'mob' (e.g. 52.14); but the plur. form ('mobs') seems unique in classical Latin (*TLL* 8.1602.12–13; *OLD* 5b). Cf. e.g. *Cat.* 4.17 (*pretio* again); Mouritsen, *PP* 58.

50.2 familiam: i.e. his slaves (*OLD* 2–3).

orabat in audaciam, ūt grĕgĕ fāctō cūm tēlīs ād sēs(e) īrrūmperent: *oro* is nowhere else constructed with *in* + acc., but, since S. uniquely constructs it with *ad* + acc. at *H.* 3.60.1, the expr. seems secure. The *ut*-clause will be either an indir. command or epexegetic of *audaciam* (*OLD ut* 39); for *audacia* see 5.4n. (*animus*). *grege facto* (again at *BJ* 58.3) is imitated at Liv. 8.24.13; for *cum telis* cf. 27.2n. (*ipse*). The dactylic rhythm is noteworthy, as often.

50.3 consul: in *Cat.* 4 Cicero lays great stress on his role as consul (e.g. §§1–2, 6, 18, 24).

ea: the escape plans mentioned in §§1–2.

dispositis praesidiis ut res atque tempus monebat: if *Sed eos... referendum censuerat* below is all a flashback to a meeting on 4 Dec., as argued, these guards will be those asked for by Nero at §4 below ('praesidiis additis'). *monere* is often used with such nouns as *res* and *tempus* as its subject (*OLD* 3a).

conuocato senatu: the famous meeting of 5 December.

refert quid de iis fieri placeat qui in custodiam traditi erant: *refert* (see 29.1n. *rem*) introduces the motion which was put before the senate on 5 December. Cicero in his *Fourth Catilinarian* refers to the putting of the motion (4.6 'referre'), but most scholars believe that that speech as a whole is 'a composite product' (Syme, *Sall.* 106n. 12) and 'combines material from various moments in the debate' (Dyck, intro. to *Cat.* 4; see also Berry, *CC* 192); and, since the speech is also said to contain revisions added some years later, it is regarded as 'an imaginative fiction' (Berry, *CC* 173; cf. 87, 150 n. 40, 177, 191–2; likewise A. W. Lintott, *Cicero as evidence* (2008) 17–18, 147–8). I have argued elsewhere, however, that the *Fourth*

Catilinarian is an accurate representation of what Cicero said when as consul he *introduced* the debate and put before the senate the motion to be debated (Woodman (2021b) 8–9; also above, 31.6n. *quam*). That motion, to which S. here refers, is in my opinion the one which Ti. Nero had proposed at an earlier meeting (4 'referendum censuerat': see next n.). *quid de iis fieri placeat* is formulaic for the request to senators for their opinion (e.g. *Cat.* 3.13 'de summa re publica quid fieri placeat'; Oakley on Liv. 8.20.11).

50.3–4 Sed eos paulo ante . . . referendum censuerat: that *Sed* introduces a parenthetical flashback is clear from *paulo ante* and the pluperfect tense (*iudicauerat*); the two following sentences also have their main verbs in the pluperfect (*decreuerat, dixerat*): how is this evidence to be interpreted? Is it more likely that the flashback continues for another two sentences, before the main narrative is resumed, as often, by *Sed* at §5? Or is it more likely that the flashback comprises only the present sentence, that the main narrative is resumed immediately with *tum*, that *decreuerat* despite its tense is part of the main narrative, but that *dixerat* has to be emended to *dixit* to preserve chronological consistency? If the matter is presented like this, it seems fairly obvious that the former hypothesis is the more plausible; yet no modern editor adopts it. Why? The fact is that scholars are wedded to a scenario in which D. Junius Silanus opened the famous debate of 5 Dec. by proposing the death penalty and was in due course followed by the more lenient proposal of Julius Caesar; but that there was an earlier meeting such as S. describes in 50.3–4 seems confirmed by passages of Cicero's *Fourth Catilinarian* (§§6–7 and 24): see Woodman (2021b) 4–12, 15–19.[90] Whether the first meeting took place earlier on 5 December or is to be identified with the meeting known to have taken place on 4 December (48.6 'frequens senatus', 50.1) cannot be ascertained, although the latter seems far more likely: S. uses the expr. *frequens senatus* of both occasions (cf. 50.3: next n.) and nowhere else; nevertheless, for the sake of clarity, I shall refer to the earlier meeting as Meeting I and to the famous meeting of 5 Dec. as Meeting II.

50.3 Sed eos paulo ante frequens senatus iudicauerat contra rem publicam fecisse: on any interpretation (see last n.), this sentence constitutes a parenthetical flashback (for *sed* to introduce a parenthesis see e.g. 8.1, 18.1, 53.2); that the crowded meeting is that of 4 Dec. is argued by D. H. Garrison, 'The events of December 4, 63 B.C. and Sallust *Cat.* 50.3–4', *CJ* 57 (1962) 360–2.

---

[90] The hypothesis of two meetings receives strong support from the relative ordering of the proposals of Nero and Caesar. Scholars infer from §4 below that Caesar spoke before Nero, yet Appian (*BC* 2.5.19–6.20) has Nero speaking before Caesar: this inconsistency is removed if there were two meetings and Caesar spoke also at the second (see further 50.5n. *Sed*).

contra rem publicam facere (again at 30.6, 51.43) is a legal expr., found in a *senatus consultum* quoted at Cic. *Fam.* 8.8.6 'eum senatum existimare contra rem publicam fecisse' and in another paraphrased at *Red. Sen.* 27 'qui impedisset, ... illum contra rem publicam ... facturum'. Since the latter *s.c.* is the same as that mentioned also at *Pis.* 35 'si quis impedisset ..., *in hostium numero* putaretur', a case can be made that a decree of anti-state activity was equivalent to declaring someone a *hostis*. A minority of scholars believe that 'the conspirators in custody were declared public enemies' (T. Rice Holmes, *The Roman republic* (1923) 1.273), but most do not (see e.g. Allély 62 (cf. 58), Straumann 94 n. 179): when Cicero at *Cat.* 4.5 lists the measures which were taken on 3–4 Dec., he makes no reference to a *hostis* declaration, a silence which most scholars regard as decisive. See further Woodman (2024) 75–7.

Stone (1999, 59) sees *iudicauerat* as 'echoing' *Cat.* 4.5 'multis iam iudiciis iudicauisti ... iudicastis'; perhaps *iudicauerat ... fecisse* looks back also to *Cat.* 4.6 'de facto quid iudicetis'.

50.4 tum D. Iunius Silanus ... decreuerat: *tum* means 'on that occasion' (*OLD* 1c): it continues the reference to Meeting I, as the tense of *decreuerat* implies, and does not resume S.'s account of Meeting II, as generally believed. That it was at Meeting I that Silanus made his proposal is clear from *Cat.* 4.7 'uideo duas *adhuc* esse sententias, unam D. Silani ...' (Woodman (2021b) 5 n. 14); for *decerno* = 'propose' see *OLD* 6.

primus sententiam rogatus quod ... consul designatus erat: consuls designate were customarily invited to speak first (App. *BC* 2.5.18 'first to speak was Silanus, who was chosen as consul in the future'; Pina Polo 247–8). Of Silanus little is otherwise known (*MRR* 2.172, *BNP* 6.1099 [I 30]) and he 'fades out after his consulship' (R. Syme, *The Augustan aristocracy* (1986) 189); he was married to Servilia, half-sister of the younger Cato (cf. S. Treggiari, *Servilia and her family* (2019) 88–119); his third daughter, Junia, wife of the Cassius who murdered Caesar, died at a great age in AD 22 (Tac. *A.* 3.76.1). Verbs such as *rogare* take a double acc., one of which is retained in the passive (*NLS* 11 §16 Note 2 (ii)).

de iis qui in custodiis tenebantur et praeterea de L. Cassio, P. Furio, P. Vmbreno, Q. Annio: i.e. a total of nine (cf. *Cat.* 3.14); for the indic. see 17.7n. (*quia*). For Cassius and Annius cf. 17.3nn.; for Umbrenus cf. 40.1n. P. Furius is mentioned at *Cat.* 3.14 as a Sullan colonist at Faesulae (cf. 59.3n.).

si deprehensi forent, supplicium sumendum: *sc. esse* or *fore*. The sentence would be a vivid future condition in direct speech (*deprehensi forent* represents a fut. perf. indic.). *supplicium* often, but not always, stands for *summum supplicium*, i.e. the death penalty (*OLD* 3a).

postea permotus oratione C. Caesaris pedibus in sententiam Ti. Neronis iturum se dixerat, qui de ea re praesidiis additis referendum censuerat: *sc. esse* with both *iturum* and *referendum*. The transmitted *dixerat* was changed to *dixit* by Bussmann and Roscher on the grounds that Silanus' statement followed Caesar's speech ('postea ... Caesaris') and hence that the pluperf. is inconsistent with *locutus est* below (5): it was assumed that *dixit* had been wrongly assimilated to the preceding pluperfects. The emendation has been accepted by almost all recent editors,[91] but they have not realised that S. is still referring to Meeting I, at which both Silanus and Caesar made proposals (above).[92] Silanus' proposal of the death penalty (*decreuerat*) was followed by Caesar's counter-proposal (*oratione*), which in turn was followed by the proposal of Ti. Nero (*censuerat*) that Cicero should increase security ('praesidiis additis') and only then put a formal motion (*referendum*) – which he did (3 *refert*).[93] It is to be noted that when the debate resumed on 5 Dec., Silanus was still regarded as the main proponent of the death penalty (*Cat.* 4.7, quoted above, 50.4n. *tum*): Caesar's speech had persuaded him of the advantage of a temporary adjournment but it had not made him change his mind about the appropriate punishment, as is clear from his inclusion in Cicero's list of those who voted in favour of execution (*Att.* 12.21.1).[94] *pedibus in sententiam alicuius ire* = 'to support the motion of X' (*OLD pes* 6b). See further nn. below. Ti. Claudius Nero was grandfather of the emperor Tiberius; since he spoke after Caesar, who was

---

[91] Kurfess in the Teubner edition does not even mention that it is an emendation but prints it as though it were the transmitted reading. He is followed by McGushin.

[92] Ramsey retains *dixerat* but explains the tense as relative to *fit* several pages later at 53.1, which seems impossible. He does not believe that there were two meetings, but the problems caused by the assumption of only a single meeting are extremely severe (summarised by Pelling on Plut. *Caes.* 8.1, pp. 166–8).

[93] Nero's proposal as reported by S. differs from what is said by Appian (intro.), the only other author to mention Nero; but, since in Appian the proposals of Nero and Caesar are very similar, it seems likely that there has been some cross-contamination and confusion.

[94] The inclusion of Silanus' name in Cicero's list must cast doubt on the story that Silanus was so shaken by Caesar's speech on 5 Dec. that at the end of it he protested bizarrely that by 'supplicium' he had not meant 'summum supplicium' at all (Suet. *DJ* 14.1, Plut. *Cic.* 21.3, *Cato Min.* 22.6), a change of heart criticised by his brother-in-law Cato in his speech (Plut. *Cato Min.* 23.1). Since Silanus is still identified with execution in the *Fourth Catilinarian* (4.7), those who believe that that speech was delivered midway through the debate on 5 Dec. are compelled to assume that Silanus' change of heart did not come immediately after Caesar's speech, when 'all' subsequent speakers agreed until Catulus and Cato (Plut. *Cato Min.* 22.5–23.1, Dio 37.36.2), but after Cicero's intervention *against* Caesar speech (so e.g. Berry, *CC* 171). That seems quite implausible.

praetor designate (below, 5n. *sed*), he must have been praetor in some earlier year (*MRR* 2.463).

praesidiis additis: in view of the circular presentation of the narrative, whereby *referendum* (last n.) relates to the motion which Cicero put at §3 (*refert*), it seems almost certain that *praesidiis additis* looks back to *dispositis praesidiis* at §3. For this sense of *p. addere* cf. Liv. 25.26.1.

50.5 Sed Caesar, ubi ad eum uentum est, rogatus sententiam a consule huiusce modi uerba locutus est: *Sed* returns us to the main narrative, as often (*OLD* 2b), and hence to Meeting II, which we left at §3 for the intervening parenthesis ('Sed eos …'); *rogatus sententiam a consule* here looks back to *consul … refert quid de iis fieri placeat* there. Since Caesar at the start of Meeting II was regarded as the principal proponent of leniency (*Cat.* 4.7 'C. Caesaris, qui mortis poenam remouet'), it follows that Caesar must have spoken in favour of leniency at Meeting I. It is therefore tempting to think that S. has transposed to Meeting II the words which he imagines Caesar spoke at Meeting I; yet in Thucydides' Mytilene episode (see intro. n.) Cleon and Diodotus each spoke at both meetings (3.36.6, 3.41), although only their speeches at the second meeting are given. For both authors it is obviously more dramatic to present the principal speeches at the decisive meeting (see also 50.3–4n. on Caesar speaking after Nero). *ubi ad eum uentum est* is a reminder that in December 63 Caesar as praetor designate was quite far down the speaking order (cf. Cic. *Att.* 12.21.1).

huiusce modi uerba: the body of Caesar's speech – i.e. excepting his proposal at the end (§43) – seems broadly structured on a ring basis: the first two paragraphs focus on the importance of dispassionateness as seen from the respective viewpoints of past (§§2–8) and future (§§9–15); the last two paragraphs concern exemplarity as seen from the respective viewpoints of future (§§25–36) and past (§§37–42). The central paragraph (§§16–24) deals with the effectiveness and status of the death penalty itself. But these are broad categorisations and there are inevitably numerous cross-currents (e.g. 21 ~ 39–40). That S.'s version of the speech is very close to what Caesar actually said has been proposed by R. F. Tannenbaum ('What Caesar said: rhetoric and history in Sallust's *Coniuratio Catilinae* 51', in K. Welch and T. W. Hillard (edd.), *Roman crossings: theory and practice in the Roman Republic* (2005) 209–23), but the unlikelihood of this is argued by Drummond 38–41 (part of a lengthy discussion of the speech, pp. 23–50).

51.1 Omnes homines … qui de rebus dubiis consultant: the opening acc. is dependent on *decet* below, and both in wording and in structure the sentence strongly resembles the start of the work as a whole (1.1), a similarity which is maintained by the subsequent deployment of *animus, ingenium, libido, dominari* and the like. The relative clause defines Caesar's speech as an example of deliberative oratory (cf. *Rhet. Herenn.* 1.2 'deliberatiuum est in consultatione', Quint. 3.8.25 'omnis ... deliberatio de dubiis est'). For such self-referential wording cf. 20.1n. (*in rem*).

ab odio, amicitia, ira atque misericordia uacuos esse decet: the two latter emotions (the one the opposite of the other) are those most relevant to the present circumstances and they feature in Caesar's two opening paragraphs, first as illustrated by the past (§§5–6), then as constituting a warning for the future (§§12–15). Cleon had begun his speech by warning against pity (Thuc. 3.37.2), Diodotus warned against anger (Thuc. 3.42.1, 43.5, 44.4). For the patterning of two sets of opposites, the first set asyndetic and both dependent on a single preposition, see Adams, *AILL* 558.

51.2 haud facile ... uerum prouidet: the verb, which seems to mean 'sees ahead to', is at first sight odd,[95] but deliberative oratory concerned itself with the future (Quint. 3.8.6 'de tempore futuro consultat'). Caesar will later expand on the topic (12–15, 25–36), which is also voiced by Diodotus (Thuc. 3.43.4, 44.3). For the contrast *prouidet ~ officiunt* cf. Plaut. *Asin.* 450–1 'non hercle te prouideram ..., | ita iracundia obstitit oculis' (compared in *TLL*), though the meaning is not quite the same.

neque quisquam omnium libidini simul et usui paruit: deliberative oratory was usually concerned with questions of expediency, *utilitas* or *utile* (Quint. 3.8.1, 22), to which *usus* here seems to be equivalent; *libido* is a generic term embracing the four emotions listed in the previous sentence. *paruit* is a gnomic perfect (11.3n. *quam*); *l. parere* is Ciceronian (*II Verr.* 1.78, *Off.* 1.92, *Fin.* 2.60).

51.3 ubi intenderis ingenium, ualet 'when you apply your intellect, it is effective': the more usual object of *intendo* is *animum* (*OLD* 9a), with which *ingenium*, as at the start of the work, is evidently synonymous; for the generalising second person subjunctive see 1.6n. (*et*).

si libido possidet, ea dominatur, animus nihil ualet: adversative asyndeton: '<but,> if passion takes possession of it, that dominates and the mind is ineffective'. For *l. dominatur* cf. Crassus, *ORF* 26, Cic. *Senec.* 41, [Sen.] *Oct.* 432, Rut. Lup. 2.2, Apul. *De Platone* 2.4.

51.4 magna mihi copia est memorandi 'I am well able to recall' (*OLD copia* 7). A deliberative speech might appeal to the past by way of *exempla* (Quint. 3.8.6, 66).

quae reges ... male consuluerint 'what bad decisions kings ... have made': *quae* is an internal accs. (*OLD consulo* 4a). *ira aut misericordia*

completes a ring with §1 and helps to round off the introductory general-
isations before the *exempla* which follow. For *ira ... impulsi* see W–M on
Tac. *A.* 3.69.5; for *misericordia i.* cf. Cic. *Part. Or.* 49.

sed ea malo dicere ...: the contrast is pointed by the wordplay *măle ~ mālo*,
which is found from Plaut. (e.g. *Poen.* 633–4) onwards: see also 37.10–11nn.
For *libidinem animi* cf. Ter. *Hec.* 534.

maiores nostri: in S.'s entire *oeuvre* 'the orations of Cato and Caesar have
the greatest concentration of historical examples' (J. D. Chaplin, *Livy's
exemplary history* (2000) 26). Caesar makes three appeals to 'our ancestors'
(cf. §§5, 37) and is matched by Cato's two (52.19, 30). In a society so
impressed by precedent as that of the Romans (intro. n. to 53.2–54.6),
such appeals were only to be expected and there are scores of examples in
the oratory of Cicero, for whom the age of *maiores nostri* begins roughly fifty
or sixty years before the present time (Morstein-Marx 108–10).

recte atque ordine: the coordination of these two words is common in
Cic. and Liv. but found nowhere else apart from Val. Max. 3.8 *init.*, where
they are in the opposite order.

51.5 bello Macedonico: the Third Macedonian War (172–168 BC),
which ended with the defeat of King Perseus at the battle of Pydna, just
off the north-western coast of the Thermaic Gulf. The abl. is temporal
(*OLS* 1.835–6), as again at 52.30 and 59.3.

Rhodiorum ciuitas ... infida atque aduersa nobis fuit: after the Romans
defeated King Antiochus III of Syria in 190 BC, they rewarded the island of
Rhodes, their ally, for its help by granting it swathes of Asia Minor in Caria
and Lycia. When Rome subsequently went to war against King Perseus (last
n.), the Rhodians' attempt at mediating between the two sides was interpreted by Rome as motivated by support for Perseus, and as a result the
island was deprived of its recently acquired territories in Asia Minor and
compelled to suffer other damage to its economy. See *CAH* 8.334–8; also
below.

opibus 'power' (causal abl.): see last n.

postquam ... de Rhodiis consultum est: it was proposed in 167 BC that
Rome should declare war on Rhodes by way of punishment for its perceived disloyalty, but the motion was opposed successfully by the elder
Cato in a famous speech which he subsequently incorporated into his
Origines (87–93C/95P: see Cornell in *FRHist* 3.132–5; Courtney, *ALP*
78–84). 'Caesar shows himself to be acting according to Catonian precedent in particular' (Levene, *OR* 235: see his whole discussion).

ne quis diuitiarum magis quam iniuriae causa bellum inceptum diceret:
sc. esse with *inceptum.* The elder Cato in his speech warned against the profit
motive (cf. Gell. 6.3.7, 52), of which a trace survives at 91C/95eP 'nos
omnia plura habere uolumus, et id nobis impune est'. For the connection
between war and wealth see Maltby on Tib. 1.10.7–8.

impunitos eos dimisere 'they left them unpunished', a set phrase (see also *OLD dimitto* 4; cf. 7b). This presumably refers only to the decision not to go to war against Rhodes, since other punishments were exacted (see above).

51.6 bellis Punicis omnibus: the three Punic Wars were 264–241, 218–201, 149–146 BC. On this *exemplum* see Levene, *OR* 237–8.

cum saepe Carthaginienses ... multa nefaria facinora fecissent: 'Punica fides' was proverbial for bad faith (Tosi 113 §245). *nefarium facinus* is a phrase beloved of Cicero, but S. may have in mind Cato, *Orat.* 59M, where it is followed (albeit not governed) by *facis* (repeated thrice).

numquam ipsi per occasionem talia fecere 'they themselves [i.e. the Romans] never acted similarly when the opportunity arose' (*OLD occasio* 1b).

magis quid se dignum foret: Cicero ranked *dignitas* above expediency in deliberative oratory (*De Or.* 2.334). For Rome acting in accordance with its *dignitas* see Oakley on Liv. 10.35.14, adding Plb. 15.4.10; Caesar was of course famously conscious of his own *dignitas* (*BC* 1.9.2 'sibi semper primam fuisse dignitatem uitaque potiorem').

51.7   uobis prouidendum est ... neu magis irae uestrae quam famae consulatis 'you must see to it that ...' (*OLD prouideo* 3b). *prouidendum*, despite its different meaning, looks back to *prouidet* (2) and *irae* to *ira* (1), while *famae* picks up the point made with *ne quis ... diceret* (5). With *irae* we have to understand a verb such as *indulgeatis* from *consulatis* by zeugma. The elder Cato in his Rhodian speech had likewise advised against a response made in anger (93C/95gP).

51.8 si digna poena pro factis eorum reperitur ...; sin magnitudo sceleris omnium ingenia exsuperat ... 'if a worthy punishment is found having regard to their deeds ...; but, if the magnitude of their crime exceeds everyone's ingenuity ...' (*OLD pro*[1] 13, *exsupero* 4a). The four present-tense verbs refer to the future (*OLS* 1.399–401). *digna poena pro factis* is a theme of Cleon's speech in Thucydides (e.g. 3.39.6, 40.4, 40.7); the nexus of novelty and ingenuity was one which appealed to Tacitus (*A.* 2.83.1, 3.57.1, 6.45.2).

nouum consilium ... iis ... quae legibus comparata sunt: Caesar's contrast resembles that of Cleon between a novel argument and one which is tried and tested (Thuc. 3.38.5). *iis ... sunt* refers to punishments.

51.9 qui ante me sententias dixerunt: on 5 Dec. every speaker before Caesar spoke in favour of the death penalty (Cic. *Att.* 12.21.1, Suet. *DJ* 14.1, Plut. *Cic.* 20.5, *Cato Min.* 22.3, Dio 37.36.1).

composite atque magnifice: each term has various literary-critical meanings (see Lausberg §1244) but it is not clear that either is being used technically here: perhaps 'in a practised and fulsome manner' (*OLD* *compositus* 4b). The adverb *composite* (again at 52.13) appears elsewhere only in Cicero (*De Or.* 1.48, 64, *Orat.* 236) before Gellius.

quae belli saeuitia esset: a verb such as *exposuere* has to be understood from *enumerauere* by zeugma.

rapi . . . compleri: the *oratio obliqua* follows *enumerauere*; the catalogue of horrors resembles those found in accounts of captured cities (cf. G. M. Paul, *Phoenix* 36 (1982) 144–55). Cicero envisages a similar catalogue, likewise mentioning *matres familias, uirgines* and *pueri* (*Cat.* 4.11–12).

quae uictoribus collibuissent 'what gave pleasure to the victors': *collibuit* is an impersonal verb, perfect in form but present in meaning; the personal use, as here, is extremely rare.

armis, c̲adaueribus, c̲ruore atque luctu: the formal pattern ABC *atque* D is the same as 51.1 (n.), but here the relationships are interlaced (weapons → bloodshed, corpses → grief). AB is the third asyndetic pairing in the sentence (Adams, *AILL* 559).

51.10 quo illa oratio pertinuit? 'what was the point of such speech?' (*OLD ille* 8, *pertineo* 2).

scilicet serves to mark irony, as often: the sentence means the opposite of what it says. The antithesis between deeds and words (here *res ~ oratio*) is conventional (e.g. 52.35 'ipsa re . . . uerba', Diod. 14.69.1; cf. Tosi 14 §25; Oakley on Liv. 7.32.12) and can be variously deployed (e.g. 58.1n.).

51.11 non ita est; neque cuiquam mortalium iniuriae suae paruae uidentur 'That is not the case; nor does any mortal consider small the injuries done to himself' (*OLD ita* 11b), as Cic. *Rab. Perd.* 29 'non est ita, Quirites, neque quisquam nostrum in rei publicae periculis cum laude ac uirtute uersatur'. The *iniuriae* which C. and his followers had intended to inflict included making war against the state (21.1–2, 26.5) as well as the murder of individuals such as consuls, magistrates and senators (18.7).

multi eas grauius aequo habuere 'many regard them more seriously than is right' (*OLD aequum* 3d). *habuere* is a gnomic perfect (11.3n. *quam*).

51.12 alia aliis licentia est 'different individuals have different freedoms'. For the related *aliud alios decet* see Tosi 255 §538.

qui demissi in obscuro uitam habent, si quid iracundia deliquere, pauci sciunt: *sc. id*: 'If the downtrodden, who have a life of obscurity, commit some offence through anger, few know of <it>'; for the perfect indic. in the protasis of a present general condition see *NLS* 150–1 §194; *quid* is an internal acc. (*OLD delinquo* 3a). Strictly *iracundia*, 'irascibility', was said to differ from *ira*, 'anger' (Cic. *TD* 4.22, Sen. *Ira* 1.4.1), but here the terms seem to be used interchangeably.

qui magno imperio praediti in excelso uitam agunt: the thought is conventional, e.g. Xen. *Ages.* 5.6 'we all know that the most distinguished

of men are those who least escape notice whatever they do'; Mayor on Juv.
8.139. Since Caesar is alluding to his fellow senators, *imperium* is being
used non-technically = 'authority'; but S., writing Caesar's speech with the
benefit of hindsight, will have intended his readers to think principally of
Cicero, who as consul exercised *imperium* in the technical sense and was
blamed for the prisoners' execution. *imperio praeditus* is an otherwise
exclusively Ciceronian phrase (*Pis.* 55, *Scaur.* 2, *Rep.* 2.56) until Suet.
Aug. 25.1.

51.13 neque studere neque odisse sed minime irasci decet: in the same
way as *odio* and *amicitia* acted as a foil for *ira atque misericordia* at 51.1, so
here, as *minime* indicates, *studere* and *odisse* (to which they correspond
chiastically) act as a foil for *irasci*: cf. Cic. *Off.* 1.89 'prohibenda quam
maxime ira in puniendo', Sen. *Ira* 1.15.3 'nil minus quam irasci punien-
tem decet'. Tacitus famously opens his *Annals* with all three terms (1.1.2–3
'odiis … sine ira et studio').

51.14 quae apud alios iracundia dicitur 'what in other people is called
anger' (*OLD apud* 13a). Anger was an ambiguous emotion whose rectitude
was much debated by intellectuals, such as S.'s contemporary, Philodemus,
in his *On Anger* (cf. V. Tsouna, *The ethics of Philodemus* (2007) 195–238); but
superbia and *crudelitas* were vices and indefensible. The three are linked at
Cic. *Fat.* 8 'iracundi aut crudeles aut superbi'.

51.15 equidem ego: this seems to be an ex. of 'contrasting *equidem*' (cf.
sed below), for which see Solodow 53–5 (who at 19–29 argues that *equidem*
and *quidem* are interchangeable). S.'s two words were used by the grammarian Priscian to argue that *equidem* cannot be a compound of *ego* and
quidem (3.103 §14). S. repeats the two at *BJ* 10.6 and 85.26, and the
combination is imitated by ps.-Sallust.

plerique mortales postrema meminere: the interlaced alliteration gives
a proverbial tone to the statement, for which cf. Tac. *A.* 6.32.4
'cesserunt … prima postremis' (and W.[4] on 6.8.5). *meminere* here = 'retain
in the mind' (*OLD* 1a).

in hominibus impiis 'in the case of wicked men' (*OLD in* 42).

51.16 D. Silanum: the first to propose the death penalty (50.4nn.).

neque illum in tanta re gratiam aut inimicitias exercere 'and he is not the
man to resort to favour or animosities in so important a matter'.

eos mores eamque modestiam uiri cognoui: probably *sc. esse*: 'I know
that such is the man's behaviour, such his restraint'. *uiri* is used instead of
eius (*OLD uir* 6); for *is* = 'such', as 31.7, see *OLD* 3.

51.17 non crudelis … sed aliena a re publica: Caesar's argument
appears to be this: Silanus' proposal is not so much cruel (~ §14) as alien
to the *res publica* (~ §6); but, since the latter is so unlikely in a *uir fortis atque
strenuus* who is characterised by *studium rei publicae* (16), the influence by
which he has been overcome must be particularly strong: the two possible

motivating factors, *metus* and *iniuria*, are given in §18. *crudelis* is regularly constructed with *in* + acc.

51.18 nam profecto aut metus aut iniuria te subegit ... genus poenae nouum decernere: according to Cicero, Silanus had in fact argued that the death penalty was traditional (*Cat.* 4.7 'hoc *genus poenae* saepe in improbos ciues in hac re publica esse usurpatum'), but Caesar contests this here (*nouum*) and will return to the point, via a series of sophistical questions, at the end of the paragraph (21–4); in between, he argues that death is not the punishment it is thought to be (20). The Roman suspicion of novelty, to which Caesar is appealing, is well illustrated by Claudius' speech to the senate in AD 48 (*ILS* 212, col. I, 1–5). *nam profecto* ('for without doubt') is a favourite of Cicero (e.g. *Cat.* 3.19); for *subigo* + infin. see 10.5n. (*ambitio*).

51.19–20 de timore ... de poena ...: of Silanus' two possible motivating factors (18), fear is dismissed immediately, perhaps appropriately in the light of his bravery (16), although Cato will capitalise on the dismissal later (52.16, 28). Instead of the second possibility, *iniuria*, Caesar focusses on its corollary – the *poena* which the wrongdoing is deemed by Silanus to deserve – and argues that execution will have exactly the opposite effect from that intended (20).

51.19 tanta praesidia: cf. 50.3 'dispositis praesidiis' (also 49.4).

51.20 de poena possum equidem dicere: since these words contrast with *de timore superuacuaneum est disserere* above (19), *equidem* here seems to have both an adversative and a limiting force: '*But* about punishment I can *at least* say ...' (for this see Solodow 92–3).

id quod res habet seems to mean 'as reality shows' (no classical parallel is given for this sense of *habere* in *TLL* 6.3.2415.31); for *id quod* see 14.1n. Caesar's appeal to reality (*OLD res* 6a) is defensive: he presents as self-evident what is merely the view of the Epicurean sect (see K. Volk, 'Caesar the Epicurean? A matter of life and death', in S. Yona and G. Davis (edd.), *Epicurus in Rome: philosophical perspectives in the Ciceronian age* (2022) 72–86, at 75–8).

luctu atque miseriis: coupled again at *Octav.* 103, 176.

mortem aerumnarum requiem, non cruciatum, esse: Caesar's point is rendered at *Cat.* 4.7 'mortem a dis immortalibus non esse supplicii causa constitutam, sed aut necessitatem naturae aut laborum ac miseriarum quietem'. For the Epicurean view cf. Lucr. 3.904–5, part of a famous passage, and 978–1023. Had S. read Lucretius? asks Stone (1999, 66 n. 63): see further below.

mortalium mala dissoluere: the verb is a favourite of Lucretius, esp. in Book 3, where his subject is death (e.g. 3.903); *mortalium* (2.8n. *multi*) is particularly appropriate in the present context: for *m. mala* cf. Plin. *NH* 2.102, 11.37.

ultra 'beyond', i.e. beyond life/after death.

51.21 per deos immortales, quam ob rem in sententiam non addidisti uti prius uerberibus in eos animaduerteretur? *addo* is regularly constructed both with *in* + acc. and with an indirect command (*OLD* 13); for the impersonal passive of *animaduerto* combined with *in* + acc. ('that punishment be inflicted on them') see *OLD* 8b (active at §39 below). Caesar supplies three possible answers to his own question ('an quia ... an quia ... sin quia ...'), each of which tries to discomfit Silanus ('at aliae leges ... quid autem ... qui conuenit ...'); but, since there was never a proposal that the conspirators be scourged, the whole syllogistic argument is rhetorical bluster (as *per deos immortales* suggests) designed to return Caesar to his original point about the status of the death penalty (17–18). For *quam ob rem* see 35.2n. (Is it just coincidence that *non addunt* appears at Lucr. 3.900? See further 51.24n. below.)

lex Porcia: Cicero once refers to three *leges Porciae* (*Rep.* 2.54) but elsewhere he, like all other authors (including S. here and at §40 below), refers to only one *lex Porcia*: since most of these references mention scourging, it is inferred that 'the most important (perhaps the first) of the *leges Porciae* probably strengthened the protection of Roman citizens against scourging' (Oakley on Liv. 10.9.3–6, p. 131, with discussion of the numerous problems involved). Since the identity of the legislator(s) is disputed, no more specific dating than the second century is agreed; but, if the elder Cato was responsible for one of the *leges*, as has been suspected, it is obviously pointed that Caesar should be made to invoke once again (see nn. above) the great-grandfather of his principal opponent.

51.22 at aliae leges item condemnatis ciuibus non animam eripi sed exilium permitti iubent: *condemnatis ciuibus* is to be taken, albeit differently, with both *eripi* and *permitti*, and *non* is to be taken with *eripi*: 'but other laws similarly order that the life of condemned citizens not be snatched away *from* them but that exile be allowed *to* them'. Caesar is choosing his words carefully, not alleging a general prohibition on capital punishment as such but reminding Silanus that *exilium* 'was institutionalised as, in effect, a substitute for the death penalty. The magistrates were required to allow a condemned person time to escape before a capital sentence was executed' (*OCD* 560; cf. Plb. 6.14.7–8 with Walbank). His point, to which he returns below (24), is that, if Silanus was influenced by the Lex Porcia in the case of scourging, why was he not similarly influenced by other laws which, instead of the immediate execution which Silanus had proposed (*animam eripi* suggests inordinate haste), allowed time for the condemned to depart into exile? As everyone must have known, however, there were no such laws, and Caesar, who repeats his point at §40 below, is not helping his case by pretending otherwise. For *animam eripere* cf. Ov. *Met.* 6.539–40, Luc. 9.788.

51.23 necari: the verb often means 'execute' and is appropriate to the method of strangulation which will eventually be used (55.5): see J. N. Adams, 'The uses of *neco* I', *Glotta* 68 (1990) 230–55, esp. 244.

51.24 sin quia leuius est 'But if because it is lighter'; *leuius* contrasts with *grauius* (23).

qui conuenit in minore negotio legem timere cum eam in maiore neglegeris 'how is it consistent to fear the law in a lesser matter when you ignore it in a greater?' Caesar returns to his first point from a different angle. In §§21–2 he was concerned with simple logic (if you are influenced by one law, why not also be influenced by another?); here he is concerned with the relative gravity of the punishments precluded by the respective laws. *qui* = 'how' (*OLD qui*² 1a), only here in S., was perhaps suggested by Lucr. 3.889 'qui non sit acerbum' (*acerbum* is in Caesar's previous sentence). For the impersonal use of *conuenit* in this sense see Cic. *Rab. Post.* 31; *OLD conuenio* 6a. *neglegeris* is another ex. of the second person generalising subjunctive (51.3n. *ubi*): the regular perfect form is *neglexeris*, but the alternative (again at *BJ* 40.1) is 'probably a deliberate imitation' of Licinius Macer 8C/22P, in whom it first appears (Briscoe in *FRHist* 1.34; also Oakley in *FRHist* 3.425, Adams, *AIL* 268–9); here it is conducive to wordplay (Cicero was himself esp. fond of the assonance of *negleg-* and *leg-*, e.g. *Cat.* 1.18 'ad neglegendas leges').

51.25–36 In this paragraph, which is framed by ring composition (*decretum, tempus, moderatur, statuatis, exempla* ~ *tempore, exemplo, decretum, statuet, moderabitur*), Caesar returns to the issue of exemplarity: the execution of the Catilinarians, however justifiable, cannot be a self-contained act but may be used as a precedent by less scrupulous rulers in the future to justify their own unjustified behaviour. Caesar's argument is not straightforward. He starts with a two-part generalisation (27), the first part of which is illustrated by the Thirty at Athens (28–31) and by Sulla at Rome (32–4); these two cases serve as a foil for the particular case of the Catilinarians, which illustrates *both* parts of the initial generalisation and to which Caesar turns at the end (35–6).

51.25 At enim quis reprehendet quod ... decretum erit? 'But who will censure what will have been decreed ...?' *At enim* introduces an imaginary objection (*OLD at*¹ 4); the question expects the answer 'no one'. For *parricidas* see 31.8n. (*hostem*).

tempus, dies: criticism will come in the future, from those who object to the Catilinarians' execution being used as a precedent for contemporary injustice. *dies* perhaps suggests that *tempus* means 'circumstances' *vel sim.*

51.26 illis merito accidet: *illis* = the imprisoned Catilinarians; *merito* aligns their case with those illustrated below (29 *merito*, 32 *merito*). For *merito accidere* + dat. see W.¹ on Vell. 118.4.

quid in alios statuatis: the words are a conceit: Caesar's listeners are
taking no decisions against anyone other than the Catilinarians; he means
that his fellow senators are setting a precedent which will be used by
a future senate to justify a decision 'against others'.

51.27 omnia mala exempla ex rebus bonis orta sunt 'All bad examples
arise from admirable circumstances' (*orta sunt* is a gnomic perfect: 11.3n.
quam). This general truth, emphasised by its chiastic word order and
alliteration, acts as a foil for the more particular *sed ... transfertur*, which
is applicable only to the case of the Catilinarians. Edd. compare Vell. 2.3.4
'non enim ibi consistunt exempla unde coeperunt, sed ... latissime euagando sibi uiam faciunt et, ubi semel recto deerratum est, in praeceps
peruenitur, nec quisquam sibi putat turpe quod alii fuit fructuosum'.

sed, ubi imperium ad ignaros eius aut minus bonos peruēnit 'but,
whenever power devolves on those unacquainted with it or on the less
good': since *ubi* = 'whenever', *peruenit* is perfect tense (*NLS* 175 §217 (2)
(*c*)); see further below, 51.33n. (*uti*). *eius* refers to *imperium*, and *ignaros
eius* refers not to persons unacquainted with wielding power but to those
who are unaware of the *effects* of wielding power – an ignorance which
Caesar fears in his present audience but which this paragraph of his speech
is designed to correct. For *peruenire* see *OLD* 5b. Caesar's statement
appears to contradict what S. said at 2.6, although the context there was
quite different (see n.).

**nouum illud exemplum ab dignis et idoneis ad indignos et non idoneos
transfertur:** the likeliest interpretation of these words (cf. 35–6n. below) is
that *nouum illud exemplum* refers to a measure introduced under admirable
circumstances (cf. *ex rebus bonis orta sunt*) by worthy and qualified leaders
('dignis et idoneis') but which is transformed into a bad precedent when
circumstances change (cf. *ubi ... peruenit*) and power devolves upon the
unworthy (*indignos ~ minus bonos*) or unqualified (*non idoneos ~ ignaros*).
Other edd. take *nouum illud exemplum* as referring to punishment and the
two sets of persons are its recipients, respectively deserving and undeserving; for *idoneus* meaning 'deserving what one gets' edd. quote Cic. *Clu.*
130.

51.28–34 Caesar illustrates his statement *omnia mala exempla ex rebus
bonis orta sunt* by means of the Thirty at Athens (28–31) and Sulla at Rome
(32–4). Both started admirably (29 *primo*, 33 *initium*) by punishing criminals and producing general happiness (29 *laetari*, 31 *laetitiae*, 34 *laetitiae*);
but afterwards (30 *post ... paulatim*, 34 *paulo post*) they turned to punishing
the innocent too.

51.28 triginta uiros: when Sparta defeated Athens at the end of the
Peloponnesian War (431–404 BC), it installed thirty men to rule the city:
although their rule lasted less than a year, their cruelty became such that it
led to their being called the Thirty Tyrants. Whether *deuictis Atheniensibus*

is dat. with *imposuere* or abl. abs. is unclear; *qui . . . tractarent* is a rel. clause of purpose.

51.29 indemnatum necare: the adj. is predicative, as Cic. *Part. Or.* 106 'ciuem euersorem ciuitatis indemnatum necare' (also *Rhet. Herenn.* 4.33, Liv. *per.* 103): 'to kill ~ uncondemned'.

ea is both internal acc. with *laetari* (*OLD laetor* 1d) and subject of *fieri*, forming an acc. + infin. after *dicere*. Both *laetari* and *dicere*, like *interficere* and *terrere* in the next sentence, are historic infinitives.

51.30 iuxta 'alike' (*OLD* 2). *libidinose* is Ciceronian apart from Liv. 3.36.7.

51.31 ciuitas seruitute oppressa: Ciceronian (*Dom.* 131, *TD* 5.57). **stulta laetitia:** cf. Sen. *Brev. Vit.* 3.3.

51.32 nostra memoria: cf. 33.2n. (*memoria*).

uictor Sulla: see 11.4n. (*postquam*).

Damasippum: as praetor in 82, L. Junius Brutus Damasippus acceded to a request from the younger Marius, the consul, that he execute the *pontifex maximus* and some other leading figures who opposed Marius; subsequently he was killed at Sulla's command after the battle of the Colline Gate (5.6n. *post*): see *MRR* 2.67, 3.113.

qui malo rei publicae creuerant 'who had grown to the detriment of the commonwealth': *malo r.p.* (again at Val. Max. 3.8.4) is abl. of attendant circumstances and equivalent to the much commoner *malo publico*.

aiebant: contemporaries of the killing; the plural is a *constructio ad sensum* after *quis non . . . laudabat?* above.

51.33 magnae initium cladis: for the ἀρχὴ κακῶν ('start of evils/disasters') motif see 11.6n (*ibi*).

uti quisque . . . concupiuerat 'whenever anyone desired . . .' (*OLD quisque* 8). In generalising clauses of repeated action, i.e. when the conjunction means 'whenever', the pluperfect is regular in past time (6.5n. *post*); and '*ut* is only so used in combination with *quisque* or *quisquis*' (*NLS* 174 §217 (2) (c)): for *uti* = *ut* see 27.2n. *uas aut uestimentum* perhaps connotes 'anything at all' (cf. Ter. *Heaut.* 141, Cato, *Orat.* 174M).

in proscriptorum numero: see 11.4nn.

51.34 laetitiae: predicative dat. (*OLD* 1a).

trahebantur: *sc. ad supplicium* or similar (*OLD traho* 1b), unless the meaning is 'were drawn in' (*OLD* 9c).

51.35–6 These sentences illustrate the qualification *sed ubi . . . transfertur* at §27 above. Cicero is a 'worthy and qualified' leader, but in a city like Rome not everyone is of similar character and in time there could be another, 'less admirable', consul, who for his own nefarious purposes might misapply the precedent of the Catilinarians' execution, which would therefore have passed to an 'unworthy and unqualified' leader.

Warnings about the future play an important part in the arguments of
both Cleon and Diodotus (Thuc. 3.38.4, 38.6, 42.2, 43.4, 44.3, 48.2).

in M. Tullio 'in the case of M. Tullius' (*OLD in* 42). See next n.

51.36 alio consule, cui item exercitus in manu sit: the clause is equivalent to a remote future condition ('if he were likewise in possession of an
army'): hence the pres. subjunc. (*NLS* 156 §200 (i)). Although it was not
Cicero himself but his colleague Antonius who had an army at his disposal
(36.3), S. is thinking of 43 BC when the young Octavian marched on Rome
with an army, was made consul, and subsequently (along with his colleagues in the Triumvirate) initiated the proscriptions, of which the
most famous victim was Cicero: 'Sallust has remodelled Caesar's protest
against Cicero in power in 63 BCE into a protest by anticipation against the
powerless Cicero's death at the hands of a regime acting in the Caesarian
name in 43 BCE' (Stone (2014) 240).

falsum aliquid pro uero credi: a future leader might fabricate or falsify
a pretext for action, as notoriously happened in the proscriptions.

ubi hoc exemplo per senatus decretum consul gladium eduxerit: *hoc
exemplo* refers to the proposal to execute the imprisoned Catilinarians. The
words *per senatus decretum consul* exactly reflect the reality of power at
Rome: it was the consul's task to consult the senate (48.6; *OLD consulo*
1b) but, at least in theory, he was under no obligation to abide by any
decision reached. 'Although the pressure on magistrates to execute what
had been decreed was considerable, many decrees contained discretion-
ary clauses' (Lintott, *CRR* 193). This explains why Cicero subsequently
could be held personally responsible for the execution of the conspirators:
writing with the benefit of hindsight, S. has given to Caesar words which
are applicable not only to 43 BC (above) but also to 58, when Cicero paid
the price for his involvement by being exiled.[96] *per ... decretum* for the
more regular *decreto* is unique to this passage and Tac. *A.* 4.44.3 'per
decretum senatus'; *educere* is a *mot juste* for drawing a sword etc. (*OLD* 4b).

illi: to be taken both with *statuet* and with *moderabitur*.

51.37 consilii ... audaciae: the two nouns are regularly combined; for
the gen. see 1.7n. (*ita*).

aliena instituta: it was a topos that 'the Romans were especially successful
at learning from, and improving on, their foes' (Walbank on Plb. 1.20.15,
with numerous refs.); see also below (38n.). *si modo* = 'provided that' (*OLD
si* 8a).

51.38 arma atque tela militaria ab Samnitibus: namely a type of shield
and javelin, according to tradition (cf. the so-called *Ineditum Vaticanum* 3,
Diod. 23.2.1, Athen. 273F); modern scholars are variously sceptical

---

[96] This seems a more likely interpretation than to assume that *senatus decretum*
refers to the *s.c.u.* (29.2-3).

(Cornell, *BR* 170–1), although the Samnite *ueru* at Virg. *Aen.* 7.665 is regarded as credible by Horsfall ad loc.

insignia magistratuum ab Tuscis pleraque sumpserunt: traditionally including the *fasces*, the *toga praetexta* and the *sella curulis* (cf. Liv. 1.8.2–3). *pleraque* is to be taken also with *arma atque tela* above; *sumere* is the technical term for borrowing customs etc. from another people (*OLD* 12b), used also by Cicero in a similar context (*Rep.* 2.30).

postremo quod ubique apud socios aut hostes idoneum uidebatur ... exsequebantur: so too Tac. *A.* 3.27.1 'accitis quae usquam egregia', 11.24.1 'transferendo huc quod usquam egregium fuerit' (Claudius' speech); see also above (37n.). *postremo* = 'in short' (*OLD* 4a); *exsequebantur* perhaps = 'put into practice'.

bonis 'good points, virtues' (*OLD bonum* 5a).

51.39 Graeciae morem imitati: both scourging and execution appear in the Twelve Tables (e.g. I.17, I.19, VIII.5: see *Rom. Stat.* 2.609–13, 684–5), which were thought to have been based on Athenian law (W–M on Tac. *A.* 3.27.1).

51.40 circumueniri 'to be framed, convicted unjustly' (16.3n. *nihilo*).

lex Porcia: 51.21n.

aliaeque leges paratae sunt quibus legibus exilium damnatis permissum est: see 51.22n. The repetition of the antecedent within the rel. clause 'has its origin in legal style, where the need for clarity calls for the removal of all ambiguity in the reference of relative pronouns ...; Caesar, who also places great store on clarity, is particularly fond of the idiom' (Courtney, *ALP* 142). The example here is thus doubly pointed: *quibus* would indeed be ambiguous otherwise, and of course the speaker is 'Caesar' himself.

51.41 hanc ego causam ... in primis magnam puto: *sc. esse*: 'I think that this is an especially important reason why we should not adopt a new policy.' The three opening words well illustrate the idiom whereby, after a demonstrative such as *hanc*, first- and second-person pronouns in the nominative (which are in a sense redundant, since the person will be evident from the verb) can function as a weak enclitic, serving to focus the demonstrative (e.g. Cic. *II Verr.* 1.14 'hanc ego causam cum agam beneficio populi Romani'): see the wide-ranging discussion of J. N. Adams, 'Wackernagel's law and the position of unstressed personal pronouns in classical Latin', *Trans. Philol. Soc.* 92 (1994) 103–78; pp. 141–51 for first- and second-person pronouns). For *causam ... quominus* cf. Cic. *Inv.* 2.132, Liv. 34.56.9, Tac. *A.* 1.14.3 (*OLD quominus* 1a). *in primis magnus* is rare (*BJ* 4.1, Cic. *Rosc. Com.* 9, Sen. *Tranq. An.* 14.4).

51.42 maior illis fuit ... quam [in] nobis: *illis* (dat.) refers to the *maiores* implied in §40. Since Caesar's speech is so often echoed by Cato's, *maior* *copia nobis quam illis est* (52.20) strongly suggests that we should delete *in*, which could so easily have intruded between -*m* and *n*-. The dat. is certainly what one would expect (e.g. Ov. *Ex P.* 1.3.91 'sit maior prudentia nobis'); the only argument against is a desire for *uariatio*.

ex paruis opibus tantum imperium: the notion 'from small beginnings' is a commonplace (see e.g. W.[5] on Tac. *A.* 4.32.2); for its application to Rome see Oakley on Liv. 6.41.8.

ea bene parta: the past passive part. of *pario* is regularly used as a noun and is often qualified by *bene* or *male* (*OLD pario*[2] 5c): 'those admirable acquisitions'.

51.43 Placet: *sc. mihi*: 'Am I recommending that . . .?' (*OLD placeo* 4; cf. 5).

ita censeo: *ita censere* is official language (e.g. 52.36, *H.* 1.67.22, Cic. *Cat.* 3.14 'ita censuerunt ut P. Lentulus . . . in custodiam traderetur', *Phil.* 5.53, 14.36 (below)). The proposal 'was in fact no more lawful than execution was' (Berry, *CC* 167, although see Stone (1999) 64 and n. 61).

publicandas eorum pecunias, ipsos in uinculis habendos per municipia quae maxime opibus ualent: *sc. esse* with both gerundives. The same two proposals are attributed to Caesar by Cic. *Cat.* 4.7, 4.10, Suet. *DJ* 14.1 and Dio 37.36.1; the qualification that the imprisonment should last only until C. had been beaten in the field is added by Plutarch (*Cic.* 21.1) and Appian (*BC* 2.6.20), the latter (*BC* 2.5.19) attributing an almost identical proposal also to Ti. Claudius Nero (contrast 50.4 above). The practice of holding prisoners in various towns, a relatively mild punishment (cf. Liv. 26.16.6), had been common but was perhaps now obsolete: see the full treatment by Oakley on Liv. 9.42.9. The stipulation *quae maxime opibus ualent* is perhaps standard (cf. *pro . . . opibus* at 30.7 (n. *uti*)).

neu quis . . . neue cum populo agat: the construction after *censeo* now changes to indir. command, a frequent variation. *referat* refers to proposing a motion in the senate (29.1n. *rem*); *cum populo agere* = 'to address the people' (*OLD ago* 39c). The wording is very similar to Dio 37.36.2.

qui aliter fecerit, senatum existimare eum contra rem publicam et salutem omnium facturum: *censeo* is now constructed with an acc. + infin., as if the governing verb were *iubeo*: the construction (again at *BJ* 24.1) is quite common (cf. *TLL* 3.793.39–77) and there is an exact parallel at Cic. *Phil.* 14.36 'ita censeo . . . senatum existimare . . .'. *senatum existimare* is itself official language, e.g. Caelius ap. Cic. *Fam.* 8.8.6 'qui impedierit prohibuerit, eum senatum existimare contra rem publicam fecisse'. Caesar's meaning is: '(I recommend) that the senate thinks that he who acts otherwise will be acting contrary to the commonwealth and the safety of everyone'. *fecerit* (perf. subjunc.) represents a fut. perf. indic. in direct speech, the *qui*-clause being equivalent to a fut. vivid condition in *oratio obliqua* (*NLS* 236 §280). For *contra rem publicam facere* cf. 50.3n. (*sed*).

52.1 ceteri uerbo alius alii uarie assentiebantur: this sentence, in which *uerbo* is abl. and *alii* dat., constitutes a proleptic contrast with the more uninhibited reaction to Cato's speech (53.1), but is not straightforward. (a) The two other exs. of *uerbo assentiri* (Liv. 3.40.6, 27.34.7) suggest assenting to the views of a previous speaker with a brief utterance without having to stand (see Oakley on Liv. 9.8.2 for the various procedures): i.e. *OLD uerbum* 3b. But *uarie* suggests that more than one method of verbal agreement was adopted. Perhaps, then, some senators said little more than 'I agree' (*placet*), while others rose to make a supporting speech: i.e. *OLD uerbum* 5d.

(b) *alius* is in apposition to *ceteri*, as at *BJ* 14.15, but what is the meaning of *alii*? (i) Perhaps the likeliest interpretation is that *alius alii* is reciprocal, as *BJ* 53.8 'milites alius alium laeti appellant', and that the meaning is: 'all the rest in different ways voiced agreement with one another' (*sc.* that Caesar's proposal was right). (ii) Ramsey thinks that S. means 'one or another of the various proposals', but, since at the meeting of 5 Dec. the senate was faced with only two proposals, those of Silanus and Caesar (*Cat.* 4.7), this is unlikely. (iii) It is possible that *alii* is being used for *alteri*, as at 54.1, and that the meaning is that some agreed with Silanus, others with Caesar: if so, this is essentially contradicted by our other sources, according to which Caesar met with unanimous or almost unanimous agreement until Cato spoke (Suet. *DJ* 14.2, Plut. *Cato Min.* 22.5–23.1, Dio 37.36.2, App. *BC* 2.6.21).[97]

M. Porcius Cato rogatus sententiam huiusce modi orationem habuit: the younger Cato, who was then tribune designate (*MRR* 2.174–5), is given his full name on his first appearance: on him see 54.1n. According to Plutarch (*Cato Min.* 23.3), who says that this was the only speech of Cato to be preserved, Cicero had instructed that the speech be taken down in shorthand (cf. M. McDonnell, 'Writing, copying and autograph manuscripts in ancient Rome', *CQ* 46 (1996) 469–91, at 474 n. 23). Whether S.'s version bears any resemblance to what Cato actually said is very doubtful (Intro. p. 19): 'Catonis uerba, siue Sallustii', as St Augustine said (*Civ. Dei* 5.12).

Cato's speech is slightly shorter than Caesar's and differently arranged. It can be seen as falling into three long sections:

---

[97] At *Cic.* 21.4 Plutarch states that the first to oppose Caesar was Catulus, followed by Cato. (Since Cicero's *Fourth Catilinarian*, which also opposes Caesar, is said by Plutarch (21.2–3) to have been delivered between the speeches of Caesar and Catulus, Plutarch is in effect contradicting himself (see Moles' n.).) The unanimity of our other source texts (including Plutarch himself at *Cato Min.* 22.5–23.1) on the almost universal approval with which Caesar's speech was received seems a strong argument against the scholarly consensus that Cicero's *Fourth Catilinarian* was delivered in mid-debate after Caesar's speech.

§§2–12 the matter is not one of punishment but of our survival;
§§13–23 Caesar's views on death and punishment are mistaken, but we do lack the moral fibre of our ancestors;
§§24–35 our present degeneracy means that we hesitate instead of acting with speed.

For *rogatus sententiam* see 50.4n. (*primus*).

52.2 Longe mihi alia mens est 'My attitude is far different' (*OLD mens* 8), as Cic. *Att.* 9.10.3 'alia res nunc tota est, alia mens mea'. Cato begins his speech by alluding closely to the start of Demosthenes' *Third Olynthiac* (1), in which the Athenians in 349 BC are urged to assist the town of Olynthus against Philip II of Macedon: Οὐχὶ ταὐτὰ παρίσταταί μοι γιγνώσκειν, ὦ ἄνδρες Ἀθηναῖοι, ὅταν τ' εἰς τὰ πράγματ' ἀποβλέψω καὶ ὅταν πρὸς τοὺς λόγους οὓς ἀκούω· τοὺς μὲν γὰρ λόγους περὶ τοῦ τιμωρήσασθαι Φίλιππον ὁρῶ γιγνομένους ('By no means the same, men of Athens, are the thoughts occurring to me when I contemplate public affairs and when <I contemplate> the speeches which I hear: for I see that the speeches are all about punishing Philip ...'). *mihi* at the start of Cato's sentence is echoed by *mecum* at the end: Thucydides' Cleon too begins his speech with the first-person pronoun (3.37.1) and repeats it later (3.39.1), but Cato far exceeds him and uses the pronoun twice as often as Caesar.

res ... pericula nostra ... sententias nonnullorum: these three items headline the following sentence.

52.3 disseruisse uidentur de poena: the motion for debate was 'de poena' (*Cat.* 4.6), but Cato is about to argue that punishment as such is beside the point.

patriae ... bellum părauere looks back to 51.25 'parricidas rei publicae'.

patriae, părentibus, āris atque focis suis: the arrangement of words is formally the same as 51.1 and 51.9 (nn.) but here comprising two sets of quasi-synonyms (see Adams, *AILL* 559–60). For the various terms see 59.5 (n.), also similarly arranged.

res autem monet cauere ab illis magis quam quid in illos statuamus consultare 'but the facts of the matter warn <us> to be on our guard against them rather than to debate what we should decide against them' (*OLD caueo* 3a). The infin. rather than an *ut*-clause after *moneo* is more common than is implied at *OLD moneo* 2d. *consultare* echoes Caesar's first sentence (51.1).

52.4 nam cetera maleficia tum persequare ubi facta sunt: Cato now switches to allude to *Against Leocrates* by the Athenian statesman and politician Lycurgus, where in 330 BC he accused his opponent of being unpatriotic when he had fled Athens (126): τῶν μὲν γὰρ ἄλλων ἀδικημάτων ὑστέρας δεῖ τετάχθαι τὰς τιμωρίας, προδοσίας δὲ καὶ δήμου καταλύσεως προτέρας ('For where other offences are concerned, the punishment should follow on the crime; but in cases of treason or the overthrow of a democracy it should precede it' [Loeb trans.]); a somewhat similar point about military discipline had been made by Cato's great-grandfather (cf. Veg. 1.13.6–7): see further Levene, *OR* 231–2. *persequare* is the generalising use of the second person potential subjunctive (1.6n. *et*), as also *prouideris* and *implores* below; for *maleficia persequi* cf. [Quint.] *Decl.* 252.23.

hoc nisi prouideris ne accidat, ubi euēnit, frustra iudicia implores '<but> unless you see to it that *this* does not happen, you invoke [*OLD imploro* 2] the courts in vain when it has taken place' (adversative asyndeton, emphasising *hoc*); the perfect tense *euēnit* (we might have expected fut. perf.) underlines the notion of 'too late'. Cato again picks up Caesar's wording (51.2 'prouidet', 7 'prouidendum', 26 'accidet ... euenerit').

capta urbe nihil fit reliqui uictis: Caesar had enumerated the horrors (51.9n.); for *nihil ... uictis* cf. 11.7 and n.

52.5 sed per deos immortales: the oath was uttered twice by Caesar in his speech (51.10, 21); *domos, uillas* (below) echoes 51.33, and *retinere* picks up 51.42.

domos, uillas, signa, tabulas uestras: for the two asyndetic pairs (dwellings ~ contents) see Adams, *AILL* 560. *uestras* takes its gender from the nearest noun (G&L 183 §286.1 (*b*)).

pluris ... fecistis 'have valued more' (*OLD facio* 18c); for the gen. of value see *NLS* 69 §87 (iv). Cato's withering statement about his listeners' disrespect for the *res publica* leads to a paradox: their luxurious way of life depends on the survival of that *res publica*.

u̲oluptatibus u̲estris ... u̲ultis: the potential for alliteration suggests that here S. perhaps wrote *uostris* and *uoltis* (Intro. p. 41).

expergiscimini aliquando 'wake up before it is too late' (*OLD aliquando* 5), a slightly different nuance from Plin. *Ep.* 1.4.3 'expergiscantur aliquando'. S. had put the same metaphor in C.'s mouth at 20.14.

52.6 non agitur de ...: either 'the issue is not ...', as §10 below (*OLD ago* 39b), or (less likely) 'this debate does not concern ...' (40a).

uectigalibus: i.e. the misappropriation of taxes, as *sociorum iniuriis* implies.

52.7 Saepenumero ... saepe perhaps derives from the opening of Cleon's speech in Thucydides (3.37.1 Πολλάκις μὲν ἤδη ... καὶ ἄλλοτε, 'On many previous occasions').

in hoc ordine 'in this order', almost 'amongst this assembly', i.e. the senate (*OLD in* 29–30). The expr. (again at §13 below) is almost exclusive to Cicero, in whom it is very common. When the lawyer Cassius Longinus advocates the deaths of a household of slaves, Tacitus makes him echo Cato's words (*A.* 14.43.1): 'Saepenumero, patres conscripti, in hoc ordine ...'.

saepe de luxuria atque auaritia nostrorum ciuium questus sum: these words are echoed by those which Livy attributes to Cato's great-grandfather

(34.4.1 '*saepe* me *querentem de* . . . [2] *auaritia et luxuria* ciuitatem laborare');
Cato returns to these two vices at §22; see also 5.8n. (*quos*).

multosque mortales: see 2.8n.

52.8 qui . . . fecissem 'since I had never given myself or my inclination
leave to commit [lit. "for"] any offence': *gratiam facere* is a set phrase (*OLD
gratia* 1b), and the verb is subjunctive because the rel. clause is causal. See
also next n.

haud facile alterius libidini malefacta condonabam: in Latin *condono* =
'pardon, forgive' (*OLD* 3) takes the acc. of the crime and the dat. of the
person, but in English we have two objects: 'I did not easily forgive some
other lustful person his misdeeds.' In our passage S. has substituted an
abstract noun + gen. for personal noun + adj. (see 8.3n. (*scriptorum*) for
this idiom). Cato in this sentence is reversing a saying of the elder Cato
(Plut. *Cato Mai.* 8.9 'he said that he pardoned every sinner except himself'): see Levene, *OR* 232–3.

52.9 ea tametsi uos parui pendebatis 'although you regarded that as of
little consideration': another gen. of value (see *OLD pendo* 6b).

opulentia neglegentiam tolerabat: *res publica* probably continues as the
subject ('<and> because of its wealth it withstood your neglect'), although
opulentia could be nom.

52.10 neque quantum . . . imperium populi Romani sit, sed haec . . .:
Cato again echoes the wording of Caesar (51.42 'tantum imperium . . .
ea . . .').

**sed haec, cuiuscumque modi uidentur, nostra an nobiscum una hostium
futura sint** 'but (the issue is) whether these things, however they seem, will
be ours or, along with ourselves, the enemy's': *-ne* has to be understood
with *nostra* in the alternative question (cf. *bonisne an* above). *haec* presumably refers to the listeners' present way of life, *cuiuscumque modi uidentur* to
the different interpretations placed upon it by its beneficiaries and by Cato
himself. The possessive genitive *hostium* implies a future of servitude.

52.11 hic mihi quisquam mansuetudinem et misericordiam nominat?
hic suggests 'in such circumstances' and/or 'at this point [*sc.* in my
speech]' (*OLD hic*² 5a, 6). *mihi* is probably a so-called 'ethic dative',
which is 'often in second position in the sentence and often preceded
by . . . a deictic pronoun' (*OLS* 1.931), exactly as here: the idiom is difficult
to translate (here perhaps 'I suppose', indicating irony). *quisquam* indicates that the expected answer to the question is negative, 'no one' (cf.
OLS 1.1167), but are we nevertheless intended to think of Cicero (cf.
Sutton 169–71)? The phrase *mansuetudo et misericordia*, which Cato repeats
later in his speech (27), is otherwise exclusively Ciceronian (*Mur.* 90, *Sull.*
93). Readers are invited to imagine Cato as saying that this trial is not the
place for the *mansuetudo et misericordia* which are urged eloquently upon
juries in other cases. The same phrase is used of Caesar at 54.2 below,

although he himself had warned against *misericordia* at 51.1. See also 34.1n.

uera *uocabula rerum* **amisimus** ... **malarum rerum** *audacia fortitudo uocatur*: a varied allusion to Thuc. 3.82.3–4 τὴν εἰωθυῖαν ἀξίωσιν τῶν ὀνομάτων ἐς τὰ ἔργα ἀντήλλαξαν τῇ δικαιώσει. τόλμα μὲν γὰρ ἀλόγιστος ἀνδρεία φιλέταιρος ἐνομίσθη ('as for the normal evaluation of *words for things*, they substituted it as they judged fit: for example, irrational *daring was considered* partisan *courage*'); cf. also Plato, *Rep.* 560E, and in general Sutton 155, 172–5. See also nn. on 10.4, 12.1, 38.3, and note *H.* 3.15.13 'nomina rerum ad ignauiam mutantes'. *audacia* + this type of gen. ('daring in/for wicked deeds') seems unusual instead of e.g. a gerund (as [Quint.] *Decl.* 252.22 'peccandi') or *ad* + acc. (as Cic. *Phil.* 13.10 'ad omne facinus').

bona aliena largiri liberalitas ... **uocatur:** Cicero remarks on this at *Off.* 1.43–4.

eo 'for that reason' (*OLD eo³* 1b), looking back to *quia*, as 20.3.

in extremo 'on the edge', as *BJ* 23.2 (*OLD extremum* 4b).

52.12 sint sane ... **sint** ...: the jussive subjunctives are concessive, as often (*OLS* 1.509; cf. 502–3): 'by all means let them be ...'.

quoniam ita se mores habent: the expr. (again at *BJ* 54.4) is imitated at Vell. 91.4.

in fūrībŭs āerārī 'in the case of treasury thieves' (*OLD in* 42). The clausula comprises a resolved molossus + cretic, common in S. (K–K 169).

ne illi sanguinem nostrum largiantur: adversative asyndeton: '<but> let them not be lavish with our blood', contrasting with *bona aliena largiri* above; for the expr. cf. Cic. *TD* 1.116. *ne* is regular with a jussive subjunc. (*NLS* 85 §109).

dum ... **parcunt:** almost causal (W–M on Tac. *A.* 3.19.2). For the contrast *scelerati ~ boni* see e.g. Cic. *Lig.* 18, *Phil.* 8.16.

perditum eant: *perditum ire* ('to set out to destroy'), after two or three appearances in comedy, recurs at 36.4 and *BJ* 31.27 and 3× in Livy, before such later authors as Gell. and Apul. (*TLL* 10.1.1274.1–5). The present passage, since *sanguinem* precedes, seems in Tacitus' mind at *A.* 4.66.2 'suum sanguinem perditum ibat'.

52.13 Bene et composite C. Caesar paulo ante in hoc ordine de uita et morte disseruit: just as Caesar had referred by name to a previous speaker (D. Silanus, 51.16), so Cato refers to Caesar, with whom he registers two points of explicit disagreement (13–16); their one point of potential agreement Cato interprets differently (19–23). *composite* echoes Caesar's wording (51.9n. *composite*). For *in hoc ordine* see 52.7n. above.

credo falsa existimans: *sc. esse*: 'thinking, I suppose, that those things are false which ...'. *credo* is parenthetic and indicates sarcasm (*OLD* 8c). Cato is disagreeing with the view Caesar expressed at 51.20.

**diuerso itinere malos a bonis loca taetra, inculta, f̲oeda atque f̲ormidu-
losa habere:** the acc. + infin. is in apposition to *ea*: 'namely, that the wicked,
by/after a different journey from the good, inhabit . . .' (*OLD habeo* 8). The
good are conventionally separated from the wicked in the Underworld
(see e.g. N–H on Hor. *C.* 2.13.23), as illustrated by the respective fates of
C. and Cato himself on Aeneas' shield (*Aen.* 8.668–70); in our passage the
separation has to be inferred from the different roads which each are
obliged to take on death (for which see e.g. Horsfall on Virg. *Aen.* 6.540–
3), but *diuerso itinere*, which looks like an abl. of route (as 50.1: see *OLS*
1.830–1), lacks a journeying word on which to depend; strictly one has to
supply e.g. *profectos* or *missos*. Yet again we have the asyndetic arrangement
ABC *atque* D (cf. 51.1, 9), the alliteration suggesting a distribution of two
pairs (see also Adams, *AILL* 573); the combination of *taeter* and *foedus* is
Ciceronian (4×).

52.14 censuit '*has* proposed', as shown by *eripiantur, sint* and *possint*
below. Cato here disagrees with Caesar's proposal for punishment
(51.43), the wording of which he repeats.

uidelicet timens . . . 'evidently fearing that . . .': Caesar's proposal, like
his belief about the afterlife (above), is conveyed by a sarcastic present
participle (cf. *OLD uidelicet* 3).

popularibus 'partners' (22.1n.).

multitudine conducta 'a hired mob' (50.1n. *duces*).

52.15 quasi . . . **sint** . . . **possit:** in unreal comparative clauses 'the
sequence of tenses is usually observed. This means that, if the tense of
the main verb is primary, the verb of the "unreal" comparative clause is
generally present, perfect or future periphrastic subjunctive' (*NLS* 210
§255).

non ibi plus possit audacia '(as if) revolutionary daring were not more
powerful there' (*OLD possum* 8b; also 2.2n. *tum*); for *audacia* cf. 5.4n.
(*animus audax*).

ubi . . . **opes minores sunt:** Cato's response to 51.43 'municipia quae
maxime opibus ualent'.

52.16 equidem: see 58.4n.

si . . . **in tanto omnium m̲etu̲ solus non t̲imet̲:** Cato is picking up on
Caesar's speech (cf. 51.19), but he may also be alluding to the rumours
that Caesar was himself a supporter of C. (cf. 49.1); indeed, according to
Plutarch, Cato insinuated such support in his actual speech (*Caes.* 8.2, *Cic.*
21.4, *Cato Min.* 23.1–2).

eo magis rēfert me mihi atque uobis timere 'it is all the more important
that I should be afraid on my own behalf and yours': an acc. + inf. as subject
of *refert* is regular (see *NLS* 170–1 §213), as is the dat. with *timere* (*OLD* 1b).

52.17 habetote: the archaising future imperative is used 'to achieve an
effect of solemnity' (*OLS* 1.517).

52.18 quanto uos attentius ea agetis 'the more carefully you deal with that matter' (*OLD ago* 38a).

illis animus infirmior … uos languere: *illis* refers to those members of the conspiracy who were still at large. The metaphor is one of illness (cf. Sen. *Ep.* 74.33 'quemadmodum in corporibus … languoris signa …, sic infirmus animus …').

iam omnes feroces aderunt 'all of them will be bearing down <on you> violently straight away' (*OLD adsum* 15); *feroces* is predicative (*NLS* 71 §88 *Note*). *iam*, idiomatic after a *si*-clause (*TLL* 7.1.106.26–30), suggests 'before you know it'.

52.19–20 Nolite existimare maiores nostros … quam illis est: Cato now, like Caesar (51.4n.), introduces the *maiores* and argues that there is no necessary correlation between military resources and national prosperity: if there were, the Roman empire would now be at its acme, given the overwhelming superiority of present-day resources to those in the past. Although Cato does not say so, he is here taking up, but reinterpreting for his own purposes, a point made by Caesar himself (51.42 'uirtus atque sapientia maior illis fuit … quam [in] nobis'). For *multo* see 36.4n. (*ea*).

52.20 quippe … maior copia nobis quam illis est: again (cf. 52.2n. *Longe*) Cato is made to sound like Demosthenes (*Phil.* 3.40 'triremes and numbers of men … everything by which one might judge our cities' strength, these we all possess today in much greater abundance and size than did those in the past').

52.21 animus in consulendo liber: *consulendo* suggests senatorial meetings (*OLD* 1b), and the freedom which Cato sees in the old-time senate (*liber*) contrasts with the enslavement to bribery and to favouritism at §23 below (*seruitis*).

52.22 luxuriam atque auaritiam: see 52.7n.

publice … priuatim …: see 9.2n. (*in suppliciis*).

omnia uirtutis praemia ambitio possidet: this sentence explains the preceding: *ambitio* affected the *boni* no less than the *mali*. S. himself had said that *ambitio*, his own downfall (3.4), was a flaw 'propius uirtutem' (11.1). *uirtutis praemia* (-*ium*) is common (e.g. *BJ* 85.20), esp. in Cicero (e.g. *Cat.* 3.26).

52.23 ubi uos separatim sibi quisque consilium capitis: now sounding like Pericles (cf. Thuc. 1.141.6–7), Cato makes an emphatic attack on individualism which comes appropriately from the great-grandson of the man who famously believed in collectivism: see J. Griffin, *Latin poets and Roman life* (1985) 178–80. In late November 63, only a couple of weeks before he spoke in favour of executing the conspirators, the younger Cato was himself being addressed by Cicero in the *Pro Murena* – a speech with which S. was certainly familiar (37.8n. *quo*, 54.4n. *sibi*; cf. 52.11n. *hic*, 24n. *supra*) – as follows: 'M. Cato, qui mihi *non tibi* sed patriae natus esse

<uideris>' (83). Interestingly *separatim . . . quisque* seems to be a pleonasm used by 'the real' Caesar (*BG* 1.19.4, *BC* 3.18.2).

hic: i.e. in the senate. For *pecuniae . . . seruitis* cf. Cic. *TD* 5.8.

eo fit ut impetus fiat in uacuam rem publicam 'hence it comes about that an attack is made on a defenceless commonwealth' (*OLD eo³* 1, *fio* 2). For *uacuam* (*OLD* 8b) cf. Liv. 23.2.7.

52.24 haec omitto: the *praeteritio* is disingenuous, since the contrast between the *maiores* and the present day provides the background to what follows, as the repetition of *maiores nostros* at §30 (cf. 19) shows.

coniurauere . . . incendere: 'the infinitive with *coniuro* is characteristic of high style', according to Mayer on Hor. *C.* 1.15.7, quoting also Virg. *G.* 1.280, seemingly the only exs. (*TLL* 4.340.41, 84).

Gallorum . . . Romano: Cato invokes esp. the Gallic attack on Rome in 390 BC and the conflict with the Cimbri and Teutoni in 105–101 BC: for the Roman fear of the Gauls see Williams, *BRRG* 170–82, Malloch 28–9; also above, 40.6n. (*pollicitos*). S.'s language is imitated at Liv. 26.27.12 'nullam . . . gentem . . . infestiorem . . . nomini Romano' (also Vell. 27.1).

dux hostium . . . [25] intra moenia: cf. *Cat.* 1.5 'ducemque hostium intra moenia' (see also 52.35n.).

supra caput denotes vulnerability (*OLD caput* 3), e.g. Liv. 3.17.2 'cum hostes supra caput sint', Tac. *H.* 4.69.1 'iamque super caput legiones'. Cicero had described the Catilinarians similarly two weeks earlier (*Mur.* 79 'in capite').

52.25 quid intra moenia deprensis hostibus faciatis 'what to do with an enemy caught inside the walls': for the idiomatic dat. see *OLD facio* 22b, though some take *deprensis hostibus* as abl.

52.26 misereamini censeo . . . atque etiam armatos dimittatis 'I think you should . . .' (for *censeo* + subjunc. see *OLD* 3a). The sentence is of course ironic: Cato means the opposite of what he says. The diminutive *adulescentuli* is mock sympathy.

52.27 ne ista uobis <u>m</u>ansuetudo et <u>m</u>isericordia, si illi arma ceperint, in <u>m</u>iseriam conuertat 'do not let your mercy and pity turn into pitiableness in your own case if they take up arms': for *ne* see 52.12n.; others understand *ne* to mean 'lest' (*sc.* 'I fear') or to be short for *dummodo ne* 'provided that . . . not . . .') or to be the affirmative particle 'assuredly' (*OLD nē²*). For the intrans. *conuerto* see *OLD* 8b. *misericordia*, now again coupled with *mansuetudo* (cf. 52.11), picks up *misereamini* without the irony; the wordplay with *miseria* is quite common (e.g. Cic. *TD* 4.18).

52.28 scilicet . . . non timetis eam: again ironical, as was Caesar's use of *scilicet* at 51.10.

immo uero maxime: *immo*, underlined by *uero*, implies 'a complete denial of the preceding remark' (*OLD* 1a); *timetis eam* has to be understood with *maxime*: 'but you *do* fear it, very greatly'.

uidelicet ... confisi: another sarcastic participial expression (cf. §14 and n.).

52.29 suppliciis muliebribus: though the adj. undoubtedly contrasts with the three 'manly' activities about to be listed, the expr. is not mere abuse: Cato has in mind a specifically female ritual for times of crisis, such as the *supplicatio* described at Liv. 25.12.14–15 (on which see C. E. Schultz, *Women's religious activity in the Roman republic* (2006) 28–33). For *suppliciis* see 9.2n.

uigilando: the watchword of Cicero in the Catilinarian crisis (e.g. *Cat.* 1.8).

ubi ... tradideris, ... implores: the main verb is the indefinite use of the second person subjunctive; whether *tradideris* is perf. subjunctive or fut. perf. indic. is unclear: for both points see 1.6n. (*et*). *socordia* and *ignauia* are coupled again at 58.4, *BJ* 31.2.

irati infestique: each adj. is regular of the gods; for both together cf. Lucr. 5.1135, Liv. 42.9.2 (in neither case of the gods, however).

52.30 A. Manlius Torquatus ... necari iussit: this famous story is told by Livy (8.7.1–22, with Oakley's nn.), who, calling the man Titus, assigns it to 340 BC and not to the 'Gallic war' of twenty years earlier (see 9.4n. *uindicatum*; R. Langlands, '"Reading for the moral" in Valerius Maximus: the case of *severitas*', *CCJ* 54 (2008) 160–87, at 170–1): see further Levene, *OR* 233–4. For *necari* see 51.23n.

52.31 parricidis: see 14.3n.

cunctamini: Cato has made this accusation twice already (§§25, 28); a dependent indir. question is first here and not common later (*TLL* 4.1395.26–9).

uidelicet cetera uita eorum huic sceleri obstat 'evidently another <aspect of> their life blocks your view of this crime of theirs': for this meaning of *obstare*, here metaphorical, see *OLD* 2b. *cetera uita* is explained by *dignitati* and *adulescentiae* below (32–3); *uidelicet* is again sarcastic (52.14n., 28n.).

52.32 dignitati Lentuli: since Lentulus had been forced to resign from his praetorship (47.3), his current rank (*OLD dignitas* 3) was that of ex-consul (cos. 71).

si ipse pudicitiae ... pepercit: in a passage which S. may be recalling (see further below), Cicero had referred to the 'insaniam libidinum ... peruersam atque impiam religionem' of Lentulus (*Sull.* 70), who had been expelled from the senate in 70 BC (17.3n.).

52.33 Cethegi adulescentiae: Cethegus' age is unknown and *adulescentia* is a flexible term (38.1n.).

nisi iterum patriae bellum fecit: S. does not mention Cethegus in connection with the first Catilinarian conspiracy (18–19): the reference seems to be to Cicero's allegation (*Sull.* 70) that in the previous decade

Cethegus had gone to Spain to murder Q. Metellus Pius, who had been sent there in 79 to fight Sertorius (see Berry ad loc.).

52.34 nam quid ego de Statilio, Gabinio, Caepario loquar?: perhaps an expansion of Cic. *Sull.* 70 'omitto ceteros, ne sit infinitum'.

quibus si quicquam umquam pensi fuisset 'if anything had ever been of importance [lit. "weight"] to them': for the expr. see 5.6n. (*neque*).

52.35 si mehercule peccato locus esset, facile paterer uos ipsa re corrigi 'if (by Hercules) there were room for a mistake, I would easily allow you to be put right by the actual events': Cato at the end of his speech returns to the point he made at the beginning (§§3–4): action is required in order to prevent disaster; if they do not act now, it will soon be too late. There is no 'room for a mistake'.

faucibus urget: *sc. nos*: 'has us by the throat', though the abl. is difficult to define: the only exact parallel is *meus me alipta* ['trainer'] *faucibus urgebat* at Fronto p. 34.1 vdH², an author very familiar with S., but cf. also Plaut. *Cas.* 943 'faucibus teneor', Cic. *Clu.* 84 'cum faucibus premeretur'. It is possible that *faucibus* means 'jaws' (*OLD* 1e) and is an abl. of instrument (C. is 'gripping us in his jaws': cf. *Cat.* 2.2 'hanc urbem quam e suis faucibus ereptam esse luget'); but *supra caput* (§24) and *in sinu urbis* (below) suggest that Rome is being seen in bodily terms, and S. may be remembering *Cat.* 1.5 'castra sunt in Italia contra populum Romanum in Etruriae faucibus collocata' ('there is in Italy a camp stationed against the Roman people at the gateway of Etruria'), as again just below.

intra moenia atque in sinu urbis sunt hostes: *atque* means 'and what is more' (*OLD* 1a) and *sinu* refers to the senate, if S. is again echoing *Cat.* 1.5 '*ducem*que *hostium* [see 52.24n.] *intra moenia atque* adeo in senatu uidemus intestinam aliquam cotidie perniciem rei p. molientem'; S. in his turn is imitated by Tac. *H.* 3.38.3 'in urbe ac sinu cauendum hostem'. *sinus urbis* is surprisingly rare in classical Latin (only Cic. *Verr.* 5.96; for *oppidi* cf. *Rep.* 3.43), but cf. Vict. *Caes.* 27.2 'inter implana urbis atque ipso sinu', Heges. 3.5.2, 4.21.1 'in medio sinu urbis, id est Romano foro', the latter an imitator of S. (Stover and Woudhuysen).

neque parari neque consuli quicquam potest occulte 'and we can make no preparations or plans in secret'.

quo magis properandum est 'speed is *therefore all the more* necessary' (1.3n. *quo*). Speed is inevitably a major consideration in the aftermath of the Mytilenean Debate (emphasised several times at Thuc. 3.49.2–4).

52.36 foeda atque crudelia facinora in ciues patriamque parauisse: the alliteration is both interlaced and sequential. The coupling of *foedus* and *crudelis* is Ciceronian (*Har. Resp.* 35, *Prov. Cons.* 3, *Phil.* 14.37).

de manifestis rerum capitalium: the gen. after *manifestus* ('plainly guilty of, caught in the act of') is regular (*OLD* 1); again at *BJ* 35.8.

supplicium: *sc. ultimum*, i.e. execution (*OLD* 3a), as 50.4.

53.1 assedit: see 31.7n.

consulares omnes: their names are listed by Cicero alongside those of Silanus and Murena, the consuls designate (*Att.* 12.21(260).1); the list excludes Crassus (cos. 70), whose absence is inferred from *Cat.* 4.10 (48.6n. *frequens*), and Q. Hortensius Hortalus (cos. 69): 'as Cicero was hardly likely to forget him it may be supposed that he was accidentally unable to attend' (Shackleton Bailey ad loc.).

uirtutem animi ad caelum ferunt: the metaphor is common (48.1n. *uirtutem*) but seems to attach itself to Cato: Cicero used it of Cato himself (*Att.* 12.21(260).1 'quae omnia ... Cato laudibus extulerat in caelum'), and then wrote a book 'quo Catonem caelo aequauit' (Tac. *A.* 4.34.4 with W.[5]).

Cato clarus atque magnus habetur: the two adjs. are often combined, but a reference to the *Origines* of Cato the Censor (2C/P 'clarorum uirorum atque magnorum') will perhaps be cued by *censuerat* in the following sentence (see also 54.6n.).

senati decretum fit sicuti ille censuerat: the death penalty had been proposed originally by Silanus (50.4n.), but our sources are agreed that Cato's speech was the decisive factor (e.g. Dio 37.36.2), and, after he had spoken, the motion was regarded as his (Cic. *Att.* 12.21(260).1 'in eius sententiam est facta discessio'), which explains why Brutus mistakenly thought that Cato had been first to propose it (ibid.). When Milo was convicted of having murdered Clodius in 52, Cato wanted to acquit him on the ground that Clodius' death was good for the *res publica*, and it was said that, if Cato had spoken up sooner, others would have followed him (Vell. 47.5). For the gen. *senati* see 30.3n.

53.2–54.6 Digression. The uirtus *and* gloria *of Caesar and Cato*

The reference to Cato as 'clarus atque magnus' (53.1) leads S. into a discussion of *uirtus* (53.2–5), which in turn leads into a comparison of the two outstanding representatives of *uirtus* in S.'s lifetime, Caesar and Cato (53.6–54.6). The doubly discursive nature of the discussion is indicated by introductory formulae at 53.2 and 53.6 (nn.). The discussion of *uirtus* allows S. not only to pick up from Cato's speech the contrast between present and past (52.19–23) but also to resume topics to which he had adverted in his preface (e.g. 53.3nn.). Yet the discussion functions merely as a foil for the comparison of the two great men. The device of comparison, for which the Greek technical term is σύγκρισις (syncrisis, in Latin *comparatio*: see Lausberg §1130), was a natural resort of historical writers, as of other types of author. Agesilaus and Artaxerxes had been compared by Xenophon (*Ages.* 9.1–5), Scipio and Lycurgus by Polybius (10.2.8–13), and Aristides and Themistocles by pseudo-Aristotle (*Ath. Pol.* 23.3–5).

The fragmentary survival of early Roman historiography means that we do not know whether the device was used by any of S.'s Latin predecessors, but a comparison of Caesar and Cato must have seemed to him quite natural. Shortly after Cato's suicide at Utica in 46 BC, Cicero wrote a work entitled *Cato* in praise of him: the work attracted considerable attention and admiration, but it annoyed Caesar, who wrote an *Anticato* in reply (Plut. *Caes.* 54.5–6).[98] The roles played by Caesar and Cato in the Catilinarian debate will have offered the author of the *Bellum Catilinae* an ideal opportunity to compare the controversial politician with his most prominent critic,[99] who had also been S.'s patron and supporter (Intro. pp. 3–4). Comparison was a standard method of dispensing praise (Arist. *Rhet.* 1368a.22–3) and according to the fourth-century AD rhetorical theorist Aphthonius (*Progymn.* 10), if you compare what is fine with what is noble, the result will be 'a double encomium' (ἡ σύγκρισις διπλοῦν ἐγκώμιόν ἐστιν). This is exactly what S. has done, distributing praise between Caesar and Cato while noting their differences. In so doing he makes an *exemplum* of each of them, thereby fulfilling one of the primary functions of Latin historiography (W.[5] on Tac. *A.* 4.33.2 'plures aliorum euentis docentur', adding R. Langlands, *Exemplary ethics in ancient Rome* (2018) and M. B. Roller, *Models from the past in Roman culture: a world of exempla* (2018)).

The syncrisis itself is elaborately written. After the first (chiastic) naming of the two parties (2 *Caesar . . . Cato*) subsequent references are varied and chiastically arranged (ABC ~ CAB: *ille . . . huic . . . Caesar . . . Cato . . . altero ~ altero . . . illius . . . huius . . . Caesar . . . Catoni . . .*). There is multiple alliteration (e.g. *mansuetudine et misericordia, miseris perfugium ~ malis pernicies*), wordplay (e.g. *negotiis amicorum intentus sua neglegere, nihil denegare quod dono dignum esset*) and chiasmus combined with wordplay (*non diuitiis cum diuite . . . sed . . . cum innocente abstinentia*). While many of the statements are triadic (e.g. *genus, aetas, eloquentia*), others are not (e.g. *esse quam uideri, quo minus ~ eo magis*), and the imperfect tense of many of the verbs is varied by others (*addiderat, adeptus est, induxerat*), including historic infinitives (*neglegere, denegare*). Scholars have debated whether S. favours one of the two parties over the other and, if so, which; but the introductory wording of 53.6 suggests that he regarded them both equally.[100]

[98] See M. Gelzer, *Caesar* (1969) 301–4, A. Corbeill, 'Anticato', in Grillo and Krebs 215–22.
[99] An *Anticato* had also been written by Hirtius, while Brutus was one of several who had written a *Cato* (details in Pelling on Plut. *Caes.* 54.6, Moles on Plut. *Brut.* 2.1).
[100] For discussion see e.g. W. W. Batstone, 'The antithesis of virtue: Sallust's "synkrisis" and the crisis of the late republic', *CA* 7 (1988) 1–29.

53.2 Sēd mĭhĭ mūltă lĕgēntī, mūlta audienti ...: the repeated *multa* agrees with *praeclara facinora* (next n.); the datives are to be taken with *libuit* below. The combination of *mihi* + present participle is a common formula, often used as an introduction and an especial favourite of Cicero (e.g. *De Or.* 1.1 'Cogitanti mihi saepenumero et memoria uetera repetenti'): S.'s version is imitated at Tac. *A.* 6.22.1 '*Sed mihi* haec ac talia *audienti*' (where see W.[4]). The combination of *legere* and *audire* (again at *BJ* 85.13) is likewise very frequent in Cicero (e.g. *Dom.* 64 'audieram et legeram clarissimos nostrae ciuitatis uiros se in medios hostes ... iniecisse'), but cf. also Imp. Aug. ap. Suet. *Tib.* 21.7, Plin. *Ep.* 3.16.2. S. is referring to works of history and, as at *BJ* 4.5 'saepe ego audiui', to oral tradition. For the dactylic rhythm cf. Stat. *Theb.* 3.714 'sed mihi multa ...' (and *multa* is repeated in the next line).

quae populus Romanus domi militiaeque mari atque terra praeclara facinora fecit: the relative clause incorporates its antecedent ('praeclara facinora'), as often (G&L 396-7 §616); we might have expected an indir. question after *legenti* and *audienti*, but rel. clauses are often used instead (20.5n. *quae*). It seems clear from §5 below (n.) that the *praeclara facinora* of §§2-4 belong to the centuries before the destruction of Carthage. *mari atque terra* as a variant for the formulaic *terra marique* (for which see Hornblower on Thuc. 1.2.2 and ref. there to Momigliano) is unparalleled (except in the quotation of this sentence at Aug. *Civ. Dei* 5.12). For *praeclara facinora* cf. 2.9n.; for *f. fecit* cf. 7.6n. (*conspici*).

forte libuit attendere quae res maxime tāntă nĕgōtĭă sūstĭnŭĭssēt 'by chance it pleased (me) to pay attention to what factor above all had kept such great activities going': here S. does use an indir. question, the answer to which is given at §4 below ('paucorum ciuium egregiam uirtutem'): the intervening §3 acts as a foil. Historians often introduce matters of intellectual curiosity by appealing to the pleasure they afford author and readers alike, for which forms of *libet* are regular (W–M on Tac. *A.* 3.55.1); here the pleasure is the author's alone, retrojected to the time of his pre-authorial reading. For *attendere* + indir. qu. see *OLD* 7. *negotia sustinere* seems not to have the sense of 'shouldering a burden' that it has at Hor. *Epi.* 2.1.1 'Cum tot sustineas et tanta negotia solus' (and Brink's n.). Skard (*ES* 61-2) used this last passage as part of his argument that *quae res ... sustinuisset* was Ennian, but *negotium/-a sustinere* is a much commoner expr. than he thought, and he seems mistakenly to have assumed that *maxime* scans as a dactyl.

53.3 parua manu cum magnis legionibus hostium contendisse: *sc. populum Romanum* from above: 'that the Roman people with a small unit had engaged with great enemy legions'. S. returns briefly to the topic for which he had no time at 7.7 (n. *quibus*). It is relatively unusual to apply the term *legio* to the enemy, although Cato is one of the authors in whom it is found (*Orig.* 95C/99P 'cum hostium legionibus').

paruis cōpiis bella gesta cum ŏpulentis regibus: *sc. esse:* 'that wars had been waged with meagre resources against wealthy kings'. *opulentis*, an adj. often used of kings and their kingdoms, dictates the meaning of *copiis*, which otherwise would simply repeat the point made in the previous sentence.

fortunae uiolentiam: the expr. recurs at Val. Max. 1.7.1, Sen. *Ep.* 66.44, [Quint.] *Decl.* 9.1. For *tolerare* see 10.2n. (*dubias*).

facundia Graecos, gloria belli Gallos ante Romanos fuisse 'that in eloquence the Greeks had been ahead of the Romans, in military glory the Gauls'. Greek eloquence and Gallic militarism have also been mentioned earlier (respectively 8.3–4 and 40.1). The superiority of Greek eloquence is a traditional theme (e.g. Hor. *Epi.* 2.1.156–7; 8.5n. *at*): it was only in the time of Cicero that Rome could be said to have achieved parity (Sen. *Contr.* 1 *praef.* 6). Gallic militarism was esp. associated with Rome's defeat at the Allia in 390 BC, together with the subsequent storming of the city, and fears of a Gallic *tumultus* were still present at the time of the Catilinarian conspiracy (40.6n. *pollicitus*, 52.24n. *Gallorum*). The reference to *facundia* here perhaps seems surprising, since the accent in §§2–3 hitherto has been on military affairs, but the whole excursus was prompted by the long speeches of Caesar and Cato (below, 6n. *quos*). *facundia* itself (5× elsewhere in S.) is absent from Cicero and Caesar but common in Ovid and in early and later imperial prose writers (see Gaertner on Ov. *Ex P.* 1.2.67); it is found only once in Livy (3.11.6). *ante* indicating superiority is likewise absent from Cicero and Caesar (*TLL* 2.135.49–136.30): S.'s expr. is imitated at Tac. *A.* 1.27.1 '*ante* alios aetate et *gloria belli*'.

53.4 ac m̲ihi m̲ulta agitanti c̲onstabat paucorum c̲iuium egregiam uir-tutem c̲uncta patrauisse 'And, as I was pondering many things, it became apparent to me that a few citizens' exceptional *uirtus* had achieved everything' (*OLD agito* 17, *consto* 9a). *uirtus* as subject of a transitive verb is striking (7.5n. *uirtus*): the combination of an abstract noun + a gen. (cf. 48.5n. *pars*) suggests elevated phraseology equivalent to 'a few exceptionally virtuous citizens', as Hor. *S.* 2.1.72 'uirtus Scipiadae' ('the brave Scipio'), *Epo.* 16.5 'uirtus Capuae' ('courageous Capua'). See also 6n. (*ingenti*) below. For *patrare* cf. 18.8n. (*quod*).

eoque factum uti diuitias p̲aupertas, multitudinem p̲aucitas superaret: *sc. esse:* 'and that for that reason it had come about that riches were overcome by poverty, masses by a few' (*OLD eo³* 1, *facio* 15). For *uti* see 27.2n.

53.5 sed postquam luxu atque desidia c̲iuitas c̲orrupta est: the nature of the corruption – luxury and idleness – suggests the period after the removal of *metus hostilis* and hence after the destruction of Carthage in

146 BC (10.1n. *Carthago*): see further next n. *desidia* is more normally coupled with *luxuria*, but S. has preferred the choicer *luxus* (13.3n. *ea*), as Lucr. 5.48, Sen. *Ep.* 71.15, Suet. *Nero* 42.2 (and note Sil. 11.33–6). For *sed postquam* see 6.3n.

rursus res publica <u>magnitudine</u> sua imperatorum atque <u>magistratuum</u> uitia sustentabat 'conversely the commonwealth because of its greatness maintained the faults of its commanders and magistrates': *rursus* (*OLD* 6a) points the contrast between *uitia sustentabat* here and *tanta negotia susti-nuisset* above (2); and for this sense of *sustentabat* (wrongly classified in *OLD* 4) cf. Sen. *Cons. Helv.* 10.7 'maiores nostri, quorum uirtus etiam nunc uitia nostra sustentat'. The greatness of the *res publica* is normally presented as a reason for its deterioration (a classic example is Liv. *praef.* 4 'ut iam magnitudine laboret sua');[101] S.'s point, determined by the upcoming focus on Caesar and Cato, is different: the greatness of the *res publica* is the reason for the deterioration of its individual leaders: the Roman empire supports their faults, by which he means the *luxus* and *desidia* and associated *uitia* which caused the socio-political corruption in the first place. See further Lintott (1972) on imperial expansion and moral decline.

sicuti †effeta parentum†: in this desperate passage the problematic words are obelised by Vretska and Reynolds. Ramsey prefers to follow those scholars who insert *ui* either before or after *parentum* and translates 'just as if the vigour of their ancestors were worn out with childbearing'; but it seems very odd indeed if, after a reference to childbearing (*effeta*), *parentum* does not mean 'parents'.[102] Kurfess prints *sicuti effeta <esset> partu* (*partu* being a modification of Kunze's *pariendo*), and he receives learned support from J. Linderski: 'we should not hesitate to deem this phrase worthy of Sallust' ('Effete Rome', *Mnem.* 52 (1999) 257–65, at 265). There are nevertheless reasons why we should hesitate.

(i) When *effetus* means 'barren, sterile' in classical Latin, it is mostly used of animals or the land; when it is applied to humans, only two examples are quoted (*TLL* 5.2.156.29–32), of which this is the first (the other is Val. Max. 7.7.4). But, if S. is saying that the *res publica* is metaphorically 'barren', this conflicts with the phrase *multis tempesta-tibus*, since it is impossible for a mother to be barren at one moment and fertile at another. (ii) The alternative is to assume that *effeta* here has its looser meaning of 'tired, exhausted', which, however, is more usually applied to the body or age (*senectus* etc.); when it is applied to

---

[101] The MSS of S. are unanimous in reading *magnitudine sua* here. Modern edd. prefer *m. sui* on the grounds that that is the reading at Aug. *Civ. Dei* 5.12; but *sua* is the universal preference in classical texts, as Livy illustrates: *sui* is post-classical and was unthinkingly substituted by Aug. when he quoted S.'s sentence.

[102] This oddity is avoided by reading *effeta parente* (with some later MSS).

persons, only two classical examples are quoted (*TLL* 5.2.157.7–9), both much later than S. (Stat. *Theb.* 6.873, Apul. *Apol.* 76). But, if S. is saying that the *res publica* is merely 'tired' or 'exhausted', this conflicts with *haud ... quisquam ... uirtute magnus*, since exhaustion would not result in one type of offspring (non-virtuous) to the exclusion of another (virtuous).

In other words, there are linguistic and logical reasons to doubt the correctness of *effeta*; a different view of the text seems required. In the first part of the sentence the *res publica* is seen as some kind of successful prop or support (*sustentabat*); since in the second part of the sentence success has been replaced by failure, we should expect an explanation of the transition: either the prop has been overwhelmed or the circumstances have become too much. Beyond this it is almost impossible to go. Since syntax requires a finite verb in the *sicuti*-clause, some scholars have supplied *esset* either before or after *effeta*; but, if we assume that *effeta* was a corruption of *esset*, that would solve two problems at a stroke. On the further assumption that *parentum* was a subsequent corruption under the influence of *effeta*, it is naturally difficult to know what S. might have written originally, but perhaps something along the lines of *sicuti esset peruentum <ad extremum>*, 'as if the end had been reached' (cf. Liv. 3.23.5 'postquam ad extremum uentum est').

multis tempestatibus haud sane quisquam Romae uirtute magnus fuit 'at many periods there was not really anyone great in *uirtus* at Rome'. Cicero often makes similar complaints (e.g. *Brut.* 2, *Rep.* 5.2); scholars have detected in S.'s statement a critical allusion to Cn. Pompeius *Magnus* (e.g. Syme, *Sall.* 113). For *tempestas* = *tempus* see 7.1n. (*ea*); for *haud sane* (again at 37.9) see *OLD sane* 4a.

53.6 memoria mea: equivalent to 'in my lifetime' (33.2n. *memoria*).

ingenti uirtute, diuersis moribus fuere uiri duo: the abls. are descriptive: both were men of great *uirtus*, illustrating the key quality mentioned above (4), but of different habits (and hence affording a basis for comparison): so too Vell. 1.13.3 'diuersi imperatoribus mores, diuersa fuere studia' (see further 54.1n.).

The elder Seneca says that the device of the obituary notice or *epitaphion*, occurring once or twice in Thucydides, was taken over by S. in a few cases and then by Livy (*Suas.* 6.21); since no formal example is found in S.'s monographs, it is normally assumed that Seneca was referring to the now fragmentary *Historiae*; but, since it is usually inferred from *fuere* that Caesar as well as Cato was now dead, the syncrisis performs a similar function.

quōs quŏnĭām rēs ōbtŭlĕrāt 'and because the context had presented them', a similar apologia to *BJ* 95.2–3 'sed quoniam nos tanti uiri res

admonuit, idoneum uisum est de natura cultuque eius paucis dicere ...
Igitur Sulla ...' (cf. *BC* 5.9 'res ipsa hortari uidetur', *BJ* 17.1 'res postulare
uidetur'). In our passage *res* refers to the speeches of the two men; *obtulerat*
is pluperf. because it is relative to *fuit* in the main clause (next n.). The
hexametrical rhythm is again notable (a rel. pronoun + *quoniam* is
a standard line-beginning, esp. in Lucr. and Ov., e.g. *M.* 1.194).

**quos ... silentio praeterire non fuit consilium quin utriusque naturam et
mores ... aperirem:** *fuit* is equivalent to an epistolary tense: S.'s intention is
seen from the viewpoint of the reader of the monograph (G&L 166–7
§252). It was a commonplace that virtue cannot be passed by in silence but
requires literary commemoration, e.g. Cic. *Sull.* 62 'ne haec quidem
P. Sullae mihi uidetur silentio praetereunda uirtus', *Marc.* 1 'tacitus praeterire nullo modo possum' (see W–M on Tac. *A.* 3.65.1 for many further
exs.). When *praeterire* is constructed with *quin*, it does not require an acc.
object (cf. Caes. ap. Cic. *Att.* 9.6A.1 'praeterire tamen non potui quin et
scriberem ad te'), but *silentio* suggests that *quos* is the object of *praeterire* as
well as of *obtulerat* ('it was not my intention to pass over them in silence
such that I did not explain the nature and behaviour of each': *OLD quin*
4a): the combination of object + *quin* is unparalleled. *silentio praeterire* is
a common expr., esp. in Cicero.

quantum ingenio possum 'to the best of my intellectual ability'. Affected
modesty is another rhetorical commonplace, e.g. Cic. *De Or.* 3.77 'quantum ingenio ... ualemus' (see W.[1] on Vell. 104.4 for many further exs.);
but the clause also serves to draw attention to the importance which
S. attaches to *ingenium* (1.3). The change to present tense (cf. last n.) is
not unusual.

54.1 genus, aetas, eloquentia aequalia fuere: Julius Caesar was born in
100; his patrician family famously claimed descent from Iulus, son of
Aeneas, and hence from the goddess Venus (Vell. 41.1 and W.[2]). He is
a popular subject for modern biographers: see e.g. M. Griffin (ed.),
A companion to Julius Caesar (2009), esp. 9–22 (family, by E. Badian).
Cato, born in 95 into a plebeian family, was a *nobilis* (5.1n. *nobili*): his
grandfather was consul in 89 and his great-grandfather (the famous Cato
the Elder) in 195; on him see Drogula, *CY*, esp. xviii (family tree), 9–22
(background), 68–85 (Catilinarian conspiracy); Volk 59–74. The alleged
parity of their oratory is determined by their speeches as presented by
S. (51–2). For the neuter *aequalia* see 5.2n. (*huic*).

aequalia ... par, item ... alia: the language of sameness and difference is
typical of syncrisis: see esp. Plut. *Mor.* 243B–C 'it is not possible to learn
better the similarity and difference between the virtues of men and women
from any other source than by putting lives beside lives and actions beside
actions ... [V]irtues acquire certain other diversities, their own colouring
as it were, due to varying natures, and they take on the likeness of the

customs on which they are founded, and of the temperament of persons
and their nurture and mode of living' (Loeb trans.).

magnitudo animi par, item gloria, sed alia alii 'their great-heartedness
was equal and likewise their glory, though different for each of them': *alii*
for *alteri* is influenced by the preceding *alia* (agreeing with *gloria*). The
remainder of the syncrisis is dedicated to illustrating the difference
between the *gloria* of the two men as stated here (see *magnus habebatur,
clarus factus, gloriam adeptus est, laudabatur, enitescere* ~ *gloriam*): both men
exemplify the acquisition of *gloria* to which S. paid such attention in the
preface (e.g. 1.3, 3.2). Individuals credited with *magnitudo animi* 'possess
the ample cognitive and affective resources that enable them to see what is
truly important ... and stir them to act accordingly'; the quality is 'a
precondition for "bravery" (*fortitudo*) and a key component of "manliness"
(*uirtus*)' (Kaster's comm. on Cic. *Sest.*, p. 421). See further Hellegouarc'h
290–4; Dyck on Cic. *Off.* 1.61–92.

54.2–3 'Here all the traits attributed to Caesar are other-directed,
radiating outward in acts of material and emotional generosity and mag-
nanimity. All the contrasting traits of Cato are self-centered and self-
contained, exercises of the will that keep the self at a safe distance from
others' (Kaster 143). 'To neither is wisdom attributed ... and ... neither is
even considered as a *statesman*' (Stone (1999) 75, his italics).

54.2 Caesar ... magnus habebatur: an inscription from Aphrodisias
refers to Caesar as 'the Great' (ὁ μέγας: see J. Reynolds, *Aphrodisias and
Rome* (1982) 159–61), but the title was due to his conquests (cf. Catull.
11.9–12) rather than to his largesse, for which see Vell. 41.1
'munificentia ... effusissimus' and W.², Pelling on Plut. *Caes.* 4.4–7, 5.8–
9. For *beneficiis ac munificentia* cf. Gell. 7.7.4.

integritate uitae: a defining quality of Cato (see W.² on Vell. 45.5 'cuius
integritatem laudari nefas est').

mansuetudine et misericordia: presumably a reference to *clementia*, with
which each noun is not uncommonly coupled: indeed Caesar, famous for
his *clementia* (Weinstock 233–43), twice refers to 'his own *clementia* and
mansuetudo' (*BG* 2.14.5, 2.31.4) and is echoed by Cicero (*Marc.* 1). But
Cato in his speech had sought to undermine these very qualities (52.11n.
(*hic*), 52.27).

huic seueritas dignitatem addiderat: Cato's famous inflexibility (see
Drogula, *CY* 346 (index)) is singled out at the very start of Plutarch's
Life of Cato (1.3 ἦθος ... ἄτρεπτον) and returned to below at §5.
Interestingly it was Caesar who was more famously associated with *dignitas*
(51.6n. *magis*). For *d. addiderat* cf. Tac. *A.* 6.27.2 and W.⁴.

54.3 dando, subleuando, ignoscendo: these seem to be further references to his munificence and clemency.

nihil largiendo: when Cato spoke in the Catilinarian debate he was tribune designate, having won the election through bribery, if the bowl intended to provide food for voters and inscribed M CATO QVEI PETIT TRIBVNV PLEBEI is as genuine as that of Cassius Longinus is thought to be (see 26.1n. *in*, 37.7n. *priuatis*; Berry, *CC* 23–5). Shortly before the present debate, in late Nov. 63, Cato had prosecuted Murena for *ambitus* (*TLRR* 111–12 no. 224); conversely he sanctioned bribery in order to get Bibulus elected consul for 59 (Suet. *DJ* 19.1; Drogula, *CY* 122).

miseris perfugium: 'He was an only (and very willing) resort for defendants or debtors or young wastrels' (Suet. *DJ* 27.2). The metaphor of the safe haven is a favourite of Cicero (e.g. *Clu.* 7 'fortunae miserae multumque iactatae portum ac perfugium').

malis pernicies: contrast Crassus at 48.8 (n. *more*).

illius facilitas, huius constantia laudabatur: *facilitas* is 'obligingness' (*OLD* 6), a quality also singled out by Suetonius (*DJ* 72 'amicos tanta semper facilitate ... tractauit'); *constantia*, a Stoic virtue, complemented Cato's *integritas* (cf. Cic. *Att.* 1.18.7).

54.4 postremo: possibly 'To sum up' (*OLD* 4a).

laborare, uigilare: virtues appropriate to the dedicated politician and military man (W.² on Vell. 79.1, 88.2).

negotiis amicorum intentus sua neglegere, nihil denegare quod dono dignum esset: *negotiis* is presumably dat. here (contrast 2.9n. *aliquo*); the infinitives are historic; the subjunctive is generic (*NLS* 114–15 §155). Privileging others' requirements over one's own is a mark of friendship (Cic. *Amic.* 57): cf. Suet. *DJ* 72. Plays on *negotium* ~ *neglegere* (again at 51.24), *neglegere* ~ *negare* and *negotium* ~ *negare* (and their affiliates) are all found elsewhere, esp. in Cicero; S. seems the only author in whom they are closely combined, although note Cic. *Q.Fr.* 3.1.1 'negari ... negari ... negotiis ... neglegentius'.

sibi magnum imperium, exercitum, bellum nouum exoptabat ubi uirtus enitescere posset: with the benefit of hindsight S. is looking forward, from the viewpoint of the late 60s, to the ten-year command in Gaul which Caesar began after his consulship in 59 (see Pelling on Plut. *Caes.* 14.10 and 29.1) and during which he not only conquered the whole of Gaul but also advanced into Britain. *ubi* = *in quo* (*sc. bello*) and introduces a rel. clause of purpose. S. has evidently been reading the *Pro Murena* (see also 52.11n. (*hic*), 52.23n. (*ubi*)), delivered in the month preceding the imprisonment of the Catilinarians, in which Cicero uses the same metaphor of the elder Cato, whom he says his great-grandson resembles (exactly as S. says of the same man at *non diuitiis ... certabat* below: see n.): cf. *Mur.* 32 'quo quidem in bello uirtus enituit egregia M. Catonis, proaui tui: quo ille, cum esset ... talis qualem te esse uideo'. *uirtus* + *enitescere* later appealed to Livy (6×; also at Sen. *Ben.* 7.15.2, *Prov.* 4.3).

54.5 decoris 'seemliness, decency' (*OLD decus* 4).

54.6 non diuitiis cum diuite ... sed cum strenuo uirtute ... certabat: Cato resembles his great-grandfather (Plut. *Cato Mai.* 10.5 'I wish to compete rather in virtue (περὶ ἀρετῆς) with the best than in money with the richest and covetous'); see also 4 above (n. *sibi*). The whole sentence forms a chiasmus, the paronomasia of the first two elements varied by the quasi-synonyms of the last three.

neque factione cum factioso 'nor in influence with the influential': for this meaning see Seager (1972) 53–4.

cum innocente abstinentia 'in financial integrity with the incorruptible' (see 12.1n. *innocentia*).

esse quam uideri bonus malebat: at Aesch. *Sept.* 592 the seer Amphiaraus 'wants not to seem but to be the best' (οὐ γὰρ δοκεῖν ἄριστος, ἀλλ' εἶναι θέλει). 'It seems obvious that Sallust must have had this very passage in mind' (Renehan, *OR* 106). Aeschylus' aphorism, which became well known (e.g. Plato, *Rep.* 361B, *Gorg.* 527B, Plut. *Quomodo adulesc.* 32D), is applied in varied form to Cato by Velleius too (35.2 'qui numquam recte fecit ut facere uideretur sed qui aliter facere non potuerat'), no doubt imitating S. in much the same way as does Livy at 6.11.7 (see Oakley's n.). A preference for reality over appearance is expressed slightly differently at Cic. *Off.* 1.65 'principemque se esse mauult quam uideri', a passage which, in view of other verbal similarities, Dyck ad loc. thinks may lie behind S.'s syncrisis of the two great men.[103]

quo minus petebat gloriam, eo magis illŭm sĕquēbātŭr: the paradox, which is proverbial (Tosi 791 §1776), constitutes an effective conclusion to the syncrisis, which ends with *gloria*, as it had begun (§1), and with Cicero's favourite clausula (K–K 176).

55.1 Postquam (ut dixi) senatus in Catonis sententiam discessit 'After the senate (as I said) had divided in favour of Cato's proposal': *discessit*, like *in sententiam* (50.4n.), is technical (*OLD* 1b). The cross-reference (5.7n. *quae*) is to 53.1.

consul optimum factu ratus noctem quae instabat antecapere: *sc. esse* or *fore* (32.1n.): 'the consul, thinking that the best thing to do <was/would be> to forestall the approaching night'. Cicero is not named because he is seen in his role as presiding magistrate; his reasoning is given in the following clause. For *optimum factu* see 32.1n.; *instare* is regular of time (*OLD* 6c); for *antecapere* see 13.3n. (*ea*).

ne quid eo spatio nouaretur 'to prevent any development in the interval' (*OLD nouo* 5c): so too App. *BC* 2.6.21 δεδιὼς ἀμφὶ τῇ νυκτὶ προσιούσῃ, μὴ τὸ συνεγνωκὼς τοῖς ἀνδράσι πλῆθος ... ἐργάσηταί τι ἄτοπον ('fearful about the

---

[103] Cicero in his *Cato* (fr. 14) wrote: 'contingebat in eo quod plerisque contra solet, ut maiora omnia re quam fama uiderentur' (ap. Macrob. 6.2.33).

approaching night lest the crowd that was in league with the men ...
should do something monstrous') and Carsana's n. Plutarch talks of
elements in the crowd who might try to help the men escape from prison
(*Cic.* 22.4).

triumuiros quae id supplicium postulabat parare iubet 'he ordered the
triumuiri to make the arrangements which their punishment demanded'.
The *triumuiri capitales* were minor magistrates in charge of night-time
policing, prisons, executions and other matters of public order (Oakley
on Liv. 9.46.3); the arrangements would consist principally in summoning
the *carnifices* (55.5n. *uindices*) along with their equipment. Almost all MSS
read *ad supplicium*, a phrase which is commonly combined with a verb of
demanding (note esp. Tac. *H.* 1.82.3 'auctores seditionis ad supplicium
ultro postulabat', 2.94.2 'postulantur ad supplicium'); but this cannot be
the case here, since in all other exs. it is a person, not a thing (*quae*), that is
demanded for punishment.[104] Many edd. simply delete *ad*, which is erased
in a couple of MSS, but to me it seems more likely that *ad* was mistakenly
written for *id* (so Gertz) than that it was inserted (as it were) out of the
blue. *id* (= *eorum*) will refer back to *triumuiros*, alluding to their particular
kind of punishment, viz. execution (cf. Tac. *A.* 6.9.2 'triumuirali suppli-
cio'). *postulare* can take a wide range of abstract subjects, although *supplicium* is unparalleled (*TLL* 10.2.268.32–270.68).

55.2 ipse ... Lentulum in carcerem deducit: 'There is no constitutional
requirement of special observance toward Lentulus now no longer in
office, and yet Cicero continues to accord him special treatment' (Stone
(1999) 74). Alone of the prisoners, Lentulus was a former consul; Cicero's
action is evidence of his 'propriety of deportment towards Lentulus, not
merely a criminal against society, but his own would-be murderer' (ibid.
75). See further Woodman (2024) 79–80. *deducere* is the *mot juste* for
escorting someone to prison (Cic. *Inv.* 2.149, Apul. *Met.* 9.42.4).

55.3 est in carcere locus quod Tullianum appellatur 'There is in the
prison an area which is called the Tullianum': the rel. pronoun takes its
gender from *Tullianum* rather than the antecedent (G&L 395 §614 R. 3
(*b*)). The *carcer* was situated at the foot of the Capitoline Hall about 100
yards NE of the Aedes Concordiae (*LTUR* 1.236–9; Vasaly 65; Berry, *CC*
247 map 1), where the senate had been meeting (*Cat.* 4.14). If the inner
area was associated with one of Rome's kings (cf. Varro, *LL* 5.151 'pars
quae sub terra Tullianum, ideo quod additum a Tullio rege'), it was
a fitting final destination for one who had aimed at *regnum* (47.2). S.'s
sentence is a classic example of the '*est locus* formula', introducing
a *descriptio loci* which is almost always concluded by a pronominal expr.

---

[104] This rules out Ahlberg's *quae ad supplicium postulabantur* and Mariotti's *quae
<res> ad supplicium postulabat.*

returning the reader to the main narrative (as here: 'in eum locum ...',
55.5). The device is as old as Homer (*Il.* 13.332–4): see e.g. van Dam on
Stat. *Silv.* 2.2.1–3; also W.[4] on Tac. *A.* 5.4.1.

**ubi paululum ascenderis ad laeuam, circiter duodecim pedes humi
depressus** '(an area), when you go up a little on the left, sunk in the
ground roughly twelve feet': *deprimo* (*OLD* 3) and *depressus* (*OLD* 1) are
technical of buildings, while *humi* can mean 'in the ground' as well as 'on'
(*TLL* 6.3.3125.48–61, *OLD humus* 1b): thus Colum. *RR* 8.15.6 'canalicu-
lus humi depressus'. S.'s meaning is by no means clear, and the topography of the prison (parts of which survive) is confusing: see T. J. Cadoux,
'The Roman *carcer* and its adjuncts', *G&R* 55 (2008) 202–21, with
illustrative figures. Evidently there were two chambers, one lower than
the other, but whether *ascenderis* refers to ascending within the prison or
to approaching from the outside is unclear. *ascenderis* is probably the
idiomatic potential use of the second person perf. subjunc. (1.6n. *et*)
rather than a fut. perf. indic.; in geographical contexts it is very common
to find second-person verbs: see K. S. Kingsley, 'Authority, experience,
and the vicarious traveller in Herodotus' *Histories*', in K. S. Kingsley,
G. Monti and T. Rood (edd.), *The authoritative historian: tradition and
innovation in ancient historiography. Essays in honour of John Marincola*
(2022) 206–23, with much bibliography.

**55.4 eum muniunt undique parietes atque insuper camera lapideis
fornicibus iuncta:** *muniunt* (*OLD* 3 'to provide with a protective wall,
covering, etc.') is difficult to translate: perhaps 'it is constructed of walls
on all sides and, above, of a vaulted roof held together by [i.e. consisting
of] stone arches'.

incultu, tenebris, odore foeda atque terribilis eius facies est 'because of
neglect, the darkness and the stench, its appearance is foul and
frightening'.

55.5 uindices rerum capitalium 'the punishers of capital matters': i.e.
the *carnifices*, who carried out the actual executions on the instructions of
the *triumuiri capitales*.

55.6 ita ille, patricius ... inuenit: for the relationship between this
'obituary' and 'the justly famous sentence'[105] at Hdt. 1.45.3 ('Adrastus,
the son of Gordias the son of Midas, this slayer [οὗτος δή] of his own
brother and slayer of his purifier, when there was a respite from people
around the grave, recognising that he was the most ill-fated of people he
had known, slew himself on the tomb') see M. D. Reeve, 'Five deaths', in
H. D. Jocelyn and H. Hurt (edd.), *Tria lustra* (1993) 261–3, who points to
the series of appositions and observes that 'Sallust uses as his subject the

---

[105] H. Immerwahr, *Form and thought in Herodotus* (1966) 52.

0

pronoun with which Herodotus introduces the appositions'. See also next
n. Lentulus had been consul in 71.

dignum moribus factisque suis exitum uitae inuenit: the majority of
MSS read *exitium*, but *exitium uitae* is not found in classical Latin; if one
wanted to retain *exitium* on the grounds that it is said to have been an
archaism for *exitus* (*OLD* 4), one would have to consider seriously the
deletion of *uitae*, which seems a step too far: it is much more plausible to
assume that *exitium* was written in error for *exitum* (the two words are
often confused). Some scholars, though printing *exitum*, have nevertheless deleted *uitae*, since (i) *exitus* alone can mean 'death', as in the
formulaic *hunc exitum habuit* (Oakley on Liv. 6.20.14), and since (ii)
the genitive is absent from some late authors who imitate S. (e.g. Aug.
Ep. 16.2 'dignum moribus factisque suis exitum ... reppererunt');[106] yet,
since *exitus uitae* is a set phrase and the genitive is present in other late
Sallustian imitators (e.g. Hegesipp. 4.20.18 'dignum meritis suis uitae
exitum tulit'), it seems gratuitous to delete it (*uitae* also produces the
more favoured spondaic clausula).

What, then, does the paradosis mean? Like *exitus uitae*, the expressions
dignus exitus and *exitum inuenire* (*OLD inuenio* 9b 'to come to an end') are
regular and individually common, although the three in combination
are found nowhere else in Latin. The most obvious meaning is 'he met
a life's end that was appropriate to the morality of his deeds', i.e.
a straightforward illustration of the topos that one gets the death one
deserves (W.[2] on Vell. 91.4). Yet the uniqueness of the combined expressions perhaps suggests that S. intended something more pointed: 'Thus
that man ... discovered that his departure from life was in keeping with
the morality of his deeds' (*OLD inuenio* 5c). This produces a *peripeteia*
which contrasts even more effectively with the two preceding cola
('patricius ... habuerat'): the distinguished Lentulus could not believe
that his manner of death was not what he had expected, an eleventh-hour
awareness which echoes that to be found in his Herodotean model (last
n.). For the loaded term *moribus* in connection with Lentulus see Stone
(1999) 73 n. 89.

de Cethego ... sumptum est: S. makes no mention of the ecstatic crowds
who are said to have accompanied Cicero to his house afterwards (Vell.
35.4, Plut. *Cic.* 22.4–7).

[106] At Vell. 112.7 'dignum furore suo habuit exitum' the reference is probably not
to death at all (see W.[1]).

56–61 CATILINE'S LAST STAND:
DECEMBER 63–EARLY 62

The brilliant set-piece description with which the monograph ends is a classic episode of ancient historiography.[107] The principal character, finding himself in a difficult and worsening situation, decides to risk everything on a battle (56–7). After delivering a pre-battle *hortatio* in direct speech (58), with numerous allusions to Thucydides (e.g. 58.3n. *ego*, 10n. *si*, 21n. *neu*), he deploys his forces for the forthcoming engagement (59.1–3). But the novice commander is faced by a veteran campaigner, whose corresponding exhortations are brief, in indirect speech, and aimed only at individuals (59.4–6). Yet, when the battle begins (60.1–4), C.'s energetic performance surprises his opponent, who is compelled to take strong counter-measures which result in the Catilinarians' defeat (60.5–7).

When Cicero urged the Catilinarian conspiracy upon the historian Lucceius as a worthy subject, he said this (*Fam.* 5.12.5):

> uiri saepe excellentis ancipites uariique casus habent admirationem, exspectationem, laetitiam, molestiam, spem, timorem; si uero exitu notabili concluduntur, expletur animus iucundissima lectionis uoluptate.

Cicero naturally saw himself as the 'outstanding man' whose handling of the various phases of the conspiracy would induce in Lucceius' readers a corresponding variety of emotions; but, if the episode has a notable outcome, such as the execution of the treasonous gang, the final emotion with which the reader is left is one of pleasure. This sequence has, as it were, been turned on its head by S. The two final paragraphs of the work are devoted to a description of the battlefield. In the first (61.1–6) there is a highly visual survey of the Catilinarian dead, whose bravery is treated with sympathy; in the second (61.7–9) S. focusses on the non-combatant loyalists, who, as they traverse the site turning over the corpses of the enemy, are shocked to find friends and relatives amongst them: 'Ita uarie per omnem exercitum laetitia, maeror, luctus atque gaudia agitabantur.' The powerful effect of this ending 'is in large measure achieved by the disquieting sense of any lack of closure', says Marincola. 'Sallust has taken two common closural devices, death and victory, and has manipulated them to produce not resolution, their usual effect, but instead the very opposite. Such a portrayal is indeed appropriate, since Sallust, writing under renewed threat of civil war, could not really consider that there had yet been an

---

[107] It seems to echo Caesar's *De Bello Gallico* (see e.g. 60.1–2nn.) and in its turn to have influenced Virgil in Book 10 of the *Aeneid* (354–79): see Woodman (2022).

ending to the conflicts between the nobles and people that had found expression in Catiline's conspiracy.'[108]

56.1 Dum ea ... geruntur: *ea* seems to refer to 36.2–55.6. The formula is a less common variant on that at 32.3 (n. *Dum*).

quam et ipse adduxerat: see 36.1nn. and 43.1n. (*cum*).

duas legiones: having already arrogated to himself the paraphernalia of a consul (36.1n. *cum*), C. now establishes two legions, the normal number in a consul's army. A legion was supposed to comprise 5,000–6,000 men, whereas we learn below that initially there were only 2,000 men in total.

<u>c</u>**ohortes pro numero militum** <u>c</u>**omplet** 'he made up cohorts having regard to the total of soldiers available' (*OLD pro* 13, *compleo* 7a). There were ten cohorts to a legion; the implication (confirmed below) is that initially the cohorts were nominal only.

56.2 ut quisque ... uenerat 'whenever anyone arrived in the camp as a volunteer or from his allies' (*OLD quisque* 8); for the generalising temporal clause see 51.33n. (*uti*). *uoluntarius* refers to men like the unfortunate Fulvius (39.5); *ex sociis* perhaps refers to men like Volturcius (45.3–47.1), though it is hard to see how they could have been very numerous.

aequaliter: between the two legions.

legiones numero hominum expleuerat: *expleuerat* = 'had made up' (*OLD* 4a): the implication is that C. now had 10,000–12,000 men, which seems hard to believe; Dio implies that he ended up with 3,000 (37.40.1), although other texts allege 20,000 (Plut. *Cic.* 16.6, App. *BC* 2.7.23). The logic of the sentence suggests that *numero* is causal, 'because of the number of men'. The tense of the verb, as of *distribuerat* above, indicates priority to the news of Antonius' approach (4).

cum 'although'.

56.3 circiter pars quarta: supply 'only' in English (cf. 6.4). The same fraction at App. *BC* 2.7.23.

ut quemque casus armauerat 'according as/depending on how chance had armed each one' (different from the idiom above at 2n. *ut quisque*).

sparos aut lanceas 'spears or lances', as Sisenna 53C/21P 'sparis ac lanceis', and perhaps also 55C/29P (cf. *LH* 119). *alii* has to be understood before *sparos*.

praeacutas sudes portabant: 'carried tip-sharpened stakes': *praeacutus* is a favourite term of Caesar (8×, e.g. *BC* 1.27.3 'sudes stipitesque praeacutos'): see also Apul. *Met.* 8.16.5, Amm. 18.7.6, 25.6.5. It is difficult to decide whether to read *portabant* with the MSS and Nonius Marcellus

---

[108] J. Marincola, 'Concluding narratives: looking to the end in classical historiography', *PLLS* 12 (2005) 285–320, at 303. For a comparison with the ending of Lucretius' *De Rerum Natura* see P. Fowler, 'Lucretian conclusions', in D. H. Roberts et al. (edd.), *Classical closure* (1997) 133–4. See also Intro. p. 18 and n. 89.

(554.13) or Servius' *portare*, the first in a series of historic infinitives (6.4n. *igitur*). For improvised weaponry see also Tac. *A.* 4.51.1 and W.[5].

56.4 postquam Antonius cum exercitu aduentabat 'after *it turned out that* Antonius was approaching with an army'. *postquam* + imperfect tense (6.3n. *sed*) here produces a special nuance: see *OLS* 1.609–10, whose way of translating is adopted here; an alternative is 'after <he realised that> A. was approaching' (G&L 360 §562, commenting 'The translation often indicates the spectator'). Antonius had been sent to pursue C. at 36.3.

Catilina per montes iter facere: the statement (the first element of a tricolon) suggests that C. was north of Faesulae, where there are routes across the Apennines to Bononia (mod. Bologna), but it is uncertain whether this is S.'s meaning and even whether he knew the regional topography. It has to be remembered that in the late first century BC maps were almost certainly unknown;[109] the difficulties of travel made it impossible for authors to acquire the kind of knowledge which we in the modern world take for granted, and, even if those difficulties were overcome, much of the evidence suggests that historians had little interest in providing genuine information for their readers. S. himself is a notorious example. He had been governor of Africa Nova and inserted into the *BJ* a substantial digression (17–19) on 'Africae situs'; yet 'nothing in what he relates conveys any suggestion of autopsy' (Syme, *Sall.* 152): S. simply repeats the same kinds of literary commonplace which other authors used (on this see Horsfall 171–91 on topography, illusion and reality in Latin topographical writing) and which readers had come to expect (cf. Cic. *Orator* 66). Sumner's speculative account of C.'s 'last journey' is based largely on the narrative at 56.4–57.4, yet the relationship of S.'s various statements to one another strongly implies that we should not place too much reliance on them (see below).

modo ad urbem, modo Galliam *uersus* castra mo*uere*: when the adv. *uersus* is used to govern a noun ('in the direction of, towards'), it follows the noun (*OLD uersus*[2] 2); failure to understand this explains why in some MSS it was taken as a participle agreeing with *Catilina*, which in turn led to the insertion of *in* or *ad* before *Galliam*. The statement is unclear, especially since S. does not specify what he means by *Galliam uersus*: is he referring to Cisalpine Gaul (as the reference to Transalpine Gaul at 57.1 might suggest), to Transalpine Gaul, or to both? Since Rome lay to the

---

[109] See e.g. A. C. Bertrand, 'Stumbling through Gaul: maps, intelligence, and Caesar's *Bellum Gallicum*', *Anc. Hist. Bull.* 11 (1997) 107–22, at 108–11, and K. Brodersen, 'Mapping (in) the ancient world', *JRS* 94 (2004) 183–90, and 'Cartography' in D. Dueck (ed.), *Geography in classical antiquity* (2012) 99–110. But the matter is controversial: see e.g. R. J. A. Talbert, 'Greek and Roman mapping', in R. J. A. Talbert and R. W. Unger (edd.), *Cartography in antiquity and the Middle Ages* (2008) 9–27.

south, there must be a suspicion that S. had no very definite area in mind but was using *Gallia* as a sort of metonymy for the opposite direction ('the north'), the polarities indicating the desperate circumstances in which C. found himself. Whatever the truth, the relationship of these directions to the *per montes iter* just mentioned is likewise unclear.

Elsewhere in S. repeated *modo* is arranged chiastically when the verb is the same (e.g. 15.5, *BJ* 23.1 'defensoribus ... praemia modo, modo formidinem ostentare'), an arrangement which he liked and seemingly invented; our passage is the only exception (cf. R. B. Steele, *Chiasmus in Sallust, Caesar, Tacitus and Justinus* (1891) 15–16).

sperabat propediem magnas copias sese habiturum, si Romae socii incepta patrauissent 'he hoped that any day he would have great forces, if his allies in Rome accomplished what they had undertaken': *patrauissent* represents a fut. perf. in direct speech. C. had earlier promised to assemble an army in the north and then to march on Rome (32.2 'sese propediem cum magno exercitu ad urbem accessurum'), a promise to which *propediem* here pointedly looks back. S. nowhere explains why C. is now expecting his allies in Rome to march northwards to him, an expectation which he repeats at 58.4, but the complete reversal of the original plan attests eloquently to the chaotic nature of the Catilinarian conspiracy. *i. patrare* recurs at *BJ* 70.5 and is varied by Tacitus at *A.* 2.66.1 'patrati quam incepti'.

56.5 seruitia repudiabat: against Lentulus' advice (44.5–6).

cuius ... magnae copiae: the antecedent is plur. *seruitia*, a remarkable lack of concord which scholars explain as a *constructio ad sensum*; but the example is significantly different from others (6.2n. *alius*, 18.1–2n., 33.1n. *uti*, 39.3n. *ubi*, 43.1n. *Lentulus*), and, if a student were to perpetrate it in a Latin prose composition, it would be adjudged a bad howler. Yet similar cases occur elsewhere (e.g. *H.* 3.15.15 'ne uos ad uirilia illa uocem quo ... maiores uostri parauere', Cic. *Div.* 1.72 'ea genera ... in quo ...') and scholars seem quite relaxed about them (see Pease on the latter). It is as if S. had written *seruitium*, 'the slave class' (*OLD* 3a).

opibus coniurationis fretus 'relying on the resources of the conspiracy'; for the sentence-appendix see 19.1n. (*adnitente*).

simul alienum suis rationibus existimans uideri causam ciuium cum seruis fugitiuis communicauisse: the most straightforward way of translating these words is 'as well as reckoning that to have shared the cause of citizens with escaped slaves seemed unhelpful to his calculations' (i.e. an acc. + infin. of which the subject is *causam ... communicauisse*), but *uideri* is arguably pleonastic with *existimans*, which perhaps explains why the usual translation is different: 'as well as reckoning that to be seen to have shared the cause of citizens with escaped slaves <was/would be> unhelpful to his calculations' (i.e. *uideri* is the subject of the acc. + infin. and *esse* or *fore* has to be supplied with *alienum*). Though other renderings of *alienum* are possible (e.g. 'unsuitable': *OLD* 8a), 'unhelpful' (*OLD* 11a) seems the likeliest: Spartacus' slave revolt was fresh in people's memory (30.2n. *Capuae*) and the involvement of slaves would be counter-productive. For *simul* see *OLD* 5a.

57.1 in castra nuntius peruenit: the news would have taken a horse-rider up to five days to deliver (43.1n. *cum*); routine travel would take longer (27.1n. *C. Manlium*); Sumner is prepared to allow up to ten days (216). The following indir. speech, in which *esse* has to be supplied with *patefactam* and *sumptum*, depends on *nuntius*.

quos supra memoraui: at 55.6; for such cross-referencing see 5.7n. (*quae*).

plerique . . . dilabuntur: so too Plut. *Cic.* 22.8, Dio 37.39.2.

reliquos Catilina *per* montes asperos magnis itineribus in agrum Pistoriensem abducit: Pistorium[110] (mod. Pistoia) is about 20 miles WNW of Faesulae along low-lying ground (*BA* Map 41: D2), a journey which would have taken no more than two days, had C. not led his remaining troops across the hills (56.4n.) to avoid detection. *magna itinera* are forced marches (*OLD magnus* 1c); *abducit* = 'withdrew' (*OLD* 2a).

eo consilio uti *per* tramites occulte *per*fugeret in Galliam Transalpinam: we are about to be told (§3) that Metellus Celer, when informed of C.'s intended route by deserters, took up position at the base of the mountains at the point where C. would descend into Gaul. This scenario makes perfect sense if C.'s intention was to cross the Apennines from south to north and descend into the Po Valley at (say) Bononia, thus reaching Cisalpine Gaul (see 56.4n. *Catilina*). Yet S. says that C. was fleeing to *Transalpine* Gaul, which is in another direction altogether; and indeed we are told that he moved his forces WNW to Pistorium for this very purpose ('eo consilio'), suggesting that, naturally enough, he was intending to make for Transalpine Gaul through Liguria along the coastal Via Aemilia Scauri. The contradiction between the present passage and §3 would be removed by Dietsch's deletion of *Transalpinam*, which has the effect of turning the journey to Pistorium into a kind of feint; but it is hard to believe that *Transalpinam* has been wrongly inserted.

per tramites = 'by means of byways' (*tramites . . . transuersa sunt . . . itinera*: Maltby 618). Conceivably S. means that C. was trying to reach the Via Aemilia Scauri not along the principal Via Quinctia towards Pisae (mod. Pisa) but along the more northerly and less obvious route through Luca (mod. Lucca); but that presupposes that S. knew the topography of the area.

---

[110] The place is also referred to as Pistoria or Pistoriae.

57.2 Q. Metellus Celer … in agro Piceno praesidebat: he had previously been despatched there (30.5n.), but returned to Rome late in 63 (Cic. *Fam.* 5.2(2).4 'cum proxime Romam uenisti') before leaving again early in 62 as proconsul of Cisalpine Gaul, which is how he described himself when he wrote to Cicero at the start of the year (*Fam.* 5.1(1).2 'qui prouinciae, qui exercitui praesum, qui bellum gero'). *praesidebat* seems to mean 'had been standing guard' (G&L 158-9 §234): the absolute use (again at e.g. Varro, *LL* 5.90) is not common.

ex difficultate rerum eadem illa existimans quae supra diximus Catilinam agitare: another sentence-appendix: 'reckoning, from the difficulty of his [i.e. C.'s] circumstances, that Catiline was contemplating those same things that we mentioned above'. Since we are about to be told (3) that Celer was informed of C.'s plans by deserters, it seems redundant to be told here that he had already read C.'s mind, something which S. cannot possibly have known. For *agitare* see *OLD* 16a.

57.3 ex perfugis: for the importance of deserters as a source of information see N. J. E. Austin and N. B. Rankov, *Exploratio: military and political intelligence in the Roman world from the Second Punic War to the battle of Adrianople* (1995) 67–73.

castra propere mouit: in anticipating C.'s speed (~ *properanti* below), Celer lives up to his *cognomen* (cf. also Cic. *Cael.* 60). His movement will have been facilitated by the Via Aemilia,[111] which goes NW from Ariminum (mod. Rimini), at the northern edge of Celer's jurisdiction, through Bononia and Mutina (Modena) to Placentia (Piacenza).

sub ipsis radicibus montium consedit, qua illi descensus erat in Galliam properanti 'took up position close to the very base of the mountains, where his [i.e. C.'s] descent would be as he hurried into Gaul' (*OLD sub* 6, *radix* 4b, *consido* 2a). *erat* illustrates the imperfect tense being used of intended actions, as Tac. *A.* 14.45.2 'iter quo damnati ad poenam ducebantur', 'along which the condemned were to be led' (G&L 158 §233); *properanti* resembles the use of dat. pres. participles in 'travelogue' contexts, e.g. Varro, *LL* 5.47 'quae est a foro eunti primore cliuo', Liv. 26.26.2 'sita Anticyra est … laeua parte sinum Corinthiacum intranti'. *sub ipsis radicibus* (*montis*) is a Caesarian expr. (*BG* 7.36.5, *BC* 1.45.6) which later recurs in Livy (36.18.3; cf. 38.20.6). *qua … properanti* is another of S.'s clauses which suggests a hexameter ('qua descensus erat ∪ ∪ – illi properanti'); for the verbal hyperbaton see 28.4n. (*egestate*).

As we have already seen (57.1n. *eo*), Celer's movements make sense if C. is hurrying to reach *Cisalpine* Gaul, but S. has already told us that he was trying to reach *Transalpine* Gaul (1). The contradiction is compounded by

---

[111] To be distinguished from the Via Aemilia Scauri.

S.'s twin statements that Celer had rightly guessed C.'s plans and in any case knew of them from deserters (2-3).

57.4 neque tamen Antonius procul aberat, utpote qui magno exercitu locis aequioribus expedit<us impedit>os in fuga sequeretur 'Yet neither was Antonius far distant, in as much as, unencumbered over more level/ favourable terrain, he was following with his large army those hampered in flight': *locis aequioribus* contrasts with C. and his followers, whose route was 'per montes asperos' (§1).

Reynolds in the OCT gives no hint that there are major problems with this sentence. The MSS read *expeditos*, a term which implies speed and manoeuvrability, either because those so described are light-armed (as, presumably, at 60.4) or lack *impedimenta* or both. It makes no sense to explain Antonius' proximity to C.'s forces if the latter are described as *expeditos* (a difficulty not countered by E. Kraggerud, *SO* 82 (2007) 55-9);[112] Antonius' advantage of 'more level ground' is entirely nullified by the size of his army and by the *impedimenta* which presumably accompanied it. The grammarian Priscian (3.343.22) quotes S.'s sentence but reads nom. *expeditus*, i.e. 'travelling light' (so Shackleton Bailey on Cic. *Att.* 8.9a (160).2 'expeditus enim antecesserat legiones'). The nominative, helpful in one sense, leaves *in fuga* high and dry and *sequeretur* without an object, but Dietsch plausibly suggested that *impeditos* should be inserted. The word could easily have been omitted through parablepsy, and, once it was omitted, *expeditus* changed to *expeditos* to provide an object for *sequeretur*. The result makes good sense ('in as much as, despite his large army, he was travelling light over more level ground and following men hampered in their flight': for the concessive use of the abl. of attendant circumstances see *OLS* 1.855 and n. 63), the chiasmus is attractive (*locis aequioribus expeditus ~ impeditos in fuga*), and there is perhaps another reminiscence of Sisenna (58C/73P 'impeditos expediti ... interficiunt'; cf. 56.3n. *sparos*).

57.5 sed Catilina ... confligere: a typically periodic sentence: subject, *postquam*-clause (including three acc. + infin. constructions), participle (*ratus*), main verb (*statuit*). For the tense of *uidet* see 20.1n. (*Catilina*).

montibus ... ullam spem: *esse* has to be supplied with each acc. + infin., which between them recapitulate the difficulties which S. has enumerated in §§1-4. For *sese* see 1.1n. (*Omnes*).

[112] *utpote qui* + subjunc. is almost always causal (*NLS* 117 §157 (1) (b) *Note*), but W. A. Camps (*CR* 9 (1959) 109) argued that the construction must here have a rare quasi-concessive meaning, which he paralleled at Plaut. *Rud.* 462 and Cic. *Att.* 2.24.4; but the sense is not much improved over that proposed by Kraggerud.

praesidii refers to reinforcements.

optimum factu ratus … temptare: *sc. esse* or *fore* (cf. 32.1, 55.1).

statuit cum Antonio quam primum confligere: S. writes as if C. were presented with a choice between Celer (2–3) and Antonius (4), each of whom was worryingly positioned, and decided that it would be more to his advantage to fight it out with the latter, his former would-be ally (21.3, 26.1).

57.6 huiusce modi orationem habuit: S. could not possibly have known what C. said, if indeed he said anything: the speech is entirely fictitious, although given 'authenticity' by the repetition of phraseology from C.'s earlier speech at 20.2–17 (8 'diuitias, decus, gloriam, praeterea liberta-tem' ~ 20.14; 18 'cum … considero' ~ 20.6; 19 'animus, aetas' ~ 20.10; 19, 21 'uirtus uestra' ~ 20.2). Much of the power of the *hortatio* 'depends on the reader recognizing how entirely conventional it is – and making the reader wonder how so perfectly wicked a man can perform the office of general' (Lendon 148, who on pp. 145–54 discusses pre-battle speeches and provides a vast bibliography).

58.1 Compertum ego habeo, milites, <u>uerba uirtutem</u> non addere: with his first three words (for which cf. 29.1n. *neque exercitus*) the bogus *imperator* affects a military experience which he was scarcely entitled to claim (see also 16.3n. *scilicet*). The theme 'words are superfluous' (as e.g. Thuc. 6.68.1, Xen. *Cyr.* 3.3.50 'no speech of admonition can be so fine that it will all at once make those who hear it good men if they are not good already', Sil. 9.184) is in various forms natural in *hortationes* (Harto Trujillo 107–11); here, as sometimes elsewhere, it functions as a *praeteritio*, since the speech does in fact follow (contrast its closural function at *BJ* 85.50 'plura dicerem, Quirites, si timidis uirtutem uerba adderent: nam strenuis abunde dictum puto'). For the opposite topos see Virg. *Aen.* 10.368 '<u>dictis</u> uirtutem accendit'. *milites*, the most frequent form of address in *hortationes*, is the first of the four vocatives with which the speech is punctuated (cf. §§4, 11, 18).

ex ignauo strenuum: these antonyms (also at Liv. 24.16.11 and [Sall.] *Ep. Caes.* 11.4) were appropriated by Tacitus (*A.* 1.70.3, *H.* 1.62.2, 2.14.3, 4.69.1): see esp. *H.* 2.46.2 'fortes et strenuos … timidos et ignauos', a reworking of our sentence.

neque fortem ex timido: contrast Hor. *Epi.* 2.2.34–6 'praetor | … hortari coepit … | uerbis quae timido quoque possent addere mentem' (where *praetor* = 'general').

oratione imperatoris: C., who had earlier appropriated the symbols of *imperium* (36.1), was called *imperator* ironically by Cicero (*Cat.* 1.5, 10).

58.2 quanta cuiusque … auribus officit: the sentences form an elaborate chiasmus (*animo … in bello ~ neque gloria neque pericula … animi*). C.'s stress on *audacia* (12, 15, 17) will be rewarded (61.1).

animo: dat. with *inest* (cf. 15.5n. *prorsus*).

patere 'to be displayed' (*OLD* 6), as *CLE* 1525c.8 'quanta patet uirtus'. It may be relevant that a battlefield could be described as a *spatium* for the display of *uirtus* (Tac. *Agr.* 8.2 with W.³).

nequiquam hortere: *sc. eum*: '<him> one would exhort in vain' (indefinite or generalising second person subjunctive: 1.6n. *et*). The verb defines the speech as a *hortatio* (20.1n. *in rem*).

58.3 **ego uos quo pauca a̲d̲monerem a̲d̲uocaui, simul uti c̲ausam mei c̲onsilii aperirem:** the combination of *admonerem*, similar in meaning (*OLD* 2a) to *hortari* (cf. Liv. 30.32.5), and *aperirem* is perhaps an allusion to Thuc. 4.126.1 διδαχὴν ἅμα τῇ παρακελεύσει, 'instruction as well as exhortation', instruction being another standard element of *hortationes* (e.g. Thuc. 5.9.2, Xen. *Anab.* 1.7.4, Amm. 23.5.16). Here the two terms itemise the remainder of the speech in reverse (chiastic) order (§§4–7 = *aperirem* and §§8–21 = *monerem*), as is often the case with headline statements: *Arma uirumque* is a classic example (see further R. Nünlist, *The ancient critic at work* (2009) 326–37 on 'reverse order'). For *quo*, varying *uti*, cf. 11.5n.; *consilii* refers to C.'s decision to fight (57.5).

58.4 **Scitis equidem** ...: their earlier knowledge (cf. *attulerit, nequiuerim*) is contrasted with their new awareness (5 'nunc uero ...'). *equidem* is equivalent to *quidem* but is rare with verbs other than first person (Solodow 19–29). Cf. 52.16.

socordia atque ignauia Lentuli quantam ipsi nobisque cladem attulerit: the two subjects of the indir. question have been placed in front of it for emphasis; for the singular verb cf. 39.4n. (*clades*). *ignauia* repeats C.'s complaint of 27.4; for the coupling with *socordia* see 52.29n. For *cladem afferre* cf. Cic. *Phil.* 3.2, *ND* 2.7, Liv. 22.7.7.

quoque modo ... **in Galliam proficisci nequiuerim:** cf. 57.3n. (*qua*). *quoque modo = et quomodo*.

dum ex urbe praesidia opperior: for the expected support cf. 56.4n. (*sperabat*). The retention of the pres. indic. with *dum* in indirect speech is 'extremely rare in classical Latin' (*NLS* 180 §221 *Note iv*).

58.5 **iuxta mecum** 'as much as me' (*OLD iuxta* 2).

58.6 **exercitus** ... **obstant:** a 'situation report', often of a grimly realistic nature, is a standard element of *hortationes* (e.g. Liv. 21.43.4 'dextra laeuaque duo maria claudunt ... circa Padus amnis ... ab tergo Alpes urgent', Curt. 4.14.11 'uentum est eo unde pulsis ne fugae quidem locus est'); compare 20.2n. (*nequiquam*). *ab* and *a* mean 'in the direction of' (*OLD* 24a).

diutius in his locis esse ... **egestas prohibet:** *sc. nos*: an acc. + inf. is the commonest construction with *prohibeo* (*NLS* 142 §187 (*a*) *Note iii*). Since staying put is not an option, they must move – but that means fighting (7).

si maxime animus ferat 'however much the spirit prompts <it>' (*OLD si* 9b, *fero* 31). *fert animus* features in the first line of Ovid's *Metamorphoses*, perhaps its most famous occurrence, but the expr. is also common in prose.

58.7 quōcūmqu(e) īrĕ plăcĕt, fērro iter aperiendum est: the opening hexameter rhythm is followed by another phrase which Virgil seems to echo (*Aen.* 10.372–3 'ferro rumpenda per hostes | est uia': see intro.). Both *quocumque ire* (cf. *Catalepton* 4.1) and *ire placet* (e.g. *Aen.* 11.332) also suit heroic verse. For Livian exs. of *ferro iter aperiendum* and the like see Oakley on 7.33.10.

58.8 quapropter uos moneo uti forti atque parato animo sitis: C. now turns to the exhortative part of his speech (cf. 3 *monerem*), his words again suggesting epic ('quāprōptēr mŏnĕō uōs ūt fōrt(i) ātquĕ părātō'). *forti atque parato animo* is abl. of description; for the two adjs. cf. Cic. *Phil.* 11.35, *Fin.* 4.72, Plancus ap. *Fam.* 10.21a.1, Sen. *Ep.* 57.5, 90.44.

memineritis uos diuitias, decus, gloriam, praeterea libertatem atque patriam in dextris uestris portare: what C.'s followers actually carry in their right hands is their weapon: he means that, if his men want the listed desirables, they must be won by fighting (cf. Hom. *Il.* 15.741, Procop. *Hist.* 3.19.2 = 8.23.21 'it has come to this, that our hope of safety is in our hands'). Compare 20.2, where C. uses a similar expr. but with a different meaning (n. *dominatio*). The rewards of victory are another convention of the *hortatio* (Harto Trujillo 127–31), and the first four items here are repeated from C.'s earlier *hortatio* (20.14). *patria* (again with *libertas* at 11 below: see n.) is the only item shared with Petreius' matching list (59.5n.), where his men too are asked to 'remember' (another topos, e.g. 58.12, Thuc. 4.95.1, 6.68.4).

58.9 si uincimus: the present tense instead of the fut. can be used for 'firm expectations' (*OLS* 1.399–401) and hence it makes the victory seem more of a reality (cf. Tac. *H.* 2.77.2 'si uincimus, honorem ... habebo'); contrast *si ... cesserimus* below.

commeatus abunde, municipia atque coloniae patebunt: the verb is probably to be taken with both cola in a slight syllepsis: 'supplies will be available in abundance, *municipia* and *coloniae* will lie open' (*OLD pateo* 5 and 3); for *abunde patere* cf. Val. Max. 4.4.1, though the sense of the verb there is different again. *municipia atque coloniae* = 'Italy' (17.4n. *ex*).

58.10 si metu cesserimus, eadem illa aduersa fient: cf. Nicias' warning that men 'should realise that, if they failed, they would find everything hostile to them' (Thuc. 6.23.2). *metu cedere* is taken over by Livy (6.24.11, 21.5.12).

neque locus neque amicus quisquam teget quem arma non texerint 'there is neither any place nor any friend that will protect <the man> whom his arms have not [lit. "will not have"] protected' (*OLD tego* 4b).

There is some similarity to Nicias' words at Thuc. 7.77.7 ('it is necessary for you to be brave men, since there is no place nearby where cowards can be saved'). C.'s statement seems to be a generalisation: cowards, simply because they are cowards, can expect no protection.

58.11 pro patria, pro libertate, pro uita: fatherland and freedom are two of the commonest rallying calls in *hortationes* (Harto Trujillo 118–21), often in the mouths of non-Romans (e.g. Tac. *A.* 1.59.6). For *libertas* see also 7.3n. (*adepta*).

illis superuacuaneum est pugnare pro potentia paucorum 'for them it is pointless to fight on behalf of the power of a few': i.e. our opponents lack the appropriate motivation. For *potentia paucorum* cf. 20.7n. (*postquam*).

58.12 quo audacius aggredimini '*Therefore* attack *all the more* boldly': for *quo* doing double duty cf. 1.3n. (*quo*).

memores pristinae uirtutis: in fact it will be C.'s opponents who show themselves mindful of *pristina uirtus* (60.3), an expr. esp. common in Cicero and Caesar (for *memor* cf. *BJ* 49.2, Nep. *Hann.* 12.5 'memor pristinarum uirtutum').

58.13 licuit uobis ... agere, potuistis ... expectare: when so-called 'modal' verbs such as *licet* and *possum* are used with an infin. to express the idea 'could have', they remain in the indic. (*NLS* 92–5 §§122–5).

cum summa turpitudine in exilio aetatem agere: Cicero repeatedly urges exile upon C., who, he said, could not live in Rome without *turpitudo*, a favourite Ciceronian word (see *Cat.* 1.13, 14, 20, 22). C. did in fact pretend at one point to be going into exile (34.2n. *Massiliam*).

amissis bonis alienas opes expectare: editors think that C. is referring principally to inheritance-hunting or *captatio*, although it has been argued that 'there is no evidence that *captatio* existed as a widespread social practice' (E. Champlin, *Final judgments* (1991) 100).

58.14 quia illa foeda atque intoleranda uiris uidebantur '<but> because those seemed foul and intolerable to real men' (adversative asyndeton); *illa* refers to the two options of the previous sentence. *uiris* is to be taken with both *intoleranda* and *uidebantur*, for the meaning 'real men', again at §21 below, cf. *OLD* 3: C. is looking back to his earlier speech (20.11 'quis mortalium cui uirile ingenium est tolerare potest ...?').

haec: i.e. going to war, as the sequence *haec ... bellum* in §15 shows.

58.15 si haec relinquere uultis 'if you want to abandon this course of action': if they want a return to peace, they are going to have to fight and win, since only the winner can end a war.

nemo nisi uictor pace bellum mutauit 'no one except the winner exchanges war for peace' (gnomic perfect: 11.3n. *quam*). *mutare* is regularly followed by an acc. and abl.: the thing given up is sometimes in the abl. (*OLD* 2a), sometimes the acc. (*OLD* 3b), as here and Val. Max. 4.2 *init.*, 5.4.1 'bellum atrox salutari pace mutauit'.

58.16 **in fuga salutem sperare** . . ., **ea uero dementia est:** '*sperare salutem* is mostly poetic and particularly frequent in the *Aeneid*' (Gaertner on Ov. *Ex P.* 1.6.37); the only recurrence in prose is Liv. 22.55.8. For the resumptive use of *ea* see 12.5n. (*proinde*).

cum . . . **auerteris:** another indefinite second person subjunctive (cf. 1.6n. *et*): 'when you turn away'.

58.17 sem*per in* *p*roelio iis m̲a̲x̲i̲m̲u̲m̲ est *p*ericulum qui m̲a̲x̲i̲m̲e̲ ti*m*ent: *semper* in initial position (cf. Tosi 859), assonance and the polyptoton of adj. ~ adv. give a proverbial cast to C.'s statement, which is the converse of the commonplace *fortissimum quemque tutissimum* (*BJ* 87.2), to which he turns in his next sentence.

audacia pro muro habetur: adversative asyndeton: '<but> boldness is regarded as being like a wall' (*OLD pro* 9, *habeo* 24c), as perhaps in the imitation at Tac. *H.* 3.73.3 'fuere qui . . . audaciam pro latebra haberent'. Some render 'is like a wall' (Batstone):[113] the sense is good but *haberi* seems not to be equivalent to *esse* (the exs. at 6.3n. (*sicuti*) are slightly different). Others compare 1.4, where *habetur* is said to mean 'is a possession'; but this is disputable (see n.). *habetur* in the sense of 'is regarded (as)' (*OLD* 24c) may at first sight seem weak in the context of a *hortatio*,[114] but can be explained as alluding to the status of C.'s statement as a truism (for which see W.[3] on Tac. *Agr.* 30.1) and thus emphasising its applicability. *murus* is an esp. common metaphor in Latin (cf. *TLL* 8.1687.60–1689.14), though nowhere else applied to *audacia* except in Hegesippus (5.4.1 'notum esset in bello plurimum audaciam posse quae uel sola sibi murus est'), on whom see further 52.35n. (*intra*).

58.18 **Cum uos** . . . **et cum facta uestra** . . .: Virgil again echoes (*Aen.* 10.369 'uos et . . . facta').

magna me spes . . . **tenet:** cf. Cic. *Clu.* 7 'magna me spes tenet', *TD* 1.97.

58.19 C. opened his speech by saying that a verbal *hortatio* would neither induce *uirtus* nor make the timid brave (§1); he ends by saying that in his own case it is his men's *uirtus* which acts as a *hortatio*, as does the constraint which makes the timid brave (ring composition).

praeterea necessitudo, quae etiam timidos f̲ortes f̲acit: with *necessitudo* we must understand *me hortatur*: the statement 'the constraint encourages me', which otherwise would seem counter-intuitive, is explained by *quae* . . . *facit*. By *necessitudo* C. means the absence of any alternative to fighting, as outlined at 57.5: see e.g. Hom. *Il.* 8.56–7 'fewer in number, but even so

---

[113] So too L. Langerwerf, '"To have daring is like a barrier": Cicero and Sallust on Catiline's *audacia*', *G&R* 62 (2015) 155–66, at 163.

[114] No one previously seems to have queried the text, but Professor M. D. Reeve suggests *audaciam pro muro habete*.

they were eager to fight in battle from dire necessity for their women and children', Thuc. 6.68.4.

58.20 nam multitudo hostium ne circumire queat prohibent angustiae loci: rather than an acc. + infin., as at 6 above, C. here constructs *prohibere* with a *ne*-clause (*OLD* 4c); *multitudo hostium* has been placed in front of the clause because, as implied by *nam*, the words constitute an elliptical explanation of *timidos* in the previous sentence: 'As for the large numbers of the enemy, <which are a reason why some of you may be afraid,> the narrowness of the place prevents them from being able to encircle us'.[115] *angustiae loci* (*-orum*) occurs often in military narratives.

58.21 quod si uirtuti uestrae Fortuna inuiderit: C. knows very well that, since his side is heavily outnumbered, the *uirtus* which he has just praised (19) will be of no avail: of course he cannot say this outright; instead he mentions a potential scenario in which his men's *uirtus* will be so exceptional that it will attract the proverbial envy of Fortune (for which see Horsfall on Virg. *Aen.* 11.43).

cauete inulti animam amittatis: *sc. ne*: 'take care that you do not lose your lives unavenged'. The injunction (cf. 33.5n. *neue*) is a commonplace, e.g. Virg. *Aen.* 2.670 'numquam omnes hodie moriemur inulti' with Horsfall.

neu ᴬcapti potius ᴮsicuti ᶜpecora trucidemini quam ᶜuirorum ᴮmore ᴬpugnantes … relinquatis: the contrast between *pecora* and *uirorum*, emphasised by the chiasmus, recalls the contrast between *homines* and *pecora* which the author himself drew at the start of the work (1.1). The relationship between the two passages, rather than suggesting transference or 'automimesis' (for which see Intro. p. 10), seems to resonate with the dual nature of C. himself, a man of evil disposition and wicked acts who is nevertheless capable of a certain heroism in his final moments.

As S. is alluding to Thuc. 2.51.4 ὥσπερ τὰ πρόβατα ἔθνῃσκον, where the first three words are 'regular Greek for "like sheep"' (Hornblower ad loc.), *pecora* is more likely to mean 'sheep' here (as Virg. *G.* 3.554) rather than simply 'animals' (as at 1.1). 'Killed like sheep' (S. has substituted *trucidemini* for the Greek 'died') occurs in extant Latin first here and at *H.* 2.96 'uicem pecorum obtruncabantur' but becomes common later (W.[1] on Vell. 119.2). Fussell describes how in 1917 French soldiers being marched up to the line 'frequently made loud *baa*-ing noises' in imitation of sheep being led to the slaughter (240).

cruentam atque luctuosam uictoriam hostibus relinquatis '(rather than) leave a bloody and grievous victory to the enemy'. C.'s followers take him at his word (61.7 'neque … incruentam uictoriam', 9 'luctus'). For *luctuosam uictoriam* cf. Amm. 14.5.2.

---

[115] It is more usual to understand a different ellipse, e.g. '<I say nothing of their superior numbers,> for …' (Summers ad loc.).

59.1–3 Haec ubi dixit ... habuisse dicebatur: his *hortatio* finished, C. arrays his troops; it is perhaps more usual for historians to place the array before the *hortatio* (see Lendon 43–5), an ordering which S. follows with C.'s opponents in §§4–6, thus effecting a chiastic arrangement overall.

59.1–3 signa canere iubet 'he ordered the trumpet calls to sound' (*OLD canere* 6d). *signa canere* is as old as Acc. *Trag.* 385R³ 'signa ... canere ... imperat'; it also recurs at *Aen.* 10.310 in the passage where Virgil seems to be alluding to S. (see intro. n.). *signa* is repeated below (2) in a different sense, the figure *distinctio* (14.3n. *conuicti*).

in locum aequum deducit: the battle was fought early in 62 (Dio 37.39.1). For the expr. cf. *BJ* 52.5 'in aequum locum deducit', *Bell. Hisp.* 5.7.

remotis omnium equis **quo militibus ex**aequato periculo a̱nimus a̱mplior **esset** 'having removed everyone's horses so that, with the danger made equal, the soldiers should have greater courage'. C. is imitating Caesar (*BG* 1.25.1 'Caesar primum suo, deinde *omnium* ex conspectu *remotis equis*, ut *aequato* omnium *periculo* spem fugae tolleret'). Although the reason is different, Virgil may again have S. in mind (*Aen.* 10.366–7 'dimittere ... equos').

ipse pedes: like Agricola (Tac. *Agr.* 35.4 'pedes ante uexilla constitit'). *pedes* is a noun used adjectivally, 'on foot' (*OLD* 1).

pro loco atque copiis 'having regard to the area and his forces' (*OLD pro* 14).

59.2 uti planities erat inter sinistros montes et ab dextra rupe asperă: this is a tricky passage. The principal MSS are agreed in reading *rupe aspera*, but some late MSS offer *rupem asperam*. The fact that the former is the more difficult reading, together with the manuscript unanimity, strongly supports *rupe aspera*; if that is correct, *aspera* must be neut. acc. plur. after *inter*. But what is the resulting meaning? Substantival *aspera* is frequently used of 'rough/difficult things' in a wide variety of contexts (e.g. *BJ* 89.3 'maiora et magis aspera aggredi'; *TLL* 2.812.61–813.9), including places (e.g. Mela 3.40 'in asperiora deuenit', Plin. *NH* 21.53 'asperis et siluestribus'; *TLL* 2.808.81–809.10); *rupe*, which means 'a steep rocky cliff, crag' (*OLD*), will be an abl. of cause ('places difficult because of a/the cliff'), although it is possible that *ab dextra*, usually understood as a set phrase = 'on the right' (as *BJ* 50.4; *OLD dextera*¹ 3), is to be taken with *rupe* and that *ab* is causal (as Vitr. 2.5.2 'saxa ... lenta sunt ab umore'; *OLD* 15). We might translate: 'because there was level ground between the leftward mountains and the hazards of a cliff on the right'. If this reasoning is correct, it is clearly very interesting that, as emended by Madvig, *asper* is again used of terrain and accompanied by an abl. at *Aen.* 10.366 'aspera aquis natura loci'. *uti* (27.2n.) in the sense of 'because', mainly a feature of early Latin which dies out after Plautus and Terence, is said to be a deliberate archaism here; the quasi-causal use at 31.7 (n. *Catilina*) is appreciably distinct (E. Karakasis, *Terence and the language of Roman comedy* (2005) 56–7). The site of the battle is traditionally identified as Campo Tizzoro, a short distance north of mod. Pistoia, but S.'s description has every sign of the conventional: 'the picture of a wide plain surrounded by hills is a stereotype' (Oakley on Liv. 9.2.6–8, p. 53) – S. has simply substituted a cliff for one set of hills.

reliquarum signa in subsidio artius collocat 'he stationed the units of the remainder [*sc.* of the cohorts] in closer formation in reserve' (for the metonymical sense of *signa* see *OLD* 11). For the importance of keeping troops in reserve see W.[3] on Tac. *Agr.* 37.1.

59.3 centuriones omnes et lectos euocatos 'all the centurions and selected veterans'; the two categories were evidently natural partners (Caes. *BC* 1.3.3, 1.17.3 'centurionibus euocatisque', 3.53.1). The MSS read *centuriones omnes lectos et euocatos*, but Servius, when quoting the passage, omits *lectos* and presents the remaining words in a different order. Since *centuriones omnes* appears to be contradicted by *lectos*, some edd. follow Servius and omit the latter; others make *omnes lectos et euocatos* stand in apposition to *centuriones*, which seems implausible. E. Courtney (*Prometheus* 38 (2012) 153), following Vretska's suggested *centuriones lectos et omnes euocatos*, proposed the transposition of *lectos* and *et*, which is both simpler and, on the assumption that *euocatus* means 'veteran' rather than 'specially summoned', better in sense: the centurions were self-selecting but the veterans were a more varied group and C. had to choose the best.

optimum quemque armatum 'all the best men who were armed'. The implication seems to be that not all the best were armed (cf. 56.3).

Faesulanum quendam: editors suggest that this may have been P. Furius (50.4n.).

curare 'to take charge, be in command', as e.g. *BJ* 60.1, 100.2 (*OLD* 4); a Sallustianism taken over by Tacitus (Goodyear on *A.* 1.31.2).

colonis: see 28.4n. (*nonnullos*).

propter aquilam assistit quam bello Cimbrico C. Marius in exercitu habuisse dicebatur 'took up position alongside the eagle which Marius was said to have had ...' (*OLD assisto* 1a). During the long war with the Cimbri and Teutoni, Marius as consul in 104 BC established the eagle as the emblem to be carried by each Roman legion (Plin. *NH* 10.16; cf. *OLD aquila* 2a). C.'s eagle was evidently well known and is twice mentioned by Cicero (*Cat.* 1.24, 2.13). It was silver and had been kept securely in C.'s house, until he sent it ahead with the armed men with whom he joined up at Forum Aurelium in November (43.1n. *cum*); its association with Marius would have appealed especially to those who had been dispossessed by the

Sullan veterans and who typically had been supporters of Marius (Berry, *CC* 27–8, 105–6).

59.4 At ex altera parte: *ex altera parte* is a set phrase, but, combined with *at* and used as a transitional formula, it occurs in *Bell. Alex.* 40.2, Liv. 3.11.1, 10.29.3. Likewise *ex alia parte* is a set phrase, but, in the form *at parte ex alia*, occurs in Catull. 64.251, Cic. *Arat.* 367, Virg. *Aen.* 10.362 and a few later authors. The likelihood is that the latter formula had occurred in Ennius (Skard, *ES* 13–14).

pedibus aeger explains *quod... nequibat*, which in turn explains the main clause. According to Dio (37.39.4) Antonius only pretended to be incapacitated, to avoid having to confront his former associate (21.3n.).

M. Petreio legato: Petreius, Antonius' deputy or staff officer (*OLD legatus* 2), was praised by Cicero for his role in the battle (*Sest.* 12). His praetorship (6 below) may have fallen in 64 (Brennan 2.753 and n. 420); between 55 and 49 he was legate under Pompey in Spain; and in 46 he was killed in a bizarre death-pact with King Juba of Numidia, whose kingdom became the province of Africa Nova under the governorship of S. (*MRR* 2.161, 220, 268, 298, 302, 600).

59.5 quas tumulti causa conscripserat: a *tumultus* was a military emergency (*OLD* 2a), usually associated with an uprising in Gaul (40.6n. *pollicitos*). The expr. *tumultūs causa* has every appearance of a set phrase (Liv. 4.27.1, 40.28.10 'tumultus causa conscriptos'), *tumultūs* being the regular gen. sing.; it is also the reading of the MSS here, but *tumulti* is an archaic form found quite commonly in early drama (see *OLD*) and Nonius quotes both our passage and Acc. 485R³ as exs. of *tumulti causa* (484, 489).

in subsidiis: see above (2n. *reliquarum*).

equo circumiens: the ideal general should ride around on horseback to encourage and direct his men as appropriate, according to the first-century AD military writer Onasander (33.6).[116]

unum quemque nominans appellat: 'an ancient technique of encouragement, universal in military historiography' (Horsfall on Virg. *Aen.* 11.731, with exs. from Hom. *Il.* 10.68 onwards, e.g. Thuc. 7.69.2 ἕνα ἕκαστον ἀνεκάλει, ... ἐπονομάζων ... αὐτοὺς ὀνομαστί, 'he called on each one, ... addressing them by name'). See also 21.4 'unum quemque nominans'.

hortatur, rogat ut meminerint ...: *hortatur* defines the *ut*-clause as a summary *hortatio* (20.1n. *in rem*).

contra latrones inermos: *latro*, an extremely common term of abuse (*OLD* 2b), is appropriately directed at opponents whose aim was widespread pillage (e.g. 20.14, 37.6, 57.1) and whose numbers included actual

---

[116] For whom see C. Petrocelli, *Onasandro. Il generale. Manuale per l'esercizio del comando* (2008).

bandits (28.4); Cicero likewise applied the term to C. and his followers (e.g. 1.23 and Dyck's n., 1.33, 2.24). *inermos* was nothing less than the truth (56.3).

pro patria, pro liberis, pro aris atque focis suis certare: appeals to children and to altars and hearths were regular (Oakley on Liv. 8.10.4 and 9.12.6, with many exs.); for *patria* cf. 58.11n.

59.6 amplius annos triginta ... in exercitu fuerat: Cicero (*Sest.* 12) praises the *mirificus usus in re militari* of Petreius, who resembles Germanicus' deputy at Tac. *A.* 1.64.4 'quadragesimum id stipendium Caecina parendi aut imperandi habebat'. For the elliptical use of *amplius* = 'more than' see *OLD* 2. A *tribunus militum* was one of six senior officers attached to a legion (*OLD tribunus* 2b); a *praefectus* was the commander of a unit of (often auxiliary) troops (*OLD* 3a); for *legatus* see 4n. above.

plerosque ipsos factaque eorum fortia nouerat: *fortia facta* (again at *BJ* 53.8, 85.4, 85.21, *H.* 2.79) is a common expr. in prose and verse and at home in epic (Skard, *ES* 35–6): see esp. Virg. *Aen.* 10.369 'per uos et *fortia facta*', where there is the same coordination with persons. The recollection of previous victories is a topos of the *hortatio* (Harto Trujillo 111–14).

accendebat: although the verb is commonly found in such contexts, note once again Virg. *Aen.* 10.368.

60.1 ubi omnibus rebus exploratis Petreius tuba signum dat 'when after a full reconnoitre ...' (for the historic present see 20.1n. *Catilina*). As also below (see nn.), S. seems to have in mind Caesar's *De Bello Gallico*: for *omnibus rebus exploratis* cf. *BG* 4.21.2; *tuba signum dare* is common in Caesar: see esp. *BG* 7.81.3 'clamore exaudito dat tuba signum'. P.'s expertise (cf. 59.6) contrasts with the seeming indecision of C. (59.1 'paululum commoratus').

60.2 postquam eo uentum est unde a ferentariis proelium committi posset 'After the point had been reached from which the battle could be started by the *ferentarii*'; the *unde*-clause is consecutive (*OLD eo²* 2). Although *proelium committere* is regular (*OLD committo* 8a), note esp. Caes. *BG* 7.88.1. *ferentarii* were so called because of the portable nature of their weaponry (Varro, *LL* 7.57 'a ferendo' and De Melo ad loc.; Maltby 228–9). In classical Latin the term occurs also at Cato, *Mil.* fr. 26 Manuwald, Plaut. *Trin.* 456 (metaphorical), Tac. *A.* 12.35.3.

maximo clamore [cum] infestis signis concurrunt: 'One should send the army into battle shouting', instructed Onasander, 'and sometimes at a run' (29.1). For shouting see further W.[3] on Tac. *Agr.* 34.1 and W.[5] on Tac. *A.* 4.48.2. *infestis signis* (always in this order apart from Cic. *Har. Resp.* 47) is a very common set phrase (Oakley on Liv. 7.37.7): 'with standards at the offensive'. The phrase is never accompanied by *cum*, which was deleted by Dietsch and emended to *cuncti* by Steuding. *concurrunt* is to be expected in any battle description (*OLD* 3) but again note Virg. *Aen.* 10.361.

pila omittunt, gladiis res geritur: C. again imitates Caesar (*BG* 7.88.3 'nostri omissis pilis gladiis rem gerunt' with Krebs' n.), although the forgoing of *pila* was a commonplace (see also Oakley on Liv. 6.12.8). *gladiis res geritur* and synonymous expressions are standard in battle descriptions: see Oakley on Liv. 9.41.18 'gladiis geritur res', where the hexametrical rhythm (derived from Enn. *Ann.* 248) makes one wonder whether S. has deliberately transposed his last two words to avoid the metrical sequence $- \mid - - \mid - \cup \cup \mid - \cup \cup \mid - -$.

60.3 ụeterani pristinae ụirtutis memores: these are P.'s veterans (59.5), although it was C.'s followers who had been urged to remember their former bravery (58.12).

illi: the Catilinarians.

maxima ui certatur: the verb is frequent in Ennius and the impersonal passive is 'the language of military historians' (Harrison on Virg. *Aen.* 10.355, where *certatur* occurs).

60.4   cum expeditis in prima acie uersari: cf. *BJ* 46.7 'ipse cum expeditis cohortibus ... apud primos erat' (of Metellus). C.'s activities are described in a series of historic infinitives (6.4n. *igitur*).

laborantibus succurrere, integros pro sauciis arcessere, omnia prouidere: the good general should 'fill up gaps, transpose a company if necessary, bring aid to the wearied, anticipate the crisis, the hour, and the outcome' (Onas. 33.6); for *omnia prouidere* cf. Liv. 3.63.3 'prouidere omnia'.

multum ipse pugnare: 'The general should fight cautiously rather than boldly, or should keep away altogether from a hand-to-hand fight with the enemy' (Onas. 33.1).

saepe hostem ferire: like the Roman soldiers of old (7.6 'hostem ferire').

strenui militis et boni imperatoris officia simul exsequebatur: C. had earlier promised his followers that he would gladly fill either of these roles (20.16); in his present desperate circumstances he combines both of them (cf. W.² on Vell. 79.1, 85.5). The change to the imperfect tense indicates that this sentence sums up the actions of the preceding historic infinitives (Chausserie-Laprée 481).

60.5   contra ac ratus erat 'otherwise than he had thought' (*OLD contra* 10c, *atque* 13b): the phrase underlines the *para prosdokian* (Intro. pp. 14–15).

magna ui tendere: the verb combines the notions of pressing ahead and straining with effort (*OLD* 8, 12); the combination of *magna* and *ui* is very common and appears as early as Enn. *Ann.* 236; an Ennian source may even be suggested by Virg. *Aen.* 12.917 'qua *ui tendat* in hostem'.

cohortem praetoriam: the general's personal bodyguard (*OLD praetorius* 1a).

in medios hostes inducit: military language, e.g. Liv. 4.32.10 'peditum-
que aciem ... in hostem inducit' (*OLD induco* 2a), but perhaps too the
source of a varied allusion by Virg. *Aen.* 10.379 'medius ... in hostes'.

eosque perturbatos atque alios alibi resistentes interficit: both participles refer to the same group of men (*eos*); *alios* is in apposition to *eos*
and, when taken with *alibi*, is explanatory of *perturbatos*: 'and killed them,
disrupted as they were, and yet resisting, some in one place, others in
another' (*OLD atque* 9). The point of the sentence, as is made clear at 61.3
below, is that, although the men in the centre were dislodged, they all
fought back.

utrimque ex lateribus: as if *ex utroque latere*, 'from each of the two flanks'.

60.6 in primis pugnantes cadunt: front-line fighting features as early as
Homer (*Il.* 9.709 αὐτὸς ἐνὶ πρώτοισι μάχεσθαι). 'It is a fine thing for a brave
man to die when he has fallen among the front ranks while fighting for his
homeland' (Tyrtaeus 10.1–2, trans. D. E. Gerber); also e.g. *Anth. Pal.*
7.304.4, 541.1.

60.7 <Catilina>, postquam ... uidet: *sc. esse* with both *fusas* and *reliquum*.
If C.'s name had been abbreviated to *ca*, it might have been interpreted as
an abortive dittography of *cadunt* and hence omitted. For the tense of *uidet*
(also at §5 above) see 20.1n. (*Catilina*).

memor generis atque pristinae suae dignitatis: C. had spoken proudly
of his background (31.7) and was sensitive about his *dignitas* (35.3n.
quod).

in confertissimos hostes incurrit: rushing into dense ranks of the
enemy is something of a topos: perhaps the most famous instance is the
deuotio of Decius Mus (Liv. 8.9.9 'se in medios hostes immisit'), but it was
not confined to Romans (e.g. Liv. 27.49.4 'se in cohortem Romanam
immisit. ibi ... pugnans cecidit', of Hasdrubal, Tac. *A.* 2.11.3 'ipse
densissimos irrumpens', of Chariovalda); again note esp. *Aen.* 10.379
'densos prorumpit in hostes'. *conferti hostes* (again at *BJ* 98.1) and variants
thereon are a staple of Livian narrative, though not exclusively (cf. e.g.
Caes. *BG* 5.44.4 'quaeque hostium pars confertissima est uisa, eam
irrumpit').

pugnans confoditur: in suffering the fate he had intended for Cicero
(28.1 'confodere'), C. dies the kind of death he had urged upon his men
(58.21 'uirorum more pugnantes').

**61.1 confecto proelio, tum uero cerneres quanta audacia ... fuisset
in exercitu Catilinae:** *tum uero* is regularly used for dramatic effect after
expressions of time (e.g. *BJ* 106.6 'quod postquam auditum est, tum uero
ingens metus nostros inuadit'; *OLD tum* 6a), esp. an abl. abs.: see
Chausserie-Laprée 520–31 (525 for this passage). The vividness is maintained by *cerneres*, yet another ex. of the second-person subjunctive (1.6n.
et, 2.3n. *neque*), which here invites the reader to visualise the scene and

draw inferences from it (Gilmartin 115–16):[117] S. begins with a panorama
(2 *quisque*), zooms in on the central area (3 *pauci*), then focusses climac-
tically on the leader in the far distance (4 *Catilina*). The *audacia* shown by
C.'s army is that which he demanded in his pre-battle speech (58.2, 12, 15,
17). *animi uis* was a feature of C. himself (5.1).

61.2 fere **^Aquem quisque** **^Buiuus** **^Cpugnando locum** **^Dceperat,** **^Aeum**
^Bamissa^anima **^Ccorpore** **^Dtegebat** 'in most cases the place which each
man when alive had seized by fighting was the one which he was protecting
with his body when his breath had left him' (*OLD tego* 4b).[118] Aided by the
use of *corpore* rather than *cadauere*, the sentence is partly a conceit, namely
that the men continued to perform their duty even after death; but it also
makes the more important point that they had not been dislodged from
the position which they had seized by their bravery in the first place (the
contrast is with *pauci ... diuersi ... conciderant* below): cf. Plaut. *Amph.* 238–
41 'sed fugam in se tamen nemo conuortitur | nec recedit loco quin statim
rem gerat: | animam amittunt prius quam loco demigrent: | quisque ut
steterat iacet optinetque ordinem'. Cf. Dio 37.40.1 ἐν χώρᾳ πάντες ἔπεσον,
'everyone fell at his post'. *fere* introduces a generalisation (*OLD* 3). *amissa
anima*, pointedly juxtaposed with *corpore*, recalls not only C.'s speech
(58.21) but also Manlius' earlier words about freedom and death (33.4).

**61.3 pauci autem ... paulo diuersius – sed omnes tamen aduersis
uulneribus – conciderant** 'however, a few ... had fallen across a slightly
wider area, but all of them with frontal wounds nevertheless' (*OLD concido*¹
1b). *diuersius ... conciderant* looks back to 60.5 'perturbatos ... interficit',
while *aduersis uulneribus* (an abl. of attendant circumstances) looks back to
resistentes. For frontal wounds cf. e.g. *BJ* 85.29, *H.* 1.76.1, Caes. *BG* 5.35.8,
Tac. *A.* 1.49.3 'pectoribus ... honesta uulnera'; *paulo* provides further
extenuation.

quos ... disiecerat: cf. 60.5.

61.4 <u>C</u>atilina uero longe a suis inter hostium <u>c</u>adauera repertus est:
cadauera looks back to 60.7 *pugnans*: C. had killed these men himself, thus

[117] The visual is a significant element in most descriptions of battlefields: see e.g.
Xen. *Ages.* 2.14 'When the battle had ended, it was possible to see (θεάσασθαι),
at the place where they had clashed, the ground stained with blood, the bodies
of friends and enemies lying alongside each other ...'. For the technique of
visualisation or *enargeia* see e.g. A. D. Walker, '*Enargeia* and the spectator in
Greek historiography', *TAPA* 123 (1993) 353–77, A. Zangara, *Voir l'histoire:
théories anciennes du récit historique* (2007), L. Huitink, 'Enactivism, *enargeia* and
the ancient readerly imagination', in M. Anderson et al. (edd.), *Distributed
cognition in classical antiquity* (2019) 169–89. For our episode cf. F. Berardi,
'L'*ekphrasis* della battaglia in Sall. *Cat.* 56–61 tra modelli letterari
e insegnamento retorico', *Pan* 10 (2021) 33–51.
[118] *pugnando* (cf. 7.7n. *quas*) indicates that *locum ceperat* does not mean merely 'had
taken up position' (*contra TLL* 3.320.64–5 and perhaps also the imitation at
Flor. 2.12(4.1).12 'quem quis in pugnando ceperat locum').

achieving the avenged death which he had urged upon his followers
(58.21).

ferociamque animi quam habuerat u̲iuus in u̲ultu retinens: for C.'s
defiance cf. 5.7 'animus ferox'; for the topos 'he died as he lived' see
55.6n. (*dignum*); for seeming to retain in death one's spirit in life cf.
Ascon. 90.3 'caput etiam tum plenum animae et spiritus', Val. Max. 9.2.1
'modo non uultum ac spiritum retinentia' (both of Marius Gratidianus:
cf. 15.2n. *timens*), Ov. *Met.* 13.478, Curt. 10.10.12, Luc. 8.665–6, Sil. 5.673,
13.733–4. Tacitus alludes to our passage in his description of Asinius
Gallus (*A.* 1.12.4 'Pollionis ... Asinii patris ferociam retineret').

61.5 postremo sums up (*OLD* 4) after the three scenes of death itemised in §§2–4 (cf. 61.1n.): the fact was that *everyone* died.

ex omni copia: C.'s forces.

ingenuus 'free-born' (*OLD* 2a).

61.6 ita cuncti suae hostiumque uitae iuxta pepercerant 'to such an
extent had everyone shown the same consideration for their own lives as
for those of their enemies' (*OLD iuxta* 2, *parco* 4). The statement is ironical,
meaning the opposite of what it says: the Catilinarians had been so intent
on killing the enemy that they knowingly ended up being killed themselves. Cf. App. *BC* 2.7.23, Dio 37.40.1 (numbering the dead at 3,000).

**61.7 Neque tamen exercitus populi Romani laetam aut incruentam
uictoriam adeptus erat:** after focussing on the *exercitus Catilinae* in §§1–6,
S. ends the monograph by concentrating on the *exercitus populi Romani* (~ 9
'per omnem exercitum') and the costly nature of its victory (cf. *tamen*): this
was the type of victory which C. had urged on his men (58.21 'cruentam
atque luctuosam uictoriam hostibus relinquatis'). Livy will often end
a battle description with a similar comment (see e.g. Liv. 7.8.7 'nec
Romanis incruenta uictoria fuit' with Oakley's n.; for the opposite see
W.[3] on Tac. *Agr.* 35.2). *laeta uictoria* is also something of a formula (e.g.
Liv. 10.36.15 'ne Romanis quidem laeta uictoria fuit'), occurring first at
Hor. *S.* 1.1.8, a passage with other examples of military (perhaps
Sallustian) language. *incruentus* is found first here and at *BJ* 92.4.

61.8 qui ... uisendi aut spoliandi gratia processerant: the
Carthaginians react similarly after Cannae (Liv. 22.51.5 'postero die ...
ad spolia legenda foedamque etiam hostibus spectandam stragem insis-
tunt'); for the desire of seeing a battlefield cf. esp. Tac. *H.* 2.70.1; for
looting cf. e.g. Liv. 32.12.10 'Romani ... insecuti caedentes spoliantesque
caesos', 37.44.3 'postero die spoliabant corpora caesorum' (also next n.).

uoluentes hostilia cadauera: *hostilia*, rather than the more usual *hostium*
(as 4 above), suggests generic classification (as Val. Max. 7.6.5 'congerie
hostilium cadauerum'; cf. Virg. *Aen.* 3.407 'hostilis facies') and hence
underlines the fact that these corpses belong to the *enemy* – which in
turn sets up the shock (παρὰ προσδοκίαν, *para prosdokian*) that amongst

them are found one's *relatives and friends*. Such shocks are associated esp. with civil wars (cf. Tac. *H.* 3.25.2, [Sen.] *Epig.* 72(69P).17–18 'dum legit exuuias hostiliaque arma reuellit, | fraternos uultus oraque maesta uidet', 73(70P).5–7) and emphasise the terrible nature of the Bellum Catilinae at the conclusion of the monograph. *uoluentes* is a particularly good detail.

pars instead of repeating *alii*, as often (2.1n. *igitur*). Both words are in apposition to *multi* and form the centre of a chiasmus.

fuere ... **qui** is further variation, as *BJ* 32.3–4 'fuere qui ... alii ... pars ...'.

61.9 laetitia, maeror, luctus atque gaudia agitabantur: the chiastic arrangement of the emotions counterpoints the confusion amongst those experiencing them (cf. *uarie*); for *agitare* = 'to experience, feel' cf. 48.1. A favoured clausula (∪ ∪ ∪ – – ∪, resolved cretic + trochee: K–K 169) features at the work's end.

SELECT BIBLIOGRAPHY

For older scholarship on Sallust the standard work is A. D. Leeman, *A systematical bibliography of Sallust (1879–1964)* (Leiden 1965). More recent are the companion website (2010) to Ramsey's commentary and the Oxford Bibliography Online (2011) by A. Ring.

COMMENTARIES AND EDITIONS

The following have been consulted:[1]

Capes, W. W. (1897). Oxford
Cook, A. M. (1884). London
Kurfess, A. (^{3}1957). Leipzig
McGushin, P. (1977). Leiden
Mariotti, I. (2007). Bologna
Merivale, C. (1870). London
Neatby, T. M. and Hayes, B. J. (1908 [?]). London
Ramsey, J. T. (1984, ^{2}2007). Oxford [referred to simply as 'Ramsey']
Ramsey, J. T. (2013). Vol. I: Loeb Classical Library 116. Cambridge, MA/London
Reynolds, L. D. (1991). Oxford
Summers, W. C. (1900). Cambridge
Vretska, K. (1976). Heidelberg

I have referred freely to standard commentaries on other texts but without providing bibliographical details here.

OTHER WORKS

As a general rule, works are referred to by author's name and page-number only. Where an author is responsible for several works, these are distinguished either by an abbreviated title or by date. Where reference is given to a reprinted work, full details of the original publication will be found in the following list.

Adams, J. N. (1973). 'The vocabulary of the speeches in Tacitus' historical works', *BICS* 20.124–44
(1982). *The Latin sexual vocabulary.* London [*LSV*]
(2013). *Social variation and the Latin language.* Cambridge [*SVLL*]

---

[1] The commentary by G. Garbugino (1998) came to my attention too late to be consulted.

(2016). *An anthology of informal Latin, 200 BC–AD 900.* Cambridge [*AIL*]

(2021). *Asyndeton and its interpretation in Latin literature.* Cambridge [*AILL*]

(2024). 'Was classical (late republican) Latin a "standard language"?', *TPS* 122.366–462

Allély, A. (2012). *La déclaration d'hostis sous la république romaine.* Bordeaux

Batstone, W. W. (2010). *Sallust:* Catiline's Conspiracy, The Jugurthine War, Histories. Oxford

Berry, D. H. (2020). *Cicero's* Catilinarians. Oxford [*CC*]

Berti, E. (2018). *Lo stile e l'uomo: quattro epistole letterarie di Seneca.* Pisa

Brennan, T. C. (2000). *The praetorship in the Roman republic.* Vols. 1–2. Oxford

Brunt, P. A. (1988). *The fall of the Roman republic and related essays.* Oxford

Cadoux, T. J. (2005). 'Catiline and the Vestal Virgins', *Historia* 54.162–79

Chausserie-Laprée, J.-P. (1969). *L'expression narrative chez les historiens latins.* Paris

Cornell, T. J. (1995). *The beginnings of Rome: Italy and Rome from the Bronze Age to the Punic Wars (c. 1000–264 BC).* London [*BR*]

Courtney, E. (1999). *Archaic Latin prose.* Atlanta [*ALP*]

(2003). *The fragmentary Latin poets.* Oxford [*FLP*]

Crawford, J. W. (1994). *M. Tullius Cicero: the fragmentary speeches.* 2nd edn. Atlanta

de Melo, W. and Scullion, S. (edd.) (forthcoming). *Oxford handbook of Greek and Latin textual criticism.* Oxford

Drogula, F. K. (2015). *Commanders and command in the Roman republic and early empire.* Chapel Hill [*CC*]

(2019). *Cato the Younger.* Oxford [*CY*]

Drummond, A. (1995). *Law, politics and power: Sallust and the execution of the Catilinarian conspirators. Historia* Einzelschriften 93. Stuttgart

Duursma, G. [see under Funari and Duursma, below]

Earl, D. C. (1961). *The political thought of Sallust.* Cambridge [*PTS*]

(1967). *The moral and political tradition of Rome.* London [*MPTR*]

Eckert, A. and Thein, A. (edd.) (2019). *Sulla: politics and reception.* Berlin/Boston

Epstein, D. F. (1987). *Personal enmity in Roman politics 218–43 BC.* London/New York

Eyben, E. (1993). *Restless youth in ancient Rome.* London/New York

Fraenkel, E. (1951). Review of M. Chouet, *Les lettres de Salluste à César* (1950), *JRS* 41.192–4

Funari, R. (2016). 'Outlines for a protohistory of Sallust's text', in J. Velaza (ed.), *From the protohistory to the history of the text* 141–64. Frankfurt am Main

Funari, R. and Duursma, G. (2019). *Lectissimus pensator verborum. Tre studi su Sallustio. Fonti sulla vita e fortuna a cura di Gerard Duursma.* Bologna [*LPV*]

Fussell, P. (1975). *The Great War and modern memory.* London/Oxford/New York

Garcea, A. (2012). *Caesar's De Analogia.* Oxford

Gilmartin, K. (1975). 'A rhetorical figure in Latin historical style: the imaginary second person singular', *TAPA* 105.99–121

Grethlein, J. (2006). 'The unthucydidean voice of Sallust', *TAPA* 136.299–327

Grillo, L. and Krebs, C. B. (edd.) (2018). *The Cambridge companion to the writings of Julius Caesar.* Cambridge

Gruen, E. S. (1974). *The last generation of the Roman republic.* Berkeley/London

Harris, W. V. (1985). *War and imperialism in republican Rome 327–70 BC.* Oxford

Harto Trujillo, M. L. (2008). *Las arengas militares en la historiografía Latina.* Madrid

Hellegouarc'h, J. (1963). *Le vocabulaire latin des relations et des partis politiques sous la république.* Paris

Horsfall, N. (2020). *Fifty years at the Sibyl's heels.* Oxford

Jenkyns, R. (2013). *God, space, and city in the Roman imagination.* Oxford

Kaster, R. A. (2005). *Emotion, restraint, and community in ancient Rome.* Oxford

Koster, S. (1983). 'Poetisches bei Sallust', in *Tessera. Sechs Beiträge zur Poesie und poetischen Theorie der Antike* 55–68. Erlangen

Krebs, C. B. (2008). 'The imagery of "the way" in the proem to Sallust's *Bellum Catilinae* (1–4)', *AJP* 129.581–94

Kroll, W. (1927). 'Die Sprache des Sallust', *Glotta* 15.280–305

La Bua, G. (2019). *Cicero and Roman education: the reception of the speeches and ancient scholarship.* Cambridge

Lausberg, H. (1998). *Handbook of literary rhetoric.* Eng. trans. Leiden

Lebek, W. D. (1970). *Verba prisca. Die Anfänge des Archaisierens in der lateinischen Beredsamkeit und Geschichtsschreibung.* Göttingen

Ledworuski, G. (1994). *Historiographische Widersprüche in der Monographie Sallusts zur Catilinarischen Verschwörung.* Frankfurt am Main

Lendon, J. E. (2017). 'Battle description in the ancient historians. Part I: structure, array, and fighting', *G&R* 64.39–64, 'Part II: speeches, results, and sea battles', *G&R* 64.145–67

Levene, D. S. (2010). *Livy on the Hannibalic War.* Oxford [*LHW*]

(2023). *Livy: The fragments and periochae.* Vols. 1–2. Oxford [*LFP*]

Levick, B. (2015). *Catiline.* London

Lintott, A. W. (1972). 'Imperial expansion and moral decline in the Roman republic', *Historia* 21.626–38
(1999). *Violence in republican Rome*. 2nd edn. Oxford [*VRR*]
(2003). *The constitution of the Roman republic*. Oxford [*CRR*]
Lowrance, W. D. (1931). 'The use of *forem* and *essem*', *TAPA* 62.169–91
Malloch, S. J. V. (2020). *The* Tabula Lugdunensis. Cambridge
Maltby, R. (1991). *A lexicon of ancient Latin etymologies*. Leeds
Marincola, J. (1997). *Authority and tradition in ancient historiography*. Cambridge
Morstein-Marx, R. (2004). *Mass oratory and political power in the late republic*. Cambridge
Mouritsen, H. (2001). *Plebs and politics in the late Roman republic*. Cambridge [*PP*]
(2022). *The Roman elite and the end of the republic: the* boni*, the nobles and* Cicero. Cambridge [*RE*]
Orbis. The Stanford geospatial network model of the Roman world (orbis.stanford.edu)
Otto, A. (1890). *Die Sprichwörter und sprichwörtlichen Redensarten der Römer*. Leipzig
Paananen, U. (1972). *Sallust's politico-social terminology*. Helsinki
Perrochat, P. (1949). *Les modèles grecs de Salluste*. Paris
Pina Polo, F. (2011). *The consul at Rome*. Cambridge
Pina Polo, F. and Díaz Fernández, A. (2019). *The quaestorship in the Roman republic*. Berlin
Rafferty, D. (2019). *Provincial allocations in Rome 123–52 BCE*. Stuttgart
Ramsey, J. T. (2015). *Sallust: Fragments of the* Histories*; Letters to Caesar*. Loeb Classical Library 522. Cambridge, MA/London
(2019). 'The date of the consular elections in 63 and the inception of Catiline's conspiracy', *HSCP* 110.213–69
Richardson, J. S. (2008). *The language of empire*. Cambridge
Rickman, G. (1980). *The corn supply of ancient Rome*. Oxford
Rosenblitt, J. A. (2019). *Rome after Sulla*. London/New York
Rüpke, J. (2008). *Fasti sacerdotum*. Oxford
Rutherford, R. B. (1989). *The* Meditations *of Marcus Aurelius: a study*. Oxford
Ryan, F. X. (1994). 'The quaestorships of Q. Curius and C. Cornelius Cethegus', *CP* 89.256–61
Scanlon, T. F. (1980). *The influence of Thucydides on Sallust*. Heidelberg
Seager, R. (1964). 'The First Catilinarian Conspiracy', *Historia* 13.338–47
(1972). '*Factio*: some observations', *JRS* 62.53–8
Shaw, E. H. (2022). *Sallust and the fall of the republic: historiography and intellectual life at Rome*. Leiden/Boston
Skard, E. (1933). *Ennius und Sallustius*. Oslo [*ES*]

(1942). 'Die Bildersprache des Sallust', in *Serta Eitremiana* 141–64. Oslo

(1956). *Sallust und seine Vorgänger.* Oslo [*SV*]

(1964). 'Zur sprachlichen Entwicklung des Sallust', *SO* 39.13–37

Solodow, J. B. (1978). *The Latin particle quidem.* University Park

Spevak, O. (2014). *The noun phrase in classical Latin prose.* Leiden/Boston

Stone, A. M. (1998). 'Was Sallust a liar? A problem in modern history', in T. W. Hillard et al. (edd.), *Ancient history in a modern university,* Vol. 1 *The ancient Near East, Greece, and Rome* 230–43. Grand Rapids/ Cambridge

(1999). 'Tribute to a statesman: Cicero and Sallust', *Antichthon* 33.48–76

(2014). 'Caesar prophesies the future', *Hermathena* 196–7.231–50

Stover, J. A. and Woudhuysen, G. (2022). '*Historiarum libri quinque*: Hegesippus between Josephus and Sallust', *Histos* 16.1–27

Straumann, B. (2016). *Crisis and constitutionalism: Roman political thought from the fall of the republic to the age of revolution.* Oxford

Sumner, G. V. (1963). 'The last journey of L. Sergius Catilina', *CP* 58.215–19

Sutton, D. (2022). *The language of revolution: a study of language change during* stasis *in ancient Greek and Roman thought.* Diss. Oxford

Syme, R. (1964). *Sallust.* Berkeley/Los Angeles/London [*Sall.*]

(2016). *Approaching the Roman revolution.* Oxford [*ARR*] ('Santangelo' refers to the Addenda)

Tatum, W. J. (2018). *Quintus Cicero: a brief handbook on canvassing for office.* Oxford

Tosi, R. (2007). *Dizionario delle sentenze latine e greche.* 16th edn. Milan

Urso, G. (2019). *Catilina: le faux populiste.* Bordeaux

Vasaly, A. (1993). *Representations: images of the world in Ciceronian oratory.* Berkeley/Los Angeles/London

Volk, K. (2021). *The Roman republic of letters: scholarship, philosophy, and politics in the age of Cicero and Caesar.* Princeton

von Albrecht, M. (1989). *Masters of Roman prose.* Eng. trans. Leeds

Walters, B. (2020). *The deaths of the republic: imagery of the body politic in Ciceronian Rome.* Oxford

Weinstock, S. (1971). *Divus Julius.* Oxford

Williams, G. (1968). *Tradition and originality in Roman poetry.* Oxford [*TORP*]

Williams, J. H. C. (2001). *Beyond the Rubicon: Romans and Gauls in republican Italy.* Oxford [*BRRG*]

Wills, J. (1996). *Repetition in Latin poetry.* Oxford

Wiseman, T. P. (1971). *New men in the Roman senate, 139 BC–AD 14.* Oxford

Woodman, A. J. (2007a). *Sallust:* Catiline's War, The Jugurthine War, Histories. London

(2007b). 'Three notes on Sallust', *CJ* 102.221–4

(2021a). 'Sallust and Catiline: conspiracy theories', *Historia* 70.55–68

(2021b). 'Cicero and Sallust: debating death', *Histos* 15.1–21

(2022). 'Virgil and Sallust: *Aeneid* 10.354–79 and *Bellum Catilinae* 58–60', *CQ* 72.944–9

(2024). 'Cicero and the end of Lentulus (cos. 71 BC)', *Historia* 73.74–81

Zair, N. (2023). *Orthographic traditions and the sub-elite in the Roman empire.* Cambridge

Zetzel, J. E. G. (2018). *Critics, compilers, and commentators: an introduction to Roman philology 800 BCE–200 CE.* Oxford/New York

INDEXES

GENERAL INDEX

All dates are BC; most Romans are listed by their *gentilicium*.

LATIN WORDS

SELECT INTERTEXTS

As allusion and influence are such significant features of S.'s writing, it seems useful to provide an illustrative conspectus of relevant texts. Since the list aims to be inclusive rather than exclusive, some examples will be more certain than others. The parallels with Cicero's *Catilinarians* (Appendix II) are not repeated here.

1.1 Enn. *Ann.* 404–5; Cato, *Orig.* 1C/P
1.3 Liv. fr. 74L
1.6 Thuc. 1.70.2
2.1 Enn. *Ann.* 307, *Euhem.* 7G–M/ 60–1V
2.2 Thuc. 1.70.8
2.3 Tac. *A.* 15.21.4
2.8 Lucr. 3.112; Sen. *Ben.* 7.2.2; Apul. *Deo Socr.* 22.3
3.1 Cato, *Orat.* 173M
3.2 Thuc. 2.35.2; Plin. *Ep.* 5.8.1; Tac. *A.* 4.33.4
3.3 Plato, *Epist.* 7.324B–C
3.5 Cic. *Font.* 30
4.1 Plato, *Epist.* 7.325E–326A; Cato, *Orat.* 128M; Cic. *Font.* 46; Tac. *A.* 1.1.3, 6.38.1
5.1–8 Liv. 21.4.2–10; Tac. *A.* 4.1.1–3
5.5 Tac. *A.* 4.38.5, 15.42.2
5.8 Liv. *praef.* 11, 34.4.1
5.9 Thuc. 2.36.2–3; Liv. *praef.* 9; Tac. *H.* 1.4.1, 2.2.2, 2.37.2, 4.48.1, *A.* 3.25.2, 16.18.1
6.1 Cato, *Orat.* 206M; Tac. *A.* 1.1.1, 2.4.2, 3.15.2
6.3 Cato, *Orig.* 117C/20P; Tac. *A.* 6.8.4
6.5 Thuc. 2.40.4; Tac. *A.* 6.2.4
6.7 Cato, *Orat.* 163M
7.3 Tac. *Agr.* 5.3
7.7 Tac. *A.* 6.22.4
8.1 Thuc. 2.41.2
8.2 Thuc. 2.41.3
8.4 Thuc. 2.35.1; Verus *ap.* Fronto p. 109.3–4 vdH²; *HA Prob.* 1.1
8.5 Liv. 34.15.9
9.4 Thuc. 2.41.4
10.1 Thuc. 2.41.4; Cic. *Font.* 12; Tac. *A.* 4.1.1
10.3 Hor. *C.* 3.24.49
10.4 Thuc. 3.82.8
10.5 Cic. *Planc.* 34; Tac. *A.* 11.1.2
11.2 Lucr. 2.11–13
11.4 Cic. *Rosc. Am.* 131

11.5 Cato, *Orat.* 163M; Tac. *H.* 2.100.2
12.1 Thuc. 2.40.1; Hor. *C.* 3.24.42
12.2 Thuc. 3.84.1
12.4 Cic. *Acad.* 2.4
13.3 Xen. *Mem.* 2.1.30; Tac. *A.* 6.4.4
13.4 Tac. *A.* 15.45.2
14.4 Theopomp. F224
14.5 Hor. *AP* 161–4
14.6 Plin. *Ep.* 9.12.1
15.2 Liv. 1.46.9; Vell. 74.3; Tac. *A.* 13.45.2
16.1 Tac. *A.* 6.45.3
16.3 Sen. *Ben.* 7.2.2
19.3–5 Tac. *A.* 4.45
20.7 Cato, *Orig.* 41C/73P, *Orat.* 18M
20.12 Hor. *Epi.* 1.1.100
23.3 Tac. *A.* 4.46.1, 13.44.1–3
23.4 Tac. *A.* 3.19.2
23.6 Tac. *Agr.* 11.3
24.3 Tac. *A.* 15.48.1
25.1–5 Tac. *A.* 13.45.1–4
25.2 Hor. *C.* 4.13.7, *Epi.* 2.1.33
25.3 Aufid. Bass. 2C/P
27.2 Tac. *A.* 11.22.1
30.4 Tac. *A.* 2.38.4
31.3 Hor. *Epi.* 1.6.30–1
33.1 Liv. 6.14.3, 6.14.5; Tac. *A.* 6.17.3
33.5 Cic. *Quinct.* 9, *Tull.* 38; Liv. 6.14.5
34.2 Tac. *A.* 3.16.3
35.3 Cic. *Verr.* 3.48, *Att.* 1.5.1, *Fam.* 5.20.4; Liv. 7.41.1
37.3 Tac. *H.* 2.8.2, 2.38.1
37.5 Tac. *A.* 5.6.2
38.1 Liv. 22.34.3; Tac. *A.* 3.27.2
38.2 Tac. *H.* 1.74.2
38.3 Thuc. 3.82.8
39.2 Tac. *A.* 1.1.2, 3.40.3, 4.33.2
40.2 Cic. *Vat.* 31, *al.*
43.1 Tac. *A.* 1.7.1, *al.*
43.3 Tac. *H.* 1.62.1
43.4 Cic. *Vat.* 4
46.2 Tac. *A.* 1.52.1

341

50.2 Liv. 8.24.13
51.2 Cic. *II Verr.* 1.78, *Off.* 1.92, *Fin.* 2.60
51.4 Cic. *Part. Or.* 49
51.12 Cic. *Pis.* 55, *Scaur.* 2, *Rep.* 2.56
51.21 Lucr. 3.900
51.24 Licin. Macer 8C/22P; Lucr. 3.889
51.31 Cic. *Dom.* 131, *TD* 5.57
51.36 Tac. *A.* 4.44.3
52.2 Dem. *Ol.* 3.1
52.4 Lycurg. *Leocr.* 126
52.7 Thuc. 3.37.1; Liv. 34.4.1; Tac. *A.* 14.43.1
52.11 Thuc. 3.82.3–4; Cic. *Mur.* 90, *Sull.* 93
52.12 Vell. 91.4; Tac. *A.* 4.66.2
52.13 Cic. *Leg.* 3.19, *Off.* 3.36, 3.83, *Rep.* 2.48
52.20 Dem. *Phil.* 3.40
52.23 Cic. *TD* 5.8
52.24 Liv. 26.27.12
52.32–4 Cic. *Sull.* 70
52.35 Cic. *Verr.* 5.96; Tac. *H.* 3.38.3
52.36 Cic. *Har. Resp.* 35, *Prov. Cons.* 3, *Phil.* 14.37

53.1 Cato, *Orig.* 2C/P
53.2 Tac. *A.* 6.22.1
53.3 Tac. *A.* 1.27.1
54.4 Cic. *Mur.* 32
54.6 Aesch. *Sept.* 592
55.6 Hdt. 1.45.3; Hegesipp. 4.20.18
56.3 Sisenna 53C/21P
56.4 Tac. *A.* 2.66.1
57.3 Caes. *BG* 7.36.5, *BC* 1.45.6
57.4 Sisenna 58C/73P (?)
58.1 Tac. *H.* 2.46.2
58.3 Thuc. 4.126.1
58.7 Virg. *Aen.* 10.372–3
58.10 Thuc. 6.23.2
58.17 Hegesipp. 5.4.1
58.18 Cic. *Clu.* 7; Virg. *Aen.* 10.369
59.1 Caes. *BG* 1.25.1; Virg. *Aen.* 10.310, 366–7
59.2 Virg. *Aen.* 10.366
59.3 Caes. *BC* 1.3.3, 1.17.3, 3.53.1
59.6 Virg. *Aen.* 10.369
60.1 Caes. *BG* 4.21.2, 7.81.3
60.2 Caes. *BG* 7.88.3
60.5 Virg. *Aen.* 10.379
60.7 Virg. *Aen.* 10.379
61.4 Tac. *A.* 1.12.4

For EU product safety concerns, contact us at Calle de José Abascal, 56–1°,
28003 Madrid, Spain or eugpsr@cambridge.org.

www.ingramcontent.com/pod-product-compliance
Ingram Content Group UK Ltd.
Pitfield, Milton Keynes, MK11 3LW, UK
UKHW022138050526
470747UK00009BA/292